D0934979

MATRIX METHODS
FOR ENGINEERING

PRENTICE-HALL INTERNATIONAL SERIES IN APPLIED MATHEMATICS

DEUTSCH, *Nonlinear Transformations of Random Processes*
DRESHER, *Games of Strategy: Theory and Applications*
EDMUNDSON, ED., *Proceedings of the National Symposium on Machine Translation, 1961*
PIPES, *Matrix Methods for Engineering*
STANTON, *Numerical Methods for Science and Engineering*

PRENTICE-HALL INTERNATIONAL, INC., *London*
PRENTICE-HALL OF AUSTRALIA, PTY., LTD., *Sydney*
PRENTICE-HALL OF CANADA, LTD., *Toronto*
PRENTICE-HALL FRANCE, S.A.R.L., *Paris*
PRENTICE-HALL OF JAPAN, INC., *Tokyo*
PRENTICE-HALL DE MEXICO, S.A., *Mexico City*

MATRIX METHODS
FOR ENGINEERING

LOUIS A. PIPES

Professor of Engineering
University of California

PRENTICE-HALL, INC.

ENGLEWOOD CLIFFS, N. J.

1963

Library of Congress Catalog Card No. 63–7545
Printed in the United States of America
56557 C

PREFACE

Although over one hundred years have elapsed since the publication of Cayley's celebrated 1858 paper on matrix theory, the total number of published treatises on matrices is not large. Most of the existing books on the subject approach the theory of matrices from the point of view of the pure mathematician and very few texts exist that develop the subject from the point of view of those interested in its applications to physical problems.

This volume is based on an amplification of a course of lectures on matrix calculus and its application to a representative group of physical problems delivered by the author over the last fifteen years to students in the Department of Engineering of the University of California at Los Angeles. The principal purpose of the book is to give the reader a working knowledge of the fundamentals of matrix calculus which he may apply to his own field of interest. Applied mathematicians, physicists, electrical engineers, as well as mechanical and aeronautical engineers will discover principles applicable to their respective fields.

The first chapter contains a brief summary of the theory of determinants. The next three chapters give an account of those properties of matrix algebra and matrix calculus which are required later for the applications. Chapter 2 is devoted to fundamental definitions and operations. In Chapter 3, a detailed discussion of the subject of eigenvalues and eigenvectors of square matrices is given. The calculus of matrices is developed in Chapter 4.

The remainder of the book is concerned with applications. Chapter 5 deals in some detail with the applications of matrix methods to the theory of elasticity. A concise discussion of the formulation of structural problems by the use of matrix algebra is given in Chapter 6. Chapter 7 contains an exposition of classical mechanics. In this chapter, the method of rotating axes and Euler's equations are developed by a matrix method. In Chapter 8 the classical theory of the vibrations of linear mechanical and electrical systems is developed. The last six chapters are devoted to applications involving problems of electric circuit analysis. Chapter 9 is concerned with a discussion of the steady-state oscillations of multiple loop electric circuits. The classical alternating current theory of circuits of a very general class is discussed in this chapter. The transient behavior of multiple loop electric circuits is developed in Chapter 10. Chapter 11 contains a detailed study of the analysis of linear conservative electric circuits. The steady-state analysis of linear four-terminal networks including the analysis of filter structures, single-phase transformers, and single-phase transmission lines is given in Chapter 12. Chapters 13 and 14 are devoted to the steady-state and transient analysis of multiconductor transmission lines. In these chapters, use is made of matrix algebra and the theory of the Laplace Transform to effect the solution of the equations of multiple transmission line theory. The book is concluded with three appendices on Laplace Transforms.

The author would like to acknowledge his gratitude to Dean L. M. K. Boelter and to Mr. John C. Dillon of the Department of Engineering of the University of California at Los Angeles for encouraging him to amplify his lecture notes into book form. My special thanks are also due to my many graduate students, and especially to Mr. Lawrence Harvill and Mr. John Staudhammer who kindly have suggested changes and additions to the manuscript, thereby improving its style and clarity. I would also like to thank my friend, Mr. Victor Rowell, for his encouragement and assistance.

Louis A. Pipes

University of California at Los Angeles

TABLE OF CONTENTS

INTRODUCTION, 1

1 THE ELEMENTS OF THE THEORY OF DETERMINANTS, 3

1. Introduction, 3.
2. Fundamental definitions and notation, 3.
3. Minors and cofactors, 4.
4. The Laplace expansion of a determinant, 5.
5. Fundamental properties of determinants, 7.
6. The expansion of numerical determinants, 8.
7. The method of pivotal condensation, 10.
8. The solution of linear equations. Cramer's rule, 13.
9. Multiplication and differentiation of determinants, 15.

2 THE FUNDAMENTALS OF MATRIX ALGEBRA, 18

1. Introduction, 18.
2. Definition of a matrix, 18.
3. Principal types of matrices, 19.
4. Equality of matrices, addition and subtraction, 20.
5. Multiplication of matrices, 21.
6. Matrix division, the inverse matrix, 24.
7. Matrix division, 28.
8. The reversal law in transposed and reciprocal products, 29.
9. Diagonal matrices and their properties, 31.
10. Partitioned matrices and partitioned multiplication, 31.
11. Matrices of special types, 32.
12. The solution of n linear equations in n unknowns, 34.

3 MATRICES AND
EIGENVALUE PROBLEMS, 38

1. Introduction, 38.
2. The eigenvalues of a square matrix, 38.
3. Geometrical interpretation of the eigenvalue problem, 40.
4. Invariants of the rotated matrix $[M]_r$, 45.
5. Algebraic discussion of the eigenvectors of a matrix, 46.
6. The eigenvalues of a real symmetric matrix are real numbers, 49.
7. Hermitian matrices, 50.
8. Orthogonal transformations, 51.
9. Symmetric matrices and quadratic forms, 53.
10. The transformation of a quadratic form into a sum of squares by means of an orthogonal transformation, 54.
11. Commutative matrices, 57.
12. Fundamental properties of the characteristic determinant and the characteristic equation of a matrix, 59.

4 THE CALCULUS
OF MATRICES, 65

1. Introduction, 65.
2. Matrix polynomials, 65.
3. Infinite series of matrices, 66.
4. The convergence of series of matrices, 67.
5. The matric exponential function, 69.
6. The matric trigonometric and hyperbolic functions, 70.
7. The matric binomial theorem (commutative matrices), 72.
8. The Cayley-Hamilton theorem, 73.
9. Reduction of polynomials by the Cayley-Hamilton theorem, 75.
10. The inversion of a matrix by the use of the Cayley-Hamilton theorem, 77.
11. Functions of matrices and Sylvester's theorem, 78.
12. Applications of Sylvester's theorem, 82.
13. The use of the characteristic equation in evaluating functions of matrices, 83.
14. Differentiation and integration of matrices, 88.
15. Association of matrices with linear differential equations, 90.
16. The solution of difference equations by the use of matrices, 94.

5 MATRIX METHODS IN THE THEORY OF ELASTICITY, 100

1. Introduction, 100.
2. Stress. Definition and notation, 100.
3. Stresses in two dimensions, 102.
4. Stresses in three dimensions, 106.
5. Infinitesimal strain in three dimensions, 111.
6. The strain energy of the medium, 117.
7. The stress-strain relations for an elastic isotropic solid, 117.
8. The principal elastic constants, 120.
9. The strain expressed in terms of the stress, 122.
10. The elastic equations of motion, 122.
11. The elastic equations of equilibrium, 125.
12. The stresses on a semi-infinite solid strained by gravitational forces, 126.

6 MATRIX METHODS IN THE ANALYSIS OF STRUCTURES, 129

1. Introduction, 129.
2. The flexibility and stiffness matrices, 130.
3. Conservative bodies and the strain energy, 134.
4. Castigliano's theorem, 135.
5. The principal directions of loading at a point of an elastic body, 135.
6. The principle of minimum potential energy, 136.
7. Determination of the flexibility matrix of a complex structure, 137.
8. The force method of stress analysis, 138.
9. The modified flexibility matrix, 142.
10. Analysis of modified structures, 144.
11. Modifications of the elements of the structure, 147.
12. The flexibility of the modified structure, 150.
13. The displacement method of stress analysis, 151.
14. The effect of the application of initial stresses p_0 with the constraint $S = 0$, 154.
15. Analysis of modifications of the structure, 155.
16. The stiffness matrix of the modified structure, 157.
17. Special types of modification of the structure, 157.

7 APPLICATIONS OF MATRICES
TO CLASSICAL MECHANICS, 163

1. Introduction, 163.
2. The matrix representation of a vector product, 163.
3. Rotation of rectangular axes, 165.
4. Kinematics and angular velocity, 166.
5. Change of reference axes in two dimensions, 170.
6. Successive rotations, 172.
7. Angular coordinates of a three-dimensional reference frame, 172.
8. The transformation matrix [L] and instantaneous angular velocities expressed in angular coordinates, 174.
9. The components of velocity and acceleration, 175.
10. The kinetic energy of a rigid body, 177.
11. Principal axes and the moments of inertia, 179.
12. Transformation of forces and couples, 181.
13. The equations of motion of a rigid body, 183.
14. Transformation of the equation of motion to moving axes, 186.
15. General form of Euler's equations, 189.
16. Motion relative to the surface of the earth, 193.
17. The plumb line, 196.
18. Motion of a free particle near the surface of the rotating earth, 198.
19. The Foucault pendulum, 201.
20. The motion of a top, 203.

8 APPLICATIONS OF MATRICES
TO VIBRATION PROBLEMS, 210

1. Introduction, 210.
2. Transformation of coordinates, 210.
3. Lagrange's equations of motion, 212.
4. Electrical and mechanical analogies, 214.
5. Systems having two degrees of freedom (conservative case), 218.
6. The general case: mass-weighted coordinates, 224.
7. The vibration of conservative systems with dynamic coupling, 227.

8 APPLICATIONS OF MATRICES TO VIBRATION PROBLEMS (Cont'd)

8. Fundamental properties of the modal matrix [A], 231.
9. The case of three coupled pendulums, 234.
10. The case of zero frequency, 238.
11. The use of functions of matrices in the theory of vibrations, 241.
12. Use of functions of matrices in the case of dynamic coupling, 247.
13. The case of multiple roots of the characteristic equation, 249.
14. The oscillations of a symmetric electric circuit, 251.
15. Nonconservative systems. Vibrations with viscous damping, 254.
16. The motion of a general damped linear dynamic system, 256.
17. The use of matrix iteration to determine the frequencies and modes of oscillation of linear conservative systems, 262.
18. Numerical example, 264.
19. Determination of the higher modes: the sweeping matrix, 267.
20. A numerical example of the iteration procedure, 270.
21. The analysis of a class of symmetric damped linear systems, 279.
22. The Routh-Hurwitz stability criterion, 282.
23. The location of the eigenvalues of a matrix, 285.

9 THE STEADY-STATE SOLUTION OF THE GENERAL n-MESH CIRCUIT, 288

1. Introduction, 288.
2. The general network, 288.
3. Formulation of the problem in terms of mesh currents, 290
4. The canonical equations and their solution, 292.
5. Steady-state solution, one applied sinusoidal electromotive force, 295.
6. Case of n sinusoidal electromotive forces of different phases, 298.
7. Voltages of different frequencies simultaneously impressed, 298.

10 THE TRANSIENT SOLUTION
OF THE GENERAL NETWORK, 305

1. Introduction, 305.
2. The heuristic process, 305.
3. The determinantal equation, 306.
4. The normal modes, 306.
5. The modal matrix, 307.
6. The relation between the amplitudes, 307.
7. Determination of the arbitrary constants, 308.
8. The case of repeated roots of the determinantal equation, 311.
9. The energy functions of the general network, 313.

11 THE DISSIPATIONLESS
NETWORK, 316

1. Introduction, 316.
2. The canonical equations and the steady-state solution, 316.
3. The transient solution, 319.
4. Determination of the fundamental frequency, 322.
5. Completion of the solution, 323.
6. Evaluation of the arbitrary constants, 325.
7. Normal coordinates, 326.
8. Illustrative example, 327.
9. Effect of small resistance terms, 333.
10. The potential function, 334.
11. Computation of the attenuation constants, 336.

12 THE STEADY-STATE ANALYSIS
OF FOUR-TERMINAL NETWORKS, 337

1. Introduction, 337.
2. The general equations, 337.
3. Alternative form of the equations, 340.
4. Interconnection of four-terminal networks, 341.
5. The chain matrices of common structures, 347.
6. The homographic transformation, 351.
7. Cascade connection of dissymmetrical networks, 352.
8. Attenuation and pass bands, 359.
9. The smooth transmission lines, 361.
10. The general ladder network, 363.

13 STEADY-STATE SOLUTION
OF MULTICONDUCTOR LINES, 365

1. Introduction, 365.
2. The coefficients of capacity and induction, 366.
3. The electromagnetic coefficients, 367.
4. The general differential equations, 368.
5. The steady-state equations, 370.
6. Solution of the equations, boundary conditions, 371.
7. The determinantal equation, 375.
8. Transformation of the basic equations, 378.
9. Solution in terms of terminal impedances, 381.
10. General considerations, 383.

14 TRANSIENT ANALYSIS
OF MULTICONDUCTOR LINES, 384

1. Introduction, 384.
2. The general equations, 384.
3. The dissipationless case, 386.
4. The general case, 390.
5. The case of ring symmetry, 392.
6. General boundary conditions, 395.
7. General considerations, 397.

APPENDIX

1 THE ELEMENTS OF THE
THEORY OF LAPLACE TRANSFORMS, 401

APPENDIX

2 THE BASIC THEOREMS OF
THE LAPLACE TRANSFORMS, 404

APPENDIX

3 TABLE OF
BASIC TRANSFORMS, 407

INDEX, 425

MATRIX METHODS
FOR ENGINEERING

INTRODUCTION

The term "matrix" in mathematics seems to have been used for the first time by the mathematician James Sylvester. In the year 1850 Sylvester applied the name "matrix" to a rectangular array of numbers "out of which determinants can be formed." The modern concept of a matrix as a hyper-complex number is due to William Rowland Hamilton. In his paper, "Linear and Vector Functions," written in 1853, Hamilton discusses the various properties of linear transformations using arrays of quantities without giving these arrays an explicit name. However, it was not until 1857 that the eminent English mathematician Cayley in his celebrated paper, "A Memoir on the Theory of Matrices," London, *Phil. Trans.*, Vol. 148, pp. 17–37 (1857), presented the modern basis of the theory of matrices.

Matrices, as shown by Cayley, provided a compact and flexible notation particularly useful in studying linear transformations, and presented an organized method for the solution of systems of linear algebraic and linear differential equations. For a long time matrices and matrix algebra were subjects studied almost exclusively by pure mathematicians, and most physicists and engineers were unaware of the existence of matrix algebra. It was not until 1925 that the physicists Heisenberg, Born, and Jordan discovered the utility of matrices in the study of problems in quantum mechanics. The subject of matrices and matrix algebra was introduced to the engineering profession by two English aeronautical engineers, W. J. Duncan and A. R. Collar. In 1934 Duncan and Collar published the paper, "A Method for the Solution of Oscillation Problems by Matrices," *Phil. Mag.*, Series 7, Vol. 17, p. 865 (1934). This paper, which is of fundamental importance in the theory of vibrations, greatly stimulated the interest in the use of matrices by engineers and physicists.

Since Cayley's original memoir, a vast literature dealing with the applications of matrices to many branches of mathematics, physics, engineering, economics, and the social sciences has developed. Matrices have been found extremely useful in the solution of many problems that arise in the different fields of engineering. Since the vast majority of engineering problems is formulated in terms of linear algebraic or linear differential equations, it is natural that their solution would be expedited by the use of matrix algebra. It might be added that the development of modern digital computing machines and the introduction of the digital viewpoint has *created* matrix problems where they did not exist before. For example, by the technique of modern numerical analysis, partial differential equations are transformed into linear algebraic equations that can be studied by the use of matrices. In the same manner, boundary-value problems become matrix problems after first passing through a reformulation in terms of integral equations.

It is the purpose of this book to develop the fundamentals of matrix algebra and the differential and integral calculus of matrices which are necessary to understand the use of matrices in typical engineering problems. The use of matrix techniques for the solution of practical engineering problems in dynamics, electric-circuit theory, heat flow, and elasticity is demonstrated by solving typical problems in each of these fields.

Since many engineers are not familar with or have forgotten some of the more useful properties of determinants, it seems advisable to review the basic ideas of the theory of determinants before the concepts of matrix algebra are developed.

1 THE ELEMENTS OF THE THEORY OF DETERMINANTS

1. INTRODUCTION

The theory of determinants is usually ascribed to G. W. Leibnitz, who stated their basic properties in a letter written to the mathematician L'Hospital in 1693. However, a Japanese mathematician, Seki Kowa, had come close to the same discovery at least as early as 1683. The work of Leibnitz seems to have been forgotten, and it was left to G. Cramer to rediscover determinants and to publish first a statement of their properties in 1750. The modern notation was introduced by A. Cayley in 1841. An excellent discussion of determinants and the historical development of their theory will be found in the work of Sir Thomas Muir[5].*

The theory of determinants is intimately connected with that of matrices. The more important definitions and properties of determinants will be developed in this chapter in order to enable the reader to refresh his memory on the fundamentals of determinant theory that are essential for the understanding of matrix algebra.

2. FUNDAMENTAL DEFINITIONS AND NOTATION

The symbol

$$(2.1) \qquad D = \begin{vmatrix} a_{11} & a_{12} \\ a_{21} & a_{22} \end{vmatrix}$$

is called a *determinant* of the second order. The quantities a_{ij} are called the

---

* Reference 5 refers to the fifth entry on the Reference at the end of Chapter 1. Each chapter has a reference list and this numbering system is used throughout to identify the entries.

elements of the determinant. The square array of quantities in (2.1) represents the following expression formed from the elements of the determinant

$$(2.2) \qquad\qquad D = a_{11}a_{22} - a_{21}a_{12}$$

The expression (2.2) is called the *expansion* of the determinant (2.1).

Determinant of the nth Order

Having considered the simple determinant of the second order given by (2.1), we now turn to the definition of the general determinant of the nth order.

A determinant of the nth order is a square array of n^2 elements, a_{ij}, arranged in n rows and n columns. When expanded, this array represents an algebraic expression of $n!$ terms that is homogeneous in the elements of the determinant. An nth-order determinant has the form:

$$(2.3) \qquad\qquad D = \begin{vmatrix} a_{11} & a_{12} & a_{13} & \cdots & a_{1n} \\ a_{21} & a_{22} & a_{23} & \cdots & a_{2n} \\ \cdot & \cdot & \cdot & \cdots & \cdot \\ a_{n1} & a_{n2} & a_{n3} & \cdots & a_{nn} \end{vmatrix}$$

The rules for expanding the general nth-order determinant will be given in a later section.

3. MINORS AND COFACTORS

Before we give the general rule for the expansion of the nth-order determinant (2.3), it is necessary to define what is meant by a *minor* and a *cofactor* of an element of a determinant.

Minor

The minor of the element a_{ij} of a determinant of order n is the determinant of order $(n - 1)$ obtained by removing the row i and the column j of the original determinant.

For example, consider the third-order determinant:

$$(3.1) \qquad\qquad D = \begin{vmatrix} a_{11} & a_{12} & a_{13} \\ a_{21} & a_{22} & a_{23} \\ a_{31} & a_{32} & a_{33} \end{vmatrix}$$

The minor of the element a_{23} is obtained by deleting the second row and the third column of D and forming the determinant M_{23} from the remaining elements. If this procedure is carried out, the following determinant is obtained:

$$(3.2) \qquad M_{23} = \begin{vmatrix} a_{11} & a_{12} \\ a_{31} & a_{32} \end{vmatrix} = \text{minor of } a_{23}$$

The Cofactor of an Element

By definition, the cofactor of a given element of a determinant is the minor of the element with either a plus or a minus sign attached to it. The sign is obtained from the following formula:

$$(3.3) \qquad \text{cofactor of } a_{ij} = C_{ij} = (-1)^{i+j} M_{ij}$$

where M_{ij} is the minor of a_{ij}.

As an example, the cofactor of the element a_{23} of the determinant (3.1) is given by

$$(3.4) \qquad C_{23} = (-1)^5 M_{23} = -M_{23}$$

The Cofactors of a Second-Order Determinant

Let D be a determinant of the second order so that

$$(3.5) \qquad D = \begin{vmatrix} a_{11} & a_{12} \\ a_{21} & a_{22} \end{vmatrix} = (a_{11}a_{22} - a_{21}a_{12})$$

As a consequence of the definitions of minors and cofactors given above it is seen that

$$(3.6) \qquad C_{11} = a_{22}, \quad C_{12} = -a_{21}, \quad C_{21} = -a_{12}, \quad C_{22} = a_{11}$$

From this it can be seen that the expansion of D may be written in the form:

$$(3.7) \qquad D = a_{11}C_{11} + a_{12}C_{12} = a_{11}C_{11} + a_{21}C_{21}$$

$$= a_{21}C_{21} + a_{22}C_{22} = a_{12}C_{12} + a_{22}C_{22}$$

From (3.7) it is seen that the expansion of (3.5) may be obtained by taking the sum of the products of the elements and their corresponding cofactors taken from a single row or a single column of the determinant D.

4. THE LAPLACE EXPANSION OF A DETERMINANT

We now come to a consideration of what may be regarded as the definition of the homogeneous polynomial of the nth order that the symbolic array of elements of the determinant of the nth order represents. In the previous section it was shown how the second-order homogeneous polynomial represented by the second-order determinant could be expanded by the equations:

(4.1)
$$D = \sum_{\substack{j=1 \\ i=1,2}}^{2} a_{ij}C_{ij} \quad \text{or} \quad D = \sum_{\substack{i=1 \\ j=1,2}}^{2} a_{ij}C_{ij}$$

(expansion by rows)　　　(expansion by columns)

By definition, the third-order determinant,

(4.2)
$$D = \begin{vmatrix} a_{11} & a_{12} & a_{13} \\ a_{21} & a_{22} & a_{23} \\ a_{31} & a_{32} & a_{33} \end{vmatrix}$$

represents the unique third-order homogeneous polynomial defined by *any one* of the six equivalent expressions:

(4.3)
$$D = \sum_{\substack{j=1 \\ i=1,2,3}}^{3} a_{ij}C_{ij} \quad \text{or} \quad D = \sum_{\substack{i=1 \\ j=1,2,3}}^{3} a_{ij}C_{ij}$$

(expansion by rows)　　　(expansion by columns)

In (4.3) the elements a_{ij} must be taken from a *single* row or a *single* column of D. The C_{ij}'s are the cofactors of the corresponding elements a_{ij} as defined in Sec. 3. As an example of the above definition, let the determinant (4.2) be expanded in terms of the first row by (4.3). This expansion gives the following result:

(4.4)
$$\begin{aligned} D &= a_{11}C_{11} + a_{12}C_{12} + a_{13}C_{13} \\ &= a_{11}(a_{22}a_{33} - a_{32}a_{23}) + a_{12}(a_{31}a_{23} - a_{21}a_{33}) \\ &\qquad\qquad + a_{13}(a_{21}a_{32} - a_{31}a_{22}) \end{aligned}$$

It can be seen that the expansion (4.4) contains six or 3! terms. Now, since one has the alternative of expanding D by using any row or any column, it may be seen that (4.2) could be expanded in six different ways by the fundamental rule (4.3). It is easy to show that all six ways lead to the same third-order homogeneous polynomial (4.4)

The definition (4.3) may be generalized to expand the nth-order determinant (2.3). The general nth-order determinant represents the nth-order homogeneous polynomial given by:

(4.5)
$$D = \sum_{\substack{j=1 \\ i=1,2,\ldots,n}}^{n} a_{ij}C_{ij} \quad \text{or} \quad D = \sum_{\substack{i=1 \\ j=1,2,\ldots,n}}^{n} a_{ij}C_{ij}$$

(rows)　　　(columns)

Equation (4.5) is the Laplace expansion of the general nth-order determinant. It can be seen from (4.5) that the determinant may be expanded by taking the sums of continued products of the elements and their corresponding cofactors along any row or along any column of the determinant. In this case the cofactors C_{ij} are determinants of the $(n - 1)$th order, but they in turn may be expanded by the rule (4.5), and so on, until the result is a homogeneous polynomial of the nth order.

The following important property of the elements of a determinant a_{ij} and their corresponding cofactors C_{ij} is easy to demonstrate.

$$(4.6) \qquad \sum_{j=1}^{n} a_{ij}C_{kj} = \sum_{j=1}^{n} a_{ij}C_{jk} = \begin{cases} D, & \text{if } i = k \\ 0, & \text{if } i \neq k \end{cases}$$

5. FUNDAMENTAL PROPERTIES OF DETERMINANTS

From the basic definition (4.5), the following properties of determinants may be deduced:

1. If *all* the elements in a row or in a column are zero, the determinant is equal to zero. This fact may be seen by expanding the determinant in terms of that row or column which contains the zero elements; then each term of the expansion contains a factor of zero.

2. If all elements but one in a row or column are zero, the determinant is equal to the product of that element and its cofactor.

3. The value of a determinant is not altered when the rows are changed to columns and the columns to rows. This fact may be proved by expanding the determinant by (4.5).

4. The interchange of any two columns or two rows of a determinant changes the sign of the determinant.

5. If two columns or two rows of a determinant are identical, the determinant is equal to zero.

6. If all the elements in any row or column are multiplied by any factor, the determinant is multiplied by that factor.

7. If each element in any column or any row of a determinant is expressed as the sum of two quantities, the determinant can be expressed as the sum of two determinants of the same order.

8. It is possible, without changing the value of a determinant, to multiply the elements of any row (or any column) by the same constant and to add the products to any other row (or column]. For example, consider the third-order determinant:

$$(5.1) \qquad D = \begin{vmatrix} a_{11} & a_{12} & a_{13} \\ a_{21} & a_{22} & a_{23} \\ a_{31} & a_{32} & a_{33} \end{vmatrix}$$

Now let the third column be multiplied by the common factor m and be added to the first column.   The resulting determinant is

(5.2) $$D_0 = \begin{vmatrix} (a_{11} + ma_{13}) & a_{12} & a_{13} \\ (a_{21} + ma_{23}) & a_{22} & a_{23} \\ (a_{31} + ma_{33}) & a_{32} & a_{33} \end{vmatrix} = D + m \begin{vmatrix} a_{13} & a_{12} & a_{13} \\ a_{23} & a_{22} & a_{23} \\ a_{33} & a_{32} & a_{33} \end{vmatrix}$$

The above decomposition of D_0 into two determinants is effected by applying principles 6 and 7.   Now, by principle 5, it can be seen that the last determinant in (5.2) must vanish, since its first and third columns are identical. It thus follows that

(5.3) $$D_0 = D$$

This establishes principle 8.

The eight properties stated above are extremely useful in the expansion of numerical determinants.   By their use, a great deal of numerical labor can frequently be avoided.

6. THE EXPANSION OF NUMERICAL DETERMINANTS

The use of Laplace's expansion and the properties of determinants given in Sec. 5 will now be illustrated by expanding determinants that have numerical elements.

EXAMPLE 1

Let it be required to expand the following determinant.

(6.1) $$D = \begin{vmatrix} 2 & 0 & 3 & 3 \\ 0 & -1 & 2 & 1 \\ 1 & -1 & 3 & 1 \\ 0 & 3 & 1 & 2 \end{vmatrix}$$

Without the use of any of the properties of Sec. 5, this determinant can be expanded conveniently by the use of the Laplace expansion in terms of the first column, since this column contains two zeros; this simplifies the expansion.   Accordingly, expanding (6.1) in terms of the first column, we have

(6.2) $$D = 2 \begin{vmatrix} -1 & 2 & 1 \\ -1 & 3 & 1 \\ 3 & 1 & 2 \end{vmatrix} + 1 \begin{vmatrix} 0 & 3 & 3 \\ -1 & 2 & 1 \\ 3 & 1 & 2 \end{vmatrix} = -16$$

The determinant (6.1) may also be expanded by the use of the properties of Sec. 5 in the following manner:

Write the last three rows of (6.1) as given.   Now form a new first row by multiplying the third row by -2 and adding it to row number one (property 8). The result of this operation is

$$(6.3) \qquad D = \begin{vmatrix} 0 & 2 & -3 & 1 \\ 0 & -1 & 2 & 1 \\ 1 & -1 & 3 & 1 \\ 0 & 3 & 1 & 2 \end{vmatrix} = \begin{vmatrix} 2 & -3 & 1 \\ -1 & 2 & 1 \\ 3 & 1 & 2 \end{vmatrix} = D_0$$

D_0 is obtained from D by expanding it in terms of its first column. Now the determinant D_0 may be transformed to a simpler one by the following operations:

(a) Writing the first row as it stands.

(b) Forming a new second row by subtracting row one from row two.

(c) Forming a new third row by multiplying row one by -2 and adding the result to row three.

By these operations, the determinant D_0 is transformed to

$$(6.4) \qquad D_0 = \begin{vmatrix} 2 & -3 & 1 \\ -3 & 5 & 0 \\ -1 & 7 & 0 \end{vmatrix}$$

This determinant may be expanded in terms of the third column so that

$$(6.5) \qquad D_0 = \begin{vmatrix} -3 & 5 \\ -1 & 7 \end{vmatrix} = -16$$

Hence, the determinant $D = D_0 = -16$.

As another example of the use of the fundamental properties of Sec. 5 in facilitating the expansion of a determinant, let it be required to expand the numerical determinant

$$(6.6) \qquad a = \begin{vmatrix} 2 & -1 & 5 & 1 \\ 1 & 4 & 6 & 3 \\ 4 & 2 & 7 & 4 \\ 3 & 1 & 2 & 5 \end{vmatrix}$$

The general procedure is to make use of property 8 in such a manner that all the elements except one in some row or column of a are equal to zero; then the determinant a is equal to the remaining element times its cofactor.

The presence of the factor -1 in the second column of (6.6) suggests the following procedure:

(a) Add four times the first row to the second row.

(b) Add two times the first row to the third row.

(c) Add the first row to the fourth row.

Since by property 8 of Sec. 5 these operations do not alter the value of the determinant, we have, after performing the operations (a), (b), and (c),

$$(6.7) \qquad a = \begin{vmatrix} 2 & -1 & 5 & 1 \\ 9 & 0 & 26 & 7 \\ 8 & 0 & 17 & 6 \\ 5 & 0 & 7 & 6 \end{vmatrix} = \begin{vmatrix} 9 & 26 & 7 \\ 8 & 17 & 6 \\ 5 & 7 & 6 \end{vmatrix} = a_0$$

The second determinant in (6.7) is obtained by expanding the first one in terms of the second column. The determinant a_0 above may be simplified by subtracting the elements of the third column from the first column. This operation results in

$$(6.8) \qquad a_0 = \begin{vmatrix} 2 & 26 & 7 \\ 2 & 17 & 6 \\ -1 & 7 & 6 \end{vmatrix}$$

The determinant (6.8) can be simplified further by the following operations:

1. Add two times the third row to the first row.

2. Add two times the third row to the second row.

These operations transform (6.8) into

$$(6.9) \qquad a_0 = \begin{vmatrix} 0 & 40 & 19 \\ 0 & 31 & 18 \\ -1 & 7 & 6 \end{vmatrix} = - \begin{vmatrix} 40 & 19 \\ 31 & 18 \end{vmatrix} = b$$

The second row of b is now subtracted from its first row. This operation gives b the form

$$(6.10) \qquad b = - \begin{vmatrix} 9 & 1 \\ 31 & 18 \end{vmatrix} = -(162 - 31) = -131$$

Hence, we have

$$(6.11) \qquad b = a_0 = a = -131$$

It is seen that the above procedure for the expansion of a is shorter than the direct use of the Laplace expansion on (6.6). It can be shown that to evaluate a determinant of order n from its algebraic definition requires $(n!)(n - 1)$ multiplications. Because of the excessive amount of labor involved in the use of the Laplace expansion, several alternative methods of expansion have been suggested.

7. THE METHOD OF PIVOTAL CONDENSATION

A very useful and efficient method for the expansion of numerical determinants will be given in this section. It appears to have been first used by

F. Chio,[2] and it has proved to be very useful for the expansion of large determinants.

Chio's method of pivotal condensation will be illustrated by applying it to the expansion of a fourth-order determinant. Before beginning the computation involved in Chio's method, the determinant under consideration is prepared by transforming it to one that has one element equal to unity. This may be done by the application of property 6 of Sec. 5. For example, if it is desired to transform a determinant whose elements are a_{rs} so that the new determinant has an element equal to unity in the third row and in the fourth column, it is necessary only to divide every element of the third row or the fourth column by a_{34} and place the number a_{34} as a factor outside of the transformed determinant. Let it be supposed that the original determinant has been transformed so that it has the form

(7.1)
$$
b = \begin{vmatrix} b_{11} & b_{12} & b_{13} & b_{14} \\ b_{21} & b_{22} & 1 & b_{24} \\ b_{31} & b_{32} & b_{33} & b_{34} \\ b_{41} & b_{42} & b_{43} & b_{44} \end{vmatrix} a_{23}
$$

To expand the determinant b, divide its various columns by b_{21}, b_{22}, 1, and b_{24} respectively; then, in view of the fact that the element b_{23} is unity, we have

(7.2)
$$
b = \begin{vmatrix} \dfrac{b_{11}}{b_{21}} & \dfrac{b_{12}}{b_{22}} & b_{13} & \dfrac{b_{14}}{b_{24}} \\ 1 & 1 & 1 & 1 \\ \dfrac{b_{31}}{b_{21}} & \dfrac{b_{32}}{b_{22}} & b_{33} & \dfrac{b_{34}}{b_{24}} \\ \dfrac{b_{41}}{b_{21}} & \dfrac{b_{42}}{b_{22}} & b_{43} & \dfrac{b_{44}}{b_{24}} \end{vmatrix} b_{21}b_{22}b_{24}
$$

The elements of the third column are now subtracted from those of the other columns and the following result is obtained:

(7.3)
$$
b = b_{21}b_{22}b_{24} \begin{vmatrix} \dfrac{b_{11}}{b_{21}} - b_{13} & \dfrac{b_{12}}{b_{22}} - b_{13} & b_{13} & \dfrac{b_{14}}{b_{24}} - b_{13} \\ 0 & 0 & 1 & 0 \\ \dfrac{b_{31}}{b_{21}} - b_{33} & \dfrac{b_{32}}{b_{22}} - b_{33} & b_{33} & \dfrac{b_{34}}{b_{24}} - b_{33} \\ \dfrac{b_{41}}{b_{21}} - b_{43} & \dfrac{b_{42}}{b_{22}} - b_{43} & b_{43} & \dfrac{b_{44}}{b_{24}} - b_{43} \end{vmatrix}
$$

This determinant is now expanded in terms of the second row to obtain

$$(7.4) \qquad b = -b_{21}b_{22}b_{24} \begin{vmatrix} \dfrac{b_{11}}{b_{21}} - b_{13} & \dfrac{b_{12}}{b_{22}} - b_{13} & \dfrac{b_{14}}{b_{24}} - b_{13} \\[2mm] \dfrac{b_{31}}{b_{21}} - b_{33} & \dfrac{b_{32}}{b_{22}} - b_{33} & \dfrac{b_{34}}{b_{24}} - b_{33} \\[2mm] \dfrac{b_{41}}{b_{21}} - b_{43} & \dfrac{b_{42}}{b_{22}} - b_{43} & \dfrac{b_{44}}{b_{24}} - b_{43} \end{vmatrix}$$

If the various columns of (7.4) are multiplied by the factors outside of the determinant, the following result is obtained:

$$(7.5) \qquad b = - \begin{vmatrix} (b_{11} - b_{21}b_{13}) & (b_{12} - b_{22}b_{13}) & (b_{14} - b_{24}b_{13}) \\ (b_{31} - b_{21}b_{33}) & (b_{32} - b_{22}b_{33}) & (b_{34} - b_{24}b_{33}) \\ (b_{41} - b_{21}b_{43}) & (b_{42} - b_{22}b_{43}) & (b_{44} - b_{24}b_{43}) \end{vmatrix}$$

By this process, the original fourth-order determinant is reduced to the third-order determinant (7.5).   This method of reducing a determinant of the nth order to one of the $(n - 1)$th order is called *pivotal condensation*.   It can be formulated in terms of the following rule:

In order to reduce the order of an nth-order determinant to one of the $(n - 1)$th order, the row and column that intersect the pivotal or unit element are deleted; then every element of the original determinant is diminished by the product of the elements which are located where the eliminated row and column are met by perpendiculars from the given element.   The resulting $(n - 1)$th-order determinant is then multiplied by $(-1)^{r+s}$, where r is the row and s is the column of the pivotal element.

By the application of this rule, the order of the original determinant is reduced by one unit.   Repeated application of the rule finally reduces the determinant to one of the second order, and its value can then be written down by inspection.

It may be mentioned that the evaluation of a large determinant of the nth order by the Laplace expansion requires, in general, $(n!)(n - 1)$ multiplications.   The number of multiplications required by the method of pivotal condensation is

$$\left(\frac{n^3}{3} + n^2 - \frac{n}{3} \right)$$

so that it is a much more efficient procedure than the classical Laplace expansion.

8. THE SOLUTION OF LINEAR EQUATIONS. CRAMER'S RULE

A great many problems that arise in applied mathematics require the solution of a system of linear algebraic equations of the form:

(8.1)

$$a_{11}x_1 + a_{12}x_2 + \cdots + a_{1n}x_n = k_1$$
$$a_{21}x_1 + a_{22}x_2 + \cdots + a_{2n}x_n = k_2$$
$$\cdot \qquad \cdot \qquad \cdots \qquad \cdot$$
$$a_{n1}x_1 + a_{n2}x_2 + \cdots + a_{nn}x_n = k_n$$

This set of equations can be solved in a very systematic manner by the use of determinants. In general, the coefficients a_{ij} are given numbers and the k_i quantities are also given, and it is required to determine the values of the unknowns x_i.

In order to show how these equations may be solved by the use of determinants, let D be the determinant of the coefficients a_{ij} so that

(8.2)

$$D = \begin{vmatrix} a_{11} & a_{12} & a_{13} & \cdots & a_{1n} \\ a_{21} & a_{22} & a_{23} & \cdots & a_{2n} \\ \cdot & \cdot & \cdot & \cdots & \cdot \\ a_{n1} & a_{n2} & a_{n3} & \cdots & a_{nn} \end{vmatrix}$$

Let the cofactor of the element a_{ij} be denoted by C_{ij} as in Sec. 3. Now, as mentioned in Sec. 4, the cofactors have the following important properties:

(8.3)

$$(a) \quad \sum_{j=1}^{n} a_{ij}C_{kj} = \begin{cases} D, & i = k \\ 0, & i \neq k \end{cases}$$

$$(b) \quad \sum_{i=1}^{n} a_{ij}C_{ik} = \begin{cases} D, & j = k \\ 0, & j \neq k \end{cases}$$

To show how these properties of the elements a_{ij} and their cofactors may be used to solve the linear system of Eqs. (8.1), consider first the second-order system:

(8.4)

$$a_{11}x_1 + a_{12}x_2 = k_1$$
$$a_{21}x_1 + a_{22}x_2 = k_2$$

Now let the first equation of (8.4) be multiplied by C_{11} and the second one by C_{21}, and let the results be added together. This procedure gives the following result:

(8.5) $\quad x_1(a_{11}C_{11} + a_{21}C_{21}) + x_2(a_{12}C_{11} + a_{22}C_{21}) = k_1C_{11} + k_2C_{21}$

Now, as a consequence of (8.3b), it can be seen that the coefficient of x_1 in

(8.5) is the determinant D of the coefficients a_{ij} of (8.4), whereas the coefficient of x_2 is equal to zero.   Hence, (8.5) may be written in the form:

$$(8.6) \qquad Dx_1 = k_1 C_{11} + k_2 C_{21} = \begin{vmatrix} k_1 & a_{12} \\ k_2 & a_{22} \end{vmatrix} = D_1$$

Hence,

$$(8.7) \qquad x_1 = \frac{D_1}{D}, \qquad D = \begin{vmatrix} a_{11} & a_{12} \\ a_{21} & a_{22} \end{vmatrix}$$

It can be seen that the determinant D_1 is obtained from the determinant D by replacing the first column of D by the quantities k_1 and k_2.

In the same manner, by multiplying the first equation of (8.4) by C_{12} and the second one by C_{22} and adding the result, it can be shown that

$$(8.8) \qquad x_2 = \frac{D_2}{D}, \quad \text{where} \quad D_2 = \begin{vmatrix} a_{11} & k_1 \\ a_{21} & k_2 \end{vmatrix}$$

The general system of Eqs. (8.1) may be treated in the same manner. For example, to obtain x_1, the first equation of (8.1) is multiplied by the co-factor C_{11}, the second one by C_{21}, the rth one by C_{r1}, etc., and the results are added.   Then, as a consequence of (8.3b), we obtain

$$(8.9) \qquad x_1 = \frac{D_1}{D}$$

In this case D_1 is the determinant formed from D by replacing the *first* column of elements of D by $(k_1, k_2, k_3, \ldots, k_n)$.   The unknown x_r can be determined by multiplying the Eqs. (8.1) by $C_{1r}, C_{2r}, C_{3r}, \ldots, C_{nr}$ and adding the results.   Then, by the use of (8.3b), the following result is obtained:

$$(8.10) \qquad x_r = \frac{D_r}{D}, \quad r = 1, 2, 3, \ldots, n \qquad \text{(Cramer's rule)}$$

where D_r is the determinant formed by replacing the elements $a_{1r}, a_{2r}, a_{3r}, \ldots, a_{nr}$ of the rth column of D by $(k_1, k_2, k_3, \ldots, k_n)$ respectively.

From (8.10) it can be seen that if the determinant of the coefficients of the system of equations D does not vanish, this equation gives the complete solution to the problem of solving the system (8.1).   However, the use of (8.10) is not practical for the solution of more than three or four simultaneous equations.

The reason for this lies in the fact that to evaluate a determinant of order n by the Laplace expansion requires $(n!)(n-1)$ multiplications.   It therefore follows that to evaluate x_r by (8.10) for a system of n equations would require $(n+1)(n!)(n-1)$ multiplications and n divisions.   More efficient methods for the solution of systems of equations will be discussed in the next chapter.

9. MULTIPLICATION AND DIFFERENTIATION OF DETERMINANTS

If A and B are determinants of order n, the *product*,

$$(9.1) \qquad C = AB$$

is a determinant of the same order. The elements of C are given by

$$(9.2) \qquad C_{ij} = \sum_{k=1}^{n} A_{ik} B_{kj}$$

If A and B are the two second-order determinants,

$$(9.3) \qquad A = \begin{vmatrix} A_{11} & A_{12} \\ A_{21} & A_{22} \end{vmatrix}, \qquad B = \begin{vmatrix} B_{11} & B_{12} \\ B_{21} & B_{22} \end{vmatrix}$$

then by (9.2) C has the following form:

$$(9.4) \qquad C = \begin{vmatrix} (A_{11}B_{11} + A_{12}B_{21}) & (A_{11}B_{12} + A_{12}B_{22}) \\ (A_{21}B_{11} + A_{22}B_{21}) & (A_{21}B_{12} + A_{22}B_{22}) \end{vmatrix}$$

It is easy to show that, by the use of the properties of determinants of Sec. 5, C can be expanded into the form:

$$(9.5) \qquad C = (A_{11}A_{22} - A_{21}A_{12})(B_{11}B_{22} - B_{21}B_{12}) = AB$$

The Derivative of a Determinant

If the determinant

$$(9.6) \qquad a = \begin{vmatrix} a_{11} & a_{12} & \cdots & a_{1n} \\ a_{21} & a_{22} & \cdots & a_{2n} \\ \cdot & \cdot & \cdots & \cdot \\ a_{n1} & a_{n2} & \cdots & a_{nn} \end{vmatrix}$$

is given, then it can be seen that as a consequence of the Laplace expansion of a given by (4.5), the partial derivative of a determinant with respect to an element equals the cofactor of that element. That is,

$$(9.7) \qquad \frac{\partial a}{\partial a_{ik}} = C_{ik}$$

PROBLEMS

1. Show that

$$\begin{vmatrix} 7 & 2 & 4 \\ 3 & -4 & 5 \\ 1 & 3 & -2 \end{vmatrix} = 25$$

2. Expand the following determinant by the method of pivotal condensation of Sec. 7.

$$D = \begin{vmatrix} 2 & 6 & -2 & 4 \\ -1 & -2 & 1 & 0 \\ 7 & 13 & 5 & 9 \\ 4 & 8 & -6 & 11 \end{vmatrix} = 308$$

3. Solve the following system of linear equations:

$$x + y + z = 2$$
$$2x - y - z = 1$$
$$x + 2y - z = -3, \qquad\qquad Ans.\ x = 1,\ y = -1,\ z = 2.$$

4. Show that

$$D = \begin{vmatrix} a & 1 & 1 & 1 \\ 1 & a & 1 & 1 \\ 1 & 1 & a & 1 \\ 1 & 1 & 1 & a \end{vmatrix} = (a - 1)^3(a + 3)$$

5. Show that

$$D = \begin{vmatrix} 1 & x & x^2 \\ 1 & y & y^2 \\ 1 & z & z^2 \end{vmatrix} = (x - y)(y - z)(z - x)$$

without expanding the determinant.

6. If the vertices of a triangle have the rectangular coordinates (x_1, y_1), (x_2, y_2), (x_3, y_3), show that the area of this triangle may be expressed by the following determinant:

$$A = \frac{1}{2} \begin{vmatrix} 1 & x_1 & y_1 \\ 1 & x_2 & y_2 \\ 1 & x_3 & y_3 \end{vmatrix}$$

7. As a consequence of the result of Problem 6, show that the equation of the straight line $ax + by + c = 0$ that passes through the points (x_1, y_1) and (x_2, y_2) can be written in the form

$$\begin{vmatrix} x & y & 1 \\ x_1 & y_1 & 1 \\ x_2 & y_2 & 1 \end{vmatrix} = 0$$

8. Given the two homogeneous linear equations,

$$a_{11}x_1 + a_{12}x_2 = 0$$
$$a_{21}x_1 + a_{22}x_2 = 0, \qquad D = \begin{vmatrix} a_{11} & a_{12} \\ a_{21} & a_{22} \end{vmatrix}$$

show by the method of Sec. 8 that $Dx_1 = 0$, $Dx_2 = 0$, and that, therefore, for a non-trivial solution $x_1 \neq 0$, $x_2 \neq 0$, the determinant of the coefficients D must vanish. Show that if $D = 0$ the *ratio* of x_1 to x_2 is given by

$$\frac{x_1}{x_2} = -\frac{a_{12}}{a_{11}} = -\frac{a_{22}}{a_{21}}$$

9. Show that, in the cases of the n homogeneous linear equations in n unknowns,

$$
\begin{array}{c}
a_{11}x_1 + a_{12}x_2 + \cdots + a_{1n}x_n = 0 \\
\cdot \qquad \cdot \qquad \cdots \qquad \cdot \qquad \cdot \\
a_{n1}x_1 + a_{n2}x_2 + \cdots + a_{nn}x_n = 0,
\end{array}
\qquad D = |a_{ij}|
$$

a necessary and sufficient condition for this system of equations to have a solution other than the trivial solution, $x_i = 0$, is that the determinant of the coefficients D must vanish.

REFERENCES

1. Aitken, A. C., *Determinants and Matrices*. New York: Interscience Publishers, Inc., 1948. (An excellent rigorous exposition of the theory of determinants from the point of view of pure mathematics.)

2. Chio, F., *Mémoire sur les fonctions connues sous le nom de résultantes ou de déterminants*. Turin: 1853, p. 11.

3. Crandall, S. H., *Engineering Analysis*. New York: McGraw-Hill Book Co., Inc., 1956. (A good exposition of modern efficient methods for the numerical evaluation of determinants.)

4. Faddeeva, V. N., *Computational Methods of Linear Algebra*. New York: Dover Publications, Inc., 1959. (This monograph contains a great deal of valuable information for the numerical evaluation of determinants and the solution of systems of linear algebraic equations.)

5. Muir, T., *The Theory of Determinants in the Historical Order of Development*. London: 1920, Vols. 1–4. (An exhaustive exposition of the theory of determinants and the historical development of the subject.)

2 THE FUNDAMENTALS OF MATRIX ALGEBRA

1. INTRODUCTION

In this chapter the basic definitions and operations of matrix algebra are given. It will be found that the introduction of matrices and matrix notation enables one to write many formulas more compactly and in a more suggestive manner. Matrix algebra has been called by some "the arithmetic of higher mathematics." The use of matrices introduces a well-designed notation that enables the underlying essence of the mathematics to be expressed without being obscured. Since matrix notation and matrix algebra was developed primarily to express linear transformations in a concise and lucid manner, it is natural that it should be employed in the formulation and the solution of linear problems.

2. DEFINITION OF A MATRIX

A matrix of order m by n is a rectangular array of mn elements having m rows and n columns. A matrix is usually denoted in the following manner:

$$(2.1) \qquad [a] = \begin{bmatrix} a_{11} & a_{12} & a_{13} & \cdots & a_{1n} \\ a_{21} & a_{22} & a_{23} & \cdots & a_{2n} \\ \cdot & \cdot & \cdot & \cdots & \cdot \\ a_{m1} & a_{m2} & a_{m3} & \cdots & a_{mn} \end{bmatrix}$$

The elements a_{ij} of the matrix $[a]$ may be real or complex numbers or functions of certain variables. A matrix such as the one given above is said to be of order (m, n). It will be noted by examining (2.1) that the element a_{rs} lies in the rth row and the sth column.

(a) Square Matrix

If in (2.1) $n = m$ so that the number of rows equals the number of columns, then the matrix is said to be a *square matrix* of order (n, n) or a square matrix of the nth order.　The determinant formed from the elements of a square matrix is called the determinant of the matrix.　The diagonal of the square matrix that contains the elements $a_{11}, a_{22}, a_{33}, \ldots, a_{nn}$ is called the *principal diagonal* of the square matrix.

(b) Transposition of Matrices

The accented matrix $[a]' = [a_{ji}]$ is obtained by a complete interchange of the rows and columns of the matrix $[a] = [a_{ij}]$ and is called the *transposed matrix of* $[a]$.　The ith row of $[a]$ is identical with the ith column of $[a]'$, etc.

3. PRINCIPAL TYPES OF MATRICES

Besides the general rectangular matrix (2.1) and the square matrix discussed above, the following principal types of matrices occur in matrix algebra:

(a) Column Vector

A set of m elements arranged in a column is a matrix of order $(m, 1)$ and is called a *column matrix* or a *column vector*.　A column vector will be denoted by a parenthesis and, to save space, it will be printed horizontally and not vertically in the following manner:

$$(3.1) \qquad (b) = (b_1 \quad b_2 \quad b_3 \quad \ldots \quad b_m), \qquad \text{(a column)}$$

(b) Row Vector

A set of n elements arranged in a row is a matrix of order $(1, n)$.　Such a matrix is called a *row matrix, line matrix*, or *row vector*.　A row vector will be denoted in the following manner:

$$(3.2) \qquad [c] = [c_1 \quad c_2 \quad c_3 \quad \ldots \quad c_n]$$

(c) A Scalar

A matrix of order $(1, 1)$ is a single element or an ordinary number.　In matrix algebra a single number is called a *scalar* to distinguish it from an array of numbers or a matrix.

(d) A Diagonal Matrix

A square matrix is said to be a *diagonal matrix* if the principal elements have the property that they are the only ones that are not zero, so that $a_{ij} = 0$, if $i \neq j$ where a_{ij} are the elements of the square matrix.

(e) *The Unit Matrix*

The unit matrix of the nth order is an nth-order square matrix whose principal diagonal elements are all equal to unity and whose other elements are equal to zero.   The unit matrix of the nth order will be denoted by U_n. For example, the third-order unit matrix is

$$(3.3) \qquad\qquad U_3 = \begin{bmatrix} 1 & 0 & 0 \\ 0 & 1 & 0 \\ 0 & 0 & 1 \end{bmatrix}$$

(f) *The Null or Zero Matrix*

A matrix of order (m, n) that has *all* of its elements equal to zero is called a zero matrix of order (m, n).

(g) *A Symmetric Matrix*

A square matrix whose elements a_{ij} are symmetric about its principal diagonal so that $a_{ij} = a_{ji}$ is said to be a *symmetric matrix*.   From this it can be seen that a symmetric matrix $[a]$ has the property that $[a]' = [a]$.

(h) *Skew-Symmetric Matrix*

If a square matrix $[a]$ has the property that $a_{ij} = -a_{ji}$ so that $[a]' = -[a]$, then $[a]$ is said to be skew symmetric.

4. EQUALITY OF MATRICES, ADDITION AND SUBTRACTION

From the above definitions it is apparent that a matrix is a mathematical entity that is entirely different from a determinant.   As was explained in Chapter 1, a determinant is a symbolic representation of a certain homogeneous polynomial formed from its elements.   A matrix, on the other hand, is merely a square or rectangular array of quantities.   Now, by defining certain rules of operation that prescribe the manner in which these arrays are to be manipulated, a certain algebra may be developed which has a formal similarity to ordinary algebra but which involves certain operations that are performed on the elements of the matrices.   It will be seen in the course of the development of matrix algebra that the fundamental rules of this algebra have been chosen in such a manner that operations involving linear transformations may be performed simply and directly.

(a) *Equality of Matrices*

The concept of equality is of fundamental importance in ordinary algebra and is likewise of fundamental importance in matrix algebra.   In matrix algebra two matrices $[a]$ and $[b]$ of the *same order* are defined to be equal if and only if their corresponding elements are identical; that is, by definition we have

(4.1) $$[a] = [b]$$

provided that $[a]$ and $[b]$ are of the same order and

(4.2) $$a_{ij} = b_{ij}, \qquad \text{for all } i \text{ and } j$$

(b) *Addition and Subtraction*

If $[a]$ and $[b]$ are matrices of the *same order*, then the sum $[a] + [b]$ is defined to be a matrix $[c]$ whose typical element c_{ij} is given by $c_{ij} = a_{ij} + b_{ij}$. In other words, by definition we have

(4.3) $$[c] = [a] + [b]$$

provided that

(4.4) $$c_{ij} = a_{ij} + b_{ij}, \qquad \text{for all } i \text{ and } j$$

Subtraction

In a similar manner, if $[a]$ and $[b]$ are matrices of the same order, then the difference $[a] - [b]$ is defined to be another matrix $[d]$ of the same order as $[a]$ and $[b]$, given by

(4.5) $$[d] = [a] - [b], \quad \text{where} \quad d_{ij} = a_{ij} - b_{ij}$$

From the above definitions it can be shown that the following operations are valid:

(4.6) $$[a] + [b] = [b] + [a]$$

(4.7) $$[a] + ([b] + [c]) = ([a] + [b]) + [c]$$

5. MULTIPLICATION OF MATRICES

(a) *Multiplication of a Matrix by a Scalar*

By definition, the multiplication of a matrix $[a]$ by an ordinary number or scalar k is effected by multiplying *each element* of $[a]$ by the number k and obtaining a new matrix whose elements are ka_{ij}. That is, by definition,

(5.1) $$[b] = k[a], \quad \text{where} \quad b_{ij} = ka_{ij}$$

For example,

(5.2) $$2\begin{bmatrix} 1 & 5 \\ 4 & 2 \end{bmatrix} = \begin{bmatrix} 2 & 10 \\ 8 & 4 \end{bmatrix}$$

(b) Multiplication of a Matrix by Another Matrix

The definition of the operation of a matrix by another matrix has been chosen in order to facilitate operations involving linear transformations by the use of matrix algebra.   The rule of multiplication bears some resemblance to that of multiplication of determinants discussed in Sec. 9 of Chapter 1.

The rule of multiplication is such that two matrices can be multiplied together only when the number of *columns* of the first is equal to the number of *rows* of the second.   That is, if $[a]$ is a matrix of order (m, n) and $[b]$ is a matrix of order (p, q), the product $[a][b]$ is not defined unless $n = p$.   If $n = p$, the matrices $[a]$ and $[b]$ are said to be *conformable*.   In matrix algebra *only* conformable matrices may be multiplied together.

Definition of Matrix Multiplication

The product of a matrix $[a]$ of order (m, p) by a matrix $[b]$ of order (p, n) is defined to be the matrix $[c]$ given by

(5.3) $$[c] = [a][b] = [c_{ij}]$$

where

(5.4) $$c_{ij} = \sum_{k=1}^{k=p} a_{ik}b_{kj}$$

It can be seen that $[c]$ is a matrix of order (m, n).   The fact that a matrix of order (m, p), when multiplied by a matrix of order (p, n), results in a matrix of order (m, n) may be expressed symbolically in the following manner:

(5.5) $$(m, p)(p, n) = (m, n)$$

This symbolic equation is useful in order to determine the order of the resulting matrix when several matrices are multiplied together.

As an example of the definition of multiplication (5.4), let

(5.6) $$[a] = \begin{bmatrix} a_{11} & a_{12} & a_{13} \\ a_{21} & a_{22} & a_{23} \\ a_{31} & a_{32} & a_{33} \end{bmatrix}, \qquad [b] = \begin{bmatrix} b_{11} & b_{12} \\ b_{21} & b_{22} \\ b_{31} & b_{32} \end{bmatrix}$$

In this case we have matrices of orders $(3, 3)(3, 2)$.   Accordingly, by (5.5) the product $[a][b]$ is a matrix of order $(3, 2)$.

In this case the elements of the product matrix $[c]$ are given by (5.4) in the form:

(5.7) $$c_{ij} = a_{i1}b_{1j} + a_{i2}b_{2j} + a_{i3}b_{3j}$$

The elements (5.7) are now arranged in the rectangular array,

(5.8) $$[c] = \begin{bmatrix} (a_{11}b_{11} + a_{12}b_{21} + a_{13}b_{31}) & (a_{11}b_{12} + a_{12}b_{22} + a_{13}b_{32}) \\ (a_{21}b_{11} + a_{22}b_{21} + a_{23}b_{31}) & (a_{21}b_{12} + a_{22}b_{22} + a_{23}b_{32}) \\ (a_{31}b_{11} + a_{32}b_{21} + a_{33}b_{31}) & (a_{31}b_{12} + a_{32}b_{22} + a_{33}b_{32}) \end{bmatrix}$$

This is the product matrix $[c] = [a][b]$. It may be seen that the result (5.8) may be obtained by taking the sum of continued products of the *rows* of $[a]$ times the corresponding *columns* of $[b]$.

It may be noted that if the matrices $[a]$ and $[b]$ are *square* and of order n, then the *determinant* of the matrix $[c]$ is the product of the *determinant* of $[a]$ and the *determinant* of $[b]$ so that

(5.9) $$|c| = |a| \, |b|$$

This follows from the definition of matrix multiplication and the rule for the multiplication of determinants given in Sec. 9, Chapter 1.

Properties of Matrix Multiplication

In general matrix multiplication is not commutative; that is, in general,

(5.10) $$[a][b] \neq [b][a]$$

This can be seen directly from the definition (5.4). The matrices (5.6) are not conformable in the order $[b][a]$ and cannot be multiplied in this order.

In matrix algebra it is necessary to distinguish between *premultiplication*, as when $[b]$ is premultiplied by $[a]$ to give the product $[a][b]$, and *postmultiplication*, as when $[b]$ is postmultiplied by $[a]$ to give the product $[b][a]$. If we have the equality,

(5.11) $$[a][b] = [b][a]$$

the matrices $[a]$ and $[b]$ are said to *commute* or to be *permutable*. The unit matrix $[U]$, it may be noted, commutes with any square matrix of the same order. That is,

(5.12) $$[U][a] = [a][U]$$

provided $[a]$ and $[U]$ are of the same order.

Continued Products of Matrices

Except for the noncommutative law, all the ordinary laws of algebra apply to the multiplication of matrices. Of particular importance is the associative law of continued products,

(5.13) $$([a][b][c]) = [a]([b][c]) = [d]$$

which allows one to dispense with parentheses and to write $[a][b][c]$ without ambiguity, since the double summation,

(5.14) $$d_{ij} = \sum_{k} \sum_{l} a_{ik} b_{kl} c_{lj}$$

can be carried out in either of the orders indicated.

However, it must be noted that the product of a chain of matrices will have meaning only if the adjacent matrices of the chain are conformable.

Positive Powers of a Square Matrix

If a square matrix $[a]$ is multiplied by itself n times, the resultant matrix is defined as $[a]^n$.   That is,

(5.15) $$[a]^n = [a][a][a]\ldots[a], \qquad \text{to } n \text{ factors}$$

6. MATRIX DIVISION, THE INVERSE MATRIX

In ordinary algebra, if the product of two quantities x and a is such that

(6.1) $$ax = 1$$

then x is said to be the *reciprocal* of a, and it is written in the following manner:

(6.2) $$x = \frac{1}{a} = a^{-1}$$

It has been mentioned that, in matrix algebra, the unit matrix $[U]$ behaves in a manner similar to unity in ordinary algebra.   That is, if $[a]$ is an nth-order square matrix and $[U]$ is the nth-order unit matrix, we have

(6.3) $$[U][a] = [a][U] = [a]$$

This is analogous to the relation $a \cdot 1 = 1 \cdot a = a$ in ordinary algebra.

The Inverse Matrix

Let $[a]$ be a *given* square matrix of the nth order and $[U]$ be the unit matrix of the nth order; then if a square matrix $[x]$ can be determined so that

(6.4) $$[a][x] = [U]$$

then $[x]$ is said to be the *reciprocal* or the *inverse* of $[a]$, and it is written in the form

(6.5) $$[x] = [a]^{-1}$$

It can be seen that Eqs. (6.4) and (6.5) are the matrix analogues of (6.1) and (6.2) of ordinary algebra.

Before discussing the general case, in which the given matrix $[a]$ is a square matrix of the nth order, let the case in which $[a]$ is a square matrix of the second order be considered.   In this case, the matrices $[x]$ and $[U]$ in (6.4) are also matrices of the second order, and Eq. (6.4) may be written in the following expanded form:

(6.6) $$\begin{bmatrix} a_{11} & a_{12} \\ a_{21} & a_{22} \end{bmatrix} \begin{bmatrix} x_{11} & x_{12} \\ x_{21} & x_{22} \end{bmatrix} = \begin{bmatrix} 1 & 0 \\ 0 & 1 \end{bmatrix}$$

In the above equation the a_{ij} elements are known, and it is required to determine the x_{ij} elements. By carrying out the indicated multiplication, Eq. (6.6) may be expanded into the four scalar equations:

(6.7) (a)
$$a_{11}x_{11} + a_{12}x_{21} = 1$$
$$a_{21}x_{11} + a_{22}x_{21} = 0,$$

(b)
$$a_{11}x_{12} + a_{12}x_{22} = 0$$
$$a_{21}x_{12} + a_{22}x_{22} = 1$$

If the determinant,

(6.8)
$$|a| \neq 0, \qquad |a| = \det [a]$$

it is possible to solve the set of equations (a) and (b) of (6.7) for the four unknowns x_{11}, x_{21}, x_{12}, and x_{22} by the use of Cramer's rule. This procedure gives the following expressions for the quantities x_{ij}:

(6.9)
$$x_{11} = \frac{C_{11}}{|a|}, \qquad x_{12} = \frac{C_{21}}{|a|}$$
$$x_{21} = \frac{C_{12}}{|a|}, \qquad x_{22} = \frac{C_{22}}{|a|}$$

The quantities C_{ij} are the cofactors of the elements a_{ij} in the determinant $|a|$. If these values of the elements x_{ij} are substituted into the matrix $[x]$, the following result is obtained:

(6.10)
$$[x] = \frac{1}{|a|} \begin{bmatrix} C_{11} & C_{21} \\ C_{12} & C_{22} \end{bmatrix} = [a]^{-1}$$

Since in this case $C_{11} = a_{22}$, $C_{22} = a_{11}$, $C_{21} = -a_{12}$, $C_{12} = -a_{21}$, the inverse matrix of $[a]$ may be written in terms of the elements of $[a]$ in the form

(6.11)
$$[a]^{-1} = [x] = \begin{bmatrix} a_{22} & -a_{12} \\ -a_{21} & a_{11} \end{bmatrix} \frac{1}{|a|}$$

The Adjoint Matrix of the Matrix [a]

The square matrix of the cofactors C_{ji} in (6.10) is called the *adjoint matrix* of the matrix $[a]$. The following notation is usually employed to denote the adjoint matrix:

(6.12)
$$\text{adj } [a] = \begin{bmatrix} C_{11} & C_{21} \\ C_{12} & C_{22} \end{bmatrix}, \qquad C_{ij} = \text{cofactor of } a_{ij}$$

As a consequence of the properties of the cofactors C_{ij} given by Eqs. (8.3) of Chapter 1, it can be shown that the adjoint of a square matrix $[a]$ has the property that

(6.13)
$$[a] \text{ adj } [a] = \text{adj } [a][a] = |a|[U]$$

where $[U]$ is the unit matrix of the same order as $[a]$. The equation is valid whether the determinant $|a|$ is zero or not.   If $|a| \neq 0$, it can be seen by substituting (6.12) into (6.10) that the inverse matrix of $[a]$ may be expressed in the form

(6.14) $$[a]^{-1} = \frac{\text{adj } [a]}{|a|}$$

Singular and Nonsingular Matrices

By definition, if the determinant of a square matrix $[a]$ *vanishes* so that $|a| = 0$, $[a]$ is said to be a *singular matrix*.

If the determinant of the square matrix $[a]$ *does not vanish*, then $|a| \neq 0$, and the matrix $[a]$ is said to be *nonsingular*.

From the discussion given above, it is seen that only nonsingular matrices possess an inverse or reciprocal matrix $[a]^{-1}$, given by (6.14).

Although the discussion of the calculation of the inverse of a matrix has been given above only for the second-order square matrix, it is easy to generalize the procedure for the case of the nth-order square matrix.   If $[a]$ is a square matrix of the nth order, then in order to find its inverse, we attempt to find an nth-order square matrix $[x]$ so that $[a][x] = [U]$, where $[U]$ is the nth-order unit matrix.   The determination of the unknown elements x_{ij} proceeds along the same lines as discussed above for the second-order case. The final result can be expressed in the form

(6.15) $$[x] = [a]^{-1} = \frac{\text{adj } [a]}{|a|}$$

The adjoint matrix of $[a]$ is given in the general nth-order case by the equation

(6.16) $$\text{adj } [a] = [C_{ji}]$$

where C_{ij} is the cofactor of the element a_{ij} in the determinant $|a|$ of the matrix $[a]$.   It should be noticed that in (6.16) the order of the letters i and j has been reversed.   In order to compute the adjoint of $[a]$ by means of its definition (6.16), it is usually convenient first to take the transpose of $[a]$ and then to replace every element of the transpose $[a]'$ by its cofactor.

As an illustration, let it be required to obtain the adjoint matrix of the third-order matrix

(6.17) $$[a] = \begin{bmatrix} a_{11} & a_{12} & a_{13} \\ a_{21} & a_{22} & a_{23} \\ a_{31} & a_{32} & a_{33} \end{bmatrix}$$

The first step in the computation of adj $[a]$ is to take the transpose of $[a]$ and thus obtain

(6.18) $$[a]' = \begin{bmatrix} a_{11} & a_{21} & a_{31} \\ a_{12} & a_{22} & a_{32} \\ a_{13} & a_{23} & a_{33} \end{bmatrix}$$

The elements of $[a]'$ are now replaced by their corresponding cofactors to obtain the adjoint matrix of $[a]$ in the form

$$(6.19) \quad \text{adj } [a] = \begin{bmatrix} (a_{22}a_{33}-a_{23}a_{32}) & (a_{13}a_{32}-a_{12}a_{33}) & (a_{12}a_{23}-a_{13}a_{22}) \\ (a_{23}a_{31}-a_{21}a_{33}) & (a_{11}a_{33}-a_{13}a_{31}) & (a_{13}a_{21}-a_{11}a_{23}) \\ (a_{21}a_{32}-a_{22}a_{31}) & (a_{12}a_{31}-a_{11}a_{32}) & (a_{11}a_{22}-a_{12}a_{21}) \end{bmatrix}$$

The inverse of $[a]$ is then obtained by dividing its adjoint matrix by the determinant of its elements $|a|$.

As a numerical example of the above general method for the determination of the inverse of a given square matrix, let it be required to determine the inverse of the following matrix:

$$(6.20) \qquad [a] = \begin{bmatrix} 2 & 2 & 0 \\ 0 & 3 & 1 \\ 1 & 0 & 1 \end{bmatrix}$$

The transposed matrix of $[a]$ is

$$(6.21) \qquad [a]' = \begin{bmatrix} 2 & 0 & 1 \\ 2 & 3 & 0 \\ 0 & 1 & 1 \end{bmatrix}$$

The adjoint matrix of $[a]$ is now obtained by replacing each element of $[a]'$ by its corresponding cofactor. If this is done, the following matrix is obtained:

$$(6.22) \qquad \text{adj } [a] = \begin{bmatrix} 3 & -2 & 2 \\ 1 & 2 & -2 \\ -3 & 2 & 6 \end{bmatrix}$$

The determinant of $[a]$ is easily computed by applying the Laplace expansion to the first column. It is

$$(6.23) \qquad |a| = 8$$

The inverse of $[a]$ is now obtained by dividing the adjoint matrix of $[a]$ by the determinant $|a|$; it is

$$(6.24) \qquad [a]^{-1} = \frac{1}{8} \begin{bmatrix} 3 & -2 & 2 \\ 1 & 2 & -2 \\ -3 & 2 & 6 \end{bmatrix}$$

Although Eq. (6.15) is formally complete for the determination of $[a]^{-1}$, it is not useful for the practical computation involved in the inversion of large matrices. The reason for this lies in the fact that to evaluate a determinant of order n from its algebraic definition requires $(n!)(n-1)$ multiplications.

The computation of the adjoint matrix requires the computation of n^2 determinants of the $(n-1)$th order, or $n^2(n-1)!(n-2)$ multiplications.

It is thus seen that the inversion of an nth-order matrix by the use of (6.15) would require $(n!)(n^2 - n - 1)$ multiplications and n^2 divisions. This is a prohibitive amount of labor. More efficient methods for the inversion of matrices will be discussed in a later section.

7. MATRIX DIVISION

The concept of matrix inversion leads to certain operations involving matrices that are similar in a formal manner to those of division in ordinary algebra.

For example, if one has the equation $ab = c$ in ordinary algebra, one can multiply both sides of this equation by a^{-1} and obtain $b = a^{-1}c = c/a$.

In matrix algebra, if one has the matrix product

$$(7.1) \qquad\qquad [a][b] = [c]$$

and if $[a]$ is a *nonsingular* matrix so that its inverse $[a]^{-1}$ exists, then it is possible to solve for the matrix $[b]$ by premultiplying both sides of (7.1) by $[a]^{-1}$ and thus obtaining

$$(7.2) \qquad\qquad [b] = [a]^{-1}[c]$$

It must be noted that there exist some differences between matrix algebra and ordinary algebra. For example, in ordinary algebra the necessary and sufficient condition that $ab = 0$ is that either $a = 0$ or $b = 0$. However, in matrix algebra, if we have

$$(7.3) \qquad\qquad [a][b] = [0]$$

it is *sufficient* that $[a] = [0]$ or $[b] = [0]$, but not *necessary*. For example,

$$(7.4) \qquad \begin{bmatrix} 1 & 0 \\ 0 & 0 \\ 1 & 0 \end{bmatrix} \begin{bmatrix} 0 & 0 & 0 \\ 1 & 1 & 0 \end{bmatrix} = \begin{bmatrix} 0 & 0 & 0 \\ 0 & 0 & 0 \\ 0 & 0 & 0 \end{bmatrix}$$

As another example, in ordinary algebra, if $ab = ad$, then $b = d$, provided that $a \neq 0$. However, in matrix algebra, if

$$(7.5) \qquad\qquad [a][b] = [a][d], \quad \text{and} \quad [a] \neq [0]$$

one *cannot* say that in general $[b] = [d]$. For example, consider the equation

$$(7.6) \qquad \begin{bmatrix} 1 & 0 & 0 \\ 0 & 1 & 0 \end{bmatrix} \begin{bmatrix} 1 & 0 \\ 0 & 1 \\ 1 & 0 \end{bmatrix} = \begin{bmatrix} 1 & 0 & 0 \\ 0 & 1 & 0 \end{bmatrix} \begin{bmatrix} 1 & 0 \\ 0 & 1 \\ 0 & 0 \end{bmatrix} = \begin{bmatrix} 1 & 0 \\ 0 & 1 \end{bmatrix}$$

However,

(7.7)
$$\begin{bmatrix} 1 & 0 \\ 0 & 1 \\ 1 & 0 \end{bmatrix} \neq \begin{bmatrix} 1 & 0 \\ 0 & 1 \\ 0 & 0 \end{bmatrix}$$

In (7.5) if $[a]$ is a *nonsingular* matrix so that its determinant $|a| \neq 0$, then it is possible to premultiply both members of (7.5) by $[a]^{-1}$ and thus obtain

(7.8) $[b] = [d]$

If we have the equation

(7.9) $[a][b] = [c][d]$

and $[a]$ is a *nonsingular* matrix, so that its inverse $[a]^{-1}$ exists, then it is possible to premultiply both members of (7.9) by $[a]^{-1}$ and thus obtain

(7.10) $[b] = [a]^{-1}[c][d]$

Negative Powers of a Matrix

If $[a]$ is a nonsingular matrix so that its inverse $[a]^{-1}$ exists, then negative powers of $[a]$ are defined by raising the inverse matrix of $[a]$, $[a]^{-1}$ to positive powers. That is, by definition,

(7.11) $[a]^{-n} = ([a]^{-1})^n, \qquad n = 0, 1, 2, 3, \ldots$

8. THE REVERSAL LAW IN TRANSPOSED AND RECIPROCAL PRODUCTS

One of the fundamental consequences of the non-commutative law of matrix multiplication is the *reversal law* exemplified in transposing or reciprocating a continued product of matrices.

(a) *Transposition*

Let $[a]$ be a matrix of order (p, n), that is, one having p rows and n columns, and let $[b]$ be an (m, p) matrix. It can be seen that the matrices $[b]$ and $[a]$ are conformable in the order $[b][a]$, and the matrix

(8.1) $[c] = [b][a], \qquad c_{ij} = \sum_{r=1}^{p} b_{ir}a_{rj}, \qquad \begin{aligned} i &= 1, 2, \ldots, m \\ j &= 1, 2, \ldots, n \end{aligned}$

By the use of the symbolic equation (5.5), the order of $[c]$ may be determined by the symbolic equation (8.2):

(8.2) $(m, p)(p, n) = (m, n)$

It is thus evident that the matrix $[c]$ is a matrix of order (m, n) and has m rows and n columns.

When the matrices $[a]$ and $[b]$ are transposed, the matrices $[a]'$ and $[b]'$ are obtained. $[a]'$ is a matrix of order (n, p), and $[b]'$ is a matrix of order (p, m). $[a]'$ and $[b]'$ are conformable when they are multiplied in the order $[a]'[b]'$. The order of this product may be obtained by the symbolic equation

(8.3) $$(n, p)(p, m) = (n, m)$$

so that the product $[a]'[b]'$ is an (n, m) matrix. It may be readily seen that $[a]'[b]'$ is the transpose of $[c]$ given by (8.1), so

(8.4) $$[c]' = [a]'[b]'$$

The typical element of $[c]'$ is given by

(8.5) $$c_{ji} = \sum_{k=1}^{p} b_{jk}a_{ki} = \sum_{k=1}^{p} a_{ki}b_{jk} = \sum_{k=1}^{p} a'_{ik}b'_{kj}$$

where a'_{ik} is the element ik in $[a]'$, and b'_{kj} is the element kj in $[b]'$.

It follows from (8.1) and (8.4) that when a matrix product is transposed, the order of the matrices forming the product must be reversed. That is,

(8.6) $$([a][b])' = [b]'[a]'$$

Similarly,

(8.7) $$([a][b][c][d])' = [d]'[c]'[b]'[a]', \text{ etc.}$$

The relation (8.7) is called the *reversal law of transposed products* in the literature of matrix algebra.

(b) *Reciprocation*

Let is be supposed that in the equation

(8.8) $$[P] = [a][b][c]$$

the matrices are square matrices and that they are *nonsingular*. Let Eq. (8.8) be multiplied by $[P]^{-1}$, the inverse matrix of $[P]$. The result is

(8.9) $$[P]^{-1}[P] = [P]^{-1}[a][b][c] = [U]$$

where $[U]$ is the unit matrix of the same order as $[P]$. If we now postmultiply (8.9) by $[c]^{-1}$, the following equation is obtained:

(8.10) $$[P]^{-1}[a][b] = [c]^{-1}$$

This equation may now be postmultiplied by $[b]^{-1}$ and the resulting equation postmultiplied by $[a]^{-1}$; the final result of these operations is

(8.11) $$[P]^{-1} = ([a][b][c])^{-1} = [c]^{-1}[b]^{-1}[a]^{-1}$$

The relation (8.11) can be extended to the product of any number of matrices; it is called the reversal law of inverse products.

9. DIAGONAL MATRICES AND THEIR PROPERTIES

A square matrix of order n that has all its non-diagonal elements equal to zero is called a *diagonal matrix*. For example, a diagonal matrix of the third order, $[a]$, has the form

$$(9.1) \qquad [a] = \begin{bmatrix} a_{11} & 0 & 0 \\ 0 & a_{22} & 0 \\ 0 & 0 & a_{33} \end{bmatrix}$$

and can be defined by the equation

$$(9.2) \qquad [a] = [a_{ij}], \qquad a_{ij} = 0, \qquad i \neq j$$

As a consequence of the definition of the product of two matrices given by (5.4), the following properties of a diagonal matrix can be established:

(a) If $[a]$ is a diagonal matrix of order (m, m) and $[b]$ is any matrix of order (m, n) the product $[a][b]$ is obtained from $[b]$ by multiplying the *rows* of $[b]$ respectively by $a_{11}, a_{22}, \ldots, a_{mm}$. In particular, if (x) is a *column vector* $(x) = (x_1, x_2, \ldots, x_m)$, then

$$[a](x) = (a_{11}x_1, a_{22}x_2, \ldots, a_{mm}x_m)$$

(b) If $[a]$ is a diagonal matrix of order (m, n) and $[b]$ is a matrix of order (p, m), the product $[b][a]$ is obtained from $[b]$ by multiplying the *columns* of $[b]$ respectively by $a_{11}, a_{22}, \ldots, a_{mm}$. In particular, if $[u]$ is a row vector $[u] = [u_1 \quad u_2 \quad \ldots \quad u_m]$, the product $[u][a] = [u_1 a_{11} \quad u_2 a_{22} \quad \ldots \quad u_m a_{mm}]$.

(c) If $[a]$ and $[b]$ are diagonal matrices of the same order, they are commutative in multiplication with each other so that $[a][b] = [b][a]$.

10. PARTITIONED MATRICES AND PARTITIONED MULTIPLICATION

It is sometimes convenient for purposes of computation to extend the use of the fundamental laws of combinations of matrices to the case in which a matrix is considered to be constructed from elements that are submatrices of minor matrices of elements. As an example, consider the matrix $[a]$ of order $(3, 3)$:

$$(10.1) \qquad [a] = \begin{bmatrix} a_{11} & a_{12} & a_{13} \\ a_{21} & a_{22} & a_{23} \\ \hline a_{31} & a_{32} & a_{33} \end{bmatrix} = \begin{bmatrix} P & Q \\ R & S \end{bmatrix}$$

This matrix has been partitioned by the introduction of a vertical and a horizontal line into the four submatrices P, Q, R, and S, where

$$(10.2) \qquad \begin{array}{cc} P = \begin{bmatrix} a_{11} & a_{12} \\ a_{21} & a_{22} \end{bmatrix}, & Q = \begin{bmatrix} a_{13} \\ a_{23} \end{bmatrix}, \\ R = (a_{31} \quad a_{32}), & S = (a_{33}) \end{array}$$

In this case, the matrix $[a]$ has been partitioned in such a manner that the diagonal submatrices P and S are square, and the partitioning is diagonally symmetrical. Now, let $[b]$ be another square matrix of the third order that is similarly partitioned:

$$(10.3) \qquad [b] = \begin{bmatrix} b_{11} & b_{12} & | & b_{13} \\ b_{21} & b_{22} & | & b_{23} \\ ----&--&|&-- \\ b_{31} & b_{32} & | & b_{33} \end{bmatrix} = \begin{bmatrix} P_1 & Q_1 \\ R_1 & S_1 \end{bmatrix}$$

Now it can easily be seen that the sum $[c] = [a] + [b]$ may be expressed in terms of the above submatrices in the form

$$(10.4) \qquad [c] = [a] + [b] = \begin{bmatrix} (P + P_1) & (Q + Q_1) \\ (R + R_1) & (S + S_1) \end{bmatrix}$$

This indicates that when two matrices of the same order are partitioned similarly, their sum may be obtained by adding their various submatrices as if they were elements.

Multiplication in Terms of Submatrices

As a consequence of the fundamental rule for the multiplication of matrices, a rectangular matrix $[b]$ may be premultiplied by another rectangular matrix $[a]$, provided the two matrices are *conformable*; that is, the number of *rows* of $[b]$ is equal to the number of *columns* of $[a]$. Now, if $[a]$ and $[b]$ are both partitioned into submatrices such that the grouping of columns in $[a]$ agrees with the grouping of rows in $[b]$, it can be shown that the product $[a][b]$ may be obtained by treating the submatrices as ordinary elements and proceeding according to the multiplication rule.

In the case of the matrices $[a]$ and $[b]$ discussed above, the partitioning is such that the product $[d] = [a][b]$ may be carried out by treating the submatrices of (10.1) and (10.3) as if they were ordinary elements and thus obtaining

$$(10.5) \qquad [d] = [a][b] = \begin{bmatrix} (PP_1 + QR_1) & (PQ_1 + QS_1) \\ (RP_1 + SR_1) & (RQ_1 + SS_1) \end{bmatrix}$$

11. MATRICES OF SPECIAL TYPES

Several types of matrices that have unique properties or symmetry frequently arise in the application of matrix algebra to physical problems. A list of the more common special matrices will be given in this section for useful reference.

(a) *Conjugate Matrices*

In several applications of matrix algebra to physical problems, matrices arise whose elements are complex numbers so that they have the form:

(11.1) $[a] = [a_{rs}]$,   where $a_{rs} = p_{rs} + jq_{rs}$, $j = (-1)^{1/2}$

A matrix $[b]$ which has the same order as $[a]$ but whose elements are the complex conjugates of $[a]$ is called the *conjugate* of $[a]$. It is usually written in the form

(11.2) $[b] = [\bar{a}]$,   where $b_{rs} = p_{rs} - jq_{rs} = \bar{a}_{rs}$

(b) *The Associate of* $[a]$

The associate of a matrix $[a]$ is the transposed conjugate of $[a]$, so

(11.3)   associate of $[a] = [\bar{a}]'$

(c) *Symmetric Matrix*

If $[a] = [a]'$, $[a]$ is a symmetric matrix.

(d) *Involutory Matrix*

If $[a] = [a]^{-1}$, $[a]$ is involutory.

(e) *Real Matrix*

If $[a] = [\bar{a}]$, $[a]$ is a real matrix.

(f) *Orthogonal Matrix*

If $[a] = ([a]')^{-1}$, $[a]$ is an orthogonal matrix.

(g) *Hermitian Matrix*

If $[a] = [\bar{a}]'$, $[a]$ is a Hermitian matrix.

(h) *Unitary Matrix*

If $[a] = ([\bar{a}]')^{-1}$, $[a]$ is unitary.

(i) *Skew-Symmetric Matrix*

If $[a] = -[a]'$, $[a]$ is skew symmetric.

(j) *Pure Imaginary*

If $[a] = -[\bar{a}]$, $[a]$ is pure imaginary.

(k) *Skew-Hermitian*

If $[a] = -[\bar{a}]'$, $[a]$ is skew Hermitian.

12. THE SOLUTION OF n LINEAR EQUATIONS IN n UNKNOWNS

The formal solution of a set of n linear equations may be expressed most elegantly and concisely by the use of matrix notation and matrix algebra.

Consider the set of n equations in the unknowns $(x_1, x_2, \ldots, x_n)$:

$$\begin{aligned}
a_{11}x_1 + a_{12}x_2 + \cdots + a_{1n}x_n &= k_1 \\
a_{21}x_1 + a_{22}x_2 + \cdots + a_{2n}x_n &= k_2 \\
&\cdots \\
a_{n1}x_1 + a_{n2}x_2 + \cdots + a_{nn}x_n &= k_n
\end{aligned}$$

(12.1)

In this set of linear algebraic equations, the coefficients a_{ij} are supposed known and the right members $k_1, k_2, \ldots, k_n$ are known quantities. It is required to determine the unknowns x_i. It can easily be seen that by constructing the square matrix $[a_{ij}] = [a]$ and the column matrices $(x) = (x_i)$ and $(k) = (k_i)$, the set of Eqs. (12.1) may be concisely written as the *single* matrix equation

$$[a](x) = (k) \tag{12.2}$$

If the determinant of the matrix $[a]$ does not vanish, then $[a]$ is a *non-singular* matrix and its inverse is given by (6.14). The solution of (12.2) for (x) may be effected by premultiplication of both members of (12.2) by $[a]^{-1}$, the inverse of $[a]$. This operation results in the solution

$$(x) = [a]^{-1}(k) \tag{12.3}$$

The inverse matrix $[a]^{-1}$ may be expressed in the form

$$(x) = [a]^{-1}(k) = \frac{\text{adj } [a](k)}{|a|} = [C_{ji}]\frac{(k)}{|a|} \tag{12.4}$$

where C_{ji} is the cofactor of the element a_{ji} in the matrix $[a]$. As a consequence of the definition of the adjoint matrix of $[a]$, adj $[a]$, and the rule of matrix multiplication, it follows that

$$x_i = \frac{1}{|a|} (k_1 C_{1i} + k_2 C_{2i} + \cdots + k_n C_{ni}), \qquad i = 1, 2, 3, \ldots, n \tag{12.5}$$

This is an alternative way of expressing *Cramer's rule* of Sec. 8 of Chapter 1.

Homogeneous Linear Equations

The case in which the right members of the set of equations (12.1) are zero arises frequently. In this case (12.2) reduces to

$$[a](x) = (0) \tag{12.6}$$

where (0) is a column matrix of n zeros. This is the corresponding *homogeneous* equation of (12.2). The two most important cases that arise in the homogeneous equation are those for which $|a| \neq 0$ and the one in which $|a| = 0$. These cases will now be discussed.

(a) *The case* $|a| \neq 0$

In this case $[a]$ is a *nonsingular* matrix and has an inverse $[a]^{-1}$, so the solution of (12.6) in this case is

$$(12.7) \qquad\qquad (x) = [a]^{-1}(0) = (0)$$

so that the only solutions are the trivial ones $x_1 = x_2 = x_3 = \cdots = x_n = 0$.

(b) *The case* $|a| = 0$

In this case let it be supposed that the cofactor $C_{ik} \neq 0$ for at least one value of i and k.

As discussed in Sec. 8 of Chapter 4, the cofactors C_{ij} of the elements of the determinant $|a|$ satisfy the following relations:

$$(12.8) \qquad \sum_{i=1}^{n} a_{ik} C_{ik} = \sum_{i=1}^{n} a_{ki} C_{ki} = |a|, \qquad (k = 1, 2, \ldots, n)$$

$$(12.9) \qquad \sum_{i=1}^{n} a_{ik} C_{ij} = \sum_{i=1}^{n} a_{ki} C_{ji} = 0, \qquad j \neq k$$

Now consider the kth equation of the set of equations represented by (12.6):

$$(12.10) \qquad\qquad a_{k1}x_1 + a_{k2}x_2 + \cdots + a_{kn}x_n = 0$$

If

$$(12.11) \qquad x_1 = pC_{j1}, \; x_2 = pC_{j2}, \; x_3 = pC_{j3}, \ldots, x_n = pC_{jn}$$

where p is *any* constant, it follows from (12.9) that (12.10) is satisfied. Even if $j = k$, (12.11) is still a solution, for then (12.10) becomes identical with (12.8), but by hypothesis $|a| = 0$.

It is thus seen that when $[a]$ is singular, the homogeneous equation has an infinite number of solutions, since j can take any value from 1 to n and p is *completely arbitrary*. It is possible, of course, that some of the solutions (12.11) may be worthless, since several of the cofactors C_{jk} may vanish. However, it can be shown that there are always enough non-vanishing cofactors so that the *ratio* of all the unknowns is determined.

The fact that the set of homogeneous equations $[a](x) = (0)$ possesses non-trivial solutions only when $|a| = 0$ is of great importance in many problems of applied mathematics.

PROBLEMS

1. Given the matrix

$$[a] = \begin{bmatrix} 1 & 1 \\ 1 & 1 \end{bmatrix}$$

show that $[a]^n = 2^{n-1}[a]$, where $n = 1, 2, 3, \ldots$.

2. Show that if

$$[a] = \begin{bmatrix} \cosh \theta & \sinh \theta \\ \sinh \theta & \cosh \theta \end{bmatrix}, \qquad [a]^n = \begin{bmatrix} \cosh n\theta & \sinh n\theta \\ \sinh n\theta & \cosh n\theta \end{bmatrix}$$

$n = 0, \pm 1, \pm 2, \ldots$.

3. Show that the matrix

$$[j] = \begin{bmatrix} 0 & -1 \\ 1 & 0 \end{bmatrix}$$

behaves in a manner similar to the unit of imaginaries $j = (-1)^{1/2}$ in the theory of complex numbers. That is, $[j]^2 = -[U]$, $[j]^3 = -[j]$, $[j]^4 = [U]$, etc. $[U]$ is the second-order unit matrix.

4. Expand $([A] + [B])([A] - [B])$. Note that the expansion is of four and not of two terms.

5. If $[a]$ is a diagonal matrix of order (m, m) and $[b]$ is any matrix of order (m, n), prove that the product $[a][b]$ is obtained from $[b]$ by multiplying the *rows* of $[b]$ by $a_{11}, a_{22}, \ldots, a_{nn}$.

6. If $[a]$ is a diagonal matrix of order (n, n), prove that $[b][a]$ is obtained from $[b]$ by multiplying the *columns* of $[b]$ respectively by $a_{11}, a_{22}, \ldots, a_{nn}$.

7. Show that diagonal matrices of the same order are commutative in multiplication with each other.

8. If $[C] = [A][A]'$, show that $[C] = [C]'$.

9. If (x) is a column vector, show that $(x)(x)' = [C]$, where $[C]$ is a square matrix with the property that $[C] = [C]'$.

10. Given the matrix

$$[A] = \begin{bmatrix} 1 & 2 & 3 \\ 1 & 3 & 5 \\ 1 & 5 & 12 \end{bmatrix}$$

find its adjoint matrix.

11. If $[A]$ is nonsingular and $[A][B] = [B][A]$, then $[A]^{-1}[B] = [B][A]^{-1}$.

12. Compute $[A]^{-1}[B]$ and $[A][B]^{-1}$, where

$$[A] = \begin{bmatrix} 1 & 2 & 3 \\ 1 & 3 & 5 \\ 1 & 5 & 12 \end{bmatrix}, \qquad [B] = \begin{bmatrix} 1 & 1 & 1 \\ 1 & 2 & 3 \\ 1 & 4 & 9 \end{bmatrix}$$

13. Show that the reciprocal of a nonsingular diagonal matrix is a diagonal matrix.

14. Given the matrix

$$[a] = \begin{bmatrix} 8 & 4 & 3 \\ 2 & 1 & 1 \\ 1 & 2 & 1 \end{bmatrix}$$

compute $[a]^{-2}$.

15. Show that the matrix

$$[A] = \begin{bmatrix} a & h \\ h & b \end{bmatrix}$$

is transformed to the diagonal form $[B] = T_\theta[A]T_\theta'$ where

$$T_\theta = \begin{bmatrix} \cos(\theta) & \sin(\theta) \\ -\sin(\theta) & \cos(\theta) \end{bmatrix} \quad \text{and} \quad \tan(2\theta) = \frac{2h}{(a - b)}$$

This is Jacobi's transformation.

REFERENCES

1. Bodewig, E., *Matrix Calculus*.   New York: Interscience Publishers, Inc., 1956.
   (A thorough discussion of basic matrix algebra and various efficient numerical
   methods for the inversion of matrices and the computation of eigenvalues.)

2. Frazer, R. A., W. J. Duncan, and A. R. Collar, *Elementary Matrices*.   New
   York and London: Cambridge University Press, 1938.   (An excellent exposition of the theory of matrices and applications to dynamics and oscillation
   problems of aeronautical engineering.)

3. Paige, L. J., and O. Taussky, Editors, *Simultaneous Linear Equations and the
   Determination of Eigenvalues*. National Bureau of Standards, Applied
   Mathematics Series 29, August, 1953.   (Contains a bibliography of over 450
   titles on the solution of linear equations and a description of useful methods
   for the determination of the eigenvalues and eigenvectors of numerical matrices
   and methods of matrix inversion.)

4. Wedderburn, J. H. M., *Lectures on Matrices*.   Ann Arbor, Michigan: J. W.
   Edwards, Publisher, Inc., 1949.   (An exposition of the classical theory of
   matrices; contains a bibliography of 661 entries covering the mathematical
   literature through 1936.)

3 MATRICES AND EIGENVALUE PROBLEMS

1. INTRODUCTION

The study of many physical systems of practical importance, such as the investigation of the elastic vibrations of a bridge or any other solid structure, the flutter vibrations of an airplane wing, the transient oscillations of an electric network, or the buckling of an elastic structure, leads to the solution of what is known in the mathematical literature as an *eigenvalue problem*. In this chapter a general mathematical discussion of the eigenvalue problem of a matrix will be given. Typical types of eigenvalue problems which arise in engineering and physics will be discussed in subsequent chapters.

2. THE EIGENVALUES OF A SQUARE MATRIX

Let $[M]$ be a square matrix of order (n, n) and (x) be a column matrix or vector of the nth order. By the rule of the multiplication of matrices discussed in Chapter 2, it is known that the multiplication of the vector (x) by the matrix $[M]$ generates a new vector (y) so that

$$(2.1) \qquad [M](x) = (y)$$

The vector (y) can be conceived as a transformation of the original vector (x). The question will now be asked whether or not it may happen that the vector (y) has the *same direction* as the vector (x). In this case (y) is simply proportional to (x), or $(y) = \mu(x)$, where μ is a scalar multiplier, and (2.1) becomes

$$(2.2) \qquad [M](x) = \mu(x)$$

The scalar multiplier μ must now be determined. To do so, the matrix equation (2.2) is expanded to the following set of n *homogeneous* algebraic equations:

$$
\begin{aligned}
M_{11}x_1 + M_{12}x_2 + \cdots + M_{1n}x_n &= \mu x_1 \\
M_{21}x_1 + M_{22}x_2 + \cdots + M_{2n}x_n &= \mu x_2 \\
&\vdots \\
M_{n1}x_1 + M_{n2}x_2 + \cdots + M_{nn}x_n &= \mu x_n
\end{aligned}
$$

(2.3)

This set of equations may be written in the form

$$
\begin{aligned}
(\mu - M_{11})x_1 - M_{12}x_2 - \cdots - M_{1n}x_n &= 0 \\
- M_{21}x_1 + (\mu - M_{22})x_2 - \cdots - M_{2n}x_n &= 0 \\
&\vdots \\
- M_{n1}x_1 - M_{n2}x_2 - \cdots + (\mu - M_{nn})x_n &= 0
\end{aligned}
$$

(2.4)

In matrix notation the set of equations (2.4) may be written in the compact form

(2.5) $$(\mu U - [M])(x) = (0)$$

where U is the nth-order unit matrix and (0) is the nth-order zero column matrix.

Now, as was discussed in Chapter 2, Sec. 12, then n homogeneous equations (2.4) in the n unknowns x_i have no solution (outside of the vanishing of all the x_i's, which means that the vector (x) does not exist) unless the determinant of the system is zero, so

(2.6) $$\det (\mu U - [M]) = p(\mu) = 0 = p(\mu)$$

In matrix algebra, the matrix

(2.7) $$[K] = \mu U - [M]$$

is called the *characteristic matrix* of the matrix $[M]$. The determinant, $\det (\mu U - [M])$, is called the *characteristic function* of $[M]$. Since $\det (\mu U - [M])$ is a polynomial in μ, it is also called the *characteristic polynomial* of $[M]$.

Equation (2.6), $p(\mu) = 0$, is the *characteristic equation* of the matrix $[M]$. In general, the characteristic polynomial $p(\mu)$ is a polynomial in μ of degree n, and the characteristic equation of the matrix $[M]$ has the form

(2.8) $$p(\mu) = \mu^n + c_1\mu^{n-1} + c_2\mu^{n-2} + \cdots + c_{n-1}\mu + c_n = 0$$

It is thus apparent that the scalar multiplier μ which we are seeking must be one of the roots of the algebraic equation (2.8). From the theory of equations it is known that an algebraic equation of the nth degree, such as (2.8), always has n roots. In general, the roots are complex numbers. It is possible that some of the roots may be multiple ones. Each multiple root must be counted according to its degree of multiplicity.

The Eigenvalues of $[M]$

The roots $\mu_1, \mu_2, \mu_3, \ldots, \mu_n$ of the characteristic equation $p(\mu) = 0$ are called the *eigenvalues* of the matrix $[M]$. In the mathematical literature the eigenvalues are also called the characteristic roots, secular values, proper values, or the latent roots of the matrix $[M]$.

The Eigenvectors of $[M]$

For every possible value of $\mu = \mu_i$, $i = 1, 2, \ldots, n$, a solution of the homogeneous equation (2.5) can be found (see Chapter 2, sec. 12). Let $(x) = (x)_i$ be the vector associated with $\mu = \mu_i$ in (2.5); we may then write

$$(2.9) \qquad (\mu_i U - [M])(x)_i = (0), \qquad i = 1, 2, \ldots, n$$

provided the characteristic equation $p(\mu) = 0$ has n *distinct roots.* The vectors $(x)_i$ are called the *eigenvectors* or *principal axes* of the matrix $[M]$. Since the eigenvectors are the solutions of a *homogeneous* set of equations, the solution is determined only up to a constant factor, and only the *ratios* of the elements in the columns $(x)_i$ are uniquely determined. The geometrical interpretation of this is that the eigenvectors are uniquely determined only in their *direction* but their *length* or absolute value is arbitrary.

3. GEOMETRICAL INTERPRETATION OF THE EIGENVALUE PROBLEM

Before we consider the general algebraic treatment of the eigenvalue problem, the geometrical significance of the eigenvalues and eigenvectors of certain special matrices will be discussed. By doing this, the operations involved in determining the eigenvalues and eigenvectors of a matrix will be found to have a very close relationship to the analytical geometry of second-order surfaces and an intuitive feeling for the results of the purely algebraic operations of the problem will be attained. In order not to obscure the main ideas with unnecessary geometrical and algebraic detail, two-dimensional problems will be considered first; the treatment will later be extended to spaces of any number of dimensions.

The Equation of a Central Ellipse

Let x_1 and x_2 be two Cartesian coordinates in a plane, as shown in Fig. 3.1. In analytic geometry of conic sections, the equation of a centrally located ellipse with reference to this Cartesian coordinate system is given in the following form:

$$(3.1) \qquad \frac{x_1^2}{a^2} + \frac{x_2^2}{b^2} = 1$$

In order to write Eq. (3.1) in matrix notation, it is necessary to introduce the following matrices:

$$(3.2) \qquad [M] = \begin{bmatrix} \dfrac{1}{a^2} & 0 \\[2mm] 0 & \dfrac{1}{b^2} \end{bmatrix}, \qquad (x) = \begin{bmatrix} x_1 \\ x_2 \end{bmatrix}$$

$[M]$ is a square matrix of the second order, and (x) is the coordinate vector. In terms of these matrices, it is easy to see that as a consequence of the rule for the multiplication of matrices, Eq. (3.1) may be written in the following form:

$$(3.3) \qquad (x_1 \quad x_2) \begin{bmatrix} \dfrac{1}{a^2} & 0 \\[2mm] 0 & \dfrac{1}{b^2} \end{bmatrix} \begin{bmatrix} x_1 \\ x_2 \end{bmatrix} = 1$$

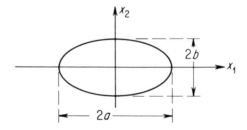

FIG. 3.1. Central Ellipse

This can be written in the more concise form,

$$(3.4) \qquad \phi(x_1 \quad x_2) = (x)'[M](x) = 1$$

In works on vector analysis, it is shown that the vector normal to the ellipse at every point of its surface is given by computing the gradient of the function $\phi(x_1 \quad x_2)$. In the notation of matrix algebra, grad ϕ may be written in the following form:

$$(3.5) \qquad \text{grad } \phi = \begin{bmatrix} \phi_{x_1} \\ \phi_{x_2} \end{bmatrix} = 2 \begin{bmatrix} \dfrac{1}{a^2} & 0 \\[2mm] 0 & \dfrac{1}{b^2} \end{bmatrix} \begin{bmatrix} x_1 \\ x_2 \end{bmatrix} = 2[M](x) = (N)$$

where ϕ_{x_1} and ϕ_{x_2} signify partial derivatives of ϕ with respect to x_1 and x_2.

Let us suppose now that the directions of the principal axes of the ellipse $\phi(x_1 \quad x_2) = 1$ are not known, and that it is required to determine these directions. The vector (x) given by (3.4) is a vector from the origin of the coordinate system to the surface of the ellipse and is, in general, not parallel to the vector (N) given by (3.5).   The vectors (x) and (N) are parallel to each other only when (x) has the direction of the principal axes.   Now, if (N) is to be parallel to (x), we must have

$$(3.6) \qquad\qquad [M](x) = \mu(x)$$

where μ is a factor of proportionality.   The relation (3.6) expresses the fact that $(N) = 2[M](x)$ and (x) have the same directions.   However, (3.6) is of the same form as Eq. (2.2), which is the fundamental equation of eigenvalue analysis.   Hence, the possible values of μ are the roots of the characteristic polynomial $p(\mu)$ of the matrix $[M]$ given by

$$(3.7) \qquad p(\mu) = \det(\mu U - [M]) = \begin{vmatrix} \left(\mu - \dfrac{1}{a^2}\right) & 0 \\ 0 & \left(\mu - \dfrac{1}{b^2}\right) \end{vmatrix} = 0$$

or

$$(3.8) \qquad\qquad p(\mu) = \left(\mu - \frac{1}{a^2}\right)\left(\mu - \frac{1}{b^2}\right) = 0$$

Hence, the two eigenvalues of $[M]$ are

$$(3.9) \qquad\qquad \mu_1 = \frac{1}{a^2}, \qquad \mu_2 = \frac{1}{b^2}$$

It is thus evident that Eq. (3.1) of the centrally located ellipse may be written in terms of the eigenvalues of $[M]$ in the form

$$(3.10) \qquad\qquad \mu_1 x_1^2 + \mu_2 x_2^2 = 1$$

The Eigenvectors of $[M]$

It remains now to find the eigenvectors of the matrix $[M]$.   These eigenvectors will give the directions of the principal axes of the ellipse.   To find them, we use Eq. (2.9), which may be written in the form

$$(3.11) \qquad\qquad [M](x)_i = \mu_i(x)_i, \qquad i = 1, 2$$

or

$$(3.12) \qquad\qquad \mu_1 x_{1i} = \mu_i x_{1i}, \qquad \mu_2 x_{2i} = \mu_i x_{2i}, \qquad i = 1, 2$$

The Eqs. (3.12) give the two eigenvectors,

$$(3.13) \qquad\qquad (x)_1 = \begin{bmatrix} r \\ 0 \end{bmatrix}, \qquad (x)_2 = \begin{bmatrix} 0 \\ s \end{bmatrix}$$

where r and s are arbitrary.   That is, the line $x_2 = 0$ is the principal axis associated with the eigenvalue μ_1, and the line $x_1 = 0$ is the principal axis associated with the eigenvalue μ_2.

In this particular example, the equation of the ellipse had the very simple form (3.1) because its principal axes coincided with the coordinate directions. In order to extend the geometrical interpretation to a more complicated case, the equation of the ellipse relative to a rotated system of axes will be considered.

Rotation of the Coordinate Axes in the Plane

Let (x_1, x_2) be a set of Cartesian coordinates in a plane, as shown in Fig. 3.2, and let (y_1, y_2) be another set of Cartesian coordinates which have the same origin as the first set of coordinates but which are inclined at an angle θ with respect to the first set, as shown.

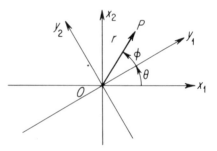

FIG. 3.2. Rotation of Axes

Let OP be a vector drawn from the origin of length r and let it make an angle of $(\theta + \phi)$ with respect to x_1 and an angle ϕ with respect to y_1. The coordinates of P with respect to x_1 and x_2 are

(3.14)
$$x_1 = r \cos (\theta + \phi) = r \cos (\theta) \cos (\phi) - r \sin (\theta) \sin (\phi)$$
$$x_2 = r \sin (\theta + \phi) = r \sin (\theta) \cos (\theta) + r \cos (\theta) \sin (\phi)$$

The coordinates of P with respect to y_1 and y_2 are

(3.15)
$$y_1 = r \cos (\phi), \qquad y_2 = r \sin (\phi)$$

If these expressions for y_1 and y_2 are substituted into (3.14), the results are

(3.16)
$$x_1 = y_1 \cos (\theta) - y_2 \sin (\theta)$$
$$x_2 = y_1 \sin (\theta) + y_2 \cos (\theta)$$

In order to express the effect of the rotation of coordinates in matrix form, it is convenient to introduce the following matrices:

(3.17) $(x) = \begin{bmatrix} x_1 \\ x_2 \end{bmatrix}, \qquad (y) = \begin{bmatrix} y_1 \\ y_2 \end{bmatrix}, \qquad [R(\theta)] = \begin{bmatrix} \cos (\theta) & \sin (\theta) \\ -\sin (\theta) & \cos (\theta) \end{bmatrix}$

In terms of these matrices, Eq. (3.16) may be written in the form

(3.18)
$$(x) = [R(-\theta)](y) = [R(\theta)]^{-1}(y)$$

This expresses the original coordinates (x) in terms of the rotated coordinates (y). If (3.18) is premultiplied by $[R(\theta)]$, the resulting equation is

(3.19)
$$(y) = [R(\theta)](x)$$

The Rotation Matrix. $[R(\theta)]$

The matrix $[R(\theta)]$ is sometimes called the *rotation matrix*. As can be seen from (3.19), premultiplication of the coordinate matrix (x) by the rotation matrix yields another coordinate matrix (y) that is inclined at an angle θ with respect to (x). The matrix $[R(\theta)]$ has the following important properties:

$$(3.20) \qquad [R(-\theta)] = [R(\theta)]' = [R(\theta)]^{-1}, \qquad \det [R(\theta)] = 1$$

As a consequence of the property (3.20), $[R(\theta)]$ is seen to be an *orthogonal matrix* [see Chapter 2, Sec. 11(f)].

The sum of the squares of the coordinates (x) and (y) are *invariant* to the transformation (3.19). That is,

$$(3.21) \quad (y_1^2 + y_2^2) = (y)'(y) = (x)'[R]'[R](x) = (x)'(x) = (x_1^2 + x_2^2)$$

The above result follows as a consequence of the reversal law of transposed products and the fact that $[R]'[R] = [U]$, the unit matrix.

The rotation matrix may be used to determine the principal axes of an ellipse when its principal axes do not coincide with the coordinates x_1 and x_2, as given by Eq. (3.1). In general, the equation of an ellipse whose center is at the origin of the coordinates x_1 and x_2 has the form

$$(3.22) \qquad\qquad Ax_1^2 + Bx_1x_2 + Cx_2^2 = 1$$

In matrix notation, Eq. (3.22) takes the form

$$(3.23) \qquad\qquad (x)' \begin{bmatrix} A & \dfrac{B}{2} \\ \dfrac{B}{2} & C \end{bmatrix} (x) = 1$$

or

$$(3.24) \qquad (x)'[M](x) = 1, \qquad [M] = \begin{bmatrix} A & \dfrac{B}{2} \\ \dfrac{B}{2} & C \end{bmatrix}$$

Let the axes now be rotated by the transformation (3.18), $(x) = [R]'(y)$. If this transformation is applied to (3.24), the result is

$$(3.25) \qquad\qquad (y)'[R][M][R]'(y) = 1$$

Now, if the new coordinates (y) coincide with the principal axes of the ellipse (3.24), Eq. (3.26) does not contain the term y_1y_2 and the matrix $[R][M][R]'$ must be a *diagonal matrix*. If the product (3.25) is carried out, the result will be seen to have the form

$$(3.26) \qquad\qquad A'y_1^2 + B'y_1y_2 + C'y_2^2 = 1$$

The coefficient of the $y_1 y_2$ term is

$$(3.27) \qquad B' = (C - A) \frac{\sin (2\theta)}{2} + \frac{B}{2} \cos (2\theta)$$

If B' is to be made to vanish, θ must be chosen so that

$$(3.28) \qquad \tan (2\theta) = \frac{B}{A - C}$$

If the matrix $[M]$ is written in the general form

$$(3.29) \qquad [M] = \begin{bmatrix} M_{11} & M_{12} \\ M_{21} & M_{22} \end{bmatrix}$$

then, by direct calculation, the transformed matrix $[M]_r = [R][M][R]'$ is given by

$$(3.30) \quad [M]_r = [R][M][R]'$$

$$= \begin{bmatrix} (M_{11} \cos^2 \theta + M_{12} \sin 2\theta + M_{22} \sin^2 \theta) & \left(M_{12} \cos 2\theta + (M_{22} - M_{11}) \dfrac{\sin 2\theta}{2} \right) \\ \left(M_{21} \cos 2\theta + (M_{22} - M_{11}) \dfrac{\sin 2\theta}{2} \right) & (M_{11} \sin^2 \theta - M_{12} \sin 2\theta + M_{22} \cos^2 \theta) \end{bmatrix}$$

4. INVARIANTS OF THE ROTATED MATRIX $[M]_r$

There are certain properties of the matrix $[M]$ that are also properties of the matrix $[M]_r$ and hence are not changed by the rotation transformation $[M]_r = [R][M][R]'$. For example, the *determinant* of $[M]$ is equal to the *determinant* of $[M]_r$. This is a consequence of the rule of multiplication of determinants and the fact that det $[R] = $ det $[R]' = 1$ so that

$$(4.1) \qquad \text{det } [M]_r = (\text{det } [R])(\text{det } [M])(\text{det } [R]') = \text{det } [M]$$

The Trace of $[M]$

The sum of the principal diagonals of $[M]$ is defined to be the trace of $[M]$, or Tr $[M]$. From (3.30) it is seen that

$$(4.2) \qquad \text{Tr } [M]_r = \text{Tr } [M] = M_{11} + M_{22}$$

It will now be shown that the characteristic polynomial of $[M]$ is the same as the characteristic polynomial of $[M]_r$ and that hence $[M]$ and $[M]_r$ have the same characteristic equation and eigenvalues. By definition, the characteristic polynomial of $[M]$, $p(\mu)$ is the determinant of the characteristic matrix of $[M]$ or $[K]$, given by

$$(4.3) \qquad [K] = \mu U - [M], \qquad p(\mu) = \text{det } [K]$$

Similarly, $[K]_r$, the characteristic matrix of $[M]_r$, is given by

$$(4.4) \qquad\qquad\qquad [K]_r = \mu U - [M]_r$$

Now, if (4.3) is premultiplied by $[R]$ and postmultiplied by $[R]'$, the result is

$$(4.5) \quad [R][K][R]' = \mu[R]U[R]' - [R][M][R]' = \mu U - [M]_r = [K]_r$$

where use has been made of the relation $[R][R]' = U$. As a consequence of the relation (4.5), the characteristic polynomials of $[M]$ and $[M]_r$, $p(\mu)$ and $p_r(\mu)$, satisfy the following equation:

$$(4.6) \qquad p_r(\mu) = \det [K]_r = \det ([R][K][R]') = \det [K] = p(\mu)$$

This relation is a consequence of the fact that

$$\det [R] = \det [R]' = 1$$

It therefore follows that the matrices $[M]$ and $[M]_r$ have the same characteristic equation,

$$(4.7) \qquad\qquad\qquad p(\mu) = p_r(\mu) = 0$$

and therefore $[M]$ and $[M]_r$ have the *same* eigenvalues. Hence, the *eigenvalues* of $[M]$ are *invariant* to the rotation transformation (4.1). Geometrically, this is evident from the fact that as seen by (3.9) the eigenvalues are the reciprocals of the squares of the semimajor and semiminor axes of the ellipse, and do not depend on the orientation of the ellipse with respect to the coordinate axes.

5. ALGEBRAIC DISCUSSION OF THE EIGENVECTORS OF A MATRIX

Before we extend the geometrical interpretation of the eigenvalue problem to a quadratic surface of n dimensions, an algebraic discussion of the eigenvalue problem will be given.

Consider a square matrix $[M]$ of order (n, n) whose elements are real numbers. It is required to determine the eigenvalues and the eigenvectors of $[M]$. By (2.6) we recall that the eigenvalues of $[M]$ are the roots of the characteristic equation,

$$(5.1) \qquad\qquad p(\mu) = \det (\mu U - [M]) = 0$$

$p(\mu)$ is the characteristic polynomial of $[M]$, and is, in general, a polynomial of the nth degree in μ. In general, the characteristic equation (5.1) will have n roots $\mu_1, \mu_2, \mu_3, \ldots, \mu_n$; in some cases, the roots may be multiple roots and must be counted according to their degree of multiplicity. The roots μ_i are the *eigenvalues* of the matrix $[M]$. This set of n numbers will be denoted symbolically by $\mu(M)$, and any particular one by $\mu_i(M)$.

The Eigenvectors of [M]

By the defining equation (2.9), the eigenvector associated with the eigenvalue μ_i is a column matrix $(A)_i$ of the nth order which satisfies the homogeneous equation

(5.2) $$(\mu_i U - [M])(A)_i = (0), \quad \text{or} \quad [M](A)_i = \mu_i(A)_i$$

Let it be assumed for the present that the characteristic equation (5.1) *does not have multiple roots*, so the eigenvalues μ_i are a set of n distinct numbers. In such a case, there are n distinct *eigenvectors* $(A)_i$ that satisfy Eq. (5.2) for the index $i = 1, 2, \ldots, n$. It must be remembered that since the elements of $(A)_i$ are solutions of the *homogeneous* equation (5.2), they are not uniquely determined, but only the *ratios* of the elements are determined. If $(A)_i$ is regarded as a vector in n-dimensional space, its *length* is not determined, but only its *direction* is uniquely determined.

The Modal Matrix of [M]

Let a square matrix [A] be constructed from the eigenvector columns $(A)_i$ in the following manner:

(5.3) $$[A] = [(A)_1 \quad (A)_2 \quad \cdots \quad (A)_n]$$

that is, the *columns* of the matrix [A] are the eigenvectors of [M]. The square matrix [A] is called the *modal matrix* of [M]. It is easy to show that the set of n equations (5.2) may be written as one equation in terms of the modal matrix. This equation has the form

(5.4) $$[M][A] = [A][D]$$

where [D] is the nth-order diagonal matrix of eigenvalues,

(5.5) $$[D] = \begin{bmatrix} \mu_1 & 0 & 0 & 0 & \cdots & 0 \\ 0 & \mu_2 & 0 & 0 & \cdots & 0 \\ 0 & 0 & \mu_3 & 0 & \cdots & 0 \\ \cdot & \cdot & \cdot & \cdot & \cdots & \cdot \\ 0 & 0 & 0 & 0 & \cdots & \mu_n \end{bmatrix}$$

If the given matrix [M] is *not* a symmetric matrix so that $[M]' = [M]$, it is possible to obtain the eigenvectors of $[M]'$ in a similar manner. The eigenvalues of $[M]'$ are the roots of the characteristic equation,

(5.6) $$\det(\mu U - [M]') = \det(\mu U - [M])' = \det(\mu U - [M]) = p(\mu) = 0$$

Equation (5.6) follows from the fact that the value of a determinant is unaltered by interchanging its rows and its columns. From (5.6) it is seen that $[M]'$ has the same characteristic equation as [M], and hence that the eigenvalues of $[M]'$ are the same as those of [M].

The Eigenvectors of $[M]'$

Let the nth-order column matrix $(B)_i$ be the eigenvector of $[M]'$ associated with the eigenvalue μ_i. This eigenvector satisfies the equation

(5.7) $$(\mu_i U - [M]')(B)_i = 0, \quad \text{or} \quad [M]'(B)_i = \mu_i(B)_i$$

where $i = 1, 2, 3, \ldots, n$.

The modal matrix of $[M]'$, $[B]$, may now be constructed from the eigenvector columns $(B)_i$ in the following manner:

(5.8) $$[B] = [(B)_1 \quad (B)_2 \quad \ldots \quad (B)_n]$$

The set of equations (5.7) may be written in terms of the diagonal matrix (5.5) in the form

(5.9) $$[M]'[B] = [B][D]$$

Equations (5.4) and (5.9) are similar to each other and will now be used to obtain a relation between the modal matrices $[A]$ and $[B]$. In the mathematical literature, the columns of the matrix $[A]$ are called the principal axes of $[M]$, and the columns of the matrix $[B]$ are called the *adjoint* axes of $[M]$.

If the eigenvalues of $[M]$ are distinct so that the characteristic equation of $[M]$ does not have multiple roots, it can be shown that the modal matrices $[A]$ and $[B]$ are non-singular matrices and therefore have inverses $[A]^{-1}$ and $[B]^{-1}$. In this case, let (5.4) be premultiplied by $[A]^{-1}$, and let (5.9) be premultiplied by $[B]^{-1}$; the results of these operations are

(5.10) $$[A]^{-1}[M][A] = [D]$$

and

(5.11) $$[B]^{-1}[M]'[B] = [D]$$

Now we take the transpose of Eq. (5.11) and obtain

(5.12) $$[B]'[M][B']^{-1} = [D]' = [D]$$

If (5.12) is compared with (5.10), it can be seen that $[B]'$ and $[A]^{-1}$ must be related to each other by the equation

(5.13) $$[B]' = [W][A]^{-1}, \quad \text{or} \quad [W] = [B]'[A]$$

where $[W]$ is a diagonal matrix. As has been mentioned above, the *lengths* of the vectors $(A)_i$ and $(B)_i$ of the modal matrices $[A]$ and $[B]$ are not determined by Eqs. (5.2) and (5.7). By multiplication with suitable constants, however, these vectors may be adjusted to satisfy the relation

(5.14) $$(B)_i'(A)_i = 1$$

Then the vectors $(B)_i$ and $(A)_i$ are said to be normalized, and the diagonal matrix $[W]$ becomes the unit matrix U, so (5.13) becomes

(5.15) $$[B]' = [A]^{-1}, \quad \text{or} \quad [B]'[A] = [A]'[B] = U$$

It is thus seen that the principal axes of the matrix $[M]$, $(A)_i$, are orthogonal to its adjoint axes $(B)_i$. If the matrix $[M]$ is a symmetric matrix so that $[M] = [M]'$, then $[A] = [B]$ and in this case (5.15) becomes

$$(5.16) \qquad\qquad [A]' = [A]^{-1}, \quad \text{or} \quad [A]'[A] = U$$

Equation (5.16) shows that the eigenvectors of a symmetric matrix are orthogonal.

The Inverse of $[M]$

If the modal matrices $[A]$ and $[B]$ of a matrix $[M]$ and its eigenvalues are known, then a simple relation may be obtained for $[M]^{-1}$. To obtain this expression, we write (5.10) in the form

$$(5.17) \qquad\qquad [M] = [A][D][A]^{-1} = [A][D][B]'$$

If the inverse of (5.17) is now taken, the result is

$$(5.18) \qquad\qquad [M]^{-1} = ([B]')^{-1}[D]^{-1}[A]^{-1} = [A][D]^{-1}[B]'$$

This relation is not very useful for obtaining the inverse of a matrix unless a complete eigenvalue analysis of the matrix has been performed.

6. THE EIGENVALUES OF A REAL SYMMETRIC MATRIX ARE REAL NUMBERS

Since the eigenvalues of a matrix are the roots of its characteristic equation, which is, in general, a high-degree algebraic equation, it might be supposed that some of the eigenvalues might be complex numbers. It will now be proved that if the matrix $[M]$ is *symmetric* so that $[M]' = [M]$, then the eigenvalues μ_i are *real numbers*.

To see this, let (A) be an eigenvector of the matrix $[M]$ associated with the eigenvalue μ; then, by definition, we have

$$(6.1) \qquad\qquad [M](A) = \mu(A)$$

If μ is a complex number, and if the elements of the matrix $[M]$ are real numbers, then the elements of (A) must be complex numbers. Now let all the complex quantities of (6.1) be replaced by their complex conjugates. If this is done, (6.1) becomes

$$(6.2) \qquad\qquad [M](\bar{A}) = \bar{\mu}(\bar{A})$$

where $\bar{\mu}$ is the complex conjugate of μ, and the elements of $(\bar{A})$ are the complex conjugates of the elements of (A). (It will be remembered that if $z = x + jy$, its complex conjugate is $\bar{z} = x - jy$, where $j = (-1)^{1/2}$ is the unit of imaginaries.)

We now premultiply (6.1) by $(\bar{A})'$ and (6.2) by $(A)'$ and thus obtain

$$(6.3) \qquad\qquad (\bar{A})'[M](A) = \mu(\bar{A})'(A)$$

$$(6.4) \qquad\qquad (A)'[M](\bar{A}) = \bar{\mu}(A)'(\bar{A})$$

Let the transpose of both members of Eq. (6.4) be taken.   The result is

(6.5) $$(\bar{A})'[M](A) = \bar{\mu}(\bar{A})'(A)$$

where use has been made of the fact that $[M]$ is symmetric and $[M]' = [M]$.
Now subtract Eq. (6.3) from Eq. (6.5) and obtain

(6.6) $$0 = (\bar{\mu} - \mu)(\bar{A})'(A)$$

Now, $(\bar{A})'(A) = |A_1|^2 + |A_2|^2 + \cdots + |A_n|^2$ is the sum of positive
quantities and cannot be zero; hence, (6.6) is satisfied if

(6.7) $$\bar{\mu} = \mu$$

Since μ is equal to its complex conjugate, it must be real.   If the eigenvalue μ
is real, then it follows that in order for (6.1) and (6.2) to be satisfied we must
have

(6.8) $$(A) = (\bar{A})$$

and the elements of the eigenvector (A) must be real numbers.   Since the
above argument holds for *any* eigenvalue and its associated eigenvector of the
matrix $[M]$, it follows that all its eigenvalues and its eigenvectors are real.
This is not generally true if the matrix is not symmetric.

7. HERMITIAN MATRICES

Sometimes it is necessary to determine the eigenvalues and eigenvectors of
matrices whose elements are complex numbers.   In quantum theory,
matrices whose elements are complex numbers but which have the property
that

(7.1) $$[\bar{M}]' = [M]$$

that is, the elements of $[M]$ are such that

(7.2) $$\bar{M}_{ij} = M_{ji}$$

are called *Hermitian matrices*.   By an argument similar to that of Sec. 6 for
symmetric matrices, it can be shown that the eigenvalues of a Hermitian
matrix are real numbers.   In this case, if (A) is an eigenvector of $[M]$
associated with an eigenvalue μ, we have

(7.3) $$[M](A) = \mu(A)$$

If the complex conjugate of Eq. (7.3) is taken, the result is

(7.4) $$[\bar{M}](\bar{A}) = \bar{\mu}(\bar{A})$$

We now premultiply (7.3) by $(\bar{A})'$ and (7.4) by $(A)'$ and thus obtain

(7.5) $$(\bar{A})'[M](A) = \mu(\bar{A})'(A)$$

(7.6) $$(A)'[\bar{M}](\bar{A}) = \bar{\mu}(A)'(\bar{A})$$

We now take the transpose of (7.6). This gives

(7.7)
$$(\bar{A})'[\bar{M}]'(A) = \bar{\mu}(\bar{A})'(A) = (\bar{A})'[M](A)$$

where use has been made of the property (7.1). If now (7.5) is subtracted from (7.7), the result is

(7.8)
$$0 = (\bar{\mu} - \mu)(\bar{A})'(A)$$

Then, since $(\bar{A})'(A) \neq 0$, it follows that

(7.9)
$$\bar{\mu} = \mu$$

and, therefore, the eigenvalues of the Hermitian matrix are *real*. The eigenvectors (A) are complex vectors. Since $[\bar{M}] = [M]'$, it follows that

(7.10)
$$\det [\bar{M}] = \det [M]' = \det [M]$$

Hence, since the determinant formed from the conjugates of the elements of $[M]$ is equal to the determinant of $[M]$, it follows that the determinant of $[M]$ must be a real number. Hermitian matrices correspond in the complex domain to symmetric matrices in the real domain. If $[M]$ is Hermitian, it follows from the fact that $[M]' = [\bar{M}]$ that if $[A]$ is the modal matrix of $[M]$ and $[B]$ is the modal matrix of $[M]'$, then

(7.11)
$$[B] = [\bar{A}]$$

and

(7.12)
$$[A]'[\bar{A}] = U$$

8. ORTHOGONAL TRANSFORMATIONS

A particular kind of transformation which plays a prominent role in applied mathematics is the *orthogonal transformation*. This transformation corresponds to a rigid rotation about the origin of a Cartesian coordinate system. An example of an orthogonal transformation in the plane has already been mentioned. The three-dimensional case will now be considered, and the treatment will later be extended to the general case of n dimensions.

Let it be supposed that all points P in three-dimensional space are subjected to the same rotation about the origin of a Cartesian coordinate system O. Each point P will be displaced to a corresponding point P' and the origin O alone will remain fixed. If we call (x_1, x_2, x_3) the coordinates of the point P and (y_1, y_2, y_3) the coordinates of the point P', we may construct a column matrix or vector (x), whose elements are the coordinates of P, and another vector (y), whose elements are the coordinates of P'. The vectors (x) and (y) will be related in a definite way in any given rotation. The relationship expresses the orthogonal transformation. Instead of supposing that the points are rotated about the origin O, we may equivalently imagine that the points of space remain fixed, but that we rotate the coordinate axes rigidly around the origin to some new position. If we call Ox_1, Ox_2, Ox_3 the original axes, the rotated axes will be represented by Oy_1, Oy_2, Oy_3. If this rotation of axes is assumed, a point P of coordinates x_1, x_2, x_3 in the original system of axes will have coordinates y_1, y_2, y_3 in the new axes. In the applications we have in view, it will be convenient to interpret an orthogonal transformation as a rotation of axes.

In order to understand the analytical properties of orthogonal transformations and of their matrices, we first consider the general linear transformation between the variables (x) and the variables (y). This transformation may be written in the form

$$
\begin{aligned}
x_1 &= s_{11}y_1 + s_{12}y_2 + s_{13}y_3 \\
(8.1) \qquad x_2 &= s_{21}y_1 + s_{22}y_2 + s_{23}y_3 \\
x_3 &= s_{31}y_1 + s_{32}y_2 + s_{33}y_3
\end{aligned}
$$

where the elements s_{ik} are constants. This transformation relates the original coordinates (x) with the rotated coordinates (y). The matrix of the transformation (8.1) is

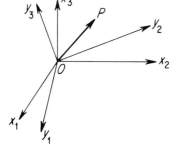

FIG. 3.3. Rotation of Coordinates

$$
(8.2) \qquad [S] = \begin{bmatrix} s_{11} & s_{12} & s_{13} \\ s_{21} & s_{22} & s_{23} \\ s_{31} & s_{32} & s_{33} \end{bmatrix}
$$

Now, since the transformation (8.1) represents a rigid rotation from the coordinates (x) to the coordinates (y), the square of the distance from the origin O to the point $P(x_1, x_2, x_3)$ or $P(y_1, y_2, y_3)$ must be the same when expressed in terms of either coordinate system. That is,

$$
(8.3) \qquad (x)'(x) = x_1^2 + x_2^2 + x_3^2 = y_1^2 + y_2^2 + y_3^2 = (y)'(y)
$$

as seen in Fig. 3.3.

In terms of the transformation matrix $[S]$, the linear transformation (8.1) may be expressed in the compact form,

$$
(8.4) \qquad (x) = [S](y)
$$

Hence, (8.3) can be expressed in terms of the transformation matrix $[S]$ by the equation

$$
(8.5) \qquad (x)'(x) = (y)'[S]'[S](y) = (y)'(y)
$$

provided the transformation matrix satisfies the relation

$$
(8.6) \qquad [S]'[S] = U, \quad \text{or} \quad [S]^{-1} = [S]'
$$

That is, if $[S]$ is to represent a rotation from the original coordinates (x)

to the new coordinates (y), it must satisfy the relation $[S]^{-1} = [S]'$. The transformation (8.4) is then said to be an *orthogonal transformation*, and the transformation matrix $[S]$ is called an *orthogonal matrix*. The numerical values of the elements of $[S]$ will, of course, depend on the particular rotation performed, but, in all cases, provided we are dealing with a rotation of the coordinates and hence with orthogonal matrices, the general relations (8.6) are satisfied. As a consequence of (8.6) we see that

$$(8.7) \qquad \det [S]' \cdot \det [S] = (\det [S])^2 = 1$$

Hence,

$$(8.8) \qquad \det [S] = \pm 1$$

The possibility of the determinant of $[S]$ having the value -1 implies that an orthogonal transformation may also represent a rotation followed by a reflection, since this transformation still keeps the distance from the origin to a given point invariant to the transformation.

If (8.1) is an orthogonal transformation, the geometrical significance of the elements s_{ik} is easily obtained. The elements of the first row of $[S]$, s_{11}, s_{12}, s_{13} are the cosines of the angles that the original axis Ox_1 makes with the three new axes Oy_1, Oy_2, Oy_3; those in the first column, namely, s_{11}, s_{21}, s_{31}, are the cosines of the angles that the new axis Oy_1 makes with the three original axes Ox_1, Ox_2, Ox_3. The other elements may be obtained in a similar manner. The properties of orthogonal matrices may be extended to matrices having any number of rows and columns. Thus, if we have a linear transformation connecting a set of n variables $x_1, x_2, \ldots, x_n$ with a set of n variables $y_1, y_2, \ldots, y_n$, the geometrical representation of the transformation will be a transformation of the rotation of the axes in a space of n dimensions. In this case, the transformation matrix $[S]$ will still satisfy the relation $[S]^{-1} = [S]'$ but will contain n rows and n columns.

9. SYMMETRIC MATRICES AND QUADRATIC FORMS

Let the following symmetric matrix with real elements be given:

$$(9.1) \qquad [a] = \begin{bmatrix} a_{11} & a_{12} & a_{13} \\ a_{21} & a_{22} & a_{23} \\ a_{31} & a_{32} & a_{33} \end{bmatrix} \quad \text{with } a_{ij} = a_{ji}$$

This symmetric matrix may be associated with the following quadratic form in the three variables, x_1, x_2, x_3:

$$(9.2) \qquad (x)'[a](x) = a_{11}x_1^2 + a_{22}x_2^2 + a_{33}x_3^2 + a_{12}x_1x_2 + a_{21}x_2x_1$$
$$+ a_{23}x_2x_3 + a_{32}x_3x_2 + a_{31}x_3x_1 + a_{13}x_1x_3$$

where (x) is a column matrix or vector whose elements are the three variables

x_1, x_2, x_3. From (9.2) we conclude that an appropriate symmetric matrix may be connected with each quadratic form. If the matrix is given, the quadratic form is determined, and vice versa.

It is advantageous to give a geometric interpretation of a quadratic form. Let the variables x_1, x_2, x_3 be the Cartesian coordinates of a point in space, and let us consider the equation obtained by equating the quadratic form to the number one. This equation is

$$(9.3) \qquad (x)'[a](x) = 1$$

It can be shown that the points P whose coordinates x_1, x_2, x_3 satisfy (9.3) lie on a quadric surface having the origin as its center. The precise nature of the quadric surface depends on the values of the elements a_{ik}. If the determinant of [a] does not vanish, the quadric surface is an ellipsoid or a hyperboloid situated in ordinary three-dimensional space. The determinant of the matrix [a] is called the *discriminant* of the quadratic form. If det [a] = 0, the quadric surface (9.3) degenerates into a cylinder of the elliptic or hyperbolic type, or else into two parallel planes symmetrically situated with respect to the origin.

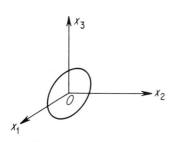

FIG. 3.4. An Ellipsoid

Let it be supposed that the quadric surface (9.3) is the equation of an ellipsoid, as shown in Fig. 3.4. This ellipsoid having the point O as center will, in general, have three principal axes. The principal axes of the ellipsoid are the three mutually perpendicular axes of symmetry that pass through the center O. It will be assumed that the principal axes differ in length. In this case, their orientation is uniquely determined.

10. THE TRANSFORMATION OF A QUADRATIC FORM INTO A SUM OF SQUARES BY MEANS OF AN ORTHOGONAL TRANSFORMATION

Let it be supposed that we wish to determine the lengths and orientation of the principal axes of the ellipsoid defined by (9.4). To do so, we shall introduce a new set of axes (y) by an orthogonal transformation (8.4) so that the axes Oy_1, Oy_2, Oy_3 coincide with the principal axes of the ellipsoid. Now, if the new axes coincide with the principal axes of the ellipsoid, its surface will be symmetrically situated with respect to them. This symmetry requires that the quadratic form, which enters into the equation of the ellipsoid in terms of these new axes, should degenerate into a sum of squares. Hence, the equation of the ellipsoid in the new axes should have the form

$$(10.1) \qquad b_1 y_1^2 + b_2 y_2^2 + b_3 y_3^2 = 1 = (y)'[b](y)$$

where

$$(10.2) \qquad [b] = \begin{bmatrix} b_1 & 0 & 0 \\ 0 & b_2 & 0 \\ 0 & 0 & b_3 \end{bmatrix}$$

The quantities b_1, b_2, b_3 are positive constants. They will be shown to be the *eigenvalues* of the matrix $[a]$ of (9.3). The *lengths* of the principal axes of the ellipsoid d_i are given by

$$(10.3) \qquad d_1 = \frac{2}{\sqrt{b_1}}, \qquad d_2 = \frac{2}{\sqrt{b_2}}, \qquad d_3 = \frac{2}{\sqrt{b_3}}$$

In order to obtain b_1, b_2, b_3, we introduce the rotated axes by means of the orthogonal transformation

$$(10.4) \qquad (x) = [S](y)$$

We now substitute this relation into (9.3) and thus obtain

$$(10.5) \qquad (y)'[S]'[a][S](y) = 1$$

If the axes have been properly rotated so that they coincide with the principal axes of the ellipsoid, then (10.5) should have the same form as (10.1) so that

$$(10.6) \qquad [S]'[a][S] = [S]^{-1}[a][S] = [b]$$

where use has been made of the orthogonal relation $[S]' = [S]^{-1}$.

If (10.6) is premultiplied by $[S]$, the resulting equation is

$$(10.7) \qquad [a][S] = [S][b]$$

Now let the transformation matrix $[S]$ be partitioned into three columns so that

$$(10.8) \qquad [S] = [(S)_1 \quad (S)_2 \quad (S)_3]$$

where $(S)_1$, $(S)_2$, and $(S)_3$ are the three columns of the square matrix $[S]$. Since $[b]$ is a diagonal matrix, it can be seen that Eq. (10.7) is equivalent to the three equations,

$$(10.9) \qquad \begin{aligned} [a](S)_1 &= b_1(S)_1 \\ [a](S)_2 &= b_2(S)_2 \\ [a](S)_3 &= b_3(S)_3 \end{aligned}$$

The form of these equations indicates that the vectors $(S)_1$, $(S)_2$, $(S)_3$ are *eigenvectors* of the matrix $[a]$ and that the numbers b_1, b_2, and b_3 are the *eigenvalues* of $[a]$ and are the three roots of the characteristic equation of $[a]$ which may be written in the form

$$(10.10) \qquad p(b) = \det(bU - [a]) = 0$$

The characteristic equation of $[a]$, in general, is a cubic equation. If (10.10) has three distinct roots b_1, b_2, b_3, then the quadric surface (9.3) has three principal axes whose lengths are given by (10.3). The matrix $[a]$ and Eq. (10.9) fix the *directions* of the vectors $(S)_i$, and the equation $[S]'[S] = U$ or

$$(10.11) \qquad\qquad (S)_i'(S) = 1, \qquad i = 1, 2, 3$$

determines the *length* of the vectors $(S)_1$, $(S)_2$, and $(S)_3$. The directions of the y_1, y_2, and y_3 axes may be determined with respect to the coordinates x_1, x_2, and x_3 by means of the equation

$$(10.11a) \qquad\qquad (x) = [S](y)$$

For example, the line y_1, $y_2 = 0$, $y_3 = 0$ may be expressed in terms of the (x) coordinates by writing (10.11) in the form

$$(10.12) \qquad \begin{bmatrix} x_1 \\ x_2 \\ x_3 \end{bmatrix} = \begin{bmatrix} s_{11} & s_{12} & s_{13} \\ s_{21} & s_{22} & s_{23} \\ s_{31} & s_{32} & s_{33} \end{bmatrix} \cdot \begin{bmatrix} y_1 \\ 0 \\ 0 \end{bmatrix}$$

If (10.12) is expanded, the result may be written in the form

$$(10.13) \qquad\qquad (x)_1 = y_1(S)_1$$

Equation (10.13) shows that the axis y_1 has the direction of the first column vector $(S)_1$ of the transformation matrix (S). It may be shown similarly that the axis y_2 has the direction of the vector $(S)_2$ and the axis y_3, the direction of the vector $(S)_3$. If (10.13) is substituted into the equation of the quadric surface,

$$(10.14) \qquad\qquad (x)_1'[a](x) = 1$$

we obtain

$$(10.15) \qquad\qquad (x)_1'[a](x)_1 = y_1(S)_1'[a](S)_1 y_1 = 1$$

But from (10.9), $[a](S)_1 = b_1(S)_1$, and hence (10.15) can be written as

$$(10.16) \qquad\qquad y_1(S)_1'(S)_1 b_1 y_1 = y_1^2 b_1 = 1$$

Equation (10.16) shows that the axis y_1 intersects the quadric surface at the distance $(b_1)^{-1/2}$ from the origin. In a similar manner, it can be shown that the axes y_2 and y_3 intersect the quadric surface (10.14) at distances of $(b_2)^{-1/2}$ and $(b_3)^{-1/2}$ from the origin.

Thus far, we have assumed that the principal axes of the ellipsoid are of unequal length. When two or all three of the principal axes of the ellipsoid have the same length (that is, when two or all three of the eigenvalues b_i are equal), the orthogonal matrix $[S]$ becomes indeterminate. The geometrical picture enables us to understand the reason for this indeterminateness. If, for example, the ellipsoid is a spheroid and the axis Ox_1 is rotated to bring it into a position Oy_1 which coincides with the axis of symmetry of the spheroid, then the axes Oy_2 and Oy_3 will always coincide with two other principal axes, no matter how much the coordinate axes are pivoted about Oy_1. In the case that the ellipsoid has all three eigenvalues equal to each other, it degenerates into a sphere. In this case *any* three mutually perpendicular diameters may serve as the principal axes of that sphere.

In the special example that has been discussed, the analysis was applied to three-dimensional ellipsoids and rotations in three-dimensional space. Exactly the same problem can be considered in a space of any number n of dimensions, although the geometrical representation now fails us unless we are able to visualize ellipsoids and rotations in a space of n dimensions. From the standpoint of matrix algebra, the problem consists in transforming a symmetric matrix of order (n, n) into a diagonal one by means of an ortho-gonal transformation, $[S]'[a][s] = [b]$, where $[b]$ is an nth-order diagonal matrix whose elements are the eigenvalues of $[a]$. In this case, the eigenvalues are the roots of an algebraic equation of the nth degree and are real numbers.

The existence of multiple roots does not invalidate the existence of n distinct and mutually perpendicular axes but only indicates that some of these axes are no longer uniquely determined but can be replaced by other equally valid axes. The multiplicity of the roots of the characteristic equation of the matrix $[a]$ introduces certain difficulties in the numerical calculations of the problem. If certain eigenvalues are almost equal to each other without collapsing into one, the associated principal axes or eigenvectors are still theoretically determined. However, to find these axes with any degree of accuracy becomes increasingly difficult as the corresponding eigenvalues approach equality.

11. COMMUTATIVE MATRICES

It has been seen that, in general, the multiplication of matrices is not a commutative operation, but it has been mentioned that in special cases matrices commute; for example, two diagonal matrices of the same order do. The general rule which determines under what conditions matrices will commute may be given a simple geometric interpretation when the matrices considered are real and symmetric. Thus, let $[A]$ and $[B]$ be two symmetric matrices which we may suppose to be of order $(3, 3)$. In this case, we may associate with each matrix a corresponding quadric surface in a space of three dimensions. We may assume that the quadric surfaces are ellipsoids. The geometric rule for the possibility of commutation of two matrices in multiplication states:

Two symmetric matrices of the same order will always commute in multi-plication when the principal axes of their associated ellipsoids coincide. The matrices will not commute when these axes do not coincide.

To see this, let the quadric surfaces associated with the matrices $[A]$ and $[B]$ be written in the form

(11.1)
$$(x)'[A](x) = 1$$

and

(11.2)
$$(x)'[B](x) = 1$$

If the principal axes of these two quadric surfaces coincide, there must exist an orthogonal matrix $[S]$ that transforms both $[A]$ and $[B]$ to the diagonal forms

(11.3)
$$[S]^{-1}[A][S] = [D]_1$$

and

(11.4)
$$[S]^{-1}[B][S] = [D]_2$$

where $[D]_1$ and $[D]_2$ are diagonal matrices whose elements are the eigenvalues of $[A]$ and $[B]$ [see Eq. (10.6)]. By premultiplication of these equations by $[S]$ and postmultiplication by $[S]^{-1}$, they can be written in the form

(11.5)
$$[A] = [S][D]_1[S]^{-1}$$

and

(11.6)
$$[B] = [S][D]_2[S]^{-1}$$

We now form the matrix product,

(11.7)
$$[A][B] = ([S][D]_1[S]^{-1})([S][D]_2[S]^{-1})$$
$$= [S][D]_1[D]_2[S]^{-1}$$

On the other hand, the product $[B][A]$ is

(11.8)
$$[B][A] = [S][D]_2[D]_1[S]^{-1}$$

Since $[D]_1$ and $[D]_2$ are diagonal matrices, they commute in multiplication so that $[D]_1[D]_2 = [D]_2[D]_1$, and the right members of (11.7) and (11.8) are equal to each other; hence,

(11.9)
$$[A][B] = [B][A]$$

This proves the rule. It is interesting to see how the rule of commutation applies in special cases.

Diagonal Matrices

Diagonal matrices may be proved to be commutative by direct multiplication; however, it is interesting to apply the commutation rule to them. It has been seen that a diagonal matrix can be associated with a quadric surface whose center is at the origin and whose principal axes coincide with the axes of coordinates. Then we consider two diagonal matrices of the same order. Since the principal axes of their associated quadric surfaces coincide with the coordinate axes, these principal axes necessarily coincide, and our geometric rule indicates that the two diagonal matrices commute.

The fact that a diagonal matrix cannot commute with an arbitrary matrix is evident, since the principal axes of an arbitrary matrix do not coincide with the coordinate axes, and hence its axes do not coincide with those of the diagonal matrix.

A *scalar matrix* is a diagonal matrix whose elements are identical and which has, consequently, three identical eigenvalues. A scalar matrix is, therefore, associated with a sphere having the origin as its center. Since the principal diagonals of a sphere are defined by any three mutually perpendicular diameters of the sphere, it follows that a certain triad of these mutually perpendicular diameters will always coincide with the principal axes of the arbitrary ellipsoid. Since the principal axes of the two surfaces always coincide, we conclude, in accordance with the geometric rule, that a scalar matrix commutes with any arbitrary matrix.

If two symmetric matrices do not commute, they cannot be simultaneously transformed into the diagonal form by means of an orthogonal transformation.

12. FUNDAMENTAL PROPERTIES OF THE CHARACTERISTIC DETERMINANT AND THE CHARACTERISTIC EQUATION OF A MATRIX

The determination of the eigenvalues and eigenvectors of a given square matrix is a problem of great importance in applied mathematics. In this section, several of the more important properties of the characteristic equation and the characteristic determinant will be discussed. These properties are very useful in the solution of matrix eigenvalue problems. The characteristic equation of a square matrix $[M]$ was defined in Sec. 2 to be

$$(12.1) \qquad \det(\mu U - [M]) = p(\mu) = 0$$

The polynomial $p(\mu)$ is the characteristic polynomial of $[M]$. If $[M]$ is an (n, n) matrix, the polynomial $p(\mu)$ is of the nth degree and has the general form

$$(12.2) \qquad p(\mu) = \mu^n + a_1\mu^{n-1} + a_2\mu^{n-2} + \cdots + a_{n-1}\mu + a_n = 0$$

If the parameter μ is placed equal to zero in (12.2), the result is

$$(12.3) \qquad p(0) = a_n$$

However, as a consequence of (12.1) we have

$$(12.4) \qquad p(0) = \det(-[M]) = (-1)^n \det[M]$$

Hence, it is apparent that the coefficient a_n of the characteristic equation is given by

(12.5) $$a_n = (-1)^n \det [M]$$

Now let it be supposed that the matrix $[M]$ has n distinct eigenvalues μ_1, μ_2, $\ldots$, μ_n. In such a case, the characteristic equation (12.2) may be written in the factored form

(12.6) $$(\mu - \mu_1)(\mu - \mu_2)\ldots(\mu - \mu_n) = p(\mu) = 0$$

If now μ is placed equal to zero in (12.6), the result is

(12.7) $$p(0) = (-1)^n \mu_1 \cdot \mu_2 \cdot \mu_3 \cdot \ldots \cdot \mu_n = a_n = (-1)^n \det [M]$$

Hence, we obtain the important relation that

(12.8) $$\mu_1 \cdot \mu_2 \cdot \mu_3 \cdot \ldots \cdot \mu_n = \det [M]$$

Since the determinant of the matrix $[M]$ is the product of its eigenvalues, it follows that if one of the eigenvalues of $[M]$ is zero, then $\det [M] = 0$ and the matrix $[M]$ is a *singular* matrix.

If now (12.6) is multiplied in order to obtain the coefficients of the various powers of μ, it will be found that the coefficient of μ^{n-1}, which is written as a_1 in (12.2), is given by

(12.9) $$a_1 = -(\mu_1 + \mu_2 + \mu_3 + \cdots + \mu_n)$$

If, on the other hand, the determinant $\det (\mu U - [M]) = p(\mu)$ is expanded in order to obtain the coefficient of μ^{n-1} in the polynomial $p(\mu)$, the result is

(12.10) $$a_1 = -(M_{11} + M_{22} + M_{33} + \cdots + M_{nn}) = -\text{Tr} [M]$$

By definition, the trace of the matrix $[M]$, $\text{Tr} [M]$, is the sum of the principal diagonal terms of $[M]$. If (12.9) and (12.10) are compared, it is seen that we have the important relation,

(12.11) $$(\mu_1 + \mu_2 + \mu_3 + \cdots + \mu_n) = \text{Tr} [M]$$

If the modal matrix $[A]$ of the matrix $[M]$ is known, it can be seen from (5.5) that the matrix $[M]$ can be written in the diagonal form,

(12.12) $$[M] = [A][D][A]^{-1}$$

where $[D]$ is the diagonal matrix whose elements are the eigenvalues μ_i of the matrix $[M]$. If (12.12) is multiplied by itself p times, the result is

(12.13) $$[M]^p = [A][D]^p[A]^{-1}$$

The diagonal matrix $[D]^p$ has as elements the quantities μ_i^p, which are the eigenvalues of $[M]$ raised to the power p. It follows, therefore, since (12.13)

is the diagonal form of $[M]^p$, that the eigenvalues of $[M]^p$ are the numbers $\mu_1^p, \mu_2^p, \ldots, \mu_n^p$, and hence, as a consequence of (12.11), we have

$$(12.14) \qquad (\mu_1^p + \mu_2^p + \mu_3^p + \cdots + \mu_n^p) = \text{Tr}\,[M]^p = S_p$$

Bôcher's Formulas for the Coefficients of the Characteristic Polynomial

The mathematician M. Bôcher has given some very useful relations for obtaining the coefficients a_i of the characteristic polynomial $p(\mu)$ of the matrix $[M]$ in terms of the quantities $S_p = \text{Tr}\,[M]^{p^1}$. These relations make it possible to obtain the polynomial (12.2) in a much more efficient manner than by direct expansion of the determinant, $\det(\mu U - [M]) = p(\mu)$.

If $S_p = \text{Tr}\,[M]^p$, Bôcher has shown that

$$a_1 = -S_1$$

$$a_2 = -\frac{1}{2}(a_1 S_1 + S_2)$$

$$(12.15) \qquad a_3 = -\frac{1}{3}(a_2 S_1 + a_1 S_2 + S_3)$$

$$\cdots \qquad \cdots \qquad .$$

$$a_n = -\frac{1}{n}(a_{n-1}S_1 + a_{n-2}S_2 + \cdots + a_1 S_{n-1} + S_n)$$

As an illustration of the use of these formulas, consider the matrix $[M]$:

$$(12.16) \qquad [M] = \begin{bmatrix} 2 & -1 & 0 \\ 9 & 4 & 6 \\ -8 & 0 & -3 \end{bmatrix}, \qquad S_1 = \text{Tr}\,[M] = 3$$

and let it be required to obtain its characteristic polynomial. Now, by direct calculation we obtain

$$(12.17) \qquad [M]^2 = \begin{bmatrix} -5 & -6 & -6 \\ 6 & 7 & 6 \\ 8 & 8 & 9 \end{bmatrix}, \qquad S_2 = \text{Tr}\,[M]^2 = 11$$

and

$$(12.18) \qquad [M]^3 = \begin{bmatrix} -16 & -19 & -18 \\ 27 & 22 & 24 \\ 16 & 24 & 21 \end{bmatrix}, \qquad S_3 = \text{Tr}\,[M]^3 = 27$$

Then, by the Bôcher formulas (12.15), we have

$$a_1 = -S_1 = -3$$

$$(12.19) \qquad a_2 = -\tfrac{1}{2}(a_1 S_1 + S_2) = -1$$

$$a_3 = -\tfrac{1}{3}(a_2 S_1 + a_1 S_2 + S_3) = 3$$

Hence, the characteristic equation of the matrix (12.16) is

$$(12.20) \quad p(\mu) = \mu^3 - 3\mu^2 - \mu + 3 = 0 = (\mu - 1)(\mu + 1)(\mu - 3)$$

In this case, the characteristic polynomial can be factored, and the eigenvalues of $[M]$ are seen to be $\mu_1 = 1$, $\mu_2 = -1$, and $\mu_3 = 3$.

The determinant of $[M]$ can be obtained if the characteristic polynomial is known, since (12.5) may be written in the form

$$(12.21) \quad \det [M] = (-1)^n a_n = -3$$

It is instructive to compute the modal matrix $[A]$ of the numerical matrix (12.16). The eigenvectors of $[M]$, $(A)_i$, satisfy the equation

$$(12.22) \quad [M](A)_i = \mu_i(A)_i, \quad i = 1, 2, 3$$

In this case, (12.22) has the explicit form,

$$(12.23) \quad \begin{bmatrix} (\mu_i - 2) & 1 & 0 \\ -9 & (\mu_i - 4) & -6 \\ 8 & 0 & (\mu_i + 3) \end{bmatrix} \begin{bmatrix} A_{1i} \\ A_{2i} \\ A_{3i} \end{bmatrix} = 0$$

If μ_i is placed equal to $\mu_1 = 1$, $\mu_2 = -1$, and $\mu_3 = 3$, the following columns are obtained:

$$(12.24) \quad (A)_1 = m \begin{bmatrix} 1 \\ 1 \\ -2 \end{bmatrix}, \quad (A)_2 = p \begin{bmatrix} 1 \\ 4 \\ -4 \end{bmatrix}, \quad (A)_3 = q \begin{bmatrix} 1 \\ -1 \\ -\frac{4}{3} \end{bmatrix}$$

where the numbers m, p, and q are arbitrary, since only the *directions* of the vectors $(A)_i$ are specified by (12.22). If $m = 1$, $p = 1$, and $q = 3$, the above columns may be assembled into a possible modal matrix $[A]$ of the matrix $[M]$, so that

$$(12.25) \quad [A] = \begin{bmatrix} 1 & 1 & 3 \\ 1 & 4 & -3 \\ -2 & -4 & -4 \end{bmatrix}$$

The inverse of $[A]$ can be calculated to be

$$(12.26) \quad [A]^{-1} = \frac{1}{8} \begin{bmatrix} 24 & 8 & 12 \\ -10 & -2 & -6 \\ -2 & -2 & -2 \end{bmatrix}$$

Direct multiplication gives the result

$$(12.27) \quad [D] = [A]^{-1}[M][A] = \begin{bmatrix} 1 & 0 & 0 \\ 0 & -1 & 0 \\ 0 & 0 & 3 \end{bmatrix}$$

The transformation relating the matrices $[D]$ and $[A]$ is called a *similarity transformation* in the mathematical literature. It is easy to see that the matrices $[D]$ and $[M]$ related by the transformation (12.27) have the following properties:

(12.28) $$\det [D] = \det [M]$$

(12.29) $$\mathrm{Tr}\,[D] = \mathrm{Tr}\,[M]$$

(12.30)   eigenvalues of $[D]$ = eigenvalues of $[M]$

PROBLEMS

1. Determine the eigenvalues and eigenvectors of the matrix
$$T = \begin{bmatrix} \cos(\theta) & \sin(\theta) \\ -\sin(\theta) & \cos(\theta) \end{bmatrix}$$

2. Determine the eigenvalues and the eigenvectors of the following matrix:
$$[M] = \begin{bmatrix} 2 & -2 & 2 \\ 1 & 1 & 1 \\ 1 & 3 & -1 \end{bmatrix}, \qquad \textit{Ans. } \mu_1 = 2,\ \mu_2 = -2,\ \mu_3 = 2.$$

3. Given the third-order circulant matrix,
$$[Z] = \begin{bmatrix} Z_0 & Z_1 & Z_2 \\ Z_2 & Z_0 & Z_1 \\ Z_1 & Z_2 & Z_0 \end{bmatrix}$$
determine its eigenvalues and its eigenvectors and reduce to the diagonal form.

4. Given the following matrix,
$$[M] = \begin{bmatrix} 0 & 1 & 0 \\ 0 & 0 & 1 \\ -a_3 & -a_2 & -a_1 \end{bmatrix}$$
show that the eigenvalues of $[M]$ are the solutions of the equation $z^3 + a_1 z^2 + a_2 z + a_3 = 0$.

5. Use Bocher's formulas to obtain the characteristic equation of the matrix
$$[M] = \begin{bmatrix} 1 & 1 & 1 \\ 1 & 2 & 2 \\ 1 & 2 & 3 \end{bmatrix}$$

6. Determine the eigenvalues and the eigenvectors of the matrix
$$[M] = \begin{bmatrix} 3 & 1+j \\ 1-j & 2 \end{bmatrix}$$

7. Given the quadric surface
$$x_1^2 + 3x_2^2 + 3x_3^2 - 2x_2 x_3 = 1$$
determine its principal axes by introducing a rotation of the coordinate axes by an orthogonal transformation.

8. Given a second-order square matrix $[M]$ that satisfies the equation $[M]^2 = U$, where U is the second-order unit matrix, show that $[M]$ is either $-U$, $+U$, or

$$[M] = \begin{bmatrix} a & r \exp(j\theta) \\ r \exp(-j\theta) & -a \end{bmatrix}$$

where $j = (-1)^{1/2}$, $a^2 + r^2 = 1$, and a, r, and θ are real.

9. Show that any orthogonal matrix of order two is necessarily of one of the following two types:

$$R_1 = \begin{bmatrix} \cos(\theta) & \sin(\theta) \\ -\sin(\theta) & \cos(\theta) \end{bmatrix}, \qquad R_2 = \begin{bmatrix} \cos(\theta) & \sin(\theta) \\ \sin(\theta) & -\cos(\theta) \end{bmatrix}$$

Show that $R_1 R_2 = R_2 R_1 = U$ and interpret this result geometrically.

10. Given the quadric surface

$$4x_1^2 + 4x_2^2 + 2x_3^2 - 4x_1x_2 + 4x_1x_3 + 4x_2x_3 = 1$$

determine the associated matrix $[M]$ of this quadric surface. By introducing an orthogonal transformation $(y) = [S](x)$, determine the directions and lengths of the principal axes of the quadric surface.

REFERENCES

1. Bôcher, M., *Introduction to Higher Algebra*. New York: The Macmillan Company, 1931, p. 296.

2. Courant, R. and D. Hilbert, *Methods of Mathematical Physics*. New York: Interscience Publishers, Inc., 1943. (A classic discussion of the matrix eigenvalue problem with geometrical and physical applications.)

3. Friedman, B., *Principles and Techniques of Applied Mathematics*. New York: John Wiley and Sons, Inc., 1956. (An excellent modern discussion.)

4. Hildebrand, F. B., *Methods of Applied Mathematics*. New York: Prentice-Hall, Inc., 1952. (An excellent, concise, but readable, account of the matrix eigenvalue problem.)

4 THE CALCULUS OF MATRICES

1. INTRODUCTION

In this chapter, the notion of a function of a matrix will be discussed, and it will be demonstrated how a matrix may be considered as a variable in direct analogy with scalar variables. The definition of a derivative and an integral of a matrix will be given, and the use of functions of matrices in the solution of linear differential equations will be discussed.

2. MATRIX POLYNOMIALS

Before we introduce the general concept of a function of a matrix, it is necessary to define what is meant by a matrix polynomial and then to define and discuss infinite series of matrices. Let us first consider a polynomial of degree n of the algebraic variable z, where z may be real or complex. Such a polynomial has the general form

$$(2.1) \qquad P(z) = a_0 + a_1 z + a_2 z^2 + \cdots + a_n z^n$$

Since the argument of the polynomial $P(z)$ is the real or complex quantity z, and since the operations of addition and multiplication of such quantities are known, it is possible to compute the value of the polynomial $P(z)$ for any given value of its argument z, since the coefficients a_i are supposed to be known quantities.

Now, if the scalar argument of the polynomial $P(z)$, z, is replaced by a square matrix $[M]$ of the nth order, and if the coefficient a_0 is multiplied by the nth-order unit matrix, we obtain

$$(2.2) \qquad P([M]) = a_0 U + a_1 [M] + a_2 [M]^2 + \cdots + a_k [M]^k$$

$P([M])$ is defined to be a polynomial of the square matrix $[M]$ of the kth degree. If the coefficients a_i and the elements of $[M]$ are known, the polynomial $P([M])$ may be computed numerically. For example, consider the following matrix polynomial:

$$(2.3) \qquad\qquad P([M]) = U + 2[M] + 5[M]^2$$

where

$$(2.4) \qquad\qquad [M] = \begin{bmatrix} 3 & 2 \\ 1 & 0 \end{bmatrix}$$

If this matrix is substituted into (2.3), the result is

$$(2.5) \qquad P([M]) = U + 2\begin{bmatrix} 3 & 2 \\ 1 & 0 \end{bmatrix} + 5\begin{bmatrix} 3 & 2 \\ 1 & 0 \end{bmatrix}^2 = \begin{bmatrix} 62 & 34 \\ 17 & 11 \end{bmatrix}$$

3. INFINITE SERIES OF MATRICES

Let

$$(3.1) \qquad\qquad F(z) = a_0 + a_1 z + a_2 z^2 + \cdots = \sum_{k=0}^{\infty} a_k z^k$$

be an infinite series of the real or complex variable z.

Let the argument z of the infinite series (3.1) be replaced by the square matrix of the nth order $[M]$, and let the coefficient a_0 be multiplied by the unit matrix U of the nth order. We then obtain

$$(3.2) \qquad F([M]) = a_0 U + a_1[M] + a_2[M]^2 + \cdots = \sum_{k=0}^{\infty} a_k [M]^k$$

This is an infinite series of the matrix $[M]$. Such a series is said to be convergent if the matrix $F([M])$ tends to a definite limit matrix $[L]$ whose elements L_{ij} are finite as the number of terms of (3.2) become infinite. That is, if

$$(3.3) \qquad\qquad F_p([M]) = \sum_{k=0}^{p} a_k [M]^k$$

and

$$(3.4) \qquad\qquad \lim_{p \to \infty} F_p([M]) = [L], \qquad L_{ij} \text{ finite}$$

then $F([M])$ is said to be a convergent series. If the series (3.2) is a convergent one, it defines a function of the matrix $[M]$.

Examples of Series of Matrices

  The Geometric Series

$$(3.5) \quad G([M]) = U + a[M] + a^2[M]^2 + a^3[M]^3 + \cdots = \sum_{k=0}^{\infty} a^k [M]^k$$

The Exponential Series

$$(3.6) \quad E([M]) = e^{[M]} = U + [M] + \frac{[M]^2}{2!} + \frac{[M]^3}{3!} + \cdots = \frac{[M]^k}{k!}$$

4. THE CONVERGENCE OF SERIES OF MATRICES

A complete discussion of the convergence of series of matrices is difficult and is given in works on pure mathematics. The convergence of an infinite series of matrices depends on the behavior of the general term $a_k[M]^k$ as k becomes indefinitely large as seen by (3.3) and (3.4). An estimate of $[M]^k$ can be obtained by a consideration of a quantity called the *norm* of the matrix $[M]$.

The Norm of a Matrix $[M]$

If the elements of a matrix $[M]$ are real numbers, where $[M]$ is a square matrix of the nth order, the norm of $[M]$ is denoted by $N(M)$ and is defined by the equation

$$(4.1) \quad N(M) = [\text{Tr}\,(MM')]^{1/2}$$

where $\text{Tr}\,(MM')$ is the trace of the product MM' of M and its transpose. If the matrix M is symmetric, then $M = M'$ and (4.1) reduces to

$$(4.2) \quad N(M) = [\text{Tr}\,(M^2)]^{1/2}$$

By direct multiplication it can be seen that

(4.3) $\text{Tr}\,(MM') = \sum\sum M_{ij}^2 = $ Sum of the squares of the elements of $[M]$

The following inequalities involving the norm of two matrices of the same order may be proved:

$$(4.4) \quad N(A + B) \leqq N(A) + N(B)$$

$$(4.5) \quad N(AB) \leqq N(A)N(B)$$

From (4.5) it follows that for any positive integer m, we have

$$(4.6) \quad N(M^m) \leqq [N(M)]^m$$

It follows from (4.6) that if $N(M) < 1$, the limit of $N(M^m)$ as m increases is zero. It therefore follows that the limit of M^k as k increases tends to the zero matrix.

The nth-order unit matrix U_n is an nth-order diagonal matrix whose principal diagonal elements are unity; hence, its norm is given by

$$(4.7) \quad N(U_n) = (n)^{1/2}$$

The scalar matrix kU_n, a diagonal matrix whose elements are all equal to k, has the norm

$$(4.8) \quad N(kU_n) = k(n)^{1/2}$$

As we demonstrated in Sec. (12) of Chapter 3, if $[A]$ is a square matrix of the nth order and its eigenvalues are μ_i, $i = 1, 2, \ldots, n$, we have the important relation,

(4.9) $$\mu_1^p + \mu_2^p + \cdots + \mu_n^p = \text{Tr}([A]^p)$$

From this equation it can be established that if $[A]$ is a real *symmetric* matrix and *all* its eigenvalues are equal to zero, then all the elements of $[A]$ must vanish, and $[A] = [0]$, the zero matrix. This can be seen by noticing that if $[A]$ is symmetric, then $[A]' = [A]$, and hence $[A][A]' = [A]^2 = AA'$. Now by the definition of the norm, (4.1), we have

(4.10) $$N^2([A]) = \text{Tr}([A][A]') = \text{Tr}([A]^2)$$
$$= \mu_1^2 + \mu_2^2 + \cdots + \mu_n^2 = \sum_i \sum_j A_{ij}^2$$

This result indicates that the sum of the squares of the elements of a symmetric matrix equals the sum of the squares of the eigenvalues of the matrix. Hence, if the eigenvalues of the symmetric matrix are zero, it follows that the elements of the matrix must be zero. This result does not hold for matrices that are not symmetric. For example, the matrix $[A]$ given by

(4.11) $$[A] = \begin{bmatrix} 2 & -1 \\ 4 & -2 \end{bmatrix}$$

has both its eigenvalues equal to zero.

From the result (4.10), it is evident that a necessary and sufficient condition that $[A]^k$ approach zero as k increases, when $[A]$ is symmetric, is that all the eigenvalues of $[A]$ be less than unity. This provides a sharper criterion of convergence than the requirement that $N([A]) < 1$, which is sufficient but not necessary for convergence. The latter criterion is more useful in most numerical work, since it is far easier to compute an estimate of $N([A])$ than the greatest eigenvalue. For example, if M_0 is the greatest absolute value of any element of $[A]$, it follows from (4.2) and (4.3) that

(4.12) $$N([A]) < nM_0$$

where n is the order of the matrix $[A]$. The test in terms of the norm (4.6) is applicable to asymmetric as well as to symmetric matrices.

If $[A]$ is not symmetric, the result (4.10) no longer holds. However, it can be easily proved that if $[A]$ is a *real* square matrix, symmetric or not, we have

(4.13) $$\mu_1^2 + \mu_2^2 + \cdots + \mu_n^2 \leq N^2([A])$$

where μ_i are the eigenvalues of $[A]$.

The relation (4.13) shows that the sum of the squares of the eigenvalues of $[A]$ is a real number, although the individual eigenvalues may be complex. The norm of a matrix is an extremely useful function, not only for investigating convergence, but also in the important problems of setting definite limits of error in certain matrix iteration processes.[4]

As an example of the use of the norm of a matrix to study the convergence of a series, consider the following geometrical progression:

(4.14) $[G]_m = U + [A] + [A]^2 + [A]^3 + \cdots + [A]^{m-1}$

If (4.14) is postmultiplied by $[A]$, the result is

(4.15) $[G]_m[A] = [A] + [A]^2 + [A]^3 + \cdots + [A]^m$

If (4.15) is subtracted from (4.14), the result is

(4.16) $[G]_m(U - [A]) = [U] - [A]^m$

If $(U - [A])$ is non-singular, (4.16) may be postmultiplied by $(U - [A])^{-1}$ and we then obtain

(4.17) $[G]_m = (U - [A]^m)(U - [A])^{-1} = (U - [A])^{-1} - [A]^m(U - [A])^{-1}$

Hence, we see that

(4.18) $(U - [A])^{-1} = [G]_m + [A]^m(U - [A])^{-1}$
$$= U + [A] + [A]^2 + [A]^3 + \cdots + [A]^{m-1}$$
$$+ [A]^m(U - [A])^{-1}$$

Let it now be supposed that $[A]$ is a square matrix of the nth order and that $N([A]) \leqq k < 1$. Then, by the use of (4.4) and (4.5) we have, on taking the norm of (4.18),

(4.19) $N[(U - A)^{-1}] \leqq n^{1/2} + k + k^2 + \cdots + k^{m-1} + k^m N[(U - [A])^{-1}]$

Since $k < 1$, we may solve for $N[(U - A)^{-1}]$. If the geometric progression in (4.19) is summed, the result is

(4.20) $N[(U - A)^{-1}] \leqq \dfrac{n^{1/2} - 1}{1 - k^m} + \dfrac{1}{1 - k}$

Since Eq. (4.20) holds for every positive integral value of m, we have, in the limit when m becomes infinite, the result

(4.21) $N[(U - A)^{-1}] \leqq n^{1/2} - 1 + \dfrac{1}{1 - k}$

whenever $N([A]) \leqq j < 1$.

It follows, therefore, that when the norm of $[A]$ satisfies this inequality, the geometric progression (4.14) converges when the number of terms becomes infinite.

5. THE MATRIC EXPONENTIAL FUNCTION

One of the most important functions that arise in the calculus of matrices is the matric exponential function. This function is of great importance in the solution of linear differential equations by the use of matrices. If $[A]$ is a square matrix of the nth order whose elements are real, we define the matric exponential function of $[A]$, $\exp([A]) = e^{[A]}$, by the following power series:

$$(5.1) \quad \exp([A]) = e^{[A]} = U + \frac{[A]}{1!} + \frac{[A]^2}{2!} + \frac{[A]^3}{3!} + \cdots = \sum_{k=0}^{\infty} \frac{[A]^k}{k!}$$

This infinite series that defines the matric exponential function, $\exp([A])$, may be shown to be convergent for all square matrices $[A]$. In order to establish the convergence of the series (5.1), let A_0 be the greatest of the numerical values of the n^2 numbers and A_{ij} be the elements of $[A]$ so that

$$(5.2) \qquad\qquad\qquad |A_{ij}| \leqq A_0$$

Then, since $[A]$ is a square matrix of the nth order, it can be seen that each element in the matrix $[A]^k$ will not exceed $n^{k-1}A_0^k$ in numerical value. Now if we let

$$(5.3) \qquad\qquad [S] = \exp([A]) = \sum_{k=0}^{\infty} \frac{[A]^k}{k!}$$

we see that all the elements S_{ij} of the matric exponential function of $[A]$ must satisfy the following inequality:

$$(5.4) \quad S_{ij} \leqq 1 + A_0 + \frac{nA_0^2}{2!} + \frac{n^2A_0^3}{3!} + \cdots + \cdots = \frac{1}{n}(e^{nA_0} - 1) + 1$$

Hence, since all the elements of $\exp[A]$ are bounded by the inequality (5.4), it follows that the matric exponential function is convergent for *all* square matrices $[A]$.

By means of the series definition for $\exp([A])$ it can be shown that if $[A]$ and $[B]$ are *commutative* matrices, so that $[A][B] = [B][A]$, we have

$$(5.5) \quad \exp([A]) \exp([B]) = \exp([B]) \exp([A]) = \exp([A]) + [B])$$

It can also be shown that,

$$(5.6) \qquad \exp([A]) \exp(-[A]) = \exp(-[A]) \exp([A]) = U$$

where U is the nth order unit matrix. These relations express the fact that $\exp(-[A])$ is the inverse of $\exp([A])$.

6. THE MATRIC TRIGONOMETRIC AND HYPERBOLIC FUNCTIONS

Every scalar power series has its matric analogue. However, the corresponding matric power series have more complicated properties. By replacing the scalar argument in the series that define the trigonometric and hyperbolic functions by a square matrix $[A]$, and realizing that $[A]^0 = U$, the unit matrix, it is possible to extend the definition of these functions to matric functions. For example, the matric sine, sin ([A]), all the matric cosine, cos ([A]), are defined by

$$
(6.1) \qquad \sin([A]) = [A] - \frac{[A]^3}{3!} + \frac{[A]^5}{5!} - \cdots
$$

$$
(6.2) \qquad \cos([A]) = U - \frac{[A]^2}{2!} + \frac{[A]^4}{4!} - \cdots
$$

The usual trigonometric identities are not always satisfied by sin ([A]) and cos ([A]) for arbitrary matrices. If the matrix [A] in the defining equation (5.1) for the exponential matric function is placed equal to $j[B]$, where j is the unit of imaginaries $(j)^{1/2}$, the following result is obtained:

$$
(6.3) \quad \exp(j[B]) = U - \frac{[B]^2}{2!} + \frac{[B]^4}{4!} - \cdots + j([B] - \frac{[B]^3}{3!} + \frac{[B]^5}{5!} - \cdots)
$$

$$
= \cos([B]) + j\sin([B])
$$

Placing [B] equal to $-[B]$ in (6.3) yields the relation

$$
(6.4) \qquad \exp(-j[B]) = \cos([B]) - j\sin([B])
$$

If the equations (6.3) and (6.4) are added and subtracted, the following relations connecting the trigonometric functions with the exponential function are obtained:

$$
(6.5) \qquad \sin([B]) = \frac{\exp(j[B]) - \exp(-j[B])}{2j}
$$

$$
(6.6) \qquad \cos([B]) = \frac{\exp(j[B]) + \exp(-j[B])}{2}
$$

The matric hyperbolic functions sinh ([A]) and cosh ([A]) are defined by the power series

$$
(6.7) \quad \sinh([A]) = [A] + \frac{[A]^3}{3!} + \frac{[A]^5}{5!} + \cdots = \frac{\exp([A]) - \exp(-[A])}{2}
$$

$$
(6.8) \quad \cosh([A]) = U + \frac{[A]^2}{2!} + \frac{[A]^4}{4!} + \cdots = \frac{\exp([A]) + \exp(-[A])}{2}
$$

It is possible to establish many of the properties of the matric trigonometric and hyperbolic functions that are similar to the ordinary scalar trigonometric and hyperbolic functions. For example, if (6.3) and (6.4) are multiplied together, the result is

$$
(6.9) \qquad \exp(j[B])\exp(-j[B]) = U = \cos^2[B] + \sin^2[B]
$$

By the use of (6.5) and (6.6), the following equations may be established:

$$
(6.10) \qquad 2\sin([B])\cos([B]) = \sin(2[B])
$$

$$
(6.11) \qquad \cos^2([B]) - \sin^2([B]) = \cos(2[B])
$$

Similarly, by the use of (6.8) and (6.7), the following result may be established:

$$(6.12) \qquad \cosh^2 ([A]) - \sinh^2 ([A]) = U$$

Other identities analogous to those satisfied by the scalar hyperbolic and trigonometric functions may be established in a similar manner.

The matrix $[J]$ defined by

$$(6.13) \qquad [J] = \begin{bmatrix} 0 & -1 \\ 1 & 0 \end{bmatrix}$$

behaves in matrix algebra in a manner similar to the unit of imaginaries $j = (-1)^{1/2}$ in ordinary algebra. By direct multiplication, we have

$$(6.14) \qquad [J]^2 = -U, \quad [J]^3 = -[J], \quad [J]^4 = U, \quad \text{etc.}$$

If in Eq. (6.1) we place $[A] = a[J]$, where a is an ordinary scalar, and compare the result with (6.7), it is easy to see that

$$(6.15) \qquad \sin (a[J]) = [J] \sinh (a)$$

If $[A] = a[J]$ is substituted in (6.2) and the results are compared with (6.8), it can be seen that

$$(6.16) \qquad \cos (a[J]) = U \cosh (a)$$

7. THE MATRIC BINOMIAL THEOREM (COMMUTATIVE MATRICES)

It is possible to establish a matric binomial theorem which is analogous to the binomial theorem of ordinary scalar algebra. For example, if $[A]$ and $[B]$ are two square matrices of the same order, then by direct multiplication we have

$$(7.1) \qquad \begin{aligned} ([A] + [B])^2 &= ([A] + [B])([A] + [B]) \\ &= [A]^2 + [B][A] + [A][B] + [B]^2 \end{aligned}$$

If the matrices $[A]$ and $[B]$ are *commutative matrices*, then $[A][B] = [B][A]$ and (7.1) becomes

$$(7.2) \qquad ([A] + [B])^2 = [A]^2 + 2[A][B] + [B]^2$$

By direct multiplication it can be seen that if n is a positive integer and $[A]$ and $[B]$ are commutative matrices, the following result is valid:

$$(7.3) \quad ([A] + [B])^n = [A]^n + n[A]^{n-1}[B] + \frac{n(n-1)}{2!} [A]^{n-2}[B]^2$$

$$+ \cdots + \frac{n(n-1)\ldots(n-p+1)}{p!} [A]^{n-p}[B]^p + \cdots + [B]^n$$

If $[B] = [A]^{-1}$, Eq. (7.3) is valid, since $[A]^{-1}$ commutes with $[A]$; in this case, (7.3) becomes

$$(7.4) \quad ([A] + [A]^{-1})^n = [A]^n + n[A]^{n-2} + \frac{n(n-1)}{2!}[A]^{n-4} + \cdots + [A]^{-n}$$

By the use of (7.4) and special matrices for $[A]$, many interesting results may be obtained. For example, let $[A]$ be the rotation matrix

$$(7.5) \qquad [A] = \begin{bmatrix} \cos\theta & -\sin\theta \\ \sin\theta & \cos\theta \end{bmatrix}, \qquad [A]^{-1} = \begin{bmatrix} \cos\theta & \sin\theta \\ -\sin\theta & \cos\theta \end{bmatrix}$$

so that

$$(7.6) \qquad\qquad\qquad [A] + [A]^{-1} = 2\cos\theta\, U$$

Now,

$$(7.7) \qquad\qquad [A]^n = \begin{bmatrix} \cos(n\theta) & -\sin(n\theta) \\ \sin(n\theta) & \cos(n\theta) \end{bmatrix}$$

It follows that if (7.6) is substituted into (7.4), and (7.7) is used, we have

$$(7.8) \quad 2^n \cos{}^n(\theta) = \cos(n\theta) + n\cos(n-2)\theta$$

$$+ \frac{n(n-1)}{2!}\cos(n-4)\theta + \cdots + \cos(-n\theta)$$

where (7.8) is obtained by equating the first element of the first row on both sides of (7.3). By placing $n = 2, 3, 4, \ldots$ the various powers of $\cos(\theta)$ may be obtained, expressed in terms of multiple angles, in the form

$$(7.9) \qquad\qquad \cos^2\theta = \tfrac{1}{2}(\cos 2\theta + 1), \qquad n = 2$$

$$(7.10) \qquad\qquad \cos^3\theta = \tfrac{1}{4}(\cos 3\theta + 3\cos\theta), \qquad n = 3$$

$$(7.11) \qquad\qquad \cos^4\theta = \tfrac{1}{8}(\cos 4\theta + 4\cos 2\theta + 3), \qquad n = 4$$

Higher powers may be obtained in the same manner.

8. THE CAYLEY-HAMILTON THEOREM

We now turn to a discussion of what is, perhaps, the most famous and important theorem in the algebra of matrices. This theorem states that if $[M]$ is a square matrix of the nth order and if $p(\mu)$ is the characteristic polynomial of $[M]$,

$$(8.1) \quad p(\mu) = \det(\mu U - [M]) = \mu^n + a_1\mu^{n-1} + a_2\mu^{n-2} + \cdots + a_n$$

then the matrix $[M]$ satisfies the polynomial equation,

$$(8.2) \quad p([M]) = [M]^n + a_1[M]^{n-1} + a_2[M]^{n-2} + \cdots + a_n U = [0]$$

where U and $[0]$ are the unit and zero matrix, respectively, with an order equal to that of $[M]$.

The Cayley-Hamilton theorem is often laconically stated in the following form:

A matrix satisfies its own characteristic equation.

In symbols, if $p(\mu)$ is the characteristic polynomial of $[M]$, then $p([M]) = [0]$. This is a very useful mnemonic device if it is properly understood.

The Eigenvalues of a Modified Matrix

Before we give a proof of the Cayley-Hamilton theorem, let us compute the eigenvalues of the matrix

$$(8.3) \qquad\qquad [N] = [M] - aU$$

when the eigenvalues of $[M]$ are supposed to be known. $[N]$ is a modification of $[M]$ obtained by subtracting the scalar quantity a from the principal diagonal of $[M]$. Now the eigenvalues of $[M]$ are the roots of its characteristic equation,

$$(8.4) \qquad\qquad p_M(\mu) = \det(\mu U - [M]) = 0$$

The eigenvalues of the modified matrix $[N]$ are the roots of its characteristic equation,

$$(8.5) \qquad p_N(z) = \det(zU - [N]) = \det[(z + a)U - [M]]$$

When we compare (8.5) and (8.4), it is seen that if $x + a = \mu$, then we have

$$(8.6) \qquad\qquad p_N(z) = p_M(\mu), \qquad z = \mu - a$$

Since the roots of $p_M(^\mu) = 0$ are the eigenvalues of $[M]$, μ_i, the roots of $p_N(z)$ are $z_i = \mu_i - a$, and these are the eigenvalues of the modified matrix $[N]$. Each eigenvalue is diminished by a.

This result may be used to establish the Cayley-Hamilton theorem for a matrix $[M]$ that has distinct eigenvalues. To do this, let it be supposed that μ_i, $i = 1, 2, 3, \ldots, n$ are the eigenvalues of $[M]$. In this case, the characteristic polynomial of $[M]$, (8.1), may be factored in the form

$$(8.7) \qquad\qquad p(\mu) = (\mu - \mu_1)(\mu - \mu_2)\ldots(\mu - \mu_n)$$

Now consider the factored matrix polynomial,

$$(8.8) \qquad p([M]) = ([M] - \mu_1 U)([M] - \mu_2 U)\ldots([M] - \mu_n)$$

where U is the nth-order unit matrix. In Chapter 3 it was shown that if an nth-order square matrix $[M]$ has n distinct eigenvalues, then its modal matrix $[A]$ may be constructed from the eigenvectors of $[M]$. The modal matrix diagonalizes $[M]$ in the form

$$(8.9) \qquad\qquad [A]^{-1}[M][A] = [D]$$

where $[D]$ is the diagonal matrix of the eigenvalues of $[M]$. We now let

$$(8.10) \qquad\qquad [N]_i = ([M] - \mu_i U)$$

With this notation, (8.8) may be written in the form

(8.11) $$p([M]) = [N]_1[N]_2[N]_3 \ldots [N]_n$$

Let (8.11) be premultiplied by $[A]^{-1}$ and postmultiplied by $[A]$, and let it be written in the form

(8.12) $[A]^{-1}p([M])[A] = [A]^{-1}[N]_1[A][A]^{-1}[N]_2[A] \ldots [A]^{-1}[N]_n[A]$

If we let

(8.13) $$[D]_i = [A]^{-1}[N]_i[A]$$

then (8.12) may be written in the form

(8.14) $$[A]^{-1}p([M])[A] = [D]_1[D]_2[D]_3 \ldots [D]_n$$

The matrices $[D]_i$ are the diagonal matrices of the modified matrices $[N]_i$. By comparing (8.10) to (8.3), we see that the modified matrix $[N]_i$ has all its eigenvalues reduced by μ_i. Hence, the ith row of the diagonal matrix $[D]_i$ has all its elements equal to zero. As a consequence of this fact, it can be seen that the product of diagonal matrices,

(8.15) $$[D]_1[D]_2[D]_3 \ldots [D]_n = [0]$$

Hence, (8.14) reduces to

(8.16) $$[A]^{-1}p([M])[A] = [0]$$

or

(8.17) $$p([M]) = [A][0][A]^{-1} = [0]$$

Equation (8.17) shows that the matrix polynomial $p([M]) = [0]$ and establishes the Cayley-Hamilton theorem of matrices which have eigenvalues that are distinct. However, it can be shown that the relation (8.17) is valid in the general case, in which some of the roots of the characteristic equation are repeated roots.[1]

9. REDUCTION OF POLYNOMIALS BY THE CAYLEY-HAMILTON THEOREM

Since a matrix satisfies its own characteristic equation in a matrix sense, as given by (8.2), it is possible to solve it for $[M]^n$ in the form

(9.1) $$[M]^n = -(a_1[M]^{n-1} + a_2[M]^{n-2} + \cdots + a_nU)$$

It is, therefore, possible to express any polynomial of the matrix $[M]$ as a polynomial of $[M]$ that does not exceed the degree $(n - 1)$, where n is the order of the matrix $[M]$.

For example, let it be required to determine the matrix given by the following polynomial:

(9.2) $$P([M]) = [M]^4 + 6[M]$$

where the matrix $[M]$ is given by

(9.3) $$[M] = \begin{bmatrix} 1 & -3 \\ 3 & 1 \end{bmatrix}$$

The characteristic equation of this matrix is

(9.4) $p(\mu) = \det(\mu U - [M]) = \mu^2 - 2\mu + 10 = 0$

Therefore, as a consequence of the Cayley-Hamilton theorem, we know that the matrix $[M]$ satisfies the equation

(9.5) $[M]^2 - 2[M] + 10U = [0]$

If Eq. (9.5) is solved for $[M]^2$, we have

(9.6) $[M]^2 = 2[M] - 10U$

Hence,

(9.7) $[M]^4 = 4[M]^2 - 40[M] + 100U$

$= 4(2[M] - 10U) - 40[M] + 100U = -32[M] + 60U$

Hence, the desired polynomial $P([M])$ is given by

(9.8) $P([M]) = [M]^4 + 6[M] = -26[M] + 60U$

It can be seen that $[M]^2, [M]^3, [M]^4, \ldots, [M]^k$, where k is an integer greater than or equal to 2, can be expressed in terms of multiples of $[M]$ and multiples of the ~~zero~~ unit matrix in the form

(9.9) $[M]^k = a_k[M] + b_k U, \quad k = 2, 3, 4, \ldots$

Negative Powers

If we premultiply $p([M])$ by $[M]^{-1}$, as given by (8.2), we obtain the equation

(9.10) $[M]^{-1}p([M]) = [M]^{n-1} + a_1[M]^{n-2} + a_2[M]^{n-3}$
$$+ \cdots + a_n[M]^{-1} = [0]$$

The equation may now be solved for $[M]^{-1}$; the result is

(9.11) $[M]^{-1} = -\dfrac{1}{a_n}([M]^{n-1} + a_1[M]^{n-2} + a_2[M]^{n-3} + \cdots + a_{n-1}U)$

This result expresses the inverse of the matrix $[M]$ in terms of the coefficients a_i of the characteristic equation of $[M]$ and the powers $[M]^{n-1}$, $[M]^{n-2}$, etc. of $[M]$. The expression (9.11) has been used as a practical method for the computation of the inverses of large matrices.[4]

In the example involving the matrix (9.3), we may write (9.5) in the form

(9.12) $[M]^{-1} = \tfrac{1}{10}(2U - [M])$

If (9.12) is multiplied by itself, the result is

(9.13) $[M]^{-2} = \tfrac{1}{100}(4U - 4[M] + [M]^2) = -\tfrac{1}{100}(2[M] + 6U)$

$= -\dfrac{1}{50}([M] + 3U)$

By repeated multiplication of (9.12) by $[M]^{-1}$ and the use of (9.6), it can be seen that negative powers of $[M]$ may be expressed in the form

$$(9.14) \qquad [M]^{-p} = c_p[M] + d_p U, \quad p = 2, 3, 4, \ldots$$

As another example of the reduction of a polynomial by the use of the Cayley-Hamilton theorem, let it be required to reduce the polynomial

$$(9.15) \qquad P([M]) = [M]^3 + 2[M]^2 - 3U$$

where the matrix $[M]$ is given by

$$(9.16) \qquad [M] = \begin{bmatrix} 4 & 5 \\ -1 & -2 \end{bmatrix}$$

The characteristic equation of this matrix is

$$(9.17) \qquad p(\mu) = \det(\mu U - [M]) = \mu^2 - 2\mu - 3 = 0$$

Hence, by the Cayley-Hamilton theorem, the matrix $[M]$ satisfies the equation

$$(9.18) \qquad [M]^2 - 2[M] - 3U = [0]$$

We have, therefore,

$$(9.19) \qquad [M]^2 = 2[M] + 3U$$

and

$$(9.20) \quad [M]^3 = 2[M]^2 + 3[M] = 2(2[M] + 3U) + 3[M] = 7[M] + 6U$$

Therefore, the required polynomial is

$$(9.21) \qquad P([M]) = [M]^3 + 2[M]^2 - 3U$$

$$= 11[M] + 9U = 11\begin{bmatrix} 4 & 5 \\ -1 & -2 \end{bmatrix} + \begin{bmatrix} 9 & 0 \\ 0 & 9 \end{bmatrix}$$

$$= \begin{bmatrix} 53 & 55 \\ -11 & -13 \end{bmatrix}$$

10. THE INVERSION OF A MATRIX BY THE USE OF THE CAYLEY-HAMILTON THEOREM

As an example of the use of (9.11) for the inversion of a matrix, let it be required to invert the following matrix:

$$(10.1) \qquad [M] = \begin{bmatrix} 2 & 2 & 0 \\ 0 & 3 & 1 \\ 1 & 0 & 1 \end{bmatrix}$$

Bôcher's formulas may be used to obtain the coefficients a_i of the characteristic equation of $[M]$. We first require the powers $[M]^2$ and $[M]^3$ of (10.1).

By direct multiplication, we obtain

$$(10.2) \qquad [M]^2 = \begin{bmatrix} 4 & 10 & 2 \\ 1 & 9 & 4 \\ 3 & 2 & 1 \end{bmatrix}$$

We now compute the following traces:

$$(10.3) \qquad S_1 = \mathrm{Tr}\,[M] = 6$$
$$(10.4) \qquad S_2 = \mathrm{Tr}\,[M]^2 = 14$$
$$(10.5) \qquad S_3 = \mathrm{Tr}\,[M]^3 = 42$$

The coefficients a_i are now computed by the equations

$$(10.6) \qquad a_1 = -S_1 = -6$$
$$(10.7) \qquad a_2 = -\tfrac{1}{2}(a_1 S_1 + S_2) = 11$$
$$(10.8) \qquad a_3 = -\tfrac{1}{3}(a_2 S_1 + a_1 S_2 + S_3) = -8$$

We now use (9.11) to compute $[M]^{-1}$, and we obtain

$$(10.9) \quad [M]^{-1} = -\frac{1}{a_3}([M]^2 + a_1[M] + a_2 U) = \frac{1}{8}\begin{bmatrix} 3 & -2 & 2 \\ 1 & 2 & -2 \\ -3 & 2 & 6 \end{bmatrix}$$

The determinant of $[M]$ is given by

$$(10.10) \qquad \det([M]) = -a_3 = 8$$

This method for the computation of the inverse of a matrix is straightforward and easily checked.   It is ideally adapted to matrix multiplication by means of punched cards.   The method has the further advantage of giving additional information besides $[M]^{-1}$. The determinant of $[M]$ and the characteristic equation of $[M]$ are obtained as by-products of the computations.

11. FUNCTIONS OF MATRICES AND SYLVESTER'S THEOREM

In Sec. 3 it was shown how a function $F(z)$ of a scalar variable z could be generalized to the analogous matric function by replacing the scalar z by the square matrix $[M]$ in the infinite series that defines $F(z)$, as indicated in Eq. (3.2).   In Sec. 9 it was shown that as a consequence of the Cayley-Hamilton theorem, a polynomial of the form

$$(11.1) \qquad P([M]) = \sum_{r=0}^{k} a_r[M]^r, \quad k > n - 1$$

may be reduced to the polynomial

$$(11.2) \qquad P([M]) = \sum_{s=0}^{s=n-1} b_s[M]^s$$

where n is the order of the matrix $[M]$.   It will now be shown that this reduction has an analogue in the case where $F([M])$ is a matric function defined by an infinite power series.

Let $[M]$ be a real square matrix of the nth order; let μ_i, $i = 1, 2, 3, \ldots, n$ be the eigenvalues of $[M]$ which are supposed to be distinct, and let $(A)_i$ be the eigenvector that corresponds to the eigenvalue μ_i. From (5.2) of Chapter 3, we have the relations

(11.3) $[M](A)_i = \mu_i(A)_i$ and $[M]^k(A)_i = \mu_i^k(A)_i$, $k = 0, 1, 2, \ldots, n$

Let (V) be an *arbitrary* column matrix or vector of the nth order. This vector may be expanded as a linear combination of the eigenvectors $(A)_i$ of the matrix $[M]$ in the following manner:

(11.4) $(V) = c_1(A)_1 + c_2(A)_2 + c_3(A)_3 + \cdots + c_n(A)_n = \sum_{k=1}^{n} c_k(A)_k$

If $[M]$ is a symmetric matrix, it can be shown [see (5.16), Chapter 3] that the vectors $(A)_i$ can be chosen as *normalized* eigenvectors of $[M]$. In this case these vectors satisfy the relation

(11.4a) $$(A)'_k(A)_i = \begin{cases} 0, & i \neq k \\ 1, & i = k \end{cases}$$

It is thus evident that the coefficient c_k in the expansion (11.4) may be obtained by premultiplying (11.4) by $(A)'_k$. The result is

(11.5) $$(A)'_k(V) = c_k$$

If $[M]$ is not a symmetric matrix, then by (5.14) of Chapter 3 it can be seen that

(11.6) $$(B)'_k(V) = c_k$$

where $(B)_k$ is the kth normalized eigenvector of $[M]'$.

Now let (11.4) be premultiplied by the sth power of $[M]$, $[M]^s$, where s is a positive integer. The result of this operation is

(11.7) $$[M]^s(V) = \sum_{k=1}^{n} c_k[M]^s(A)_k = \sum_{k=1}^{n} c_k\mu_k^s(A)_k$$

as a consequence of (11.3). It follows, therefore, that if $P([M])$ is any polynomial of the matrix $[M]$, we have

(11.8) $$P([M])(V) = \sum_{k=1}^{n} c_k P(\mu_k)(A)_k$$

We may generalize this result to continuous matric functions of $[M]$ that are defined by convergent power series of $[M]$. If $g([M])$ is such a function, we have

(11.9) $$g([M])(V) = \sum_{k=1}^{n} c_k g(\mu_k)(A)_k$$

If the function $g([M])$ is such that its elements g_{ir} are functions of a parameter μ, we define the integral of the matric function $g([M])$ with respect to μ as the matrix obtained by integrating each element $g_{ir}(\mu)$ with respect to μ. That is, by definition,

(11.10) $$\int_a^b g([M])\, d\mu = \int_a^b [g_{ir}(\mu)\, d\mu]$$

Now let

(11.11) $$g([M]) = (\mu U - [M])^{-1}$$

and consider the following contour integral in the μ plane:

(11.12) $$I_0 = \frac{1}{2\pi j} \oint (\mu U - [M])^{-1}(v)\, d\mu$$

where the closed path of integration encloses all the singularities of the integrand. In order to carry out the integration, we see that as a consequence of (11.9) we have

(11.13) $$(\mu U - [M])^{-1}(V) = \sum_{k=1}^{n} c_k(\mu - \mu_k)^{-1}(A)_k$$

If (11.13) is substituted into (11.12), the integral takes the form

(11.14) $$I_0 = \frac{1}{2\pi j} \oint \sum_{k=1}^{n} c_k(\mu - \mu_k)^{-1}(A)_k\, d\mu$$

The integrand is seen to have simple poles at $\mu = \mu_i$, $i = 1, 2, \ldots, n$. Since the residue at each of these poles is one, and the integral is equal to $2\pi j$ times the sum of the residues of the integrand by Cauchy's residue theorem, we have

(11.15) $$I_0 = \sum_{k=1}^{n} c_k(A)_k = (V)$$

If we compare (11.12) with (11.15), we may write

(11.16) $$\left\{ \frac{1}{2\pi j} \oint (\mu U - [M])^{-1}\, d\mu \right\}(V) = (V)$$

Since this result is valid for any *arbitrary* vector (V), we must have

(11.17) $$\frac{1}{2\pi j} \oint (\mu U - [M])^{-1}\, d\mu = U$$

where U is the nth-order unit matrix.

Let us now consider the following matric function:

(11.18) $$g([M]) = F(\mu)(\mu U - [M])^{-1}$$

and the integral

(11.19) $$J_0 = \frac{1}{2\pi j} \oint F(\mu)(\mu U - [M])^{-1}(V)\, d\mu$$

As a result of (11.9), we have

(11.20) $$F(\mu)(\mu U - [M])^{-1}(V) = \sum_{k=1}^{n} c_k F(\mu)(\mu - \mu_k)^{-1}(A)_k$$

If this expression is substituted into (11.19), we obtain

(11.21) $$J_0 = \frac{1}{2\pi j} \oint \sum_{k=1}^{n} c_k F(\mu)(\mu - \mu_k)^{-1}(A)_k \, d\mu$$

In order to evaluate this integral, we notice that the integrand has simple poles at $\mu = \mu_k$, $k = 1, 2, 3, \ldots, n$. If we evaluate the sum of the residues at these poles and multiply by $2\pi j$, we have

(11.22) $$J_0 = \sum_{k=1}^{n} c_k F(\mu_k)(A)_k = F([M])(V)$$

where the second equality of (11.22) is a consequence of (11.9). If we now compare (11.19) with (11.22) and realize that (V) is an *arbitrary* vector, we see that we must have

(11.23) $$F([M]) = \frac{1}{2\pi j} \oint F(\mu)(\mu U - [M])^{-1} \, d\mu$$

This formula expresses the matric function $F([M])$ in terms of a contour integral. This contour integral may now be evaluated in the following manner.

It may be noticed that (11.23) has a marked similarity to Cauchy's integral formula in the theory of the complex variable.[8]

In order to evaluate (11.23) we notice that $(\mu U - [M])$ is the *characteristic matrix* of $[M]$ [see (2.7) of Chapter 3]; we thus have

(11.24) $$(\mu U - [M]) = [K] = [K(\mu)]$$

The inverse of the characteristic matrix is

(11.25) $$[K(\mu)]^{-1} = (\mu U - [M])^{-1} = \frac{[A(\mu)]}{p(\mu)}$$

where $[A(\mu)]$ is the *adjoint* of $[K(\mu)]$ and $p(\mu)$ is the characteristic polynomial of $[M]$. If we now substitute (11.25) into (11.23) we have

(11.26) $$F([M]) = \frac{1}{2\pi j} \oint \frac{F(\mu)}{p(\mu)} [A(\mu)] \, d\mu$$

Since $p(\mu) = 0$ is the characteristic equation of $[M]$, the polynomial $p(\mu)$ has simple zeros at $\mu = \mu_k$, $k = 1, 2, 3, \ldots, n$, the eigenvalues of $[M]$. Hence, by Cauchy's residue theorem, the integral may be evaluated and the result written in the form

(11.27) $$F([M]) = \sum_{k=1}^{n} \frac{F(\mu_k)}{p'(\mu_k)} [A(\mu_k)]$$

where the notation $p'(\mu_k)$ signifies

$$\frac{dp}{d\mu}(\mu)$$

evaluated at $\mu = \mu_k$. The relation (11.27) is known in the mathematical literature as Sylvester's theorem. In the proof of Sylvester's theorem given here, it was assumed that the matrix $[M]$ has *distinct* eigenvalues μ_k. A different proof of Sylvester's theorem, as well as the confluent form valid for the case of repeated eigenvalues, will be found in the book by Frazer, Duncan, and Collar.[2]

12. APPLICATIONS OF SYLVESTER'S THEOREM

When the characteristic matrix and the eigenvalues of the matrix are known, Sylvester's theorem enables one to obtain simple expressions for matric polynomials and matric functions. For example, let it be required to determine the exponential function exp ($[M]$) when

$$[M] = \begin{bmatrix} 1 & 0 \\ 0 & 2 \end{bmatrix}$$

In this case we have

$$(12.1) \qquad F([M]) = \exp([M]) = e^{[M]}$$

In this case, the characteristic matrix of $[M]$ is

$$(12.2) \qquad [K] = (\mu U - [M]) = \begin{bmatrix} (\mu - 1) & 0 \\ 0 & (\mu - 2) \end{bmatrix}$$

The adjoint of $[K]$ is

$$(12.3) \qquad [A(\mu)] = \begin{bmatrix} (\mu - 2) & 0 \\ 0 & (\mu - 1) \end{bmatrix}$$

The characteristic polynomial of $[M]$ is

$$(12.4) \qquad p(\mu) = (\mu - 1)(\mu - 2) = \mu^2 - 3\mu + 2$$

Now since $p'(1) = 1$ and $p'(2) = +1$, we have, as a consequence of (11.27),

$$(12.5) \qquad \exp([M]) = e^2 \begin{bmatrix} 0 & 0 \\ 0 & 1 \end{bmatrix} - e \begin{bmatrix} -1 & 0 \\ 0 & 0 \end{bmatrix} = \begin{bmatrix} e & 0 \\ 0 & e^2 \end{bmatrix}$$

As another example, let it be required to compute $[M]^{256}$, where the matrix

$$[M] = \begin{bmatrix} 1 & 0 \\ 0 & 3 \end{bmatrix}$$

To do this by direct multiplication would be a very laborious task. However, the required power may be computed by Sylvester's theorem very simply. In this case, the characteristic matrix of $[M]$ is

$$(12.6) \qquad [K] = \mu U - [M] = \begin{bmatrix} (\mu - 1) & 0 \\ 0 & (\mu - 3) \end{bmatrix}$$

The characteristic polynomial of $[M]$ is

$$(12.7) \qquad p(\mu) = (\mu - 1)(\mu - 3) = \mu^2 - 4\mu + 3$$

The eigenvalues of $[M]$ are, therefore, $\mu_1 = 1$ and $\mu_2 = 3$. The adjoint of the characteristic matrix $[M]$ is given by

$$(12.8) \qquad [A(\mu)] = \begin{bmatrix} (\mu - 3) & 0 \\ 0 & (\mu - 1) \end{bmatrix}$$

The derivative of the characteristic polynomial is, in this case,

$$(12.9) \qquad p'(\mu) = 2\mu - 4$$

Therefore, by Sylvester's theorem (11.27) we have

$$(12.10) \qquad \begin{bmatrix} 1 & 0 \\ 0 & 3 \end{bmatrix}^{256} = 1^{256} \begin{bmatrix} 1 & 0 \\ 0 & 0 \end{bmatrix} + 3^{256} \begin{bmatrix} 0 & 0 \\ 0 & 1 \end{bmatrix} = \begin{bmatrix} 1 & 0 \\ 0 & 3^{256} \end{bmatrix}$$

13. THE USE OF THE CHARACTERISTIC EQUATION IN EVALUATING FUNCTIONS OF MATRICES

The evaluation of functions of matrices by the use of Sylvester's theorem is usually quite a laborious procedure. In this section it will be shown that a function of a matrix can be evaluated by the use of the characteristc equation satisfied by the matrix. In the case of matric polynomials, this procedure is a generalization of the "remainder theorem" of ordinary algebra.

Let $F(x)$ be a given polynomial. Let $F(x)$ be divided by a polynomial $p(x)$ of lesser degree than $F(x)$. Now let the result of this division be expressed in the form

$$(13.1) \qquad \frac{F(x)}{p(x)} = Q(x) + \frac{R(x)}{p(x)}$$

where $R(x)$ is the remainder of the division. Now, if (13.1) is multiplied by $p(x)$, the result is

$$(13.2) \qquad F(x) = p(x)Q(x) + R(x)$$

Now let $p(a) = 0$; then if $x = a$ in (13.2) we have

$$(13.3) \qquad F(a) = R(a)$$

The result (13.3) may be used to evaluate matric polynomials. As an example, let

(13.4)
$$[M] = \begin{bmatrix} 1 & -3 \\ 3 & 1 \end{bmatrix}$$

and let it be required to evaluate the polynomial $[M]^4 + 6[M]$. The characteristic equation of $[M]$ is

(13.5) $p(\mu) = \det(\mu U - [M]) = \mu^2 - 2\mu + 10 = 0$

Now consider the scalar polynomial $F(x) = x^4 + 6x$ and divide it by the polynomial $p(x) = x^2 - 2x + 10$, the characteristic polynomial of $[M]$. The result of this division is

(13.6) $$\frac{F(x)}{p(x)} = x^2 + 2x - 6 + \frac{(-26x + 60)}{p(x)}$$

If (13.6) is multiplied by $p(x)$, the result is

(13.7) $F(x) = (x^2 + 2x - 6)p(x) + (-26x + 60)$

Now if the matrix $[M]$ is substituted into (13.7), we have $p([M]) = 0$ by the Cayley-Hamilton theorem, and, therefore,

(13.8) $F([M]) = [M]^4 + 6[M] = -26[M] + 60U$

This example suggests the following method for evaluating matric polynomials:

If $F([M])$ is a polynomial of the arbitrary nth order matrix $[M]$ and if the characteristic equation of $[M]$ is $p(\mu) = 0$, then $F([M])$ is equal to $R([M])$, where $R(\mu)$ is the remainder when $F(\mu)$ is divided by $p(\mu)$.

The proof of this method follows from a consideration of the identity (13.2). If the scalar x is replaced by the matrix $[M]$, the identity still holds, and since $p([M]) = [0]$ by the Cayley-Hamilton theorem, we have $F([M]) = R([M])$.

The above method applies only to the evaluation of matric polynomials.

Matric Functions

Now let it be supposed that it is desired to evaluate $F([M])$ where $F(\mu)$ is an analytic function of μ and, therefore, has an infinite power series expansion in μ. To evaluate this function, let us follow a procedure similar to that of (13.2). That is, we look for a polynomial $R(\mu)$ of degree $(n - 1)$ such that

(13.9) $F(\mu) = p(\mu)Q(\mu) + R(\mu)$

where $p(\mu)$ is the characteristic polynomial of $[M]$ and $Q(\mu)$ is an analytic function of μ.

The polynomial $R(\mu)$ will have the general form

$$(13.10) \qquad R(\mu) = a_0 + a_1\mu + a_2\mu^2 + \cdots + a_{n-1}\mu^{n-1}$$

where the coefficients a_i are to be determined by the following procedure: In (13.9) we substitute the eigenvalues of $[M]$, $\mu_1, \mu_2, \mu_3, \ldots, \mu_n$ for μ. Now, since $p(\mu)$ is the characteristic polynomial of $[M]$, we have $p(\mu_i) = 0$ for $i = 1, 2, 3, \ldots, n$; by this procedure, we obtain the following equations from (13.9):

$$
\begin{aligned}
F(\mu_1) &= R(\mu_1) \\
F(\mu_2) &= R(\mu_2) \\
&\ \ \cdot \\
F(\mu_n) &= R(\mu_n)
\end{aligned}
$$

(13.11)

These are n linear equations that enable the n coefficients a_i of the polynomial $R(\mu)$ of (13.10) to be determined. Having determined $R(\mu)$ by this procedure, we may now solve (13.9) for $Q(\mu)$ in the form

$$(13.12) \qquad Q(\mu) = \frac{F(\mu) - R(\mu)}{p(\mu)}$$

$Q(\mu)$ is seen to be an analytic function of μ, since the zeros of the denominator are also the zeros of the numerator in (13.12). Now, since (13.9) holds for all values of μ in the region of convergence of $F(\mu)$, we may substitute the matrix $[M]$ for μ in (13.9) and get the following identity:

$$(13.13) \qquad F([M]) = p([M])Q([M]) + R([M])$$

If we now use the fact that $p([M]) = [0]$ as a consequence of the Cayley-Hamilton theorem, we find that

$$(13.14) \qquad F([M]) = R([M])$$

The use of this technique for the evaluation of matric functions will now be illustrated by some examples.

EXAMPLE 1

Let the function (12.1) be evaluated by the method of this section. To do this, we assume that

$$(13.15) \qquad e^{[M]} = a_0 U + a_1[M], \qquad [M] = \begin{bmatrix} 1 & 0 \\ 0 & 2 \end{bmatrix}$$

In this case, the eigenvalues are $\mu_1 = 2$, $\mu_2 = 1$. Hence, the two equations to determine a_0 and a_1 are

$$
\begin{aligned}
e^2 &= a_0 + 2a_1 \\
e &= a_0 + a_1
\end{aligned}
$$

(13.16)

Hence,

$$a_1 = e^2 - e, \qquad a_0 = 2e - e^2$$

Therefore,

(13.17) $\qquad e^{[M]} = (2e - e^2)U + (e^2 - e)[M] = \begin{bmatrix} e & 0 \\ 0 & e^2 \end{bmatrix}$

This is the result given by (12.5), obtained in a simpler manner.

EXAMPLE 2

As a second example, consider the problem of obtaining the power $[M]^{256}$ of the matrix

$$[M] = \begin{bmatrix} 1 & 0 \\ 0 & 3 \end{bmatrix}$$

as discussed in Sec. 12.   To obtain this power, we write

(13.18) $\qquad [M]^{256} = a_0 U + a_1[M] = \begin{bmatrix} (a_0 + a_1) & 0 \\ 0 & (a_0 + 3a_1) \end{bmatrix}$

Since the eigenvalues of $[M]$ are $\mu_1 = 1$ and $\mu_2 = 3$, we have the following two equations to determine the constants a_0 and a_1:

(13.19)
$$1 = a_0 + a_1$$
$$3^{256} = a_0 + 3a_1$$

If (13.19) is substituted into (13.18), the result is

(13.20) $\qquad [M]^{256} = \begin{bmatrix} 1 & 0 \\ 0 & 3^{256} \end{bmatrix}$

This is the same result given by (12.10), obtained in a simpler manner.

EXAMPLE 3

As a third example, let it be required to evaluate the matric exponential function $e^{[M]}$ when the matrix

$$[M] = \begin{bmatrix} 0 & 1 \\ 1 & 0 \end{bmatrix}$$

In this case, the characteristic equation of $[M]$ is $p(\mu) = \mu^2 - 1 = 0$, and the eigenvalues are $\mu_1 = 1$ and $\mu_2 = -1$.   To evaluate $e^{[M]}$, we write

(13.21) $\qquad\qquad e^{[M]} = a_0 U + a_1[M]$

In this case, the two equations to determine a_0 and a_1 are

(13.22)
$$e = a_0 + a_1$$
$$e^{-1} = a_0 - a_1$$

If we solve for a_0 and a_1 in the above equations, we obtain

(13.23) $a_0 = \dfrac{e + e^{-1}}{2} = \cosh(1)$ $a_1 = \dfrac{e - e^{-1}}{2} = \sinh(1)$

If these values of a_0 and a_1 are now substituted into (13.21), the result is

(13.24) $$e^{[M]} = \begin{bmatrix} \cosh(1) & \sinh(1) \\ \sinh(1) & \cosh(1) \end{bmatrix}$$

EXAMPLE 4

As a last example, let it be required to obtain the positive integral powers of the matrix

$$[T] = \begin{bmatrix} A & B \\ C & D \end{bmatrix}$$

whose determinant is unity, so that $\det [T] = (AD - BC) = 1$.   To do this, we assume

(13.25) $[T]^n = a_0 U + a_1[T]$

Since the determinant of $[T]$ is unity, the characteristic equation of $[T]$ is

(13.26) $p(\mu) = \det(\mu U - [T]) = \mu^2 - \mu(A + D) + 1 = 0$

The eigenvalues of $[T]$, therefore, satisfy the equations

(13.27)
$$\mu_1 + \mu_2 = (A + D) = \text{Tr } [T]$$
$$\mu_1 \cdot \mu_2 = 1 = \det [T]$$

It is convenient to let $\mu_1 = e^a$ and $\mu_2 = e^{-a}$.   In this notation, the second equation in (13.27) is satisfied and the first equation in (13.27) may be written in the form

(13.28) $\dfrac{e^a + e^{-a}}{2} = \dfrac{(A + D)}{2} = \cosh(a) = \dfrac{1}{2}\text{Tr } [T]$

In order to obtain the constants a_0 and a_1 in the expansion (13.25) we write the equations

(13.29)
$$e^{an} = a_0 + a_1 e^a$$
$$e^{-an} = a_0 + a_1 e^{-a}$$

The solutions of these equations are

(13.30) $$a_1 = \frac{\sinh(na)}{\sinh(a)}, \qquad a_0 = -\frac{\sinh[(n-1)a]}{\sinh(a)}$$

If these values for a_0 and a_1 are substituted into (13.25), we obtain the convenient expression for the positive integral powers of the matrix $[T]$.

(13.31) $$[T]^n = \frac{\sinh(an)}{\sinh(a)}[T] - \frac{\sinh[(n-1)a]}{\sinh(a)}U$$

It may be shown that this expression is valid for $n = 0, \pm 1, \pm 2, \pm 3$, etc. This result is very useful in the study of certain types of electric circuits.

14. DIFFERENTIATION AND INTEGRATION OF MATRICES

Let $[A(t)]$ be a matrix whose elements $A_{rs} = A_{rs}(t)$ are functions of the scalar variable t.

(14.1) $$[A(t)] = \begin{bmatrix} A_{11}(t) & A_{12}(t) & \cdots & A_{1n}(t) \\ A_{21}(t) & A_{22}(t) & \cdots & A_{2n}(t) \\ \cdot & \cdot & \cdots & \cdot \\ A_{n1}(t) & A_{n2}(t) & \cdots & A_{nn}(t) \end{bmatrix}$$

Then we define the derivative of $[A(t)]$ with respect to the variable t, and write it

$$\frac{d}{dt}[A(t)]$$

by

(14.2) $$\frac{d}{dt}[A(t)] = \begin{bmatrix} \dfrac{dA_{11}}{dt}(t) & \dfrac{dA_{12}}{dt}(t) & \cdots & \dfrac{dA_{1n}}{dt}(t) \\ \cdot & \cdot & \cdots & \cdot \\ \dfrac{dA_{n1}}{dt}(t) & \dfrac{dA_{n2}}{dt}(t) & \cdots & \dfrac{dA_{nn}}{dt}(t) \end{bmatrix}$$

That is, the derivative of a matrix whose elements are functions of a scalar variable t is defined to be the matrix of the derivatives of the original matrix with respect to the variable t.

The integral of the matrix $[A(t)]$ of (14.1) is defined as the matrix of the integrals of the various elements of the matrix. That is, if we define Q to be the *integral operator* $Q = \int (\ )dt$, then we define the integral of $[A(t)]$ to be

(14.3) $$Q[A(t)] = \int [A(t)]\,dt = \begin{bmatrix} QA_{11}(t) & QA_{12}(t) & \cdots & QA_{1n}(t) \\ QA_{21}(t) & QA_{22}(t) & \cdots & QA_{2n}(t) \\ \cdot & \cdot & \cdots & \cdot \\ QA_{n1}(t) & QA_{n2}(t) & \cdots & QA_{nn}(t) \end{bmatrix}$$

By the use of the definition of the derivative of a matrix it is easy to show that

(14.4) $$\frac{d}{dt}[A(t) + B(t)] = \frac{d}{dt}A(t) + \frac{dB}{dt}(t)$$

(14.5) $$\frac{d}{dt}[A(t)B(t)] = \frac{d}{dt}A(t)B(t) + A(t)\frac{d}{dt}B(t)$$

(14.6) $$\frac{d}{dt}A^2(t) = \frac{d}{dt}A(t)A(t) + A(t)\frac{d}{dt}A(t)$$

(14.7) $$\frac{d}{dt}A^{-1}(t) = -A^{-1}(t)\frac{d}{dt}A(t)A^{-1}(t)$$

If t is a real variable and $[M]$ is a matrix whose elements are constants, then one obtains

(14.8) $$\frac{d}{dt}t^k[M] = kt^{k-1}[M]$$

Consider the following matric exponential function:

(14.9) $$e^{t[M]} = U + t[M] + \frac{t^2[M]^2}{2!} + \frac{t^3[M]^3}{3!} + \frac{t^4[M]^4}{4!} + \cdots$$

Then, if (14.9) is differentiated with respect to t, one obtains

(14.10) $$\frac{d}{dt}e^{t[M]} = [M] + t[M]^2 + \frac{t^2[M]^3}{2!} + \frac{t^3[M]^4}{3!} + \cdots$$

$$= [M]e^{t[M]} = e^{t[M]}[M]$$

This result is of importance in the solution of linear differential equations with constant coefficients by the use of matrices.

As a consequence of (14.10), one can establish many interesting results which have their scalar analogues. For example, let $[A(t)]$ be a matrix that is conformable with the constant matrix $[M]$ of (14.9). Then, if $D = d/dt$, we have

(14.11) $$D[e^{Mt}A] = e^{Mt}DA + e^{Mt}MA = e^{Mt}(UD + M)A$$

where U is the unit matrix of the same order as $[M]$. If (14.11) is differentiated $(m - 1)$ times, the result may be written in the form

(14.12) $$D^m[e^{Mt}A] = e^{Mt}(UD + M)^m A$$

Hence, if $P(D)$ is any polynomial of the differential operator D, we have

(14.13) $$P(D)[e^{Mt}A] = e^{Mt}P(UD + M)A$$

as a consequence of (14.12). This result is valid when $[M]$ is a matrix of constants, and $[A(t)]$ is a matrix that does not necessarily commute with $[M]$.

15. ASSOCIATION OF MATRICES WITH LINEAR DIFFERENTIAL EQUATIONS

Matrix algebra provides a most concise notation for the formulation of linear differential equations that involve several dependent variables. The advantage of concise expression is very important in intricate problems that involve several dependent variables. Such problems are now receiving extensive treatment in the theory of vibrations of structures, electrical circuits, etc. These problems involve linear differential equations; the application of matrices to the solution of these equations will now be discussed.

Any set of differential equations can be easily changed into another set involving only first-order differential coefficients by writing the highest-order coefficient as the differential coefficient of a new dependent variable. All other differential coefficients are regarded as separate dependent variables, and, for each new variable introduced, another equation must be added to the set. These added equations are merely the mathematical statement that each new variable is the differential coefficient of the variable that represents the next differential coefficient of lower order.

As a very simple example, consider the following equation:

$$(15.1) \qquad \frac{d^2x}{dt^2} + x = 0$$

In order to express this equation as a set of first-order equations, let $x = x_1$ and

$$(15.2) \qquad \frac{dx_1}{dt} = x_2$$

With this notation (15.1) becomes

$$(15.3) \qquad \frac{dx_2}{dt} = -x_1$$

Therefore, the original second-order differential equation (15.1) may be written in the following matrix form:

$$(15.4) \qquad \frac{d}{dt}\begin{bmatrix} x_1 \\ x_2 \end{bmatrix} = \begin{bmatrix} 0 & 1 \\ -1 & 0 \end{bmatrix}\begin{bmatrix} x_1 \\ x_2 \end{bmatrix}$$

By following the procedure suggested above, it can be shown that any set of homogeneous linear differential equations with constant coefficients can be written in the form

$$(15.5) \qquad \begin{aligned} Dx_1 &= u_{11}x_1 + u_{12}x_2 + u_{13}x_3 + \cdots + u_{1n}x_n \\ Dx_2 &= u_{21}x_1 + u_{22}x_2 + u_{23}x_3 + \cdots + u_{2n}x_n \\ &\quad \cdot \qquad \cdot \qquad \cdot \qquad \cdots \qquad \cdot \\ Dx_n &= u_{n1}x_1 + u_{n2}x_2 + u_{n3}x_3 + \cdots + u_{nn}x_n \end{aligned}$$

where $D = d/dt$, the differential operator. If we let (x) represent the column matrix of the nth order whose elements are the dependent variables $x_i(t)$, and

[u] the nth-order square matrix of the constant coefficients u_{ij}, the set of differential equations (15.5) may be expressed in the following compact form:

$$(15.6) \qquad\qquad D(x) = [u](x)$$

In the case we are considering, the elements u_{ij} of the square matrix [u] are constants. In the general case of linear differential equations, the elements of [u] are functions of the independent variable t so that $u_{ij} = u_{ij}(t)$. In the general case in which the elements of [u] are functions of t, we may write [u(t)], so the set of linear equations with *variable* coefficients may be written in the form

$$(15.7) \qquad\qquad D(x) = [u(t)](x)$$

Since the case of constant coefficients is a special case of the more general one in which the coefficients are variable, the integration of (15.7) will be considered. This set of differential equations may be integrated by a procedure which is known in the mathematical literature as the Peano-Baker method of integration.[5]

The principle of the Peano-Baker method is quite simple. Let the initial values of the elements of the column matrix (x) be given at $t = 0$ so that

$$(15.8) \qquad\qquad (x) = (x)_0 \quad \text{at } t = 0$$

where $(x)_0$ is a column vector of the *initial* values of the elements of (x). Then, by direct integration of (15.7) with respect to the independent variable t, we obtain

$$(15.9) \qquad\qquad (x) = (x)_0 + \int_0^t [u(\phi)](x)d\phi$$

This is an integral equation to determine (x). The variable ϕ is a subsidiary variable of integration. This integral equation may now be solved by an iterative scheme involving repeated substitution of (x) from the left member of (15.9) into the integral. If the following integral operator is introduced,

$$(15.10) \qquad\qquad Q = \int_0^t (\ )d\phi$$

then (15.9) may be written in the form

$$(15.11) \qquad\qquad (x) = (x)_0 + Q[u](x)$$

By repeated substitution, the following equation is obtained:

$$(15.12) \quad (x) = (U + Q[u] + Q[u]Q[u] + Q[u]Q[u]Q[u] + \cdots)(x)_0$$

In the series (15.12) U is the unit matrix of order n, and the second term is the integral of [u] taken between the limits 0 and t. To obtain $Q[u]Q[u]$, [u] and $Q[u]$ are multiplied in the order $uQ[u]$, and the product is then integrated between 0 and t. The remaining terms are formed in the same manner. If the elements of the matrix $[u]$ remain bounded in the range from 0 to t, it may be shown that the series (15.12) is absolutely and uniformly convergent and that it defines a square matrix $G([u])$, given by

$$(15.13) \quad G([u]) = U + Q[u] + Q[u]Q[u] + Q[u]Q[u]Q[u] + \cdots$$

The matrix $G([u])$ has been called the *matrizant* of $[u]$. In terms of the matrizant, the solution of the set of differential equations (15.7) is given by

$$(15.14) \qquad\qquad (x) = G([u])(x)_0$$

If the series (15.13) is differentiated with respect to t, the result is

$$(15.15) \qquad\qquad \frac{d}{dt} G([u]) = [u]G([u])$$

(15.15) expresses the fundamental property of the matrizant.

In the special case in which the elements of the matrix $[u]$ are *constants*, we have, by direct integration of the series (15.13),

$$(15.16) \quad G([u]) = U + [u]\frac{t}{1!} + [u]^2 \frac{t^2}{2!} + [u]^3 \frac{t^3}{3!} + \cdots = e^{[u]t}$$

Therefore, the solution of the set of differential equations with constant coefficients (15.6) may be expressed in the convenient form,

$$(15.17) \qquad\qquad (x) = e^{[u]t}(x)_0$$

in terms of the *initial* values of the variables (x) at $t = 0$.

In order to apply the result (15.17) to special cases, it is necessary to evaluate $e^{[u]t}$ when the elements of the matrix $[u]$ are known. This may be done by the use of the method of Sec. 13. In order to evaluate $e^{[u]t}$, we first determine the eigenvalues of the matrix $[u]$, $\mu_1, \mu_2, \mu_3, \ldots, \mu_n$ by solving its characteristic equation,

$$(15.18) \qquad\qquad p(\mu) = \det(\mu U - [u]) = 0$$

We then expand $e^{[u]t}$ in the form

$$(15.19) \qquad e^{[u]t} = a_0 U + a_1[u] + a_2[u]^2 + \cdots + a_{n-1}[u]^{n-1}$$

and determine the coefficients a_i of the above expansion by the use of the eigenvalues of $[u]$ and the relations (13.11).

As an example of the general procedure, let it be required to solve by this method the following system of equations:

$$(15.20)$$
$$\frac{dx_1}{dt} = u_{11}x_1 + u_{12}x_2$$
$$\frac{dx_2}{dt} = u_{21}x_1 + u_{22}x_2$$

subject to the initial conditions

$$(x)_0 = \begin{bmatrix} x_{10} \\ x_{20} \end{bmatrix}$$

where x_{10} and x_{20} are the values of x_1 and x_2 at $t = 0$.

In this case, the matrix $[u]$ is given by

(15.21)
$$[u] = \begin{bmatrix} u_{11} & u_{12} \\ u_{21} & u_{22} \end{bmatrix}$$

The eigenvalues of $[u]$ are the roots of its characteristic equation,

(15.22)
$$p(\mu) = \det(\mu U - [u])$$
$$= \mu^2 - \mu(u_{11} + u_{22}) + (u_{11}u_{22} - u_{12}u_{21}) = 0$$

If we let

(15.23)
$$u_{11} + u_{22} = \mathrm{Tr}\,[u] = T$$

and

(15.24)
$$(u_{11}u_{22} - u_{12}u_{21}) = \det[u] = D_0$$

then the roots of the characteristic equation (15.22) or the eigenvalues of $[u]$ are

(15.25)
$$\mu_1 = \frac{T}{2} + \left[\left(\frac{T}{2} \right)^2 - D_0 \right]^{1/2} = a + b$$
$$\mu_2 = \frac{T}{2} - \left[\left(\frac{T}{2} \right)^2 - D_0 \right]^{1/2} = a - b$$

Since in this case the matrix $[u]$ is a square matrix of the second order, the expansion (15.19) takes the following form:

(15.26)
$$e^{[u]t} = a_0 U + a_1[u]$$

We have, therefore, the following two equations for the determination of the unknown coefficients a_0 and a_1:

(15.27)
$$e^{(a+b)t} = a_0 + a_1(a + b)$$
$$e^{(a-b)t} = a_0 + a_1(a - b)$$

If these two equations are solved for a_0 and a_1, the results are

(15.28)
$$a_0 = e^{at} [\cosh(bt) - \frac{a}{b} \sinh(bt)], \qquad a_1 = \frac{e^{at}}{b} \sinh(bt)$$

Hence, $e^{[u]t}$ has the expansion

(15.29)
$$e^{[u]t} = e^{at} [\cosh(bt) - \frac{a}{b} \sinh(bt)U + \frac{e^{at}}{b} \sinh(bt)[u]$$

The solution of the differential equations (15.20) is then given by (15.17).

16. THE SOLUTION OF DIFFERENCE EQUATIONS BY THE USE OF MATRICES

In this section it will be shown that the solution of difference equations with constant coefficients may be simply effected by the use of matrix multiplication. To illustrate the general procedure, consider the following system of difference equations with constant coefficients:

(16.1)
$$p_{n+1} = 3p_n + 4q_n$$
$$q_{n+1} = p_n + 3q_n$$

It is required to determine p_n and q_n in terms of the initial values p_0 and q_0. In order to do this, let p_n and q_n be regarded as the component of a vector $(x)_n$ defined by

(16.2)
$$(x)_n = \begin{bmatrix} p_n \\ q_n \end{bmatrix}$$

With this notation, the difference equations (16.1) may be written in the form

(16.3)
$$(x)_{n+1} = \begin{bmatrix} 3 & 4 \\ 1 & 3 \end{bmatrix} (x)_n$$

If we now define the vector $(x)_0$ to be the vector of the initial values p_0, q_0, we have, as a consequence of (16.3),

(16.4)
$$(x)_1 = [M](x)_0, \quad \text{where} \quad [M] = \begin{bmatrix} 3 & 4 \\ 1 & 3 \end{bmatrix}$$

Since by (16.3), $(x)_{n+1} = [M](x)_n$, it is, therefore, clear that

(16.5)
$$(x)_n = [M]^n(x)_0$$

This equation gives the required solution of the problem expressed in terms of the nth power of the matrix $[M]$. To evaluate $[M]^n$, we use the method of Sec. 13. That is, we expand $[M]^n$ in the form

(16.6)
$$[M]^n = a_0 U + a_1[M]$$

In this example the eigenvalues of $[M]$ are found to be $\mu_1 = 5$ and $\mu_2 = 1$; we therefore have the following two equations to determine a_0 and a_1:

(16.7)
$$5^n = a_0 + 5a_1, \quad 1^n = a_0 + a_1$$

The solutions of these equations are

(16.8)
$$a_0 = \frac{(5 - 5^n)}{4}, \quad a_1 = \frac{(5^n - 1)}{4}$$

Consequently, the matrix $[M]^n$ may be expressed in the following form:

(16.9)
$$[M]^n = \begin{bmatrix} \frac{1}{2}(5^n + 1) & (5^n - 1) \\ \frac{1}{4}(5^n - 1) & \frac{1}{2}(5^n + 1) \end{bmatrix}$$

Hence, if the matrix equation (16.5) is expanded, the following solution for the system of difference equations (16.1) is obtained:

(16.10)
$$p_n = \tfrac{1}{2}(5^n + 1)p_0 + (5^n - 1)q_0$$
$$q_n = \tfrac{1}{4}(5^n - 1)p_0 + \tfrac{1}{2}(5^n + 1)q_0$$

As a more general example of the use of matrices to solve a system of linear difference equations with constant coefficients, consider the following system:

(16.11)
$$p_{n+1} = Ap_n + Bq_n$$
$$q_{n+1} = Cp_n + Dq_n$$

where the coefficients A, B, C, and D are given numbers. It is required to solve the system of difference equations for p_n and q_n in terms of the initial values p_0 and q_0. This problem is a generalization of (16.1). If we follow the same procedure that was used in solving the system (16.1), the problem reduces to that of obtaining an expression for $[M]^n$, where $[M]$ is the matrix

(16.12)
$$[M] = \begin{bmatrix} A & B \\ C & D \end{bmatrix}$$

The procedure for obtaining $[M]^n$ is similar to that used in Example 4 of Sec. 13. Let the determinant of $[M]$ be denoted by D_0 so that

(16.13)
$$D_0 = \det [M] = (AD - BC)$$

The matrix $[M]$ may be written in the following form:

(16.14)
$$[M] = D_0^{1/2} \begin{bmatrix} \dfrac{A}{D_0^{1/2}} & \dfrac{B}{D_0^{1/2}} \\ \dfrac{C}{D_0^{1/2}} & \dfrac{D}{D_0^{1/2}} \end{bmatrix} = D_0^{1/2} \begin{bmatrix} P & Q \\ R & S \end{bmatrix} = D_0^{1/2}[N]$$

The elements of the matrix $[N]$ are obtained from the elements of $[M]$ by dividing each element of $[M]$ by the square root of the determinant of $[M]$. The determinant of the matrix $[N]$ is given by

(16.15)
$$\det [N] = (PS - RQ) = \frac{(AD - BC)}{D_0} = 1$$

In order to obtain the nth power of the matrix $[N]$, we may now use the result (13.31), since the determinant of $[N]$ is unity. Hence,

(16.16)
$$[N]^n = \frac{\sinh (an)}{\sinh (a)}[N] - \frac{\sinh [a(n - 1)]}{\sinh (a)}U$$

where

(16.17)
$$\cosh (a) = \frac{(P + S)}{2} = \frac{(A + D)}{2D_0^{1/2}} = \frac{1}{2D_0^{1/2}} \operatorname{Tr} [M]$$

As a consequence of (16.14) we see that

$$(16.18) \qquad [N] = D_0^{-1/2}[M]$$

If this result is now substituted into (16.16), we have

$$(16.19) \qquad [M]^n = D_0^{(n-1)/2}\frac{\sinh (an)}{\sinh (a)}[M] - D_0^{n/2}\frac{\sinh [a(n-1)]}{\sinh (a)}U$$

where U is the second-order unit matrix and the quantity a is given by (16.17). The expression (16.19) is very useful in electric circuit theory. It may be written in terms of the Tchebychev polynomial $S_{n-1}(x)$ in the following form:

$$(16.20) \qquad [M]^n = D_0^{(n-1)/2}S_{n-1}(x)[M] - D_0^{n/2}S_{n-2}(x)U$$

where

$$(16.21) \qquad S_{n-1}(x) = \frac{\sinh (na)}{\sinh (a)}, \qquad x = 2\cosh (a) = \frac{\text{Tr } [M]}{D_0^{1/2}}$$

The solution of the system of difference equations (16.11) is

$$(16.22) \qquad \begin{bmatrix} p_n \\ q_n \end{bmatrix} = [M]^n \begin{bmatrix} p_0 \\ q_0 \end{bmatrix}$$

where $[M]^n$ is given by either (16.19) or (16.20).

Difference Equations of Higher Order

In many applications of difference equations to practical problems, it is necessary to solve one difference equation of a higher order than the first, rather than a system of first-order difference equations. For example, let it be required to solve the second-order difference equation

$$(16.23) \qquad p_{n+1} = 5p_n - 6p_{n-1}$$

In order to solve this equation, the initial values p_0 and p_1 must be given, and p_n obtained from (16.23). The solution is most easily effected if a new variable q_{n+1} is introduced by the relation $q_{n+1} = p_n$. By this device, the problem is now reduced to solving the two simultaneous difference equations of the first order,

$$(16.24) \qquad p_{n+1} = 5p_n - 6q_n$$

$$(16.25) \qquad q_{n+1} = p_n$$

The initial value p_0 corresponds to q_1, and, therefore, if we introduce the square matrix $[M]$ given by

$$(16.26) \qquad [M] = \begin{bmatrix} 5 & -6 \\ 1 & 0 \end{bmatrix}$$

and the column matrix

$$(x)_n = \begin{bmatrix} p_n \\ q_n \end{bmatrix}$$

then it can be seen that

(16.27) $$(x)_{n+1} = [M]^n(x)_1$$

Since $(x)_1$ is now the column of the given initial values, the problem is therefore reduced to that of raising the matrix $[M]$ to the integral power $[M]^n$. In this case the eigenvalues of $[M]$ are $\mu_1 = 3$ and $\mu_2 = 2$. If $[M]^n$ is evaluated by the method of (16.6) and (16.27) is expanded, the resulting solution may be expressed in the form

(16.28) $$p_{n+1} = (3^{n+1} - 2^{n+1})p_1 - 6(3^n - 2^n)p_0$$

This is the solution of the difference equation (16.23) subject to the *initial* values p_1 and p_0. The method illustrated by this example may be generalized to solve the difference equation of the kth order with constant coefficients,

(16.29) $$P_{k+n} + a_1 p_{n+k-1} + \cdots + a_k p_n = 0$$

when the *initial* values $p_0, p_1, p_2, \ldots, p_{k-1}$ are given. To do this, construct the kth-order column matrix $(x)_{n+1}$ whose elements are $p_{n+k}, p_{n+k-1}, \ldots, p_{n+1}$. The difference equation (16.29) is then equivalent to the following matrix equation:

(16.30) $$(x)_{n+1} = [A](x)_n$$

where the matrix $[A]$ has the form

(16.31) $$[A] = \begin{bmatrix} -a_1 & -a_2 & \cdots & -a_{k-1} & -a_k \\ 1 & 0 & \cdots & 0 & 0 \\ 0 & 1 & \cdots & 0 & 0 \\ \cdot & \cdot & \cdots & \cdot & \cdot \\ 0 & 0 & \cdots & 1 & 0 \end{bmatrix}$$

The solution of the difference equation (16.29) may then be obtained by expanding the matrix equation

(16.32) $$(x)_{n+1} = [A]^n(x)_1$$

PROBLEMS

1. Given the algebraic equation of the third degree,

$$z^3 + a_1 z^2 + a_2 z + a_3 = 0$$

construct a matrix $[M]$ whose characteristic equation is the given algebraic equation.

2. Solve the equation $D^2 u + w^2 u = 0$ by the Peano-Baker method, subject to the initial conditions $y(0) = y_0$ and $y(0) = v_0$.

3. Evaluate the matrix polynomial $P([M]) = [M]^3 - [M] + 4U$, where

$$[M] = \begin{bmatrix} 2 & 0 \\ 0 & 1 \end{bmatrix}$$

4. Evaluate the matric function $\sin([M])$ if

$$[M] = \begin{bmatrix} 2 & 1 \\ 1 & 2 \end{bmatrix}$$

5. Evaluate the matric function $\sinh([M])$ if

$$[M] = \begin{bmatrix} 2 & -2 & 3 \\ 1 & 1 & 1 \\ 1 & 3 & -1 \end{bmatrix}$$

6. Evaluate $[M]^{500}$ if

$$[M] = \begin{bmatrix} 2 & -2 & 3 \\ 1 & 1 & 1 \\ 1 & 3 & -1 \end{bmatrix}$$

7. Evaluate $[M]^n$ if

$$[M] = \begin{bmatrix} \cosh(\theta) & \sinh(\theta) \\ \sinh(\theta) & \cosh(\theta) \end{bmatrix} \quad \text{and} \quad n = 0, \pm 1, \pm 2, \text{ etc.}$$

8. Solve the difference equation $A_{k+1} - cA_k + A_{k-1} = 0$, subject to the *given* initial conditions A_0 and A_1.

9. Given the third order *circulant matrix*

$$[C] = \begin{bmatrix} a_1 & a_2 & a_3 \\ a_3 & a_1 & a_2 \\ a_2 & a_3 & a_1 \end{bmatrix}$$

determine the eigenvalues and eigenvectors of $[C]$.

10. Solve the following system of difference equations:

$$I_{k-1} = I_k + Y(V_k + V_{k-1})$$
$$V_{k-1} = V_k + Z(I_{k-1} - YV_{k-1})$$

subject to the initial conditions that I_0 and V_0 are given quantities.

REFERENCES

1. Bôcher, M., *Introduction to Higher Algebra*. New York: The Macmillan Company, 1931.

2. Frazer, R. A., W. J. Duncan, and A. R. Collar, *Elementary Matrices*. New York: Cambridge University Press, 1938. (Contains a detailed discussion of Sylvester's theorem and the reduction of matric polynomials and matric functions; the solution of linear differential equations is discussed in detail.)

3. Hildebrand, F. B., *Methods of Applied Mathematics.* Englewood Cliffs, N.J.: Prentice-Hall, Inc., 1952. (A thorough and clear presentation of most of the material presented in this chapter.)

4. Hotelling, H., "Some New Methods in Matrix Calculation," *The Annals of Mathematical Statistics*, Vol. XVI, No. 1 (March, 1943), pp. 1–34.

5. Ince, E. L., *Ordinary Differential Equations.* New York: Longmans, Green and Company, 1927, pp. 408–415.

6. Kaufmann, A. and M. Denis-Papin, *Cours de Calcul Matriciel Applique.* Paris, France: Editions Albin Michel, 1957. (This text contains an excellent exposition of the reduction of matrix polynomials and functions.)

7. Michal, A. D., *Matrix and Tensor Calculus.* New York: John Wiley and Sons, Inc., 1946. (This text contains a short but clear discussion of matric polynomials, matric functions, and the solution of differential equations by the use of matrices.)

8. Pipes, L. A., *Applied Mathematics for Engineers and Physicists*, 2nd Ed. New York: McGraw-Hill Book Company, Inc., 1958, p. 520.

5 MATRIX METHODS IN THE THEORY OF ELASTICITY

1. INTRODUCTION

Although the tensor calculus is the most natural and powerful mathematical method for the treatment of the fundamental principles of the elastic deformation of bodies, the matrix calculus can also be used to advantage in formulating the basic principles of stress and strain which are the foundations of the mathematical theory of elasticity. Since the classical theory of stress and strain involves linear transformations, a matrix formulation of the basic principles involved leads to a short and neat treatment of the subject.

2. STRESS. DEFINITION AND NOTATION

The analysis of stress is essentially a branch of statics which is concerned with the detailed description of the way in which the stress at a point of a body varies.

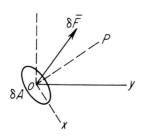

FIG. 5.1. Elementary Area

In order to specify the forces acting within a body, we proceed as follows: at the point O in which we are interested we take a definite direction OP and a small flat surface of area δA perpendicular to OP and containing the point O, as shown in Fig. 5.1. OP is called the normal to the surface δA; the side of the surface in the direction OP will be called the "positive side," and that in the opposite direction will be called the "negative side."

At each point of the surface δA, the material on one side of the surface exerts a definite force upon the material on the other side, so that conditions in the solid as a whole would be unaltered if a cut were made across the surface δA and these forces inserted.

The resultant of all the forces exerted by the material on the positive side of A upon the material on the other side will be a force $\delta\bar{F}$. Actually, there will also be a couple but, as the area δA is supposed to be infinitesimally small, this couple may be neglected.

The limit of the ratio $\delta\bar{F}/\delta A$ as δA tends to zero is called the *stress* at the point O across the plane whose normal is in the direction OP. This stress will be denoted by $\bar{P}_{op}$ and defined by

$$(2.1) \qquad\qquad \bar{P}_{op} = \lim_{\delta A \to 0} \frac{\delta\bar{F}}{\delta A}$$

$\bar{P}_{op}$ is a vector whose magnitude has the dimensions of force per unit area. From the way that $\bar{P}_{op}$ has been defined, it can be seen that the material on the *negative side* of the elementary area of Fig. 5.1 exerts a force $-\bar{P}_{op}\delta A$ upon the material on the positive side of the area.

Let a right-handed Cartesian coordinate system now be introduced through the point O and let the area δA be oriented so that the normal OP coincides with the x axis of the Cartesian coordinate system, as shown in Fig. 5.2. The area δA now lies in the yz plane. The vector $\bar{P}_{ox}$ can be resolved into components in the form

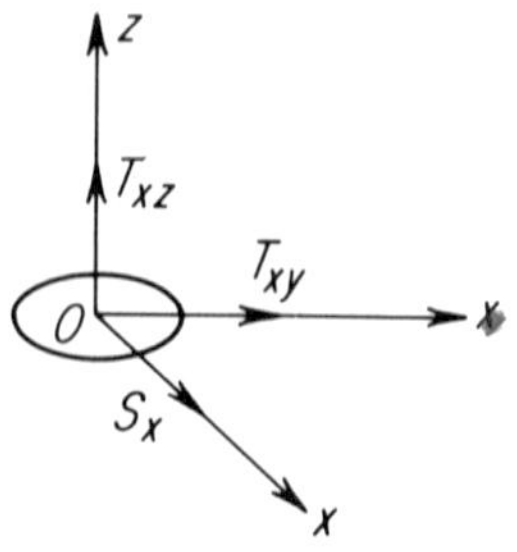

$$(2.2) \qquad (p)_{ox} = \begin{bmatrix} S_x \\ T_{xy} \\ T_{xz} \end{bmatrix}$$

FIGURE. 5.2

The component S_x, which is in the direction Ox and normal to the area δA, is called the *direct* or *normal* component of stress. The components T_{xy} and T_{xz} are in the plane of δA and are called transverse or shear stresses. The notation S for normal stresses and T for shear stresses will be used in this discussion. In the case of the shear stresses, T_{xy} and T_{xz}, the first suffix denotes the direction of the normal to the small area δA and the second suffix denotes the direction in which the component acts. In this discussion the convention will be taken that if the normal component of the stress across a surface is positive, it is called a *tensile* stress, since it tends to pull the material on the positive side of the surface away from the negative side. If the normal component of the stress is negative, it will be called a *compressive* stress.

The vector $\bar{P}_{oy}$ can be resolved into the three components along the x, y, and z axes and can be written in the form

$$(2.3) \qquad (p)_{oy} = \begin{bmatrix} T_{yx} \\ S_y \\ T_{yz} \end{bmatrix} = \text{stress across a plane normal to } oy$$

Similarly, the vector P_{oz} may be resolved into components in the form

$$(2.4) \qquad (p)_{oz} = \begin{bmatrix} T_{zx} \\ T_{zy} \\ S_z \end{bmatrix} = \text{stress across a plane normal to } oz$$

A square matrix $[T]$ can be constructed from the three vectors $(p)_{ox}$, $(p)_{oy}$, and $(p)_{oz}$ in the following manner:

$$(2.5) \qquad [T]_0 = [(p)_{ox} \quad (p)_{oy} \quad (p)_{oz}] = \begin{bmatrix} S_x & T_{yx} & T_{zx} \\ T_{xy} & S_y & T_{zy} \\ T_{xz} & T_{yz} & S_z \end{bmatrix}$$

The matrix $[T]$ is called the *stress matrix*. The nine elements of $[T]$ are called the stress components, or components of stress at the point O. It can be shown that the stress across any plane through O can be expressed in terms of the elements of $[T]$ so that they give a complete specification of the stress at the point.

3. STRESSES IN TWO DIMENSIONS

Before we discuss the general theory of stress in three dimensions, it is instructive to study the corresponding two-dimensional problems. In order to do this, we first consider the forces on a very small square of material $OABCO$, whose side length $OA = OC = a$ is very small. This square is shown in Fig. 5.3. The forces on the side AB of the square (per unit length perpendicular to the plane of the paper) are aS_x and aT_{xy}. The forces on the face CO are $-aS_x$ and $-aT_{xy}$, etc. It can be seen that the forces are in equilibrium. However, if moments are taken about the point O, it is seen that there is a couple of moment

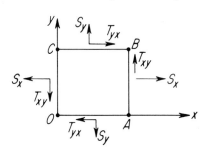

FIG. 5.3. A Square Element in Equilibrium

$$(3.1) \qquad M = a(T_{xy} - T_{yx})$$

In order to preserve equilibrium, this moment must vanish. Therefore, we must have

$$(3.2) \qquad T_{xy} = T_{yx}$$

In two dimensions, the general stress matrix $[T]$ reduces to the second-order square matrix

$$(3.3) \qquad [T]_0 = \begin{bmatrix} S_x & T_{yx} \\ T_{xy} & S_y \end{bmatrix}$$

and as a consequence of (3.2) we see that it is a symmetric matrix.

We now consider Fig. 5.4. This figure depicts a triangular slab of material in equilibrium. It is desired to calculate the normal and shear stresses S and T across the plane face AB. It is assumed that the triangular figure is so small that the stresses on AB differ very little from those across a parallel plane through O. Let $AB = a$, $OA = b$, and $OB = c$.

Let p_x and p_y be the components of stress across the face AB of the triangular slab of Fig. 5.4 (it is assumed that the slab has unit height perpendicular to the paper). For equilibrium we must have

(3.4) $$ap_x = cS_x + bT_{yx}$$

(3.5) $$ap_y = cT_{xy} + bS_y$$

From the geometry, we have $c = a \cos \theta$, $b = a \sin \theta$; hence, if these relations are substituted into (3.4) and (3.5) and the result is divided by a, we obtain

(3.6) $$\begin{bmatrix} p_x \\ p_y \end{bmatrix} = \begin{bmatrix} S_x & T_{yx} \\ T_{xy} & S_y \end{bmatrix} \cdot \begin{bmatrix} \cos \theta \\ \sin \theta \end{bmatrix}$$
$$= (p)$$

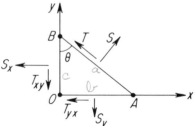

FIG. 5.4. Stress Across a Plane

In order to compute the normal stress S on the plane AB of Fig. 5.4, it is necessary only to resolve the vector (3.6) in the direction of the normal to the plane AB. The direction cosines of this normal with respect to the x and y axes are $\cos \theta$ and $\sin \theta$; hence, S is given by

(3.7) $$S = p_x \cos (\theta) + p_y \sin (\theta)$$

Since p_x and p_y are given by (3.6), S may be obtained by the relation

(3.8) $$\begin{bmatrix} \cos (\theta) \\ \sin (\theta) \end{bmatrix}' \begin{bmatrix} S_x & T_{yx} \\ T_{xy} & S_y \end{bmatrix} \begin{bmatrix} \cos (\theta) \\ \sin (\theta) \end{bmatrix}$$

If the vector of direction cosines of the normal is written in the following form:

(3.9) $$(n) = \begin{bmatrix} \cos (\theta) \\ \sin (\theta) \end{bmatrix}$$

then the normal stress S may be written in the compact form

(3.10) $$S = (n)'[T]_0(n)$$

where $[T]_0$ is the stress matrix (3.3). It can be seen that if (u) is a unit vector whose direction cosines are u_x and u_y so that

(3.11) $$(u) = \begin{bmatrix} u_x \\ u_y \end{bmatrix}$$

then the stress in the direction of the unit vector (u) is

(3.12) $S_u = (u)'[T]_0(n) = $ stress in the (u) direction

In order to get the shear stress T on the face AB, it is necessary only to orient the unit vector (u) in the direction AB. If this is done, the direction cosines of (u) are $u_x = -\sin\theta$, $u_y = \cos\theta$. If these values for the direction cosines of (u) are substituted into (3.12), the following expression for the shear stress T on the plane AB is obtained:

(3.13) $$T = \begin{bmatrix} -\sin\theta \\ \cos\theta \end{bmatrix} [T]_0(n)$$

If the expressions for S and for T are expanded, the following results are obtained:

(3.14) $S = S_x \cos^2\theta + 2T_{xy}\sin\theta\cos\theta + S_y\sin^2\theta$

(3.15) $T = (S_y - S_x)\sin\theta\cos\theta + T_{xy}(\cos^2\theta - \sin^2\theta)$

If the expression for the normal stress S is differentiated with respect to the angle θ, the following result is obtained:

(3.16) $\dfrac{dS}{d\theta} = 2(S_y - S_x)\sin\theta\cos\theta + 2T_{xy}(\cos^2\theta - \sin^2\theta) = 2T$

It can be seen from this result that the normal stress S is a maximum or a minimum when the angle θ is given by

(3.17) $$\tan 2\theta = \frac{2T_{xy}}{(S_x - S_y)}$$

For this value of the angle θ, the shear stress T vanishes. Equation (3.17) defines two directions at right angles to each other such that the normal stresses over them are the greatest and least and the shear stresses over them are zero. These are called the *principal axes of stress.*

The significance of the principal axes of stress can be easily understood if one studies the manner in which the stress matrix is transformed when one rotates the coordinate system from the original set of axes x, y to a system of Cartesian coordinates x', y' that are obtained from the original ones by a rotation through an angle θ, as shown in Fig. 5.5.

Rotation of the Coordinate Axes

As we have seen in Chapter 3, a rotation of the coordinate axes may be expressed by the equation

(3.18) $$\begin{bmatrix} x \\ y \end{bmatrix} = \begin{bmatrix} \cos\theta & -\sin\theta \\ \sin\theta & \cos\theta \end{bmatrix} \begin{bmatrix} x' \\ y' \end{bmatrix}, \qquad [S] = \begin{bmatrix} \cos\theta & -\sin\theta \\ \sin\theta & \cos\theta \end{bmatrix}$$

where the transformation matrix $[S]$ is an orthogonal matrix with the property that $[S]^{-1} = [S]'$. If the axes x-y are rotated to the axes x'-y' by the orthogonal transformation (3.18), then all vectors expressed in terms of components along the x-y axes are transformed to vectors whose components are expressed along the x'-y' axes by the transformations

(3.19) $$(p) = [S](\bar{p})', \quad (n) = [S](\bar{n})^{\bullet}$$

Equation (3.6) may be written in the compact form,

(3.20) $$(p) = [T]_0(n)$$

As a consequence of (3.19), Eq. (3.20) is transformed in the new coordinate system to

(3.21) $$[S](\bar{p})' = [T]_0[S](\bar{n})^{\bullet}$$

or, if (3.21) is premultiplied by $[S]^{-1} = [S]'$, the result is

(3.22) $$(\bar{p})' = [S]'[T]_0[S](\bar{n})^{\bullet}$$

The stress matrix $[T]_0$ is, therefore, transformed by the equation

(3.23) $$[\bar{T}]_0 = [S]'[T]_0[S]$$

Then Eq. (3.6) has the form

(3.24) $$(\bar{p}) = [\bar{T}]_0(\bar{n})$$

in the rotated coordinate system.

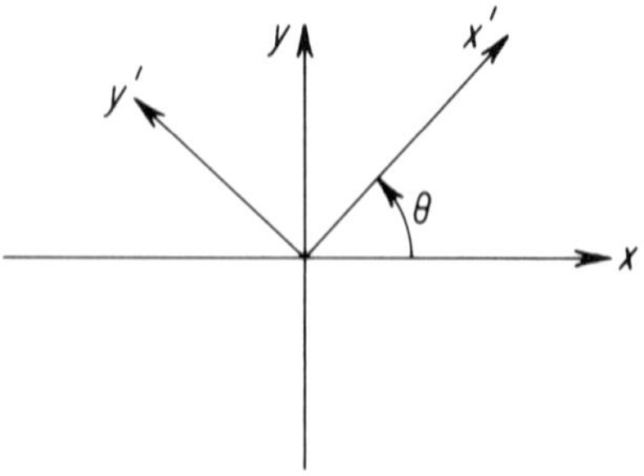

FIG. 5.5. Rotated Coordinate System

If Eq. (3.23) is expanded by carrying out the indicated matrix multiplication, the result is

(3.25) $$[\bar{T}]_0 = \begin{bmatrix} (S_x \cos^2\theta + T_{xy}\sin 2\theta + S_y \sin^2\theta) & (S_y - S_x)\dfrac{\sin 2\theta}{2} + T_{xy}\cos 2\theta \\ (S_y - S_x)\dfrac{\sin 2\theta}{2} + T_{xy}\cos 2\theta & (S_x \sin^2\theta - T_{xy}\sin 2\theta + S_y \cos^2\theta) \end{bmatrix}$$

$$= \begin{bmatrix} \bar{S}_x & \bar{T}_{xy} \\ \bar{T}_{xy} & \bar{S}_y \end{bmatrix}$$

This is the stress matrix in the rotated coordinate system. It is seen, therefore, that if the angle of rotation of the axes is given by

(3.26) $$\tan 2\theta = \frac{2T_{xy}}{(S_x - S_y)}$$

the matrix $[\bar{T}]_0$ has the diagonal form, since for this angle $T'_{xy} = 0$. The coordinate axes x' and y' are now principal axes of stress. Since the symmetric matrix $[T]_0$ is reduced to the diagonal form by the transformation (3.23) when the angle θ satisfies (3.26), it is evident that $[S]$ is in this case the modal matrix of $[T]_0$, and that the diagonal elements S'_x and S'_y are the *eigenvalues* of the matrix $[T]_0$.

The Eigenvalues of the Stress Matrix

The eigenvalues of the stress matrix $[T]_0$ are the roots of the characteristic equation

$$(3.27) \qquad \det (\mu U - [T]_0) = \begin{vmatrix} (\mu - S_x) & -T_{xy} \\ -T_{xy} & (\mu - S_y) \end{vmatrix}$$

$$= \mu^2 - \mu(S_x + S_y) + S_x S_y - T_{xy}^2 = 0$$

The roots of (3.27) are the eigenvalues S_1 and S_2 of the stress matrix $[T]_0$ and are given by

$$(3.28) \qquad S_1 = \frac{(S_x + S_y)}{2} + \frac{[(S_x - S_y)^2 + 4T_{xy}^2]^{1/2}}{2}$$

and

$$(3.29) \qquad S_2 = \frac{(S_x + S_y)}{2} - \frac{[(S_x - S_y)^2 + 4T_{xy}^2]^{1/2}}{2}$$

These eigenvalues of $[T]_0$ are the principal stresses. Since the trace and the determinant of a matrix are *invariant* under a rotation transformation of the type (3.23), we have

$$(3.30) \qquad S_1 + S_2 = S_x + S_y = \text{Tr } [T]_0$$

and

$$(3.31) \qquad S_1 S_2 = \det [T]_0 = S_x S_y - T_{xy}^2$$

That is, if the axes are rotated, these quantities remain unchanged. These invariants are of great importance in the theory of elasticity.

4. STRESSES IN THREE DIMENSIONS

In three dimensions the stress matrix $[T]_0$ is given by

$$(4.1) \qquad [T]_0 = \begin{bmatrix} S_x & T_{yx} & T_{zx} \\ T_{xy} & S_y & T_{zy} \\ T_{xz} & T_{yz} & S_z \end{bmatrix}$$

where the elements of $[T]_0$ are the stress components discussed in Sec. 2. By considering the equilibrium of a rectangular parallelepiped whose faces are perpendicular to the x, y, and z axes of the Cartesian coordinate system, it can be shown by taking couples about the x, y, and z axes that

$$(4.2) \qquad T_{xy} = T_{yx}, \qquad T_{yz} = T_{zy}, \qquad T_{zx} = T_{xz}$$

We next calculate the stress across a plane through O whose normal has the direction cosines (n_x, n_y, n_z) relative to the x, y, and z axes. In order to do this, we consider the equilibrium of a small tetrahedron $OABC$, shown in Fig. 5.6. The face ABC is normal to the unit vector (n) and has an area W. Since the direction cosines of the normal to the face ABC are n_x, n_y, and n_z, the areas of the faces OAB, OBC, and OCA are Wn_z, Wn_x, and Wn_y, respectively. If now p_x, p_y, and p_z are the components of stress across the face ABC in the direction of the x, y, and z axes, and then if the forces acting on the tetrahedron are resolved in the x direction, the following result is obtained:

$$(4.3) \qquad Wp_x = Wn_xS_x + Wn_yT_{yx} + Wn_zT_{zx}$$

or

$$(4.4) \qquad p_x = n_xS_x + n_yT_{yx} + n_zT_{zx}$$

In a similar manner, if the forces are resolved in the y and z directions, the following equations are obtained:

$$(4.5) \quad p_y = n_xT_{xy} + n_yS_y + n_zT_{zy}$$

$$(4.6) \quad p_z = n_xT_{xz} + n_yT_{yz} + n_zS_z$$

If we let (p) denote a vector whose components are p_x, p_y, and p_z, and (n) the unit normal vector of components n_x, n_y, and n_z, then Eqs. (4.4), (4.5), and (4.6) may be written in the compact form

$$(4.7) \qquad (p) = [T]_0(n)$$

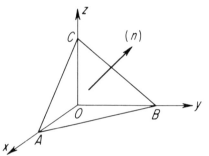

FIG. 5.6. Tetrahedron in Equilibrium

The normal stress S across the plane face ABC is obtained by resolving the vector (p) in the direction of the normal by taking the scalar product of the vectors (n) and (p). If this is done, one obtains

$$(4.8) \quad S = (n)'(p) = (n)'[T]_0(n)$$
$$= n_x^2S_x + n_y^2S_y + n_z^2S_z + 2n_yn_zT_{yz} + 2n_zn_xT_{zx} + 2n_xn_yT_{xy}$$

If a direction is specified by the unit vector (u) whose direction cosines with respect to the x, y, z axes are u_x, u_y, and u_z, then the vector (p) may be resolved in the direction (u) by taking the scalar product of the vectors (u) and (p). If $(p)_u$ is the component of (p) in the direction of (u), we have

$$(4.9) \qquad (p)_u = (u)'(p) = (u)'[T]_0(n)$$

If two unit vectors, say (u) and (v), are chosen so that they are normal to (n) and to each other, then they lie in a plane parallel to the plane ABC. If now (p) is resolved in the direction of these unit vectors, they are components of the shear stress T across ABC, and we may write

(4.10) $T_u = (u)'[T]_0(n)$ and $T_v = (v)'[T]_0(n)$

Since the vectors (n), (u), and (v) are *orthogonal* unit vectors, they satisfy the following relationships:

(4.11) $(n)'(n) = 1,$ $(u)'(u) = 1,$ $(v)'(v) = 1$

and

(4.12) $(n)'(u) = 0,$ $(n)'(v) = 0,$ $(u)'(v) = 0$

The square of the shear stress across ABC T^2 is given by

(4.13) $T^2 = T_u^2 + T_v^2$

This, however, is not the simplest method of calculating the shear stress.

The Stress Quadric

Let the position vector (R) of a point P in the x, y, z Cartesian coordinate system of Fig. 5.6 be given by

(4.14) $(R) = S^{-1/2}(n) = \begin{bmatrix} x \\ y \\ z \end{bmatrix}$

where S is the normal stress given by (4.8). The unit vector (n) may then be expressed in the form

(4.15) $(n) = S^{1/2}(R)$

If this value for (n) is substituted into Eq. (4.8), the following result is obtained:

(4.16) $(R)'[T]_0(R) = 1$

This equation has the expanded form

(4.17) $x^2 S_x + y^2 S_y + z^2 S_z + 2yzT_{yz} + 2zxT_{zx} + 2xyT_{xy} = 1$

The point P, therefore, lies on this quadric surface. In Chapter 3, Sec. 10, it was shown that it is possible to introduce a rotated coordinate system (x', y', z') by means of an orthogonal matrix $[M]$ in the form

(4.18) $\begin{bmatrix} x \\ y \\ z \end{bmatrix} = [M] \begin{bmatrix} x' \\ y' \\ z' \end{bmatrix}$,   where $[M]^{-1} = [M]'$

so that in the x', y', z' coordinate system, (4.17) has the form

(4.19) $S_1 x'^2 + S_2 y'^2 + S_3 z'^2 = 1$

The x', y', z' axes are the principal axes of the quadric surface (4.17).

The Principal Stresses

The quantities S_1, S_2, and S_3 of (4.19) are the principal stresses. These quantities are the *eigenvalues* of the stress matrix $[T]_0$. Since the stress matrix is a symmetric matrix whose elements are all real, it has real eigenvalues. The principal stresses are, therefore, the solutions of the characteristic equation of the stress matrix $[T]_0$. This equation has the form

$$(4.20) \qquad \det(\mu U - [T]_0) = \begin{bmatrix} (\mu - S_x) & -T_{xy} & -T_{xz} \\ -T_{yx} & (\mu - S_y) & -T_{yz} \\ -T_{zx} & -T_{zy} & (\mu - S_z) \end{bmatrix}$$

This is a cubic in μ, and its three real roots are the principal stresses $\mu_1 = S_1$, $\mu_2 = S_2$, and $\mu_3 = S_3$.

The Invariants of the Stress Matrix

If the characteristic equation of the matrix $[T]_0$, (4.20), is expanded, it may be written in the following form:

$$(4.21) \qquad \mu^3 - \theta\mu^2 + I_2\mu - I_3 = 0$$

The coefficients of this equation have the following values:

$$(4.22) \qquad \theta = \operatorname{Tr}[T]_0 = (S_x + S_y + S_z) = (S_1 + S_2 + S_3)$$

$$(4.23) \qquad I_2 = S_x S_y + S_y S_z + S_z S_x - T_{xy}^2 - T_{yz}^2 - T_{zx}^2$$
$$= S_1 S_2 + S_2 S_3 + S_3 S_1$$

and

$$(4.24) \qquad I_3 = \det[T]_0 = S_1 S_2 S_3$$

The quantity θ in (4.22) is called the *bulk stress*. If a definite stress at a point is under consideration, and if the directions of the axes of x, y, and z are changed, the values of the six components of stress S_x, S_y, ..., T_{zx} will change, but the principal stresses S_1, S_2, and S_3 must retain the same values; therefore, Eq. (4.21) will remain unchanged, and, therefore, its coefficients θ, I_2, and I_3 must remain constant. These coefficients are the *invariants* of the stress matrix. It can be seen that the bulk stress θ is the sum of the three principal stresses.

The Shear Stresses

If a Cartesian coordinate system x, y, z is taken along the principal axes of the stress quadric (4.17), then with respect to these axes the stress matrix has the following form:

$$(4.25) \qquad [T]_0 = \begin{bmatrix} S_1 & 0 & 0 \\ 0 & S_2 & 0 \\ 0 & 0 & S_3 \end{bmatrix}$$

where S_1, S_2, and S_3 are the principal *stresses*.

If (n) is a unit vector normal to a plane in the x, y, z space, the components of stress across this plane are given by (4.7) in the form

(4.26)
$$p_x = n_x S_1$$
$$p_y = n_y S_2, \quad \text{or} \quad (p) = [T]_0(n)$$
$$p_z = n_z S_3$$

where n_x, n_y, n_z are the direction cosines of the normal (n). The normal stress across this plane is, by (4.8),

(4.27) $$S = (n)'[T]_0(n) = n_x^2 S_1 + n_y^2 S_2 + n_z^2 S_3$$

The magnitude R of the stress across the plane under consideration is given by

(4.28) $$R = (p_x^2 + p_y^2 + p_z^2)^{1/2} = (n_x^2 S_1^2 + n_y^2 S_2^2 + n_z^2 S_3^2)^{1/2}$$

Let it be assumed that the vectors (p) and (n) are oriented as shown in Fig. 5.7. The shear stress vector (T) lies in the plane of (n) and (p) and is normal to the vector (n). Let the magnitude of the shear stress vector be denoted by T. Then if the stress vector (p) across the plane is resolved into its components T and S in and perpendicular to the plane of Fig. 5.7, the following relation is obtained:

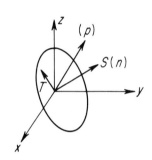

FIGURE 5.7

(4.29) $$R^2 = T^2 + S^2$$

where $R^2 = (p)'(p)$ is the square of the magnitude of the stress vector (p). This equation may be solved for the square of the magnitude of the shear vector or T^2 in the form

(4.30) $$T^2 = R^2 - S^2 = n_x^2 S_1^2 + n_y^2 S_2^2 + n_z^2 S_3^2 - (n_x^2 S_1 - n_y^2 S_2 + n_z^2 S_3)^2$$
$$= (S_1 - S_2)^2 n_x^2 n_y^2 + (S_2 - S_3)^2 n_y^2 n_z^2$$
$$+ (S_3 - S_1)^2 n_z^2 n_x^2$$

In the special case in which $S_1 = S_2 = S_3 = -p$, we have, by (4.27), $S = -p$, and from (4.30) we have $T = 0$. This is the case of *hydrostatic pressure* p.

The square of the magnitude of the shear stress T^2 given in (4.30) may also be written in the compact matrix form

(4.31) $$T^2 = R^2 - S^2 = (p)'(p) - [(n)'[T]_0(n)]^2$$
$$= (n)'[T]_0^2(n) - [(n)'[T]_0(n)]^2$$

In order to determine the maximum value of T with a variation of the direction of the normal (n), it is necessary to differentiate either (4.30) or (4.31) with respect to the direction cosines of the normal (n), n_x, n_y, and n_z, subject to the condition that since (n) is a unit vector, we must have $n_x^2 + n_y^2 + n_z^2 = 1$, and, therefore, these quantities cannot all vary independently.

If the expression (4.30) is differentiated with respect to the direction cosines n_x, n_y, and n_z of the normal vector (n) subject to the condition that $n_x^2 + n_y^2 + n_z^2 = 1$, the direction cosines along which the stationary values of T lie may be determined. These quantities define three directions that the unit vector (n) must have so that the shear stress has a stationary value. If these three directions $(n)_1$, $(n)_2$, and $(n)_3$ are then substituted into (4.30) or (4.31), three different values T_1, T_2, and T_3 for the shear stress are obtained. The three directions $(n)_i$ and the corresponding shear stresses T_i are found to be

$$(4.32) \qquad (n)_1 = \begin{bmatrix} 0 \\ 2^{-1/2} \\ 2^{-1/2} \end{bmatrix}, \qquad T_1 = \tfrac{1}{2}(S_2 - S_3)$$

$$(4.33) \qquad (n)_2 = \begin{bmatrix} 2^{-1/2} \\ 0 \\ 2^{-1/2} \end{bmatrix}, \qquad T_2 = \tfrac{1}{2}(S_1 - S_3)$$

$$(4.34) \qquad (n)_3 = \begin{bmatrix} 2^{-1/2} \\ 2^{-1/2} \\ 0 \end{bmatrix}, \qquad T_3 = \tfrac{1}{2}(S_1 - S_2)$$

If the principal stresses S_1, S_2, and S_3 are written in order of decreasing magnitude so that S_1 is the greatest and S_3 is the least (algebraically), we have $S_1 > S_2 > S_3$, and we see that $T_2 = \tfrac{1}{2}(S_1 - S_3)$ is the greatest principal shear stress. The principal shear stresses T_1, T_2, and T_3 lie in the directions $(n)_1$, $(n)_2$, and $(n)_3$ with respect to the principal axes. If the normal stresses are computed in these directions by (4.27), the following results are obtained:

$$(4.35) \qquad (n)_1'[T]_0(n)_1 = \tfrac{1}{2}(S_3 + S_2)$$

$$(4.36) \qquad (n)_2'[T]_0(n)_2 = \tfrac{1}{2}(S_3 + S_1)$$

$$(4.37) \qquad (n)_3'[T]_0(n)_3 = \tfrac{1}{2}(S_1 + S_2)$$

These are the normal stresses corresponding to T_1, T_2, and T_3.

It can be seen that the directions $(n)_1$, $(n)_2$, and $(n)_3$ bisect the angles between the principal axes and that the greatest shear stress, $T_2 = \tfrac{1}{2}(S_1 - S_3)$, is across a plane whose normal bisects the angle between the directions of the greatest and least principal stresses.

5. INFINITESIMAL STRAIN IN THREE DIMENSIONS

Consider an elastic medium to be acted on by deforming forces. Such a medium is said to be in a state of *strain*. In order to describe the state of deformation of the medium, let a fixed Cartesian coordinate system be introduced, as shown in Fig. 5.8.   In this fixed Cartesian coordinate system, let a particle P_0 of the medium have the position vector $(P)_0$ given by

$$(5.1) \qquad (P)_0 = \begin{bmatrix} x \\ y \\ z \end{bmatrix}$$

before the medium has been deformed or strained.   Let the position vector of a neighboring particle Q_0 have the following position vector:

$$(5.2) \qquad (Q)_0 = \begin{bmatrix} x + x' \\ y + y' \\ z + z' \end{bmatrix}$$

before the medium is strained.   After the medium is deformed or is in a state of strain, let the particle P_0 move to the position P_s and let the new position vector of the particle P_0 be given by

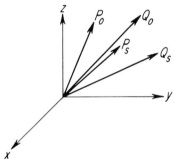

FIGURE 5.8

$$(5.3) \qquad (P)_s = \begin{bmatrix} x + u \\ y + v \\ z + w \end{bmatrix} = (P)_0 + (R)$$

The vector (R) is called the *displacement vector* of the point P_0; its Cartesian components are u, v, w so that

$$(5.4) \qquad (R) = \begin{bmatrix} u \\ v \\ w \end{bmatrix}$$

For convenience, let the following notation be introduced:

$$(5.5) \qquad (Q)_0 - (P)_0 = (L)_0 = \begin{bmatrix} x' \\ y' \\ z' \end{bmatrix}$$

That is, $(L)'_0(L) = L_0^2$ is the square of the distance from the point P_0 to the point Q_0 before the medium has been deformed.   After the medium is in a state of strain, let the position vector of the point Q_s be given by

$$(5.6) \qquad (Q)_s = \begin{bmatrix} (x + x' + u + u') \\ (y + y' + v + v') \\ (z + z' + w + w') \end{bmatrix} = (Q)_0 + (R) + (DR)$$

where the vector (DR) is the vector

$$(5.7) \qquad (DR) = \begin{bmatrix} u' \\ v' \\ w' \end{bmatrix}$$

This vector is the increment that must be given to the displacement vector (R) in order to obtain the displacement vector at the point (Q) after the medium has been strained. Since it is assumed that the points $(P)_0$ and $(Q)_0$ are very close together, the components of the vector $(L)_0$, x', y', z' are small quantities, and we may write

$$(5.8) \qquad (DR) = \begin{bmatrix} u' \\ v' \\ w' \end{bmatrix} = \begin{bmatrix} u_x & u_y & u_z \\ v_x & v_y & v_z \\ w_x & w_y & w_z \end{bmatrix} \begin{bmatrix} x' \\ y' \\ z' \end{bmatrix}$$

where u_x, u_y, u_z, etc. are the partial derivatives of $u(x, y, z)$ with respect to x, y, and z, respectively. Equation (5.8) is a Taylor's expansion of the functions $u(x, y, z)$, $v(x, y, z)$, and $w(x, y, z)$ at the neighboring point $(x + x', y + y', z + z')$. Since x', y', z' are assumed to be small quantities, terms of order x'^2, $x'y'$, etc. are neglected.

If we let the square matrix of partial derivatives in (5.8) be denoted by

$$(5.9) \qquad [M] = \begin{bmatrix} u_x & u_y & u_z \\ v_x & v_y & v_z \\ w_x & w_y & w_z \end{bmatrix}$$

Eq. (5.8) may be written in the compact form

$$(5.10) \qquad (DR) = [M](L)_0$$

Now let the following notation be introduced:

$$(5.11) \qquad e_x = u_x, \quad e_y = v_y, \quad e_z = w_z$$

$$(5.12) \qquad e_{yz} = e_{zy} = w_y + v_z, \quad e_{zx} = e_{xz} = u_z + w_x, \quad e_{xy} = e_{yx} = v_x + u_y$$

$$(5.13) \qquad 2\theta_x = w_y - v_z, \quad 2\theta_y = u_z - w_x, \quad 2\theta_z = v_x - u_y$$

With this notation, the matrix $[M]$ of (5.9) may be written in the following form:

$$(5.14) \qquad [M] = \frac{1}{2} \begin{bmatrix} 2e_x & e_{xy} & e_{xz} \\ e_{yx} & 2e_{yy} & e_{yz} \\ e_{zx} & e_{zy} & 2e_{zz} \end{bmatrix} + \begin{bmatrix} 0 & -\theta_z & \theta_y \\ \theta_z & 0 & -\theta_x \\ -\theta_y & \theta_x & 0 \end{bmatrix}$$

Let the first square matrix of the right member of (5.14) be denoted by $[S]$ and the second square matrix by $[\theta]$; then (5.14) may be written in the compact form

$$(5.15) \qquad [M] = [S] + [\theta]$$

In terms of these two matrices, (5.8) may be written in the form

$$(5.16) \qquad (DR) = [M](L)_0 = [S](L)_0 + [\theta](L)_0$$

It can be shown that the vector $[\theta](L)_0$ has for components the displacement of the vector $(L)_0$, due to a small rotation of components $(\theta_x, \theta_y, \theta_z)$. From the definition of θ_x, θ_y, and θ_z given by (5.13), it can be shown that, in the language of vector analysis, we may write

$$(5.17) \qquad \begin{bmatrix} \theta_x \\ \theta_y \\ \theta_z \end{bmatrix} = \frac{1}{2} \operatorname{curl} \begin{bmatrix} u \\ v \\ w \end{bmatrix} = \frac{1}{2} \begin{bmatrix} 0 & -D_z & D_y \\ D_z & 0 & -D_x \\ -D_y & D_x & 0 \end{bmatrix} \begin{bmatrix} u \\ v \\ w \end{bmatrix}$$

where D_x, D_y, and D_z are partial derivatives with respect to x, y, and z. If $\theta_x = \theta_y = \theta_z = 0$, the strain is said to be *irrotational*.

The Extension of the Medium

Let the square of the distance between the points P_s and Q_s be denoted by L_s^2 and the following notation introduced:

$$(5.18) \qquad (Q)_s - (P)_s = (L)_s$$

With this notation, we have $L_s^2 = (L)_s'(L)_s$. If we subtract (5.3) from (5.6) and use (5.5) to simplify the result, we have

$$(5.19) \qquad (Q)_s - (P)_s = (L)_0 + (DR) = (L)_s$$

The square of the distance between the points P_s and Q_s is, therefore, given by

$$(5.20) \qquad \begin{aligned} L_s^2 = (L)_s'(L)_s &= [(L)_0' + (DR)'][(L)_0 + (DR)] \\ &= (L)_0'(L) + 2(L)_0'(DR) + (DR)'(DR) \end{aligned}$$

The quantity $(DR)'(DR)$ may be computed by the use of (5.10) and is given by

$$(5.21) \qquad (DR)'(DR) = (L)_0'[M]'[M](L)_0$$

If (5.21) is expanded, this quantity is seen to contain squares and products of the derivatives u_x, u_y, etc. which are the elements of the matrix $[M]$. In the theory of infinitesimal strain, these quantities are neglected. The term $(DR)'(DR)$ in (5.20) is, therefore, neglected in the theory of infinitesimal strain, and L_s^2 is given by

$$(5.22) \qquad L_s^2 = (L)_0'(L)_0 + 2(L)_0'(DR)$$

The quantity $(L)_0'(L)_0 = L_0^2$ is the square of the distance between the points P_0 and Q_0 in the unstrained state of the medium. We now compute

$$(5.23) \qquad 2(L)_0'(DR) = 2(L)_0'[M](L)_0 = 2(L)_0'([S] + [\theta])(L)_0$$

It can be shown by direct computation that

$$(5.24) \qquad (L)_0'[\theta](L)_0 = 0$$

This result is to be expected, since, as we have mentioned, the vector $[\theta](L)_0$ represents a small rotation.   Equation (5.23), therefore, reduces to

$$(5.25) \qquad\qquad 2(L)'_0(DR) = 2(L)'_0[S](L)_0$$

and (5.22) may be written in the form

$$(5.26) \qquad\qquad L^2_s = (L)'_0(L)_0 + 2(L)'_0[S](L)_0$$

Let the vector $(L)_0$ have the length L_0 and be oriented in the direction of the *unit* vector (a) whose direction cosines are a_x, a_y, a_z so that

$$(5.27) \qquad\qquad (L)_0 = L_0(a) = L_0 \begin{bmatrix} a_x \\ a_y \\ a_z \end{bmatrix}$$

If this expression for $(L)_0$ is substituted into (5.26), the result may be written in the form

$$(5.28) \qquad\qquad L^2_s = L^2_0[1 + 2(a)'[S](a)]$$

If the square roots of both sides of (5.28) are taken and if the squares of $(a)'[S](a)$ are neglected, the result is

$$(5.29) \qquad\qquad L_s = L_0[1 + (a)'[S](a)]$$

The extension e corresponding to the direction (a) in the unstrained state at P is, by definition,

$$(5.30) \qquad e = \frac{L_s - L_0}{L_0} = (a)'[S](a)$$
$$= a^2_x e_x + a^2_y e_y + a^2_z e_z + a_y a_z e_{yz} + a_z a_x e_{zx} + a_x a_y e_{xy}$$

If a point R_0 has the position vector $(R)_0$ given by

$$(5.31) \qquad\qquad (R)_0 = e^{-1/2}(a) = \begin{bmatrix} x \\ y \\ z \end{bmatrix}$$

so that the position vector of the point R_0 has the same direction as the unit vector (a) and a distance from the origin $e^{-1/2}$, then we have, as a consequence of (5.31),

$$(5.32) \qquad\qquad (a) = e^{1/2}(R)_0$$

If this expression for the unit vector (a) is now substituted into (5.30), the following equation is obtained:

$$(5.33) \qquad\qquad e = e(R)'_0[S](R)_0$$

If (5.33) is divided by e and the matrix product is expanded, the following equation is obtained:

(5.34) $(R)'[S](R)_0 = x^2 e_x + y^2 e_y + z^2 e_z + yz e_{yz} + zx e_{zx} + xy e_{xy} = 1$

This is the equation of the *strain quadric*. The square matrix $[S]$ of this quadric is the *strain matrix*. In expanded form, the stress matrix $[S]$ is

(5.35) $$[S] = \frac{1}{2} \begin{bmatrix} 2e_x & e_{xy} & e_{xz} \\ e_{yx} & 2e_y & e_{yz} \\ e_{zx} & e_{zy} & 2e_z \end{bmatrix}$$

Since, by (5.12), $e_{xy} = e_{yx}$, $e_{xz} = e_{zx}$, and $e_{yz} = e_{zy}$, it is seen that $[S]$ is a *symmetric* matrix. The elements of the strain matrix are the *components of strain*. The quantities e_x, e_y, e_z are the extensions of lines in the directions of the axes. The quantities e_{xy}, e_{zx}, e_{yz} are called the *shearing strains* or *detrusions*. It can be shown that

$$\left(\frac{\pi}{2} - e_{yz} \right)$$

is the angle in the strained state between lines that were initially parallel to the y and z axes in the unstrained state. Similar relations hold for e_{xy} and e_{zx}.

If (k) is a unit vector, the vector strain in the direction of this unit vector e_k is given by the equation

(5.36) $e_k = [S](k)$

It is possible to diagonalize the strain matrix $[S]$ by an orthogonal transformation in a manner similar to that demonstrated in (4.18) for the stress quadric.

The Principal Strains

The eigenvalues of the strain matrix $[S]$ are the roots of the characteristic equation of the matrix $[S]$. This equation is

(5.37) $p(\mu) = \det(\mu U - [S]) = 0$

The three roots of this cubic equation in u are the eigenvalues μ_1, μ_2, μ_3 of the matrix $[S]$. In the theory of elasticity, these eigenvalues are written in the form

(5.38)
$$\mu_1 = e_1$$
$$\mu_2 = e_2$$
$$\mu_3 = e_3$$

The eigenvalues of $[S]$, e_1, e_2, e_3 are called the *principal strains*. The eigenvectors of $[S]$ are the principal axes of strain. It can be seen that e_1, e_2, e_3 are extensions in the directions of the principal axes of strain.

Since the trace of a matrix is invariant under an orthogonal transformation, we have the following invariant quantity:

$$(5.39) \qquad \Delta = \mathrm{Tr}\,[S] = (e_x + e_y + e_z) = (e_1 + e_2 + e_3)$$

The quantity Δ is called the *dilatation*, or the increase in volume per unit volume, of the medium. The dilatation may be expressed in terms of the displacement vector (R) of (5.4) in the following manner:

$$(5.40) \qquad \Delta = (e_x + e_y + e_z) = (u_x \times v_y + w_z) = \mathrm{div}\,(R)$$

6. THE STRAIN ENERGY OF THE MEDIUM

The potential energy per unit volume stored in a medium by elastic straining is a quantity of great theoretical importance. In order to obtain an expression for this energy, consider a small cube of side length a with its faces perpendicular to the principal axes of stress (and strain). (In Sec. 7 the fact that the principal axes of stress and the principal axes of strain are identical in the medium is isotropic.) Let the final state of stress be such that S_1, S_2, S_3 are the principal stresses and e_1, e_2, e_3 are the principal strains. Let it be assumed that this final state of stress and strain is produced by a gradual increase during which the stresses are kS_1, kS_2, kS_3 and the strains are ke_1, ke_2, ke_3, where k is a variable that increases from 0 to 1. Then, at any stage, the force applied to the surface of the cube perpendicular to the S_1 axis is $ka^2 S_1$, and when k increases from k to $k + dk$, the displacement of this surface is $ae_1 dk$, so that the total work done by the forces in the S_1 direction in producing the final state of strain is

$$(6.1) \qquad S_1 e_1 a^3 \int_0^1 k\,dk = \tfrac{1}{2} S_1 e_1 a^3$$

There will be similar contributions from the other directions, and adding these and dividing by the volume a^3 gives the following result for W, the strain energy per unit volume:

$$(6.2) \qquad W = \tfrac{1}{2}(S_1 e_1 + S_2 e_2 + S_3 e_3)$$

It is evident that since the elastic medium is assumed to be one in which energy is conserved, it does not matter by what process the final state of stress and strain is reached. The linear increase described above was chosen because it is the simplest to calculate.

7. THE STRESS-STRAIN RELATIONS FOR AN ELASTIC ISOTROPIC SOLID

Consider an isotropic elastic medium; that is, one whose characteristics at any point are independent of direction. If such a medium is stressed so that it is in a state of strain, its state of stress may be specified by a stress matrix $[T]_0$, and its state of strain may be specified by a strain matrix $[S]$.

The eigenvectors of $[T]_0$ define the principal axes of stress, and the eigenvectors of $[S]$ define the principal axes of strain. These two sets of principal axes must be identical if the solid is isotropic. This fact follows because the stresses are purely normal in the direction of the principal axes of stress, and thus must produce a system of displacements which are symmetrical with respect to these axes, since no asymmetrical displacement is to be preferred to any other. Now the displacements are symmetrical about the principal axes of strain, so the two sets of axes must coincide.

If S_1, S_2, S_3 are the *principal stresses* and e_1, e_2, e_3 are the *principal strains* of the medium, the following relations may be assumed as the stress-strain equations referred to principal axes:

$$(7.1) \qquad \begin{bmatrix} S_1 \\ S_2 \\ S_3 \end{bmatrix} = \begin{bmatrix} (n + 2G) & n & n \\ n & (n + 2G) & n \\ n & n & (n + 2G) \end{bmatrix} \begin{bmatrix} e_1 \\ e_2 \\ e_3 \end{bmatrix}$$

The quantities n and G are constants. In the literature of the theory of elasticity they are known as *Lamé's parameters*. These quantities are the most convenient elastic constants to use in theoretical work when it is required that stress be expressed in terms of strain. It can be seen that, in Eq. (7.1), $(n + 2G)$ relates stress and strain in the same direction, and that the constant n relates them in perpendicular relations. The Lamé parameters n and G are related to other commonly occurring elastic constants. These relations will be discussed in the next section.

The relations (7.1) may be written in a more compact form if they are expressed in terms of the *dilatation* $e_0 = \Delta$. By definition, the dilatation is

$$(7.2) \qquad \Delta = e_0 = e_1 + e_2 + e_3$$

If the matrix equation (7.1) is expanded, it can be seen that the relations between the principal stresses and the principal strains may be written in the form

$$(7.3) \qquad S_1 = ne_0 + 2Ge_1, \quad S_2 = ne_0 + 2Ge_2, \quad S_3 = ne_0 + 2Ge_3$$

These relations express the principal stresses in terms of the principal strains referred to principal axes. It is now desired to obtain the relations between stresses and strains referred to a general Cartesian coordinate system. In order to effect the required transformation, let us call the principal axes x_p, y_p, z_p and denote these axes by the column matrix,

$$(7.4) \qquad (x)_p = \begin{bmatrix} x_p \\ y_p \\ z_p \end{bmatrix}$$

Let the general axes be denoted by x, y, z and expressed as the elements of the column matrix,

$$(7.5) \qquad (x) = \begin{bmatrix} x \\ y \\ z \end{bmatrix}$$

Now let it be supposed that the axes x, y, z are inclined to the principal axes so that they are related to each other by an orthogonal transformation of the form $(x) = [a](x)_p$ of the form

$$(7.6) \qquad \begin{bmatrix} x \\ y \\ z \end{bmatrix} = \begin{bmatrix} l_1 & m_1 & n_1 \\ l_2 & m_2 & n_2 \\ l_3 & m_3 & n_3 \end{bmatrix} \begin{bmatrix} x_p \\ y_p \\ z_p \end{bmatrix}, \qquad [a] = \begin{bmatrix} l_1 & m_1 & n_1 \\ l_2 & m_2 & n_2 \\ l_3 & m_3 & n_3 \end{bmatrix}$$

The elements l_i, m_i, n_i of the orthogonal matrix $[a]$ are the direction cosines of the x, y, z axes with respect to the principal axes x_p, y_p, z_p. The stress quadric expressed in terms of principal axes has the form

$$(7.7) \qquad (x)_p'[T]_p(x)_p = 1, \qquad [T]_p = \begin{bmatrix} S_1 & 0 & 0 \\ 0 & S_2 & 0 \\ 0 & 0 & S_3 \end{bmatrix}$$

Since the orthogonal transformation (7.6) may be expressed in the form

$$(7.8) \qquad (x)_p = [a]'(x)$$

the stress quadric expressed in the axes (x) has the form

$$(7.9) \qquad (x)'[a][T]_p[a]'(x) = 1$$

Therefore, the stress matrix referred to the coordinates (x) has the form

$$(7.10) \qquad [T]_0 = [a][T]_p[a]' = \begin{bmatrix} S_x & T_{xy} & T_{xz} \\ T_{yx} & S_y & T_{yz} \\ T_{zx} & T_{zy} & S_z \end{bmatrix}$$

If the *strain quadric* referred to the principal axes $(x)_p$

$$(7.11) \qquad (x)_p'[S]_p(x)_p = 1$$

is transformed to the axes (x), it takes the form

$$(7.12) \qquad (x)'[a][S]_p[a]'(x) = 1$$

Therefore, the strain matrix $[S]$ referred to the coordinates (x) has the form

$$(7.13) \qquad [S] = [a][S]_p[a]' = \frac{1}{2} \begin{bmatrix} 2e_x & e_{xy} & e_{xz} \\ e_{yx} & 2e_y & e_{yz} \\ e_{zx} & e_{zy} & 2e_z \end{bmatrix}$$

where

(7.14)
$$[S]_p = \begin{bmatrix} e_1 & 0 & 0 \\ 0 & e_2 & 0 \\ 0 & 0 & e_3 \end{bmatrix}$$

It is, therefore, possible by matrix multiplication to obtain the elements of the stress matrix $[T]_0$ from (7.10) and the strain matrix $[S]$ from (7.13). If the matrix multiplication is carried out, one obtains

(7.15)
$$S_z = l_1^2 S_1 + m_1^2 S_2 + n_1^2 S_3,$$
$$e_z = l_1^2 e_1 + m_1^2 e_2 + n_1^2 e_3$$
$$T_{yz} = S_1 l_1 l_2 + S_2 m_1 m_2 + S_3 n_1 n_2,$$
$$e_{yz} = 2(e_1 l_1 l_2 + e_2 m_1 m_2 + e_3 n_1 n_2)$$
etc.

If the expressions for S_1, S_2, and S_3 given in (7.3) are substituted into the expression for S_z in (7.15), the following result is obtained:

(7.16)
$$S_z = (l_1^2 + m_1^2 + n_1^2)ne_0 + 2G(l_1^2 e_1 + m_1^2 e_2 + n_1^2 e_3)$$
$$= ne_0 + 2Ge_z$$

The last result is evident, since the sum of the squares of the direction cosines l_1, m_1, and n_1 equals unity and the coefficient of $2G$ is e_z, as given by (7.15). In a similar manner, if we substitute (7.3) into the expression for T_{yz} of (7.15), we obtain

(7.17) $T_{yz} = (l_1 l_2 + m_1 m_2 + n_1 n_2)ne_0 + 2G(l_1 l_2 e_1 + m_1 m_2 e_2 + n_1 n_2 e_3)$

Since the vectors (l_1, m_1, n_1) and (l_2, m_2, n_2) are perpendicular, the coefficient of ne_0 in (7.17) must vanish, since it is the scalar product of these two vectors. The coefficient of G in Eq. (7.17) is e_{yz} given in (7.15). Therefore, we have

(7.18)
$$T_{yz} = Ge_{yz}$$

In a similar manner, the relations between the elements of the stress matrix $[T]_0$ of (7.10) and the strain matrix $[S]$ of (7.13) may be obtained. The complete set of equations connecting the stress and strain is found to be

(7.19) $S_x = ne_0 + 2Ge_x, \quad S_y = ne_0 + 2Ge_y, \quad S_z = ne_0 + 2Ge_z$

(7.20) $T_{yz} = Ge_{yz}, \quad T_{zx} = Ge_{zx}, \quad T_{xy} = Ge_{xy}$

If we add Eqs. (7.19) and use the relation $(e_x + e_y + e_z) = e_0$, we obtain

(7.21) $S_x + S_y + S_z = (3n + 2G)e_0$

8. THE PRINCIPAL ELASTIC CONSTANTS

The relations between stress and strain have been formulated above in terms of the Lamé parameters n and G. We now proceed to define the other commonly occurring elastic constants and to express them in terms of n and G.

(a) The Modulus of Rigidity G

The modulus of rigidity is defined as the ratio of shear stress to shear strain in simple shear. It can be seen by (7.20), therefore, that the modulus of rigidity is the quantity G.

(b) The Bulk Modulus or Incompressibility K

This modulus is defined as the ratio of hydrostatic pressure to the dilatation it produces. In this case we have

(8.1) $$S_x = S_y = S_z = -p$$

Therefore, by (7.21), we have

(8.2) $$(3n + 2G)e_0 = -3p$$

Hence, by the definition of K, we have

(8.3) $$K = -\frac{p}{e_0} = \left(n + \frac{2G}{3}\right)$$

The reciprocal of K is called the *compressibility*.

(c) The Young's Modulus E

Young's modulus E is defined as the ratio of tension to extension in a cylinder which is under axial tension and which is not restricted laterally. In this case we have $S_2 = S_3 = 0$ in (7.1). If the matrix equation (7.1) is solved for e_2 and e_3 in terms of e_1, we obtain

(8.4) $$e_2 = e_3 = -\frac{n}{2(n + G)} e_1$$

From (7.1) we have

(8.5) $$S_1 = (n + 2G) + ne_2 + ne_3$$

Hence,

(8.6) $$E = \frac{S_1}{e_1} = \frac{G(3n + 2G)}{(n + G)}$$

(d) Poisson's Ratio ν

Poisson's ratio ν is defined as the ratio of lateral contraction to longitudinal extension for the cylinder in the case above; that is, by (8.4),

(8.7) $$\nu = \frac{n}{2(n + G)}$$

(e) *Relations Between the Elastic Constants*

Many relations between the basic elastic constants defined above may be obtained. The following ones are frequently useful:

(8.8)
$$n = \frac{E}{(1 + \nu)(1 - 2\nu)}, \quad G = \frac{E}{2(1 + \nu)}$$

(8.9)
$$K = \frac{2(1 + \nu)G}{3(1 - 2\nu)} = \frac{E}{3(1 - 2\nu)}$$

(8.10)
$$E = \frac{9KG}{3K + G}, \quad \nu = \frac{(3K - 2G)}{2(3K + G)}, \quad \frac{n}{G} = \frac{2\nu}{(1 - 2\nu)}$$

9. THE STRAIN EXPRESSED IN TERMS OF THE STRESS

Equations (7.19) and (7.20) related the stress of the medium in terms of the strain. If these equations are solved for the strains and the relation (8.8) is used, the following expressions are obtained:

(9.1)
$$\begin{aligned} Ee_x &= S_x - \nu(S_y + S_z), \\ Ee_y &= S_y - \nu(S_x + S_z), \\ Ee_z &= S_z - \nu(S_x + S_y) \end{aligned}$$

(9.2) $\quad Ee_{yz} = 2(1 + \nu)T_{yz}, \quad Ee_{zx} = 2(1 + \nu)T_{zx}, \quad Ee_{xy} = 2(1 + \nu)T_{xy}$

10. THE ELASTIC EQUATIONS OF MOTION

The Equations of Equilibrium

The differential equations of equilibrium for an elastic medium may be obtained by considering the conditions for the static equilibrium of an infinitesimal rectangular parallelepiped located at the general point (x, y, z) of the medium. Let a system of body forces (F_x, F_y, F_z) per unit volume be acting on the body. Then the equations for the equilibrium of the small parallelepiped are

(10.1)
$$\begin{aligned} D_x S_x + D_y T_{xy} + D_z T_{xz} &= -F_x \\ D_x T_{yx} + D_y S_y + D_z T_{yz} &= -F_y, \quad D_x = \frac{\partial}{\partial x}, \text{ etc.} \\ D_x T_{zx} + D_y T_{zy} + D_z S_z &= -F_z \end{aligned}$$

If we denote by (F) a column matrix whose elements are the components of the body forces F_x, F_y, F_z per unit volume, and a column matrix (D) of derivative operators,

(10.2)
$$(D) = \begin{bmatrix} D_x \\ D_y \\ D_z \end{bmatrix}$$

then Eq. (10.1) may be written in the form

(10.3) $(D)'[T] = -(F)'$

where $[T]$ is the stress matrix.

The stress-strain relations (7.19) and (7.20) may be written in the compact matrix form

(10.4) $[T] = 2G[S] + ne_0[U]$

where $[T]$ is the stress matrix, $[S]$ is the strain matrix, and $[U]$ is the third-order unit matrix.

Equation (10.3) expresses the equilibrium conditions in terms of the stress matrix. If (10.4) is substituted into (10.3), the following equation is obtained:

(10.5) $(D)'(2G[S] + ne_0[U]) = -(F)'$

By the definition of e_x, e_y, e_{yz}, etc. given in (5.11) and (5.12), it can be seen that the strain matrix $[S]$ may be written in the form

(10.6) $[S] = \dfrac{1}{2}\begin{bmatrix} 2e_x & e_{xy} & e_{xz} \\ e_{yx} & 2e_y & e_{yz} \\ e_{zx} & e_{zy} & 2e_z \end{bmatrix} = \begin{bmatrix} 2u_x & (u_y + v_x) & (u_z + w_x) \\ (v_x + u_y) & 2v_y & (v_z + w_y) \\ (w_x + u_z) & (w_y + v_z) & 2w_z \end{bmatrix}$

The dilatation e_0 may be written in the form

(10.7) $e_0 = (e_x + e_y + e_z) = (u_x + v_y + w_z) = \operatorname{div}(R)$

where (R) is the displacement vector defined by (5.4).

If the differentiations indicated in the matrix equation (10.5) are carried out and the transpose of the resulting equation is taken, the following result is obtained:

(10.8) $(n + G)\begin{bmatrix} D_x e_0 \\ D_y e_0 \\ D_z e_0 \end{bmatrix} + G\begin{bmatrix} \nabla^2 u \\ \nabla^2 v \\ \nabla^2 w \end{bmatrix} = \begin{bmatrix} -F_x \\ -F_y \\ -F_z \end{bmatrix}$

where ∇^2 is the Laplace operator defined by

(10.9) $\nabla^2 = D_x^2 + D_y^2 + D_z^2 = (D)'(D)$

The matrix equation (10.8) may be written in the more compact form

(10.10) $(n + G)(D)e_0 + G\nabla^2(R) = -(F)$

If m is the *mass per unit volume* of the medium, then, by Newton's second law, if the system of forces expressed by (10.10) are not in equilibrium, we may write

(10.11) $(n + G)(D)e_0 + G\nabla^2(R) + (F) = mD_t^2(R)$

where (R) is the displacement vector and D_t^2 is the second partial derivative with respect to the time t. Equation (10.11) is the equation of motion of the medium.   An alternative form of the equation of motion (10.11) may be obtained by premultiplying by the transpose of the operator (D).   If (10.11) is premultiplied by $(D)'$, the following result is obtained:

(10.12) $(n + G)(D)'(D)e_0 + G\nabla^2(D)'(R) + (D)'(F) = mD_t^2(D)'(R)$

As a consequence of (10.7), the dilatation e_0 may be written in the form

(10.13) $e_0 = (u_x + v_y + w_z) = (D)'(R) = \text{div } (R)$

We also have

(10.14) $(D)'(F) = D_x F_x + D_y F_y + D_z F_z = \text{div } (F)$

If Eqs. (10.9), (10.13), and (10.14) are used to simplify (10.12), this equation may be written in the form

(10.15) $(n + 2G)\nabla^2 e_0 + \text{div } (F) = mD_t^2 e_0$

If the body forces are such that $(F) = (0)$ or $\text{div } (F) = 0$, then the scalar equation (10.15) takes the form

(10.16) $\nabla^2 e_0 = \dfrac{1}{c^2} D_t^2 e_0, \quad \text{where} \quad c^2 = \dfrac{(n + 2G)}{m}$

This is the classical wave equation.   The solution of this equation indicates that waves of dilatation e_0 are propagated through the elastic medium with a velocity of c given by

(10.17) $c = \left[\dfrac{(n + 2G)}{m} \right]^{1/2}$

These waves are called the *P-waves* in seismology.   It can be shown that they are longitudinal waves and correspond to *irrotational* motion of the medium.

The S-Waves (Waves of Zero Dilatation)

If the body force vector (F) is zero so that there are no body forces acting on the medium, and if the dilatation e_0 is placed equal to zero in Eq. (10.11) then this equation reduces to the vector wave equation

(10.18) $G\nabla^2(R) = mD_t^2(R), \quad \text{div } (R) = 0$

This equation indicates that each component of the displacement vector (R), u, v, and w, is propagated as a wave in the medium with a velocity of $(G/m)^{1/2}$.   It can be shown that these are transverse or shear waves.   They are propagated in such a manner that the dilatation is zero, and they are called equivoluminal, or *S-waves* in seismology.

11. THE ELASTIC EQUATIONS OF EQUILIBRIUM

The equations of equilibrium of the medium may be regarded as special cases of the matrix equation (10.11) in which all particles of the medium are at rest. If we place $D_t^2(R) = (0)$ in (10.11), the following equation is obtained:

$$(11.1) \qquad (n + G)(D)e_0 + G\nabla^2(R) + (F) = (0)$$

This matrix equation is the equation of equilibrium in terms of the displacements of the medium. If the body forces (F) are such that div $(F) = 0$, it can be seen that Eq. (10.15) reduces in the static case to

$$(11.2) \qquad \nabla^2 e_0 = 0$$

This indicates that if the body forces are constant, the dilatation e_0 satisfies Laplace's equation.

The Strain Potential ϕ

If there are no body forces acting on the medium, then $(F) = (0)$, and Eq. (11.1) reduces to

$$(11.3) \qquad (n + G)(D)e_0 + G\nabla^2(R) = (0)$$

To solve this equation, let the displacement vector (R) be expressed as the gradient of a scalar function $\phi(x, y, z)$ in the form

$$(11.4) \qquad (R) = \frac{1}{2G} \text{grad } \phi = \frac{1}{2G}(D)\phi$$

The function ϕ is called the strain potential function in the theory of elasticity. Since $e_0 = \text{div } (R) = (D)'(R)$, (11.3) may be written in the alternative form

$$(11.5) \qquad (n + G)(D)(D)'(R) + G(D)'(D)(R) = (0)$$

If we substitute (11.4) into (11.5), we obtain

$$(11.6) \qquad \frac{(n + G)}{2G}(D)(D)'(D)\phi + (D)'(D)(D)\frac{\phi}{2} = (0)$$

In order to interpret the operator $(D)'(D)(D)$ that occurs in (11.6), it must be realized that $(D)'(D) = \nabla^2$, a scalar operator, so that

$$(11.7) \qquad (D)'(D)(D) = \nabla^2 \begin{bmatrix} D_x \\ D_y \\ D_z \end{bmatrix} = (D)\nabla^2$$

Therefore, (11.6) may be written in the form

$$(11.7a) \qquad \left(\frac{n}{2G} + 1\right)(D)\nabla^2\phi = (0)$$

This equation requires that

(11.8) $$(D)\nabla^2\phi = 0$$

or that $\nabla^2\phi$ be a constant.

Since the objective is to obtain some solutions rather than the general solution, the choice is made to specify that

(11.9) $$\nabla^2\phi = 0$$

This is one way to satisfy Eq. (11.7). If ϕ is chosen to satisfy Laplace's equation (11.9), then we have

(11.10) $$e_0 = (D)'(R) = (D)'(D)\frac{\phi}{2G} = \nabla^2\frac{\phi}{2G} = 0$$

Therefore, this choice of ϕ gives a state of strain in which the dilatation e_0 is zero. The stresses in the medium may then be computed by (7.19) and (7.20) and are found to be given by

(11.11) $$S_x = D_x^2\phi, \quad T_{xy} = D_xD_y\phi, \quad \text{etc.}$$

Therefore, in this case, the stress matrix takes the form

(11.12) $$[T] = \begin{bmatrix} S_x & T_{xy} & T_{xz} \\ T_{yx} & S_y & T_{yz} \\ T_{zx} & T_{zy} & S_z \end{bmatrix} = \begin{bmatrix} D_x^2 & D_xD_y & D_xD_z \\ D_yD_x & D_y^2 & D_yD_z \\ D_zD_x & D_zD_y & D_z^2 \end{bmatrix}\phi$$

12. THE STRESSES ON A SEMI-INFINITE SOLID STRAINED BY GRAVITATIONAL FORCES

In order to illustrate the use of the general Eq. (11.1) in the solution of a definite problem of elasticity, it will be applied to obtain the state of stress

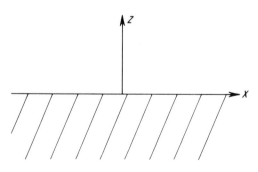

FIGURE 5.9

in a semi-infinite region under the influence of gravity. In order to formulate this problem mathematically, introduce a Cartesian coordinate system, as shown in Fig. 5.9. The x and y axes are taken in the surface of the semi-infinite region, and the z axis is taken vertically upwards; the region considered is $z < 0$, and the body force is $F_z = -mg$, where m is the mass per unit volume of the medium and g the gravitational constant. It is evident from the conditions of the problem that there can be no displacement in the x and y directions so that

(12.1) $$u = 0, \quad v = 0$$

The displacement vector (R) has, therefore, only one component, so it has the form

(12.2) $$(R) = \begin{bmatrix} 0 \\ 0 \\ w \end{bmatrix}$$

Therefore,

(12.3) $$e_0 = \text{div}\,(R) = w_z$$

In this case, the matrix equation (11.1) reduces to the scalar equation

(12.4) $$(n + G)D_z^2 w + G(D_x^2 + D_y^2 + D_z^2)w = -F_z = mg$$

Because of the symmetry of the system, the displacement w does not vary with respect to x or y; therefore, (12.4) simplifies to the form

(12.5) $$(n + 2G)D_z^2 w = mg$$

Hence,

(12.6) $$\frac{dw}{dz} = \frac{mgz}{(n + 2G)} = e_0 = e_z$$

where the constant of integration is zero, since $dw/dz = 0$ at $z = 0$. Another integration yields the result

(12.7) $$w = \frac{mgz^2}{2(n + 2G)} + \text{Constant}$$

The stresses in the medium may now be obtained by Eqs. (7.19) and (7.20). In this case, the strains e_z and e_y are both zero, so Eq. (7.19) reduces to

(12.8) $$S_x = ne_0 = \frac{nmgz}{(n + 2G)}$$

(12.9) $$S_y = ne_0 = \frac{nmgz}{(n + 2G)}$$

(12.10) $$S_z = ne_0 + 2Ge_z = (n + 2G)e_0 = mgz$$

The strains e_{yz}, e_{zx}, e_{xy} are all zero as a consequence of (5.12). Therefore, (7.20) reduces to

(12.11) $$T_{yz} = T_{zx} = T_{xy} = 0$$

Equations (12.8), (12.9), and (12.10) give the stresses at a depth z within the medium. These stresses S_x, S_y, S_z are principal stresses. If this analysis is applied to the stresses at shallow depths below the earth's surface, it can be seen that the vertical stress S_z is just the load or the weight of a column of rock of unit area above the point considered. If the constants n and G are given values for granite rock, it is found that the horizontal stresses are approximately one-third of the magnitude of the vertical stress.

REFERENCES

1. Love, A. E. H., *A Treatise on the Mathematical Theory of Elasticity*. New York: Dover Publications, 1944. (The classical theory of the mathematical theory of the subject.)

2. Sokolnikoff, I. S., *Mathematical Theory of Elasticity*, 2nd ed. New York: McGraw-Hill Book Company, Inc., 1956. (An excellent exposition of the theory of stress and strain and a complete survey of the general mathematical theory. The use of tensor notation permits an elegant and concise formulation of the general theory.)

3. Timoshenko, S. and J. N. Goodier, *Theory of Elasticity*, 2nd ed. New York: McGraw-Hill Book Company, Inc., 1951. (This is the standard treatise of the engineering applications of the subject; it contains a clear and elementary exposition of the mathematical theory.)

4. Westergaard, H. M., *Theory of Elasticity and Plasticity*. New York: John Wiley and Sons, Inc., 1952. (This book presents an interesting historical discussion of the theory of elasticity and a clear discussion of stress and strain using vector notation. The classical problems of the theory of elasticity are discussed in a detailed manner.)

6 MATRIX METHODS IN THE ANALYSIS OF STRUCTURES

1. INTRODUCTION

The calculation of the stresses and strains in complex elastic structures has received a great impetus since the end of World War II. This has been the result of two principal factors: first, the development of new techniques of analysis to meet the increasing requirements of greater accuracy, and, second, the revolutionary development of the electronic digital computer. Complex structural problems occur in mechanical and civil engineering; however, the motivation for the development of new and better methods of analysis has been the need for such methods for the stress analysis of modern aeronautical structures. Since the analysis of even a relatively simple structure composed of linear elastic members undergoing small deformations leads to a number of simultaneous linear equations in the static case and a corresponding number of linear differential equations in the dynamic case, it is not surprising that these equations may be simply formulated in matrix form. During recent years the advantage of the matrix formulation of structural problems has been widely recognized and has led to what is now known as "the matrix analysis of structures."[1]

It has been found that it is possible to express structural theory in matrix language and to carry out the required computations by using matrix techniques. This procedure has led to the following two advantages:

1. The use of matrices allows a systematization and simplification of the calculations that is not possible by other methods. Also, since matrix algebra is the ideal "language" for the electronic digital computer, operations involving matrix algebra require the minimum amount of programming time to direct the machine to perform the required matrix operations.

2. The second advantage gained by the use of matrices is that it introduces an exceptional conciseness and transparency into the mathematics of

stress analysis which are not possible if the standard longhand notation is used.

During the last ten years a vast literature on the general subject of the matrix analysis of structures has appeared. An excellent summary of this literature up to the year 1958 will be found in an article by J. H. Argyris.[2]

It is impossible in this chapter to go into an extensive discussion of the general methods of analysis that have been developed to study the stresses and deformations of special structures; therefore, only the basic principles and definitions fundamental to the analysis of structures by the use of matrices will be presented.

2. THE FLEXIBILITY AND STIFFNESS MATRICES

The elementary meaning of the terms flexibility and stiffness can be illustrated by considering an experiment in which a load or force F parallel to the axis of a coil spring, as shown in Fig. 6.1, is applied to the free end of an anchored helical spring. If the displacement of the point of application is x, then the flexibility ϕ of the spring is defined by the quotient,

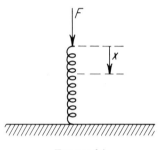

FIGURE 6.1

$$(2.1) \qquad \phi = \frac{x}{F}$$

It is, therefore, apparent that the flexibility ϕ is the displacement produced by a unit load, $F = 1$. The deflection x may be written in the form

$$(2.2) \qquad x = \phi F$$

That is, the displacement is the product of the load and the flexibility.

The Stiffness

The reciprocal of the flexibility is called the stiffness. Hence, if k is the stiffness of the spring of Fig. 2.1, then

$$(2.3) \qquad k = \frac{1}{\phi}$$

The force is, therefore, related to the displacement by the equation

$$(2.4) \qquad F = kx$$

The Elastic Energy

If the stiffness k is a constant, so that the spring satisfies Hooke's law, the elastic energy necessary to compress the spring by an amount x, U, may be computed by the following equation:

$$(2.5) \qquad U = \int_0^x F dx = \int_0^x k x dx = \frac{kx^2}{2} = \frac{1}{2}\frac{Fx}{2} = \frac{x^2}{2\phi}$$

Generalization of the Flexibility and Stiffness Concept

It is necessary to generalize the flexibility and stiffness concepts in order to express properly the relation between a force and the displacement produced by this force when it is applied to a point of an elastic body. Consider the elastic body shown in Fig. 6.2. Let the body be constrained so that it cannot move as a rigid body, and let a force be applied to the body at the point P, as shown. Since the applied force is a vector, it may be written as a column matrix (F) in the form

$$(2.6) \qquad (F)_p = \begin{bmatrix} F_x \\ F_y \\ F_z \end{bmatrix}$$

where F_x, F_y, F_z are the components of (F) in the x, y, z directions of a Cartesian reference. Let it be supposed that the elastic body satisfies Hooke's law. Then the deflection (R) can be obtained by summing the deflections caused by the three components of the force (F). Let the components of the deflection vector $(R)_p$ be

$$(2.7) \qquad (R)_p = \begin{bmatrix} x_p \\ y_p \\ z_p \end{bmatrix}$$

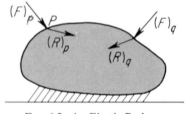

FIG. 6.2. An Elastic Body

Evidently, as a consequence of Hooke's law, the general relation connecting the force or load (F) with the displacement which it produces at its point of application can be written in the form

$$(2.8) \qquad \begin{aligned} x_p &= \phi_{11}F_x + \phi_{12}F_y + \phi_{13}F_z \\ y_p &= \phi_{21}F_x + \phi_{22}F_y + \phi_{23}F_z \\ z_p &= \phi_{31}F_x + \phi_{32}F_y + \phi_{33}F_z \end{aligned}$$

If we denote the square matrix of the coefficients of these equations by $[\phi]$, then these equations may be written in the concise matrix form,

$$(2.9) \qquad (R)_p = [\phi](F)_p$$

The square matrix $[\phi]$ is called the flexibility matrix of the elastic body at the point P. Equation (2.9) is a generalization of the scalar equation (2.2).

The elements of the matrix $[\phi]$ that have the same suffixes, such as ϕ_{11}, ϕ_{22}, ϕ_{33}, are called *direct flexibilities*. The other elements, such as ϕ_{12}, etc., are called *cross*, or *compound, flexibilities*.

The Case of Several Loads

Let another force or load be applied at another point Q of the elastic body of Fig. 6.2.   Let the displacement of the point Q be denoted by $(R)_q$ and the load applied to the point Q be $(F)_q$.   The general relations between the forces $(F)_p$ and $(F)_q$ and the corresponding displacements $(R)_p$ and $(R)_q$ produced at the points p and q may be written in the convenient matrix form,

$$(2.10) \qquad \begin{bmatrix} (R)_p \\ (R)_q \end{bmatrix} = \begin{bmatrix} [\phi]_{pp} & [\phi]_{pq} \\ [\phi]_{qp} & [\phi]_{qq} \end{bmatrix} \begin{bmatrix} (F)_p \\ (F)_q \end{bmatrix}$$

The matrices $[\phi]_{pp}$, $[\phi]_{pq}$, $[\phi]_{qp}$, and $[\phi]_{qq}$ are matrices of order $(3, 3)$ of direct and cross flexibilities.   These matrices enable one to compute the displacements $(R)_p$ and $(R)_q$ at the points p and q when the systems of forces $(F)_p$ and $(F)_q$ are acting simultaneously or when only one force system or the other is acting alone.   For example, if no force is acting at the point Q, then $(F)_q = (0)$; if the matrix equation (2.10) is multiplied to obtain $(R)_p$ and $(R)_q$, we have

$$(2.11) \qquad (R)_p = [\phi]_{pp}(F)_p$$

and

$$(2.12) \qquad (R)_q = [\phi]_{qp}(F)_p$$

This last equation gives the displacement of the point Q produced by the force $(F)_p$ acting at the point P.   If the load at p is zero, then $(F)_p = (0)$; if there is a load $(F)_q$ acting at the point q, the deflections $(R)_p$ and $(R)_q$ are again obtained by expanding (2.10).

As the number of loading points increases, the notation of (2.10) becomes increasingly clumsy; it is then more convenient to introduce the following notation:

Let there be n loading points on the structure 1, 2, 3, ..., n.   Let

$(R)_k$ = the deflection vector at the loading point k.

$(F)_k$ = the force vector acting at the loading point k.

$[\phi]_{jk}$ = a third-order direct- or cross-flexibility matrix of the points j and k.   (If $j = k$, the matrix is a direct flexibility matrix; if $j \neq k$, the matrix is a cross flexibility matrix.)

With this notation, the relations between the deflection vectors and the load vectors of the structure may be written in the form

$$(2.13) \qquad \begin{bmatrix} (R)_1 \\ (R)_2 \\ \vdots \\ (R)_n \end{bmatrix} = \begin{bmatrix} [\phi]_{11} & [\phi]_{12} & \cdots & [\phi]_{1n} \\ [\phi]_{21} & [\phi]_{22} & \cdots & [\phi]_{2n} \\ \vdots & \vdots & \cdots & \vdots \\ [\phi]_{n1} & [\phi]_{n2} & \cdots & [\phi]_{nn} \end{bmatrix} \begin{bmatrix} (F)_1 \\ (F)_2 \\ \vdots \\ (F)_n \end{bmatrix}$$

This matrix equation may be written in the compact form,

$$(2.14) \qquad (R) = [\phi](F)$$

It is, therefore, seen that the column matrix (R) is a partitioned matrix that contains the n deflection vectors of the structure; hence, it contains $3n$ elements. The square matrix $[\phi]$ is a square partitioned matrix of flexibilities. It contains $9n^2$ elements. The column matrix (F) is a partitioned matrix of the n load vectors. It is customary to call (R) the deflection matrix, $[\phi]$ the flexibility matrix, and (F) the force, or load, matrix.

The Representation of the Elastic Properties of a Body by a Flexibility Matrix

When static loads are applied and displacements measured only at a finite number of points of a body or system, such as an extended body of elastic material, all problems on deflection can be completely solved when the elements of the flexibility matrix $[\phi]$ are known. In general, the number of degrees of freedom which any given loading point possesses is three when it is not directly constrained, but may be two or one when it is constrained or as a consequence of a particular kind of load (symmetry, etc.). In general, therefore, the number of degrees of freedom of a structure loaded at n points is $3n$, and the flexibility matrix $[\phi]$ is a square matrix of order $3n$ and, therefore, contains $9n^2$ elements.

When the loads are not strictly applied only at a finite number of points, it may still be sufficiently accurate for many purposes to treat the system as if it had only a definite finite set of loading points. For example, the system may be supposed to be divided up into regions, each of which surrounds and is associated with a definite loading point. Then any load applied within a given region is treated as if it were applied directly to the associated loading point. Clearly, the higher the accuracy of representation required, the smaller must the regions be and the more numerous the loading points.

The Stiffness Matrix

If the flexibility matrix $[\phi]$ is nonsingular and has an inverse $[\phi]^{-1}$, it is possible to premultiply Eq. (2.14) by $[\phi]^{-1}$ and obtain the equation

$$(2.15) \qquad (F) = [\phi]^{-1}(R)$$

The matrix $[\phi]^{-1} = [k]$ is called the stiffness matrix of the system or the structure. In terms of the stiffness matrix, (2.15) takes the form

$$(2.16) \qquad (F) = [k](R)$$

This equation expresses the loads (F) in terms of the deflections (R) produced by the loads.

3. CONSERVATIVE BODIES AND THE STRAIN ENERGY

In order to compute the work done by the various forces acting on a body to produce a final deformation denoted by the displacement vector (R), consider the work done by the ith force F_i during the elastic deformations. Let it be assumed that all the forces acting on the structure are applied simultaneously and are increased from zero to their final value at such a slow rate that equilibrium between loads and internal stresses is continuously maintained. The average value of the force F_i during the loading process is $\frac{1}{2}F_i$, the total displacement through which this force acts is R_i, and, therefore, the work done by the force is $\frac{1}{2}F_iR_i$. The total work done by all the forces, W, can, therefore, be obtained by the following summation:

$$(3.1) \qquad W = U = \tfrac{1}{2}(R)'(F) = \tfrac{1}{2}(F)'(R)$$

This expression for W depends only upon the *final* values of the deformations (R) and the forces (F), and does not depend upon the manner in which this final configuration is reached. This is a property of a conservative system, and, therefore, the work done upon the body is the strain energy U stored in it in the form of strain energy. By means of (2.14) the expression (3.1) for the strain energy of the body may be expressed in terms of the flexibility matrix in the following form:

$$(3.2) \qquad U = \tfrac{1}{2}(F)'[\phi]'(F) = \tfrac{1}{2}(F)'[\phi](F)$$

In order for these two expressions for U to be equal, we must have

$$(3.3) \qquad [\phi] = [\phi]' \quad \leftarrow \text{not proven} \atop (\text{assumr})$$

Therefore, the flexibility matrix $[\phi]$ is a symmetric matrix, and its elements must satisfy the symmetry condition

$$(3.4) \qquad \phi_{rs} = \phi_{sr}$$

This relation is known in the literature of the theory of structures as *Maxwell's reciprocal theorem*.

The strain energy U may also be expressed in terms of the deflections (R) by the use of Eq. (2.16) to eliminate (F) from (3.2). If this is done, the following expression results:

$$(3.5) \qquad U = \tfrac{1}{2}(R)'[k](R) = \tfrac{1}{2}(R)'[k]'(R)$$

This relation indicates that the stiffness matrix $[k]$ must have the property that

$$(3.6) \qquad [k] = [k]' \quad \text{or} \quad k_{rs} = k_{sr}$$

and hence must also be a symmetric matrix. This is, of course, a consequence of Maxwell's reciprocal theorem, since, by definition, $[k] = [\phi]^{-1}$; it follows that if $[\phi]$ is symmetric, its inverse $[k]$ must also be a symmetric matrix.

4. CASTIGLIANO'S THEOREM

This theorem enables the displacements (R) to be obtained by means of differentiating the potential energy expression with respect to the forces (F). In order to establish this theorem, let the following vector operator be introduced:

$$(4.1) \qquad (D_F) = \begin{bmatrix} D_{F_1} \\ D_{F_2} \\ \cdots \\ D_{F_n} \end{bmatrix}, \quad \text{where} \quad D_{F_i} = \frac{\partial}{\partial F_i}$$

Then if the operator (D_F) is applied to the scalar potential function V, the result is

$$(4.2) \qquad (D_F)V = (D_F)\frac{(F)'[\phi](F)}{2} = [\phi](F) = (R)$$

This theorem is very important in the theory of structures.

5. THE PRINCIPAL DIRECTIONS OF LOADING AT A POINT OF AN ELASTIC BODY

Consider a single force (F) applied at a point P of an elastic body. Then, as mentioned in Sec. 2, this force produces a displacement of the point P which may be denoted by the vector (R). In general, the vectors (F) and (R) do not have the same directions, but their components satisfy Eq. (2.8). This equation may be written in the matrix form

$$(5.1) \qquad (R) = [\phi](F)$$

where $[\phi]$ is the $(3, 3)$ flexibility matrix of the body at the point P.

A *principal direction* of loading at a point P of an elastic body is such that a force applied at P in the principal direction produces a displacement in the same direction. In order to determine the principal direction, let us introduce a unit vector (u) whose direction is that of the principal direction. Now, if a load is applied in the principal direction, it may be expressed in the form

$$(5.2) \qquad (F) = F_0(u)$$

where F_0 is the *magnitude* of the load. The displacement in the principal direction produced by the load (5.2) may be expressed in the form

$$(5.3) \qquad (R) = R_0(u)$$

where R_0 is the magnitude of the displacement. Now if (5.2) and (5.3) are substituted into (5.1), the result is

$$(5.4) \qquad F_0[\phi](u) = R_0(u)$$

Now let

(5.5)
$$\mu = \frac{R_0}{F_0}$$

so that μ is the *flexibility* measured in the principal direction. With this notation, (5.4) may be written in the form

(5.6)
$$(\mu U - [\phi])(u) = (0)$$

It is, therefore, seen that in order to satisfy (5.6) we must have

(5.7)
$$\det (\mu U - [\phi]) = 0$$

Therefore, the permissible values of μ are the three eigenvalues of the flexibility matrix $[\phi]$. Since $[\phi]$ is a symmetric matrix, the three eigenvalues μ_1, μ_2, μ_3 are real. These quantities are the *flexibilities* measured in the principal directions. The relation (5.6) enables us to compute the three *eigenvectors* $(u)_1$, $(u)_2$, $(u)_3$ of the matrix $[\phi]$. These three unit vectors have the directions of the principal directions of loading. These directions are orthogonal, since $[\phi]$ is a symmetric matrix.

This analysis indicates that there are always three real and mutually orthogonal principal directions of loading at any point of a conservative body or system, and that associated with each direction there is a flexibility μ_i. The three flexibilities along the principal directions are the eigenvalues of the flexibility matrix $[\phi]$.

6. THE PRINCIPLE OF MINIMUM POTENTIAL ENERGY

Energy methods find a wide application in the solution of structural problems in the determination of deformations of structures under the influence of static and dynamic loads and in the calculation of the elements of the flexibility and stiffness matrices. The principle of *minimum potential energy* is a useful tool in computing the displacements of conservative elastic systems, and it is based on the *principle of virtual work*.[16] The principle of virtual work applied to deformable bodies can be stated as follows:

If a body is in equilibrium under the action of prescribed external forces, the work (virtual work) done by these forces in a small additional displacement compatible with the geometric constraints (virtual displacement) is equal to the change in the strain energy of the body.

The principle of virtual work can be stated in the following mathematical form:

(6.1)
$$\delta W_e = \delta U$$

where δW_e is the virtual work done by the external forces and δU is the change in strain energy resulting from a small virtual displacement of the body.

If we define V, the *potential energy*, by the equation

(6.2) $$V = U - W_e$$

then it can be seen by transposing Eq. (6.1) that

(6.3) $$\delta U - \delta W_e = \delta V = 0$$

This equation is a mathematical statement of the *minimum potential energy principle*; it is applicable only to conservative systems. The principle of minimum potential energy is usually stated in the following manner:

Among all possible deformation configurations compatible with the geometric constraints, the configuration which satisfies the equations of equilibrium is the one which minimizes the potential energy $V = U - W_e$.

As a simple application of this general principle, consider the problem of determining the deflection of the spring, shown in Fig. 6.3, produced by the load W which it supports. In this simple case we have, if k is the spring stiffness, $U = \int_0^x kx$

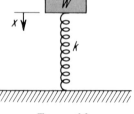

(6.4) $$U = \tfrac{1}{2}kx^2$$

This is the strain energy of the spring when it is compressed by a distance x. The work done by the force of gravity when the weight W is lowered a distance x is

FIGURE 6.3

(6.5) $$W_e = Wx$$

In this example, the potential energy V of the system is

(6.6) $$V = U - W_e = \frac{kx^2}{2} - Wx$$

If we now minimize V with respect to the deflection x, we obtain

(6.7) $$\frac{dV}{dx} = kx - W = 0$$

Therefore, the deflection of the spring is given by

(6.8) $$x = \frac{W}{k}$$

7. DETERMINATION OF THE FLEXIBILITY MATRIX OF A COMPLEX STRUCTURE

An elastic structure, no matter how complex, is fundamentally a group of elastic elements joined together to form a system that is often statically indeterminate. The structure under consideration can usually be idealized so that it consists of structural elements whose strain energy can be computed in terms of internal stresses. This idealization is a process of replacing a continuous system by an equivalent lumped parameter system. The success of the equivalent lumped parameter method of analysis depends upon the ability of the analyst to replace the actual structure by a simpler idealized structure which retains the essential features of the actual structure. At the present time, there are two general methods that have been developed for the stress analysis of complex structures. These two methods are as follows:

(a) *The Force Method of Analysis*

In this method of analysis, the complex structure is viewed as an assemblage of a finite number of elastic components. The original structure is cut or "exploded" into its basic components, and each component is placed in equilibrium under the action of an internal force system. The various *forces* acting on the components of the exploded structure are regarded as the unknown quantities. If the structure is statically determinate, the generalized force system can be computed from the equations of equilibrium, and the deflections can be obtained by applying Castigliano's theorem. If the structure is *statically indeterminate*, the correct internal force system must be obtained by the principle of minimum strain energy. This is equivalent to imposing the requirements that the deformation of each element is *compatible* with the deformation of every other element.

(b) *The Displacement Method of Analysis*

In this method, the structure is again viewed as an assemblage of a finite number of interconnected elastic components. However, now the *generalized displacements*, or deformations, of the various discrete components of the structure are regarded as the unknown quantities, instead of the generalized forces acting on the various components. The deformation of each elastic component is required to be compatible with the deformation of every other component. The correct deformation pattern is obtained by applying the principle of minimum potential energy. This is equivalent to the requirement that every component of the structure should be in static equilibrium. This method is sometimes called the method of direct stiffness calculation. We now turn to a detailed discussion of these two general methods of analysis.

8. THE FORCE METHOD OF STRESS ANALYSIS

Let the original structure, which is shown as a block in Fig. 6.4, be divided, or "exploded," into the structures shown in Fig. 6.5. In this schematic drawing the original structure has been exploded into four elementary structures. The *external force system* impressed on the original structure is denoted by a column matrix (F), and the *internal force system* of the exploded

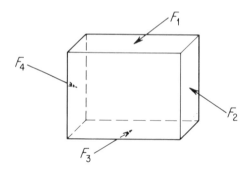

FIG. 6.4. Original Structure

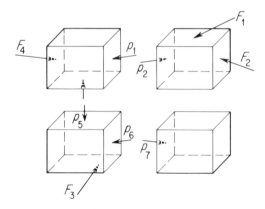

FIG. 6.5. Exploded Structure

structure is denoted by a column matrix (p). In order to discuss the force method in general, let the following notation be introduced:

General Notation

 n = the number of internal forces or stresses in the structural elements of the exploded structure.

 m = the number of external generalized forces (including couples) that are applied to the original structure.

 r = the number of redundant internal forces of the exploded structure.

 F = a column matrix whose elements are the generalized forces or loads applied to the original structure. An $(m, 1)$ matrix.

 X = a column matrix whose elements are the r redundancies or the r unknown self-equilibrating system of internal forces of the exploded structure. A matrix of order $(r, 1)$.

 D = the (n, n) flexibility matrix of the structural elements of the exploded structure.

ϕ = the (m, m) flexibility matrix for the generalized external force system F of the original structure.

p = a column matrix whose n elements are the generalized forces on the structural elements of the exploded structure. A matrix of order $(n, 1)$.

S = a matrix whose elements are the m generalized displacements in the directions of the applied generalized forces F of the original structure. A matrix of order $(m, 1)$.

v = a column matrix whose elements are the generalized strains or displacements of the structural elements of the exploded structure. A matrix of order $(n, 1)$.

f_0 = a transfer matrix of order (n, m) of the exploded structure for unit applied external loads.

f_z = a transfer matrix of order (n, r) of the exploded structure for unit redundant forces.

U = the strain energy of the structure.

$d_{00} = f'_0 D f_0$ = a matrix of order (m, m).

$d_{z0} = f'_z D f_0$ = a matrix of order (r, m).

$d_{zz} = f'_z D f_z$ = a matrix of order (r, r).

In order to begin the force method of analysis, the stresses or internal forces of the exploded structure are expressed by the following matrix equation:

(8.1) $$p = f_0 F + f_z X$$

The exploded system is chosen so that the calculations of the transfer matrix f_0 are as elementary as possible. Equation (8.1) expresses the principle of static equilibrium of the exploded structure.

The total strain energy of the exploded structure may be expressed in the following form:

(8.2) $$U = \tfrac{1}{2}(p'Dp)$$

If the expression for the internal forces p given by (8.1) is substituted into (8.2), the result is

(8.3) $$2U = (F'f'_0 + X'f'_z)[D](f_0 F + f_z X)$$

This result may also be written in the convenient form

(8.4) $$2U = (F' \quad X') \begin{bmatrix} (f'_0 D f_0) & (f'_0 D f_z) \\ (f'_z D f_0) & (f'_z D f_z) \end{bmatrix} \begin{bmatrix} F \\ X \end{bmatrix}$$

If the following notation is now introduced:

(8.5) $$d_{00} = (f'_0 D f_0), \quad \text{an } (m, m) \text{ matrix}$$

(8.6) $$d_{z0} = (f'_z D f_0), \quad \text{an } (r, m) \text{ matrix}$$

(8.7) $$d_{zz} = (f'_z D f_z), \quad \text{an } (r, r) \text{ matrix}$$

then Eq. (8.4) may be written in the following concise form:

$$(8.8) \qquad U = \tfrac{1}{2}(F' \quad X') \begin{bmatrix} d_{00} & d'_{x0} \\ d_{x0} & d_{xx} \end{bmatrix} \begin{bmatrix} F \\ X \end{bmatrix}$$

The strain energy U of the exploded structure is now in a convenient form, so the column of redundant forces X may be determined by the principle of minimum strain energy. Accordingly, the strain energy U, as given by (8.8), is now minimized with respect to the redundant forces X_i by the expression

$$(8.9) \qquad \frac{\partial U}{\partial X_i} = 0, \qquad i = 1, 2, 3, \ldots, r \text{ (8)}$$

After some algebraic manipulations, the result of the differentiation (8.9) enables the column of redundant forces X to be expressed in the form

$$(8.10) \qquad X = - d_{xx}^{-1} d_{x0} F$$

The n generalized forces of the exploded structure p may now be obtained by the use of Eq. (8.1). The internal forces are, therefore, given by

$$(8.11) \qquad p = (f_0 - f_x d_{xx}^{-1} d_{x0}) F$$

This is a very convenient expression for the generalized forces of the elements of the exploded structure in terms of the generalized external forces F applied to the original structure.

Computation of the Flexibility Matrix ϕ of the Original Structure

The result (8.11) may be more concisely expressed by the introduction of the matrix

$$(8.12) \quad b = (f_0 - f_x d_{xx}^{-1} d_{x0}) = \text{an } (n, m) \text{ rectangular transfer matrix}$$

With this notation, (8.11) takes the concise form

$$(8.13) \qquad p = bF$$

Now, if ϕ is the (m, m) flexibility matrix of the structure in terms of the m applied generalized forces F, then the strain energy U of the structure may be expressed by the equations

$(8.14) \quad U = \tfrac{1}{2}(p'Dp),$ in terms of the internal generalized forces p of the exploded structure

$(8.15) \quad U = \tfrac{1}{2}(F'\phi F),$ in terms of the generalized applied forces F

As a consequence of (8.13) we have $p' = F'b'$. Therefore, (8.14) may be written in the form

$$(8.16) \qquad U = \tfrac{1}{2}(F'b'DbF) = \tfrac{1}{2}F'(b'Db)F$$

If we now compare (8.15) with (8.16), it is seen that the flexibility matrix ϕ must have the form

$$(8.17) \qquad \phi = (b'Db), \quad \text{an } (m, m) \text{ matrix}$$

Equation (8.17) gives the flexibility matrix ϕ of the original structure in terms of the generalized external applied forces F.

The Generalized Displacements

If we let S be a column matrix whose elements are the m generalized displacements (including linear and angular displacements) produced by the m generalized external forces F, we have, as a consequence of the definition of the flexibility matrix ϕ, the following equation:

$$(8.18) \qquad S = \phi F \quad \text{(a column of } m \text{ generalized displacements)}$$

The Generalized Strains

If we let v be a column matrix whose elements are the n generalized strains or displacements of the structural elements of the exploded structure, we have, by the definition of the flexibility matrix D of the structural elements of the exploded structure,

$$(8.19) \qquad v = Dp = DbF$$

since by (8.13) $p = bF$.

A relation between the displacements S and the displacements v may be obtained by writing (8.18) in the form

$$(8.20) \qquad S = \phi F = (b'Db)F = b'(DbF)$$

If we now compare (8.19) with (8.20), we notice that S may be expressed in terms of v by the equation

$$(8.21) \qquad S = b'v$$

This equation is an important relation, because it gives the generalized displacements S of the original structure due to the application of the generalized forces F in terms of the generalized displacements v of the elements of the exploded structure in a very simple and compact manner.

9. THE MODIFIED FLEXIBILITY MATRIX

In certain applications of the force method of structural analysis, it is necessary to find the modification of the flexibility matrix ϕ of the structure if certain constraints or modifications are imposed on the original structure without having to start the calculations giving the new flexibility matrix from the very beginning. In this section we will assume that we are given the flexibility matrix ϕ of the original structure for m of its points as discussed above, and we now are required to find a new flexibility matrix ϕ_1 for k points of the structure, where k is less than m, when the remaining $p = m - k$ points of the structure are fixed in space.

In order to obtain the required modified flexibility matrix ϕ_1, we write the flexibility matrix of the original structure in the following partitioned form:

$$(9.1) \qquad \phi = \begin{bmatrix} \phi_{kk} & \phi_{kp} \\ \phi_{pk} & \phi_{pp} \end{bmatrix}$$

where $p =$ the number of points to be fixed in space, and $p + k = m$. Since ϕ is a symmetric matrix, it is noted that

$$(9.2) \qquad \phi_{pk} = \phi'_{kp}$$

Now let the displacement matrix S be partitioned in the form

$$(9.3) \qquad S = \begin{bmatrix} S_k \\ S_p \end{bmatrix}$$

Equation (8.17) may now be written in the form

$$(9.4) \qquad S = \phi F = \begin{bmatrix} \phi_{kk} & \phi_{kp} \\ \phi_{pk} & \phi_{pp} \end{bmatrix} \begin{bmatrix} F_k \\ F_p \end{bmatrix} = \begin{bmatrix} S_k \\ S_p \end{bmatrix}$$

where the column of generalized forces F has been partitioned into the columns F_k and F_p. If the multiplication indicated in (9.4) is performed, the results may be written in the form

$$(9.5) \qquad \phi_{kk}F_k + \phi_{kp}F_p = S_k$$

$$(9.6) \qquad \phi_{pk}F_k + \phi_{pp}F_p = S_p = 0$$

In (9.6) we have placed the elements of the displacement S_p equal to zero, since by hypothesis the p points of the original structure are now not permitted to move and are to be fixed. Equation (9.6) may now be solved for F_p to obtain

$$(9.7) \qquad F_p = -\phi_{pp}^{-1}\phi_{pk}F_k$$

If this value of F_p is now substituted into (9.5), the resulting equation is

$$(9.8) \qquad (\phi_{kk} - \phi_{kp}\phi_{pp}^{-1}\phi_{pk})F_k = S_k$$

This result is of the form

$$(9.9) \qquad \phi_1 F_k = S_k$$

ϕ_1 is now recognized to be the desired modified flexibility matrix of the constrained structure. If (9.8) and (9.9) are compared, it is seen that ϕ_1 is given by

$$(9.10) \qquad \phi_1 = (\phi_{kk} - \phi_{kp}\phi_{pp}^{-1}\phi_{pk})$$

It is, therefore, seen that the new flexibility matrix ϕ_1 may be simply obtained by (9.10) without having to start the analysis from the beginning. The result (9.10) is very useful in the analysis of structures when constraints of the form $S_p = 0$ are introduced.

10. ANALYSIS OF MODIFIED STRUCTURES

A method will now be described for finding the redistribution of stresses and deflections caused by a subsequent modification of the original structure without having to repeat all the computations ab initio.

The basic idea of the method is to fill in the removed elements of the original structure by the introduction of fictitious elements. For computational purposes it is preferable to select the dimensions of these fictitious elements to conform to those of the surrounding structure. In order to obtain the same stress and strain distribution in the assumed continuous structure and in the actual structure, *initial strains* v_0 are imposed on the additional elements of such magnitudes that their total stresses p_h, caused by the effect of the external loads F and the initial strains, become zero. By this procedure, the effect of the fictitious elements is cancelled, and the uniform pattern of the basic equation is retained.

Notation

h = the number of elements to be removed.

g = the number of elements of the original structure to be retained.

H = the column of the h *initial strains* to be impressed on the elements to be removed.

p_h = the stresses in the h elements to be removed.

p_g = the stresses in the elements of the structure with cutouts.

$v_0 = \begin{bmatrix} 0 \\ H \end{bmatrix}$ = the column of the initial strains impressed on the elements of the structure.

Before the initial strains v_0, are applied, the stresses on the various structural elements of the system are given by (10.1) in the form

(10.1) $p = f_0F + f_zX$

After the imposition of the initial strains v_0 on the structural elements, the stresses are given by

(10.2) $p = f_0F + f_z(X + X_0)$

The elements of the column X_0 represent the increase of the self-equilibrating system of stresses caused by the initial strains v_0.

In order to obtain an expression for X_0, regard the effect of the initial strains as being produced by fictitious external loads F_0 which will produce the same stresses as the initial strains.   Then, as a consequence of (8.19) and (10.1), we have

$$(10.3) \qquad p_0 = D^{-1}v_0 = f_0 F_0$$

The unknown X_0 may now be obtained by the use of (8.10) which in this case may be written in the form

$$(10.4) \qquad X_0 = -d_{xx}^{-1}d_{x0}F_0 = -d_{xx}^{-1}f'_x D(f_0 F_0) = -d_{xx}^{-1}f'_x DD^{-1}v_0$$
$$= -d_{xx}^{-1}f'_x v_0$$

The total redundant force matrix is now given by

$$(10.5) \qquad (X + X_0) = -d_{xx}^{-1}d_{x0}F_0 - d_{xx}^{-1}f'_x v_0$$

The first term of the right member of (10.5) is produced by the external loads F, and the second term is the effect of the initial strains v_0.

The total stress distribution produced by the combined effect of the external loads and the initial strains is obtained by substituting (10.5) into (10.2).   This gives the expression

$$(10.6) \qquad p = (f_0 - f_x d_{xx}^{-1}d_{x0})F - f_x d_{xx}^{-1}f'_x v_0$$

To determine the effect of the removed elements, let the initial strain matrix be written in the following partitioned form:

$$(10.7) \qquad v_0 = \begin{bmatrix} 0 \\ H \end{bmatrix}$$

where H is a column matrix of the h initial strains to be imposed on the elements to be removed.   Now write the f_x matrix in the following partitioned form:

$$(10.8) \qquad f_x = \begin{bmatrix} f_{xg} \\ f_{xh} \end{bmatrix}$$

The matrix f_{xh} is a rectangular transfer matrix of order (h, r); it is the submatrix of f_x whose rows correspond to the elements of the structure to be removed.

With this notation, we have

$$(10.9) \qquad f'_x v_0 = f'_{xh} H$$

The stress matrix (10.6) may now be written in the form

$$(10.10) \qquad p = bF - f_x d_{xx}^{-1}f'_{xh} H$$

where the (n, m) matrix b is given by

$$(10.11) \qquad b = (f_0 - f_x d_{xx}^{-1}d_{x0})$$

This matrix may now be partitioned in the form

$$(10.12) \qquad b = \begin{bmatrix} b_g \\ b_h \end{bmatrix}$$

where b_h is an (h, m) matrix.

By the use of (10.8) and (10.12), the stress matrix (10.10) may now be written in the form

$$(10.13) \qquad \begin{bmatrix} p_g \\ p_h \end{bmatrix} = \begin{bmatrix} b_g \\ b_h \end{bmatrix} \cdot F - \begin{bmatrix} f_{xg} \\ f_{xh} \end{bmatrix} \cdot d_{xx}^{-1} f'_{xh} H = p$$

p_g are the stresses in the structure with cutouts, and p_h are the stresses in the elements to be removed. In order to determine the magnitudes of the h initial strains H, the stresses p_h are put equal to zero. If (10.13) is expanded, the results are

$$(10.14) \qquad p_g = b_g F - f_{xg} d_{xx}^{-1} f'_{xh} H$$

$$(10.15) \qquad p_h = b_g F - f_{xh} d_{xx}^{-1} f'_{xh} H = 0$$

H may be determined from (10.15) in the form

$$(10.16) \qquad H = [f_{xh} d_{xx}^{-1} f'_{xh}]^{-1} b_h F$$

If this result is now substituted into (10.14), the following expression is obtained:

$$(10.17) \qquad p_g = [b_g - (f_{xg} d_{xx}^{-1})(f_{xh} d_{xx}^{-1} f'_{xh})^{-1} b_h] F$$

This expression gives the true stress distribution in the $(n - h)$ elements of the cut structure. By this procedure, the stresses in the cut structure are obtained in terms of the stresses already computed for the fictitious continuous structure.

It is to be noted that the matrix to be inverted in (10.17) is the matrix

$$(10.18) \qquad M_h = (f_{xh} d_{xx}^{-1} f'_{xh}), \quad \text{an } (h, h) \text{ matrix}$$

The order of this matrix is equal to the number of linearly independent stresses to be nullified. If one shear panel is removed, the order is one and the matrix is a scalar number. If a flange between two adjoining nodal points is removed, the order is two, etc.

The stresses in the cut structure may also be written in the form (10.13) with H expressed by (10.16). This formulation gives

$$(10.19) \qquad p_c = \begin{bmatrix} p_g \\ 0 \end{bmatrix} = [b - (f_x d_{xx}^{-1} f'_{xh}) M_h^{-1} b_h] F$$

or

$$(10.20) \qquad p_c = b_c F,$$

where

$$(10.21) \qquad b_c = b - (f_x d_{xx}^{-1} f'_{xh}) M_h^{-1} b_h$$

The Flexibility Matrix of the Cut Structure $= \phi$

The flexibility matrix d of the original structure is given by (8.17) in the form

$$(10.22) \qquad\qquad \phi = b'Db$$

The displacements S of the original structure are given by (8.20) in the form

$$(10.23) \qquad\qquad S = \phi F$$

If we let ϕ_c be the flexibility matrix of the cut structure, the displacements S_c of the cut structure are now given by

$$(10.24) \qquad\qquad S_c = \phi_c F$$

Since the cut structure is assumed to have the initial strains v_0, (5.20) gives the following relation for the displacements of the cut structure:

$$(10.25) \qquad\qquad S_c = \phi F + b'v_0 = \phi F + b'_h H$$

This equation is obtained by noting that v_0 is given by (10.7). If (10.24) and (10.25) are set equal to each other, the following equation is obtained:

$$(10.26) \qquad\qquad S_c = \phi_c F = [d + b'_h M_h^{-1} b_h]\phi$$

From this equation, it is seen that

$$(10.27) \qquad\qquad \phi_c = d + b'_h M_h^{-1} b_h$$

This expression gives a very simple and symmetrical relation between the flexibility of the cut structure ϕ_c and the flexibility ϕ of the original homogeneous structure.

11. MODIFICATIONS OF THE ELEMENTS OF THE STRUCTURE

In Sec. 10, the effects of removing certain elements of the original structure were considered. In many applications of practical importance, it is desired to determine the alterations of the stresses and strains of the structure when h structural elements are modified without starting the analysis ab initio. Modification of the h elements under consideration may involve either making the elements more rigid or more flexible.

For purposes of analysis, the effect of the modification of the original structure will be regarded as equivalent to the introduction of H fictitious *initial strains* on the h elements to be modified so that their total strains v_{ho} are identical to those in the modified elements in the new structure v_{hm}. The stresses in the original structure p_0 are then the same as those of the altered structure p_m but without the effect of the initial strains.

Notation

h = the number of structural elements to be altered.

g = the number of unaltered structural elements.

$n = (h + g)$ = the total number of structural elements.

D_g = the (g, g) flexibility matrix of the g unassembled elements in the original structure.

D_h = the (h, h) flexibility matrix of the h unassembled elements of the original structure.

$D_0 = \begin{bmatrix} D_g & 0 \\ 0 & D_h \end{bmatrix}$, the (n, n) flexibility matrix of the unassembled structural elements of the original structure.

$D_m = \begin{bmatrix} D_g & 0 \\ 0 & D_{hm} \end{bmatrix}$, the (n, n) flexibility matrix of the unassembled structural elements of the modified structure.

$\Delta D_h = D_{hm} - D_h$ = the change in the D_h matrix of the original structure.

v_{h0} = the total strains in the h elements of the original structure, including the effect of the fictitious assumed initial strains H.

v_{hm} = the total strains of the modified structure.

p_0 = the stresses in the elements of the original structure.

p_m = the stresses in the elements of the modified structure.

$b = \begin{bmatrix} b_g \\ b_h \end{bmatrix}$, the (n, m) rectangular transfer matrix for stresses in the original structure.

$f_x = \begin{bmatrix} f_{xg} \\ f_{xh} \end{bmatrix}$, the (n, r) stress transfer matrix of the original structure for unit redundancies.

H = the $(h, 1)$ fictitious column matrix of the h strains introduced in the h elements to be modified in the original structure.

$v_0 = \begin{bmatrix} 0 \\ H \end{bmatrix}$ = the $(n, 1)$ initial strain column.

F = the $(m, 1)$ column of external loads (both systems).

$M_h = (f_{xh}d_{xx}^{-1}f'_{xh}), \; d_{xx} = (f'_x D_0 f_x)$.

The modifications of the h elements of the original structure are assumed to be caused by an increase or a decrease of the flange cross-sectional areas, sheet thickness, etc. These modifications can be regarded as a change in the flexibility matrix D_0 of the original structural elements.

By a suitable rearrangement of the order in which the elements are assembled, the matrix D_0 can always be written in the following partitioned form:

$$(11.1) \qquad\qquad D_0 = \begin{bmatrix} D_g & 0 \\ 0 & D_h \end{bmatrix}$$

In applications of the method, actual rearrangement is not required, since it is only necessary to extract the submatrix D_h.

The problem is to determine the alteration of the stress and strain distribution of the original structural elements when the matrix D_0 is changed to

$$(11.2) \quad D_m = \begin{bmatrix} D_g & 0 \\ 0 & (D_h + \Delta D_h) \end{bmatrix} = \begin{bmatrix} D_g & 0 \\ 0 & D_m \end{bmatrix}, \quad D_{hm} = D_h + \Delta D_h$$

By a suitable choice of the fictitious initial strains H, the stress matrices p_0 and p_m of the original and modified structures are given by Eq. (10.10) in the form

$$(11.3) \quad p_0 = p_m = b\dot{\phi} - f_z d_{zz}^{-1} f'_{zh} H, \quad d_{zz} = (f'_z D_0 f_z)$$

The equivalent strains v_{h0} in the h elements of the original structure are given by (8.19) in the form

$$(11.4) \quad v_{h0} = D_{h0} F_0 + v_0 = D_h[b_h\dot{\phi} - f_{zh}d_{zz}^{-1} f'_{zh} H] + H$$

The strains v_{hm} in the modified structure are given by (5.19) in the form

$$(11.5) \quad v_{hm} = D_{hm}[b_h F - f_{zh}d_{zz}^{-1} f'_{zh} H]$$

The fictitious initial strains may be determined by the condition that $v_{h0} = v_{hm}$, or

$$(11.6) \quad D_h[b_h F - f_{zh}d_{zz}^{-1} f'_{zh} H] + H = D_{hm}[b_h F - f_z d_{zz}^{-1} f'_{zh} H]$$

After some algebraic reductions (11.6) may be solved for H in the form

$$(11.7) \quad H = [M_h + (\Delta D_h)^{-1}]^{-1} b_h F$$

The stresses p_m in the modified structure are now given by (11.3) in the concise form

$$(11.8) \quad p_m = b_m F$$

where the (n, m) rectangular matrix b_m has the form

$$(11.9) \quad b_m = b - f_z d_{zz}^{-1} f'_{zh} [M_h + (\Delta D_h)^{-1}]^{-1} b_h$$

It is to be noted that the order of the matrix to be inverted to obtain b_m is (h, h).

If the original elements are made *stiffer*, $\Delta D_h < 0$, whereas if they are made more *flexible* $\Delta D_h > 0$.

The following three important special cases frequently arise in practice.

(a) *Modification of the Structure by the Elimination of h Elements*

This is the case of the cut structure discussed in Sec. 10. If h elements are removed, we have $\Delta D_h \to \infty$ and $(\Delta D_h)^{-1} \to 0$; hence, in this case, (11.9) reduces to

$$(11.10) \quad b_m = b - f_z d_{zz}^{-1} f'_{zh} M_h^{-1} b_h$$

This equation corresponds to Eq. (10.21).

(b) *Modification of the Structure by Making h Elements Rigid*

In this case $D_{hm} = 0$, and hence $\Delta D_h = -D_h$. Equation (11.9) now reduces to

$$(11.11) \qquad b_m = b - f_x d_{xx}^{-1} f'_{xh}[M_h - D_h^{-1}]^{-1} b_h$$

It is noted that $D_h^{-1} = k_h$ = the original stiffness matrix of h unassembled elements.

(c) *Modification of the Structure Keeping h Elements Geometrically Similar*

In many cases of practical importance, the h elements of the altered structure are geometrically similar to the original elements. In such cases the flexibility matrix D_{hm} has the form

$$(11.12) \qquad D_{hm} = a_h D_h$$

where a_h is a diagonal matrix of order (h, h). For this type of modification, we have

$$(11.13) \qquad \Delta D_h = D_{hm} - D_h = (a_h - I_h) D_h$$

where I_h is the unit matrix of the hth order. Hence,

$$(11.14) \qquad (\Delta D_h)^{-1} = D_h^{-1}(a_h - I_h)^{-1} = k_h(a_h - I_h)^{-1}$$

For this case, (11.9) reduces to

$$(11.15) \qquad b_m = b - (f_x d_{xx}^{-1} f_{xh}^{-1})[M_h + k_h(a_h - I_h)^{-1}]^{-1} b_h$$

12. THE FLEXIBILITY OF THE MODIFIED STRUCTURE

The flexibility matrix ϕ_m of the modified structure is now given by Eq. (5.17) in the form

$$(12.1) \qquad \phi_m = b'_m D_m b_m$$

where D_m is the flexibility matrix of the unassembled elements of the modified structure

$$(12.2) \qquad D_m = \begin{bmatrix} D_g & 0 \\ 0 & D_{hm} \end{bmatrix} = \begin{bmatrix} D_g & 0 \\ 0 & (D_h + \Delta D_h) \end{bmatrix}$$

The displacements S_m of the modified structure are given by (5.20) in the form

$$(12.3) \qquad S_m = \phi_m F$$

These displacements may also be written in terms of the flexibility matrix d_0 of the original structure and the fictitious initial strains in the form

$$(12.4) \qquad \begin{aligned} S_m &= \phi_0 F + b' v_0 = \phi_0 F + b'_h H \\ &= (\phi_0 + b'_h[M_h + (\Delta D_h)^{-1}]^{-1} b_h) F \end{aligned}$$

Hence, if (12.3) is compared with (12.4) we see that

$$(12.5) \qquad \phi_m = \phi_0 + b'_h[M_h + (\Delta D_h)^{-1}]^{-1}b_h$$

This relation gives the flexibility matrix ϕ_m of the modified structure in terms of the flexibility matrix ϕ_0 of the original structure in a very simple and concise manner.

13. THE DISPLACEMENT METHOD OF STRESS ANALYSIS

The second most important method of stress analysis is generally called the displacement method of stress analysis. In this method, the structure under consideration is again "exploded" and regarded as an assemblage of a finite number of interconnected elastic components. However, in this method, the generalized displacements or deformations of the various discrete components of the structure are regarded as the unknown quantities instead of as the generalized forces acting on the various components of the exploded structure, as is done in the force method.

In the displacement method of analysis, the deformation of each elastic component is required to be compatible with the deformation of every other component. The correct deformation pattern is obtained by applying the principle of minimum potential energy. This is equivalent to the requirement that every component of the exploded structure should be in static equilibrium. The displacement method of analysis is sometimes called the method of direct stiffness calculation in the technical literature.

The displacement method can be regarded as *the dual* of the force method; therefore, every equation used in the force method of analysis has its counterpart in the displacement method. This duality that exists between both methods has been discussed in some detail by Professor J. H. Argyris.[1] The duality that exists between the two methods is summarized in the tables at the end of this chapter.

Notation Used in the Displacement Method of Analysis

A concise derivation of the displacement method of analysis will now be given and the procedure compared with that of the force method which has already been discussed.

$n =$ the number of strains in the structural elements.

$m =$ the number of external generalized forces applied to the structure.

$i =$ the number of kinematically indeterminate displacements of the structure.

$F =$ the $(m, 1)$ column of external forces.

$S_i =$ the $(i, 1)$ column of kinematically indeterminate displacements.

$K =$ the (n, n) stiffness matrix of the unassembled elements of the structure.

$k =$ the (m, m) stiffness matrix of the structure.

S = the $(m, 1)$ column of displacements in the direction of F.

v = the $(n, 1)$ column of strains of the n structural elements.

a_0 = the (n, m) strain matrix for unit S and $S_i = 0$.

a_i = the (n, i) strain matrix for unit S_i and $S = 0$.

a = the (n, m) final strain matrix for unit S.

p = the $(n, 1)$ column of stresses of the n structural elements.

$C_{i0} = a_i'Ka_0$ = an (i, m) matrix.

$C_{ii} = a_i'Ka_i$ = an (i, i) matrix.

$C_{00} = a_o'Ka_0$ = an (m, m) matrix.

The Fundamental Equations

By the application of the principles of statics to the elements of the structure, the following equation for the strains v of the structural elements may be written.

(13.1) $$v = a_0S + a_iS_i$$

where S is the column of impressed displacements in the direction of the external forces F, and S_i is the column of the i kinematically indeterminate displacements of the structure.

If K is the (n, n) stiffness matrix of the unassembled structural elements, the strain energy U of the structure may be written in the form

(13.2) $$U = \tfrac{1}{2}v'Kv$$

The transpose of (13.1) gives

(13.3) $$v' = S'a_o' + S_i'a_i'$$

If this is substituted into (13.2), the result is

(13.4) $$U = \tfrac{1}{2}(S'a_o' + S_i'a_i')K(a_0S + a_iS_i)$$

$$= \tfrac{1}{2}(S' \quad S_i')\begin{bmatrix} a_o' \\ a_i' \end{bmatrix}K(a_0 \quad a_i)\begin{bmatrix} S \\ S_i \end{bmatrix}$$

$$= \tfrac{1}{2}(S' \quad S_i')\begin{bmatrix} (a_o'Ka_0) & (a_o'Ka_i) \\ (a_i'Ka_0) & (a_i'Ka_i) \end{bmatrix} \cdot \begin{bmatrix} S \\ S_i \end{bmatrix}$$

Let the following notation be introduced:

(13.5) $\qquad\qquad C_{i0} = (a_i'Ka_0)$,   an (i, m) matrix

(13.6) $\qquad\qquad C_{ii} = (a_i'Ka_i)$,   an (i, i) matrix

(13.7) $\qquad\qquad C_{00} = (a_o'Ka_0)$,   an (m, m) matrix

With this notation, the expression (13.4) for the strain energy U of the structure may be written in the form

(13.8) $$U = \tfrac{1}{2}(S \quad S_i')\begin{bmatrix} C_{00} & C_{i0}' \\ C_{i0} & C_{ii} \end{bmatrix} \cdot \begin{bmatrix} S \\ S_i \end{bmatrix}$$

In order to compute the kinematically indeterminate displacements S_i, we minimize the strain energy U by taking the derivatives.[8]

$$(13.9) \qquad \frac{\partial U}{\partial S_{ip}} = 0, \qquad p = 1, 2, 3, \ldots, i$$

After some algebraic reductions, the result of the differentiation (13.9) gives the following expression for the kinematically indeterminate displacements:

$$(13.10) \qquad S_i = -C_{ii}^{-1}C_{i0}S$$

If this expression is substituted into (13.1), the result may be written in the form

$$(13.11) \qquad v = aS$$

where

$$(13.12) \qquad a = (a_0 - a_i C_{ii}^{-1}C_{i0})$$

Equation (13.11) expresses the strains of the n structural elements v in terms of the impressed displacements S.

The Stiffness Matrix of the Structure k

In terms of the displacements S, the strain energy U of the structure may be written in the form

$$(13.13) \qquad U = \tfrac{1}{2}S'kS = \tfrac{1}{2}v'Kv$$

where k is the (m, m) stiffness matrix of the structure. As a consequence of (13.11), we have $v' = S'a'$, and hence (13.13) may be expressed in the form

$$(13.14) \qquad U = \tfrac{1}{2}S'(a'Ka)S = \tfrac{1}{2}S'kS$$

By inspection of (13.14), it is seen that the stiffness matrix k has the form

$$(13.15) \qquad k = (a'Ka) = (a_0 - a_i C_{ii}^{-1}C_{i0})'K(a_0 - a_i C_{ii_j}^{-1}C_{i0})$$

If the product in (13.15) is carried out, it can be seen that the result may be written in the form

$$(13.16) \qquad k = C_{00} - (C_{i0}'C_{ii}^{-1}C_{i0})$$

The Displacement S

In terms of the stiffness matrix of the structure k, the displacements S are related to the external forces F by the equation

$$(13.17) \qquad F = kS = (a'Ka)S = a'Kv$$

The last member of (13.17) is a consequence of (13.11). The stresses p on the elements of the structure are given by

$$(13.18) \qquad p = Kv = KaS$$

If this is substituted into (13.17), we obtain the important relation

$$(13.19) \qquad F = a'p$$

This equation relates the m applied forces to the structure F and the n stresses p of the structural elements.

14. THE EFFECT OF THE APPLICATION OF INITIAL STRESSES p_0 WITH THE CONSTRAINT $S = 0$

Before we discuss methods for the analysis of the modified structure, it is necessary to obtain a relation for the kinematically indeterminate displacements S_i when initial stresses p_0 are applied to the n structural elements and the constraint that the displacements S should remain zero.

As a consequence of the constraint $S = 0$, the application of the initial strains p_0 to the elements of the structure will induce strains v in the structural elements. The stress matrix of the system will, therefore, have the form

$$(14.1) \qquad p = Kv + p_0$$

Since it is assumed that $S = 0$, Eq. (13.1) now takes the form

$$(14.2) \qquad v = a_i S_i$$

and hence the stress matrix (14.1) in this case is

$$(14.3) \qquad p = p_0 + Ka_i S_i$$

The internal strain energy of the structure may be expressed in the form

$$(14.4) \qquad U = \tfrac{1}{2}F'DF, \qquad D = K^{-1}$$

where D is the flexibility matrix of the unassembled structural elements.

It is now required to determine the kinematically indeterminate displacements S_i as a consequence of the impressed initial strains and the constraint $S = 0$. These displacements may be obtained by minimizing the strain energy U.

If (14.3) is substituted into (14.4), the result may be written in the form

$$(14.5) \qquad U = \tfrac{1}{2}F'DF = (p_0' + S_i'a_i'K)D(p_0 + Ka_i S_i)$$

$$= \tfrac{1}{2}(p_0' \quad S_i') \begin{bmatrix} D & a_i \\ a_i' & C_{ii} \end{bmatrix} \cdot \begin{bmatrix} p_0 \\ S_i \end{bmatrix}$$

The kinematically indeterminate displacements S_i may now be determined by the condition of minimum strain energy. This condition takes the form

$$(14.6) \qquad \frac{\partial U}{\partial S_{ip}} = 0, \qquad p = 1, 2, 3, \ldots, i$$

After some algebraic reductions,[8] the result of the differentiations (14.6) may be expressed in the form

$$(14.7) \qquad\qquad S_i = -C_{ii}^{-1}a_i'p_0$$

This expression gives the kinematically indeterminate displacements under the restriction that the displacements S are constrained to remain zero, whereas the initial stresses p_0 are applied to the n structural elements.

The strains v under these conditions are given by (14.2) in the form

$$(14.8) \qquad\qquad v = a_i S_i = -a_i C_{ii}^{-1}a_i'p_0$$

The stress matrix p is given by (14.2) in the form

$$(14.9) \qquad\qquad p = p_0 + Kv = p_0 - Ka_i C_{ii}^{-1}a_i'p_0$$

The forces acting on the m points of restraint ($S = 0$) are given by (13.19) in the form

$$(14.10) \qquad\qquad F = a'p_0$$

15. ANALYSIS OF MODIFICATIONS OF THE STRUCTURE

In many applications of practical importance, it is desired to determine the alterations of the stresses and strains of the structural elements when certain parts of the structure are modified.   In this section, a method of analysis is presented that enables the new state of stress and strain to be determined without starting the analysis ab initio when certain component parts of the original structure are altered by the introduction of cutouts, and without making certain structural elements more rigid or more flexible.

Notation

Let

$h =$ the number of structural elements to be altered.

$g =$ the number of structural elements to remain unaltered.

$n = (g + h) =$ the total number of structural elements.

$K_g =$ the (g, g) stiffness matrix of the g unassembled elements of the original structure that are to remain unaltered.

$K_h =$ the (h, h) stiffness matrix of the h unassembled elements of the original structure that are to be altered.

$$K_0 = \begin{bmatrix} K_g & 0 \\ 0 & K_h \end{bmatrix}$$

$K_m = \begin{bmatrix} K_g & 0 \\ 0 & K_{hm} \end{bmatrix}$, the (n, n) stiffness matrix of the unassembled structural elements of the modified structure.

The effect of the modification of the structure will be considered to be equivalent to introducing an initial fictitious stress matrix J on the h elements to be modified.

Let the matrix a_i be partitioned in the form

$$(15.1) \qquad\qquad a_i = \begin{bmatrix} a_{ig} \\ a_{ih} \end{bmatrix}$$

The effect of the introduction of the initial stresses J on the h elements to be modified is to give the following strain matrix as a consequence of (14.8):

$$(15.2) \qquad\qquad v_m = v_0 - a_i C_{ii}^{-1} a'_{ih} J$$

where the initial stress matrix is given by

$$(15.3) \qquad\qquad p_0 = \begin{bmatrix} 0 \\ J \end{bmatrix}$$

and v_0 is the strain matrix of the original structure. By the use of (14.1), the modified stress matrix of the h elements to be altered is

$$(15.4) \qquad P_{mh} = K_h v_{mh} + J = K_h(v_{0h} - a_{ih} C_{ii}^{-1} a'_{ih} F_h) + J$$

Another way of writing p_{mh} in terms of the modified stiffness matrix is

$$(15.5) \qquad\qquad p_{mh} = K_{mh}(v_{0h} - a_{ih} C_{ii}^{-1} a'_{ih} J)$$

If we let

$$(15.6) \qquad\qquad K_{mh} = K_h + \Delta K_h$$

then (15.5) may be written in the form

$$(15.7) \qquad\qquad p_{mh} = (K_h + \Delta K_h)(v_{0h} - a_{ih} C_{ii}^{-1} a'_{ih} J)$$

If (15.7) is equated to (15.4), the resulting equation may be solved for the unknown J. After some algebraic reductions, this procedure gives

$$(15.8) \qquad\qquad J = Q^{-1} v_{0h} = Q^{-1} a_h S$$

where

$$(15.9) \qquad\qquad Q = [a_{ih} C_{ii}^{-1} a'_{ih} + (\Delta K_h)^{-1}]$$

The modified strain matrix is now given by (15.2) in the form

$$(15.10) \qquad\qquad v_m = v_0 - a_i C_{ii}^{-1} a'_{ih} Q^{-1} a_h S$$

Since $v_0 = aS$, (15.10) may be written in the convenient form,

$$(15.11) \qquad\qquad v_m = a_m S$$

where

$$(15.12) \qquad\qquad a_m = (a - a_i C_{ii}^{-1} a'_{ih} a_h)$$

16. THE STIFFNESS MATRIX OF THE MODIFIED STRUCTURE

The stiffness matrix of the modified structure, k_m, relates the force and displacement matrices by the equation

$$(16.1) \qquad\qquad F_m = k_m S$$

The stiffness matrix of the modified structure is given by (13.15) in the form

$$(16.2) \qquad\qquad k_m = a_m' K_m a_m$$

A simple method for calculating the modified stiffness matrix k_m is to write the modified force matrix in the form

$$(16.3) \qquad\qquad F_m = F_0 + \Delta F$$

By the use of Eq. (13.19) we obtain

$$(16.4) \qquad\qquad F_0 = a' F_0 = k_0 S$$

$$(16.5) \qquad\qquad \Delta F = a_h' J = \Delta k S$$

Hence, if (16.4) and (16.5) are substituted into (16.3), the result is

$$(16.6) \qquad F_m = a' F_0 + a_h' J = (k_0 + \Delta k) S = k_m S$$

Hence,

$$(16.7) \qquad\qquad k_m = (k_0 + \Delta k)$$

As a consequence of (16.5), we have

$$(16.8) \qquad\qquad a_h' J = a_h' Q^{-1} a_h S = \Delta k S$$

Therefore,

$$(16.9) \qquad\qquad \Delta k = a_h' Q^{-1} a_h$$

Hence, the stiffness matrix of the modified structure is given by

$$(16.10) \qquad k_m = (k_0 + \Delta k) = (k_0 + a_h' Q^{-1} a_h)$$

where k_0 is the stiffness matrix of the original structure before modification.

17. SPECIAL TYPES OF MODIFICATION OF THE STRUCTURE

The following two types of modification of the original structure are of considerable practical importance:

(a) *Making h Elements of the Original Structure Rigid*

In this case, we have the condition

$$(17.1) \qquad\qquad \Delta k_h \to \infty \quad \text{or} \quad (\Delta k_h)^{-1} = 0$$

The appropriate Q matrix for this type of modification is

$$(17.2) \qquad\qquad Q = a_{ih} C_{ii}^{-1} a_{ih}'$$

(b) *The Elimination of h Elements*

In this case, we have

(17.3) $$K_{hm} = 0 \quad \text{or} \quad \Delta K_h = -K_h$$

For this case, the Q matrix reduces to

(17.4) $$Q = [a_{ih} C_{ii}^{-1} a'_{ih} - K_h]$$

Table 1

DUALITY OF FORCE AND DISPLACEMENT METHODS

Force Method	Displacement Method
n = number of strains	n = number of stresses
m = number of external forces	m = number of external forces
r = number of redundancies	i = number of indeterminate displacements
F = column of m external forces	F = column of m external forces
S = column of m displacements	S = column of m displacements
X = column of r redundant forces	S_i = column of i indeterminate displacements
$D = (n, n)$ flexibility matrix of unassembled structural elements	$K = (n, n)$ stiffness matrix of unassembled structural elements
v = column of n strains of the structural elements	v = column of n strains of the structural elements
$f_0 = (n, m)$ stress matrix of the basic structure for unit external loads	$a_0 = (n, m)$ strain matrix of the basic structure for unit displacements S
$f_z = (n, r)$ stress matrix of the basic structure for unit redundancies	$a_i = (n, i)$ strain matrix of the basic structure for unit S_i
p = column of n stresses in the structural elements	p = column of n stresses in the structural elements
ϕ = the (m, m) flexibility matrix of the structure	k = the (m, m) stiffness matrix of the structure
The Strain Energy U	The Strain Energy U
$U = 1/2 F'DF = 1/2\phi'd\phi$	$U = 1/2 v'Kv = 1/2 S'kS$

Table 2

DUALITY OF FORCE AND DISPLACEMENT METHODS
ANALOGOUS BASIC EQUATIONS

Force Method	Displacement Method
$p = f_0 F + f_z X$	$v = a_0 S + a_i S_i$
$X = -d_{zz}^{-1} d_{z0}\phi, \quad (r, 1)$	$S_i = -C_{ii}^{-1} C_{i0} S, \quad (i, 1)$
$d_{zz} = (f'_z D f_z), \quad (r, r)$	$C_{ii} = (a'_i K a_i), \quad (i, i)$
$d_{z0} = (f'_z D f_0), \quad (r, m)$	$C_{i0} = (a'_i K a_0), \quad (i, m)$
$d_{00} = (f'_0 D f_0), \quad (m, m)$	$C_{00} = (a'_0 K a_0), \quad (m, m)$
$p = bF$	$v = aS$
$b = (f_0 - f_z d_{zz}^{-1} d_{z0}), \quad (n, m)$	$a = (a_0 - a_i C_{ii}^{-1} C_{i0}), \quad (n, m)$

$d = (b'Db), \quad (m, m)$ $k = (a'Ka), \quad (m, m)$

$d = d_{00} - (d'_{z0}d_{zz}^{-1}d_{z0})$ $k = C_{00} - (C'_{i0}C_{ii}^{-1}C_{i0})$

$S = \phi F$ $F = kS$

$\phi = k^{-1}$ $k = \phi^{-1}$

$v = Dp$ $p = Kv$

$D = K^{-1}$ $K = D^{-1}$

$S = b'v$ $F = a'p$

$ab' = I_n$ (unit matrix or order n) $ba' = I_n$ (unit matrix of order n)

$a'b = I_m$ (unit matrix of order m) $b'a = I_m$ (unit matrix of order m)

Table 3   Part 1

DUALITY OF FORCE AND DISPLACEMENT METHODS
STRUCTURAL MODIFICATIONS

Force Method	Displacement Method
h = number of structural elements to be modified	h = number of structural elements to be modified
g = the number of unaltered structural elements	g = the number of unaltered structural elements
$n = (h + g)$ = total number of structural elements	$n = (h + g)$ = total number of structural elements
$D_0 = \begin{bmatrix} D_g & 0 \\ 0 & D_h \end{bmatrix} = (n, n)$ flexibility matrix of the unassembled structural elements of the original structure	$K_0 = \begin{bmatrix} K_g & 0 \\ 0 & K_h \end{bmatrix} = (n, n)$ stiffness matrix of the unassembled structural elements of the original structure
D_g = the (g, g) flexibility matrix of the g unassembled elements of the original structure that remain unaltered	K_g = the (g, g) stiffness matrix of the g unassembled elements of the original structure that remain unaltered
D_h = the (h, h) flexibility matrix of the h unassembled elements of the original structure that are to be altered	K_h = the (h, h) stiffness matrix of the h unassembled structural elements of the original structure that are to be altered
$D_{hm} = D_h + \Delta D_h$, the (h, h) flexibility matrix of the h unassembled elements of the modified structure	$K_{hm} = K_h + K_h$ = the (h, h) stiffness matrix of the h unassembled elements of the modified structure
$\Delta D_h = D_{hm} - D_h$ = the change of the D_h matrix produced by the modification of the system	$\Delta K_h = K_{hm} - K_h$ = the change of the K_h matrix produced by the modification of the system
H = a column matrix of h fictitious strains introduced to take into account the modification of the h altered structural elements	J = a column of h initial fictitious stresses introduced to take into account the modification of the h altered structural elements

Table 3   Part 2

Force Method	*Displacement Method*
$b = \begin{bmatrix} b_g \\ b_h \end{bmatrix} = $ the partitioned (n, m) rectangular matrix for stresses of the original structure	$a = \begin{bmatrix} a_g \\ a_h \end{bmatrix} = $ the partitioned (n, m) rectangular matrix for strains of the original structure
$f_z = \begin{bmatrix} f_{zg} \\ f_{zh} \end{bmatrix} = $ the partitioned (n, r) stress matrix for unit redundancies of the original structure	$a_i = \begin{bmatrix} a_{ig} \\ a_{ih} \end{bmatrix} = $ the partitioned (n, i) strain matrix for unit indeterminate displacements of the original structure
$p_m = bF - f_z d_{zz}^{-1} f'_{zh} H = $ the modified stress matrix in the presence of the initial strains H	$v_m = aS - a_i C_{ii}^{-1} a'_{ih} J = $ the modified strain matrix in the presence of the initial stresses J
$p_h = b_h F - f_{zh} d_{zz}^{-1} f'_{zh} H = $ the total stresses in the h elements to be modified	$v_h = a_h S - a_{ij} C_{ii}^{-1} a'_{ih} J = $ the total strains in the h elements to be modified
$v_h = D_h F_h + H$ $= D_h (b_h F - f_{zh} d_{zz}^{-1} d'_{zh} H) + H$ $= $ the total strains calculated for the h elements on the basis of the original structure	$p_h = K_h v_h + J$ $= K_h (a_h S - a_{ih} C_{ii}^{-1} a'_{ih} J) + J$ $= $ the total stresses calculated for the h elements on the basis of the original structure
$v_h = D_{hm} p_h = D_{hm} (b_h F - f_{zh} d_{zz}^{-1} f'_{zh} H)$ $= $ the total strains for the h elements on the basis of the modified structure	$p_h = k_{hm} v_h = k_{hm} (a_h S - a_{ih} C_{ii}^{-1} a'_{ih} J)$ $= $ the total stresses for the h elements on the basis of the modified structure
$H = P^{-1} b_h F = $ the initial strain matrix obtained by equating the two expressions in Part II for v_h	$J = Q^{-1} a_h S = $ the initial stress matrix obtained by equating the two expressions for F_h in Part II
$P = [f_{zh} d_{zz}^{-1} f'_{zh} + (\Delta D_h)^{-1}]$	$Q = [a_{ih} C_{ii}^{-1} a'_{ih} + (\Delta K_h)^{-1}]$
$p_m = b_m \phi$ the stress matrix of the modified structure	$v_m = a_m S = $ the strain matrix of the modified structure
$b_m = b - f_z d_{zz}^{-1} f'_{zh} P^{-1} b_h$ $= $ the modified (n, m) matrix for stresses of the altered structure	$a_m = a - a_i C_{ii}^{-1} a'_{ih} Q^{-1} a_h$ $= $ the modified (n, m) matrix for strains of the altered structure
$S_m = \phi_m F = $ the modified displacement matrix	$F_m = k_m S = $ the modified force matrix
$\phi_m = \phi_0 + b'_h P^{-1} b_h = $ the (m, m) flexibility matrix of the modified structure	$k_m = k_0 + a'_h Q^{-1} a_h = $ the (m, m) stiffness matrix of the modified structure

Elimination of h Elements
$$\Delta D_h \to \infty, \quad (\Delta D_h)^{-1} = 0$$
$$P = f_{zh} d_{zz}^{-1} f'_{zh}$$

Making h Elements Rigid
$$\Delta K_h \to \infty, \quad (\Delta K_h)^{-1} = 0$$
$$Q = a_{ih} C_{ii}^{-1} a'_{ih}$$

Making h Elements Rigid
$$D_{hm} = 0, \quad \Delta D_h = -D_h$$
$$P = [f_{zh} d_{zz}^{-1} f'_{zh} - D_h^{-1}]$$

Elimination of h Elements
$$K_{hm} = 0, \quad \Delta K_h = -K_h$$
$$Q = [a_{ih} C_{ii}^{-1} a'_{ih} - k_h]$$

REFERENCES

1. Argyris, J. H., "Energy Theorems and Structural Analysis," *Aircraft Engineering*, Vol. XXVI (Oct., Nov., 1954), Vol. XXVII (Feb., Mar., Apr., May, 1955), pp. 89–94.

2. Argyris, J. H., "On the Analysis of Complex Elastic Structures," *Applied Mechanics Reviews*, Vol. 11, No. 7 (July, 1958), pp. 331–338.

3. Cicala, P., "Effects of Cut-Outs in Semi-Monocoque Structures," *J. Ae. Sci.*, Vol. 15, No. 3 (March, 1948), pp. 171–179.

4. Denke, P. H., "A Matric Method of Structural Analysis," *Proc. Second U.S. National Congress of Applied Mechanics* (1955).

5. Denke, P. H., and I. V. Boldt, "A General Digital Computer Program for Static Stress Analysis," *Proc. Western Joint Computer Conference* (1955), pp. 72–78.

6. Denke, P. H. and C. K. Wang, "Matric Analysis of Statically Indeterminate Structures by the Displacement Method," Report of the Douglas Aircraft Co., Inc. (Oct., 1957).

7. Falkenheimer, H., "Systematic Analysis of Redundant Elastic Structures by Means of Matrix Calculus," *Jour. Ae. Sci.*, Vol. 20 (Apr., 1953), p. 293.

8. Frazer, R. A., W. J. Duncan, and A. R. Collar, *Elementary Matrices*. London: Cambridge University Press, 1938, p. 43.

9. Goodey, W. J., "Notes on a General Method of Treatment of Structural Discontinuities," *Journ. Roy. Ae. Sci.*, Vol. 59, No. 538 (Oct., 1955), p. 695.

10. Hunt, P. M., "The Electronic Digital Computer in Aircraft Structural Analysis," *Aircraft Engineering*, Vol. XXVIII (Feb., Mar., Apr., May, 1956).

11. Lang, A. L. and R. L. Bisplinghoff, "Some Results of Swept-Back Wing Structural Studies," *Jour. Ae. Sci.*, Vol. 18, No. 11 (Nov., 1951), pp. 705–717.

12. Langefors, B., "Analysis of Elastic Structures by Matrix Transformation with Special Regard to Semimonocoque Structures," *Jour. Ae. Sci.*, Vol. 19, No. 7 (July, 1952), pp. 451–458.

13. Langefors, B., "Matrix Methods for Redundant Structures," *Jour. Ae. Sci.*, Vol. 20 (Apr., 1953), p. 292.

14. Levy, S., "Computation of Influence Coefficients for Aircraft Structures with Discontinuities and Sweepback," *Jour. Ae. Sci.*, Vol. 14, No. 10 (Oct., 1947), pp. 547–560.

15. Levy, S., "Structural Analysis and Influence Coefficients for Delta Wings," *Jour. Ae. Sci.*, Vol. 20, No. 7 (July, 1953), pp. 449–454.

16. Sokolnikoff, I. S., *Mathematical Theory of Elasticity*, 2nd ed. New York: McGraw-Hill Book Co., Inc., 1956, pp. 382–386.

17. Turner, M. J., R. W. Clough, H. C. Martin, and L. J. Topp, "Stiffness and Deflection Analysis of Complex Structures." Paper presented at the Jan., 1954, Annual Meeting of the Institute of Aeronautical Sciences, New York.

18. Wehle, L. B. and W. Lansing, "A Method for Reducing the Analysis of Complex Redundant Structures to a Routine Procedure," *Jour. Ae. Sci.*, Vol. 19, No. 10 (Oct., 1952), pp. 677–684.

19. Williams, D., "Development in the Structural Approach to Aero-Elastic Problems," *Aircraft Engineering*, Vol. 26, No. 307 (Sept., 1954), pp. 303–307.

20. Williams, D., "A General Method for Deriving the Structural Influence Coefficients of Aeroplane Wings," Farnborough Report No. Structures 168 (Nov., 1954).

21. Williams, D., "Notes on the Practical Applications of the Method of R.A.E. Report No. Structures 168," R.A.E. Report No. Structures 209 (May, 1956).

22. Williams, D., "Relative Accuracy of Deflections and Bending Moments Derived by the Method of R.A.E. Report No. Structures 168," R.A.E. Technical Note No. Structures 188 (Mar., 1956).

23. Williams, D., "Solution of Aeroelastic Problems by Means of Influence Coefficients," *Jour. Roy. Aero. Soc.*, (Apr., 1957), pp. 247–251.

7 APPLICATIONS OF MATRICES TO CLASSICAL MECHANICS

1. INTRODUCTION

The theory of kinematics and dynamics of three-dimensional mechanical systems may be expressed in a very clear and compact manner by the use of matrix notation. Such topics as the rotation of coordinate systems, relative velocities and accelerations, and the dynamics of rigid bodies are somewhat simplified when discussed in the language of matrix algebra. This chapter is intended as an introduction to the use of matrices in problems in classical mechanics, and it is hoped that the simplicity of the matrix notation will stimulate the student to pursue the subject further.

2. THE MATRIX REPRESENTATION OF A VECTOR PRODUCT

Before we discuss the kinematics and dynamics of mechanical systems, it is necessary to discuss the manner by which the ordinary vector product of two vectors is represented in matrix algebra. Let two column matrices or vectors (u) and (v) be given. Let the elements of (u) be (u_1, u_2, u_3) and the elements of (v) be (v_1, v_2, v_3).

We have already defined the *scalar product* of ordinary vector theory by the equation

$$(2.1) \qquad (u) \cdot (v) = (v) \cdot (u) = (u)'(v) = (v)'(u) = u_1 v_1 + u_2 v_2 + u_3 v_3$$

We note here that $(v)'(u)$ is the transpose of $(u)'(v)$, and since these products give a scalar or a $(1, 1)$ matrix, it is clear that the transpose equals itself.

Although the notation $(u) \times (v)$ is not usually used in matrix theory it is sometimes useful to do so in certain applications. In ordinary vector analysis the *vector product* of the vectors (u) and (v) is designated by the notation

$$(2.2) \qquad\qquad (w) = (u) \times (v)$$

In this notation (w) is said to be the vector, or cross product, of the vectors (u) and (v).

By the definition of the vector product $(u) \times (v) = (w)$, (w) is a vector with three components given by the column

$$(2.3) \qquad (w) = (u) \times (v) = \begin{bmatrix} (u_2 v_3 - u_3 v_2) \\ (u_3 v_1 - u_1 v_3) \\ (u_1 v_2 - u_2 v_1) \end{bmatrix}$$

It can be seen that the column (w) may be obtained by writing the following product:

$$(2.4) \qquad (w) = \begin{bmatrix} 0 & -u_3 & u_2 \\ u_3 & 0 & -u_1 \\ -u_2 & u_1 & 0 \end{bmatrix} \begin{bmatrix} v_1 \\ v_2 \\ v_3 \end{bmatrix}$$

For convenience, let the square matrix in (2.4) be designated by $[U]$ so that

$$(2.5) \qquad [U] = \begin{bmatrix} 0 & -u_3 & u_2 \\ u_3 & 0 & -u_1 \\ -u_2 & u_1 & 0 \end{bmatrix}$$

With this notation, we may write the vector product (2.3) in the compact form,

$$(2.6) \qquad (w) = [U](v)$$

In a similar manner, let us define the square matrix $[V]$ by the equation

$$(2.7) \qquad [V] = \begin{bmatrix} 0 & -v_3 & v_2 \\ v_3 & 0 & -v_1 \\ -v_2 & v_1 & 0 \end{bmatrix}$$

By means of the square matrix $[V]$ we may now write the vector product $(v) \times (u)$ in the form

$$(2.8) \qquad (v) \times (u) = [V](u) = -[U](v) = -(w)$$

The matrices $[U]$ and $[V]$ are two skew-symmetric matrices. We shall say that $[U]$ is the skew-symmetric matrix associated with the vector (u) and $[V]$ is the skew-symmetric matrix associated with the vector (v). It should be noticed that this definition only holds for matrices of order $(3, 3)$.

With this notation, the triple scalar product may be written in the following form:

$$(2.9) \qquad (u) \times (v) \cdot (w) = (w)'[U](v) = (v)'[U]'(w)$$

It can be shown that the *triple vector product* may be written in the form

$$(2.10) \qquad (w) \times (v) \times (u) = [W][V](u) = (v)(w)'(u) - (w)'(v)(u)$$

3. ROTATION OF RECTANGULAR AXES

In discussing the kinematics of motion, it is frequently necessary to introduce coordinate systems that are rotated with respect to fixed coordinate systems. The analysis of the rotation of axes lends itself to a concise matrix formulation.

Let us designate a fixed Cartesian coordinate system by $O-x_1$, $O-x_2$, and $O-x_3$, as shown in Fig. 7.1. Let $O-y_1$, $O-y_2$, $O-y_3$ be a second right-handed coordinate system possessing the same origin as the first system, but rotated with respect to the first system. Let us introduce the notation

(3.1) $S_{ij} = $ the cosine of the angle between $O-x_i$ and $O-y_j$

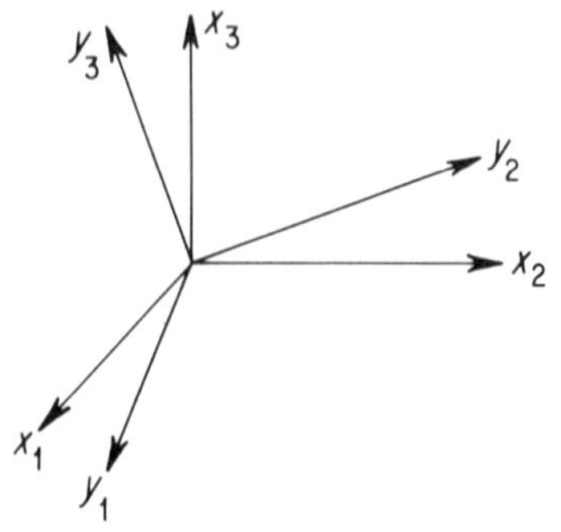

Then the relationships between the coordinates are

(3.2) $\begin{aligned} x_1 &= S_{11}y_1 + S_{12}y_2 + S_{13}y_3 \\ x_2 &= S_{21}y_1 + S_{22}y_2 + S_{23}y_3 \\ x_3 &= S_{31}y_1 + S_{32}y_2 + S_{33}y_3 \end{aligned}$

FIGURE 7.1

If we designate the coordinates by the columns (x) and (y) and the square matrix of direction cosines by $[S]$, we may write (3.2) in the compact form

(3.3) $$(x) = [S](y)$$

It is evident that $[S]$ is an orthogonal matrix, for

(3.4) $$S_{1j}^2 + S_{2j}^2 + S_{3j}^2 = 1, \qquad (j = 1, 2, 3)$$

and

(3.5) $$S_{1i}S_{1j} + S_{2i}S_{2j} + S_{3i}S_{3j} = 0, \qquad (i \neq j)$$

These equations follow, since (3.4) represents the cosines of the angles between the y_j and y_j axes and (3.5) represents the cosines of the angles between y_i and y_j axes, respectively. It follows from (3.4) and (3.5) that

(3.6) $$[S]^{-1} = [S]'$$

and hence $[S]$ is an orthogonal matrix.

It can be shown that because (x) and (y) are two right-handed system of axes, we have

(3.7) $$\det [S] = 1$$

The (y) coordinates may be expressed in terms of the (x) coordinates by the equation

(3.8) $$(y) = [S]^{-1}(x) = [S]'(x)$$

Distances are preserved under a general orthogonal transformation. The distance from the origin to the point (x) is given by

$$(3.9) \qquad r^2 = (x)'(x) = (y)'[S]'[S](y) = (y)'(y)$$

The square of the distance between the two points $(x)_1$ and $(x)_2$, R^2, is given by

$$(3.10) \quad R^2 = [(x)'_2 - (x)'_1][(x)_2 - (x)_1)] = [(y)'_2 - (y)'_1]S'S[(y)_2 - (y)_1]$$
$$= [(y)'_2 - (y)'_1][(y)_2 - (y)_1]$$

If a_x is the representation of a unit vector in the (x) system, its representation in the (y) system is given by

$$(3.11) \qquad (a)_y = [S]'(a)_x$$

If a_x and b_x are two unit vectors in the (x) system, and if a_y and b_y are their corresponding representation in the (y) system, then, if θ is the angle between the vectors a_x and b_x, we have

$$(3.12) \qquad \cos(\theta) = (a)'_x(b)_x = (a)'_y[S]'[S](b)_y = (a)'_y(b)_y$$

Therefore, the angle between the directions $(a)_x$ and $(b)_x$ is *invariant* under the orthogonal transformation.

4. KINEMATICS AND ANGULAR VELOCITY

The position vector of a particle at a point P whose coordinates with respect to a fixed Cartesian reference system are (x_1, x_2, x_3) is the column vector

$$(4.1) \qquad (x) = \begin{bmatrix} x_1 \\ x_2 \\ x_3 \end{bmatrix}$$

The velocity vector (v) and the acceleration vector (a) are given by the rates of change of the elements of the vector (x) in the form

$$(4.2) \qquad (v) = (\dot{x})$$

and

$$(4.3) \qquad (a) = (\dot{v}) = (\ddot{x})$$

The concept of angular velocity will now be introduced. It is assumed that the reader is already acquainted with the physical concept of angular velocity, and perhaps with its representation in ordinary vector theory.

Let us suppose that in addition to the fixed system of axes (x) we are also given a second set of rectangular axes (y) related to the fixed system at any given time by the orthogonal transformation (see Fig. 7.1)

$$(4.4) \qquad (x) = [S](y)$$

Now let it be assumed that the point P is a fixed point relative to the (y) system of axes and that the (y) axes are rotating with respect to the fixed axes (x) so that the elements of the orthogonal transformation matrix $[S]$ are functions of the time t. Then the velocity of the point P relative to the fixed (x) system is given by

(4.5) $$(\dot{x}) = (v) = [\dot{S}](y)$$

since by hypothesis the coordinates (y) of P in the rotating system are constant. Since, as a consequence of (4.4), we have

(4.6) $$(y) = [S]^{-1}(x) = [S]'(x)$$

we can use (4.6) to eliminate (y) from (4.5) and write

(4.7) $$(\dot{x}) = [\dot{S}][S]'(x) = (v)$$

Let

(4.8) $$[W] = [\dot{S}][S]'$$

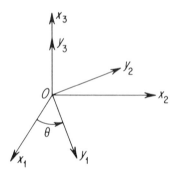

The matrix $[W]$ is a $(3, 3)$ matrix which we shall call the *angular velocity matrix* of the (y) system with respect to the fixed (x) system. The velocity of P with respect to the fixed system given by (4.7) may be expressed in the form

FIG. 7.2. Rotating Coordinate System

(4.9) $$(v) = [W](x)$$

It should be noted that the three elements of (v) refer to the components of the velocity in the direction of the axes of the fixed x system.

The definition of $[W] = [\dot{S}][S]'$ is quite in keeping with the usual concept of angular velocity. As an example of the use of this notation, consider a set of coordinates (y) that rotate about the x_3 axis of a fixed set of coordinates (x_1, x_2, x_3), as shown in Fig. 7.2. The coordinates (x_1, x_2, x_3) are fixed in space, whereas the coordinates (y_1, y_2, y_3) rotate. The y_3 axis coincides with the x_3 axis, and the coordinates y_1 and y_2 rotate about the x_3 axis with angular velocity $\dot{\theta}$.

It is easy to see that the transformation equations between the (x) system and the (y) system are given by

(4.10) $$\begin{bmatrix} x_1 \\ x_2 \\ x_3 \end{bmatrix} = \begin{bmatrix} \cos\theta & -\sin\theta & 0 \\ \sin\theta & \cos\theta & 0 \\ 0 & 0 & 1 \end{bmatrix} \begin{bmatrix} y_1 \\ y_2 \\ y_3 \end{bmatrix} = [S](y)$$

The matrix $[S]$ in this case is the square matrix in Eq. (4.10). The matrix $[\dot{S}]$ in this case is

(4.11) $$[\dot{S}] = \begin{bmatrix} -\sin\theta\,\dot{\theta} & -\cos\theta\,\dot{\theta} & 0 \\ \cos\theta\,\dot{\theta} & -\sin\theta\,\dot{\theta} & 0 \\ 0 & 0 & 0 \end{bmatrix}$$

The matrix $[S]'$ is

$$(4.12) \qquad [S]' = \begin{bmatrix} \cos\theta & \sin\theta & 0 \\ -\sin\theta & \cos\theta & 0 \\ 0 & 0 & 1 \end{bmatrix}$$

The angular velocity matrix $[W]$ may now be obtained by direct matrix multiplication of $[\dot{S}]$ and $[S]'$. We thus obtain

$$(4.13) \qquad [W] = [\dot{S}][S]' = \begin{bmatrix} 0 & -\dot{\theta} & 0 \\ \dot{\theta} & 0 & 0 \\ 0 & 0 & 0 \end{bmatrix}$$

If we let $\dot{\theta} = w_3$ be the angular velocity of the rotating system about the x_3 axis, then the matrix $[W]$ takes the form

$$(4.14) \qquad [W] = [\dot{S}][S]' = \begin{bmatrix} 0 & -w_3 & 0 \\ w_3 & 0 & 0 \\ 0 & 0 & 0 \end{bmatrix}$$

In ordinary vector theory, angular velocity is usually regarded as a vector (w). In this particular case, the vector (w) has components given by

$$(4.15) \qquad (w) = \begin{bmatrix} 0 \\ 0 \\ w_3 \end{bmatrix}$$

It can be seen that in terms of the vector (w), Eq. (4.9) for the velocity (v) may be written in the form

$$(4.16) \qquad (v) = [W](x) = (w) \times (x)$$

It is, therefore, apparent that the multiplication $[W](x)$ is the same as the vector product of (w) and (x).

It can be shown that the angular velocity matrix $[W]$ is always a skew-symmetric matrix. In order to do this, we start with the identity

$$(4.17) \qquad [S][S]' = U, \text{ the unit matrix}$$

If we differentiate (4.17) with respect to the time, we obtain

$$(4.18) \qquad [\dot{S}][S]' + [S][\dot{S}]' = [0]$$

Hence,

$$(4.19) \qquad [\dot{S}][S]' = [W] = -[S][\dot{S}]' = -([\dot{S}][S]')' = -[W]'$$

Since $[W] = -[W]'$, it is a skew-symmetric matrix.

In the general case in which the (y) axes rotate with respect to the (x) axes in a general manner, the angular velocity matrix $[W]$ has the general form

$$(4.20) \qquad [W] = [\dot{S}][S]' = \begin{bmatrix} 0 & -w_3 & w_2 \\ w_3 & 0 & -w_1 \\ -w_2 & w_1 & 0 \end{bmatrix}$$

where w_1, w_2, w_3 are the angular velocities of the (y) axes with respect to the x_1, x_2, and x_3 axes.

The Transformation of the Angular Velocity Matrix

In order to determine how to find the components of the angular velocity in directions other than along the axes of the original (x) system, let us introduce another fixed coordinate system through the origin O of Fig. 7.2. Let this new fixed Cartesian coordinate system be denoted by (z), and let it be related to the original fixed system by the transformation

$$(4.21) \qquad (x) = [M](z)$$

where $[M]$ is a constant orthogonal matrix. If we differentiate (4.21) with respect to the time, we obtain

$$(4.22) \qquad (\dot{x}) = (v) = [M](\dot{z}) = [W](x)$$

If we now substitute (4.21) into (4.22), we obtain

$$(4.23) \qquad [M](\dot{z}) = [W][M](z)$$

This may be written in the form

$$(4.24) \qquad (\dot{z}) = [M]'[W][M](z)$$

We may, therefore, write

$$(4.25) \qquad [W]_z = [M]'[W][M], \quad (\dot{z}) = [W]_z(z)$$

where $[W]_z$ is the angular velocity matrix referred to the (z) system. Equation (4.25) enables us to find the components of the angular velocity in directions other than along the axes of the original (x) system.

Transformation of the Angular Velocity Vector

From the elements w_1, w_2, w_3 we may form the angular velocity vector (w) given by

$$(4.26) \qquad (w) = \begin{vmatrix} w_1 \\ w_2 \\ w_3 \end{vmatrix}$$

If the system of coordinates (x) and (z) are fixed and are related by the orthogonal transformation $(x) = [M](z)$, then the angular velocity vector

(w) in the (x) system is related to the angular velocity vector in the (z) system by the transformation

$$(4.27) \qquad\qquad (w) = [M](w)_z$$

This relation enables us to find the elements of $[W]$ rapidly when we are referred to any desired coordinate system.

5. CHANGE OF REFERENCE AXES IN TWO DIMENSIONS

In order to clarify the principal ideas, let us consider first reference axes in two dimensions. For this purpose, let us consider a fixed Cartesian reference frame (x) and an auxiliary reference frame (y), as shown in Fig. 7.3. The position of the auxiliary frame of reference at any instant t can be specified completely by the Cartesian coordinates (a) of O' referred to the fixed axes, and by the inclination of ϕ of $O'y_1$ to Ox_1, as shown in the figure.

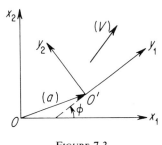

FIGURE 7.3

Let (x) and (y) denote, respectively, the columns of the components of any vector (V) in the plane, measured parallel to the fixed and rotated or auxiliary axes. Let the rotation transformation between the rotated axes (y) and the fixed axes (x) be given by

$$(5.1) \qquad (y) = [S]'(x) = [L](x)$$

where, for convenience, we write

$$(5.2) \qquad\qquad [L] = [S]'$$

The matrix $[L]$ is a second-order square orthogonal matrix given by

$$(5.3) \qquad [L] = \begin{bmatrix} \cos\phi & \sin\phi \\ -\sin\phi & \cos\phi \end{bmatrix} = [S]'$$

The matrix $[L]$ is orthogonal, since

$$(5.4) \qquad [L]^{-1} = \begin{bmatrix} \cos\phi & -\sin\phi \\ \sin\phi & \cos\phi \end{bmatrix} = [L]' = [S]$$

By differentiation, we obtain

$$(5.5) \quad [L][\dot{L}]' = -[\dot{L}][L]' = \dot{\phi} \begin{bmatrix} \cos\phi & \sin\phi \\ -\sin\phi & \cos\phi \end{bmatrix} \begin{bmatrix} -\sin\phi & -\cos\phi \\ \cos\phi & -\sin\phi \end{bmatrix}$$

$$= \begin{bmatrix} 0 & -w \\ w & 0 \end{bmatrix} = [W]$$

where $w = \dot{\phi}$ is the angular velocity of the moving frame (y). $[W]$ is the angular velocity matrix of the moving frame. If we now differentiate (5.1), we obtain

(5.6) $$(\dot{y}) = [L](\dot{x}) + [\dot{L}](x)$$

If we solve (5.5) for $[\dot{L}]$, we obtain

(5.7) $$[\dot{L}] = -[W][L]$$

Hence, if this value of $[\dot{L}]$ is substituted into (5.6), we have

(5.8) $$(\dot{y}) = [L](\dot{x}) - [W][L](x)$$

Since $[L](x) = (y)$, we may eliminate (x) from (5.8) and write

(5.9) $$[L](\dot{x}) = (\dot{y}) + [W](y) = (UD + [W])(y)$$

where U is the second-order unit matrix, and D is the derivative operator with respect to the time.

Now, as a consequence of Eq. (5.1), $[L](\dot{x})$ represents the components of the time-rate of change of the vector (V), measured in the direction of the *moving* axes (y) at time t. We see from this fact that the components of the time-rate of change of any vector measured in the directions of the moving axes are obtained from the components (y) of the vector itself in the same directions by the application of the operator $(UD + [W])$ on (y).

For example, if (V) represents the absolute position of a general point P of the plane whose coordinates are (x), then we have

(5.10) $$(x) = (a) + (x)_r$$

where $(x)_r$ are the absolute coordinates of P relative to the point O'. We thus have

(5.11) $$(x)_r = (x) - (a)$$

The (y) coordinates of the point P are given by the transformation

(5.12) $$(y) = [L](x)_r = [L](x - a)$$

We have, therefore,

(5.13) $$[L](x) = [L](a) + (y)$$

Hence, the components of the velocity of P measured parallel to the (y) axes, (v), are given by

(5.14) $$(v) = (UD + [W])([L]a + y)$$

If the components of the velocity of O' measured along the (y) axes are denoted by (u), then we see from (5.14) that (u) is given by

(5.15) $$(u) = (UD + [W])[L](a)$$

In terms of the velocity (u) we may write (5.14) in the form

(5.16) $$(v) = (u) + (UD + [W])(y)$$

It can be seen by similar reasoning that the components of the *acceleration* of P measured parallel to the moving axes (y), $(\dot{v})$, is given by

(5.17) $(\dot{v}) = (UD + [W])(v)$

These formulas for the velocity and acceleration will be generalized to three dimensions in a later section.

6. SUCCESSIVE ROTATIONS

Let it be supposed that the angle ϕ of Fig. 7.3 is increased to $\phi + \phi_1$. Then the transformation matrix (5.3) becomes the matrix $[L]_1$ given by

(6.1) $[L]_1 = \begin{bmatrix} \cos(\phi + \phi_1) & \sin(\phi + \phi_1) \\ -\sin(\phi + \phi_1) & \cos(\phi + \phi_1) \end{bmatrix}$

$= \begin{bmatrix} \cos\phi_1 & \sin\phi_1 \\ -\sin\phi_1 & \cos\phi_1 \end{bmatrix}[L]$

If we let

(6.2) $R(\phi_1) = \begin{bmatrix} \cos\phi_1 & \sin\phi_1 \\ -\sin\phi_1 & \cos\phi_1 \end{bmatrix}$

we see that premultiplication of the matrix $[L]$ by the matrix $R(\phi_1)$ is equivalent to a rotation of the coordinate system (y) through an angle ϕ_1 about the axis O'. From Eq. (6.2) it can be seen that any succession of such rotations through angles $\phi_1, \phi_2, \ldots, \phi_n$ will be represented by the transformation matrix $[L]_n$, where $[L]_n$ is given the equation

(6.3) $[L]_n = R(\phi_n)R(\phi_{n-1})\ldots R(\phi_1)[L] = R(\phi_n + \phi_{n-1} + \cdots + \phi_1)[L]$

If the angles $\phi_i = 2s\pi/n$, where s is any integer, then after the complete cycle of rotations, the frame of reference (y) is returned to its original position. In this case we have

(6.4) $[L]_n = \left[R\left(\frac{2s\pi}{n}\right)\right]^n = U$

where U is the second-order unit matrix. We see, therefore, that the matrices $R(2s\pi/n)$ are all nth roots of $[L]_n$.

7. ANGULAR COORDINATES OF A THREE-DIMENSIONAL REFERENCE FRAME

In order to specify the orientation of a frame of reference (y) in space, three independent parameters are required. These parameters may be chosen in various manners. In this discussion we shall introduce angles which are usually used in the investigation of the motion of aeroplanes rather than the system of angular coordinates which were originally introduced by Euler.

Let (x) represent the coordinates x_1, x_2, x_3 of a Cartesian reference system *fixed* in space and (y) another Cartesian coordinate system y_1, y_2, y_3 rotated with respect to the first system.   Since we are at the moment concerned with the question of the relative orientation of these two frames, we will suppose that the origin O of the (x) system and the origin O' of the (y) system coincide. We shall later assume that the origin O' can move relative to the origin O. The relative orientations of the fixed system (x) and the rotated system (y) is shown in Fig. 7.4.

The rotated coordinates (y) are related to the fixed coordinates (x) by an orthogonal transformation of the form

$$(7.1) \qquad\qquad (y) = [L](x)$$

The matrix $[L]$ is an orthogonal matrix.   In order to obtain the elements of $[L]$, we can suppose that originally the axes (y) coincide with the axes (x) and that by applying three rotations to the axes (y) relative to the axes (x) we arrive at the final orientation of the axes (y).

Consider the transformation

$$(7.2) \qquad (y) = \begin{bmatrix} \cos\phi_3 & \sin\phi_3 & 0 \\ -\sin\phi_3 & \cos\phi_3 & 0 \\ 0 & 0 & 1 \end{bmatrix}(x) = R_3(\phi_3)(x)$$

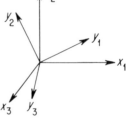

FIGURE 7.4

This is an orthogonal transformation that rotates the coordinate system (y) through an angle ϕ_3 about the x_3 axis.   The transformation

$$(7.3) \qquad (y) = \begin{bmatrix} \cos\phi_2 & 0 & -\sin\phi_2 \\ 0 & 1 & 0 \\ \sin\phi_2 & 0 & \cos\phi_2 \end{bmatrix}(x) = R_2(\phi_2)(x)$$

is an orthogonal transformation that rotates the coordinate system (y) through an angle ϕ_2 about the axis x_2.   Finally, the transformation

$$(7.4) \qquad (y) = \begin{bmatrix} 1 & 0 & 0 \\ 0 & \cos\phi_1 & \sin\phi_1 \\ 0 & -\sin\phi_1 & \cos\phi_1 \end{bmatrix}(x) = R_1(\phi_1)(x)$$

is an orthogonal transformation that rotates (y) through an angle ϕ_1 about the axis x_1.

In order to obtain the desired final orientation of the axes (y) relative to the axes (x), we shall assume that originally the axes (y) and the axes (x) coincided and then we applied the sequence of rotations $R_3(\phi_3)$, $R_2(\phi_2)$, and $R_1(\phi_1)$ in succession.   In this manner we obtain the final transformation matrix $[L]$ given by

$$(7.5) \qquad\qquad [L] = R_1(\phi_1)R_2(\phi_2)R_3(\phi_3)$$

In terms of this matrix, the final relation between the fixed axes (x) and the rotated axes (y) is

$$(7.6) \qquad (y) = [L](x)$$

In the aeronautical literature the following notation is used for the angular displacements ϕ_3, ϕ_2, and ϕ_1:

$$(7.7) \qquad \begin{aligned} \phi_3 &= \text{rotation in yaw} \\ \phi_2 &= \text{rotation in pitch} \\ \phi_1 &= \text{rotation in roll} \end{aligned}$$

8. THE TRANSFORMATION MATRIX [L] AND INSTANTANEOUS ANGULAR VELOCITIES EXPRESSED IN ANGULAR COORDINATES

If we introduce the notation

$$(8.1) \qquad C_i = \cos(\phi_i), \quad S_i = \sin(\phi_i), \quad i = 1, 2, 3$$

to express the cosine and sine of the angles ϕ_1 defined by (7.7), (7.2), (7.3), and (7.4), then if the indicated matrix multiplication (7.5) is performed, the transformation matrix $[L]$ is found to be

$$(8.1a) \qquad [L] = \begin{bmatrix} (C_2 C_3) & (C_2 S_3) & (-S_2) \\ (S_1 S_2 C_3 - C_1 S_3) & (C_1 C_3 + S_1 S_2 S_3) & (S_1 C_2) \\ (S_1 S_3 + C_1 S_2 C_3) & (C_1 S_2 S_3 - S_1 C_3) & (C_1 C_2) \end{bmatrix}$$

The angular velocity matrix $[W]$ is now given by

$$(8.2) \qquad \begin{aligned} [W] &= [L][\dot{L}]' \\ &= \begin{bmatrix} 0 & (S_1\dot\phi_2 - C_2 C_1 \dot\phi_3) & (C_2 S_1 \dot\phi_3 + C_1 \dot\phi_2) \\ (C_2 C_1 \dot\phi_3 - S_1 \dot\phi_2) & 0 & (S_2 \dot\phi_3 - \dot\phi_1) \\ (-C_2 S_1 \dot\phi_3 - C_1 \dot\phi_2) & (\dot\phi_1 - S_2 \dot\phi_3) & 0 \end{bmatrix} \\ &= \begin{bmatrix} 0 & -w_3 & w_2 \\ w_3 & 0 & -w_1 \\ -w_2 & w_1 & 0 \end{bmatrix} \end{aligned}$$

where w_1, w_2, w_3 are the angular velocities of the moving reference frame (y) about the axes y_1, y_2, and y_3.

From Eq. (8.2) it is evident that

$$(8.3) \qquad \begin{aligned} w_1 &= \dot\phi_1 = \dot\phi_3 \sin\phi_2 \\ w_2 &= \dot\phi_2 \cos\phi_1 + \dot\phi_3 \sin\phi_1 \cos\phi_2 \\ w_3 &= -\dot\phi_2 \sin\phi_1 + \dot\phi_3 \cos\phi_1 \cos\phi_2 \end{aligned}$$

It is convenient to write (w) for a vector whose elements are w_1, w_2, w_3 and to represent by $(\dot{\phi})$ a vector whose elements are $\dot{\phi}_1$, $\dot{\phi}_2$, $\dot{\phi}_3$; with this notation, Eqs. (8.3) may be written in the compact matrix form

(8.4) $$(w) = [K](\dot{\phi})$$

where $[K]$ is the square matrix

(8.5) $$[K] = \begin{bmatrix} 1 & 0 & -\sin\phi_2 \\ 0 & \cos\phi_1 & \sin\phi_1\cos\phi_2 \\ 0 & -\sin\phi_1 & \cos\phi_1\cos\phi_2 \end{bmatrix}$$

The matrix $[K]$ has the inverse

(8.6) $$[K]^{-1} = \sec\phi_2 \begin{bmatrix} \cos\phi_2 & \sin\phi_1\sin\phi_2 & \cos\phi_1\sin\phi_2 \\ 0 & \cos\phi_1\cos\phi_2 & -\sin\phi_1\cos\phi_2 \\ 0 & \sin\phi_1 & \cos\phi_1 \end{bmatrix}$$

Corresponding equations may be obtained when other systems of angular coordinates are used.

9. THE COMPONENTS OF VELOCITY AND ACCELERATION

In order to obtain the components of velocity and acceleration measured in the directions of the moving axes (y), consider Fig. 7.5. In this figure, (x)

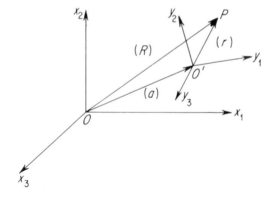

FIGURE 7.5

represents a column matrix whose elements are the *fixed* Cartesian co-ordinates x_1, x_2, x_3. The column matrix (y) has for its elements the *moving* Cartesian coordinates y_1, y_2, y_3. The relative directions of a unit vector $(\hat{y})$ in the moving coordinate frame and a unit vector $(\hat{x})$ in the fixed frame are given by the equation

(9.1) $$(\hat{y}) = [L](\hat{x})$$

where $[L]$ is the rotation matrix given by (7.5).

In the fixed coordinate system (x), the position vector of a point P may be written in the form

$$(9.2) \qquad\qquad (R)_x = (a)_x + (r)_x$$

where $(a)_x$ is the position vector of the origin O' of the moving coordinates (y) relative to the origin of the fixed coordinates O. The position vector $(r)_x$ is the position vector of the point P relative to the origin O' of the moving coordinate system. The subscript x is used to express the fact that these vectors are expressed in the (x) coordinate system in Eq. (9.2). Since the transformation matrix $[L]$ is an orthogonal matrix, we have $[L]^{-1} = [L]'$, and we may express the vector $(r)_x$ measured in the directions of the moving system by $(r)_y$, where, because of the transformation (9.1), we have

$$(9.3) \qquad\qquad (r)_x = [L]'(r)_y$$

If this is substituted from $(r)_x$ in (9.2), we obtain

$$(9.4) \qquad\qquad (R)_x = (a)_x + [L]'(r)_y$$

The absolute velocity of the point P is $(V)_x = (\dot{R})_x$. Therefore, if we differentiate (9.3) with respect to the time t, we obtain the following expression for the absolute velocity of the point P:

$$(9.5) \qquad\qquad (V)_x = (\dot{a})_x + [\dot{L}]'(r)_y + [L]'(\dot{r})_y$$

The absolute velocity of the point P measured in the direction of the moving axes (y) is $(V)_y = [L](V)_x$. Hence, the absolute velocity of P measured in the direction of the moving axes (y) is

$$(9.6) \qquad (V)_y = [L](V)_x = [L](\dot{a})_x + [L][\dot{L}]'(r)_y + [L][L]'(\dot{r})_y$$
$$= [L](\dot{a})_x + [W](r)_y + (\dot{r})_y$$

where $[W] = [L][\dot{L}]'$ is the angular velocity matrix. Now let

$$(9.7) \quad [L](\dot{a})_x = (U)_y = \text{the velocity of the origin } O' \text{ in the direction of the}$$
$$\text{moving axes}$$

With this notation, we may write Eq. (9.6) in the form

$$(9.8) \qquad\qquad (V)_y = (U)_y + ([W] + UD)(r)_y$$

In Eq. (9.8) D is the derivative operator with respect to the time, and U is the unit matrix of the third order.

If P is a point of a rigid body, and the axes (y) are fixed in the body (body axes), then the coordinates of $(r)_y$ do not change as the body moves, and $(\dot{r})_y = (0)$. In this case, the velocity $(V)_y$ reduces to

$$(9.9) \qquad\qquad (V)_y = (U)_y + [W](r)_y$$

The Absolute Acceleration

The absolute acceleration of the point P measured in the direction of the moving axes (y) may be obtained by applying the operator $([W] + UD)$ to the absolute velocity vector $(V)_y$. If we denote the absolute acceleration of P measured in the direction of the moving axes by $(A)_y$, we then have

$$(9.10) \quad (A)_y = ([W] + UD)(V)_y = ([W] + UD)(U)_y + ([W] + UD)^2(r)_y$$

If the point P does not move relative to the coordinates (y) so that $(\dot{r})_y = (0)$, the expression (9.10) for the acceleration reduces to

$$(9.11) \qquad (A)_y = ([W] + UD)(U)_y + ([W]^2 + D[W])(r)_y$$

The angular velocity matrix $[W]$ is given by Eq. (8.2). In terms of the column matrix (w) whose elements are given by (8.3) we may write the expression for the absolute velocity of the point P fixed relative to the (y) coordinate frame, as given by (9.9) in the alternative form

$$(9.12) \qquad (V)_y = (U)_y + (w) \times (r)_y = (U)_y - (r)_y \times (w)$$

where $(w) \times (r)_y$ is the vector product of the angular velocity vector (w) and the position vector of the point P, $(r)_y$, relative to the moving coordinate system (y). If we denote the position vector $(r)_y$ of the point P relative to the moving origin O' of Fig. 7.5 in terms of its components in the (y) reference frame by the equation

$$(9.13) \qquad\qquad (r)_y = \begin{bmatrix} y_1 \\ y_2 \\ y_3 \end{bmatrix}$$

we can construct the following matrix:

$$(9.14) \qquad\qquad [Y] = \begin{bmatrix} 0 & -y_3 & y_2 \\ y_3 & 0 & -y_1 \\ -y_2 & y_1 & 0 \end{bmatrix}$$

In terms of this matrix the vector product $(r)_y \times (w)$ may be expressed in the following form:

$$(9.15) \qquad\qquad (r)_y \times (w) = [Y](w)$$

With this notation, Eq. (9.12) can be written in the form

$$(9.16) \qquad\qquad (V)_y = (U)_y - [Y](w)$$

10. THE KINETIC ENERGY OF A RIGID BODY

We will now assume that the moving coordinates (y) are fixed in the body [(y) are the body axes] and that the origin O' is at the center of mass of the rigid body whose motion we wish to study. The rigid body may be regarded as composed of a collection of particles whose relative distances from each other are constant. If we denote by m the mass of a typical particle, and its position vector with respect to the origin O' of the moving coordinate system attached to the body by

(10.1) $$(r)_y = (y)$$

we can then express the absolute velocity of the particle by (9.16) written in the form

(10.2) $$(v) = (u) - [Y](w)$$

where $(v) = (V)_y$ is the absolute velocity of the particle measured in the direction of the moving axes and (u) is the absolute velocity $(U)_y$ of the origin O' of the moving coordinate system measured in the direction of the moving axes.

The kinetic energy T_p of the typical particle of mass m is given by the equation

(10.3) $$2T_p = m(v)'(v)$$

The kinetic energy T of the entire rigid body may be expressed as the sum of the kinetic energies of all of its particles. This may be expressed in the form

(10.4) $$2T = \sum m(v)'(v)$$

If we take the transpose of Eq. (10.2), we obtain

(10.5) $$(v)' = (u)' - (w)'[Y]' = (u)' + (w)'[Y]$$

since $[Y]$ is a skew-symmetric matrix and, therefore, $[Y]' = -[Y]$. The scalar product $(v)'(v)$ may, therefore, be expressed in the form

(10.6)
$$(v)'(v) = \{(u)' + (w)'[Y]\}\{(u) - [Y](w)\}$$
$$= (u)'(u) - 2(u)'[Y](w) - (w)'[Y]^2(w)$$

If this expression is substituted into (10.4), the result is

(10.7) $$2T = \sum m(u)'(u) - 2(u)' \sum m[Y](w) - \sum (w)'m[Y]^2(w)$$

Since the origin O' of the moving coordinate system is the center of mass of the body, it can be shown that

(10.8) $$\sum m[Y] = [0]$$

We also have

(10.9) $$\sum m(u)'(u) = M(u)'(u)$$

where M is the total mass of the body.

The Inertia Matrix

Let us expand the term $[J] = -\sum m[Y]^2$ in the last member of Eq. (10.7). The expanded form for $[J]$ is

(10.10) $[J] = -\sum m[Y]^2$

$$= \begin{bmatrix} \sum m(y_2^2 + y_3^2) & \sum -my_1y_2 & \sum -my_1y_3 \\ \sum -my_2y_1 & \sum m(y_3^2 + y_1^2) & \sum -my_2y_3 \\ \sum -my_3y_1 & \sum -my_3y_2 & \sum m(y_1^2 + y_2^2) \end{bmatrix}$$

The square matrix $[J]$ is a symmetric matrix. This matrix is called the inertia matrix of the rigid body. The elements of the principal diagonal are the *moments of inertia* of the body about the axes y_1, y_2, and y_3 of the coordinate axes (y) that are moving with the body. The terms not on the principal diagonal are the *products of inertia* of the body.

If we use the relations (10.8), (10.9), and (10.10) to simplify Eq. (10.7), we obtain the final expression for the kinetic energy T of the moving rigid body in the form

(10.11) $$T = \tfrac{1}{2}M(u)'(u) + \tfrac{1}{2}(w)'[J](w)$$

The first term of (10.11) is the kinetic energy of the body due to the velocity (u) of the center of mass of the body O', and the second term involves the kinetic energy of the body which is due to the rotation of the body about the body axes (y).

11. PRINCIPAL AXES AND THE MOMENTS OF INERTIA

The inertia matrix $[J]$ may be written in the alternative form

(11.1) $$[J] = \sum m[(y)'(y)U - (y)(y)']$$

where U is the unit matrix of the third order. The fact that this form for the inertia tensor is equivalent to the form (10.10) may be seen by expanding the expression $[(y)'(y)U - (y)(y)']$. If this is done, one obtains

(11.2) $$[(y)'(y)U - (y)(y)'] = (y_1^2 + y_2^2 + y_3^2)U - \begin{bmatrix} y_1^2 & y_1y_2 & y_2y_3 \\ y_2y_1 & y_2^2 & y_2y_3 \\ y_3y_1 & y_3y_2 & y_3^2 \end{bmatrix}$$

$$= \begin{bmatrix} (y_2^2 + y_3^2) & -y_1y_2 & -y_1y_3 \\ -y_2y_1 & (y_1^2 + y_3^2) & -y_2y_3 \\ -y_3y_1 & -y_3y_2 & (y_1^2 + y_2^2) \end{bmatrix}$$

The square matrix (11.2) is thus seen to be of the same form as that of (10.10), and the expression (11.1) is exactly the same as that given for the inertia matrix $[J]$ in (10.10). Let the square matrix $[G]$ be defined by the equation

(11.3) $$[G] = \sum m(y)(y)'$$

and let us define the matrix $[P]$ by the equation

(11.4) $$[P] = \sum m(y)'(y)U$$

With this notation, we have, as a consequence of (11.1), the relation

(11.5) $$[J] = [P] - [G]$$

We may, therefore, express the matrix $[G]$ in terms of the inertia matrix $[J]$ and the diagonal matrix $[P]$ in the form

(11.6) $$[G] = [P] - [J]$$

It will be noticed that the elements of the matrix $[G]$ not on the principal diagonal are the products of inertia with positive signs. Let it now be required to find another set of axes (z) fixed in the body with origin at O' oriented in such a manner that the products of inertia vanish. To do this, let us introduce the new coordinate axes (z) by means of the transformation

(11.7) $$(y) = [N](z), \quad \text{or} \quad (z) = [N]'(y)$$

where $[N]$ is an orthogonal matrix.

It can be seen that the axes (z) are another set of Cartesian coordinate axes that have the same origin O' as the axes (y) but are rotated with respect to (y) by the orthogonal transformation matrix $[N]$. If we now substitute (y) as given by (11.7) into (11.3), we obtain

(11.8) $$[G] = \sum m[N](z)(z)'[N]' = [N] \sum m(z)(z)'[N]'$$

If we now introduce the notation

(11.9) $$[G]_z = \sum m(z)(z)'$$

where $[G]_z$ is the matrix $[G]$ transformed to the coordinates (z), we may then write (11.8) in the form

(11.10) $$[G] = [N][G]_z[N]'$$

This equation may be solved for $[G]_z$ to obtain

(11.11) $$[G]_z = [N]'[G][N]$$

Now let Eq. (11.5) be premultiplied by $[N]'$ and postmultiplied by $[N]'$ to obtain

(11.12) $$[N]'[J][N] = [N]'[P][N] - [N]'[G][N]$$

If we introduce the notation

(11.13) $$[J]_z = [N]'[J][N]$$

$[J]_z$ is the transformed inertia matrix in the new (z) coordinates. As a consequence of Eq. (11.4) we have

(11.14) $$[N]'[P][N] = [P]$$

since $[N]'(y)'(y)[N] = (y)'(y)[N]'[N] = (y)'(y)U$, where U is the third-order unit matrix. Accordingly, we may write (11.12) in the form

(11.15) $$[J]_z = [P] - [G]_z$$

If for the transformation matrix $[N]$ we choose the matrix

(11.16) $$[N] = [(k)_1 \quad (k)_2 \quad (k)_3]$$

where the column matrices $(k)_1$, $(k)_2$, and $(k)_3$ are the three normalized eigenvectors of the inertia matrix $[J]$, then the transformation $[N]'[J][N]$ diagonalizes the inertia matrix, and we have, by (11.13), the transformed inertia matrix $[J]_z$ in the form

(11.17) $$[J]_z = [N]'[J][N] = \begin{bmatrix} \mu_1 & 0 & 0 \\ 0 & \mu_2 & 0 \\ 0 & 0 & \mu_3 \end{bmatrix} = \begin{bmatrix} I_1 & 0 & 0 \\ 0 & I_2 & 0 \\ 0 & 0 & I_3 \end{bmatrix}$$

where μ_1, μ_2, and μ_3 are the eigenvalues of the inertia matrix $[J]$. In this case the eigenvalues are the solutions of the characteristic equation of the matrix $[J]$ or solutions of the equation

(11.18) $$\det (\mu U - [J]) = 0$$

Since the diagonal matrix $[P]$ is invariant to the transformation (11.7) because

$$(y)'(y) = (z)'[N]'[N](z) = (z)'(z)$$

we may write (11.15) in the form

(11.19) $$[J]_z = [P]_z - [G]_z = \begin{bmatrix} \sum m(z_2^2 + z_3^2) & 0 & 0 \\ 0 & \sum m(z_3^2 + z_1^2) & 0 \\ 0 & 0 & \sum m(z_1^2 + z_2^2) \end{bmatrix}$$

The quantities

(11.20) $$\begin{aligned} \mu_1 &= I_1 = \sum m(z_2^2 + z_3^2) \\ \mu_2 &= I_2 = \sum m(z_3^2 + z_1^2) \\ \mu_3 &= I_3 = \sum m(z_1^2 + z_2^2) \end{aligned}$$

are called the *principal moments of inertia* and the axes z_1, z_2, z_3 are the *principal axes of inertia*.

12. TRANSFORMATION OF FORCES AND COUPLES

It is an experimental fact that forces are vectors and are, therefore, transformed from one Cartesian coordinate system of axes to another in the same manner as the coordinates themselves. This is the usual idea used in resolving forces. Let $(F)_x$ be a column matrix whose elements are the three components of force measured in the (x) system of coordinates, and let $(F)_y$ be a column matrix whose elements are the components of the force vector

$(F)_x$ measured in the rotated (y) system. Then, if the coordinates (x) and (y) are related by the transformation matrix equation,

$$(12.1) \qquad (x) = [S](y) = [L]'(y), \quad [S] = [L]'$$

then the vectors $(F)_x$ and $(F)_y$ are related by the equation

$$(12.2) \qquad (F)_x = [S](F)_y$$

where $[S]$ is the orthogonal matrix of transformation.

The differentials of the coordinates satisfy the same transformation equation as the coordinates themselves, so

$$(12.3) \qquad d(x) = [S]d(y)$$

where the matrix $[S]$ is a constant. The element of work dW done by a force $(F)_x$ in a small displacement is the scalar product of the vectors $(F)_x$ and $d(x)$. These elements are expressed in matrix notation by the equation

$$(12.4) \qquad dW = (F)'_x \, d(x)$$

In the (y) system of coordinates, this equation is

$$(12.5) \qquad dW = (F)'_y[S]'[S] \, d(y) = (F)'_x \, d(y)$$

It is thus seen that dW is an invariant to the rotation transformation, (12.1).

Transformation of Moments or Couples

Consider a force $(F)_x$ expressed in terms of components along the fixed coordinate system (x). If $(r)_x$ is a vector from the origin of the fixed coordinate system to the line of action of the force, then the moment or couple of the force $(F)_x$ about the origin O is expressed by the vector $(g)_x$. This vector is given by the following vector product:

$$(12.6) \qquad (g)_x = (r)_x \times (F)_x$$

The vector product of (12.6) may be expressed in matrix notation by the method discussed in Sec. 2 of this chapter. If the vector $(r)_x$ has the form

$$(12.7) \qquad (r)_x = \begin{bmatrix} x_1 \\ x_2 \\ x_3 \end{bmatrix}$$

we construct the square matrix $[X]$ given by

$$(12.8) \qquad [X] = \begin{bmatrix} 0 & -x_3 & x_2 \\ x_3 & 0 & -x_1 \\ -x_2 & x_1 & 0 \end{bmatrix}$$

In terms of this matrix, the vector product in (12.6) may be expressed in matrix form, and we have

(12.9) $$(g)_x = [X](F)_x$$

If we now transform to the rotated system of axes (y), the force $(F)_x$ transforms to the (y) system by the relation $(F)_x = [S](F)_y$. It can be shown that the square matrix $[X]$ transforms into a corresponding matrix $[Y]$ in the (y) system by the equation

(12.10) $$[X] = [S][Y][S]'$$

If this is substituted into (12.9), we obtain

(12.11) $$(g)_x = [S][Y][S]'[S](F)_y = [S][Y](F)_y$$

However, in the (y) system of coordinates, the moment is represented by $(g)_y$, where

(12.12) $$(g)_y = [Y](F)_y$$

Therefore, we may write (12.11) in the form

(12.13) $$(g)_x = [S](g)_y$$

We see, therefore, that the couple $(g)_x$ transforms to the rotated system according to the same law of transformation as the coordinates themselves.

13. THE EQUATIONS OF MOTION OF A RIGID BODY

Let P be an arbitrary particle of a rigid body. Let the mass of the particle be m, and let its position vector with respect to a fixed system of Cartesian coordinates be (x). If we let (p) be the vector whose elements are the components of the total *external* forces acting on P, and $(p)_i$ be the vector representing the total internal force acting on P, then the equation of motion of the particle is

(13.1) $$(p) + (p)_i = m(\ddot{x})$$

If we sum this equation for all the particles that compose the body, the summation $\sum (p)_i$ vanishes, since the internal forces must occur in equal and opposite pairs. We therefore obtain the equation

(13.2) $$\sum (p) = \sum m(\ddot{x})$$

Let $\sum (p)$ be denoted by (P). Hence, (P) is a vector that represents the *total external force* applied to the body.

The Center of Mass

Let the position vector of the *center of mass* of the rigid body be denoted by the matrix $(x)_c$. By definition, this position vector is given by

(13.3) $$(x)_c = \sum \frac{m(x)}{M}$$

where M is the total mass of the body. If we differentiate this equation twice with respect to the time, we obtain

(13.4) $M(\ddot{x})_c = \sum m(\ddot{x})$

However, we see from (13.2) that this must equal the total external force exerted on the rigid body, and, therefore, we have

(13.5) $(P) = M(\ddot{x})_c$

This equation shows that the body moves as a whole, as if all the mass were concentrated at the center of mass and all the forces acted there.

The rotational motion of the rigid body requires a more elaborate analysis. Let us begin this analysis by considering again the Eq. (13.1) for the motion of an individual particle P of the body. We will now take moments about a point $(x)_0$ that is *fixed* in the body, but which may be moving in space, as shown in Fig. 7.6. The position vector of an arbitrary point P in the body (x) may be expressed in the form

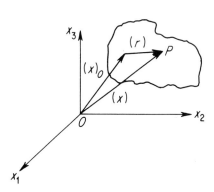

(13.6) $(x) = (x)_0 + (r)$

We will now take the moments of the forces $(p) + (p)_i$ about the point $(x)_0$. This is done by taking the vector product of (r) and the forces $(p) + (p)_i$. In order to express this vector product in matrix notation, let

Fig. 7.6. Motion of a Rigid Body   (13.7) $(r) = (x) - (x)_0 = \begin{bmatrix} r_1 \\ r_2 \\ r_3 \end{bmatrix}$

and construct the square matrix $[R]$ by the equation

(13.8) $[R] = \begin{bmatrix} 0 & -r_3 & r_2 \\ r_3 & 0 & -r_1 \\ -r_2 & r_1 & 0 \end{bmatrix}$

The vector product of (r) and $(p) + (p)_i$ may now be expressed in the matrix form $[R](p + p_i)$. If we substitute (13.6) into (13.1), we obtain

(13.9) $(p) + (p)_i = m(\ddot{x})_0 + m(\ddot{r})$

The vector product of (r) and the forces $(p) + (p)_i$ is now obtained by premultiplication of (13.9) by $[R]$ to obtain

(13.10) $[R](p) + [R](p)_i = m[R](\ddot{x})_0 + m[R](\ddot{r})$

To simplify this expression, let us use the identity

(13.11) $\dfrac{d}{dt}[R](\dot{r}) = [R](\ddot{r}) + [\dot{R}](\dot{r}) = [R](\ddot{r})$

since it can be shown by direct multiplication that $[\dot{R}](\dot{r}) = (0)$. If $[W]$ is the angular velocity matrix of the rigid body, we have

$$(13.12) \qquad\qquad (\dot{r}) = [W](r)$$

As a consequence of (13.11), we see that

$$(13.13) \qquad\qquad [R](\ddot{r}) = \frac{d}{dt}[R][W](r)$$

Hence, Eq. (13.10) may be written in the form

$$(13.14) \qquad [R](p) + [R](p)_i = m[R](\ddot{x})_0 + \frac{dm}{dt}[R][W](r)$$

We now sum these equations for all the particles of the body. The sum $\sum [R](p)_i$ vanishes, since all the forces occur in equal and opposite pairs. Let

$$(13.15) \qquad\qquad (G) = \sum [R](p)$$

where (G) is the *total moment* of the external forces about the point $(x)_0$. With this notation, Eq. (13.14) may be written in the form

$$(13.16) \qquad (G) = \sum m[R](\ddot{x})_0 + \frac{d}{dt}[\sum m[R][W](r)]$$

This equation may be simplified by taking the location of $(x)_0$ at either of the following two special positions:

(a) The point $(x)_0$ is the fixed origin O. In this case, $(x)_0$ is a point fixed in the body and in space so that the body rotates about a fixed point.

(b) The point $(x)_0$ is chosen to be $(x)_c$, the center of mass of the body which is, in general, a moving point. In this case, the summations $m(r)$ and $m(R)$ both vanish, since all the elements of these matrices vanish.

We see, therefore, that if $(x)_0$ is chosen in *either* of the two special positions (a) or (b), Eq. (13.16) reduces to

$$(13.17) \qquad\qquad (G) = \frac{d}{dt}[\sum m[R][W](r)]$$

If we now let the vector (H) be the *angular momentum* of the body about the point $(x)_0$ given by

$$(13.18) \qquad\qquad (H) = \sum m[R][W](r)$$

then Eq. (13.17) may be written in the form

$$(13.19) \qquad\qquad (G) = \frac{d}{dt}(H)$$

This is the basic equation of motion of the rigid body.

14. TRANSFORMATION OF THE EQUATION OF MOTION TO MOVING AXES

Unfortunately, the basic equation (13.19) is not very useful as it stands, because the vector (r) varies continuously as the body moves, since it is referred to axes whose directions remain fixed. Because of the variation of (r) with time, it is very difficult to compute the angular momentum (H), as given by (13.18). It is, therefore, convenient to introduce the system of fixed axes (y), as shown in Fig. 7.7. The system of Cartesian coordinates (y) is fixed in the body. The origin O' of the (y) coordinate system is at the center of mass of the moving body. Let a unit vector (a) have the components $(a)_x$ with respect to the fixed (x) system of coordinates and the components $(a)_y$ in the (y) system of coordinates. Now, if the system of coordinates (y) is rotated with respect to the coordinates (x) by an orthogonal transformation, then the components $(a)_x$ of the unit vector (a) are related to the components $(a)_y$ by the transformation

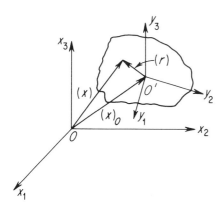

FIG. 7.7. Transformation of Axes

$$\text{(14.1)} \qquad (a)_x = [S](a)_y$$

where $[S]$ is the orthogonal transformation matrix.

Transformation of the Angular Momentum Vector

In the fixed system of coordinates, (x), the angular momentum vector (H) is given by Eq. (13.18) in the form

$$\text{(14.2)} \qquad (H)_x = \sum m[R]_x[W]_x(r)_x$$

where all the matrices are expressed in terms of the directions of (x). If we let the corresponding matrices in the directions of (y) be $[R]_y$, $[W]_y$, $(r)_y$, we have the transformation equations

$$\text{(14.3)} \qquad [R]_x = [S][R]_y[S]'$$

$$\text{(14.4)} \qquad [W]_x = [S][W]_y[S]'$$

and

$$\text{(14.5)} \qquad (r)_x = [S](r)_y$$

Hence, if these expressions are substituted into (14.2), the result is

$$\text{(14.6)} \qquad (H)_x = \sum m[S][R]_y[S]'[S][W]_y[S]'[S](r)_y$$
$$= \sum m[S][R]_y[W]_y(r)_y = [S](H)_y$$

The simplification of (14.6) is made possible because $[S]$ is orthogonal, and, therefore, $[S]'[S] = U$, the third-order unit matrix.

Transformation of the Basic Equation of Motion

The basic equation of motion (13.19) is expressed in terms of the fixed coordinate system of axes (x). We therefore write this equation in the form

$$(14.7) \qquad (G)_x = \frac{d}{dt}(H)_x = (\dot{H})_x$$

We have just demonstrated that the angular momentum vector $(H)_x$ transforms according to the rule

$$(14.8) \qquad (H)_x = [S](H)_y$$

If we differentiate this equation with respect to the time t, we obtain

$$(14.9) \qquad (\dot{H})_x = [\dot{S}](H)_y + [S](\dot{H})_y$$

The basic equation of motion (14.7) may, therefore, be written in the form

$$(14.10) \qquad (G)_x = [\dot{S}](H)_y + [S](\dot{H})_y$$

If we denote the components of the total moment vector $(G)_x$ expressed in the (y) directions by $(G)_y$, we have the relation

$$(14.11) \qquad (G)_x = [S](G)_y$$

Hence (14.11) may be written in the form

$$(14.12) \qquad [S](G)_y = [\dot{S}](H)_y + [S](\dot{H})_y$$

If we premultiply this by $[S]'$, we obtain

$$(14.13) \qquad (G)_y = [S]'[\dot{S}](H)_y + (\dot{H})_y$$

The quantity

$$(14.14) \qquad [W]_y = [S]'[\dot{S}]$$

is the angular velocity matrix referred to axes instantaneously coinciding with the rotating axes (y). With this notation (14.13) may be written in the form

$$(14.15) \qquad (G)_y = [W]_y(H)_y + (\dot{H})_y$$

This is the basic equation of the motion of the body referred to the moving directions of the axes (y) fixed in the body with their origin at the center of mass of the body, as shown in Fig. 14.1. Now, since $(r)_y$ and $[R]_y$ are measured in terms of the moving directions of the axes fixed in the body, they are constant with respect to the time.

The angular momentum vector $(H)_y$ is given by (14.6) in the form

$$(14.16) \qquad (H)_y = \sum m[R]_y[W]_y(r)_y$$

If $(w)_y$ is the angular velocity vector with respect to the moving axes, we have

(14.17) $[W]_y(r)_y = (w)_y \times (r)_y = -(r)_y \times (w)_y = -[R]_y(w)_y$

by the rules of transformation of vector products. We may, therefore, express (14.16) in the form

(14.18) $$(H)_y = -\sum m[R]_y^2(w)_y$$

The matrix

(14.19) $$[J]_y = -\sum m[R]_y^2$$

is the inertia matrix of the body about its center of mass expressed in terms of the coordinates (y) fixed in the body. This matrix was discussed in Sec. 10. In terms of the inertia matrix, the angular momentum $(H)_y$ by (14.18) may be expressed in the form

(14.20) $$(H)_y = [J]_y(w)_y$$

Since the inertia matrix $[J]_y$ is a constant, we have

(14.21) $$(\dot{H})_y = [J]_y(\dot{w})_y$$

The basic equation of motion (14.15) may, therefore, be written in the form

(14.22) $$(G)_y = [J]_y(\dot{w})_y + [W]_y[J]_y(w)_y$$

The Kinetic Energy of Rotation

In Sec. 10 it was shown in Eq. (10.11) that the kinetic energy of rotation T_r may be expressed in the notation of this section by the equation

(14.23) $$T_r = \tfrac{1}{2}(w)_y'[J]_y(w)_y$$

If the (y) axes are chosen to coincide with the principal axes of the body, then the inertia matrix in these coordinates has the diagonal form

(14.24) $$[J]_y = \begin{bmatrix} A & 0 & 0 \\ 0 & B & 0 \\ 0 & 0 & C \end{bmatrix}$$

where A, B, and C are the moments of inertia about the principal axes y_1, y_2, and y_3. In this case, if we write the angular velocity vector in the form

(14.25) $$(w) = \begin{bmatrix} w_1 \\ w_2 \\ w_3 \end{bmatrix}$$

the kinetic energy of rotation (14.23), when expanded, takes the simple form

(14.26) $$T_r = \tfrac{1}{2}(Aw_1^2 + Bw_2^2 + Cw_3^2)$$

In this case, the equations of motion, when expanded, take the form

$$(14.27) \qquad \begin{bmatrix} G_1 \\ G_2 \\ G_3 \end{bmatrix} = \begin{bmatrix} A\dot{w}_1 + (C - B)w_2 w_3 \\ B\dot{w}_2 + (A - C)w_3 w_1 \\ C\dot{w}_3 + (B - A)w_1 w_2 \end{bmatrix}$$

where G_1, G_2, G_3 are the external moments applied to the body about the principal axes y_1, y_2, y_3. Equations (14.27) are known as Euler's equations of motion for the rigid body.

15. GENERAL FORM OF EULER'S EQUATIONS

When the moving axes (y) are fixed in the body, as shown in Fig. 7.7, and the center of the (y) coordinates O' is either a fixed point in space or located at the center of mass $(x)_c$ of the body, the basic equations of motion are given by (14.22) in the general form

$$(15.1) \qquad (G)_y = [J]_y(\dot{w})_y + [W]_y[J]_y(w)_y$$

$(G)_y$ is the *total moment* of the external forces acting on the body about the origin O' of the (y) coordinate system. $[J]_y$ is the inertia matrix of the body about the point O' expressed in the coordinate system (y). $(w)_y$ is the angular velocity vector whose elements are the components of the angular velocity of the body about the axes y_1, y_2, and y_3. These components are given by (14.25). The angular velocity matrix $[W]_y$ has the form

$$(15.2) \qquad [W]_y = \begin{bmatrix} 0 & -w_3 & w_2 \\ w_3 & 0 & -w_1 \\ -w_2 & w_1 & 0 \end{bmatrix}$$

If the body coordinates (y) are chosen so that they coincide with the principal axes of the body, then the inertia matrix $[J]_y$ has the diagonal form given by (14.24). Equation (15.1), when expanded into components, yields three equations for the motion of the rigid body. These are Euler's equations in the general form. If the body axes are chosen to be principal axes of inertia, then $[J]_y$ is the diagonal matrix (14.24) and Euler's equations take the form (14.27).

In order to relate Euler's equations with the kinetic energy of rotation of the rigid body, let us premultiply Eq. (15.1) by $(w)'_y$ to obtain

$$(15.3) \qquad (w)'_y(G)_y = (w)'_y[J]_y(\dot{w})_y + (w)'_y[W]_y[J]_y(w)_y$$

From the definition of the vector product, we have

$$(15.4) \qquad [W]_y(w)_y = (w)_y \times (w)_y = (0)$$

Hence, the transpose of (15.4) is

$$(15.5) \qquad (w)'_y[W]'_y = -(w)'_y[W]_y = (0)'$$

Since $(w)'_y[W]_y$ vanishes, Eq. (15.3) reduces to

(15.6) $$(w)'_y(G)_y = (w)'_y[J]_y(\dot{w})_y$$

The kinetic energy of rotation T_r of the rigid body is given by (14.23) in the form

(15.7) $$T_r = \tfrac{1}{2}(w)'_y[J]_y(w)_y$$

If (15.7) is differentiated with respect to the time t, the result is

(15.8)
$$\dot{T}_r = \tfrac{1}{2}(\dot{w})'_y[J]_y(w)_y + \tfrac{1}{2}(w)'_y[J]_y(\dot{w})_y$$
$$= (w)'_y[J]_y(\dot{w})_y$$

If this is substituted into the right member of (15.6), we obtain

(15.9) $$(w)'_y(G)_y = \dot{T}_r = \frac{d}{dt}T_r$$

Therefore, the left-hand side of (15.9) represents the power furnished by the couple $(G)_y$ to increase the kinetic energy of rotation T_r of the body.

If the body does not experience a couple, then $(G)_y = (0)$, and the Euler equation (15.1) reduces to

(15.10) $$(0) = [J]_y(\dot{w})_y + [W]_y[J]_y(w)_y$$

Let us premultiply this equation by the row matrix $(w)'_y[J]_y$ to obtain

(15.11) $$(0) = (w)'_y[J]^2(\dot{w})_y + (w)'_y[J]_y[W]_y[J]_y(w)_y$$

If we take the transpose of this equation, we obtain

(15.12) $$(0) = (\dot{w})'_y[J]^2_y(w)_y - (w)'_y[J]_y[W]_y[J]_y(w)_y$$

We now add (15.11) and (15.12) to obtain

(15.13) $$(0) = (w)'_y[J]^2(\dot{w})_y + (\dot{w})'_y[J]^2(w)_y = \frac{d}{dt}[(w)'_y[J]^2_y(w)_y]$$

The angular momentum vector of the body about the point O' is

(15.14) $$(H)_y = [J]_y(w)_y$$

Hence, if we multiply (15.14) by its transpose, we obtain

(15.15) $$(H)'_y(H)_y = (w)'_y[J]^2_y(w)_y$$

If we compare this with (15.13), we see that

(15.16) $$\frac{d}{dt}(H)'_y(H)_y = 0$$

Therefore, this indicates that in the absence of an applied external couple $(G)_y$ to the body, the square of the resultant angular momentum is a constant.

Conditions for Permanent Rotation About a Fixed Axis in the Body

The conditions under which the body rotates permanently about an axis fixed in the body will now be examined in the case in which the body is rotating freely without the influence of any external torque. The body is supposed to be rotating about its center of mass, and the coordinates (y) fixed in the body have their origin O' at the center of mass and the directions of the principal axes of the body. The equations of motion for this case are

(15.17) $$(G)_y = [J]_y(\dot{w})_y + [W]_y[J]_y(w)_y = (0)$$

Since the (y) axes are principal axes of the body, the inertia matrix $[J]_y$ has the form

(15.18) $$[J]_y = \begin{bmatrix} A & 0 & 0 \\ 0 & B & 0 \\ 0 & 0 & C \end{bmatrix}$$

Let the body be rotating about an axis fixed in the body. Let this axis have the direction of the unit vector $(u)_y$ measured in the (y) coordinate system. The angular velocity vector $(w)_y$ will, therefore, have the form

(15.19) $$(w)_y = w(u)_y$$

since $(u)_y$ is a constant unit vector directed along the permanent axis of rotation. The expanded form of Eq. (15.19) is

(15.20) $$(w)_y = w\begin{bmatrix} u_1 \\ u_2 \\ u_3 \end{bmatrix}$$

where u_1, u_2, u_3 are the components of the unit vector $(u)_y$ in the directions of the coordinate axes y_1, y_2, y_3. With this notation, the angular velocity matrix $[W]_y$ may be written in the form

(15.21) $$[W]_y = w\begin{bmatrix} 0 & -u_3 & u_2 \\ u_3 & 0 & -u_1 \\ -u_2 & u_1 & 0 \end{bmatrix} = w[U]_y$$

If the expressions (15.19) and (15.21) are substituted into the equations of motion of the rigid body (15.17), the resulting equation is

(15.22) $$(0) = \dot{w}[J]_y(u)_y + w^2[U]_y[J]_y(u)_y$$

If we now premultiply this equation by $(u)'_y$, the result is

(15.23) $$(0) = \dot{w}(u)'_y[J]_y(u)_y$$

since the product $(u)'_y[U]_y$ vanishes. The product $(u)'_y[J]_y(u)_y$ cannot vanish, because it is a sum of positive terms. In order for (15.23) to be satisfied, therefore, we must have

(15.24) $\dot{w} = 0$

The previous equation shows that w is a constant, and Eq. (15.22) reduces to

(15.25) $[U]_y[J]_y(u)_y = (0)$

If this equation is expanded, we obtain

$$(C - B)u_2u_3 = 0$$

(15.26) $(A - C)u_1u_3 = 0$

$$(B - A)u_1u_2 = 0$$

If the moments of inertia A, B, and C are distinct, we must have

(15.27) $u_2u_3 = 0, \quad u_1u_3 = 0, \quad u_1u_2 = 0$

In order for these equations to be satisfied, it is necessary for *two* of the quantities u_1, u_2, u_3 to vanish. Accordingly, the unit vector (u) must have the same direction as one of the axes y_1, y_2, or y_3. It therefore follows that the permanent axis of rotation of the body must coincide with one of the principal axes of the body, y_i.

The Stability of the Permanent Rotation About a Fixed Axis

The stability of the permanent rotation discussed above demands special attention. To investigate the stability of this motion, let it be assumed that the body is rotating about the principal axis y_1 with angular velocity w, so that initially

(15.28) $(w)_y = \begin{bmatrix} w \\ 0 \\ 0 \end{bmatrix}$

Let the body be slightly disturbed from its original motion, so that, after the disturbance, the angular velocity vector $(w)_y$ has the form

(15.29) $(w)_y = \begin{bmatrix} w + e_1 \\ e_2 \\ e_3 \end{bmatrix}$

where e_1, e_2, e_3 are small increments of angular velocity along the y_1, y_2, y_3 directions. If the equation of motion (15.17) is expanded with $(w)_y$ expressed in the form (15.29), the result is

$$A(\dot{w} + \dot{e}_1) - (B - C)e_2e_3 = 0$$

(15.30) $B(\dot{e}_2) - (C - A)e_3w = 0$

$$C(\dot{e}_3) - (A - B)e_2w = 0$$

where we have neglected the small quantities of the second-order e_1e_3 and e_1e_2.

If the quantity e_3 is eliminated between the second and third equations of (15.30), the following equation in e_2 is obtained:

(15.31) $$BC\ddot{e}_2 + w^2(C - A)(B - A)e_2 = 0$$

This is a linear differential equation of the second order in e_2. In order to insure the stability of the motion, e_2 must remain a small quantity. If the coefficient of e_2 in the differential equation (15.31) is positive, e_2 oscillates with simple harmonic motion but does not increase indefinitely. Therefore, for *stability* we must have

(15.32) $$(C - A)(B - A) > 0$$

In the stability analysis we have assumed that the permanent axis of rotation is the y_1 axis. A is the moment of inertia associated with this axis. We notice that the stability criterion (15.32) is satisfied, provided A is either the greatest or the least of the three moments of inertia A, B, or C.

16. MOTION RELATIVE TO THE SURFACE OF THE EARTH

To illustrate the use of the general equations of motion of a particle expressed in matrix notation, we shall consider in this section the motion of a free particle near a point O' at the surface of the earth. Since the earth has a rotation whose period is approximately 23 hours, 56 minutes, 4.1 seconds, or 86,164.1 mean solar seconds, a system of axes which are fixed relatively to the surface of the earth are in rotation with respect to a system of fixed axes. It is of interest to see in what manner the apparent motions on the surface of the earth depend upon the rotation of the earth.

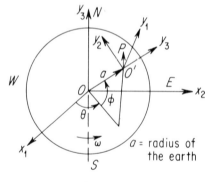

FIG. 7.8. Coordinate System on the Rotating Earth

Let (y) be a Cartesian coordinate axes system having its origin at the point O' of the earth's surface, as shown in Fig. 7.8. Let the rotating coordinate system (y) have the following orientation:

(16.1) $$(y) = \begin{bmatrix} y_1 \\ y_2 \\ y_3 \end{bmatrix} = \begin{matrix} \text{toward the east} \\ \text{toward the north} \\ \text{vertical at } O' \end{matrix}$$

Let (x) be a fixed Cartesian reference system with the x_3 axis coinciding with the axis of rotation of the earth. The x_1 and x_2 axes are in the plane of the equator and have fixed directions with respect to the stars.   With respect to the (x) axes, the earth is rotating with the angular speed w given by

(16.2) $$w = \frac{2\pi}{86164.1} = 7.2921 \times 10^{-5} \text{ sec}^{-1}$$

This quantity is so small that its square can generally be neglected.

Let the polar coordinates of the point O' with respect to the (x) axes be

(16.3)
$$\begin{aligned} x_{1_{0'}} &= a \cos (\phi) \cos (\theta) \\ x_{2_{0'}} &= a \cos (\phi) \sin (\theta) \\ x_{3_{0'}} &= a \sin (\phi) \end{aligned} \quad \text{or} \quad (x)_0 = \begin{bmatrix} x_{1_{0'}} \\ x_{2_{0'}} \\ x_{3_{0'}} \end{bmatrix}$$

where a is the radius of the earth.   In this system of polar coordinates we have

(16.4) $$\phi = \text{the angle of latitude of } O'$$

(16.5) $$\theta = \text{the angle of longitude of } O'$$

The transformation matrix $[S]$ expressing the directions of coordinate system (x) with respect to the coordinate system (y) in the form

(16.6) $$(x) = [S](y)$$

may be obtained from Fig. 7.8 by noting that the coordinate y_1 coincides with the θ direction, the coordinate y_2 coincides with the ϕ direction, and the coordinate y_3 coincides with the radial direction.   The direction cosines of the angles which the axes of the (x) system make with the axes of the (y) system are the elements of the orthogonal matrix $[S]$.   Therefore, we obtain

(16.7)
$$\begin{bmatrix} x_1 \\ x_2 \\ x_3 \end{bmatrix} = \begin{bmatrix} -\sin (\theta) & -\sin (\phi) \cos (\theta) & \cos (\phi) \cos (\theta) \\ \cos (\theta) & -\sin (\phi) \sin (\theta) & \cos (\phi) \sin (\theta) \\ 0 & \cos (\phi) & \sin (\phi) \end{bmatrix} \begin{bmatrix} y_1 \\ y_2 \\ y_3 \end{bmatrix}$$

Since O' is fixed on the surface of the earth, the angle ϕ is constant, and θ is equal to wt.   Expression (16.7) would give the relations between the axes (x) and the axes (y) if the two coordinate systems had a common origin.   Since origin O' has the coordinates $(x)_0$ given by (16.3) in the (x) system, the equations of transformation from the system (x) to the system (y) of Fig. 7.8 may be written in the matrix form

(16.8) $$(x) = (x)_0 + [S](y)$$

where $(x)_0$ is given by (16.3), and $[S]$ is the square matrix of (16.7).

The absolute velocity of the point P whose coordinates are (y) in the moving system of axes is obtained by differentiating (16.8) with respect to the time.   Before we do this, it is more convenient to express $(x)_0$ in the form

(16.9) $$(x)_0 = [S](a)$$

where $(x)_0$ is the position vector of the origin O' with respect to the origin O

expressed in the directions of the axes (x). The vector a has a component only along the y_3 direction, and, therefore, has the form

$$(16.10) \qquad (a) = \begin{bmatrix} 0 \\ 0 \\ a \end{bmatrix}$$

With this notation, (16.8) has the form

$$(16.11) \qquad (x) = [S](a) + [S](y)$$

These are the coordinates of the point P expressed in terms of the fixed co-ordinate system (x). The absolute velocity of P is, therefore,

$$(16.12) \qquad (v)_x = (\dot{x}) = [\dot{S}](a) + [\dot{S}](y) + [S](\dot{y})$$

The absolute velocity of P measured in the direction of the coordinates (y) we will call $(v)_y$. This vector is obtained by the premultiplication of (16.12) by $[S]'$. This operation gives the result

$$(16.13) \qquad (v)_y = [S]'(v)_x = [S]'[\dot{S}](a) + [S]'[\dot{S}](y) + (\dot{y})$$

The matrix $[W]$ is the angular velocity matrix

$$(16.14) \qquad [W] = [S]'[\dot{S}]$$

In terms of the angular velocity matrix, (16.13) may be written in the form,

$$(16.15) \qquad (v)_y = [W](a) + ([W] + UD)(y)$$

where U is the third-order unit matrix and D is the time derivative operator d/dt.

The *absolute acceleration* $(A)_y$ of the point P measured in the direction of the moving coordinate axes (y) is given by the equation

$$(16.16) \quad (A)_y = ([W] + UD)(v)_y = ([W] + UD)[W](a) + ([W] + UD)^2(y)$$

The Angular Velocity Matrix $[W]$

The angular velocity matrix $[W] = [S]'[\dot{S}]$ for the coordinate system under consideration. In this case, the transformation matrix $[S]$ is given by Eq. (16.7) in the form

$$(16.17) \qquad [S] = \begin{bmatrix} -\sin(\theta) & -\sin(\phi)\cos(\theta) & \cos\phi\cos(\theta) \\ \cos(\theta) & -\sin(\phi)\sin(\theta) & \cos(\phi)\sin(\theta) \\ 0 & \cos(\phi) & \sin(\phi) \end{bmatrix}$$

This matrix has the transpose $[S]'$ given by

$$(16.18) \qquad [S]' = \begin{bmatrix} -\sin(\theta) & \cos(\theta) & 0 \\ -\sin(\phi)\cos(\theta) & -\sin(\phi)\sin(\theta) & \cos(\phi) \\ \cos(\phi)\cos(\theta) & \cos(\phi)\sin(\theta) & \sin(\phi) \end{bmatrix}$$

As we see by examining Fig. (7.8), the angle θ is given by $\theta = wt$ so that $\dot{\theta} = w$, where w is the angular speed of the earth's rotation given by Eq. (16.2). The derivative of the transformation matrix $[S]$ with respect to the time, $[\dot{S}]$, is obtained by differentiating (16.17). Since $\theta = wt$ and ϕ is constant, we obtain $[\dot{S}]$ in the form

$$(16.19) \quad [\dot{S}] = \begin{bmatrix} -\cos(\theta) & \sin(\phi)\sin(\theta) & -\cos(\phi)\sin(\theta) \\ -\sin(\theta) & -\sin(\phi)\cos(\theta) & \cos(\phi)\cos(\theta) \\ 0 & 0 & 0 \end{bmatrix} W$$

In order to obtain the angular velocity matrix $[W] = [S]'[\dot{S}]$, we pre-multiply (16.19) by (16.18) and obtain the matrix

$$(16.20) \quad [W] = [S]'[\dot{S}] = \begin{bmatrix} 0 & -w\sin(\phi) & w\cos(\phi) \\ w\sin(\phi) & 0 & 0 \\ -w\cos(\phi) & 0 & 0 \end{bmatrix}$$

From the elements of $[W]$, we may construct the angular velocity vector

$$(16.21) \quad (w) = \begin{bmatrix} 0 \\ w\cos(\phi) \\ w\sin(\phi) \end{bmatrix} = \begin{bmatrix} w_1 \\ w_2 \\ w_3 \end{bmatrix}$$

Since the angular speed w of the rotating earth is constant, the elements of the angular velocity matrix $[W]$ given by (16.20) are constant. Therefore, terms of the form $UD[W]$ in the expression for the absolute acceleration (16.16) vanish, and the expression for the absolute acceleration is given by

$$(16.22) \quad (A)_y = [W]^2(a) + ([W]^2 + 2[W]D + UD^2)(y)$$

If the matrix $[W]$ given by (16.20) is multiplied by itself, the following result is obtained:

$$(16.23) \quad [W]^2 = \begin{bmatrix} -w^2 & 0 & 0 \\ 0 & -w^2\sin^2(\phi) & w^2\sin\phi\cos(\phi) \\ 0 & w^2\sin(\phi)\cos(\phi) & -w^2\cos^2(\phi) \end{bmatrix}$$

17. THE PLUMB LINE

Let a sphere of mass m be suspended from a point on the y_3 axis, as shown in Fig. 7.9, by a string in which the tension is T. It will be assumed that the sphere is at rest at the origin. The plumb line will coincide with the y_3 axis, since, by definition, the y_3 axis is vertical, and vertical means the direction of the plumb line. Let the vector (G) denote the acceleration of the gravitational attraction of the earth on the sphere. The earth is assumed to be symmetrical with respect to the y_2-y_3 plane, which is a meridian plane of the earth, and, therefore, the vector (G) will lie in this plane. Let (G) have the elements given by

$$(17.1) \qquad (G) = \begin{bmatrix} 0 \\ G_2 \\ -G_3 \end{bmatrix}$$

Since the sphere is relatively at rest at the origin, its coordinates satisfy the equations

$$(17.2) \qquad (y) = (0), \quad (\dot{y}) = (0), \quad (\ddot{y}) = (0)$$

The absolute acceleration of the particle is given by (16.22) to be

$$(17.3) \qquad (A)_y = [W]^2(a) = \begin{bmatrix} A_1 \\ A_2 \\ A_3 \end{bmatrix}$$

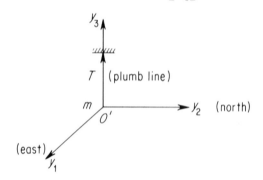

FIG. 7.9. The Plumb Line

If we denote by $(F)_y$ the force acting on the particle, we have

$$(17.4) \qquad (F)_y = m(G) + \begin{bmatrix} 0 \\ 0 \\ T \end{bmatrix}$$

By Newton's law, this force is related to the acceleration of the particle by the equation

$$(17.5) \qquad (F)_y = m(A)_y = m[W]^2(a) = m(G) + \begin{bmatrix} 0 \\ 0 \\ T \end{bmatrix}$$

If this equation is expanded, the following equations are obtained:

$$(17.6) \qquad \begin{aligned} mA_1 &= 0 \\ mA_2 &= mw^2 a \sin(\phi) \cos(\phi) = mG_2 \\ mA_3 &= -mw^2 a \cos^2(\phi) = -mG_3 + T \end{aligned}$$

We have, therefore,

(17.7)
$$G_2 = w^2 a \sin(\phi) \cos(\phi)$$
$$T = mG_3 - mw^2 a \cos^2(\phi) = m(G_3 - w^2 a \cos^2 \phi)$$

If the earth were not rotating, $w = 0$, G_2 would vanish and the value of T/m would be G. Since we have

(17.8) $$G^2 = G_2^2 + G_3^2$$

or

(17.9) $$G_3 = (G^2 - G_2^2)^{1/2} = G[1 - a^2 w^4 \sin^2(\phi) \cos^2(\phi)]^{1/2}$$
$$= G - \frac{1 a^2 w^4}{2G} \sin^2(\phi) \cos^2(\phi)$$

It is seen that T is slightly diminished by the rotation of the earth. The quantity g, which is the usual acceleration of gravity, is given by

(17.10) $$g = \frac{T}{m} = (G_3 - w^2 a \cos^2 \phi)$$

The angular speed of the earth w is given by Eq. (16.2) and is of the order of 1/14,000. This number is so small that, for regions in which g can be regarded as constant, the remaining terms in the acceleration Eqs. (16.22) which have w^2 as a factor are wholly inappreciable and may be dropped from further consideration.

18. MOTION OF A FREE PARTICLE NEAR THE SURFACE OF THE ROTATING EARTH

The equations for the acceleration of a free particle referred to the rotating system of axes (y) are

(18.1) $$(A)_y = (\ddot{y}) + 2[W](\dot{y}) = (g)$$

where the vector (g) has the elements

(18.2) $$(g) = \begin{bmatrix} 0 \\ 0 \\ -g \end{bmatrix}$$

These equations are obtained by discarding the terms involving the square of the angular velocity matrix $[W]^2$ in (16.22) with the exception of the term appearing in g given by (17.10). These are the equations of motion of a free particle near the earth's surface. The terms in the solution of (18.1) that do not involve the small quantity w are the general terms of the solution of the equation

(18.3) $$(\ddot{y})_0 = (g)$$

The general solution of the matrix differential equation (18.3) is

(18.4) $$(y)_0 = (g)\frac{t^2}{2} + (b)t + (c)$$

where (b) and (c) are arbitrary column vectors

Now let the solution of (18.1) be given by

(18.5) $$(y) = (y)_0 + (z)$$

where (z) is a column vector whose elements are small. If this form of solution is substituted into (18.1), the result is

(18.6) $$(\ddot{y})_0 + (\ddot{z}) + 2[W](\dot{y})_0 + 2[W](\dot{z}) = (g)$$

Since $(y)_0$ satisfies (18.3), we may subtract (18.3) from (18.6), and we see that (z) must satisfy the equation

(18.7) $$(\ddot{z}) + 2[W](\dot{y})_0 + 2[W](\dot{z}) = (0)$$

The term $2[W](\dot{z})$ is a vector whose elements are small quantities of the second order and may be neglected. Hence, in order to determine (z), we must solve the equation

(18.8) $$(\ddot{z}) = -2[W](\dot{y})_0 = -2[W][(g)t + (b)]$$

If we integrate twice with respect to t, we obtain

(18.9) $$(z) = -2[W]\left[(g)\frac{t^3}{6} + (b)\frac{t^2}{2}\right]$$

If this is substituted into (18.6), we obtain the following solution for (y):

(18.10) $$(y) = (y)_0 + (z) = (g)\frac{t^2}{2} + (b)t + (c) - [W]\left[(g)\frac{t^3}{3} + (b)t^2\right]$$

The arbitrary vectors (b) and (c) must now be determined from the initial conditions of the motion. Let the particle start from the origin O' at $t = 0$ with the initial velocity (v) so that the initial conditions are

(18.11) $$(y) = (0), \quad (\dot{y}) = (v), \quad \text{at } t = 0$$

With these initial conditions, we find that

(18.12) $$(c) = (0), \quad (b) = (v)$$

For these initial conditions, we obtain the solution,

(18.13) $$(y) = (v)t + (g)\frac{t^2}{2} - [W]\left[(g)\frac{t^3}{3} + (v)t^2\right]$$

Let

(18.14) $$(v) = \begin{bmatrix} v_1 \\ v_2 \\ v_3 \end{bmatrix}$$

where v_1, v_2, and v_3 are the components of the initial velocity in the y_1, y_2, y_3 directions; then if (18.13) is expanded, we obtain

$$(18.15) \qquad \begin{bmatrix} y_1 \\ y_2 \\ y_3 \end{bmatrix} = \begin{bmatrix} v_1 t + w(v_2 \sin \phi - v_3 \cos \phi)t^2 + \dfrac{w \cos \phi g t^3}{3} \\ v_2 t - w \sin \phi v_1 t^2 \\ v_3 t - \left(\dfrac{g}{2} - w v_1 \cos \phi \right) t^2 \end{bmatrix}$$

If the particle is projected in the meridian plane $O'y_2 y_3$, we have $v_1 = 0$; then the solution (18.15) reduces to

$$(18.16) \qquad \begin{bmatrix} y_1 \\ y_2 \\ y_3 \end{bmatrix} = \begin{bmatrix} w(v_2 \sin \phi - v_3 \cos \phi)t^2 + \dfrac{w \cos \phi g t^3}{3} \\ v_2 t \\ v_3 t - g\dfrac{t^2}{2} \end{bmatrix}$$

Therefore, as far as the y_2 and y_3 coordinates are concerned, the motion to this order of approximation is independent of the earth's rotation. However, there is a small deviation in the y_1 direction. The time of flight of the particle is given by

$$(18.17) \qquad t = \frac{2y_3}{g}$$

The total deviation in the y_1 direction during the flight of the particle is obtained by substituting the value of time given by (18.17) into the first equation of (18.16). This deviation is

$$(18.18) \qquad y_1 = \frac{4wv_3^2(v_2 \sin \phi - \tfrac{1}{3}v_3 \cos \phi)}{g^2}$$

It can be seen that if

$$(18.19) \qquad v_2 \sin \phi = v_3 \frac{\cos \phi}{3}$$

or

$$(18.20) \qquad 3 \tan \phi = \frac{v_3}{v_2} = \tan b$$

where b is the *initial* angle of elevation of the path of the particle; then the deviation y_1 vanishes.

Therefore, at any latitude ϕ there is a certain angle of projection b in the meridian plane such that the deviation over the whole path vanishes. If the angle of projection is *greater* than that specified by (18.20), the deviation is negative, whereas if the angle of projection b is smaller, the deviation is positive.

If the particle is projected upwards, then $v_2 = 0$. In this case, (18.16) becomes

$$(18.21) \qquad \begin{bmatrix} y_1 \\ y_2 \\ y_3 \end{bmatrix} = \begin{bmatrix} -wv_3 \cos \phi t^2 + w \cos \phi g \dfrac{t^3}{3} \\ 0 \\ v_3 t - g \dfrac{t^2}{2} \end{bmatrix}$$

The deviation is now

$$(18.22) \qquad y_1 = -\frac{4wv_3^3 \cos \phi}{3g^2}$$

The particle, therefore, lands at a point west of the point from which it started.

19. THE FOUCAULT PENDULUM

The Foucault pendulum differs from an ordinary spherical pendulum in that the Foucault pendulum is started from a position of rest relative to the surface of the earth, and the effects of the rotation of the earth are taken into account. Let the pendulum be of length S, and let it be suspended from the origin of the (y) coordinate system, as shown in Fig. 7.10. Let the pendulum bob have a mass m, and let mT be the tension in the wire that suspends the bob from the point O'. The equations of motion of the pendulum are

$$(19.1) \quad (y) + 2[W](\dot{y}) = -\frac{T}{S}(y) - (g)$$

where the vector (g) has the elements

$$(19.2) \qquad (g) = \begin{bmatrix} 0 \\ 0 \\ g \end{bmatrix}$$

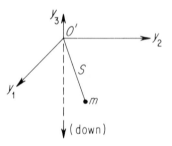

FIG. 7.10. Foucault Pendulum

Let it be supposed that the motion is restricted to very small oscillations about the vertical point of equilibrium. In such a case the quantities y_2/S and y_1/S may be regarded as small quantities, and their squares can be neglected. In such a case we may take

$$(19.3) \qquad y_3 = -S$$

and

$$(19.4) \qquad T = g$$

If we make these approximations and expand the matrix equation (19.1), the first two equations of the expansion are

(19.5)
$$\ddot{y}_1 - 2w_1 \dot{y}_2 = -\frac{g}{S} y_1$$

$$\ddot{y}_2 + 2w_1 \dot{y}_1 = -\frac{g}{S} y_2$$

where we have written

(19.6)
$$w_1 = w \sin \phi$$

If we now introduce two new coordinates z_1 and z_2 by the transformation

(19.7)
$$\begin{bmatrix} y_1 \\ y_2 \end{bmatrix} = \begin{bmatrix} \cos(w_1 t) & \sin(w_1 t) \\ -\sin(w_1 t) & \cos(w_1 t) \end{bmatrix} \begin{bmatrix} z_1 \\ z_2 \end{bmatrix}$$

The relation between the y coordinates and the z coordinates given by the orthogonal transformation (19.7) is shown in Fig. 7.11. As shown in the figure, the coordinates z rotate in the mathematical negative directions with respect to the coordinates y which are fixed to the earth with the angular velocity $w_1 = w \sin(\phi)$, where ϕ is the angle of latitude. If the differential equations (19.5) are expressed in terms of the z coordinates by the transformation (19.7), they become

(19.8)
$$\ddot{z}_1 + \left(w_1^2 + \frac{g}{S}\right) z_1 = 0$$

$$\ddot{z}_2 + \left(w_1^2 + \frac{g}{S}\right) z_2 = 0$$

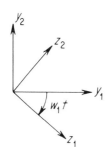

FIG. 7.11.   Rotating Coordinate System

If we now let

(19.9)
$$w_0 = \left[\frac{g}{S} + w_1^2\right]^{1/2} = \left(\frac{g}{S}\right)^{1/2}$$

where we can neglect the very small term w_1^2 in comparison with g/S, then the solution of the two differential equations (19.8) may be expressed in the form

(19.10)
$$z_1 = A \sin(w_0 t + b_1), \quad z_2 = B \sin(w_0 t + b_2)$$

where A and B are arbitrary constants and b_1 and b_2 are arbitrary phase angles. A, B, b_1, and b_2 may be determined from the initial conditions and, therefore, depend on how the motion of the pendulum begins. The coordinates z_1 and z_2 oscillate independently of each other with the period P_0 given by

(19.11)
$$P_0 = \frac{2\pi}{w_0}$$

This is the period of oscillation of a simple pendulum of length S. Regardless of the initial conditions, the pendulum bob describes an elliptical path relative to the rotating coordinates z_1 and z_2. This ellipse rotates with an angular velocity of $w_1 = \sin \phi$ in the direction indicated in Fig. 7.10. In order to keep the pendulum in motion for as long a time as possible, it is desirable to have the bob as heavy and the wire as long as possible. In the original experiment of Foucault in the Pantheon in Paris in 1851, the pendulum had the following dimension:

$$(19.12) \qquad\qquad S = 67 \text{ meters}$$

The period of the pendulum P_0 given by (19.11) for this pendulum was 16 seconds; the period P_r of the rotation of the z coordinate system is given by

$$(19.13) \qquad\qquad P_r = \frac{2\pi}{w_1} = \frac{2\pi}{w \sin \phi} = \frac{24 \text{ hours}}{\sin \phi}$$

The period P_r depends only upon the latitude and not at all upon the initial conditions or the length and weight of the pendulum. In the original experiment of Foucault, $P_r = 32$ hours.

20. THE MOTION OF A TOP

We shall now illustrate the use of the general equations of motion (15.1) to study the motion of a top. It will be assumed that the base of the top is in contact with a fixed horizontal table, as shown in Fig. 7.12. The surface of the table is supposed to be rough enough so that the top does not slip.

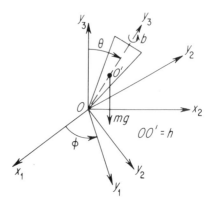

In order to describe the motion of the spinning top, we will take a fixed reference coordinate system x_1, x_2, x_3. The coordinates x_1 and x_2 lie in the plane of the horizontal table, and the x_3 axis is vertical. The apex point of the top is in contact with the table at the origin of the Cartesian coordinate system (x). We shall choose the moving coordinate axes y_1, y_2, y_3 to be only partially fixed with respect to the top.

FIG. 7.12. A Spinning Top

Let y_3 lie along the axes of symmetry of the top; let y_1 lie in the plane $x_3 O y_3$ and be perpendicular to y_3. The axis y_2 completes the right-handed coordinate system (y). The angle between the x_3 and y_3 axes will be denoted by θ. The angle ϕ is the angle that the plane $x_3 O y_3$ makes with the fixed plane $x_1 O x_3$. Finally, let the angular velocity of the top measured in the direction of its axis of rotation be denoted by $\dot{b}$.

The angular velocity vector of the (y) axes, (w), has the following elements:

$$(20.1) \qquad (w)_y = \begin{bmatrix} -\dot{\phi} \sin \theta \\ \dot{\theta} \\ \dot{\phi} \cos \theta \end{bmatrix}$$

The angular velocity vector of the top, $(w)_t$, contains the additional component produced by the rotation of the top about the y_3 axis. The *total* angular velocity of the top about the y_3 axis will be denoted by n and is given by

$$(20.2) \qquad n = \dot{\phi} \cos \theta + b$$

where b is the angular velocity resulting from the spin of the top. The angular velocity vector $(w)_t$ for the top is, therefore,

$$(20.3) \qquad (w)_t = \begin{bmatrix} -\dot{\phi} \sin \theta \\ \dot{\theta} \\ \dot{\phi} \cos \theta + b \end{bmatrix} = \begin{bmatrix} -\dot{\phi} \sin \theta \\ \dot{\theta} \\ n \end{bmatrix}$$

Since Oy_3 is an axis of symmetry in the top, the (y) axes are principal axes, so the inertia matrix is

$$(20.4) \qquad [J]_y = \begin{bmatrix} A & 0 & 0 \\ 0 & A & 0 \\ 0 & 0 & C \end{bmatrix}$$

where C is the moment of inertia of the top about the y_3 axis. A is the moment of inertia about any axis perpendicular to y_3. Because of the symmetry of the top, the moment of inertia about the y_1 and y_2 axes is always A, despite the fact that these axes are not fixed in the body. Relative to the moving axes, the angular momentum of the top is given by (14.20) in the form

$$(20.5) \qquad (H)_y = [J]_y(w)_t$$

The couple $(G)_y$ is given by Eq. (14.15) in the form

$$(20.6) \qquad (G)_y = [W]_y(H)_y + (\dot{H})_y$$

where $[W]_y$ is the angular velocity matrix associated with the angular velocity matrix of the (y) axes, $(w)_y$.

If the center of mass of the top, O', is located at a distance h from the origin O, as shown in Fig. 7.12, we have

$$(20.7) \qquad (G)_y = \begin{bmatrix} 0 \\ mgh \sin \theta \\ 0 \end{bmatrix}$$

The equation of motion is obtained by substituting (20.5) into (20.6) and thus obtaining

(20.8) $$(G)_y = [W]_v[J]_v(w)_t + [J]_v(\dot{w})_t$$

If this matrix equation is multiplied out, the third element of the resultant column is found to be

(20.9) $$C\dot{n} = 0$$

Hence, the spin n about the y_3 axis is constant throughout the motion.

Steady Precessional Motion

For *steady precessional* motion θ and $\dot{\phi}$ remain constants. In such a case, the vector $(w)_t$ is given by

(20.10) $$(w)_t = \begin{bmatrix} -\dot{\phi}\sin\theta \\ 0 \\ n \end{bmatrix}$$

This vector is now a constant, so $(\dot{w})_t = (0)$, and Eq. (20.8) reduces to

(20.11) $$(G)_y = [W]_v[J]_v(w)_t$$

The expanded form of this equation is

(20.12) $$\begin{bmatrix} 0 \\ mgh\sin\theta \\ 0 \end{bmatrix} = \begin{bmatrix} 0 & -\dot{\phi}\cos\theta & 0 \\ \dot{\phi}\cos\theta & 0 & \dot{\phi}\sin\theta \\ 0 & -\dot{\phi}\sin\theta & 0 \end{bmatrix} \begin{bmatrix} A & 0 & 0 \\ 0 & A & 0 \\ 0 & 0 & C \end{bmatrix} \begin{bmatrix} -\dot{\phi}\sin\theta \\ 0 \\ n \end{bmatrix}$$

Upon multiplication, this reduces to

(20.13) $$\begin{bmatrix} 0 \\ mgh\sin\theta \\ 0 \end{bmatrix} = \begin{bmatrix} 0 \\ -A\dot{\phi}^2\sin\theta\cos\theta + Cn\dot{\phi}\sin\theta \\ 0 \end{bmatrix}$$

Therefore, in this case the equation of motion reduces to the single equation

(20.14) $$A\dot{\phi}^2\cos\theta - Cn\dot{\phi} + mgh = 0$$

where we have excluded the possibility that $\sin\theta = 0$. Hence, steady precessional motion is possible either when $\theta = 0$ (in this case $\dot{\phi}$ has no meaning) or are the precessional angular velocities given by solving (20.14) for $\dot{\phi}$. The two possible values for $\dot{\phi}$ are, therefore,

(20.15) $$\dot{\phi} = \frac{Cn}{2A\cos\theta} \pm \frac{[C^2n^2 - +mghA\cos\theta]^{1/2}}{2A\cos\theta}$$

If the top is spinning very rapidly so that n is large, we may approximate the two roots given by (20.15) by

(20.16) $$\dot{\phi}_1 = \frac{Cn}{A \cos \theta}, \quad \text{or} \quad \dot{\phi}_2 = \frac{mgh}{Cn}$$

These two values of $\dot{\phi}$ are called the *rapid* and the *slow* precessional angular velocities.

The Vertical, or Sleeping, Top

If $\theta = 0$, we have the case of the vertical, or "sleeping," top. The stability of this type of motion of the top will now be examined. To examine the stability in the neighborhood of $\theta = 0$, we will examine the solution of Eq. (20.8) under the assumption that the angle θ and its derivative $\dot{\theta}$ are both small quantities so that the squares of these quantities can be neglected.

The equation of motion (20.8) takes the following form when it is expanded:

(20.17)
$$\begin{bmatrix} 0 \\ mgh\,\theta \\ 0 \end{bmatrix} = \begin{bmatrix} A & 0 & 0 \\ 0 & A & 0 \\ 0 & 0 & C \end{bmatrix} \begin{bmatrix} -\ddot{\phi} - \dot{\phi}\dot{\theta} \\ \ddot{\theta} \\ 0 \end{bmatrix}$$

$$+ \begin{bmatrix} 0 & -\dot{\phi} & \dot{\theta} \\ \dot{\phi} & 0 & \dot{\phi}\theta \\ -\dot{\theta} & -\dot{\phi}\theta & 0 \end{bmatrix} \begin{bmatrix} A & 0 & 0 \\ 0 & A & 0 \\ 0 & 0 & C \end{bmatrix} \begin{bmatrix} -\dot{\phi}\theta \\ \dot{\theta} \\ n \end{bmatrix}$$

If the matrix multiplication is performed, this equation reduces to

(20.18)
$$\begin{bmatrix} 0 \\ mgh \\ 0 \end{bmatrix} = \begin{bmatrix} -A\ddot{\phi}\theta - 2A\dot{\phi}\dot{\theta} + Cn\dot{\theta} \\ A\ddot{\theta} - A\dot{\phi}^2\theta + Cn\dot{\phi}\theta \\ 0 \end{bmatrix}$$

The motion of the center of mass of the top will now be projected on a horizontal plane by the introduction of the transformation

(20.19)
$$\begin{bmatrix} z_1 \\ z_2 \end{bmatrix} = h \sin \theta \begin{bmatrix} \cos \phi \\ \sin \phi \end{bmatrix}$$

This transformation may be written in the complex form when θ is small so that $\sin \theta = \theta$ by the introduction of the complex quantity $z = z_1 + jz_2$, where $j = (-1)^{1/2}$. If this is done, we may write the transformation (20.19) in the alternative form,

(20.20) $$z = z_1 + jz_2 = h\theta\,(\cos \phi + j \sin \phi) = h\theta e_j{}^{\phi}$$

for small values of θ. If we now take the first and second derivatives of (20.20) with respect to time, we obtain the following results:

(20.21) $$\dot{z} = he^{j\phi}(\dot{\theta} + j\dot{\phi}\theta)$$

(20.22) $$\ddot{z} = he^{j\phi}(\ddot{\theta} - \dot{\phi}^2\theta + 2j\dot{\phi}\dot{\theta} + j\ddot{\phi}\theta)$$

If Eq. (20.18) is now premultiplied by the row matrix $[-j \quad 1 \quad 0]$, the following result is obtained:

$$(20.23) \qquad mgh\theta = A(\ddot{\theta} - \dot{\phi}^2\theta + j\ddot{\phi}\theta + 2j\dot{\phi}\dot{\theta}) + Cn(\dot{\phi}\theta - j\dot{\theta})$$

If this equation is now multiplied by $he^{j\phi}$, the result may be written in the following form:

$$(20.24) \qquad\qquad mghz = A\ddot{z} - jCn\dot{z}$$

This is a linear differential equation of the second order with constant coefficients in the variable z. If we try a solution of the form

$$(20.25) \qquad\qquad z = Ke^{st}$$

where K is an arbitrary constant, then s is determined by the quadratic equation

$$(20.26) \qquad\qquad As^2 - jCns - mgh = 0$$

This is the characteristic equation of the differential equation (20.24). The two roots of this equation are

$$(20.27) \qquad\qquad s_{1,\,2} = \frac{j[Cn \pm (C^2n^2 - 4Amgh)^{1/2}]}{2A}$$

Hence, the solution for z is of the form

$$(20.28) \qquad\qquad z = K_1e^{s_1t} + K_2e^{s_2t} = z_1 + jz_2$$

For stability, z_1 and z_2 must remain small. This means that the two roots s_1 and s_2 of the characteristic equation of (20.24) must be pure imaginary numbers. In order for this to be the case, we see by examining (20.27) that we must have

$$(20.29) \qquad\qquad C^2n^2 > 4Amgh$$

This is the condition for the stability of the vertical, or "sleeping," top. If the top slows down, then n decreases to the point where the condition (20.29) is not satisfied, and the top cannot maintain the vertical position as a position of equilibrium.

PROBLEMS

1. By the use of the equations of Sec. 18, show that a projectile which has a flat trajectory seems to deviate toward the right in the northern hemisphere and toward the left in the southern hemisphere.

2. A particle of mass m is released at a height h above the origin O' of the (y) coordinate system of axes of Sec. 18.   Find the position of the point at which the particle lands on the surface of the earth.

3. A pendulum of length S is suspended from a point in the northern hemisphere whose latitude is ϕ. The pendulum is released from rest at a small displacement a to the east. Show that it comes to rest instantaneously after a complete swing at a distance $2\pi aw \sin \phi (S/g)^{1/2}$ to the south of its initial position.

4. A uniform plate of sides $2h$ and $2k$ and mass M rotates with constant angular velocity w about one of its diagonals. For this motion to be maintained, show from Euler's equations that the couple which must act on the plate has a magnitude of

$$\frac{\frac{1}{3}Mw^2hk(h^2 - k^2)}{(h^2 + k^2)}$$

and that it is perpendicular to the plate at any moment.

5. A rigid body is freely hinged at its center of gravity G. The principal moments of inertia at G are in the ratio $6:5:2$, the principal axes being designated by Gy_1, Gy_2, Gy_3. The body is set in rotation with angular velocity w about a line in the plane Gy_1y_3 inclined to the axes at 45 deg. Assuming that eventually the rotation becomes steady about an axis fixed in the body, show by the use of Euler's equations and their two integrals that this axis must be Gy_2, and that the angular velocity is then $2w/(5)^{1/2}$.

6. Show that the component of the angular velocity of a body moving under no forces, about the direction of constant angular momentum, is constant and equal to $2T/|H|$.

7. If a body having kinetic symmetry about the axis of greatest moment be subject to a retarding couple about the instantaneous axis, whose magnitude varies as the angular velocity, then the instantaneous axis will approach asymptotically the axis of symmetry.

8. A body is compelled to rotate about its center of mass with uniform angular velocity $w(u)$ about an axis along a unit vector (u) that does not coincide with a principal axis of inertia. Determine the components of the required applied couple about the principal axes of inertia.

9. It is required to determine the couple necessary to compel a body having symmetry about an axis to move in such a way that the axis of symmetry precesses uniformly about a fixed direction.

10. A Foucault pendulum is started at $t = 0$ with no initial velocity, and with an initial displacement of a toward the north. Integrate the differential equations of motion of the pendulum, and study the motion of the bob of the pendulum, projected on the ground plane.

REFERENCES

1. Ames, J. S. and F. D. Murnaghan, *Theoretical Mechanics*. New York: Dover Publications, 1958. (A very clear presentation expressed in vector notation.)

2. Frazer, R. A., W. J. Duncan, and A. R. Collar, *Elementary Matrices.* New York: Cambridge University Press, 1938. (Chapter VIII of this treatise has an excellent but somewhat terse discussion of the applications of matrix notation to kinematics and rigid body dynamics.)

3. Goldstein, H., *Classical Mechanics.* Cambridge, Massachusetts: Addison-Wesley Press, Inc., 1951. (This text contains an excellent exposition of the theory of classical mechanics; matrix and vector notation are used.)

4. Milne, E. A., *Vectorial Mechanics.* New York: Interscience Publishers Inc., 1948. (This treatise contains a very concise discussion of classical mechanics expressed in vector and tensor notation.)

5. Webster, A. G., *Dynamics.* New York: Stechert Publications, 1912. (Vector notation is not used in this book; Part II contains a clear discussion of the motion of the symmetrical top under the action of no forces and a comprehensive discussion of the top under the action of gravitational forces.)

8 APPLICATIONS OF MATRICES TO VIBRATION PROBLEMS

1. INTRODUCTION

The theory of vibrations is one of the most important subjects in the general area of applied mathematics. From the practical engineering standpoint, this subject includes the linear vibrations of mechanical and acoustical systems, the oscillations of electrical circuits or electromechanical systems, the vibrations of bridges and other structures, and the flutter of aircraft wings. In the study of the majority of vibration problems, the mathematical formulation involves the solution of a set of linear differential equations with constant coefficients. This is true when the system contains a finite number of degrees of freedom. The vibrations of continuous systems, such as the vibration of strings, beams, plates, etc., leads to a mathematical formulation involving partial differential equations. In this chapter, only systems with a finite number of degrees of freedom will be considered. The analysis is based on Lagrange's equations of motion because of their generality and the fact that they unify the treatment of vibrating systems of different types.

2. TRANSFORMATION OF COORDINATES

In the study of the dynamics of vibrating systems, it is frequently useful to introduce coordinates other than the usual Cartesian, cylindrical, spherical, or other common types of coordinates. This section presents a discussion of transformation of coordinates expressed in matrix notation. By the use of the transformation expressions derived in this manner, the significance of Lagrange's equations is clarified.

Let the position vector of a point mass, m, in a fixed Cartesian coordinate system, Fig. 8.1, be (x). The vector (x) has the form

$$(2.1) \qquad (x) = \begin{bmatrix} x_1 \\ x_2 \\ x_3 \end{bmatrix}$$

where x_1, x_2, x_3 are the Cartesian coordinates of the particle m. Let us now introduce the three variables q_1, q_2, q_3, and let the coordinates x_i be functions of the variables q_i so that

$$
\begin{aligned}
x_1 &= x_1(q_1, q_2, q_3) \\
x_2 &= x_2(q_1, q_2, q_3) \\
x_3 &= x_3(q_1, q_2, q_3)
\end{aligned}
$$

(2.2)

If we introduce the following partial derivative operators:

$$
\begin{aligned}
D_1 &= \frac{\partial}{\partial q_1} \\
D_2 &= \frac{\partial}{\partial q_2} \\
D_3 &= \frac{\partial}{\partial q_3}
\end{aligned}
$$

(2.3)

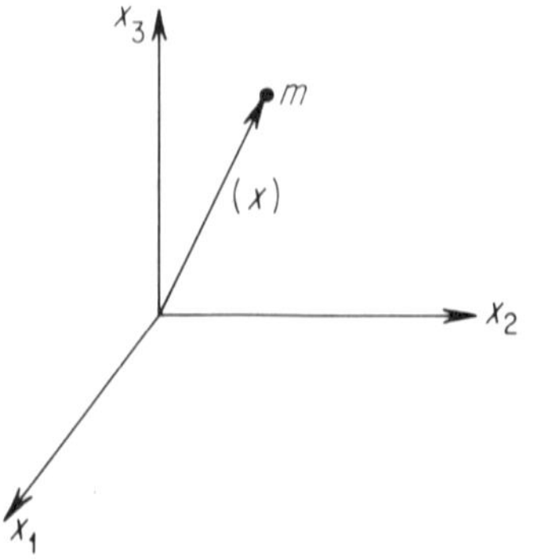

then the differentials dx_1, dx_2, dx_3 may be expressed in the following form:

$$
\begin{bmatrix} dx_1 \\ dx_2 \\ dx_3 \end{bmatrix} = \begin{bmatrix} D_1 x_1 & D_2 x_1 & D_3 x_1 \\ D_1 x_2 & D_2 x_2 & D_3 x_2 \\ D_1 x_3 & D_2 x_3 & D_3 x_3 \end{bmatrix} \begin{bmatrix} dq_1 \\ dq_2 \\ dq_3 \end{bmatrix}
$$

(2.4)

FIGURE 8.1

If we denote the vector having elements dx_1, dx_2, dx_3 by (dx), the vector having elements dq_1, dq_2, dq_3 by (dq), and the vector operator having elements D_1, D_2, D_3 by D, then it may be easily seen that Eq. (2.4) may be written in the compact form

$$
(dx) = \operatorname{tr} [Dx'](dq)
$$

(2.5)

where D is the vector (D), x' is the vector (x) transposed, and the notation $\operatorname{tr} [Dx']$ denotes the transpose of the product Dx'. From (2.5) it can be seen that $\operatorname{tr} [Dx']$ is the Jacobian matrix of the transformation. It is the square matrix in (2.4).

By the use of the ordinary rules of partial differentiation, it can easily be shown that the matrix $\operatorname{tr} [Dx']$ has the following properties:

$$
\operatorname{tr} [\dot{D}\dot{x}'] = \operatorname{tr} [Dx']
$$

(2.6)

$$
\frac{d}{dt} \operatorname{tr} [Dx'] = \operatorname{tr} [\dot{D}\dot{x}']
$$

(2.7)

In (2.6) $\dot{D}$ stands for the vector whose elements are $\partial/\partial \dot{q}_1$, $\partial/\partial \dot{q}_2$, $\partial/\partial \dot{q}_3$. If T_0 stands for the scalar quantity,

$$
T_0 = \tfrac{1}{2}(\dot{x})'(\dot{x})
$$

(2.8)

it can also be shown that

(2.9) $$(\dot{x})' \operatorname{tr} [\dot{D}\dot{x}'] = \dot{D}'T_0$$

and

(2.10) $$(\dot{x})' \operatorname{tr} [D\dot{x}'] = D'T_0$$

The relations (2.5) through (2.10) are very useful in effecting changes of variable in dynamical problems.

3. LAGRANGE'S EQUATIONS OF MOTION

The basic relations involved in the change in variables by (2.2) will now be used to deduce the Lagrange equations of motion from the Newtonian equations of motion expressed in Cartesian coordinates. In order to do this, we return to Fig. 2.1, and consider the motion of the particle m when it is acted upon by a force (F). Since (x) is the position vector of the particle, its Newtonian equation of motion is

(3.1) $$(F) = m(\ddot{x})$$

where $(\ddot{x})$ is the acceleration vector of the particle. If we are to consider the motion of n particles in a system, we require a total of $3n$ coordinates to specify the state of the system at any time. In practical cases, however, a smaller number of coordinates is required to specify the configuration of the system. Some of the coordinates may be lengths, and others may be angles. Let it be supposed that only n such coordinates are required, and let these coordinates be denoted by the n elements of the column matrix (q). Then every coordinate of every particle is a function of the n coordinates $q_1, q_2, \ldots, q_n$.

The work done by the force (F) in a small displacement (dx) is

(3.2) $$dW = (F)'(dx)$$
$$= m(\ddot{x})'(dx), \quad \text{as a consequence of (3.1)}$$

Since $(dx) = \operatorname{tr} [Dx'](dq)$ by (2.5), we may write (3.2) in the form

(3.3) $$dW = m(\ddot{x})' \operatorname{tr} [Dx'] dq$$

By differentiation, we obtain

(3.4) $$\frac{d}{dt}\{(\dot{x})' \operatorname{tr} [Dx']\} = (\ddot{x})' \operatorname{tr} [Dx'] + (\dot{x})' \frac{d}{dt} \operatorname{tr} [Dx']$$

or, hence,

(3.5) $$(\ddot{x})' \operatorname{tr} [Dx'] = \frac{d}{dt}\{(\dot{x})' \operatorname{tr} [Dx']\} - (\dot{x}) \frac{d}{dt} \operatorname{tr} [Dx']$$

However, by the use of (2.6) and (2.7), this may be written in the form

$$(3.6) \qquad (\ddot{x})' \operatorname{tr} [Dx'] = \frac{d}{dt} \{(\dot{x})' \operatorname{tr} [D\dot{x}']\} - (\dot{x}) \operatorname{tr} [D\dot{x}']$$

$$= \frac{d}{dt} \dot{D}'T_0 - D'T_0$$

This last transformation is made by the use of (2.9) and (2.10).   If (3.6) is now substituted into (3.3), we obtain the following expression for the work done by the force (F):

$$(3.7) \qquad dW = \left[\frac{d}{dt} \dot{D}'T - D'T \right] (dq)$$

where

$$(3.8) \qquad T = mT_0 = \frac{m}{2} (\dot{x})'(\dot{x})$$

T is the kinetic energy of the particle.

If we now add all the equations of the type (3.7) for all the particles of the system, we obtain on the left-hand side the total work done in the displacement, and on the right-hand side T becomes the total kinetic energy of the system.   If the system is a conservative one, then the total work done by the forces (F) may be derived for the change of a potential energy function V where $V = -W$ so that

$$(3.9) \qquad -dW = dV = (D'V)\, dq$$

If this is substituted into (3.7) summed for all the particles of the system, the result is

$$(3.10) \qquad \left[\frac{d}{dt} \dot{D}'T - D'T + D'V \right] (dq) = 0$$

Now if the n differentials contained in the column (dq) are independent, it is necessary that the n elements of the row matrix of (3.10) must vanish, and hence we have

$$(3.11) \qquad \frac{d}{dt} \dot{D}'T - D'T + D'V = [0]$$

These equations are the n generalized equations of motion of the system under the action of conservative forces.   If expanded, these equations have the form

$$(3.12) \qquad \frac{d}{dt}\frac{\partial T}{\partial \dot{q}_i} - \frac{\partial T}{\partial q_i} + \frac{\partial V}{\partial q_i} = 0$$

for $i = 1, 2, 3, \ldots, n$.   This system of equations is known as Lagrange's equations for a dynamical system under the action conservative forces.   In the literature of dynamics, the q_i's are called generalized coordinates, and the $\dot{q}_i$'s are known as generalized velocities. Since the generalized coordinates may be angular coordinates as well as linear coordinates, the generalized velocities may be angular velocities as well as linear velocities.

A more general form of Lagrange's equations which takes into account frictional forces proportional to the generalized velocities and the effect of nonconservative generalized forces Q_i is the following one:

$$(3.13) \qquad \frac{d}{dt}\left(\frac{\partial T}{\partial \dot{q}_i}\right) - \frac{\partial T}{\partial q_i} + \frac{\partial V}{\partial q_i} + \frac{\partial F}{\partial \dot{q}_i} = Q_i$$

where $i = 1, 2, 3, \ldots, n$. The function F is called the *dissipation function*; its derivatives with respect to the generalized velocities take into account the generalized retarding forces caused by viscous-type friction. The functions Q_i are called generalized forces. They include all other forces acting on the system, such as time-dependent disturbing forces.

The use of Lagrange's equations in the formulation of the equations of motion of vibrating systems leads usually to a simpler procedure than the use of the Newtonian equations of motion. This is particularly true if the vibrating system is a complex one with many coupled parts. In the Newtonian formulation, the principle of action and reaction has to be invoked; this is a difficult procedure in the case of complex systems. On the other hand, the Lagrange formulation centers the attention on the energy functions of the entire system, and in this case the action and reaction of the component parts of the system need not be considered and the equations of motion are determined directly by differentiation of the energy functions of the system.

The Lagrange formulation of vibration problems is particularly valuable in the study of electromechanical systems. In systems of this type, electrical oscillations are coupled to mechanical oscillations of the whole system so that some of the generalized coordinates are distances and angles, whereas other coordinates may be charges and currents. The energy functions will contain mechanical kinetic and potential energy and also electrical kinetic and potential energy. The use of the Lagrange's equations in studying these systems presents an elegant and unifying method.

4. ELECTRICAL AND MECHANICAL ANALOGIES

One of the most important vibrating systems from a practical standpoint is the electrical circuit. The differential equations of motion of linear mechanical vibrating systems and linear electrical circuits are identical in form. This can be seen by considering the behavior of the mechanical system of Fig. 8.3 and the oscillations of the electrical circuit of Fig. 8.2.

In Fig. 8.2 is depicted a mechanical system composed of a mass m free to move on a frictionless horizontal plane. The mass is attached to a linear spring of spring constant k and to a viscous damping device, or "dashpot," of coefficient c.   The electrical circuit of Fig. 8.2 consists of a series connection of a resistance R, an inductance L, and an elastance S.   The elastance S is the reciprocal of the capacitance C of the capacitor of Fig. 8.3.   The basic differential equations that govern the oscillations of these two simple systems may be obtained by applying Kirchhoff's second law to the electrical circuit and Newton's law of motion to the mechanical system.   The equation for the oscillation of the current $i(t)$ of the electrical circuit is

(4.1) $$L\frac{di}{dt} + Ri + Sq = e(t)$$

where $e(t)$ is the applied electromotive force and $q(t)$ is the circulating charge in the circuit.   The current i is related to q by the equation

(4.2) $$i = \frac{dq}{dt}$$

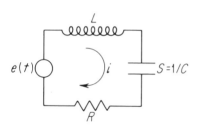

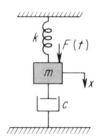

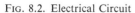

FIG. 8.2. Electrical Circuit   FIG. 8.3. Mechanical System

The equation of motion of the mechanical system in terms of the displacement x of the mass m measured from the position of equilibrium is

(4.3) $$m\ddot{x} + c\dot{x} + kx = F(t)$$

where $F(t)$ is the external applied force to the mass m.   The damping device impedes the motion of m by a viscous force $c\dot{x}$.   If the equation for the circuit is formulated in terms of the charge $q(t)$ by the use of Eq. (4.2), then it is seen that Eq. (4.1) is equivalent to

(4.4) $$L\ddot{q} + R\dot{q} + Sq = F(t)$$

This equation is of a form identical to that of (4.3).   If the various terms in Eqs. (4.3) and (4.4) are placed in analogous relationship with each other, we obtain the classical analogy between electrical circuits and mechanical vibrating systems.   Before we do so, it is important to notice that the torsional system of Fig. 8.4 has an equation of motion of the same form as (4.3) and (4.4).   The system of Fig. 8.4 is composed of a flywheel of moment of inertia J attached to a rigid support by a shaft whose stiffness in torsion is k_t.   The flywheel is impeded in its motion by a torque proportional to its angular velocity $\dot{\theta}$ by a damping device.

The torsional oscillations of the system of Fig. 8.4 may be expressed in terms of the angle of twist θ measured with respect to the equilibrium position of the system. The equation of motion of the system of Fig. 8.3 is the torsional analogue of (4.3), and, therefore, has the form

$$(4.5) \qquad J\ddot{\theta} + B\dot{\theta} + k_t\theta = \tau(t)$$

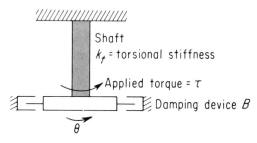

Shaft
k_t = torsional stiffness

Applied torque = τ

Damping device B

θ

FIG. 8.4. Torsional System

By comparing the terms of Eqs. (4.3), (4.4), and (4.5), we can construct the following table of analogues:

TABLE OF ANALOGUES

Mechanical (linear)	Mechanical (torsional)	Electrical
mass m	moment of inertia J	inductance L
stiffness k	torsional stiffness k_t	elastance S
damping c	torsional damping B	resistance R
impressed force $F(t)$	impressed torque $\tau(t)$	potential $e(t)$
displacement x	angular displacement θ	charge q
velocity $\dot{x} = v$	angular velocity $\dot{\theta}$	current i
kinetic energy $\dfrac{mv^2}{2}$	kinetic energy $\dfrac{J\dot{\theta}^2}{2}$	kinetic energy $\dfrac{Li^2}{2}$
potential energy $\dfrac{kx^2}{2}$	potential energy $\dfrac{k_t\theta^2}{2}$	potential energy $\dfrac{Sq^2}{2}$
dissipation $\dfrac{c\dot{x}^2}{2}$	dissipation $\dfrac{B\dot{\theta}^2}{2}$	dissipation $\dfrac{Ri^2}{2}$

Energy Considerations

The energy balance of the electric circuit of Fig. 8.1 may be obtained by first multiplying both members of Eq. (4.1) by the current $i = dq/dt$ to obtain

$$(4.6) \qquad Li\frac{di}{dt} + Ri^2 + Sq\frac{dq}{dt} = ei = P(t)$$

where $P(t) = ei$ is the *power* delivered by the source of potential $e(t)$ to the electric circuit. If it is now supposed that, before $t = 0$, the current $i = 0$ and the charge $q = 0$, and that at $t = 0$ the potential $e(t)$ is applied to the circuit, then the energy $W(t)$ which is furnished to the circuit by the source of potential $e(t)$ may be obtained by integrating Eq. (4.6) from $t = 0$ to $t = t$. If this is done, the following result is obtained:

$$(4.7) \quad W(t) = \int_0^t \left[Li \frac{di}{dt} + Ri^2 + Sq \frac{dq}{dt} \right] dt = \int_0^t ei \, dt = \int_0^t P(t) \, dt$$

If the integration is performed, the result is

$$(4.8) \quad W(t) = \frac{Li^2}{2} + \int_0^t Ri^2 \, dt + \frac{Sq^2}{2} = \int_0^t ei \, dt = \int_0^q e \, dq$$

This equation is interpreted physically by noting that $Li^2/2$ is the energy stored in the inductance L in the form of magnetic energy, $Sq^2/2$ is the energy stored in the elastance S in the form of electric energy, and $\int_0^t Ri^2 \, dt$ represents the energy dissipated in the resistance R in the form of heat energy.

If the equation for the mechanical system of Fig. 8.3, (4.3), is multiplied by $\dot{x}$ and integrated from $t = 0$ to $t = t$, we obtain the following expression for the mechanical work $W_m(t)$ performed by the force $F(t)$ acting on the mass m:

$$(4.9) \quad W_m(t) = \frac{mv^2}{2} + \int_0^t cv^2 \, dt + \frac{kx^2}{2} = \int_0^t Fv \, dt = \int_0^x F \, dx, \quad v = \dot{x}$$

In this case, $mv^2/2$ is the kinetic energy of the mass m, $kx^2/2$ is the strain or potential energy of the spring k, and $\int_0^t cv^2 \, dt$ is the energy dissipated by the damping device, or "dashpot," in the form of heat. By comparing (4.8) with (4.9) the analogous energy functions of the electric circuit and the mechanical system may be seen.

The classical analogy between the electrical system and the mechanical system given in the above table of analogues is usually called the mass-inductance analogy. There is another analogy in common use called the mass-capacitance analogy. In this second analogy, the mechanical force is placed in analogy with the current, and the mechanical velocity is placed in analogy with the potential. This analogy will not be used in this discussion, although in certain special cases it presents some advantages over the classical analogy.[2]

The Lagrange Equation for the Electric Circuit

It can be seen that if we regard the electric circuit as a dynamical system with the following energy functions:

$$(4.10) \qquad T = \frac{Li^2}{2} = \frac{L\dot{q}^2}{2} \qquad \text{(the magnetic energy)}$$

(4.11) $V = \dfrac{Sq^2}{2}$ (the electric energy)

(4.12) $F = \dfrac{Ri^2}{2} = \dfrac{R\dot{q}^2}{2}$ (the dissipation function)

and

(4.13) $Q = e$ (the generalized force)

then it is apparent that the Lagrange equation (3.13) gives the Kirchhoff equation (4.1) for the electric circuit. It is thus apparent that from the Lagrangian point of view, the linear electrical circuit is a dynamical system whose energy functions are the magnetic energy, the electric energy, and one-half the rate of dissipation of electric energy into heat energy by the resistance.

5. SYSTEMS HAVING TWO DEGREES OF FREEDOM (CONSERVATIVE CASE)

Before we discuss the general case of the vibrations of a linear system having n degrees of freedom, it is instructive to discuss the simple case of a simple system that has no resistance or friction, whose motion is specified by

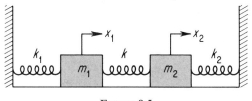

FIGURE 8.5

two coordinates. The free oscillations of the system will be studied. In order to fix the general ideas, let us consider the motion of the system of Fig. 8.5. This system consists of two masses m_1 and m_2 free to move on a frictionless horizontal plane. The masses are attached to each other by a

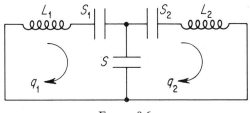

FIGURE 8.6

linear spring k and to two walls by linear springs k_1 and k_2. The position of the masses is specified by the two Cartesian coordinates x_1 and x_2 measured from the position of equilibrium of the system. It is evident that the classical electric circuit analogue of this system is the electric circuit depicted in Fig. 8.6. We shall center our attention on the mechanical system, realizing that the analysis of the oscillations of the circuit follows an exactly similar procedure.

The kinetic energy of the mechanical system is

$$(5.1) \qquad T = \tfrac{1}{2}(m_1 \dot{x}_1^2 + m_2 \dot{x}_2^2)$$

The potential energy of the system is the strain energy of the springs when the two masses are displaced by distances x_1 and x_2 from the equilibrium position. This energy is

$$(5.2) \qquad V = \tfrac{1}{2}[k_1 x_1^2 + k_2 x_2^2 + k(x_1 - x_2)^2]$$

It is convenient to introduce the coordinate vector

$$(5.3) \qquad (x) = \begin{bmatrix} x_1 \\ x_2 \end{bmatrix}$$

and the two square matrices

$$(5.4) \qquad [m] = \begin{bmatrix} m_1 & 0 \\ 0 & m_2 \end{bmatrix}$$

and

$$(5.5) \qquad [k] = \begin{bmatrix} (k_1 + k) & -k \\ -k & (k_2 + k) \end{bmatrix}$$

The matrix $[m]$ is the inertia matrix, and the matrix $[k]$ is the stiffness matrix. Both of these square matrices are symmetric. In terms of the coordinate vector (x) and the matrices $[m]$ and $[k]$, the kinetic energy T and the potential energy V may be written in the compact forms

$$(5.6) \qquad T = \tfrac{1}{2}(\dot{x})'[m](\dot{x})$$

and

$$(5.7) \qquad V = \tfrac{1}{2}(x)'[k](x)$$

We thus see that T and V are two quadratic forms. Before we obtain the Lagrangian equations of motion of the system, it is instructive to transform to new coordinates by a linear transformation so that in the new coordinates the quadratic forms T and V have a simpler form.

Introduction of Mass-Weighted Coordinates

In order to simplify the quadratic form T, let us introduce the new coordinates (z) by the transformation

$$(5.8) \qquad (z) = [m]^{1/2}(x)$$

where $[m]^{1/2}$ is a square matrix given by

$$(5.9) \qquad [m]^{1/2} = \begin{bmatrix} m_1^{1/2} & 0 \\ 0 & m_2^{1/2} \end{bmatrix}$$

The matrix $[m]^{1/2}$ has the property that

(5.10) $$[m]^{1/2}[m]^{1/2} = [m]$$

The Cartesian coordinates (x) are obtained by inverting the transformation (5.8) and thus obtaining

(5.11) $$(x) = [m]^{-1/2}(z)$$

The kinetic energy of the system has a very simple form in terms of the mass-weighted coordinates (z). If (5.11) is substituted into (5.6), we obtain

(5.12) $$T = \tfrac{1}{2}(\dot{x})'[m](\dot{x}) = \tfrac{1}{2}(\dot{z})'[m]^{-1/2}[m][m]^{-1/2}(\dot{z}) = \tfrac{1}{2}(\dot{z})'(\dot{z})$$

We see from Eq. (5.12) that the transformation to mass-weighted coordinates reduces the kinetic energy to the squares of the velocities as if the masses were unity.

If (5.11) is substituted into (5.7), the result is

(5.13) $$V = \tfrac{1}{2}(z)'[m]^{-1/2}[k][m]^{-1/2}(z)$$

We now let

(5.14) $$[K] = [m]^{-1/2}[k][m]^{-1/2} = \begin{bmatrix} \dfrac{(k_1 + k)}{m_1} & \dfrac{-k}{\sqrt{m_1 m_2}} \\ \dfrac{-k}{\sqrt{m_1 m_2}} & \dfrac{(k_2 + k)}{m_2} \end{bmatrix} = \begin{bmatrix} K_{11} & K_{12} \\ K_{21} & K_{22} \end{bmatrix}$$

In terms of the symmetric matrix $[K]$, the potential energy takes the form

(5.15) $$V = \tfrac{1}{2}(z)'[K](z)$$

Let us now introduce the orthogonal transformation

(5.16) $$(z) = \begin{bmatrix} \cos\theta & -\sin\theta \\ \sin\theta & \cos\theta \end{bmatrix} \begin{bmatrix} y_1 \\ y_2 \end{bmatrix} = L(y)$$

where $[L]$ is the square matrix of the transformation (5.16). Since $[L]$ is an orthogonal matrix, it has the fundamental property that

(5.17) $$[L]^{-1} = [L]'$$

If (5.16) is substituted into (5.12), the result is

(5.18) $$T = \tfrac{1}{2}(\dot{y})'[L]'[L](\dot{y}) = \tfrac{1}{2}(\dot{y})'(\dot{y})$$

The potential energy V is transformed to

(5.19) $$V = \tfrac{1}{2}(y)'[L]'[K][L](y)$$

In the second-order system which we are considering, we know that orthogonal transformation (5.16) is a transformation from the coordinates (z) to the coordinates (y), which may be interpreted as a rotation of axes, as shown in Fig. 8.7. By direct matrix multiplication, we obtain

$$(5.20) \qquad [K]_0 = [L]'[K][L] = \begin{bmatrix} A & B \\ B & C \end{bmatrix}$$

where

$$(5.21) \qquad A = K_{11} \cos^2 \theta + K_{12} \sin (2\theta) + K_{22} \sin^2 \theta$$

$$(5.22) \qquad B = (K_{22} - K_{11}) \frac{\sin (2\theta)}{2} + K_{12} \cos (2\theta)$$

$$(5.23) \qquad C = K_{11} \sin^2 \theta - K_{12} \sin (2\theta) + K_{22} \cos^2 (\theta)$$

It can be seen from (5.22) that the element B of the matrix $[K]_0$ can be made to vanish if the angle of rotation θ is chosen to be such that the following equation is satisfied:

$$(5.24) \quad \tan (2\theta) = \frac{2K_{12}}{(K_{11} - K_{22})}$$

For this angle of rotation, the potential energy V as given by (5.19) takes the form

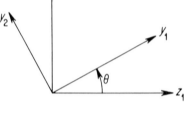

FIG. 8.7. Rotation of Axes

$$(5.25) \qquad V = \tfrac{1}{2}(y)'[K]_0(y)$$
$$= \tfrac{1}{2}(Ay_1^2 + Cy_2^2)$$

The kinetic energy T is given by (5.18) in the form

$$(5.26) \qquad T = \tfrac{1}{2}(\dot{y})'(\dot{y}) = \tfrac{1}{2}(\dot{y}_1^2 + \dot{y}_2^2)$$

The Lagrange equations of motion (3.13) now take the form

$$(5.27) \qquad \frac{d}{dt}\left(\frac{T}{\dot{y}_i}\right) + \frac{\partial V}{\partial y_i} = 0, \qquad i = 1, 2$$

If the differentiations are carried out, the results are

$$(5.28) \qquad \ddot{y}_1 + Ay_1 = 0, \quad \ddot{y}_2 + Cy_2 = 0$$

The coordinates y_1 and y_2 are seen to be uncoupled, and they perform independent oscillations. These coordinates are called the *normal coordinates* of the system.

Normal Coordinates in the Symmetrical Case

Before we proceed to the general solution, it is instructive to discuss the case of symmetry in which the system has the properties that

$$(5.29) \qquad m = m_1 = m_2 \quad \text{and} \quad k_1 = k_2 = k_0$$

In this case it is seen that $K_{11} = K_{22}$, and Eq. (5.24) reduces to

$$(5.30) \qquad \tan (2\theta) = \frac{2K_{12}}{0} = \infty, \quad \tan (2\theta) = \frac{\pi}{2}$$

Hence, the angle that uncouples the normal coordinates is the angle

(5.31) $$\theta = \frac{\pi}{4}$$

Hence,

$$\cos(\theta) = \sin(\theta) = (2)^{-1/2}$$

In this case we obtain A and C from (5.21) and (5.23) in the forms

(5.32) $$A = K_{11} + K_{12} = \frac{k_0}{m} = w_1^2$$

(5.33) $$C = K_{11} - K_{12} = \frac{(k_0 + 2k)}{m} = w_2^2$$

The system performs oscillations of simple harmonic types of angular frequencies w_1 and w_2.

The General Case of Two Degrees of Freedom

If the system has no symmetry, K_{11} and K_{22} will not be equal. If the angle θ is chosen to satisfy (5.24), then the normal coordinates satisfy the differential equations (5.28), whose solutions may be written in the form

(5.34) $$y_1 = a_1 \cos(w_1 t) + b_1 \sin(w_1 t), \quad y_2 = a_2 \cos(w_2 t) + b_2 \sin(w_2 t)$$

where $w_1 = A^{1/2}$, $w_2 = C^{+1/2}$, and a_i and b_i are arbitrary. The solution (5.34) may be conveniently represented in matrix form by introducing the two diagonal matrices $[C]$ and $[S]$, defined by

(5.35) $$[C] = \begin{bmatrix} \cos(w_1 t) & 0 \\ 0 & \cos(w_2 t) \end{bmatrix}, \quad [S] = \begin{bmatrix} \sin(w_1 t) & 0 \\ 0 & \sin(w_2 t) \end{bmatrix}$$

and two column matrices (a) and (b) of arbitrary constants of the form

(5.36) $$(a) = \begin{bmatrix} a_1 \\ a_2 \end{bmatrix}, \quad (b) = \begin{bmatrix} b_1 \\ b_2 \end{bmatrix}$$

The solution that describes the oscillations of the normal coordinates, (5.34), may be written in the compact form

(5.37) $$(y) = [C](a) + [S](b)$$

This form may be extended to the case of n degrees of freedom. By the use of the transformations (5.8) and (5.16), we can revert back to the original Cartesian coordinates (x) and obtain

(5.38) $$(x) = [m]^{-1/2}[L](y) = [m]^{-1/2}[L][C](a) + [m]^{-1/2}[L][S](b)$$

In order to determine the column matrices of arbitrary constants (a) and (b), it is necessary to know the initial displacements $(x)_0$ and velocities $(v)_0$ of the system.

At $t = 0$, the matrix $[C]$ becomes the unit matrix and $[S]$ vanishes, so

$$(5.39) \qquad (x)_0 = [m]^{-1/2}[L](a)$$

or, therefore,

$$(5.40) \qquad (a) = [L]'[m]^{1/2}(x)_0$$

This equation determines the arbitrary column matrix (a).

We notice also that at $t = 0$, $d/dt\,[C]$ vanishes, whereas $d/dt\,[S] = [w]$ where $[w]$ is the diagonal matrix with the elements w_i arranged down its leading diagonal. Therefore,

$$(5.41) \qquad (v)_0 = [m]^{-1/2}[L][w](b)$$

or, therefore,

$$(5.42) \qquad (b) = [w]^{-1}[L]'[m]^{1/2}(v)_0$$

This equation determines the arbitrary column matrix (b). If we introduce the notation

$$(5.43) \qquad [P] = [m]^{-1/2}[L]$$

then (5.40) and (5.43) may be substituted into (5.38) and the solution obtained in the form

$$(5.44) \qquad (x) = [P][C][P]^{-1}(x)_0 + [P][S][w]^{-1}[P]^{-1}(v)_0$$

In the case of symmetry (5.29), the matrix $[P]$ has the form

$$(5.45) \qquad [P] = m^{1/2}[L]$$

The general solution in this case becomes

$$(5.46) \qquad (x) = [L][C][L]'(x)_0 + [L][S][w]^{-1}[L]'(v)_0$$

where, in this case, the matrix $[L]$ has the form

$$(5.47) \qquad [L] = 2^{-1/2}\begin{bmatrix} 1 & -1 \\ 1 & 1 \end{bmatrix}$$

If the system starts from rest so that $(v)_0 = (0)$, the solution is

$$(5.48) \qquad (x) = \frac{1}{2}\begin{bmatrix} 1 & -1 \\ 1 & 1 \end{bmatrix}\begin{bmatrix} \cos(w_1 t) & 0 \\ 0 & \cos(w_2 t) \end{bmatrix}\begin{bmatrix} 1 & 1 \\ -1 & 1 \end{bmatrix}\begin{bmatrix} x_{01} \\ x_{02} \end{bmatrix}$$

If the matrix multiplication is performed, the result is

$$(5.49) \qquad \begin{aligned} x_1 &= (x_{01} + x_{02})\frac{\cos}{2}(w_1 t) + (x_{01} - x_{02})\frac{\cos}{2}(w_2 t) \\[2mm] x_2 &= (x_{01} + x_{02})\frac{\cos}{2}(w_1 t) - (x_{01} - x_{02})\frac{\cos}{2}(w_2 t) \end{aligned}$$

6. THE GENERAL CASE: MASS-WEIGHTED COORDINATES

The general case of n degrees of freedom, in which the system's behavior is expressed in mass-weighted coordinates, is a direct generalization of the simple two degrees of freedom discussed in detail in Sec. 5. Mass-weighted coordinates are particularly suitable when it is desired to find the normal coordinates (y), because the transformation connecting the mass-weighted coordinates (z) and the normal coordinates (y) is an orthogonal one of the form

$$(6.1) \qquad (z) = [L](y), \quad \text{where } [L]^{-1} = [L]'$$

in the general case. Equation (6.1) is a generalization of (5.16). Although mass-weighted coordinates simplify the analysis necessary to obtain the normal coordinates, they can be introduced only if the inertia matrix $[m]$ has the diagonal form

$$(6.2) \qquad [m] = \begin{bmatrix} m_1 & 0 & \dots & 0 \\ 0 & m_2 & \dots & 0 \\ . & . & \dots & . \\ 0 & 0 & \dots & m_n \end{bmatrix}$$

This is the case when the system under consideration involves no *dynamic coupling* terms. Terms involving dynamic coupling give rise to off-diagonal terms in the inertia matrix (6.2). Systems involving dynamic coupling will be discussed in the next section.

In practical applications, many systems have inertia matrices of the form (6.2) and they therefore merit special consideration. Such systems have kinetic energy functions of the general form

$$(6.3) \qquad T = \tfrac{1}{2}(\dot{x})'[m](\dot{x})$$

where (x) is the coordinate matrix, a column matrix of the nth order, and $(\dot{x})$ is the time derivative of the coordinate matrix, or the velocity matrix. If $[m]$ has the diagonal form (6.2), then (6.3), if expanded, is seen to be a sum of squares of the velocities multiplied by the inertia coefficients. If we now introduce a matrix $[m]^{1/2}$, a diagonal matrix similar to (5.9) whose elements are the square roots of the elements of the inertia matrix (6.2), then the mass-weighted coordinates (z) are introduced by the transformation

$$(6.4) \qquad (z) = [m]^{1/2}(x)$$

This transformation enables the kinetic energy (6.3) to be expressed in the form

$$(6.5) \qquad T = \tfrac{1}{2}(\dot{z})'(\dot{z})$$

as shown in (5.12).

In the general case of n degrees of freedom, the stiffness matrix $[k]$ has the form

$$
(6.6) \qquad [k] = \begin{bmatrix}
k_{11} & k_{12} & k_{13} & \cdots & k_{1n} \\
k_{21} & k_{22} & k_{23} & \cdots & k_{2n} \\
\cdot & \cdot & \cdot & \cdots & \cdot \\
k_{n1} & k_{n2} & k_{n3} & \cdots & k_{nn}
\end{bmatrix}
$$

where $k_{ij} = k_{ji}$ so that $[k]' = [k]$; that is, $[k]$ is a symmetric matrix. The potential energy is now given by the quadratic function V of the form

$$
(6.7) \qquad V = \tfrac{1}{2}(x)'[k](x)
$$

As indicated in (5.13), the transformation (6.4) transforms (6.7) into

$$
(6.8) \qquad V = \tfrac{1}{2}(z)'[K](z)
$$

where the new matrix $[K]$ is given by

$$
(6.9) \qquad [K] = [m]^{-1/2}[k][m]^{-1/2}
$$

The elements of the matrix $[K]$ are seen to be

$$
(6.10) \qquad K_{ij} = \frac{k_{ij}}{(m_i m_j)^{1/2}}
$$

$[K]$ is a symmetric matrix. To determine the normal coordinates (y) in this general case, it is necessary to obtain an orthogonal matrix $[L]$ that diagonalizes the symmetric matrix $[K]$ in the form

$$
(6.11) \qquad [L]'[K][L] = \begin{bmatrix}
\mu_1 & 0 & 0 & \cdots & 0 \\
0 & \mu_2 & 0 & \cdots & 0 \\
0 & 0 & \mu_3 & \cdots & 0 \\
\cdot & \cdot & \cdot & \cdots & \cdot \\
0 & 0 & 0 & \cdots & \mu_n
\end{bmatrix} = [K]_0
$$

Once the matrix $[L]$ is obtained, then the transformation

$$
(6.12) \qquad (z) = [L](y)
$$

applied to the kinetic energy T of (6.5) and the potential energy V of (6.8) reduces these two expressions to

$$
(6.13) \qquad T = \tfrac{1}{2}(\dot{y})'(\dot{y})
$$

and

$$
(6.14) \qquad V = \tfrac{1}{2}(y)'[K]_0(y)
$$

The kinetic and potential energy expressions are, therefore, reduced to sums of squares of the velocities $\dot{y}_i$ and the coordinates y_i. These coordinates satisfy the Lagrange equations

(6.15) $$\ddot{y}_i + \mu_i y_i = 0, \quad i = 1, 2, 3, \ldots, n$$

These are the Eqs. (5.28) for the two-degrees-of-freedom case. The co-ordinates (y) are the normal coordinates of the system.

In order to obtain the required orthogonal matrix $[L]$ of (6.11), we first begin by reducing $[K]$ to the diagonal form. This can be done by selecting a column vector (A) that satisfies the equation

(6.16) $$[K](A) = \mu(A)$$

This may also be written in the form

(6.17) $$(\mu U - [K])(A) = (0)$$

where U is the nth-order unit matrix. Since this is a set of homogeneous linear equations in the elements of the vector (A), we have

(6.18) $$\det (\mu U - [K]) = 0$$

This is the characteristic equation of the symmetric matrix $[K]$. The roots of this equation μ_i, $i = 1, 2, 3, \ldots, n$, are, therefore, the eigenvalues of $[K]$. Since

$$p(\mu) = \det (\mu U - [K])$$

is the characteristic polynomial of $[K]$, to each eigenvalue μ_i, there is as-sociated a column matrix $(A)_i$ or eigenvector of $[K]$ that satisfies (6.17) or

(6.19) $$[K](A)_i = \mu_i(A)_i, \quad i = 1, 2, 3, \ldots, n$$

From these n eigenvectors $(A)_i$, we construct the square matrix

(6.20) $$[A] = [A_{ji}],$$

where the subscript i refers to the particular eigenvalue μ_i. With this nota-tion, the set of equations (6.18) may be written as a single equation of the form

(6.21) $$[K][A] = [A][K]_0$$

where $[K]_0$ is the diagonal matrix of the eigenvalues of $[K]$ given by (6.11). In order to obtain the required orthogonal matrix $[L]$ from the square matrix $[A]$, write $[A]$ in the partitioned form

(6.22) $$[A] = [(A)_1 \ (A)_2 \ (A)_3 \ \ldots \ (A)_n] = [A_{ji}]$$

where $(A)_i$ is the typical eigenvector associated with the eigenvalue μ_i. We now construct a square matrix $[L]$ whose typical element L_{ji} is given by the equation

(6.23) $$[L] = [L_{ji}], \quad L_{ji} = \frac{A_{ji}}{[(A)_i'(A)_i]^{1/2}}$$

It is easy to show that $[L]$ is an orthogonal matrix with the property that

(6.24) $$[K][L] = [L][K]_0$$

and

(6.25) $$[L]^{-1} = [L]'$$

If (6.24) is premultiplied by $[L]'$, Eq. (6.11) is satisfied. Therefore, $[L]$ is the desired matrix. In computing the elements of $[L]$ from the eigenvectors of $[K]$, it is convenient to place $A_{1i} = 1$; this can be done, since the eigenvectors are not determined uniquely by (6.19), but only the *ratios* of the numbers A_{ji} are determined. Once the matrix $[L]$ has been determined, the solution of the problem in terms of the initial conditions $(x)_0$ and $(v)_0$ is given by (5.44). The matrices $[C]$ and $[S]$ are now diagonal matrices of the form (5.35) of the nth order. The natural angular frequencies of the system w_i are given in terms of the eigenvalues of $[K]$ in the form

(6.26) $$w_i = (\mu_i)^{1/2}, \qquad i = 1, 2, 3, \ldots, n$$

7. THE VIBRATION OF CONSERVATIVE SYSTEMS WITH DYNAMIC COUPLING

In Secs. 5 and 6, we have considered the vibration of systems whose potential energy function V contained coupling terms; that is, it contained terms involving products of the coordinates. However, the kinetic energy function T contained only a sum of squares of the velocities multiplied by certain inertia coefficients. In this section the oscillation of systems that contain products of the velocities will be considered. Terms involving the products of the velocities of the system are called *dynamic coupling terms*. The system in this case is said to have *dynamic coupling* between the degrees of freedom defined by the generalized coordinates. Such systems are characterized by having kinetic energy functions of the form

(7.1) $$T = \tfrac{1}{2}(\dot{q})'[m](\dot{q})$$

where $(\dot{q})$ is a vector whose n elements are the generalized velocities, and $[m] = [m_{rs}]$ is an nth-order square matrix of inertia coefficients. The inertia matrix is a symmetric matrix so that $[m]' = [m]$, but it is no longer a diagonal matrix as in the case of systems that do not contain dynamic coupling terms.

The potential energy function V is a quadratic form involving the stiffness elements of the matrix $[k]$ which may be written as

(7.2) $$V = \tfrac{1}{2}(q)'[k](q)$$

In this expression, (q) is a vector whose elements are the n generalized coordinates q_i, and $[k]$ is the square stiffness matrix of the nth order. $[k]$ is a symmetric matrix.

It can be seen that the only difference between systems having dynamic coupling and systems of the type discussed in Sec. 6 is that the square inertia matrix $[m]$ now contains elements that are not on the principal diagonal. If the kinetic energy function T and the potential energy function V are now differentiated as indicated by the Lagrange equations,

$$(7.3) \qquad \frac{d}{dt}\left(\frac{\partial T}{\partial \dot{q}_i}\right) - \frac{\partial T}{\partial q_i} + \frac{\partial V}{\partial q_i} = 0, \qquad i = 1, 2, 3, \ldots, n$$

the following equations of motion are obtained:

$$(7.4) \qquad [m](\ddot{q}) + [k](q) = (0)$$

The Dynamical Matrix $[D]$

In many systems of practical importance, it is simpler to obtain the inverse stiffness, or flexibility, matrix $[k]^{-1} = [\phi]$ than it is to obtain the stiffness matrix itself either by direct measurement or by calculation. In such cases all the necessary information relative to the system can be expressed in the form of the matrix $[D]$, which is called the *dynamical matrix* in the modern literature of vibration theory. This matrix is defined by

$$(7.5) \qquad [D] = [k]^{-1}[m] = [\phi][m], \quad \text{(the dynamical matrix)}$$

If the matrix differential equation (7.4) is premultiplied by $[k]^{-1}$, the result may be written in the form

$$(7.6) \qquad [D](\ddot{q}) + (q) = (0)$$

The Inverse Dynamical Matrix $[W]$

Sometimes in the analysis of dynamical systems, it happens that the matrix $[k]$ is a singular matrix and, therefore, $[k]^{-1}$ does not exist. In this case the dynamical matrix $[D]$ cannot be obtained. In such cases it is convenient to introduce the *inverse dynamical matrix* $[W] = [D]^{-1}$. This matrix is given by

$$(7.7) \qquad [W] = [m]^{-1}[k] = [D]^{-1}, \quad \text{(the inverse dynamical matrix)}$$

To obtain the equations of motion of the system in terms of the inverse dynamical matrix, it is necessary only to premultiply Eq. (7.4) by $[m]^{-1}$ and obtain

$$(7.8) \qquad (\ddot{q}) + [W](q) = (0)$$

It is, therefore, seen that the differential equations of the system may be expressed in the equivalent alternative forms (7.6) and (7.8). In general, the matrices $[D]$ and $[W]$ are not symmetric matrices.

The Classical Solution: The Natural Frequencies and Modes

In order to study the oscillations of the general system formulated in terms of the inverse dynamical matrix $[W]$ by (7.8), let us search for an oscillatory solution of this matrix differential equation of the form

$$(7.9) \qquad\qquad (q) = (A) \sin (wt + \theta)$$

where (A) is a column matrix of n unknown amplitudes, w is an angular frequency to be determined, and θ is a phase angle. If this assumed solution is substituted into (7.8), the following result is obtained:

$$(7.10) \qquad\qquad -w^2(A) + [W](A) = (0)$$

after the trigonometric function $\sin (wt + \theta)$ has been divided from both terms. If we let

$$(7.11) \qquad\qquad w^2 = \mu$$

Eq. (7.10) may be written in the following alternative form:

$$(7.12) \qquad (\mu U - [W])(A) = (0), \qquad U = n\text{th-order unit matrix}$$

This equation represents a set of linear homogeneous equations in the elements of the column matrix (A). In order for a nontrivial solution of these equations to be permissible, it is necessary that the determinant of the coefficients of the elements of (A) vanish. We have, therefore,

$$(7.13) \qquad\qquad \det (\mu U - [W]) = 0$$

This equation is recognized as the characteristic equation of the inverse dynamical matrix $[W]$. In general, it is an equation of the nth degree. Let it be assumed that the n roots of (7.13) are distinct and have the values, $\mu_1, \mu_2, \ldots, \mu_n$. These roots are the eigenvalues of $[W]$. To each eigenvalue μ_i there corresponds a natural frequency of oscillation w_i given by (7.11) in the form

$$(7.14) \qquad\qquad w_i = (\mu_i)^{1/2}, \qquad i = 1, 2, 3, \ldots, n$$

The Modal Columns

From (7.12) it can be seen that to each eigenvalue μ_i there corresponds a column $(A)_i$ or eigenvector of the matrix $[W]$ that satisfies the equation

$$(7.15) \qquad\qquad [W](A)_i = \mu_i(A)_i, \qquad i = 1, 2, 3, \ldots, n$$

In the literature of vibration theory, the eigenvectors $(A)_i$ are called *modal columns*.

Orthogonality of the Modal Columns

Since $[W] = [m]^{-1}[k]$, Eq. (7.15) may also be written in the form

(7.16) $$[k](A)_i = \mu_i[m](A)_i$$

Let us write the same equation with subscript j so that

(7.17) $$[k](A)_j = \mu_j[m](A)_j$$

If we now premultiply (7.16) by $(A)'_j$ and (7.17) by $(A)'_i$, we obtain

(7.18) $$(A)'_j[k](A)_i = \mu_i(A)'_j[m](A)_i$$

(7.19) $$(A)'_i[k](A)_j = \mu_j(A)'_i[m](A)_j$$

We recall that $[k]$ and $[m]$ are symmetric matrices; hence, if we take the transpose of both sides of (7.19), we obtain

(7.20) $$(A)'_j[k](A)_i = \mu_j(A)'_j[m](A)_i$$

If we now subtract (7.20) from (7.18), the result is

(7.21) $$0 = (\mu_i - \mu_j)(A)'_j[m](A)_i$$

Since, by hypothesis, μ_i and μ_j are two *distinct* eigenvalues, we must have

(7.22) $$(A)'_j[m](A)_i = 0, \qquad i \neq j$$

If this is now substituted into (7.20), we see that we must also have

(7.23) $$(A)'_j[k](A)_i = 0, \qquad i \neq j$$

The relations (7.22) and (7.23) are a form of generalized orthogonal relations satisfied by the modal columns or eigenvectors of the inverse dynamical matrix $[W]$.

The Modal Matrix $[A]$

We now construct a partitioned square matrix $[A]$ by placing the modal columns or eigenvectors $(A)_i$ side by side to form a square array of numbers in the form

(7.24) $$[A] = [(A)_1 \quad (A)_2 \quad \ldots \quad (A)_n] = [A_{ji}]$$

This square matrix $[A]$ is called *the modal matrix* of the matrix $[W]$.

The set of equations (7.15) may be written as a single equation in terms of the modal matrix. This equation has the form

(7.25) $$[W][A] = [A][d]$$

where $[d]$ is a diagonal matrix whose elements are the eigenvalues μ_i. $[d]$ has the form

(7.26) $$[d] = \begin{bmatrix} \mu_1 & 0 & 0 & \ldots & 0 \\ 0 & \mu_2 & 0 & \ldots & 0 \\ . & . & . & \ldots & . \\ 0 & 0 & 0 & \ldots & \mu_n \end{bmatrix}$$

If the eigenvalues of $[W]$ are distinct, $[A]$ can be shown to be nonsingular and, therefore, to have an inverse $[A]^{-1}$. If (7.25) is postmultiplied by $[A]^{-1}$, the result is

$$(7.27) \qquad\qquad [W] = [A][d][A]^{-1}$$

Therefore, the modal matrix $[A]$ reduces the inverse dynamical matrix $[W]$ to the diagonal form.

The Eigenvectors of the Dynamical Matrix $[D]$

Equation (7.15) indicates that the column $(A)_i$ is an eigenvector of the inverse dynamical matrix $[W]$ associated with the eigenvalue μ_i. It is instructive to determine what relations exist between the eigenvectors of $[W]$ and the eigenvectors of the dynamical matrix $[D]$. In order to discover these relations, we may write (7.15) in the form

$$(7.28) \qquad\qquad [D]^{-1}(A)_i = \mu_i(A)_i$$

or, if (7.28) is premultiplied by $[D]$, the result may be written in the form

$$(7.29) \qquad\qquad [D](A)_i = \frac{1}{\mu_i}(A)_i = z_i(A)_i$$

where $z_i = 1/\mu_i$. It is, therefore, evident from (7.29) that the column $(A)_i$ is also an eigenvector of the dynamical matrix $[D]$ but is associated with the eigenvalue $1/\mu_i = z_i$ of the matrix $[D]$. The angular frequency w_i of the system corresponding to the eigenvalue μ_i is given by (7.14) in the form

$$(7.30) \qquad\qquad w_i = (\mu_i)^{1/2} = \left(\frac{1}{z_i}\right)^{1/2}, \qquad i = 1, 2, 3, \ldots, n$$

We see, therefore, that the eigenvector $(A)_i$ is the modal column associated with the angular frequency w_i regardless of whether the analysis is formulated in terms of the inverse dynamical matrix $[W]$ or the dynamical matrix $[D]$. It is seen from (7.30) that the largest eigenvalue of $[D]$ gives the lowest frequency of oscillation, whereas the largest eigenvalue of $[W]$ gives the highest frequency of the system.

8. FUNDAMENTAL PROPERTIES OF THE MODAL MATRIX [A]

The modal matrix $[A]$ is defined by (7.24) as the square matrix formed from the n eigenvectors or modal columns $(A)_i$. If the eigenvalues of the inverse dynamical matrix $[W]$ are distinct, we have shown that the modal columns $(A)_i$ satisfy the *orthogonality* relations (7.22) and (7.23). Let us now take the transpose of $[A]$ and form the product $[A]'[m][A]$. Then, by direct multiplication we obtain

$$(8.1) \quad [A]'[m][A] = \begin{bmatrix} (A)'_1[m](A)_1 & (A)'_1[m](A)_2 & \cdots & (A)'_1[m](A)_n \\ & \cdot & & \cdot \\ & \cdot & \cdots & \cdot \\ (A)'_n[m](A)_1 & (A)'_n[m](A)_2 & \cdots & (A)'_n[m](A)_n \end{bmatrix}$$
$$= [P] = [P_{ii}]$$

where

(8.2)
$$P_{ii} = (A)'_i[m](A)_i$$

It is thus evident that the matrix $[P]$ is a diagonal matrix, since by the orthogonality relation (7.22) all the elements of (8.1) that are not on the principal diagonal are equal to zero. By direct multiplication, it can also be shown that the product $[A]'[k][A]$ has the diagonal form

(8.3)
$$[A]'[k][A] = [S] = [S_{ii}], \qquad i = 1, 2, 3, \ldots, n$$

where

(8.4)
$$S_{ii} = (A)'_i[k](A)_i = \mu_i(A)'_i[m](A)_i = \mu_i P_{ii}$$

This is a consequence of the orthogonality relation (7.23) and the relation (7.18). Therefore, $[S]$ is a diagonal matrix.

If (8.1) is premultiplied by $[P]^{-1}$, the result is

(8.5)
$$[P]^{-1}[A]'[m][A] = [U]$$

where $[U]$ is the nth-order unit matrix. If we now postmultiply (8.5) by $[A]^{-1}$, the result is

(8.6)
$$[A]^{-1} = [P]^{-1}[A]'[m]$$

This is a convenient expression for the inverse of the modal matrix. The inverse $[P]^{-1}$ is easily obtained, since $[P]$ is a diagonal matrix.

Normal Coordinates

Let us now introduce the new coordinates (y) related to the generalized coordinates (q) by the transformation

(8.7)
$$(q) = [A](y)$$

It is instructive to transform the kinetic energy function T and the potential energy function V to the new coordinates (y). The kinetic energy is transformed by the equation

(8.8)
$$T = \tfrac{1}{2}(\dot{q})'[m](\dot{q}) = \tfrac{1}{2}(\dot{y})'[A]'[m][A](\dot{y}) = \tfrac{1}{2}(\dot{y})'[P](\dot{y})$$

Since $[P]$ is a diagonal matrix, T is now expressed as the sum of terms of the form $P_{ii}\dot{y}_i^2/2$.

The potential energy function is transformed by the equation

(8.9)
$$V = \tfrac{1}{2}(q)'[k](q) = \tfrac{1}{2}(y)'[A]'[k][A](y) = \tfrac{1}{2}(y)'[S](y)$$

The matrix $[S]$ is a diagonal matrix, so it is seen from (8.9) that V is also expressed in a simple manner as the sum of terms of the form $S_{ii}y_i^2/2$. If now the Lagrange equations are applied to the functions T and V expressed in terms of the coordinates (y), the following equations are obtained:

(8.10)
$$P_{ii}\ddot{y}_i + S_{ii}y_i = 0, \qquad i = 1, 2, 3, \ldots; n$$

However, by (8.4) we see that $S_{ii} = \mu_i P_{ii} = w_i^2 P_{ii}$. Hence, if this expression for S_{ii} is substituted into (8.10) and the result is divided by P_{ii}, we obtain

(8.11) $\ddot{y}_i + w_i^2 y_i = 0$, $i = 1, 2, 3, \ldots, n$

It is thus evident that the coordinates y_i perform simple harmonic oscillations of the form

(8.12) $y_i = a_i \cos(w_i t) + b_i \sin(w_i t)$, $i = 1, 2, 3, \ldots, n$

where a_i and b_i are arbitrary constants. The coordinates y_i may, therefore, be taken as the *normal coordinates* of the system. If it is desired to obtain a complete solution of the problem in terms of the initial conditions, it is possible to proceed in a manner similar to that described in Sec. 5. If a diagonal matrix $[C]$ whose elements are the functions $\cos(w_i t)$ and another diagonal matrix $[S]$ whose elements are the functions $\sin(w_i t)$ are introduced, then it is possible to express the set of Eq. (8.12) in the form

(8.13) $(y) = [C(t)](a) + [S(t)](b)$

where (a) and (b) are columns of the arbitrary constants a_i and b_i. The generalized coordinates of the problem (q) may now be obtained by (8.7) in the form

(8.14) $(q) = [A](y) = [A][C(t)](a) + [A][S(t)](b)$

Let the given initial conditions at $t = 0$ be expressed in the form

(8.15) $(q)_{t=0} = (q)_0$, $(\dot{q})_{t=0} = (v)_0$

At $t = 0$, we have

$[C(0)] = [U]$,   the unit matrix. $[S(0)] = [0]$

(8.16)
$$\frac{d}{dt}[C(t)]_{t=0} = [0], \quad \frac{d}{dt}[S(t)]_{t=0} = [w_i]$$

where $[w_i]$ is a diagonal matrix whose elements are w_i arranged down its principal diagonal. If these properties of the matrices $[C(t)]$ and $[S(t)]$ are used, we have

(8.17) $(q)_{t=0} = [A][C(0)](a) = [A](a) = (q)_0$

or

(8.18) $(a) = [A]^{-1}(q)_0$

and

(8.19) $(\dot{q})_{t=0} = (v)_0 = [A][w_i](b)$

hence,

(8.20) $(b) = [w_i]^{-1}[A]^{-1}(v)_0$

Equations (8.18) and (8.20) determine the arbitrary constants (*a*) and (*b*). If these expressions for (*a*) and (*b*) are substituted into the solution (8.14), the result is

(8.21) $(q) = [A][C(t)][A]^{-1}(q)_0 + [A][S(t)][w_i]^{-1}[A]^{-1}(v)_0$

This is the complete solution of the vibration problem in terms of the initial displacements and velocities.   The inverse of the dynamical matrix [*A*] may be obtained by the use of (8.6) in the form $[A]^{-1} = [P]^{-1}[A]'[m]$.

Although (8.21) gives the general solution of the problem for the case of distinct eigenvalues μ_i of the inverse dynamical matrix [*W*], in most of the vibration problems which are encountered in engineering the interest is not in the general solution, but the attention of the investigator is usually centered in discovering the spectrum of natural frequencies and the nature of the various normal modes.   In such cases it is necessary only to find the w_i's and the corresponding $(A)_i$'s.   An iterative procedure for determining these quantities is given in a later section.

9. THE CASE OF THREE COUPLED PENDULUMS

In order to illustrate the general theory discussed in the last two sections, we shall consider the case of three identical pendulums, as shown in Fig. 8.8.

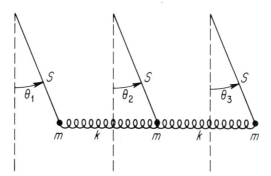

FIG. 8.8. Three Coupled Pendulums

The three pendulums are coupled by two identical springs of stiffness *k* attached to the masses of the pendulums.   Each pendulum has a length *S* and consists of a weightless rod from which is suspended a mass *m*.   The three masses are attached to each other by two springs of stiffness *k* and of negligible weight.   In order to discuss the oscillations of this system, it is convenient to choose the angles θ_1, θ_2, and θ_3 measured from the vertical, as shown in Fig. 8.7 as the generalized coordinates.   It will be assumed that the oscillations are small so that we may make the following approximations:

(9.1) $\sin \theta_i \doteq \theta_i, \quad \cos \theta_i \doteq 1 - \dfrac{\theta_i^2}{2}, \quad i = 1, 2, 3$

The kinetic energy of the system is given by

(9.2) $$T = \tfrac{1}{2}mS^2(\dot{\theta}_1^2 + \dot{\theta}_2^2 + \dot{\theta}_3^2)$$

It will be assumed that when $\theta_i = 0$, $i = 1, 2, 3$, the system is in equilibrium and the springs are not strained. If the angles θ_i are assumed to be small (less than 7 deg.), then the potential energy V is given by the following expression to a high degree of accuracy.

(9.3) $$V = \tfrac{1}{2}mgS(\theta_1^2 + \theta_2^2 + \theta_3^2) + \tfrac{1}{2}kS^2[(\theta_2 - \theta_1)^2 + (\theta_3 - \theta_2)^2]$$

The expressions for the kinetic energy T and the potential energy V may be written in the form

(9.4) $$T = \tfrac{1}{2}(\dot{\theta})'[M](\dot{\theta}) \quad \text{and} \quad V = \tfrac{1}{2}(\theta)'[K](\theta)$$

where (θ) is a column matrix of the three angular coordinates, and $(\dot{\theta})$ is a column matrix whose elements are the three angular velocities $\dot{\theta}_i$. The matrices $[M]$ and $[K]$ are square matrices given by

(9.5) $$[M] = mS^2[U]$$

where $[U]$ is the unit matrix of the third order.

(9.6) $$[K] = \begin{bmatrix} (mgS + kS^2) & -kS^2 & 0 \\ -kS^2 & (mgS + 2kS^2) & -kS^2 \\ 0 & -kS^2 & (mgS + kS^2) \end{bmatrix}$$

The Lagrangian equations of the system are

(9.7) $$[M](\ddot{\theta}) + [K](\theta) = (0)$$

The inverse dynamical matrix of the system $[W] = [M]^{-1}[K]$ is

(9.8) $$[W] = [M]^{-1}[K] = \frac{1}{mS^2}[K] = \begin{bmatrix} \left(\dfrac{g}{S} + \dfrac{k}{m}\right) & -\dfrac{k}{m} & 0 \\ -\dfrac{k}{m} & \left(\dfrac{g}{S} + \dfrac{2k}{m}\right) & -\dfrac{k}{m} \\ 0 & -\dfrac{k}{m} & \left(\dfrac{g}{S} + \dfrac{k}{m}\right) \end{bmatrix}$$

The matrix $[W]$ may be written in the more compact form

(9.9) $$[W] = \begin{bmatrix} (a + b) & -b & 0 \\ -b & (a + 2b) & -b \\ 0 & -b & (a + b) \end{bmatrix}$$

where

(9.10) $$a = \frac{g}{S}, \quad b = \frac{k}{m}$$

The characteristic equation of the inverse dynamical matrix is

$$(9.11) \quad \det(\mu U - [W]) = \begin{bmatrix} \mu - (a+b) & b & 0 \\ b & \mu - (a+2b) & b \\ 0 & b & \mu - (a+b) \end{bmatrix}$$

$$= (\mu - a)[\mu - (a+b)][\mu - (a+3b)]$$

The eigenvalues of $[W]$ are, therefore,

$$(9.12) \qquad \mu_1 = a, \quad \mu_2 = (a+b), \quad \mu_3 = (a+3b)$$

The eigenvectors $(A)_i$, or modal columns, satisfy the equation

$$(9.13) \qquad [W](A)_i = \mu_i(A)_i, \quad i = 1, 2, 3$$

If the first element of each modal column $(A)_i$ is placed equal to unity and Eq. (9.13) is expanded, it is easily seen that the modal columns are then given by the equations

$$(9.14) \qquad (A)_1 = \begin{bmatrix} 1 \\ 1 \\ 1 \end{bmatrix}, \quad (A)_2 = \begin{bmatrix} 1 \\ 0 \\ -1 \end{bmatrix}, \quad (A)_3 = \begin{bmatrix} 1 \\ -2 \\ 1 \end{bmatrix}$$

These are the modes of oscillation of the three pendulums that correspond to the natural angular frequencies

$$w_1 = (\mu_1)^{1/2} = \left(\frac{g}{S}\right)^{1/2}$$

$$w_2 = (\mu_2)^{1/2} = \left(\frac{g}{S} + \frac{k}{m}\right)^{1/2}$$

$$w_3 = (\mu_3)^{1/2} = \left(\frac{g}{S} + \frac{3k}{m}\right)^{1/2}$$

If the system is oscillating in mode $(A)_1$, the three pendulums swing back and forth in synchronism with the angular frequency w_1. In this mode the springs preserve their natural length, and the restoring force is entirely due to gravity. When the system is oscillating in mode $(A)_2$, the two pendulums at the left and at the right swing in opposition, whereas the middle pendulum stands still. In this second mode of oscillation, the angular frequency of the motion is w_2. When the system is oscillating in its third mode $(A)_3$, the pendulums at the left and at the right swing in unison, whereas the middle pendulum swings in opposition with twice the amplitude. This motion takes place with the angular frequency of w_3.

Orthogonality of the Modes

The orthogonality relation of the modal columns (7.22) in this special case takes the following form:

$$(9.15) \qquad (A)'_j[M](A)_i = mS^2(A)'_j(A)_i = 0, \qquad i \neq j$$

so that

$$(9.16) \qquad (A)'_j(A)_i = 0, \qquad i \neq j$$

This simplification is effected because the inertia matrix $[M]$ in this case has the simple form $[M] = mS^2[U]$ given by (9.5).

The Modal Matrix

The square modal matrix $[A]$ may now be constructed from the three modal columns (9.14) in the form

$$(9.17) \qquad [A] = \begin{bmatrix} 1 & 1 & 1 \\ 1 & 0 & -2 \\ 1 & -1 & 1 \end{bmatrix}$$

The transpose of the modal matrix $[A]$ is, in this case,

$$(9.18) \qquad [A]' = \begin{bmatrix} 1 & 1 & 1 \\ 1 & 0 & -1 \\ 1 & -2 & 1 \end{bmatrix}$$

Equation (8.1) now takes the form

$$(9.19) \qquad [A]'[m][A] = mS^2[A]'[A] = mS^2 \begin{bmatrix} 3 & 0 & 0 \\ 0 & 2 & 0 \\ 0 & 0 & 6 \end{bmatrix} = [P]$$

Therefore, we have

$$(9.20) \qquad [P]^{-1} = \frac{1}{mS^2} \begin{bmatrix} \frac{1}{3} & 0 & 0 \\ 0 & \frac{1}{2} & 0 \\ 0 & 0 & \frac{1}{6} \end{bmatrix}$$

Hence, by (8.6) we have $[A]^{-1}$ in the form

$$(9.21) \qquad [A]^{-1} = [P]^{-1}[A]'[M] = \frac{1}{6} \begin{bmatrix} 2 & 2 & 2 \\ 3 & 0 & -3 \\ 1 & -2 & 1 \end{bmatrix}$$

The normal coordinates, (y) coordinates, are related to the coordinates (θ) by (8.7). In this case this equation takes the form

$$(9.22) \qquad (\theta) = [A](y) = \begin{bmatrix} 1 & 1 & 1 \\ 1 & 0 & -2 \\ 1 & -1 & 1 \end{bmatrix} \begin{bmatrix} y_1 \\ y_2 \\ y_3 \end{bmatrix} = \begin{bmatrix} \theta_1 \\ \theta_2 \\ \theta_3 \end{bmatrix}$$

or

$$(9.23) \qquad (y) = [A]^{-1}(\theta) = \frac{1}{6} \begin{bmatrix} 2 & 2 & 2 \\ 3 & 0 & -3 \\ 1 & -2 & 1 \end{bmatrix} \begin{bmatrix} \theta_1 \\ \theta_2 \\ \theta_3 \end{bmatrix} = \begin{bmatrix} y_1 \\ y_2 \\ y_3 \end{bmatrix}$$

If the system is started with no initial angular velocity but with initial angular displacements $(\theta)_0$, the solution is then given by (8.21) in the form

$$(9.24) \qquad (\theta) = [A][C(t)][A]^{-1}(\theta)_0$$

If this equation is expanded, it has the form

$$(9.25) \quad \begin{bmatrix} \theta_1 \\ \theta_2 \\ \theta_3 \end{bmatrix}$$

$$= \begin{bmatrix} 1 & 1 & 1 \\ 1 & 0 & -2 \\ 1 & -1 & 1 \end{bmatrix} \begin{bmatrix} \cos w_1 t & 0 & 0 \\ 0 & \cos w_2 t & 0 \\ 0 & 0 & \cos w_3 t \end{bmatrix} \begin{bmatrix} 2 & 2 & 2 \\ 3 & 0 & -3 \\ 1 & -2 & 1 \end{bmatrix} \begin{bmatrix} \theta_{10} \\ \theta_{20} \\ \theta_{30} \end{bmatrix} \frac{1}{6}$$

The equation, therefore, gives the motion of the three pendulums when the motion is started with zero angular velocity at $t = 0$, and each pendulum is given an initial displacement θ_{10}, θ_{20}, and θ_{30} at $t = 0$. It can be seen that, in general, all the normal coordinates are excited, and the resulting motion of the system is very complicated.

10. THE CASE OF ZERO FREQUENCY

If one of the eigenvalues of the inverse dynamical matrix $[W]$ μ_i is zero, the system under consideration has one frequency w_i equal to zero. This situation arises when the system under consideration has at least one degree of unrestrained freedom of motion. In such a case, the stiffness matrix $[k]$ is a *singular matrix*, and the dynamical matrix $[D] = [k]^{-1}[m]$ cannot be constructed. The principal features of this type of motion may be illustrated by a simple example.

Consider the motion of a short train composed of three cars, each of mass m, coupled to each other by elastic coupling of stiffness k, as shown in Fig. 8.9. The train is assumed to be able to roll along the track without any frictional forces acting upon it. The coupling is represented by two linear springs of stiffness coefficients k. The kinetic energy T and the potential energy V of the system are given by

(10.1) $T = \frac{1}{2}(\dot{x})'[m](\dot{x}), \quad V = \frac{1}{2}(x)'[k](x)$

where (x) is the coordinate vector, $(\dot{x})$ is the velocity vector, and $[m]$ and $[k]$ are the inertia and stiffness matrices given in this case by

(10.2) $[m] = m[U] \quad \text{and} \quad [k] = \begin{bmatrix} k & -k & 0 \\ -k & 2k & -k \\ 0 & -k & k \end{bmatrix}$

where $[U]$ is the unit matrix of the third order. It can be seen by inspection that the determinant of the stiffness matrix vanishes and, therefore, $[k]$ is a

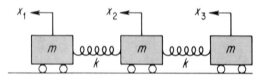

FIG. 8.9. A Short Train

singular matrix. The inverse dynamical matrix $[W] = [m]^{-1}[k]$ has the form

(10.3) $[W] = \frac{1}{m}[k] = \begin{bmatrix} b & -b & 0 \\ -b & 2b & -b \\ 0 & -b & b \end{bmatrix}, \quad \text{where} \quad b = \frac{k}{m}$

The characteristic equation of $[W]$ is

(10.4) $\det(\mu U - [W])$

$$= \begin{bmatrix} (\mu - b) & b & 0 \\ b & (\mu - 2b) & b \\ 0 & b & (\mu - b) \end{bmatrix} = \mu(\mu - b)(\mu - 3b)$$

The eigenvalues of $[W]$ are

(10.5) $\mu_1 = 0, \quad \mu_2 = b, \quad \mu_3 = 3b$

These eigenvalues correspond to the following natural frequencies of the system,

(10.6) $w_1 = 0, \quad w_2 = \left(\frac{k}{m}\right)^{1/2}, \quad w_3 = \left(\frac{3k}{m}\right)^{1/2}$

The eigenvectors $(A)_i$, or modes, satisfy the equation

(10.7) $[W](A)_i = \mu_i(A)_i, \quad i = 1, 2, 3$

If the first element of each modal column is chosen to be unity, the modal columns are given by

$$(10.8) \qquad (A)_1 = \begin{bmatrix} 1 \\ 1 \\ 1 \end{bmatrix}, \quad (A)_2 = \begin{bmatrix} 1 \\ 0 \\ -1 \end{bmatrix}, \quad (A)_3 = \begin{bmatrix} 1 \\ -2 \\ 1 \end{bmatrix}$$

The modal matrix of the system $[A]$ is, therefore,

$$(10.9) \qquad [A] = \begin{vmatrix} 1 & 1 & 1 \\ 1 & 0 & -2 \\ 1 & -1 & 1 \end{vmatrix}$$

This is the same modal matrix obtained for the system of coupled pendulums of Sec. 9. In this case the normal coordinates y_i satisfy the following differential equations:

$$(10.10) \qquad \ddot{y}_1 = 0, \quad \ddot{y}_2 = w_2^2 y_2, \quad \ddot{y}_3 = w_3^2 y_3$$

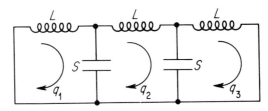

FIG. 8.10. Electric Circuit Equivalent of Fig. 8.9

The solutions of these equations have the forms

$$(10.11) \qquad \begin{aligned} y_1 &= a_1 t + b_1, \\ y_2 &= a_2 \cos w_2 t + b_2 \sin w_2 t, \\ y_3 &= a_3 \cos w_3 t + b_3 \sin w_3 t \end{aligned}$$

where the a's and b's are arbitrary constants. Since $(x) = [A](y)$ or

$$(10.12) \qquad \begin{bmatrix} x_1 \\ x_2 \\ x_3 \end{bmatrix} = \begin{bmatrix} 1 & 1 & 1 \\ 1 & 0 & -2 \\ 1 & -1 & 1 \end{bmatrix} \begin{bmatrix} y_1 \\ y_2 \\ y_3 \end{bmatrix}$$

it can be seen that if only the coordinate y_1 is excited, then y_2 and y_3 are zero and we have from (10.12)

$$x_1 = y_1, \quad x_2 = y_1, \quad x_3 = y_1$$

This indicates that the train moves as a rigid body along the track without oscillating. Since $\ddot{y}_1 = 0$, the train either remains at rest or continues to move with constant velocity as a rigid body along the track.

It is instructive to notice that the electrical circuit that is equivalent to the train of Fig. 8.9 has the form shown in Fig. 8.10. The energy functions T

and V of this circuit are given by

(10.12a) $$T = \tfrac{1}{2}(\dot{q})'[L](\dot{q})$$

(10.13) $$V = \tfrac{1}{2}(q)'[S](q)$$

where (q) is the column matrix whose elements are the circulating charges, $(\dot{q})$ is the column matrix whose elements are the circulating currents, and $[L]$ and $[S]$ are the square inductance and elastance matrices given by

(10.14) $$[L] = L[U]$$

where $[U]$ is the third-order unit matrix.

(10.15) $$[S] = \begin{bmatrix} S & -S & 0 \\ -S & 2S & -S \\ 0 & -S & S \end{bmatrix}$$

The equations of motion for the charges q_i, therefore, have the same form as the equations for the displacements of the cars x_i.

It may be noted that if the Kirchhoff electromotive force law is applied to the outside loop of the circuit of Fig. 8.10, we obtain

(10.16) $$L(\dot{q}_1 + \dot{q}_2 + \dot{q}_3) = 0$$

This equation is satisfied if we let

(10.17) $$q_1 + q_2 + q_3 = 0$$

It is possible to use this relation to eliminate one of the coordinates, say q_3, and write

(10.18) $$q_3 = -(q_1 + q_2)$$

We are now left with a system of two degrees of freedom. Since the relation (10.17) removes the first normal coordinate, which is the one that oscillates with $w_1 = 0$, the modified system contains the remaining two modes and frequencies, but the zero frequency mode has been removed.

11. THE USE OF FUNCTIONS OF MATRICES IN THE THEORY OF VIBRATIONS

Let us consider the simple harmonic oscillator shown in Fig. 8.11. This oscillator has a single degree of freedom; it consists of a unit mass attached to a fixed point by a linear spring of stiffness k. The motion of the oscillator

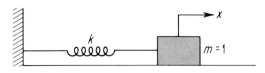

FIG. 8.11. Simple Harmonic Oscillator

may be specified by the coordinate x measured from the position of equilibrium. The kinetic energy T and the potential energy V of this simple oscillator are given by

(11.1) $$T = \tfrac{1}{2}\dot{x}^2, \quad V = \tfrac{1}{2}kx^2$$

The equation of motion of the oscillator is, therefore,

(11.2) $$\ddot{x} + kx = 0$$

If we let $k = w^2$, the solution, appropriate to the initial conditions,

(11.3) $$x = x_0, \quad \dot{x} = v_0 \quad \text{at } t = 0$$

is conveniently written in the form

(11.4) $$x = x_0 \cos (wt) + \frac{v_0}{w} \sin (wt)$$

The problem of the oscillations of a conservative dynamical system of n degrees of freedom about a position of stable equilibrium is a generalization of the problem of the simple oscillator; in seeking a generalization of the solution (11.4), matrix notation suggests itself.

If the system under consideration *does not* possess dynamic coupling, the use of mass-weighted coordinates x, as explained in Sec. 6, enables us to express the energy functions of the system T and V in the forms

(11.5) $$T = \frac{(\dot{x})'(x)}{2}$$

and

(11.6) $$V = \frac{(x)'[K](x)}{2}$$

These expressions are generalizations of (11.1). The kinetic energy T is a positive definite quadratic form, $[K]$ is a symmetric square matrix, and the potential energy V is a nonnegative quadratic form. The Lagrangian equations of motion of the system are

(11.7) $$(\ddot{x}) + [K](x) = (0)$$

The standard method for the solution of these equations has been given in Sec. 6. It consists of determining the eigenvalues μ_i of the matrix $[K]$, which will be assumed to be positive and distinct, and constructing the orthogonal matrix $[L]$ by means of (6.23). The columns of the square matrix $[L]$ are the normalized eigenvectors of the symmetric matrix $[K]$. Then $[L]'[K][L]$ is the diagonal matrix $[K]_0$ given by (6.11). The normal coordinates (y) are given by

(11.8) $$(y) = [L]'(x)$$

The equation of motion of the normal coordinates is

(11.9) $$(\ddot{y}) + [K]_0(y) = (0)$$

Since $[K]_0$ is a diagonal matrix, the normal coordinates are uncoupled, and Eq. (11.9) may be expanded into n equations of the form

(11.10) $$\ddot{y}_r + w_r^2 y_r = 0, \quad \mu_r = w_r^2, \quad r = 1, 2, 3, \ldots, n$$

If we now define the two square matrices $[C]$ and $[S]$ in the following manner:

(11.11) $$[C] = \begin{bmatrix} \cos(w_1 t) & 0 & \cdots & 0 \\ 0 & \cos(w_2 t) & \cdots & 0 \\ \cdot & & \cdots & \cdot \\ 0 & 0 & \cdots & \cos(w_n t) \end{bmatrix}$$

(11.12) $$[S] = \begin{bmatrix} \dfrac{\sin}{w_1}(w_1 t) & 0 & \cdots & 0 \\ 0 & \dfrac{\sin}{w_2}(w_2 t) & \cdots & 0 \\ \cdot & \cdot & \cdots & \cdot \\ 0 & 0 & \cdots & \dfrac{\sin}{w_n}(w_n t) \end{bmatrix}$$

In terms of these matrices, the normal coordinates (y) may be expressed concisely in the form

(11.13) $$(y) = [C](a) + [S](b)$$

where (a) and (b) are arbitrary columns. Since $(x) = [L](y)$, we have

(11.14) $$(x) = [L][C](a) + [L][S](b)$$

If $(x) = (x)_0$ and $(\dot{x}) = (v)_0$ at $t = 0$, it is easy to see that (a) and (b) may be determined, and the final solution for (x) may be written in the following manner:

(11.15) $$(x) = [L][C][L]'(x)_0 + [L][S][L]'(v)_0$$

It has been shown in Chapter 4 that the transformation $[L]'[K][L]$ which reduces $[K]$ to the diagonal form, with diagonal elements μ_i, $i = 1, 2, 3, \ldots, n$, as given by (6.11), will reduce any function of $[K]$, $F([K])$ to a diagonal form with diagonal elements $F(\mu_i)$, $i = 1, 2, 3, \ldots, n$.

Now let $[B]^2 = [K]$; with this notation, the matrix differential Eq. (11.7) takes the form

(11.16) $$(\ddot{x}) + [B]^2(x) = (0)$$

This equation is analogous to the equation for the single-degree-of-freedom case written in the form

(11.17) $$\ddot{x} + w^2 x = 0$$

The solution of (11.16) may be written in terms of the matrix cosine and sine functions in the form

(11.18) $\qquad (x) = \cos([B]t)(x)_0 + [B]^{-1} \sin([B]t)(v)_0$

This is exactly analogous to the solution (11.4) for the simple one-degree-of-freedom case. To interpret the significance of the matrix functions of (11.18), we have the result

(11.19) $\quad [L]'[F(B)][L] = [L]'[F(K^{1/2})][L] = \begin{bmatrix} F(w_1) & 0 & \cdots & 0 \\ 0 & F(w_2) & \cdots & 0 \\ \cdot & & \cdot & \cdots \\ 0 & 0 & \cdots & F(w_n) \end{bmatrix}$

since $(\mu_i)^{1/2} = w_i$. As a consequence of the result (11.19) we have

(11.20) $\qquad [L]' \cos([B]t)[L] = [C]$

and

(11.21) $\qquad [L]'[B]^{-1} \sin([B]t)[L] = [S]$

Therefore, the matrix functions $\cos([B]t)$ and $[B]^{-1} \sin([B]t)$ may be defined by the relations

(11.22) $\qquad \cos([B]t) = [L][C][L]'$

and

(11.23) $\qquad [B]^{-1} \sin([B]t) = [L][S][S]'$

It is thus apparent that the solutions (11.23) and (11.18) are identical. The solution (11.18) is a direct generalization of the one for the single degree of freedom. It may be interpreted by expanding the matric functions $\cos([B]t)$ and $[B]^{-1} \sin([B]t)$ using the method of Sec. 11, Chapter 4. To illustrate the use of this technique, let us consider the case of three degrees of freedom. Let it be assumed that the matrix $[K]$ has the three distinct eigenvalues μ_1, μ_2, and μ_3. In order to expand an analytic function $F([K])$ of the square matrix $[K]$ by the method of Chapter 4, we write

(11.24) $\qquad F([K]) = a_0 U + a_1[K] + a_2[K]^2$

The three constants a_0, a_1, and a_2 are determined by the matrix equation

(11.25) $\qquad \begin{bmatrix} a_0 \\ a_1 \\ a_2 \end{bmatrix} = \begin{bmatrix} 1 & \mu_1 & \mu_1^2 \\ 1 & \mu_2 & \mu_2^2 \\ 1 & \mu_3 & \mu_3^2 \end{bmatrix}^{-1} \begin{bmatrix} F(\mu_1) \\ F(\mu_2) \\ F(\mu_3) \end{bmatrix} = \begin{bmatrix} D_0 \\ D_1 \\ D_2 \end{bmatrix} \frac{1}{D}$

In (11.25) D is the determinant

(11.26) $\qquad D = \begin{vmatrix} 1 & 1 & 1 \\ \mu_1 & \mu_2 & \mu_3 \\ \mu_1^2 & \mu_2^2 & \mu_3^2 \end{vmatrix} = (\mu_1 - \mu_2)(\mu_1 - \mu_3)(\mu_3 - \mu_2)$

Determinants of this form are called *alternant determinants*. The quantities D_r, $r = 0, 1, 2$ in (11.25) are obtained from D. D_r is derived from D by replacing the elements of the $(r + 1)$th row of D by $F(\mu_1)$, $F(\mu_2)$, $F(\mu_3)$. If the values of a_0, a_1, and a_2 given by (11.25) are substituted into (11.3) and some algebraic reductions are made, the matrix function $F([K])$ may be written in the symmetric form

$$(11.27) \qquad F([K]) = \frac{([K] - \mu_2 U)([K] - \mu_3 U)F(\mu_1)}{D_{12}D_{13}}$$

$$+ \frac{([K] - \mu_3 U)([K] - \mu_1 U)F(\mu_2)}{D_{23}D_{21}}$$

$$+ \frac{([K] - \mu_1 U)([K] - \mu_2 U)F(\mu_3)}{D_{31}D_{32}}$$

where $[U]$ is the third-order unit matrix, and

$$(11.28) \qquad D_{rs} = \mu_r - \mu_s$$

Equation (11.27) for the expansion of a matrix function $F([K])$ in terms of its eigenvalues μ_i is called Sylvester's matrix analogue of Lagrange's interpolation formula.[3]

A concise expression for the expansion of a matrix function $F([K])$ for the case in which the eigenvalues μ_i of $[K]$ are distinct may be expressed in a symbolic determinantal form. If $[K]$ is a matrix of the fourth order, this symbolic expression is

$$(11.29) \qquad \begin{vmatrix} 1 & 1 & 1 & 1 & U \\ \mu_1 & \mu_2 & \mu_3 & \mu_4 & [K] \\ \mu_1^2 & \mu_2^2 & \mu_3^2 & \mu_4^2 & [K]^2 \\ \mu_1^3 & \mu_2^3 & \mu_3^3 & \mu_4^3 & [K]^3 \\ F(\mu_1) & F(\mu_2) & F(\mu_3) & F(\mu_4) & F(K) \end{vmatrix} = 0$$

If this symbolic determinant is expanded in terms of the last row, the desired expansion for $F([K])$ is obtained. In general, the form (11.27) is more convenient. In order to use (11.27) to obtain the expansion for $\cos([B]t)$, it must be realized that $[B] = [K]^{1/2}$ and that $\mu_i^{1/2} = w_i$; therefore, as a consequence of (11.27) we have

$$(11.30) \quad \cos([B]t) = \cos([K]^{1/2}t) = \frac{([K] - \mu_2 U)([K] - \mu_3 U)\cos(w_1 t)}{D_{12}D_{13}}$$

$$+ \frac{([K] - \mu_3 U)([K] - \mu_1 U)\cos(w_2 t)}{D_{23}D_{21}}$$

$$+ \frac{([K] - \mu_1 U)([K] - \mu_2 U)\cos(w_3 t)}{D_{31}D_{32}}$$

A similar expression may be obtained for the matrix function $[B]^{-1} \sin([B]t)$ by the use of (11.27) and by replacing $F(\mu_i)$ in this equation with $\sin(w_i t)/w$ for $i = 1, 2, 3$.

Application to the Oscillations of a Loaded String

To illustrate the general procedure, consider the oscillations of three equal masses m spaced at equal intervals of a along a light string under constant tension τ, as shown in Fig. 8.12. The masses are supposed to be vibrating transversely to the line AB and in the plane of the paper. The equations of motion of the three masses are of the form (11.7) with the matrix $[K]$ given by

$$(11.31) \qquad [K] = b^2 \begin{bmatrix} 2 & -1 & 0 \\ -1 & 2 & -1 \\ 0 & -1 & 2 \end{bmatrix}, \quad b^2 = \frac{\tau}{am}$$

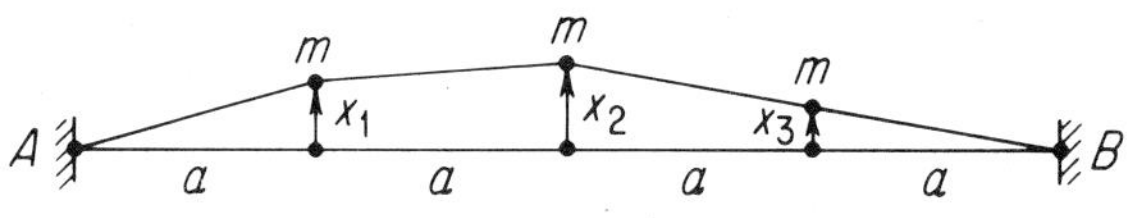

FIGURE 8.12

The eigenvalues of $[K]$, μ_i are

$$(11.32) \qquad \begin{aligned} \mu_1 &= (2 - \sqrt{2})b^2 \\ \mu_2 &= 2b^2 \\ \mu_3 &= (2 + \sqrt{2})b^2 \end{aligned}$$

The expression for $\cos([B]t)$ is now obtained by (11.30) in the form:

$$\cos([B]t) = \frac{1}{4} \begin{bmatrix} 1 & \sqrt{2} & 1 \\ \sqrt{2} & 2 & \sqrt{2} \\ 1 & \sqrt{2} & 1 \end{bmatrix} \cos(w_1 t) + \frac{1}{2} \begin{bmatrix} 1 & 0 & -1 \\ 0 & 0 & 0 \\ -1 & 0 & 1 \end{bmatrix} \cos(w_2 t)$$

$$(11.33)$$

$$+ \frac{1}{4} \begin{bmatrix} 1 & -\sqrt{2} & 1 \\ -\sqrt{2} & 2 & -\sqrt{2} \\ 1 & -\sqrt{2} & 1 \end{bmatrix} \cos(w_3 t)$$

A similar expression, with the same matrix coefficients, holds for the function $[B]^{-1} \sin([B]t)$; therefore, the general solution (11.18) may be written down at once. If the matrix $[L]$ of (11.8) is required, it can be constructed by taking a nonvanishing column from each of the square matrices of (11.33) and normalizing each column to unity. This procedure gives

$$(11.34) \qquad [L] = \frac{1}{2} \begin{bmatrix} 1 & -2 & 1 \\ 2 & 0 & -2 \\ 1 & 2 & 1 \end{bmatrix}$$

12. USE OF FUNCTIONS OF MATRICES IN THE CASE OF DYNAMIC COUPLING

If the system under consideration is one that has *dynamic coupling*, then the kinetic energy function T and the potential energy function V have the forms

$$(12.1) \qquad T = \tfrac{1}{2}(\dot{x})'[m](\dot{x}), \quad V = \tfrac{1}{2}(x)'[k](x)$$

where $[m]$ is the symmetric inertia matrix and $[k]$ is the symmetric stiffness matrix; T is positive definite, and V is nonnegative. In this case the Lagrangian equations of motion are

$$(12.2) \qquad [m](\ddot{x}) + [k](x) = (0)$$

These equations may be expressed in terms of the inverse *dynamical matrix* $[W] = [m]^{-1}[k]$, in the form

$$(12.3) \qquad (\ddot{x}) + [W](x) = (0)$$

The inverse dynamical matrix $[W] = [m]^{-1}[k]$ is not, in general, a symmetric matrix. The properties of the eigenvectors of $[W]$ were discussed at some length in Sec. 7; it was there shown that the modal matrix of $[W]$ in the case in which the eigenvalues μ_i of $[W]$ are distinct has the property that

$$(12.4) \qquad [A]'[m][A] = [P], \quad [A]'[k][A] = [S]$$

where the matrices $[P]$ and $[S]$ are *diagonal matrices*. The following notation is now introduced:

$$(12.5) \qquad (H)_i = \frac{(A)_i}{\{(A)_i'[m](A)_i\}^{1/2}}, \quad i = 1, 2, 3, \ldots, n$$

The columns $(H)_i$ are recognized to be the *normalized eigenvectors* of $[W]$ with respect to $[m]$. As a consequence of (8.2) and (8.4), it is easy to show that the vectors $(H)_i$ have the following properties:

$$(12.6) \qquad (H)_i'[m](H)_j = \begin{cases} 0, & i \neq j \\ 1, & i = j \end{cases}$$

and

$$(12.7) \qquad (H)_i'[k](H)_j = \begin{cases} 0, & i \neq j \\ \mu_i, & i = j \end{cases}$$

If a square matrix $[H]$ is now constructed from the n columns $(H)_i$, $i = 1, 2, 3, \ldots, n$, then $[H]$ is the *normalized modal matrix*, and it has the properties that

$$(12.8) \qquad [H]'[m][H] = U$$

where U is the nth-order unit matrix, and

$$(12.9) \qquad [H]'[k][H] = [d]$$

where $[d]$ is the diagonal matrix of the eigenvalues μ_i of $[W]$.

From Eq. (12.8) it is possible to obtain the matrix $[H]'$ in the form

$$(12.10) \qquad [H]' = [H]^{-1}[m]^{-1}$$

If this is now substituted into (12.9), the result is

$$(12.11) \qquad [H]'[k][H] = [H]^{-1}[m]^{-1}[k][H] = [d]$$

However, since $[m]^{-1}[k] = [W]$, the inverse dynamical matrix, we have, as a consequence of (12.11),

$$(12.12) \qquad [H]^{-1}[W][H] = [d]$$

If the inverse of the normalized modal matrix $[H]$ is required, it may be obtained from (12.8) in the form

$$(12.13) \qquad [H]^{-1} = [H]'[m]$$

If we define a new square matrix $[V]$ by the equation

$$(12.14) \qquad [V] = [W]^{1/2}, \quad \text{or} \quad [W] = [V]^2$$

in terms of $[V]$, the differential equations of the system (12.3) have the form

$$(12.15) \qquad (\ddot{x}) + [V]^2(x) = (0)$$

In terms of matrix functions, the solution of this equation may be expressed in the form

$$(12.16) \qquad (x) = \cos([V]t)(x)_0 + [V]^{-1}\sin([V]t)(v)_0$$

where $(x)_0$ is a column of initial displacements and $(v)_0$ is a column of initial velocities. Since the normalized modal matrix $[H]$ reduces $[W]$ to the diagonal form by the transformation $[H]^{-1}[W][H]$, this transformation will also reduce any function of $[W]$ to a diagonal form, and, therefore,

$$(12.17) \quad [H]^{-1}F([V])[H] = [H]^{-1}F([W]^{1/2})[H]$$

$$= \begin{bmatrix} F(w_1) & 0 & \cdots & 0 \\ 0 & F(w_2) & \cdots & 0 \\ \cdot & \cdot & \cdots & \cdot \\ 0 & 0 & \cdots & F(w_n) \end{bmatrix}$$

Therefore, if we use the notation

$$(12.18) \qquad [C] = \begin{bmatrix} \cos(w_1 t) & 0 & \cdots & 0 \\ 0 & \cos(w_2 t) & \cdots & 0 \\ \cdot & \cdot & \cdots & \cdot \\ 0 & 0 & \cdots & \cos(w_n t) \end{bmatrix}$$

and

$$(12.19) \qquad [S] = \begin{bmatrix} \dfrac{\sin}{w_1}(w_1 t) & 0 & \cdots & 0 \\ 0 & \dfrac{\sin}{w_2}(w_2 t) & \cdots & 0 \\ \cdot & \cdot & \cdots & \cdot \\ 0 & 0 & \cdots & \dfrac{\sin}{w_n}(w_n t) \end{bmatrix}$$

Then, since $w_i = (\mu_i)^{1/2}$, we have

$$(12.20) \qquad\qquad [H]^{-1} \cos([V]t)[H] = [C]$$

$$(12.21) \qquad\qquad [H]^{-1}[V]^{-1} \sin([V]t)[H] = [S]$$

as a consequence of (12.17).

In terms of the diagonal matrices $[C]$ and $[S]$, we have the following explicit relations for the functions $\cos([V]t)$ and $[V]^{-1} \sin([V]t)$:

$$(12.22) \qquad\qquad \cos([V]t) = [H][C][H]^{-1}$$

and

$$(12.23) \qquad\qquad [V]^{-1} \sin([V]t) = [H][S][H]^{-1}$$

These functions may also be computed by the use of (11.29) by substituting $[W]$ for the matrix $[K]$. The eigenvalues μ_i in the resulting equation are the eigenvalues of the matrix $[W]$.

13. THE CASE OF MULTIPLE ROOTS OF THE CHARACTERISTIC EQUATION

Consider the case in which the Lagrangian equations of motion of the vibrating system are given by

$$(13.1) \qquad\qquad (\ddot{x}) + [K](x) = (0), \quad \text{where} \quad [K] = [B]^2$$

Let it be supposed that the characteristic equation of the system,

$$(13.2) \qquad\qquad \det(\mu U - [K]) = 0$$

has a certain number of multiple roots, or, in other words, the matrix $[K]$ has a certain number of multiple eigenvalues.

It is apparent that if the equations of motion are of the form (13.1), each coordinate x_r will satisfy an equation, obtained by elimination of the remaining variables, which is simply

$$(13.3) \quad (D^2 + w_1^2)(D^2 + w_2^2)\ldots(D^2 + w_n^2)x_r = 0, \quad D^2 = \frac{d^2}{dt^2}, \quad w_i = (\mu_i)^{1/2}$$

$$\text{for} \quad i = 1, 2, 3, \ldots, n$$

Now if some of the eigenvalues of the matrix $[K]$ are assumed to coincide, some of the w^2's coincide, and, in general, it might be expected to contain "secular" terms of the form $h(t) \cos(wt)$ and $k(t) \sin(wt)$ corresponding to a repeated root w, where $h(t)$ and $k(t)$ are polynomials of degree one less than the multiplicity of the root, in addition to the usual terms in $\cos(wt)$ and $\sin(wt)$ for the single roots. This is what Lagrange and others who followed him supposed. It turns out, however, that when the assumed solutions are substituted into the original differential equations (13.1) in accordance with the usual procedure for determining the relations between the arbitrary constants of the solution, all the coefficients in $h(t)$ and $k(t)$ vanish identically, with the exception of their constant terms. The reason for this is not directly obvious, although, of course, the matter has been well understood since Weierstrass discussed it in 1858. The matrix solution (11.18) concisely demonstrates the disappearance of the "secular" terms in the dynamical problem, as will now be shown.

When repeated roots occur, (11.18) is still formally the solution of (13.1), but as there is now a certain arbitrariness in the matrix $[L]$ in the definitions (11.22) and (11.23), the trigonometric functions $\cos([B]t)$ and $[B]^{-1} \sin([B]t)$ will be assumed to be defined by Sylvester's theorem, in its confluent form.

Let it be assumed that the matrix $[K]$ is of the fourth order and that its eigenvalues are

$$(13.4) \quad \mu_1 = a, \quad \mu_2 = b, \quad \mu_3 = b, \quad \mu_4 = b$$

The peculiarity of the dynamical case is that if the matrix $[K]$ has repeated eigenvalues, it satisfies an identical equation which is of lower degree than the order of $[K]$. This equation is called the *reduced Cayley-Hamilton equation*, and it is obtained by counting each distinct linear factor in the ordinary Cayley-Hamilton equation once only. In the above example, the ordinary Cayley-Hamilton equation has the form

$$(13.5) \quad ([K] - aU)([K] - bU)^3 = [0]$$

where U is the fourth-order matrix. The *reduced* Cayley-Hamilton equation is, in this case,

$$(13.6) \quad ([K] - aU)([K] - bU) = [0]$$

The fact that $[K]$ satisfies the reduced equation follows at once from the fact that $[K]$ can be reduced to the diagonal form whether it contains repeated eigenvalues or not.   From a knowledge of the reduced Cayley-Hamilton equation, an analytic function $F([K])$ of the matrix $[K]$ may be expanded in the form

(13.7) $F([K]) = c_0 U + c_1[K]$, $U =$ the fourth-order unit matrix

where the constants c_0 and c_1 may be obtained from the equations

(13.8)
$$F(a) = c_0 + c_1 a$$
$$F(b) = c_0 + c_1 b$$

If Eqs. (13.8) are solved for the constants c_0 and c_1 and the results are substituted into (13.7), then the matrix function $F([K])$ may be written in the form

(13.9) $$F([K]) = \frac{[bF(a) - aF(b)]U}{(b - a)} + \frac{[F(b) - F(a)][K]}{(b - a)}$$

14. THE OSCILLATIONS OF A SYMMETRIC ELECTRICAL CIRCUIT

An example that illustrates the occurrence of a vanishing eigenvalue, a pair of repeated eigenvalues, and a single eigenvalue of the matrix $[K]$ will now be given in order to clarify the ideas discussed in Sec. 13.

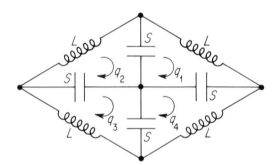

FIG. 8.13. Symmetric Electrical Circuit

Consider the electrical circuit of Fig. 8.13.   It consists of four equal inductances L and four equal elastances S connected in the symmetric arrangement shown in the figure.   The generalized coordinates q_1, q_2, q_3, q_4 of the system may be taken as the four circulating charges in the four internal loops of the circuit as shown.

If we introduce the coordinate vector (q) whose elements are the four circulating charges, the square inductance matrix $[L]$, and the square elastance matrix $[S]$, then the differential equations governing the oscillations of the system may be written in the compact matrix form,

(14.1) $[L](\ddot{q}) + [S](q) = (0)$

In this case the inductance matrix $[L]$ has the simple diagonal form

(14.2) $[L] = LU$

where U is the fourth-order unit matrix.

The elastance matrix $[S]$ has the symmetric form

(14.3) $[S] = S\begin{bmatrix} 2 & -1 & 0 & -1 \\ -1 & 2 & -1 & 0 \\ 0 & -1 & 2 & -1 \\ -1 & 0 & -1 & 2 \end{bmatrix} = S[B]$

where $[B]$ is the fourth-order numerical matrix in (14.3).

If the matrix differential equation (14.1) is premultiplied by $[L]^{-1}$, the result is

(14.4) $(\ddot{q}) + [L]^{-1}[S](q) = (0)$

or

(14.5) $(\ddot{q}) + [K](q) = (0)$,   where $[K] = [L]^{-1}[S] = \dfrac{S}{L}[B]$

The differential equation of the circuit now has the form (13.1). The characteristic equation of the matrix $[K]$ is

(14.6) $\det(\mu U - [K]) = 0$

If we introduce the notation

(14.7) $a^2 = \dfrac{S}{L}$

then

(14.8) $[K] = a^2[B]$

If (14.8) is substituted into (14.6), it is seen that the characteristic equation of $[K]$ may be written in the alternative form,

(14.9) $\det\left(U\dfrac{\mu}{a^2} - [B]\right) = 0$

or if we let

(14.10) $\phi = \dfrac{\mu}{a^2}$

then (14.9) takes the form

(14.11) $\det(\phi U - [B]) = 0$

This is the characteristic equation of the numerical matrix $[B]$. If Eq. (14.10) is expanded, it will be found that the resulting polynomial in ϕ can be factored, and the eigenvalues of $[B]$ are found to be

(14.12) $\phi_1 = 0, \quad \phi_2 = 2, \quad \phi_3 = 2, \quad \phi_4 = 4$

As a consequence of the relation (14.10), these eigenvalues of $[B]$ correspond to the following eigenvalues of $[K]$:

(14.13) $\mu_1 = 0, \quad \mu_2 = 2a^2, \quad \mu_3 = 2a^2, \quad \mu_4 = 4a^2$

If (14.8) is substituted into (14.5), the differential equation of the circuit is seen to have the form

(14.14) $(\ddot{q}) + a^2[B](q) = (0)$

The solution of this matrix differential equation may now be written in the form

(14.15) $(q) = \cos(at[B]^{1/2})(q)_0 + a[B]^{-1/2}\sin(at[B]^{1/2})(i)_0$

The vectors $(q)_0$ and $(i)_0$ have as elements the initial charges and initial currents in the circuit at $t = 0$. Since the matrix $[B]$ has the eigenvalues (14.12), it has a reduced Cayley-Hamilton equation of the form.

(14.16) $[B]([B] - 2U)([B] - 4U) = [0]$

If the same technique given in Sec. 13 in order to compute a function of the matrix $[K]$ is now applied to compute a function of the matrix $[B]$, the following result is obtained:

(14.17) $F([B]) = \frac{1}{8}([B] - 2U)([B] - 4U)F(0) - \frac{1}{4}[B]([B] - 4U)F(2)$
$$+ \frac{1}{8}[B]([B] - 2U)F(4)$$

This result may now be used to expand the two matrix functions of the right member of (14.15) to obtain

(14.18) $(q) = \frac{1}{4}[C_1 + 2C_2\cos(2^{1/2}at) + C_3\cos(2at)](q_0)$
$$+ \frac{1}{4}\left[C_1 t + 2C_2\sin\frac{(2^{1/2}at)}{(2^{1/2}a)} + C_3\sin\frac{(2at)}{(2a)}\right](i)_0$$

C_1, C_2, and C_3 are the following square matrices:

(14.19)

$$C_1 = \begin{bmatrix} 1 & 1 & 1 & 1 \\ 1 & 1 & 1 & 1 \\ 1 & 1 & 1 & 1 \\ 1 & 1 & 1 & 1 \end{bmatrix}, \quad C_2 = \begin{bmatrix} 1 & 0 & -1 & 0 \\ 0 & 1 & 0 & -1 \\ -1 & 0 & 1 & 0 \\ 0 & -1 & 0 & 1 \end{bmatrix}$$

$$C_3 = \begin{bmatrix} 1 & -1 & 1 & -1 \\ -1 & 1 & -1 & 1 \\ 1 & -1 & 1 & -1 \\ -1 & 1 & -1 & 1 \end{bmatrix}$$

The ratios of the coordinates q_i in the various vibrational modes can be read off from the elements of the matrices C_i to give

$$\begin{bmatrix} 1 \\ 1 \\ 1 \\ 1 \end{bmatrix} \text{ (zero frequency),} \qquad \begin{bmatrix} 1 \\ 0 \\ -1 \\ 0 \end{bmatrix} \text{ or } \begin{bmatrix} 0 \\ 1 \\ 0 \\ -1 \end{bmatrix} \text{ (degenerate modes of frequency } = 2^{1/2}a)$$

(14.20)

$$\begin{bmatrix} 1 \\ -1 \\ 1 \\ -1 \end{bmatrix} \text{ (frequency } 2a)$$

15. NONCONSERVATIVE SYSTEMS. VIBRATIONS WITH VISCOUS DAMPING

In the last few sections, the general theory of conservative systems has been considered. These systems, which are characterized completely by their kinetic and potential energy functions, are of great importance; since, in many problems that arise in practice, the frictional forces involved in the system are relatively small, they may be disregarded in the analysis, and the system may be treated as if it were a conservative one.

The mathematical analysis of vibrating systems that involve frictional forces of a general nature leads to a formulation involving *nonlinear* differential equations. However, in a great many practical problems, the frictional forces involved are proportional to the velocities or to the relative velocities of the moving parts of the system. Frictional forces of this type are present in systems that contain viscous friction. In the analogous electrical problems, these forces are the potential drops caused by the various resistances of the system, as indicated by the discussion of Sec. 4. The mathematical analysis of vibration problems of systems involving viscous friction leads usually to the solution of *linear* differential equations and is relatively simple.

The Dissipation Function

Consider a particle of mass m that may move along a horizontal plane, as shown in Fig. 8.14. Let it be assumed that as the particle moves, its motion

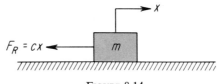

FIGURE 8.14

is resisted by viscous force proportional to the velocity of the mass, $F_R = c\dot{x}$. When the particle moves through a small distance dx, the work, dW, dissipated in friction is

$$(15.1) \qquad dW = F \, dx = cv \, dx$$

where $v = \dot{x}$ is the velocity of the particle. The time rate at which energy is dissipated is

$$(15.2) \qquad \frac{dW}{dt} = P = cv \frac{dx}{dt} = cv^2$$

This represents the power lost in friction as the mass is forced to move along the plane. The *dissipation function* D is defined to be one-half this power loss, or

$$(15.3) \qquad D = \frac{P}{2} = \frac{cv^2}{2} = \frac{c\dot{x}^2}{2}$$

It is evident that the frictional force F_r may be obtained by the equation

$$(15.4) \qquad F_r = -\frac{dD}{d\dot{x}} = -c\dot{x}$$

By an extension of the above analysis to the case of a system having n degrees of freedom undergoing viscous friction, it can be shown that the dissipation function for this general system has the form

$$(15.5) \qquad D = \tfrac{1}{2}(\dot{q})'[c](\dot{q})$$

where $(\dot{q})$ is a vector whose elements are the n generalized velocities $\dot{q}_i$ of the system. $[c]$ is an nth-order square symmetric matrix whose elements c_{ij}, in general, depend on the configuration of the system. In the case of small vibrations in the neighborhood of a configuration of stable equilibrium, these coefficients may be treated as constants with good accuracy. The symmetric matrix $[c]$ is called the *damping matrix* in the modern literature of mechanical vibrations.

The dissipation function D given by (15.5) represents *half* the rate at which energy is being dissipated in the entire system as it moves under the influence of viscous friction. The generalized forces that arise from the viscous friction of the system, F_i, are given by

$$(15.6) \qquad F_i = -\frac{\partial D}{\partial \dot{q}_i}, \qquad i = 1, 2, 3, \ldots, n$$

The Lagrangian equations of the system now have the form

$$(15.7) \qquad \frac{d}{dt}\left(\frac{\partial T}{\partial \dot{q}}\right) - \frac{\partial T}{\partial q_i} = -\frac{\partial V}{\partial q_i} - \frac{\partial D}{\partial \dot{q}_i} + Q_i, \qquad i = 1, 2, 3, \ldots, n$$

where T is the kinetic energy, V the potential energy, and D the dissipation function of the system.

The left-hand member of (15.7) represents the effect of the inertia terms of the system; the terms of the right-hand member are the various generalized forces of the system:

(a) The term $-\partial V/\partial q_i$ takes into account forces that may be derived from a potential function V, such as gravitational forces, forces caused by elastic springs, etc.

(b) The term $-\partial D/\partial \dot{q}_i$ takes into account the effect of retarding force due to viscous friction.

(c) The term Q_i includes all other forces acting on the system, such as time-dependent disturbing forces.

In terms of the inertia matrix $[m]$, the stiffness matrix $[k]$, and the damping matrix $[c]$ of the system, the Lagrangian equations (15.7) may be written in the following concise form:

$$(15.8) \qquad [m](\ddot{q}) + [c](\dot{q}) + [k](q) = (Q)$$

The elements of the column matrix (Q) are the generalized forces Q_i of the system.

A general linear electrical network may be regarded as a dynamical system that is characterized by the following functions:

$$(15.9) \qquad T = \tfrac{1}{2}(\dot{q})'[L](\dot{q}), \quad V = \tfrac{1}{2}(q)'[S](q), \quad D = \tfrac{1}{2}(\dot{q})'[R](\dot{q})$$

In these expressions, the $(\dot{q})$ elements are the various mesh currents of the circuit, the elements of (q) are the various mesh charges of the circuit, and the square matrices $[L]$, $[S]$, and $[R]$ are symmetric matrices and are called the inductance, elastance, and resistance matrices of the circuit. In this case T represents the magnetic energy of the circuit, V is the electric energy, and D is one-half the power dissipated by the resistances of the circuit. The Lagrangian equations (15.7) now take the following form:

$$(15.10) \qquad [L](\ddot{q}) + [R](\dot{q}) + [S](q) = (e)$$

The elements of the vector (e) are the various mesh potentials applied to the electrical circuit.

16. THE MOTION OF A GENERAL DAMPED LINEAR DYNAMIC SYSTEM

We now consider a general method for the solution of the equations of motion of a linear damped dynamical system whose motion is governed by the following differential equation:

$$(16.1) \qquad [m](\ddot{q}) + [c](\dot{q}) + [k](q) = (Q)$$

This is the basic equation of motion of the general nonconservative system discussed in Sec. 15, under the influence of viscous damping forces.

The elements of the vector (q) are the n generalized coordinates of the system, whereas the vector (Q) has for elements the n generalized forces

$Q_i(t)$ which are, in general, functions of the time t. The inertia matrix $[m]$, damping matrix $[c]$ and stiffness matrix $[k]$ are symmetric square matrices of the nth order.

The classical method of solving these equations in the absence of damping so that $[c] = [0]$ is to find the normal modes of oscillation of the homogeneous equation

$$(16.2) \qquad [m](\ddot{q}) + [k](q) = (0)$$

by one of the methods of this chapter and then to determine the normal coordinates. As has been discussed in the above sections, the normal coordinates satisfy a set of differential equations that contain no inertial or elastic coupling between them.

In the case of the homogeneous equation with damping,

$$(16.3) \qquad [m](\ddot{q}) + [c](\dot{q}) + [k](q) = (0)$$

However, unless the damping matrix happens to be *proportional* to either the inertia matrix $[m]$ or the stiffness matrix $[k]$, velocity coupling exists, and the chief object of using normal coordinates is defeated unless the coupling terms are small and can be neglected.

In this section it will be shown how orthogonal relations between the solutions of the homogeneous equation (16.3) may be obtained and how from these relations a set of uncoupled coordinates may be constructed.

The Reduced Equation

Let the following square partitioned matrices be introduced:

$$(16.4) \qquad [A] = \begin{bmatrix} [0] & [m] \\ [m] & [c] \end{bmatrix}, \qquad [B] = \begin{bmatrix} -[m] & [0] \\ [0] & [k] \end{bmatrix}$$

The matrices $[A]$ and $[B]$ are square matrices of order $2n$. Since $[m]$, $[c]$, and $[k]$ are symmetric matrices, it is evident that the matrices $[A]$ and $[B]$ are symmetric matrices and $[B]$ is a diagonal matrix. We now introduce the following partitioned vectors:

$$(16.5) \qquad (y) = \begin{bmatrix} (\dot{q}) \\ (q) \end{bmatrix} \quad \text{and} \quad (F) = \begin{bmatrix} (0) \\ (Q) \end{bmatrix}$$

The vectors (y) and (F) are vectors of order $2n$. In terms of this notation, it is easy to show that Eq. (16.3) may be written in the equivalent form,

$$(16.6) \qquad [A](\dot{y}) + [B](y) = (F)$$

Equation (16.6) is called the *reduced equation*. If the indicated matrix multiplication involving the partitioned matrices is performed, it will be found that the reduced equation is equivalent to (16.1). For purposes of analysis, the reduced equation is preferable to the original equation (16.1), because it is a matrix differential equation of the first order and the co-efficient matrices $[A]$ and $[B]$ are symmetric matrices.

The Solution of the Homogenous Reduced Equation

Before we solve the complete reduced equation, the solution of the homogeneous reduced equation will be undertaken. This equation has the form

$$(16.7) \qquad [A](\ddot{y}) + [B](y) = (0)$$

In general, $[A]$ is a nonsingular matrix and has the following inverse:

$$(16.8) \qquad [A]^{-1} = \begin{bmatrix} -[m]^{-1}[c][m]^{-1} & [m]^{-1} \\ [m]^{-1} & [0] \end{bmatrix}$$

Let (16.7) be premultiplied by $[A]^{-1}$; the result of this operation is

$$(16.9) \qquad (\ddot{y}) + [A]^{-1}[B](y) = (0)$$

Now let us define the square matrix $[M]$ by the equation

$$(16.10) \qquad [M] = -[A]^{-1}[B] = \begin{bmatrix} -[m]^{-1}[c] & -[m]^{-1}[k] \\ U & [0] \end{bmatrix}$$

where U is the nth-order unit matrix. The square matrix $[M]$ is a matrix of the $2n$th order. In terms of $[M]$, (16.9) may be written in the form

$$(16.11) \qquad (\ddot{y}) - [M](y) = (0)$$

In order to solve (16.11), we attempt to find a solution of the form

$$(16.12) \qquad (y) = e^{\mu t}(v)$$

where μ is a parameter to be determined and (v) is a column matrix of $2n$ constants. If (16.12) is substituted into (16.11) and the exponential $e^{\mu t}$ divided from both members of the resulting equation, the following set of homogeneous equations in the constants v_i is obtained expressed in matrix form:

$$(16.13) \qquad (\mu U - [M])(v) = (0)$$

where U is the unit matrix of the nth order. In order for (16.13) to have a nontrivial solution, the determinant of the elements of (v) must vanish, and hence we must have

$$(16.14) \qquad \det (\mu U - [M]) = 0$$

This equation is recognized as the characteristic equation of the matrix $[M]$. The $2n$ roots of (16.14) are the *eigenvalues* μ_i of the matrix $[M]$. In general, the matrix $[M]$ will have $2n$ eigenvalues, μ_i, $i = 1, 2, 3, \ldots, 2n$.

For a stable system, each μ_i is either real and negative or complex with a negative real part. The complex roots occur as complex conjugate pairs with corresponding complex conjugate eigenvectors or modal columns $(v)_i$. A procedure by which the eigenvalues and eigenvectors of $[M]$ by a matrix iteration scheme will be described in a later section. Let it be assumed that the eigenvalues μ_i are distinct. As can be seen as a consequence of (16.13), the eigenvalue μ_r associated with the eigenvector $(v)_r$ satisfies an equation of the form

$$(16.15) \qquad \mu_r(v)_r - [M](v)_r = (0), \qquad r = 1, 2, 3, \ldots, 2n$$

However, by (16.10) we have $[M] = -[A]^{-1}[B]$, so (16.15) may be written in the form

$$(16.16) \qquad \mu_r(v)_r + [A]^{-1}[B](v)_r = (0)$$

If this equation is premultiplied by $[A]$, the result is

$$(16.17) \qquad \mu_r[A](v)_r + [B](v)_r = (0)$$

The sth eigenvalue and eigenvector satisfy an equation of the same form as (16.17), or

$$(16.18) \qquad \mu_s[A](v)_s + [B](v)_s = (0)$$

Now let (16.17) be premultiplied by $(v)'_s$ and (16.18) be premultiplied by $(v)'_r$; the resulting equations are

$$(16.19) \qquad \mu_r(v)'_s[A](v)_r + (v)'_s[B](v)_r = (0)$$

and

$$(16.20) \qquad \mu_s(v)'_r[A](v)_s + (v)'_r[B](v)_s = (0)$$

We now take the transpose of Eq. (16.20) and use the fact that the matrices $[A]$ and $[B]$ are *symmetric* matrices; we thus obtain

$$(16.21) \qquad \mu_s(v)'_s[A](v)_r + (v)'_s[B](v)_r = 0$$

Let us now subtract (16.21) from (16.19) to obtain

$$(16.22) \qquad (\mu_r - \mu_s)(v)'_s[A](v)_r = 0, \qquad r \neq s$$

Now, since by hypothesis the eigenvalues μ_r and μ_s are *distinct*, it follows that in order for (16.22) to be satisfied, it is necessary that

$$(16.23) \qquad (v)'_s[A](v)_r = 0, \qquad r \neq s$$

As a consequence of (16.21) this also implies that

$$(16.24) \qquad (v)'_s[B](v)_r = 0, \qquad r \neq s$$

Hence, the eigenvectors $(v)_i$ satisfy *orthogonality relations* of the form (16.23) and (16.24).

The Solution of the Inhomogeneous Equation

The orthogonality relations satisfied by the eigenvectors or modal columns of $[M]$ are very useful in effecting a solution of the inhomogeneous equation,

(16.25) $$[A](\dot{y}) + [B](y) = (F)$$

In order to solve this equation, we expand (y) into a modal series of the form

(16.26) $$(y) = \sum_{i=1}^{2n} (v)_i x_i(t)$$

where $(v)_i$ are the eigenvectors of $[M]$, and the $x_i(t)$ functions are scalar functions of the time t to be determined. This method of solution is equivalent to Lagrange's method of variation of parameters. We now substitute (16.26) into (16.25) and thus obtain

(16.27) $$\sum_{i=1}^{2n} [A](v)_i \dot{x}_i(t) + \sum_{i=1}^{2n} [B](v)_i x_i(t) = (F)$$

Let us now premultiply (16.27) by $(v)_r'$ to obtain

(16.28) $$\sum_{i=1}^{2n} (v)_r'[A](v)_i \dot{x}_i + \sum_{i=1}^{2n} (v)_r'[B](v)_i x_i = (v)_r'(F)$$

As a consequence of the orthogonality conditions (16.23) and (16.24), the only terms that survive in the series of (16.28) are the ones for which $i = r$ and, therefore, (16.28) reduces to

(16.29) $\quad (v)_r'[A](v)_r \dot{x}_r + (v)_r'[B](v)_r x_r = (v)_r'(F), \qquad r = 1, 2, 3, \ldots, 2n$

Now, as a consequence of (16.19) we have

(16.30) $$(v)_r'[B](v)_r = -\mu_r(v)_r'[A](v)_r$$

Hence, if this relation is substituted into (16.29), the result is

(16.31) $\quad (v)_r'[A](v)_r(\dot{x}_r - \mu_r x_r) = (v)_r'(F), \qquad r = 1, 2, 3, \ldots, 2n$

If the eigenvectors $(v)_r$ are normalized with respect to $[A]$, then

(16.32) $$(v)_r'[A](v)_r = 1$$

In this case, (16.31) reduces to the simple form

(16.33) $$\dot{x}_r - \mu_r x_r = F_r, \qquad r = 1, 2, 3, \ldots, n$$

where

(16.34) $$F_r = (v)_r'(F), \qquad r = 1, 2, 3, \ldots, 2n$$

It can be seen from (16.33) that the functions $x_i(t)$ satisfy simple first-order differential equations. The $x_i(t)$ functions are not coupled to each other, but play a role somewhat similar to normal coordinates in the case of conservative dynamical systems.

Completing the Solution

Before we obtain the final solution for the inhomogeneous equation, it is useful to notice that since (y) is the partitioned vector given by (16.5), the solution of the form (16.12) implies that the coordinate vector varies in the form

$$(16.35) \qquad (q) = e^{\mu t}(\phi), \quad \text{and} \quad (\dot{q}) = e^{\mu t}\mu(\phi)$$

where (ϕ) is an nth-order column vector; then by the definition of (y) we have

$$(16.36) \qquad (y) = \begin{bmatrix} (\dot{q}) \\ (q) \end{bmatrix} = \begin{bmatrix} \mu(\phi) \\ (\phi) \end{bmatrix} e^{\mu t} = (v)e^{\mu t}$$

Hence, for the ith mode, the modal column has the form

$$(16.37) \qquad (v)_i = \begin{bmatrix} \mu_i(\phi)_i \\ (\phi)_i \end{bmatrix}$$

If the system starts its motion with zero initial displacement and zero initial velocity at $t = 0$, then $(q)_0 = (0)$ and $(\dot{q})_0 = (0)$ so that we must have

$$(16.38) \qquad (y) = (0) \quad \text{at} \quad t = 0$$

Hence, it can be seen that as a consequence of (16.26) we must have

$$(16.39) \qquad x_i(t) = 0 \quad \text{for} \quad i = 1, 2, 3, \ldots, n$$

Hence, the set of differential equations (16.33) must be solved subject to the condition that all the x's are zero at time zero. Such a solution is

$$(16.40) \qquad x_r(t) = \int_0^t e^{\mu_r (t-u)} F_r(u) \, du, \qquad r = 1, 2, 3, \ldots, 2n$$

The solution for (y) is obtained by substituting the expressions for x_r in (16.26). The result of this substitution is

$$(16.41) \qquad (y) = \sum_{i=1}^{2n} (v)_i \int_0^t e^{\mu_i(t-u)} F_i(u) \, du = \begin{bmatrix} (\dot{q}) \\ (q) \end{bmatrix}$$

Now the functions $F_i(t)$ are given by (16.34). If the eigenvector $(v)_r$ is expressed in the form (16.37), then we obtain

$$(16.42) \qquad F_i = (v)_i'(F) = [\mu_i(\phi)_i' \quad (\phi)_i'] \begin{bmatrix} 0 \\ Q(t) \end{bmatrix} = (\phi)_i'(Q(t))$$

Since the typical eigenvector has the form (16.37), it can be substituted into (16.41) and the following expressions for the displacements (q) and the velocities $(\dot{q})$ of the system obtained:

(16.43)
$$(q) = \sum_{i=1}^{2n} (\phi)_i \int_0^t e^{\mu_i(t-u)} F_i(u) \, du$$

and

(16.44)
$$(\dot{q}) = \sum_{i=1}^{2n} \mu_i(\phi)_i e^{\mu_i(t-u)} F_i(u) \, du$$

This is the solution for the forced motion of the system subject to the zero initial conditions of (16.38). The functions $F_i(u)$ are obtained from the generalized forces $(Q(t))$ by Eq. (16.42).

17. THE USE OF MATRIX ITERATION TO DETERMINE THE FREQUENCIES AND MODES OF OSCILLATION OF LINEAR CONSERVATIVE SYSTEMS

The use of an iterative procedure in order to determine the frequencies and modes of systems having a finite number of degrees of freedom by the use of matrix algebra appears to have first been suggested in a fundamental paper by R. von Mises and H. Geiringer in 1929.[2]   In 1934 W. J. Duncan and A. R. Collar[1] gave a number of practical applications of iteration using matrix notation in the calculations.

In this section, a brief discussion of the method will be given for the case of conservative systems and the method illustrated by applying it to typical systems.

In Sec. 7 it was shown that the equations of motion governing the free oscillations of a linear conservative system can be written in the two alternative forms

(17.1)
$$[D](\ddot{q}) + (q) = (0)$$

or

(17.2)
$$(\ddot{q}) + [W](q) = (0)$$

where $[D] = [k]^{-1}[m]$ is the *dynamical matrix* of the system and $[W] = [D]^{-1}$ or $[W] = [m]^{-1}[k]$ is the *inverse dynamical* matrix of the system.

If an oscillatory solution of either (17.1) or (17.2) of the form

(17.3)
$$(q) = (A) \sin (wt + \theta)$$

is assumed, then the substitution of (17.3) into (17.1) leads to the equation

(17.4)
$$(zU - [D])(A) = (0) \quad \text{where} \quad z = 1/w^2$$

On the other hand if (17.3) is substituted into (17.2), then the following equation is obtained

(17.5)
$$(\mu U - [W])(A) = (0) \quad \text{where} \quad \mu = w^2$$

Equations (17.4) and (17.5) lead to the following characteristic equations

(17.6) $\det (zU - [D]) = 0$

(17.7) $\det (\mu U - [W]) = 0$

From these two equations it is seen that the eigenvalues of $[D]$, $z_1, z_2, z_3, \ldots,$ z_n are related to the natural angular frequencies of the system by the equations

(17.8) $w_i = (1/z_i)^{1/2}, \qquad i = 1, 2, 3, \ldots, n$

If we call z_1 the *largest eigenvalue* of the dynamical matrix $[D]$, then $w_1 = (1/z_1)^{1/2}$ is the *lowest* natural frequency of the system.

The eigenvalues of the inverse dynamical matrix $[W]$, μ_i, on the other hand, are related to the natural angular frequencies w_i or the system by the equations

(17.9) $w_i = (\mu_i)^{1/2}, \qquad i = 1, 2, 3, \ldots, n$

It is thus seen that the *largest* eigenvalue of $[W]$ corresponds to the *greatest* natural frequency of the system.

To each eigenvalue z_i of $[D]$, there corresponds a *modal column* or *eigenvector* $(A)_i$ that satisfies the equation

(17.10) $[D](A)_i = z_i(A)_i, \qquad i = 1, 2, 3, \ldots, n$

A similar relation exists between the eigenvectors of $[W]$ and its eigenvalues.

The Basis of the Matrix Iteration Method

The fundamental ideas on which the matrix iteration methods are based will now be explained. The procedure will be illustrated by the use of the dynamical matrix $[D]$. It is realized that a similar procedure can be carried out in which the matrix $[W]$ instead of $[D]$ is used. Let it be assumed that the dynamical matrix has n eigenvectors $(A)_1, (A)_2, \ldots, (A)_n$. In this case the modal matrix of $[D]$ formed by assembling the columns $(A)_i$ in the form

(17.11) $[A] = [(A)_1, (A)_2, \ldots, (A)_n],$ (the modal matrix of $[D]$)

is non-singular. Therefore we know that

(17.12) $\det [A] = \det [(A)_1 \quad (A)_2 \quad \ldots \quad (A)_n] \neq 0$

Therefore the vectors $(A)_i$, $i = 1, 2, 3, \ldots, n$ form a linearly independent set of vectors in an n-dimensional space. It is possible to expand an arbitrary vector $(x)_0$ in this space as a linear combination of the vectors $(A)_i$, $i = 1, 2, 3, \ldots, n$, in the form

(17.13) $(x)_0 = c_1(A)_1 + c_2(A)_2 + c_3(A)_3 + \cdots + c_n(A)_n$

However, it is easily seen that as a consequence of (17.10), we have the result

(17.14) $[D]^s(A)_i = z_i^s(A)_i, \qquad i = 1, 2, 3, \ldots, n$
$$s = 1, 2, 3, 4, \ldots$$

Let us now call the largest eigenvalue of $[D]$, z_1 the next largest z_2, etc., so that

(17.15) $$z_1 > z_2 > z_3 > \cdots > z_n$$

Now let the Eq. (17.13) be multiplied by the dynamical matrix $[D]$ s times. As a consequence of (17.14), the result is

(17.16) $[D]^s(x)_0 = (x)_s = c_1 z_1^s(A)_1 + c_2 z_2^s(A)_2 + \cdots + c_n z_n^s(A)_n$

$$= z_1^s \left[c_1(A)_1 + c_2 \left(\frac{z_2}{z_1}\right)^s (A)_2 + \cdots + c_n \left(\frac{z_n}{z_1}\right)^s (A)_n \right]$$

Now since the eigenvalues z_i of $[D]$ are, by hypothesis, distinct and z_1 is the *largest eigenvalue*, it is apparent that after multiplying the arbitrary vector $(x)_0$ by $[D]$ or *iterating* with $[D]$ a sufficient number of times s, the coefficients of the eigenvectors $(A)_2, (A)_3, \ldots, (A)_n$ in the sum (17.16) become very small compared to the coefficient of $(A)_1$. It can therefore be seen that we have the following result

(17.17) $(x)_s = [D]^s(x)_0 \approx z_1^s c_1(A)_1$ (for a sufficiently large s)

If one more iteration is performed, it can be seen that the result is

(17.18) $$(x)_{s+1} = z_1(x)_s$$

In other words, when the iteration procedure has proceeded so that the first term in the sum (17.16) is dominant, then one more iteration produces a vector $(x)_{s+1}$ that is a mere multiple of the preceding vector $(x)_s$. This multiple is z_1 the *largest eigenvalue* of the dynamical matrix $[D]$. The number of iterations required in order for the stage (17.17) to be reached is of course determined by how widely separated the magnitudes of the eigenvalues z_i happen to be. If the first two eigenvalues are of nearly the same magnitude, for example, it may require a large number of iterations before the first term of the sum (17.17) becomes dominant.

When the stage expressed by (17.17) has been reached, it is noted that the vector $(x)_s$ is proportional to the eigenvector $(A)_1$ associated with the eigenvalue z_1. This enables the mode of oscillation when the system is executing vibrations at its lowest natural frequency to be determined.

18. NUMERICAL EXAMPLE

To illustrate the general principles discussed in Sec. 17, let the lowest frequency and corresponding mode of oscillation of the conservative dynamical system of Fig. 8.15 be determined. The dynamical system of Fig. 8.15 consists of three disks or fly-wheels of identical moments of inertia J. The three disks are free to rotate and are connected to each other by shafting of negligible mass and torsional stiffness k. The last shaft on the left is connected to a rigid wall. The kinetic energy function T and the potential energy function V for the system are

$$(18.1) \qquad T = \frac{J}{2}(\dot\theta_1^2 + \dot\theta_2^2 + \dot\theta_3^2)$$

$$(18.2) \qquad V = \frac{k}{2}[\theta_1^2 + (\theta_2 - \theta_1)^2 + (\theta_3 - \theta_2)^2]$$

the coordinates θ_1, θ_2, θ_3 are angular displacements of the disks measured from positions of equilibrium. As a consequence of the kinetic and potential

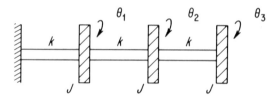

FIG. 8.15.   Torsional Dynamical System

energy functions, it is easy to see that the inertia and stiffness matrices $[m]$ and $[k]$ in this case have the following forms

$$(18.3) \qquad [m] = J \begin{bmatrix} 1 & 0 & 0 \\ 0 & 1 & 0 \\ 0 & 0 & 1 \end{bmatrix} \qquad \text{(inertia matrix)}$$

and

$$(18.4) \qquad [k] = k \begin{bmatrix} 2 & -1 & 0 \\ -1 & 2 & -1 \\ 0 & -1 & 1 \end{bmatrix}$$

The Dynamical Matrix

The dynamical matrix $[D]$ of the system may now be constructed from the matrices (18.3) and (18.4), it has the form

$$(18.5) \qquad [D] = [k]^{-1}[m] = \frac{J}{k}\begin{bmatrix} 1 & 1 & 1 \\ 1 & 2 & 2 \\ 1 & 2 & 3 \end{bmatrix} = \frac{J}{k}[a]$$

where $[a]$ is the numerical matrix

$$(18.6) \qquad [a] = \begin{bmatrix} 1 & 1 & 1 \\ 1 & 2 & 2 \\ 1 & 2 & 3 \end{bmatrix}$$

The characteristic equation of the system (17.6) now has the form

(18.7) $$\det(zU - [D]) = \det\left(zU - \frac{J}{k}[a]\right) = 0$$

If we now let

(18.8) $$\frac{kz}{J} = p$$

then the characteristic equation (18.7) is

(18.9) $$\det(pU - [a]) = 0$$

The eigenvalues of the matrix $[a]$, p_1, p_2, p_3 are related to the eigenvalues of the dynamical matrix $[D]$ by the Eq. (18.8) or

(18.10) $$z_i = \frac{J}{k}p_i, \qquad i = 1, 2, 3$$

The natural angular frequencies w_i of the system are given by (17.8) in the form

(18.11) $$w_i = \left(\frac{1}{z_i}\right)^{1/2} = \left(\frac{k}{Jp_i}\right)^{1/2}, \qquad i = 1, 2, 3$$

The largest eigenvalue of the matrix $[a]$, p_1, therefore gives the lowest angular frequency of the system.

The Determination of the Lowest Frequency and Mode by Matrix Iteration

The largest eigenvalue p_1 of the matrix $[a]$ will now be determined by the process of matrix iteration described in Sec. 17.   For this purpose, we select

(18.12) $$(x)_0 = \begin{bmatrix} 1 \\ 1 \\ 1 \end{bmatrix}$$

for the *arbitrary vector*.   The first iteration with the matrix $[a]$ produces the following vector

(18.13) $$[a](x)_0 = \begin{bmatrix} 1 & 1 & 1 \\ 1 & 2 & 2 \\ 1 & 2 & 3 \end{bmatrix} \begin{bmatrix} 1 \\ 1 \\ 1 \end{bmatrix} = \begin{bmatrix} 3 \\ 5 \\ 6 \end{bmatrix} = 6 \begin{bmatrix} 0.500 \\ 0.833 \\ 1.000 \end{bmatrix} = (x)_1$$

Since it is only the *ratios* of the elements of the vector $(x)_1$ that are of importance, we may discard the number 6 and take for $(x)_1$ the column that remains in (18.13) after the six has been discarded.   Therefore the next iteration gives

(18.14) $$[a](x)_1 = \begin{bmatrix} 1 & 1 & 1 \\ 1 & 2 & 2 \\ 1 & 2 & 3 \end{bmatrix} \begin{bmatrix} 0.500 \\ 0.833 \\ 1.000 \end{bmatrix} = \begin{bmatrix} 2.333 \\ 4.167 \\ 5.167 \end{bmatrix} = 5.167 \begin{bmatrix} 0.451 \\ 0.806 \\ 1.000 \end{bmatrix} = (x)_2$$

we now discard the number 5.167 and take the column remaining to be the vector $(x)_2$. The third iteration produces the following result

$$(18.15) \quad [a](x)_2 = \begin{bmatrix} 1 & 1 & 1 \\ 1 & 2 & 2 \\ 1 & 2 & 3 \end{bmatrix} \begin{bmatrix} 0.451 \\ 0.806 \\ 1.000 \end{bmatrix} = \begin{bmatrix} 2.257 \\ 4.063 \\ 5.063 \end{bmatrix} = 5.063 \begin{bmatrix} 0.445 \\ 0.802 \\ 1.000 \end{bmatrix} = (x)_3$$

we now discard the number 5.063 and proceed to the fourth iteration

$$(18.16) \quad [a](x)_3 = \begin{bmatrix} 1 & 1 & 1 \\ 1 & 2 & 2 \\ 1 & 2 & 3 \end{bmatrix} \begin{bmatrix} 0.445 \\ 0.802 \\ 1.000 \end{bmatrix} = \begin{bmatrix} 2.247 \\ 4.049 \\ 5.049 \end{bmatrix} = 5.049 \begin{bmatrix} 0.445 \\ 0.802 \\ 1.000 \end{bmatrix} = (x)_4$$

A further iteration merely repeats the factor 5.049. Therefore, we conclude that the iteration process has been carried far enough and that the dominant eigenvalue of the matrix $[a]$ is

$$(18.17) \qquad\qquad\qquad p_1 = 5.049$$

This corresponds to the following value of ω_1

$$(18.18) \qquad\qquad \omega_1 = \left(\frac{k}{5.049J}\right)^{1/2} = 0.446\left(\frac{k}{J}\right)^{1/2}$$

The corresponding mode is proportional to

$$(18.19) \qquad\qquad (\chi)_4 = \begin{pmatrix} 0.445 \\ 0.802 \\ 1.000 \end{pmatrix}$$

That is, when the system is oscillating at its lowest natural angular frequency (18.18), the first, second, and third disks are oscillating in the relative amplitudes $0.445 : 0.802 : 1.000$.

19. DETERMINATION OF THE HIGHER MODES: THE SWEEPING MATRIX

The highest natural frequency and mode of the system of the last section could be determined by carrying out the matrix-iteration process in terms of the inverse dynamical matrix $[\omega]$. We now turn to a method by which the intermediate modes and frequencies may be determined.

The general solution of the matrix differential equation

$$(19.1) \qquad\qquad [D](\ddot{q}) + (q) = (0)$$

may be written in the convenient form

$$(19.2) \qquad\qquad (q) = \sum_{i=1}^{n} Ci(A)_i \sin(\omega_i t + \theta_i)$$

where C_i and θ_i are arbitrary constants $(A)_i$ the ith eigenvector of the dynamical matrix $[D]$ and ω_i is related to the ith eigenvalue Z_i of the dynamical matrix $[D]$ by the equation

(19.3) $$\omega_i = \left(\frac{1}{Z_i}\right), \qquad i = 1, 2, 3, \ldots, n$$

The general solution (19.2) may also be written in the convenient matrix form

(19.4) $$(q) = [A] \begin{bmatrix} \sin(\omega_1 t + \theta_1) & 0 & \cdots & 0 \\ 0 & \sin(\omega_2 t + \theta_2) & \cdots & 0 \\ \cdot & \cdot & \cdots & \cdot \\ 0 & & \cdots & 0 \quad \sin(\omega_n t + \theta_n) \end{bmatrix} (C)$$

where $[A]$ is the modal matrix of $[D]$ and (C) is a column whose elements are the n arbitrary constants C_i of (19.2).

Equation (8.6) gives a convenient expression for the inverse $[A]^{-1}$ of the modal matrix $[A]$ in the form

(19.5) $$[A]^{-1} = [P]^{-1}[A]^1[M] = [B]$$

The *normal coordinates* (y) of the dynamical system may be obtained by the relation

(19.6) $$(y) = [A]^{-1}(q) = [B](q) \quad \text{where} \quad [B] = [A]^{-1}$$

If (19.4) is now premultiplied by $[B] = [A]^{-1}$, the result is

(19.7) $$(y) = [B](q) = \begin{bmatrix} \sin(\omega_1 t + \theta_1) & \cdots & 0 \\ 0 & \sin(\omega_2 t + \theta_2) & \cdots \\ \cdot & \cdots & \cdot \\ 0 & \cdots & \sin(\omega_n t + \theta_n) \end{bmatrix}$$

If (19.7) is expanded, we obtain

(19.8) $$y_i = C_i \sin(\omega_i t + \theta_i), \qquad i = 1, 2, 3, \ldots, n$$

The y_i quantities perform independent oscillations and are therefore the normal coordinates of the system.

Continuing the Solution

Let the ith row of the matrix $[B] = [A]^{-1}$ as given by (19.5) be denoted by $[B]_i$, then it is easy to see that since the matrix $[P]$ given by (8.1) in the form

(19.9) $$[P] = [A]^1[M][A] = \begin{bmatrix} P_{11} & 0 & \cdots & 0 \\ 0 & P_{22} & \cdots & 0 \\ \cdot & \cdot & \cdots & \cdot \\ 0 & 0 & \cdots & P_{nn} \end{bmatrix}$$

is a diagonal matrix, it follows from (19.5) that the ith row of $[B]$ may be expressed in the form

$$(19.10) \qquad [B]_i = P_{ii}(A)_i^1 [M]$$

In particular, the first row of $[B]$, $[B]_1$ is given by

$$(19.11) \qquad [B]_1 = P_{11}(A)_i^1 [M]$$

Since $[B] = [A]^{-1}$ or $[B] \cdot [A] = U$ where U is the nth order unit matrix, it follows that the rows of $[B]$ are related to the eigenvectors $(A)_i$ by the equations

$$(19.12) \qquad [B]_i(A)_j = \begin{Bmatrix} 0 & j & i \neq j \\ 1 & j & i = j \end{Bmatrix}$$

From this, it follows that the normal coordinate y_1 is given by the equation

$$(19.13) \qquad [B]_1(q) = C_1 \sin(\omega_1 t + \theta_1) = y_1$$

If now, the fundamental mode is to be absent, the following condition is necessary

$$(19.14) \qquad [B]_1(q) = 0$$

If (19.14) is expanded, the following result is obtained

$$(19.15) \qquad B_{11}q_1 + B_{12}q_2 + \cdots + B_{1n}q_n = 0$$

Therefore, we obtain the following equations of constraint between the coordinates

$$
(19.16) \qquad
\begin{aligned}
q_1 &= \frac{-B_{12}}{B_{11}} q_2 \frac{B_{13}}{B_{11}} q_3 \cdots \frac{-B_{1n}}{B_{11}} q_n \\
q_2 &= q_2 \\
q_3 &= q_3 \\
&\cdots \\
q_n &= q_n
\end{aligned}
$$

This set of equations may be written in the convenient matrix form

$$(19.17) \qquad (q) = [S]_1(q)$$

where the square matrix $[S]$ is given by

$$(19.18) \qquad [S]_1 = \begin{bmatrix} 0 & \dfrac{-B_{12}}{B_{11}} & \dfrac{-B_{13}}{B_{11}} & \cdots & \dfrac{-B_{1n}}{B_{11}} \\ 0 & 1 & 0 & \cdots & 0 \\ \cdot & \cdot & \cdot & \cdots & \cdot \\ 0 & 0 & 0 & \cdots & 1 \end{bmatrix}$$

Equation (19.17) constrains the coordinates in such a manner that the fundamental mode has been removed. The matrix $[S]_1$ is called the "sweeping matrix." The product of the original dynamical matrix and the sweeping matrix $[S]$ gives a new dynamical matrix $[D]$, which is so constructed as to have the fundamental mode removed. This new dynamical matrix is given by

$$(19.19) \qquad [D]_1 = [D][S]_1$$

The iteration procedure carried out with the modified dynamical matrix $[D]_1$ will yield the frequency and corresponding modal column or eigenvector corresponding to the second mode of oscillation. That is, iterating with the modified dynamical matrix $[D]_1$ will yield a column proportional to $(A)_2$ the second eigenvector of $[D]$ and the next largest eigenvalue Z_2 of $[D]$. The second natural frequency of the system, ω_2, is then given by (19.3) in the form

$$(19.20) \qquad \omega_2 = \left(\frac{1}{Z_2}\right)^{1/2}$$

Having obtained the second eigenvector $(A)_2$, then by (19.10) it is possible to obtain the second row of $[B]_1[B]_2$ in the form

$$(19.21) \qquad [B]_2 = P_{22}(A)_2^1[M]$$

If we now introduce the constraint

$$(19.22) \qquad [B]_2(q) = 0$$

this constraint insures that the second mode of oscillation is suppressed. If we now eliminate q_1 between the equation $[B]_1(q) = 0$ and (19.22), we can construct a second "sweeping matrix" $[S]_2$. By the use of the equation

$$(19.23) \qquad [D]_2 = [D]_1[S]_2$$

we construct a new dynamical matrix that has the fundamental and just overtone modes absent. The iteration procedure is now continued with $[D]_2$ and the modal column $(A)_2$ and eigenvalue Z_2 obtained. From $(A)_2$ the row $[B]_2$ can now be obtained from (19.10) and this may be used to suppress the second overtone mode. A third sweeping matrix $[S]_3$ can now be constructed, etc. until all the eigenvectors and eigenvalues of the original dynamical matrix are obtained.

20. A NUMERICAL EXAMPLE OF THE ITERATION PROCEDURE

The entire analysis described in Sec. 19 is perhaps best illustrated by an example. For this, let us consider the oscillations of a triple pendulum under gravity in a vertical plane. This example is given by W. J. Duncan and A. R. Collar in their fundamental paper published in 1934.[3]

The dynamical system under consideration is depicted by Fig. 8.16.

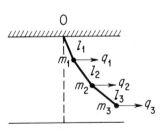

FIG. 8.16.   Triple Pendulum

The system consists of three masses, m_1, m_2, and m_3. The mass m_1 is suspended from a fixed point by a weightless rod of length l_1. The mass m_2 is suspended from m_1 by a weightless rod of length l_2 and similarly, the mass m_3 is suspended from m_2 by a weightless rod of length l_3. The system executes lateral oscillations in a vertical plane.

The case of small oscillations will be considered. In order to specify the motion of the system, the lateral displacements q_1, q_2, q_3 of the masses from the vertical will be used as coordinates. The first step in the analysis of the motion is to compute the dynamical matrix $[D]$ of the system.

The Flexibility Matrix

If a set of horizontal static forces F_1, F_2, F_3 are applied in the direction of the displacements q_1, q_2, and q_3, the relation between the forces and the displacements may be written in the form

(20.1)
$$\begin{pmatrix} F_1 \\ F_2 \\ F_3 \end{pmatrix} = \begin{bmatrix} k_{11} & k_{12} & k_{13} \\ k_{21} & k_{22} & k_{23} \\ k_{31} & k_{32} & k_{33} \end{bmatrix} \begin{pmatrix} q_1 \\ q_2 \\ q_3 \end{pmatrix}$$

where the square matrix in (20.1) is the stiffness matrix $[k]$. If (20.1) is premultiplied by the inverse of $[k]$, $[k]^{-1}$, the result may be written in the form

(20.2)
$$\begin{pmatrix} q_1 \\ q_2 \\ q_3 \end{pmatrix} = \begin{bmatrix} \phi_{11} & \phi_{12} & \phi_{13} \\ \phi_{21} & \phi_{22} & \phi_{23} \\ \phi_{31} & \phi_{32} & \phi_{33} \end{bmatrix} \begin{pmatrix} F_1 \\ F_2 \\ F_3 \end{pmatrix} = [\phi](F)$$

The matrix $[\phi] = [k]^{-1}$ is the flexibility matrix. Since the stiffness matrix is a symmetric matrix, so is the flexibility matrix $[\phi]$ so that

(20.3)
$$\phi_{rs} = \phi_{sr}$$

In terms of the flexibility matrix $[\phi]$, the dynamical matrix $[D]$ is given by the equation

(20.4)
$$[D] = [k]^{-1}[m] = [\phi][m]$$

To determine the elements of the first column of the flexibility matrix, it is necessary only to impose a horizontal unit force F_1 on the first mass of the pendulum system and compute or measure the corresponding deflections (q_1, q_2, q_3); this gives the *first column* of $[\phi]$. If a unit force F_2 is now applied to the mass m_2, the corresponding deflections give the second column of $[\phi]$, etc.

If a static unit force is applied horizontally to the mass m_1, then the three masses will each be displaced a distance a given by

(20.5)
$$a = \frac{l_1}{g(m_1 + m_2 + m_3)}$$

Hence the first column of the flexibility matrix is given by

(20.6)
$$a = \phi_{11} = \phi_{21} = \phi_{31}$$

If a unit force F_2 is now applied horizontally to m_2, m_1 will again be displaced a distance a, but m_2 and m_3 will each be displaced a distance $(a + b)$, where

$$(20.7) \qquad b = \frac{l_2}{g(m_2 + m_3)}$$

Hence, the elements of the second column of the matrix $[\phi]$ are given by

$$(20.8) \qquad \phi_{12} = a, \qquad \phi_{22} = \phi_{32} = (a + b)$$

Finally, if a unit horizontal force F_3 is applied to m_3, then m_1 is displaced a distance a, m_2 is displaced a distance $(a + b)$ and m_3 a distance $(a + b + c)$, where

$$(20.9) \qquad c = \frac{l_3}{gm_3}$$

The elements of the third column of $[\phi]$ are, therefore

$$(20.10) \qquad \phi_{13} = a, \qquad \phi_{23} = (a + b), \qquad \phi_{33} = (a + b + c)$$

Therefore, the flexibility matrix is given by

$$(20.11) \qquad [\phi] = \begin{bmatrix} a & a & a \\ a & (a + b) & (a + b) \\ a & (a + b) & (a + b + c) \end{bmatrix}$$

The inertia matrix $[m]$ in this case has the diagonal form

$$(20.12) \qquad [m] = \begin{bmatrix} m_1 & 0 & 0 \\ 0 & m_2 & 0 \\ 0 & 0 & m_3 \end{bmatrix}$$

Therefore, the dynamical matrix $[D]$ of the pendulum system has the form

$$(20.13) \qquad [D] = [\phi][m] = \begin{bmatrix} m_1 a & m_2 a & m_3 a \\ m_1 a & m_2(a + b) & m_3(a + b) \\ m_1 a & m_2(a + b) & m_3(a + b + c) \end{bmatrix}$$

As a numerical example, let us take the case where all the masses are equal and the lengths of the pendulums are equal. That is, we consider the case for which

$$(20.14) \qquad m_1 = m_2 = m_3 = m, \qquad l_1 = l_2 = l_3 = l$$

For this special case, the quantities a, b and c defined above reduce to

$$(20.15) \qquad a = \frac{l}{3mg}, \qquad b = \frac{l}{2mg}, \qquad c = \frac{l}{mg}$$

With these values of a, b, c, the dynamical matrix (20.13) becomes,

$$(20.16) \qquad [D] = \frac{l}{6g} \begin{bmatrix} 2 & 2 & 2 \\ 2 & 5 & 5 \\ 2 & 5 & 11 \end{bmatrix} = \frac{l}{6g} [N]$$

where the matrix $[N]$ is the square matrix in (20.16). The characteristic equation of the dynamical matrix $[D]$ is

$$(20.17) \qquad \det(ZU - [D]) = 0$$

If we let

$$(20.18) \qquad p = \frac{6g}{l} Z$$

then the characteristic equation (20.17) is equivalent to the equation

$$(20.19) \qquad \det(pU - [N]) = 0$$

This is the characteristic equation of the numerical matrix $[N]$.

The eigenvalues of $[N]$, p_1, p_2, p_3 are related to the eigenvalues of $[D]Z_1$, Z_2, Z_3 by the Eq. (20.18) or

$$(20.20) \qquad Z_i = \frac{l}{6g} p_i = \frac{1}{\omega_i^2}, \qquad i = 1, 2, 3$$

where the ω_i quantities are the natural angular frequencies of the oscillating pendulums. Therefore, once the eigenvalues p_i of $[N]$ have been determined, the angular frequencies ω_i are given by

$$(20.21) \qquad \omega_i = \sqrt{\frac{6g}{lp_i}}$$

The eigenvectors of $[N]$ are the same as the eigenvectors of $[D]$.

The Iteration Procedure

The iteration procedure will now be carried out with the matrix $[N]$. First the largest eigenvalue p_i of $[N]$ will be determined with its corresponding eigenvector. This will determine the smallest or fundamental angular frequency ω_1 of the pendulum system.

We choose for the arbitrary vector $(\chi)_0$ to begin the procedure, the vector

$$(20.22) \qquad (\chi)_0 = \begin{pmatrix} 1 \\ 1 \\ 1 \end{pmatrix}$$

and begin the iteration sequence.

$$(20.23) \qquad [N](\chi)_0 = \begin{bmatrix} 2 & 2 & 2 \\ 2 & 5 & 5 \\ 2 & 5 & 11 \end{bmatrix} \begin{pmatrix} 1 \\ 1 \\ 1 \end{pmatrix} = \begin{pmatrix} 6 \\ 12 \\ 8 \end{pmatrix}$$

$$= 18 \begin{pmatrix} \frac{1}{3} \\ \frac{2}{3} \\ 1 \end{pmatrix}$$

It is unnecessary to carry the common factor 18 in the further computations since it is the ratios of the successive elements in the multiplications that are important. The factor 18 is therefore dropped and the process continued. We thus obtain

$$(20.24) \qquad \begin{bmatrix} 2 & 2 & 2 \\ 2 & 5 & 5 \\ 2 & 5 & 11 \end{bmatrix} \begin{pmatrix} \frac{1}{3} \\ \frac{2}{3} \\ 1 \end{pmatrix} = \begin{pmatrix} 4 \\ 9 \\ 15 \end{pmatrix} = 15 \begin{pmatrix} 0.26 \\ 0.6 \\ 1 \end{pmatrix}$$

$$\begin{bmatrix} 2 & 2 & 2 \\ 2 & 5 & 5 \\ 2 & 5 & 11 \end{bmatrix} \begin{pmatrix} 0.26 \\ 0.6 \\ 1 \end{pmatrix} = 14.53 \begin{pmatrix} 0.25688 \\ 0.58716 \\ 1.00000 \end{pmatrix}$$

After nine multiplications, we obtain

$$(20.25) \qquad \begin{bmatrix} 2 & 2 & 2 \\ 2 & 5 & 5 \\ 2 & 5 & 11 \end{bmatrix} \begin{pmatrix} 0.254885 \\ 0.584225 \\ 1.000000 \end{pmatrix} = 14.4309 \begin{pmatrix} 0.254885 \\ 0.584225 \\ 1.000000 \end{pmatrix}$$

If the process is repeated, the last column matrix is merely multiplied by the factor 14.4309 and we therefore conclude that this is the dominant eigenvalue of the matrix $[N]$ so that

$$(20.26) \qquad p_1 = 14.4309$$

The fundamental frequency $F_1 = \omega_1/2\pi$ of the oscillation is obtained by the use of (20.22) and it is

$$(20.27) \qquad F_1 = \frac{\omega_1}{2\pi} = \frac{1}{2\pi} \sqrt{\frac{6g}{lp_1}} = 0.102624 \sqrt{\frac{g}{l}} \text{ cycles per second}$$

The eigenvector or fundamental modal column, $(A)_1$, is proportional to the column matrix in the right member of (20.25) so that we have

$$(20.28) \qquad (A)_1 \approx \begin{pmatrix} 0.254885 \\ 0.584225 \\ 1.000000 \end{pmatrix}$$

Determination of the First Overtone

To obtain the frequency of the first overtone $F_2 = \omega_2/2\pi$ we first use Eq. (19.11) to obtain the row $[B]_1$. In this case, the inertia matrix $[m]$ has the simple form

$$
(20.29) \qquad [m] = \begin{bmatrix} m & 0 & 0 \\ 0 & m & 0 \\ 0 & 0 & m \end{bmatrix} = mU
$$

where U is the third-order unit matrix, so that (19.11) reduces to

$$
(20.30) \qquad\qquad [B] = mp_{11}(A)_1^1
$$

Since we are interested only in a row proportional to $[B]_1$ we may take $[B]_1$ to be equal to $(A)_1^1$, so that

$$
(20.31) \qquad [B]_1 = (A)_1^1 = [0.254885,\ 0.584225,\ 1.000000]
$$

The condition (19.14) insuring that the fundamental mode is not present is now given by

$$
(20.32) \qquad [B]_1(q) = 0.254885q_1 + 0.584225q_2 + q_3 = 0
$$

or

$$
(20.33) \qquad\qquad q_1 = -2.29211q_2 - 3.92334q_3
$$

Accordingly, the "sweeping matrix" (19.18) for the pendulum system is

$$
(20.34) \qquad [S]_1 = \begin{bmatrix} 0 & -2.29211 & -3.92334 \\ 0 & 1 & 0 \\ 0 & 0 & 1 \end{bmatrix}
$$

The new dynamical matrix $[D]_1$ is given by (19.19) in the form

$$
(20.35) \qquad [D]_1 = [D][S]_1
$$

$$
= \begin{bmatrix} 2 & 2 & 2 \\ 2 & 5 & 5 \\ 2 & 5 & 11 \end{bmatrix} \begin{bmatrix} 0 & -2.29211 & -3.92334 \\ 0 & 1 & 0 \\ 0 & 0 & 1 \end{bmatrix}
$$

$$
= \begin{bmatrix} 0 & -2.58422 & -5.84668 \\ 0 & 0.41578 & -2.84668 \\ 0 & 0.41578 & 3.15332 \end{bmatrix}
$$

$[D]_1$ is the dynamical matrix from which the fundamental mode has been removed. We now repeat the iterative procedure by choosing a vector

$$
(\chi)_0 = \begin{pmatrix} 1 \\ 1 \\ 1 \end{pmatrix}
$$

and compute the product $[D]_1(\chi)_0$, etc. In the process of iteration, it is not necessary to compute the leading element of any column, since this is always multiplied by zero in the next step of iteration. In this way, we find

$$[D]_1(\chi)_0 = \begin{pmatrix} \cdots \\ -2.4309 \\ 3.5691 \end{pmatrix} = 3.5691 \begin{pmatrix} \cdots \\ -0.68110 \\ 1 \end{pmatrix}$$

(20.36)

$$[D]_1 \begin{pmatrix} \cdots \\ -0.68110 \\ 1 \end{pmatrix} = \begin{pmatrix} \cdots \\ -3.1299 \\ 2.8701 \end{pmatrix} = 2.8701 \begin{pmatrix} \cdots \\ -1.09049 \\ 1 \end{pmatrix}$$

After fifteen multiplications, the column repeats itself, and the scalar factor is found to be

(20.37) $$p_2 = 2.6152$$

At this stage, a computation of the leading element gives

(20.38) $$[D]_1 \begin{pmatrix} -0.95670 \\ -1.29429 \\ 1 \end{pmatrix} = 2.6152 \begin{pmatrix} -0.95670 \\ -1.29429 \\ 1 \end{pmatrix}$$

Hence, the mode of the first overtone is

(20.39) $$(A)_2 = \begin{pmatrix} -0.95670 \\ -1.29429 \\ 1 \end{pmatrix}$$

The frequency F_2 of the first overtone is determined (20.21) and is found to be

(20.40) $$F_2 = \frac{\omega_2}{2\pi} = \frac{1}{2\pi}\sqrt{\frac{6g}{2.6152l}} = 0.24107\sqrt{\frac{g}{l}} \text{ cycles per second}$$

Determination of the Second Overtone

To determine the frequency and mode of the second overtone, we first find a row proportional to $[B]_2$ by Eq. (19.21). Since the inertial matrix has the simple form (20.29) we may take

(20.41) $$[B]_2 = (A)_2^1$$

The condition for the absence of the second overtone is

(20.42) $$[B]_2(q) = [-0.95670, -1.29429, 1](q) = (0)$$

If this equation is solved for q, the result is

(20.43) $$q_1 = -1.35287q_2 + 1.04526q_3$$

If q_1 is now eliminated between (20.43) and (20.33), we obtain

$$(20.44) \qquad 0 = 0.93924q_2 + 4.96860q_3$$

or

$$(20.45) \qquad q_2 = -5.2900q_3$$

From this result, we now construct a second sweeping matrix $[S]_2$ that has the form,

$$(20.46) \qquad [S]_2 = \begin{bmatrix} 1 & 0 & 0 \\ 0 & 0 & -5.2900 \\ 0 & 0 & 1 \end{bmatrix}$$

The dynamical matrix $[D]_2$ that has the fundamental and first overtone modes absent is given by (19.23) in the form

$$(20.47)\ [D]_2 = [D]_1[S]_2 = \begin{bmatrix} 0 & -2.58422 & -5.84668 \\ 0 & 0.41578 & -2.84668 \\ 0 & 0.41578 & 3.15332 \end{bmatrix} \begin{bmatrix} 1 & 0 & 0 \\ 0 & 0 & -5.2900 \\ 0 & 0 & 1 \end{bmatrix}$$

$$= \begin{bmatrix} 0 & 0 & 7.8238 \\ 0 & 0 & -5.0461 \\ 0 & 0 & 0.9539 \end{bmatrix}$$

We now repeat the iterative process with $[D]_2$ and obtain

$$(20.48) \qquad [D]_2(x)_0 = \begin{bmatrix} 0 & 0 & 7.8238 \\ 0 & 0 & -5.0461 \\ 0 & 0 & 0.9539 \end{bmatrix} \begin{pmatrix} 1 \\ 1 \\ 1 \end{pmatrix} = \begin{pmatrix} 7.8238 \\ -5.0461 \\ 0.9539 \end{pmatrix}$$

$$= 0.9539 \begin{pmatrix} 8.2019 \\ -5.2900 \\ 1 \end{pmatrix}$$

If the process is repeated, the factor 0.9539 is again obtained, so that it is unnecessary to continue further. We, therefore, have obtained the smallest eigenvalue p_3 of the matrix $[N]$; it is

$$(20.49) \qquad p_3 = 0.9539$$

The highest frequency F_3 of oscillation of the pendulum system is therefore

$$(20.50) \qquad f_3 = \frac{1}{2\pi} \sqrt{\frac{6g}{p_3 l}} = \frac{1}{2\pi} \sqrt{\frac{6g}{0.9539 l}} = 0.39916 \sqrt{\frac{g}{l}}$$

The mode $(A)_3$ that corresponds to this frequency is

$$(20.51) \qquad\qquad (A)_3 = \begin{pmatrix} 8.2019 \\ -5.2900 \\ 1 \end{pmatrix}$$

The modal matrix $[A]$ of the pendulum system may be taken to be

$$(20.52) \qquad [A] = \begin{bmatrix} 0.254885 & -0.95670 & 8.2019 \\ 0.584225 & -1.29429 & -5.2900 \\ 1 & 1 & 1 \end{bmatrix}$$

The second overtone could have been obtained directly by iterating with the inverse dynamical matrix $[D]^{-1} = [\omega]$ discussed in Sec. 7.

The characteristic equation of $[\omega]$ is

$$(20.53) \qquad\qquad \det(\mu U - [\omega]) = 0$$

If the largest eigenvalue of $[\omega]$, μ_1, is determined, then the largest angular frequency ω_3 is given by the equation

$$(20.54) \qquad\qquad \omega_3 = \sqrt{\mu_1}$$

In the case under consideration, the dynamical matrix $[D]$ has the form (20.16), or

$$(20.55) \qquad\qquad [D] = \frac{l}{6g}[N]$$

The inverse dynamical matrix $[\omega]$ in this case, is therefore

$$(20.56) \qquad\qquad [D]^{-1} = \frac{6g}{l}[N]^{-1} = [\omega]$$

The inverse of $[N]$ is easily computed and has the following form

$$(20.57) \quad [N]^{-1} = \begin{bmatrix} 2 & 2 & 2 \\ 2 & 5 & 5 \\ 2 & 5 & 11 \end{bmatrix}^{-1} = \frac{1}{6}\begin{bmatrix} 5 & -2 & 0 \\ -2 & 3 & -1 \\ 0 & -1 & 1 \end{bmatrix} = [H]$$

Hence

$$(20.58) \qquad\qquad [\omega] = \frac{6g}{l}[H]$$

If (20.58) is now substituted into the characteristic equation (20.53), the following equation is obtained

$$(20.59) \qquad\qquad \det\left(\mu U - \frac{6g}{l}[H]\right) = 0$$

or if we introduce the notation

(20.60) $$\frac{\mu l}{6g} = \phi$$

then (20.60) can be written in the form

(20.61) $$\det(\phi U - [H]) = 0$$

This is the characteristic equation of the numerical matrix $[H]$. If the largest eigenvalue ϕ_1 of $[H]$ is obtained, then the largest eigenvalue μ_1 of $[\omega]$ is given by (20.60) to be

(20.62) $$\mu_1 = \frac{6g\phi_1}{l} = \omega_3^2$$

Therefore, the greatest natural frequency $f_3 = \omega_3/2\pi$ is related to ϕ_1 by the equation

(20.63) $$f_3 = \frac{1}{2\pi}\sqrt{\frac{6g\phi_1}{l}}$$

The iterative process when applied to the matrix $[H]$ yields the following results

(20.64) $$\phi_1 = 1.048323$$

for the largest eigenvalue of $[H]$. The eigenvector associated with this eigenvalue is found to be

(20.65) $$(A)_3 = \begin{pmatrix} 8.20180 \\ -5.28994 \\ 1 \end{pmatrix}$$

The frequency f_3 may now be computed by using (20.63) and its numerical value is given by

(20.66) $$f_3 = \frac{\omega_3}{2\pi} = \frac{1}{2\pi}\sqrt{\frac{6gx/0.048323}{l}} = 0.399157\sqrt{\frac{g}{l}}$$

These results agree quite well with those given by (20.50) and (20.51).

21. THE ANALYSIS OF A CLASS OF SYMMETRIC DAMPED LINEAR SYSTEMS

The motion of a general damped linear system has been discussed in some detail in Sec. 16. The free oscillations of such a system are determined by the solution of the differential equation

(21.1) $$[m](\ddot{q}) + [C](\dot{q}) + [k](q) = (0)$$

An important class of damped oscillatory systems that arise in practice have the property that the damping matrix $[C]$ is a linear combination of the stiffness matrix $[k]$ and the inertia matrix $[m]$, that is these systems exhibit a degree of symmetry in that

$$(21.2) \qquad [C] = a[m] + b[k]$$

where a and b are two real constants. If the relation (21.2) is substituted into (21.1) and the symbolic derivative operator

$$(21.3) \qquad D = \frac{d}{dt}, \qquad D^2 = \frac{d^2}{dt^2}$$

is introduced, the resulting equation may be written in the form

$$(21.4) \qquad [m](D^2 + aD)(q) + [k](bD + 1)(q) = (0)$$

In order to solve (21.4), we search for a solution of the type

$$(21.5) \qquad (q) = (A)e^{pt}$$

where (A) is a column of n constants and p is a constant to be determined. If (21.5) is substituted into (21.4), the result is

$$(21.6) \qquad [m](p^2 + ap)(A) + [k](bp + 1)(A) = (0)$$

This equation may be divided by the scalar $(bp + 1)$ to obtain

$$(21.7) \qquad \left(\frac{p^2 + ap}{1 + bp}\right)[m](A) + [k](A) = (0)$$

Now, if the system were devoid of damping, then $[C] = [0]$ and the Eq. (21.1) would reduce to

$$(21.8) \qquad [m](\ddot{q}) + [k](q) = (0)$$

This is the equation that governs the oscillations of a linear conservative system. The classical method for solving (21.8) has been discussed in Sec. 7 and consists of searching for a solution of the form

$$(21.9) \qquad (q) = (A)\sin(\omega t + \phi)$$

If this is substituted into (21.8), the resulting equation is

$$(21.10) \qquad -\omega^2[m](A) + [k](A) = (0)$$

If (21.10) and (21.7) are compared, it is seen that the two equations are identical in form. If we let

$$(21.11) \qquad \left(\frac{p^2 + ap}{1 + bp}\right) = -\omega^2$$

Now let

$$(21.12) \qquad \omega^2 = \mu$$

in (21.11). Then we have

$$(21.13) \qquad \mu[m](A) = [k](A)$$

or if (21.13) is premultiplied by $[m]^{-1}$ we obtain

$$(21.14) \qquad [\omega](A) = \mu(A)$$

where $[\omega] = [m]^{-1}[k] = [D]^{-1}$, the inverse dynamical matrix.

The possible values of $\mu, \mu_1, \mu_2, \mu_3, \ldots, \mu_n$ are the eigenvalues of $[\omega]$ and are the roots of the characteristic equation

$$(21.15) \qquad \det (\mu U - [\omega]) = (0)$$

The n columns (A) of (21.5) are thus seen to be the eigenvectors of the inverse dynamical matrix.

The possible values of p, p_i can be obtained from the Eq. (21.11) written in the form

$$(21.16) \qquad \frac{pi^2 + ap_i}{1 + bp_i} = -\mu_i, \qquad i = 1, 2, 3, \ldots, n$$

The quadratic (21.16) can be solved for p_i and the result written in the form

$$(21.17) \qquad p_i = -\alpha_i \pm j\beta_i, \qquad j = \sqrt{-1}, \qquad i = 1, 2, 3, \ldots, n$$

where

$$(21.18) \qquad \alpha_i = \frac{a + \mu_i b}{2}$$

$$(21.19) \qquad \beta_i = \sqrt{\mu_i - \alpha_i^2}$$

Equations (21.18) give the damping factor α_i and the natural frequency for any principal mode when the condition (21.2) holds. It is thus seen that a necessary and sufficient condition for the *dynamic stability* of the system is that all the α_i's be *positive* or that

$$(21.20) \qquad a + \mu_i b \geqslant 0, \qquad i = 1, 2, 3, \ldots, n$$

for each eigenvalue μ_i. It can be seen that this equation can be satisfied even in cases when either a or b (but not both) are negative.

Equation (21.16) gives $2n$ values of P_i. A solution $(q)_i$ of (21.4) that corresponds to the following two values of P_i

$$(21.21) \qquad P_i = -C_i + j\beta_i \quad \text{and} \quad \bar{P}_i = -\alpha_i - j\beta_i$$

may be written in the following form

$$(21.22) \qquad (q)_i = (A)_i[C_i e^{P_i t} + D_i e^{\bar{P}_i t}]$$
$$= (A)_i[C_i e^{-\alpha_i t} e^{j\beta_i t} + D_i e^{-\alpha_i t} e^{-j\beta_i t}]$$

where $(A)_i$ is the ith eigenvector of $[W]$ and the quantities C_i, D_i are arbitrary constants. This form of solution is a consequence of Eq. (21.5). Equation (21.21) may be written in the alternative form

$$(21.23) \qquad (q)_i = (A)_i e^{-\alpha_i t}[P_i \cos(\beta_i t) + D_i \sin(\beta_i t)]$$

where P_i and D_i are two new arbitrary constants. The general solution of (21.4) may now be obtained by summing all the particular solutions (21.23) in the form

$$(21.24) \qquad (q) = \sum_{i=1}^{n} (A)_i e^{-\alpha_i t}[P_i \cos(\beta_i t) + D_i \sin(\beta_i t)]$$

The arbitrary constants P_i, $i = 1, 2, \ldots, n$, may be obtained from the *initial displacements* of the system and the arbitrary constants D_i may be obtained from a knowledge of the *initial velocities* of the system.

The motion of systems that possess the symmetry expressed by Eq. (21.2) have been discussed by Lord Rayleigh.[10]

22. THE ROUTH-HURWITZ STABILITY CRITERION

Consider a linear dynamical system that has n degrees of freedom. If the various parameters of the system are constant, the differential equations of motion of the system when it is performing free oscillations may be written in the following matrix form

$$(22.1) \qquad (m)(\ddot{x}) + (c)(\dot{x}) + (k)(x) = (0)$$

where (x) is a column matrix whose n elements x_i, $(i = 1, 2, 3, 4, \ldots, n)$ are the n coordinates of the system. The matrices (m), (c) and (k) are square matrices of the nth order whose elements are known constants. The dots indicate differentiation with respect to the time in the usual manner.

In order to investigate the behavior of the given system, let a solution of (22.1) having the form

$$(22.2) \qquad (x) = (A)e^{pt}$$

be assumed. In the assumed solution (A) is a column of constants, and e^{pt} is the scalar exponential function. The quantity p is to be determined. If (22.2) is now substituted into (22.1) the result is

$$(22.3) \qquad \{(m)p^2 + (c)p + (k)\}(A) = (0)$$

where the scalar factor e^{pt} has been divided out. Equation (22.3) represents a set of linear homogeneous algebraic equations in the elements A_i of the column matrix (A).

If the following notation is introduced

$$(22.4) \qquad (g) = (m)p^2 + (c)p + (k)$$

then the Eq. (22.3) may be written in the compact form

$$(22.5) \qquad (g)(A) = (0)$$

In order for (22.5) to have a non-trivial solution, it is necessary for the *determinant* of the matrix (g) to vanish. That is, it is necessary that

$$(22.6) \qquad D(p) = \det (g) = 0$$

The determinant $D(p)$ can be expressed in the following form

$$(22.7) \qquad D(p) = \det (g) = \begin{vmatrix} g_{11}(p) & g_{12}(p) & \cdots & g_{1n}(p) \\ g_{21}(p) & g_{22}(p) & \cdots & g_{2n}(p) \\ \cdot & \cdot & \cdots & \cdot \\ g_{n1}(p) & g_{n2}(p) & \cdots & g_{nn}(p) \end{vmatrix}$$

If the determinant $D(p)$ is expanded, a polynomial in p of degree $2n$ is obtained in the general case. Equation (22.6), therefore, has the following form

$$(22.8) \qquad D(p) = a_0 p^{2n} + a_1 p^{2n-1} + a_2 p^{2n-2} + \cdots + a_{2n-1} p + a_{2n} = 0$$

where the constants a_i, $i = 0, 1, 2, 3, \ldots, 2n$, are functions of the elements of the matrices (m), (c), and (k) and are therefore characteristic of the dynamical system under consideration. They are real numbers.

The stability or instability of the dynamical system depends on the location of the zeros of the polynomial $D(p)$. These zeros are the roots of the algebraic equation (22.8).

In general, the $2n$ roots of the algebraic equation $D(p) = 0$ will be complex numbers. Since the coefficients a_i, $i = 0, 1, 2, 3, \ldots, 2n$, of the Eq. (22.8) are real numbers, the roots of this equation occur in conjugate complex pairs of the form

$$(22.9) \qquad p_i = b_i + jw_i, \qquad \bar{p}_i = b_i - jw_i \quad \text{for} \quad i = 1, 2, 3, \ldots, n$$

If the real parts, b_i of *all* the roots of (22.8) are *negative numbers*, the solution (22.2) will contain *decrement factors* of the form $e^{b_i t}$. If this is the case, then when the system is disturbed from its equilibrium position $(x) = (0)$, it will return to this position and the dynamical system is said to be a *stable system*.

If, on the other hand, one or more of the b_i quantities happens to be *positive*, the displacement (x) of the system will increase indefinitely with the time t once the system is displaced from the position $(x) = 0$. In such a case the system is said to be *unstable*. If one or more of the b_i quantities are zero and all the others negative, then the system will execute oscillations once it is disturbed from the position $(x) = (0)$. These oscillations will be of finite amplitude. The system is therefore capable of executing free oscillations of bounded amplitudes.

From the above discussion it is therefore apparent that a linear system whose equations of motion are of the form (22.1) is a *stable system* if all the roots of the Eq. (22.8) have *negative real parts*.

It is thus apparent that the stability or instability of the dynamical system under consideration can be determined by obtaining the roots of the characteristic equation of the system (22.8). When the numerical values for the coefficients a_i, $i = 0, 1, 2, 3, \ldots, 2n$ are known, the roots of the equation $D(p) = 0$ may be determined by some iterative procedure such as Graeffe's root-squaring method. Iterative methods for solving high degree algebraic equations are discussed in books on numerical analysis.[7] The solution of the equation $D(p) = 0$ is a laborious procedure in all but the simplest cases. Fortunately information concerning the *stability* of the system may be obtained without solving the characteristic equation (22.8) by the application of a criterion which is known in the mathematical literature as the *Routh-Hurwitz stability criterion*.

The Routh-Hurwitz criterion will be stated here without proof. The reader interested in the method of proof of this criterion is referred to the paper written by Hurwitz in 1895.[8]

Let $2n = k$. With this notation, the characteristic equation (22.8) of the system under consideration may be written in the following form

(22.10) $\quad D(p) = a_0 p^k + a_1 p^{k-1} + a_2 p^{k-2} + \cdots + a_{k-1} p + a_k = 0$

Let it be assumed that (22.9) is written in such a manner that the first coefficient a_0 is *positive*.

The necessary and sufficient conditions for the real parts of all the roots of (22.10) to be negative may be stated in the following form:

1. All the coefficients a_i, $i = 1, 2, 3, \ldots, k$, must be positive. [This condition, that all the coefficients a_i must have the same sign, is a necessary but not a sufficient condition for the real parts of all the roots of (22.10) to be negative.]

2. A necessary and sufficient condition for stability is that the following *test functions* T_i are all *positive* when $D(p) = 0$ has been put in to such a form that a_0 is *positive*.

$$T_0 = a_0, \qquad T_1 = a_1, \qquad T_2 = \begin{vmatrix} a_1 & a_0 \\ a_3 & a_2 \end{vmatrix}$$

$$T_3 = \begin{vmatrix} a_1 & a_0 & 0 \\ a_3 & a_2 & a_1 \\ a_5 & a_4 & a_3 \end{vmatrix}, \qquad T_4 = \begin{vmatrix} a_1 & a_0 & 0 & 0 \\ a_3 & a_2 & a_1 & a_0 \\ a_5 & a_4 & a_3 & a_2 \\ a_7 & a_6 & a_5 & a_4 \end{vmatrix}$$

(22.11)

$$T_5 = \begin{vmatrix} a_1 & a_0 & 0 & 0 & 0 \\ a_3 & a_2 & a_1 & a_0 & 0 \\ a_5 & a_4 & a_3 & a_2 & a_1 \\ a_7 & a_6 & a_5 & a_4 & a_3 \\ a_9 & a_8 & a_7 & a_6 & a_5 \end{vmatrix}, \qquad T_i = \begin{vmatrix} a_1 & a_0 & 0 & 0 & \cdots & \cdot \\ a_3 & a_2 & a_1 & a_0 & \cdots & \cdot \\ a_5 & a_4 & a_3 & a_2 & \cdots & \cdot \\ \cdot & \cdot & \cdot & \cdot & \cdots & \cdot \\ a_{2i-1} & a_{2i-2} & \cdot & \cdot & \cdots & a_i \end{vmatrix}$$

In constructing the test functions T_i all the coefficients a_r with $r > k$ or $r < 0$ are replaced by zeros. It is thus evident that the elements of the bottom row of the kth determinant are all zero except for the last term. Hence

$$(22.12) \qquad\qquad T_k = a_k T_{k-1}$$

Consequently, if $a_k > 0$, then T_k has the same sign as T_{k-1} and it is therefore necessary to test the determinants only from T_0 to T_{k-1}. If any of the determinants T_i, $i = 0, 1, 2, 3, k - 1$, have negative values, the system under consideration is *unstable*.

If the test determinant T_{k-1} vanishes, so that

$$(22.13) \qquad\qquad T_{k-1} = 0$$

it may be shown that the characteristic equation (22.10) has a pair of purely imaginary roots or else it has a pair of equal and opposite real roots.

23. THE LOCATION OF THE EIGENVALUES OF A MATRIX

The following theorems relating to the location of the eigenvalues of a matrix (M) with real or complex elements are sometimes useful: Let the typical eigenvalue of (M) be denoted as $\mu = a + jw$.

(a) If (M) is a Hermitian matrix, and in particular if (M) is real and symmetrical, then all its eigenvalues are real.

(b) If (M) is a matrix of a general type, a lies between the greatest and smallest eigenvalue of the Hermitian matrix $\frac{1}{2}\{(M) + (\overline{M})'\}$, and w lies between the greatest and least eigenvalue of the Hermitian matrix $j\{(M) - (\overline{M})'\}/2$.

Theorem (b) is useful in estimating the magnitudes of the real and imaginary parts of the eigenvalues of a matrix of general type.[11]

PROBLEMS

1. A light horizontal string of length $9a$ has its ends fixed. Two small particles of masses $2m$ and m are attached to this string at distances a and $5a$ from one end. Find the normal modes of transverse horizontal vibration, and prove that the periods are $4\pi(2ma/3T)^{1/2}$ and $4\pi(ma/3T)^{1/2}$, where T is the tension in the string.

2. A double pendulum consists of a bob A of mass $3m$ suspended from a fixed point O by a light inextensible string of length a and a second bob B of mass m suspended from A by a light inextensible string also of length a. If OA makes a small angle θ to the vertical, and if AB makes a small angle ϕ to the vertical, where the points O, A, and B lie in a fixed vertical plane, prove that the kinetic energy and the potential energy are respectively given by

$$T = 2ma\dot{\theta}^2 + \tfrac{1}{2}ma^2\dot{\phi}^2 + ma^2\dot{\theta}\dot{\phi}$$
$$V = 2mga\theta^2 + \tfrac{1}{2}mga\phi^2$$

to terms of the second order. Write down Lagrange's equations, and deduce that the periods of the two normal modes are given by $2\pi/n$, where $n^2 = 2g/a$ and $n^2 = 2g/3a$. Find the ratios of the values of θ and ϕ in these two normal modes.

3. A shaft carries four identical disks each of moment of inertia J. If the shaft is flexible and the four disks are equally spaced, show that the kinetic energy T and the potential energy V of the system are given by the following expressions

$$T = J\left(\frac{\dot{\theta}_1^2 + \dot{\theta}_2^2 + \dot{\theta}_3^2 + \dot{\theta}_4^2}{2}\right)$$

$$V = \tfrac{1}{2}C\{(\theta_1 - \theta_2)^2 + (\theta_2 - \theta_3)^2 + (\theta_3 - \theta_4)^2\}$$

where c is the torsional stiffness of the length of shaft between the disks and θ_i are angular coordinates. Write the Lagrange equations of the system and show that the coordinates θ_i satisfy the following equation, $\dot{\theta}_1 + \dot{\theta}_2 + \dot{\theta}_3 + \dot{\theta}_4 = $ const. Show that $w = 0$ is one of the angular frequencies of the system. If $p = Jw^2/c$, show that the characteristic equation of the system is

$$p(p^3 - 6p^2 + 10p - 4) = 0$$

4. A cube of mass m rests on four equal springs attached to its lower corners. The spring constant of each spring is k (pounds/ft.). If the length of one side of the cube is s ft., determine the principal modes of vibration. Neglect the horizontal motion of the springs.

5. A uniform shaft that is free to rotate in bearings carries five equidistant disks. The moments of inertia of four disks are equal to J, while the moment of inertia of one of the end disks is equal to $2J$. Calculate the lowest frequency and the corresponding mode of the system by the use of matrix iteration.

6. A four story building has an elastic frame structure. The mass of the building is concentrated at each floor; one-half at the second floor; the other half equally distributed between the third and fourth floors. Assume the shearing rigidities between the floors to be the same. Determine the natural frequencies of the building and its modes of vibration.

7. Determine the nature of the forced oscillations of the building of Problem 6 if the ground vibrates horizontally in a pure harmonic motion given by $x = x_0 \sin(wt)$.

8. A train is composed of ten identical cars each of mass m. The effect of the coupling between the cars may be assumed to be represented by identical stiff springs of stiffness k. Determine the smallest value of the damping factor of identical shock absorbers placed between the cars and acting by viscous friction such that the relative motion of the cars will not be oscillatory.

9. A massless string is stretched under a large tensile force F. The string is loaded with ten point masses. The string is fastened at $x = 0$ to a fixed support. A point mass m is located at $x = a$, the second point mass is located at $x_2 = a(1 + r)$ and its mass is mr. At the point $x_3 = a(1 + r + r^2)$

is located a point mass mr^2 and so on.   The point masses and their spacing thus decreases as a geometric progression.   The string is fastened to a fixed support at a distance ar^{10} units from the tenth mass.   Study the transverse vibrations of the loaded string and determine the modes and frequencies of the system if $r < 1$.

REFERENCES

1. Bisplinghoff, R. L., H. Ashley and R. L. Halfman, *Aeroelasticity.* Cambridge, Mass.: Addison-Wesley Publishing Co., Inc., 1955.

2. Den Hartog, J. P., *Mechanical Vibrations*, 3rd Ed.   New York: McGraw-Hill Book Co., Inc., 1940.

3. Duncan, W. J. and A. R. Collar, "A Method for the Solution of Oscillation Problems by Matrices," Phil. Mag., Series 7, Vol. 17 (1934), pp. 865–909.

4. Frazer, R. A., W. J. Duncan and A. R. Collar, *Elementary Matrices and Some Applications to Dynamics and Differential Equations.*   New York: Cambridge University Press, 1938.

5. Gardner, M. S. and J. L. Barnes, *Transients in Linear Systems.*   New York: John Wiley and Sons, Inc., 1942.

6. Goldstein, H., *Classical Mechanics.*   Cambridge, Mass.: Addison-Wesley Publishing Co., Inc., 1951.

7. Hartree, D. R., *Numerical Analysis.*   New York: Oxford University Press, 1952.

8. Hurwitz, A., "Ueber die Bedingungen unter welchen eine Gleichung nur Wurzeln nit negativen reelen Theilen besitzt," Mathematische Annalen, Vol. 46 (1895), pp. 273–284.

9. Kármán, T. and M. A. Biot, *Mathematical Methods in Engineering.*   New York: McGraw-Hill Book Co., Inc., 1940.

10. Rayleigh, J. W. S., *The Theory of Sound*, Vol. 1, New York: Dover Publications, Inc., 1945.

11. Timoshenko, S., *Vibration Problems in Engineering.*   Princeton, N.J.: D. Van Nostrand Co., Inc., 1937.

12. Turnbull, H. W. and A. C. Aitken, *An Introduction to the Theory of Canonical Matrices.*   London: Blackie and Son, Ltd. (1932), pp. 76–79.

13. von Mises, R. and H. Geiringer, "Praktische Verfahred der Gleichungsauflosung," Z. angew. Math. u. Mech., Vol. 9 (1929), pp. 152–164.

9 THE STEADY-STATE SOLUTION OF THE GENERAL n-MESH CIRCUIT

1. INTRODUCTION

The mathematical analysis of linear electric circuits whose parameters are lumped and constant leads to a set of linear differential equations with constant coefficients. It is natural that the study of this set of differential equations should be facilitated by the use of the notation of matrix algebra. Not only is the analysis of complex circuits made simpler and more systematic but the introduction of linear transformations frequently gives the electrical engineer a greater insight in the synthesis of design of certain types of electric structures.

For example, in an entire class of electric circuits which are known in the literature of communication engineering as four-terminal networks, it has been found that there exists an intimate connection between the eigenvalues and eigenvectors of certain matrices of the second order and the propagation constants and characteristics and iterative impedances of circuits of this type. In recent years, certain properties of matrices have aided the synthesis of filter circuits and other types of electrical structures whose behavior has to conform with certain prescribed characteristics.

In this chapter some of the fundamental principles and properties of linear, invariable electric circuits whose parameters are lumped are discussed with the use of the notation of matrix algebra. The chapter is concluded with references to the literature where fuller and more advanced exposition may be found.

2. THE GENERAL NETWORK

(a) *Definition*

By the "general network" is meant a system consisting of a finite number of meshes linked together in the most general conceivable manner and excited by means of electromotive forces of arbitrary form.   Each mesh is made up of a general assemblage of resistances, inductances, and capacitances, and, in general, the linkage of each element with every other element is arbitrary.

(b) Definition of "Lumped System"

By regarding a system as "lumped," we mean that if an electromotive force is impressed upon the system, the effects of this electromotive force are felt instantaneously throughout the system.   That is, the physical dimensions of the system are such that the finite velocity of electromagnetic phenomena may be regarded as infinite.   Since an arbitrary electromotive force may be considered to be composed of a linear superposition of simple harmonic components of various frequencies, we may formulate the criterion of regarding a system as lumped, in the following manner:

Let f be the frequency of the highest frequency component of the impressed arbitrary electromotive force in cycles per second.   Then if λ is the shortest essential wave length in the disturbance given by the relation

$$(2.1) \qquad\qquad \lambda = \frac{c}{f}$$

where $c = 3 \times 10^{10}$ cm/sec is the velocity of light in a vacuum, and λ is large compared with the maximum dimension of the system (say 50 or 100 times), then we may consider the electrical system to be "lumped."

As an example, let us suppose that we have a system which consists of an arrangement of coils and condensers in the laboratory and that the highest component frequency of the impressed electromotive force is 100,000 cycles a second.   In this case, we have

$$(2.2) \qquad\qquad \lambda = \frac{3 \times 10^{10}}{10^5} = 3 \times 10^5 = 3 \text{ kilometers}$$

Hence, the system under consideration may be regarded as a lumped system. Such a system will be called a "quasi-stationary" system.   The development of this criterion follows from a consideration of the electromagnetic equations.[5]

(c) Definition of "Linear"

By a linear network is meant one whose component parts, such as resistances, inductances, and capacitances, are either constant or vary with the time.   In this discussion, we shall consider circuits whose elements are *constants*.

(d) Definition of "Bilateral"

By a bilateral network is meant one whose component parts have the property that they will pass currents with equal facility in either direction.

An electrolyte, in general, is an example of an element that is not bilateral, since current flows through it in only one direction.

3. FORMULATION OF THE PROBLEM IN TERMS OF MESH CURRENTS

The general problem of circuit analysis may be formulated in the following manner:

We are given a general, linear, bilateral, lumped, electrical network with initial charges in the various capacitances and initial currents in the various component parts; it is required to determine the behavior of the system due to these initial conditions which may be specified at $t = 0$ and to the application of general applied electromotive forces on the various meshes at $t = 0$.

We shall base our discussion of this problem on the two laws of Kirchhoff.

The First Law

Kirchhoff's first law states that the sum of the voltages about any closed contour or mesh in a network is zero. This means that at any instant the sum of all the applied electromotive forces acting on the mesh or closed contour and the various electromotive force drops across the various component elements of the mesh under consideration must be equal to zero.

The Second Law

Kirchhoff's second law states that the sum of the currents flowing into any junction or nodal point of the network must be equal to zero at all instants.

If we are able to trace n distinct closed contours in the network, then we have a network of n independent meshes, and the first law of Kirchhoff enables us to write n voltage equations. In any multimesh network, however, there will be more branches than meshes, and the voltage equations will be insufficient in number to determine all the branch currents.

To solve the problem in terms of branch currents requires that we write enough additional relations between the currents by invoking the second law to make the total number of equations equal to the number of unknowns.

There is, however, a method due to Maxwell by means of which it is possible to solve an n-mesh problem by the solution of n simultaneous equations. Maxwell postulates the existence of fictitious, circulating mesh currents, one current for each mesh. When a given branch is part of one mesh only, then the current in the branch is identical to the mesh current. If, however, a given branch is part of both of two adjacent meshes, then both mesh currents will flow through the same branch, and the branch current is the algebraic sum of the mesh currents.

It is convenient to adopt the convention that the clockwise direction of mesh currents is positive. Since Maxwell's method reduces the number of unknown currents to n, the number of independent meshes in the network, it is clear that the n voltage equations of Kirchhoff's first law are always sufficient to solve the problem.

Setting up Kirchhoff's First Law

Let us consider the general network of Fig. 9.1. Such a network may be schematically represented as shown in the diagram. It is assumed that each mesh contains a combination of resistances, capacitances, and inductances, and that these elements are coupled in a general manner to all the other elements of the network. Let us set up Kirchhoff's laws for the system. Since we are specifying the system by means of circulating currents, it is necessary to set up only the first law. Consider mesh 1; the counter voltage $E_{11}(t)$ induced in it due to its own current is

$$(3.1) \qquad E_{11}(t) = \frac{L_{11}di_1}{dt} + R_{11}i_1 + S_{11}\int_{-\infty}^{t} i_1\,dt$$

where L_{11} represents the sum of the mesh inductance coefficients, R_{11} is the sum of the mesh resistance coefficients, and S_{11} is the sum of the mesh

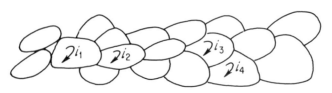

FIGURE 9.1

elastance coefficients. Since it is assumed that every mesh is coupled to every other mesh, the countervoltage which is induced into mesh 1 by mesh k is

$$(3.2) \qquad E_{1k}(t) = \frac{L_{1k}di_k}{dt} + R_{1k}i_k + S_{1k}\int_{-\infty}^{t} i_k\,dt$$

where L_{1k} is the sum of the mutual inductance coefficients between meshes 1 and k, R_{1k} is the sum of the mutual resistance coefficients between meshes 1 and k, and S_{1k} is the sum of the mutual elastance coefficients between meshes 1 and k. If now $E_1(t)$ represents the sum of the electromotive forces impressed on mesh 1, then by Kirchhoff's first law we must have

$$(3.3) \qquad \sum_{k=1}^{n} \frac{L_{1k}di_k}{dt} + R_{1k}i_k + S_{1k}\int_{-\infty}^{t} i_k\,dt = E_1(t)$$

where n is the total number of meshes of the system, and we suppose that $E_1(t)$ represents the total impressed electromotive force on mesh 1, which is supposed to be an arbitrary function of the time t. Kirchhoff's first law, when applied to mesh 2, yields the equation

$$(3.4) \qquad \sum_{k=1}^{n} \frac{L_{2k}di_k}{dt} + R_{2k}i_k + S_{2k}\int_{-\infty}^{t} i_k\,dt = E_2(t)$$

Applying Kirchhoff's first law to the various meshes yields n such equations. If we now introduce the following "differential-integral operators" defined as follows:

(3.5)
$$Z_{mn}(D) = L_{mn}D + R_{mn} + \frac{S_{mn}}{D}$$

where

$$D = \frac{d}{dt}$$

$$\frac{1}{D} = \int_{-\infty}^{t} (\ )\, dt$$

We may write this set of equations in the form

(3.6)
$$Z_{11}(D)i_1 + Z_{12}(D)i_2 + \cdots + Z_{1n}(D)i_n = E_1(t)$$
$$Z_{21}(D)i_1 + Z_{22}(D)i_2 + \cdots + Z_{2n}(D)i_n = E_2(t)$$
$$\phantom{Z_{11}(D)i_1}\cdot\phantom{+ Z_{22}(D)i_2}\cdot\cdots\phantom{+ Z_{2n}(D)i_n}\cdot$$
$$Z_{n1}(D)i_1 + Z_{n2}(D)i_2 + \cdots + Z_{nn}(D)i_n = E_n(t)$$

This is a set of equations of n linear integro-differential equations with constant coefficients.

If we now introduce the following matrices:

(3.7)
$$[Z(D)] = \begin{bmatrix} Z_{11}(D) & Z_{12}(D) & \ldots & Z_{1n}(D) \\ Z_{21}(D) & Z_{22}(D) & \ldots & Z_{2n}(D) \\ & \cdot & \ldots & \\ Z_{n1}(D) & Z_{n2}(D) & \ldots & Z_{nn}(D) \end{bmatrix}$$

(3.8)
$$(i) = (i_r), \qquad r = 1, 2, \ldots, n$$

(3.9)
$$(e) = (e_r), \qquad r = 1, 2, \ldots, n$$

then we may write the set of Eqs. (3.6) as one matrix equation:

(3.10)
$$[Z(D)](i) = (e)$$

The set of Eqs. (3.10) is called the "canonical" equations of the general electric circuit.

4. THE CANONICAL EQUATIONS AND THEIR SOLUTION

We have seen how, by a straightforward application of Kirchhoff's first law, we have obtained the set of integro-differential equations that may be concisely written in the matrix form (3.10).

The Operational Impedance Matrix $[Z(D)]$

We shall call the matrix $[Z(D)]$, whose elements are differential operators, the "operational impedance matrix" of the system. By definition, we see that

(4.1) $$[Z(D)] = [L]D + [R] + [S]\frac{1}{D}$$

As we shall see later, the following relations hold between the elements of $[R]$, $[L]$, and $[S]$:

(4.2) $$L_{mn} = L_{nm}, \quad R_{mn} = R_{nm}, \quad S_{mn} = S_{nm}$$

and hence $[R]$, $[L]$, and $[S]$ are symmetric matrices with the property that

(4.3) $$[L]' = [L], \quad [R]' = [R], \quad [S]' = [S]$$

where the accents denote transposition. Since $[Z(D)]$ is the sum of symmetric matrices, it follows that

(4.4) $$[Z(D)]' = [Z(D)]$$

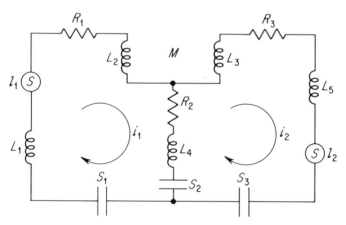

FIGURE 9.2

It may be noted that the elements of the matrices $[L]$, $[R]$, and $[S]$ may be written down by inspection of the wiring diagram of the circuit. As an example, consider the circuit shown in the following diagram of Fig. 9.2.

For this circuit, we have

$$[L] = \begin{bmatrix} (L_1 + L_2 + L_4) & (-L_4 + M) \\ (-L_4 + M) & (L_3 + L_4 + L_5) \end{bmatrix}$$

$$[R] = \begin{bmatrix} (R_1 + R_2) & -R_2 \\ -R_2 & (R_2 + R_3) \end{bmatrix} \qquad [S] = \begin{bmatrix} (S_1 + S_2) & -S_2 \\ -S_2 & (S_2 + S_3) \end{bmatrix}$$

If the convention of calling all the mesh currents positive when they are taken in a clockwise sense is adhered to, then the mutual parameters L_{mn}, S_{mn}, and R_{mn} will, in general, have negative numerical values.

When a mutual inductance M occurs as in the above example, its sign cannot, in general, be determined. One must then be guided by the direction in which the voltages are induced. In general, if the mutual inductance between any two meshes causes the introduction of a positive counter voltage in one mesh for a positive rate of change of current in the other, according to the positive assumed directions, then that mutual inductance is numerically positive with regard to the mutual parameter. In practical cases, measurements must be made to determine the sign of M, unless it is obvious from the winding of the coils.

The Particular Integral

We are now confronted with the problem of solving the canonical equations of the circuit. To do this, let us use a heuristic process of assuming the form of the solution. If we are able to carry our solution through, then by invoking the principle of uniqueness, which states that under certain general conditions that are always met in practical cases the solution of the canonical equations is unique, we are assured that we have obtained the solution without regard to our initial assumption. It may be mentioned that we are here following the classical method, in contrast to the operational method of solving these equations discussed in Chapter 10.

Accordingly, let us *assume* that the solution of the matrix integro-differential equation

$$(4.5) \qquad\qquad [Z(D)](i) = (e)$$

is

$$(4.6) \qquad\qquad (i) = (i)_t + (i)_s$$

where $(i)_t$ and $(i)_s$ are columnar matrices whose elements are functions of t to be determined. On substituting the assumed form of the solution into (4.5), we have

$$(4.7) \qquad\qquad [Z(D)](i)_t + [Z(D)](i)_s = (e)$$

Let us now specify that

$$(4.8) \qquad\qquad [Z(D)](i)_t = (0)$$

and that

$$(4.9) \qquad\qquad [Z(D)](i)_s = (e)$$

As we shall see, the elements of $(i)_t$ are the various complementary functions of the differential equation and represent the so-called "transient" terms. The elements of $(i)_s$ are the particular integrals of the differential equations, and these elements are called the "steady-state" currents when the various electromotive forces are of a periodic nature. It is to a study of these "steady-state" terms that we now turn.   The method of solution discussed in this chapter is the so-called "classical method."

5. STEADY-STATE SOLUTION, ONE APPLIED SINUSOIDAL ELECTROMOTIVE FORCE

Let us suppose, for simplicity, that our general n-mesh system has impressed upon it one electromotive force of instantaneous value $E_1 \cos (wt)$ in mesh 1, and that there are no impressed electromotive forces in the other meshes of the network.   In this case, our matrix (e) reduces to

$$(e) = \begin{bmatrix} E_1 \cos (wt) \\ 0 \\ 0 \\ \cdot \\ 0 \end{bmatrix}$$

(5.1)

Now since $e^{jwt} = \cos (wt) + j \sin (wt)$, where $j = \sqrt{-1}$, we may write

(5.2)
$$E_1 \cos (wt) = \text{Re } E_1 e^{jwt}$$

where Re means "the real part of."   Hence, we can write

(5.3)
$$(e) = \text{Re } (E)e^{jwt}$$

where

(5.4)
$$(E) = \begin{bmatrix} E_1 \\ 0 \\ \cdot \\ 0 \end{bmatrix}$$

In order to solve the equation $[Z(D)](i)_s = (e)$, let us assume that

(5.5)
$$\begin{aligned} i_1 &= \text{Re } I_1 e^{jwt} \\ i_2 &= \text{Re } I_2 e^{jwt} \\ &\quad \cdots \\ i_n &= \text{Re } I_n e^{jwt} \end{aligned}$$

where $I_1, I_2, \ldots, I_n$ are complex constants to be determined.   We may thus write

(5.6)
$$(i)_s = \text{Re } (I)e^{jwt}$$

where (I) is the matrix of complex constant elements:

(5.7)
$$(I) = \begin{bmatrix} I_1 \\ I_2 \\ \cdot \\ I_n \end{bmatrix}$$

Now,

$$[Z(D)] = [L]D + [R] + [S]\frac{1}{D}$$

and

$$De^{jwt} = jwe^{jwt}, \quad \frac{1}{D}e^{jwt} = \frac{e^{jwt}}{jw}$$

Therefore,

(5.8) $\qquad [Z(D)] \text{ Re } (I)e^{jwt} = \text{Re}\left(jw[L] + [R] + \frac{[S]}{jw}\right)(I)e^{jwt}$

$$= \text{Re } (E)e^{jwt}$$

Suppressing the "Re" symbol, we have

(5.9) $\qquad \left(jw[L] + [R] + \frac{[S]}{jw}\right)(I)e^{jwt} = (E)e^{jwt}$

or

(5.10) $\qquad \left(jw[L] + [R] + \frac{[S]}{jw}\right)(I) = (E)$

If we let

(5.11) $\qquad [Z(jw)] = jw[L] + [R] + \frac{[S]}{jw}$

be the impedance matrix of the network, then the complex current magnitudes are given by

(5.12) $\qquad (I) = [Z(jw)]^{-1}(E)$

where $[Z(jw)]^{-1}$ is the inverse of the impedance matrix $[Z(jw)]$. If we let $[A(jw)]$ be the "adjoint" matrix of the impedance matrix $[Z(jw)]$ then we may write (5.12) in the form

(5.13) $\qquad (I) = \frac{[A(jw)](E)}{|Z(jw)|}, \quad |Z(jw)| = \det [Z(jw)]$

Since $[Z(jw)]$ is a symmetrical matrix, the elements of its adjoint, $[A(jw)]$, are obtained by replacing the various elements of $[Z(jw)]$ by their corresponding cofactors. As an example, let us consider the simple two-mesh network of Fig. 9.2. We will suppose that $e_2 = 0$ and that $e_1(t) = E_1 \cos (wt)$, where E_1 is the maximum value of the impressed electromotive force. In this example, we have

(5.14) $[Z(jw)] = jw[L] + [R] + \dfrac{[S]}{jw}$

$$= \begin{bmatrix} R_{11} + j\left(L_{11}w - \dfrac{S_{11}}{w}\right) & R_{12} + j\left(L_{12}w - \dfrac{S_{12}}{w}\right) \\ R_{21} + j\left(L_{21}w - \dfrac{S_{21}}{w}\right) & R_{22} + j\left(L_{22}w - \dfrac{S_{22}}{w}\right) \end{bmatrix}$$

where $R_{12} = R_{21}$, $L_{12} = L_{21}$, $S_{12} = S_{21}$.

(5.15) $(e) = \begin{bmatrix} E_1 \cos(wt) \\ 0 \end{bmatrix}$, $(E) = \begin{bmatrix} E_1 \\ 0 \end{bmatrix}$

(5.16) $[A(jw)] = \begin{bmatrix} R_{22} + j\left(wL_{22} - \dfrac{S_{22}}{w}\right) & -R_{21} - j\left(L_{21}w - \dfrac{S_{21}}{w}\right) \\ -R_{12} - j\left(wL_{12} - \dfrac{S_{12}}{w}\right) & R_{11} + j\left(L_{11}w - \dfrac{S_{11}}{w}\right) \end{bmatrix}$

In this case, (5.13) becomes

(5.17) $\begin{bmatrix} I_1 \\ I_2 \end{bmatrix} = \dfrac{\begin{bmatrix} R_{22} + j\left(L_{22}w - \dfrac{S_{22}}{w}\right) & -R_{21} - j\left(L_{21}w - \dfrac{S_{21}}{w}\right) \\ -R_{12} - j\left(L_{12}w - \dfrac{S_{12}}{w}\right) & R_{11} + j\left(L_{11}w - \dfrac{S_{11}}{w}\right) \end{bmatrix}}{|Z(jw)|} \cdot \begin{bmatrix} E_1 \\ 0 \end{bmatrix}$

Hence

(5.18) $\begin{bmatrix} I_1 \\ I_2 \end{bmatrix} = E_1 \dfrac{\begin{bmatrix} R_{22} + j\left(L_{22}w - \dfrac{S_{22}}{w}\right) \\ -R_{11} - j\left(L_{12}w - \dfrac{S_{12}}{w}\right) \end{bmatrix}}{|Z(jw)|}$

It may be noted that if E_1 is given in rms volts, then I_1 and I_2 are in rms complex amperes. If E_1 is the maximum value of the applied voltage, then in order to get the instantaneous values of the currents $i_1(t)$ and $i_2(t)$, we must use the expression

(5.19) $(i)_s = \text{Re}\,(I)e^{jwt}$

If, in general, $I_1 = I_1 e^{j\theta_1}$ and $I_2 = I_2 e^{j\theta_2}$, where I_1 and I_2 are the moduli of I_1 and I_2, then

(5.20)
$$i_{1s} = I_1 \cos(wt + \theta_1)$$
$$i_{2s} = I_2 \cos(wt + \theta_2)$$

where θ_1 and θ_2 are phase angles given by the equations

(5.21) $\theta_1 = \tan^{-1} \dfrac{\text{Im } I_1}{\text{Re } I_1}$, $\theta_2 = \tan^{-1} \dfrac{\text{Im } I_2}{\text{Re } I_2}$

where "Im" means "imaginary part of."

6. CASE OF n SINUSOIDAL ELECTROMOTIVE FORCES OF DIFFERENT PHASES

In this case, our voltage matrix has the form

$$
(6.1) \qquad (e) = \begin{bmatrix} E_1 \cos (wt + \theta_1) \\ E_2 \cos (wt + \theta_2) \\ \cdots \\ E_n \cos (wt + \theta_n) \end{bmatrix}
$$

where the E_i's are the maximum values of the applied electromotive forces and the θ_i's are the various phase angles. Following the same procedure as that used in Sec. 5, let us write

$$
(6.2) \qquad E_k \cos (wt + \theta_k) = \mathrm{Re}\ E_k e^{jwt} e^{j\theta_k}
$$

Therefore, we may write

$$
(6.3) \qquad (e) = \mathrm{Re} \begin{bmatrix} E_1 e^{j\theta_1} \\ E_2 e^{j\theta_2} \\ \cdots \\ E_n e^{j\theta_n} \end{bmatrix} e^{jwt} = \mathrm{Re}\ (E e^{j\theta}) e^{jwt}
$$

where we define

$$
(6.4) \qquad (E e^{j\theta}) = \begin{bmatrix} E_1 e^{j\theta_1} \\ E_2 e^{j\theta_2} \\ \cdots \\ E_n e^{j\theta_n} \end{bmatrix}
$$

If we follow the same algebraic manipulations as those in Sec. 4, we obtain

$$
(6.5) \qquad (I) = \frac{[A(jw)](E e^{j\theta})}{|z(jw)|}
$$

where $[A(jw)]$ is the adjoint of $[Z(jw)]$ as before, and $(E e^{j\theta})$ is defined by (6.4). If we are interested in instantaneous values, we have

$$
(6.6) \qquad (i) = \mathrm{Re}\ (I) e^{jwt}
$$

as before.

7. VOLTAGES OF DIFFERENT FREQUENCIES SIMULTANEOUSLY IMPRESSED

Thus far, we have concerned ourselves with obtaining the steady-state solution to the general n-mesh circuit when the various impressed electromotive forces are of the same frequency. Let us now consider the case where the impressed voltages are of different frequencies in the various meshes. For generality, let us assume that the impressed voltage in the kth mesh is of the form

$$
(7.1) \qquad e_k(t) = E_k^{(1)} \cos w_1 t + E_k^{(2)} \cos w_2 t + \cdots + E_k^{(m)} \cos w_m t
$$

Then we may write our voltage matrix in the form

(7.2) $$(e) = (E^{(1)} \cos w_1 t) + \cdots + (E^{(m)} \cos w_m t)$$

where

(7.3) $$(E^{(r)} \cos w_r t) = \begin{bmatrix} E_1^{(r)} \cos w_r t \\ E_2^{(r)} \cos w_r t \\ \cdots \\ E_n^{(r)} \cos w_r t \end{bmatrix}$$

or, more concisely,

(7.4) $$(e) = \sum_{r=1}^{m} (E^{(r)} \cos w_r t)$$

$$= \operatorname{Re} \sum_{r=1}^{m} (E^{(r)}) e^{jw_r t}$$

Let us now assume

(7.5) $$(i)_s = \operatorname{Re} \sum_{r=1}^{m} (I^{(r)}) e^{jw_r t}$$

where

(7.6) $$(I^{(r)}) = \begin{bmatrix} I_1^{(r)} \\ I_2^{(r)} \\ \cdots \\ I_n^{(r)} \end{bmatrix}$$

is the solution of the matrix equation $[Z(D)](i)_s = (e)$.   Now we have

(7.7) $$\sum_{r=1}^{r=m} [Z(jw_r)](I^{(r)}) e^{jw_r t} = \sum_{r=1}^{r=m} (E^{(r)}) e^{jw_r t}$$

Since this equality is to be satisfied for all values of time, the coefficients of like powers of e must be equal.   Hence, we have

(7.8) $$[Z(jw_r)](I^{(r)}) = (E^{(r)}), \quad \text{for} \quad r = 1, 2, 3, \ldots, m$$

or

(7.9) $$(I^{(r)} = [Z(jw_r)]^{-1}(E^{(r)}) = \frac{[A(jw_r)]^{-1}(E^{(r)})}{|Z(jw_r)|}$$

where $[A(jw_r)]$ is the adjoint matrix of $[Z(jw_r)]$.   We thus have the solution for the instantaneous currents produced by the general system of electromotive forces:

(7.10) $$(i)_s = \operatorname{Re} \sum_{r=1}^{r=m} \frac{[A(jw_r)](E^{(r)}) e^{jw_r t}}{|Z(jw_r)|}$$

This result shows that the principle of superposition holds for different frequencies, as well as for various voltages of the same frequency, if the various electromotive forces are periodic functions.

Periodic Electromotive Forces

If the impressed electromotive forces are periodic functions of fundamental period T, they may be represented within certain restrictions on continuity in the complex Fourier series form:

$$(7.11) \qquad e_k(t) = \sum_{n=-\infty}^{+\infty} a_{kn} e^{jnwt} \quad \text{where} \quad w = \frac{2\pi}{T}$$

The coefficients a_{kn} are given by

$$(7.12) \qquad a_{kn} = \frac{w}{2\pi} \int_0^{2\pi/w} e_k(t) e^{-inwt} \, dt$$

If we introduce a column matrix $(a)_r$ defined by the equation

$$(7.13) \qquad (a)_r = \begin{bmatrix} a_{1r} \\ a_{2r} \\ \cdots \\ a_{nr} \end{bmatrix}$$

we may write the electromotive force matrix in the form

$$(7.14) \qquad (e) = \sum_{r=-\infty}^{r=+\infty} (a)_r e^{jrwt}$$

Now, in order to obtain the steady-state solution from the equation

$$(7.15) \qquad [Z(D)](i)_s = (e)$$

let

$$(7.16) \qquad (i)_s = \sum_{r=\infty}^{\infty} (i)_r e^{jrwt}$$

Substituting this into (7.15), we obtain

$$(7.17) \qquad \sum_{r=-\infty}^{+\infty} [Z(jwr)](i)_r e^{jrwt} = \sum_{r=-\infty}^{+\infty} (a)_r e^{jrwt}$$

Equating the coefficients of like harmonic terms, we have

$$(7.18) \qquad [Z(jwr)](i)_r = (a)_r$$

or

$$(7.19) \qquad (i)_r = [Z(jwr)]^{-1}(a)_r = \frac{[A(jwr)]}{Z(jwr)}(a)_r$$

where $[A(jwr)]$ is the adjoint matrix of $[Z(jwr)]$. Substituting (7.19) into (7.16), we have for the steady-state solution

$$(7.20) \qquad (i)_s = \sum_{r=-\infty}^{+\infty} \frac{[A(jwr)]}{Z(jwr)} (a)_r e^{jwrt}$$

This is the steady-state solution for impressed voltages of a fundamental period $T = 2\pi/w$.

Remarks on Complex Fourier Series

In the analysis of electrical networks, it is quite a common problem to compute the effective, or root mean square, value of irregular but periodic currents and voltages. It may be mentioned that the expression for the effective value of an irregular periodic function has great symmetry in terms of the complex coefficients of the Fourier series expansion of the function. As an example, consider that a certain periodic current is expressed in the complex Fourier series form

$$(7.21) \qquad i(t) = \sum_{n=-\infty}^{+\infty} A_n e^{jnwt}$$

and let us find the effective value of this function, i_f, defined by the equation

$$(7.22) \qquad i_f^2 = \frac{w}{2\pi} \int_0^{2\pi/w} i^2 \, dt$$

Now, from the series (7.21), we have

$$(7.23) \qquad i^2 = \left(\sum_{n=-\infty}^{+\infty} A_n e^{jnwt} \right) \left(\sum_{n=-\infty}^{+\infty} A_n e^{jnwt} \right)$$

This product may be written as a double summation in the form

$$(7.24) \qquad i_f^2 = \sum_{\substack{r=-\infty \\ n=-\infty}}^{+\infty} A_n A_r e^{j(n+r)wt}$$

If we substitute this into the integral (7.22), we have

$$(7.25) \qquad i_f^2 = \frac{w}{2\pi} \int_0^{2\pi/w} \sum_{\substack{r=-\infty \\ n=-\infty}}^{\infty} A_r A_n e^{j(n+r)wt} \, dt$$

Now, since all the integrals vanish except those for which $n = -r$ because of the relation

$$(7.26) \qquad \int_0^{2\pi/w} e^{jnwt} \, dt = 0$$

we have

$$(7.27) \qquad i_f^2 = \frac{w}{2\pi} \sum_{r=-\infty}^{+\infty} A_r A_{-r} \int_0^{2\pi/w} dt = \sum_{r=-\infty}^{+\infty} A_r A_{-r}$$

and hence

$$(7.28) \qquad i_f = \sqrt{\sum_{r=-\infty}^{+\infty} A_r A_{-r}}$$

This is a very convenient expression for calculating the effective value of a periodic function if the complex Fourier coefficients of the function are known. Since A_r is the conjugate of A_{-r}, we also have

$$(7.29) \qquad i_{eff}^2 = 2 \sum_{r=1}^{\infty} |A_r|^2$$

The Average Power Delivered to a Circuit

Let us consider that a circuit has impressed upon it the irregular electromotive force:

$$(7.30) \qquad e(t) = \sum_{n=-\infty}^{+\infty} A_n e^{jnwt}$$

and that the current flowing in the circuit is

$$(7.31) \qquad i(t) = \sum_{r=-\infty}^{+\infty} B_r e^{jrwt}$$

Then the average power consumed in the circuit is

$$(7.32) \qquad \bar{P} = \frac{w}{2\pi} \int_0^{2\pi/w} ei \, dt = \frac{w}{2\pi} \sum_{\substack{r=-\infty \\ n=-\infty}}^{\infty} A_n B_r \int_0^{2\pi/w} e^{j(n+r)wt} \, dt$$

Using (7.26), we obtain

$$(7.33) \qquad \bar{P} = \sum_{n=-\infty}^{+\infty} A_n B_{-n}$$

a particularly convenient result. In general, it may be stated that the complex form of Fourier series is to be preferred to the real form in the calculation of the steady-state currents in networks produced by the application of irregular periodic electromotive forces.

REFERENCES

1. Baker, H. F., "On Certain Linear Differential Equations of Astronomical Interest," *Philosophical Transactions of the Royal Society*, Series A, Vol. 216 (1916).

2. Brillouin, L., "Les Filtres électriques et la théorie des matrices," *Revue générale de l'électricité* (Jan. 4, 1936), pp. 3–16.

3. Brillouin, L., *Wave Propagation in Periodic Structures*. New York: Dover Publications, 1953, Ch. IX.

4. Brown, J. S. and F. D. Bennett, "The Application of Matrices to Vacuum Tube Circuits," *Proc. IRE*, Vol. 36 (July, 1948), p. 844.

5. Carson, J. R., "Electromagnetic Theory and the Foundations of Circuit Theory," *Bell System Tech. Jour.*, Vol. 6 (Jan., 1927), p. 1.

6. Cauer, W., "Vierpole," *Elektrische Nachrichten-Technik*, Vol. 6 (May, 1929), p. 272.

7. Cauer, W., "Vierpole mit vorgeschriebenen Dämpfungsverhalten," *Telegraphen-Fernsprecht-Technik*, Vol. 29 (Oct., 1940), p. 185.

8. Cayley, A., "A Memoir on the Theory of Matrices," *Transactions of the London Philosophical Society*, Vol. 148 (1857), pp. 17–37.

9. Cocci, G., "Funzioni di trasmissione di quadripole di pure reattanze inserti tra due restenze," *Alta Frequenza*, Vol. 7 (Aug., 1938), p. 804.

10. Cocci, G., "Progetto di quadripole di pure reattanze con funzione di trasmissione data," *Alta Frequenza*, Vol. 10 (Nov., 1941), p. 470.

11. Darlington, S., "Synthesis of Reactance Four-Poles Which Produce Prescribed Insertion Loss Characteristics," *Journal of Mathematics and Physics*, Vol. 18 (1939), p. 257.

12. Denis-Papin, M. and A. Kaufmann, *Cours de Calcul Matriciel Applique*. Paris: Editions Albin Michel, 1951.

13. Frazer, R. A., W. J. Duncan, and A. R. Collar, *Elementary Matrices and Some Applications to Dynamics and Differential Equations*. London: Cambridge University Press, 1938.

14. Gewertz, C. M., "Synthesis of a Finite Four-Terminal Network from Its Prescribed Driving-Point Functions and Transfer Functions," *Journal of Mathematics and Physics*, Vol. 12 (July, 1933), p. 1.

15. Howitt, N., "Group Theory and the Electric Circuit," *Physical Review*, Vol. 37 (Dec., 1931), p. 1538.

16. Kemble, E. C., *The Fundamental Principles of Quantum Mechanics*. New York: McGraw-Hill Book Co., Inc., 1937, Ch. X.

17. Piloty, H., "Kanonische Kettenschaltungen für Reaktanzvierpole mit vorgeschriebenen Betriebseigenshaften," *Telegraphen-Fernsprecht-Technik*, Vol. 29 (July, 1940), p. 185.

18. Pipes, L. A., *Applied Mathematics for Engineers and Physicists*. New York: McGraw-Hill Book Co., Inc., 1946, Ch. IV and X.

19. Pipes, L. A., "Matrices in Engineering," *Electrical Engineering*, Vol. 56 (Sept., 1937), pp. 1977–1990.

20. Pipes, L. A., "The Matrix Theory of Four-Terminal Networks," *Philosophical Magazine*, Ser. 7, Vol. 30 (Nov., 1940), pp. 370–395.

21. Richards, P. I., "Applications of Matrix Algebra to Filter Theory," *Proc. IRE*, Vol. 34 (Mar., 1946), p. 145.

22. Shea, R. F. ed., *Principles of Transistor Circuits*. New York: John Wiley and Sons, Inc., 1953, Ch. XV.

23. Shekel, J., "Matrix Representation of Transistor Circuits," *Proc. IRE*, Vol. 40 (Nov., 1952), pp. 1493–1497.

24. Stigant, A. S., *Modern Electrical Engineering Mathematics*. London: Hutchinson's Scientific and Technical Publications, 1946.

25. Strecker, F. and R. Feldtkeller, "Grundlagen der Theorie des allgemeinen Vierpoles," *Elektrische Nachrichten-Technik*, Vol. 6 (Feb., 1929), p. 93.

26. Talbot, A., *A New Method of Synthesis of Reactance Networks*. Monograph No. 77, Institution of Electrical Engineers (Oct., 15, 1953).

27. Tellegen, B. D. H., *The Gyrator, a New Electric Network Element*. Phillips Research Report 3 (1948), pp. 81–101.

28. Vowels, R. E., "Matrix Methods in the Solution of Ladder Networks," *Journal of the Institution of Electrical Engineers*, Vol. 95, Part III (Jan., 1948), pp. 40–50.

29. Wedderburn, J. H. M., *Lectures on Matrices*. New York: American Mathematical Society, 1934.

30. Zurmühl, R., *Matrizen*. Berlin: Julius Springer, 1950.

10 THE TRANSIENT SOLUTION OF THE GENERAL NETWORK

1. INTRODUCTION

In this chapter the classical procedure of solving the set of equations of the general network will be developed. To save writing and to keep the equations concise, the equations will be written in matrix form. In the last chapter, the so-called "steady-state" solution of the general network subject to the application of general periodic electromotive forces was given. We now turn to the solution of the equation

(1.1) $$[Z(D)](i)_t = (0)$$

2. THE HEURISTIC PROCESS

In order to solve Eq. (1.1), let us adopt the heuristic procedure of assuming a solution of the form

(2.1) $$(i)_t = (k)e^{mt}$$

Here e^{mt} is a scalar multiplier to be determined, and (k) is a column matrix of constants to be determined. Since

(2.2) $$[Z(D)] = [L]D + [R] + \frac{[S]}{D}$$

we therefore have

(2.3) $$[Z(D)]e^{mt} = \left(m[L] + [R] + \frac{[S]}{m}\right)e^{mt}$$
$$= [Z(m)]e^{mt}$$

Hence, upon substituting the assumed form of the solution into Eq. (1.1), we obtain

(2.4) $$e^{mt}[Z(m)](k) = (0)$$

305

or

(2.5) $$[Z(m)](k) = (0)$$

where the scalar multiplier e^{mt} has been divided out, since it cannot be equal to zero for a finite value of m or t.

3. THE DETERMINANTAL EQUATION

Equation (2.5) represents a set of homogeneous linear equations. In order for the set of equations to have a consistent solution other than $(k) = (0)$, we must have

(3.1) $$D(m) = |Z(m)| = 0$$

that is, the determinant of the system (2.5) must vanish.   Since

(3.2) $$Z_{mn}(m) = mL_{mn} + R_{mn} + \frac{S_{mn}}{m}$$

and since in the general n-mesh case, the determinant $D(m)$ has n rows and n columns, it follows that the determinant $D(m)$ is a polynomial in m of degree $2n$.

Equation (3.1) is the determinantal equation of the system.   Since it is of degree $2n$, it will, in general, have $2n$ roots, which for the present we will regard as distinct.   These roots, which we will denote by $(m_1, m_2, \ldots, m_{2n})$, are, in general, complex numbers.   It may be shown that for an electrical network, the roots occur in conjugate complex pairs and have negative real parts.   The occurrence of repeated roots is rare and will be discussed in a later section.   The quantities m_i are called the generalized natural frequencies of the system.

4. THE NORMAL MODES

Returning to the set of homogeneous algebraic equations

(4.1) $$[Z(m)](k) = (0)$$

we have seen that the consistency condition yields $2n$ different values of the constant m.   It thus appears that we may write altogether $2n$ solutions of the form

(4.2) $$(i)_t = (k)e^{mt}$$

one solution for each value of m.   The form of the transient solution, is, therefore,

(4.3)
$$i_{1t} = k_{11}e^{m_1 t} + k_{12}e^{m_2 t} + \cdots + k_{1,\,2n}e^{m_{2n}t}$$
$$i_{2t} = k_{21}e^{m_1 t} + k_{22}e^{m_2 t} + \cdots + k_{2,\,2n}e^{m_{2n}t}$$
$$\vdots$$
$$i_{nt} = k_{n1}e^{m_1 t} + k_{n2}e^{m_2 t} + \cdots + k_{n,\,2n}e^{m_{2n}t}$$

This set of equations may be written in the concise matrix form

(4.4)
$$(i)_t = \sum_{r=1}^{2n} (k_r)e^{m_r t}$$

where

(4.5)
$$(k_r) = \begin{bmatrix} k_{1r} \\ k_{2r} \\ \cdots \\ k_{nr} \end{bmatrix}$$

The first subscript in the elements of the matrix (k_r) refers to the particular mesh current to which the term belongs. The second subscript denotes the mode to which the term belongs and corresponds to the subscript of m in the corresponding exponential term. The column matrices (k_r) will be spoken of as the "modal columns" or "eigenvectors." The modal columns have the fundamental property that

(4.6)
$$[Z(m_r)](k_r) = (0)$$

5. THE MODAL MATRIX

The $(n \times 2n)$ matrix formed from the modal columns is of great importance in further theory. It will be called the "modal matrix," and it will be denoted by

(5.1)
$$[k] = \begin{bmatrix} k_{11} & k_{12} & k_{13} & \cdots & k_{1,\,2n} \\ k_{21} & k_{22} & k_{23} & \cdots & k_{2,\,2n} \\ \cdot & \cdot & \cdot & \cdots & \cdot \\ k_{n1} & k_{n2} & k_{n3} & \cdots & k_{n,\,2n} \end{bmatrix}$$

In the case of distinct roots of the determinantal equation, the elements of the modal matrix are constants.

6. THE RELATION BETWEEN THE AMPLITUDES

As we have seen, our heuristic method of solution has led us to a consideration of $2n$ modal columns with the relation

(6.1)
$$[Z(m_r)](k_r) = (0)$$

Now, since there are $2n$ modal columns, each containing n elements, it would appear that we must determine $2n^2$ arbitrary constants. However, from the general theory of differential equations, we are assured that our set of n differential equations of the second order may be completely solved in terms of $2n$ arbitrary constants. We must, therefore, obtain certain relations between the constants of the modal matrix.

The Adjoint Matrix of the Modal Impedance Matrix

We shall call the matrix $[Z(m)]$ the modal impedance matrix. Let us now introduce the matrix $[A(m)]$, the adjoint of the modal impedance matrix. Then, by definition,

$$(6.2) \qquad [Z(m)][A(m)] = [A(m)][Z(m)] = D(m)U_n$$

where $D(m)$ is the determinant of $[Z(m)]$ and U_n is the unit matrix of order n. Let us consider the original set of differential equations:

$$(6.3) \qquad [Z(D)](i)_t = (0)$$

Now, we have seen that this equation led to the equations satisfied by the modal columns, which are equations of the type

$$(6.4) \qquad [Z(m_r)](k_r) = (0), \qquad r = 1, 2, \ldots, 2n$$

Now, if we place $m = m_r$ in Eq. (6.2), we obtain

$$(6.5) \qquad [Z(m_r)][A(m_r)] = (0)$$

because $D(m_r) = 0$. It thus appears that the columns of $[A(m_r)]$ are all proportional to (k_r). Now, since $[Z(m_r)]$ is a symmetric matrix, the elements A_{mn} of the adjoint matrix $[A(m_r)]$ are obtained from the matrix $[Z(m_r)]$ by replacing the various elements in the latter matrix by their corresponding cofactors. Comparing (6.4) and (6.5), we see that, in general, if

$$(6.6) \qquad [A(m)] = \begin{bmatrix} A_{11}(m) & A_{12}(m) & \cdots & A_{1n}(m) \\ \cdot & \cdot & \cdots & \cdot \\ A_{n1}(m) & A_{n2}(m) & \cdots & A_{nn}(m) \end{bmatrix}$$

Then the modal column (k_r) may be written in the form

$$(6.7) \qquad (k_r) = C_r \begin{bmatrix} A_{1m}(m_r) \\ A_{2m}(m_r) \\ \cdots \\ A_{nm}(m_r) \end{bmatrix} = C_r\{A_m(m_r)\}$$

where C_r is a constant of proportionality, and m denotes an *arbitrary* column of $[A(m)]$.

From this we see that the ratios of the elements of the modal columns are determined by the ratios of the elements of the columns of the adjoint matrix, $[A(m)]$, where m is placed equal to its proper value for the particular mode under consideration.

7. DETERMINATION OF THE ARBITARY CONSTANTS

Let us return to our solution:

$$(7.1) \qquad (i)_t = \sum_{r=1}^{r=2n} (k_r)e^{m_r t}$$

By the last section, we have seen that we could determine the elements of the modal columns (k_r) to within an arbitrary constant by the relation (6.7). Since the elements of the modal columns are determined to an arbitrary constant and there are $2n$ modal columns, it appears that we have only $2n$ arbitrary constants, as required by the general theory of differential equations. To determine these constants, let us introduce the matrix $[M(t)]$, which we shall call the eigenvalue matrix and which is defined by the equation

$$(7.2) \qquad [M(t)] = \begin{bmatrix} e^{m_1 t} & 0 & \cdots & 0 \\ 0 & e^{m_2 t} & \cdots & 0 \\ \cdot & \cdot & \cdots & \cdot \\ 0 & 0 & \cdots & e^{m_{2n} t} \end{bmatrix}$$

We see from this that the matrix $[M(t)]$ is a diagonal matrix of order $(2n) \times (2n)$. In terms of this matrix, we can write the solution for the transient currents in the form

$$(7.3) \qquad (i)_t = [k][M(t)](c)$$

where (c) is a matrix of $2n$ arbitrary constants.

The performance of the general electric network is completely determined if the values of the initial n-mesh currents and charges are given together with the character of the electromotive forces which are impressed on the system. For simplicity, the time t may be taken as zero when the various electromotive forces are first impressed on the system. From the preceding chapter, we have seen that solution of the general equations specifying the network behavior may be written in the form

$$(7.4) \qquad (i) = (i)_t + (i)_s$$

where $(i)_s$ is the particular integral or the "steady-state" part of the solution, provided the impressed electromotive forces are periodic in nature, and $(i)_t$ represents the solution of the complementary function or "transient" part of the solution and is the natural or "force-free" behavior of the system. This part of the solution is represented by (7.3). The problem is now to determine the arbitrary constants that are the $2n$ elements of the column matrix (c). In order to carry out this determination, let us introduce the matrices (i^0) and (q^0), where (i^0) is a column matrix whose n elements are the known initial mesh currents flowing in the network at $t = 0$ and (q^0) is a column matrix whose n elements are the known initial mesh charges of the system at $t = 0$. The charge matrix is the integral of the current matrix and may be written in the form

$$(7.5) \qquad \int_0^t (i)\, dt = (q)$$

Now

$$(7.6) \qquad \int_0^t (i)_t\, dt = \int_0^t [k][M(t)](c)\, dt$$

and since the matrices $[k]$ and (c) are matrices of constants, the integration involves only an integration with respect to time of the matrix $[M(t)]$ defined by (7.2). Let $[N(t)]$ be the integral of the matrix $[M(t)]$ determined by the equation:

$$(7.7) \qquad [N(t)] = \begin{bmatrix} \dfrac{e^{m_1 t}}{m_1} & 0 & \cdots & 0 \\ 0 & \dfrac{e^{m_2 t}}{m_2} & \cdots & 0 \\ \cdot & \cdot & \cdots & \cdot \\ 0 & 0 & \cdots & \dfrac{e^{m_{2n} t}}{m_{2n}} \end{bmatrix}$$

That is, $[N(t)]$ is a diagonal matrix of order $(2n \times 2n)$ whose principal diagonal contains the elements $e^{m_j t}/m_j$. Hence, we obtain

$$(7.8) \qquad (q)_t = [k][N(t)](c)$$

The steady-state distribution of charge is obtained from the steady-state current matrix by the equation

$$(7.9) \qquad (q)_s = \int_{-\infty}^{t} (i)_s \, dt$$

Now let us suppose that at $t = 0$, we know the initial charges and currents and we wish to evaluate the $2n$ arbitrary constants that constitute the elements of the matrix (c). Placing $t = 0$, we have

$$(7.10) \qquad \begin{aligned} (i^0) &= [k][M(0)](c) + (i^0)_s \\ (q^0) &= [k][N(0)](c) + (q^0)_s \end{aligned}$$

where $(i^0)_s$ and $(q^0)_s$ are nth-order columnar matrices whose elements are the values obtained by placing $t = 0$ in the steady-state solution. If we transpose the matrices $(i^0)_s$ and $(q^0)_s$ to the other side of Eq. (7.10), we obtain

$$(7.11) \qquad \begin{aligned} [k][M(0)](c) &= (i^0) - (i^0)_s \\ [k][N(0)](c) &= (q^0) - (q^0)_s \end{aligned}$$

Now

$$(7.12) \qquad [k][M(0)] = \begin{bmatrix} k_{11} & k_{12} & \cdots & k_{1,\,2n} \\ \cdot & \cdot & \cdots & \cdot \\ k_{n1} & k_{n2} & \cdots & k_{n,\,2n} \end{bmatrix}$$

and

$$(7.13) \qquad [k][N(0)] = \begin{bmatrix} \dfrac{k_{11}}{m_1} & \cdots & \dfrac{k_{1,\,2n}}{m_{2n}} \\ \cdot & \cdots & \cdot \\ \dfrac{k_{n1}}{m_1} & \cdots & \dfrac{k_{n,\,2n}}{m_{2n}} \end{bmatrix}$$

From these two ($n \times 2n$) matrices, we can construct a ($2n \times 2n$) matrix $[W]$ partitioned in the following manner:

$$(7.14) \qquad [W] = \begin{bmatrix} [k][M(0)] \\ [k][N(0)] \end{bmatrix} = \begin{bmatrix} k_{11} & \cdots & k_{1,\,2n} \\ \cdot & \cdots & \cdot \\ k_{n1} & \cdots & k_{n,\,2n} \\ \dfrac{k_{11}}{m_1} & \cdots & \dfrac{k_{1,\,2n}}{m_{2n}} \\ \cdot & \cdots & \cdot \\ \dfrac{k_{n1}}{m_1} & \cdots & \dfrac{k_{n,\,2n}}{m_{2n}} \end{bmatrix}$$

We note that $[W]$ is a square matrix and, in general, has an inverse. If we now form a column matrix (v) as follows:

$$(7.15) \qquad (v) = \begin{bmatrix} (i^0) & \cdots & (i^0)_s \\ (q^0) & \cdots & (q^0)_s \end{bmatrix}$$

where (v) is a partitioned column matrix of order $2n$. Then we may write Eqs. (7.11) in the form

$$(7.16) \qquad [W](c) = (v)$$

and we finally obtain

$$(7.17) \qquad (c) = [W]^{-1}(v)$$

Equation (7.17) gives a formal expression for the $2n$ arbitrary constants in terms of the initial conditions of the system. This is the classical solution of the general lumped network problem expressed in matrix symbolism. It is a most compact formulation, but the amount of work required to carry out the solution is considerable when a large number of meshes is involved. A great deal of the labor involved is that required to solve the determinantal equation of the system. Another tedious task is the calculation of the inverse matrix $[W]^{-1}$ and the resulting multiplication to obtain the matrix of arbitrary constants, (c). Once (c) has been determined, the transient part of the solution is given by (7.3) and the complete solution by (7.4).

8. THE CASE OF REPEATED ROOTS OF THE DETERMINANTAL EQUATION

So far in our discussion, we have considered that the determinantal equation has n *distinct* roots, m_j. The case of repeated roots may be treated as follows: In the case of distinct roots, we have seen by Eq. (6.7) that we may take the modal column (k_r) corresponding to the mode m_r as a column proportional to any *arbitrary* column of the adjoint of the matrix $[Z(m_r)]$, $[A(m_r)]$. Let us consider that the determinantal equation has m_s as a double root. Now consider the two matrices:

(8.1) $[B_0(t, m_s)] = e^{m_s t}[A(m_s)]$

(8.2) $[B_1(t, m_s)] = \left[\dfrac{d}{dm} e^{m_s t} A(m)\right]_{m = m_s} = e^{m_s t}\left[\dfrac{(1)}{A(m_s)} + t[A(m_s)]\right]$

where

(8.3) $\left[\dfrac{(1)}{A(m_s)}\right] = \dfrac{d}{dm}[A(m)]_{m = m_s}$

Now by (6.5) it can be easily seen that the matrix (8.1) satisfies the fundamental equation of the system

(8.4) $[Z(D)][B_0(t, m_s)] = [0]$

and hence any of its columns may be taken to be a solution of Eq. (6.3). Let us now operate with the operator $[Z(D)]$ on the matrix (8.2). We obtain

(8.5) $[Z(D)][B_1(t, m)] = [Z(D)]\left[\dfrac{d}{dm} e^{mt} A(m)\right]$

$$= \dfrac{d}{dm}[Z(D)][e^{mt} A(m)]$$

$$= \dfrac{d}{dm}(e^{mt}[Z(m)][A(m)])$$

$$= e^{mt}\left(\dfrac{d}{dm} + t\right)\Delta(m)I$$

Now, since m_s is assumed to be a double root of (m), both $\Delta(m)$ and $(d\Delta(m)/dm)$ vanish when $m = m_s$. We therefore have

(8.6) $[Z(D)][B_1(t, m_s)] = [0]$

It is thus clear that for the double root $m = m_s$, we can take one modal column proportional to any column of $[A(m_s)]$ as in the case of distinct roots, and we may take another modal column proportional to any of the columns of

(8.7) $U_1(t, m_s) = \dfrac{(1)}{[A(m_s)]} + t[A(m_s)]$

By a similar argument it may be shown that if m_s represents a member of a set of s equal roots of the determinantal equation, the appropriate solution for m_s may be written in the form

(8.8) $(i)_t = [k_s(t)]$

where the modal column $[k_s(t)]$ may be chosen proportional to any s linearly independent columns of the family of matrices

$$U_0(t, m_s) = [A(m_s)]$$

$$U_1(t, m_s) = \frac{(1)}{[A(m_s)]} + t(A(m_s))]$$

(8.9)

$$\cdots$$

$$U_{s-1}(t, m_s) = \frac{(s-1)}{[A(m_s)]} + (s-1)t\frac{(s-2)}{[A(m_s)]}$$

$$+ \frac{(s-1)(s-2)}{2!} t^2 \frac{(s-3)}{[A(m_s)]} + \cdots + t^{s-1}[A(m_s)]$$

We note from this that in the case of equal roots, the modal matrix $[k]$ will have certain columns whose elements are functions of the time, and care must be used in noting this fact in computing $[W]$ by (7.14). The rest of the solution proceeds in the same manner as in the case of distinct roots.

9. THE ENERGY FUNCTIONS OF THE GENERAL NETWORK

We shall now consider the fundamental question of the distribution of energy in the electrical network. In order to obtain these expressions, let us consider that the network is inert at $t = 0$, and that at this instant suitable electromotive forces are introduced in the various meshes, and that at time $t = t_0$ charges have accumulated in the various condensers and currents are flowing in the various meshes. We shall consider that the final charges in the various mesh condensers are given by the n elements of the column matrix

(9.1) $(Q) = (Q_j)$ $j = 1, 2, \ldots, n$

The final currents in the various meshes of the network at the time t_0 are given by the n elements of the column matrix

(9.2) $(I) = (I_j)$ $j = 1, 2, \ldots, n$

Since the state of energy of the system at $t = t_0$ will depend only upon the current and charge distribution at that instant, we can, without loss of generality, assume that at any instant between $0 \gtrless t \gtrless t_0$ each charge is the same fraction θ of its final value; that is

(9.3) $(q) = \theta(Q)$

where the elements of the matrix (q) are the various mesh-charges at any time $0 \gtrless t \gtrless t_0$, and θ is a scalar multiplier. In the same way, we shall assume that during this interval we have

(9.4) $(i) = \phi(I)$

where ϕ is a scalar multiplier. Both θ and ϕ will have the values 0 at $t = 0$ and 1 at $t = t_0$. During this charging process, the batteries will have furnished a certain energy to the system which we will denote by W.   From elementary considerations we may write

(9.5) $$W = \int_0^{t_0} (e_1 i_1 + e_2 i_2 + \cdots + e_n i_n)\, dt$$

since $e_j i_j$ denotes the amount of *power* furnished by the battery in mesh j, etc. The integral of the power gives the total energy.   Now Eq. (9.5) may be written in the matrix form

(9.6) $$W = \int_0^{t_0} (i)'(e)\, dt$$

where $(i)'$ is a line matrix obtained by transposing the column matrix (i). Let us now substitute the basic equation for the electromotive force (e),

(9.7) $$(e) = [L]\frac{d}{dt}(i) + [R](i) + [S](q)$$

into Eq. (9.6).   We then have

(9.8) $$W = \int_0^{t_0} \left\{ (i)'[L]\frac{d}{dt}(i) + (i)'[R](i) + (i)'[S](q) \right\} dt$$

Let

(9.9) $$T = \int_0^{t_0} (i)'[L]\frac{d}{dt}(i)\, dt$$

From (9.4) we may eliminate (i) and $(i)'$ and obtain

(9.10) $$T = \int_0^{t_0} (I)'[L](I)\phi\,\frac{d\phi}{dt}\, dt = \int_{\phi=0}^{\phi=1} (I)'[L](I)\phi\, d\phi = \frac{(I)'[L](I)}{2}$$

This represents the part of the energy which the batteries have supplied in building up the final currents (I) in the various inductances of the system. It thus represents magnetically stored energy.   Returning to (9.8), let us place

(9.11) $$V = \int_0^{t_0} (i)'[S](q)\, dt$$

Using (9.3), we may write this in the form

(9.12) $$V = \int_0^{t_0} (Q)'[S](Q)\theta\,\frac{d\theta}{dt}\, dt = \int_{\theta=0}^{\theta=1} (Q)'[S](Q)\theta\, d\theta = \frac{(Q)'[S](Q)}{2}$$

This represents the electric energy which is stored in the various condensers of the network.   Returning to (9.8), let us place

(9.13) $$W_r = \int_0^{t_0} (i)'[R](i)\, dt$$

This represents the energy which has been dissipated in the various resistances of the network in the form of heat.   If we let

(9.14) $$F = (i)'[R](i)$$

we see that this represents the instantaneous power consumed by the resistances of the network.

The expressions (9.10), (9.12), and (9.14) are called quadratic forms and have the important property of being positive for all values of the variables. We thus see from our general analysis that the general circuit is characterized by three fundamental functions: its instantaneous magnetic energy, T; its instantaneous electric energy, V; and its dissipation function, F.

The Lagrangian Equations

If the energy and dissipation functions of a network are known, it is a simple matter to write the Kirchhoff's equations of the network. To do this, we note that

$$(9.15) \qquad e_{Lk} = \frac{d}{dt}\left(\frac{\partial T}{\partial \dot{q}_k}\right) \qquad k = 1, 2, \ldots, n$$

is the inductive counter voltage on the contour of mesh k. We also note that

$$(9.16) \qquad e_{ck} = \frac{\partial V}{\partial q_k} \qquad k = 1, 2, \ldots, n$$

denotes the capacitive counter voltage on the contour of mesh k. Similarly,

$$(9.17) \qquad e_{rk} = \frac{1}{2}\frac{\partial F}{\partial \dot{q}_k} \qquad k = 1, 2, 3, \ldots, n$$

Hence, the Kirchhoff electromotive-force equation for the kth mesh may be written in the form

$$(9.18) \qquad e_{Lk} + e_{rk} + e_{ck} = e_k \qquad k = 1, 2, 3, \ldots, n$$

Or in terms of the energy and dissipation functions, we have

$$(9.19) \qquad \frac{d}{dt}\left(\frac{\partial T}{\partial \dot{q}_k}\right) + \frac{1}{2}\frac{\partial F}{\partial \dot{q}_k} + \frac{\partial V}{\partial q_k} = e_k, \qquad k = 1, 2, \ldots, n$$

These are the Lagrangian equations of the general electrical network.

REFERENCES

1. Frazer, R. A., W. J. Duncan, and A. R. Collar, *Elementary Matrices.* London: Cambridge University Press, 1938.

2. Guillemin, E. A., *Communication Networks*, Vol. 1. New York: John Wiley and Sons, 1931.

3. Pipes, L. A., "Transformation Theory of General Static Polyphase Networks," *Trans. A.I.E.E.*, Vol. 59 (1940).

11 THE DISSIPATIONLESS NETWORK

1. INTRODUCTION

In the last two chapters the general classical procedure involved in the solution of the transient and steady-state behavior of the general n-mesh lumped circuit was considered. It was there seen that the treatment of the general case was most concise, provided that matrix algebra was used in its formulation. In this chapter, the solution of the so-called "dissipationless" network will be considered. This type of network is characterized by the fact that its resistance elements are negligible. Networks of this type are used extensively in communication engineering and are sometimes also called "oscillatory networks." In this chapter it will be demonstrated that by the use of a matrix multiplication process the solution of the determinantal equation of the system is avoided and the modal columns of the network are obtained in a very direct manner.

2. THE CANONICAL EQUATIONS AND THE STEADY-STATE SOLUTION

The differential equations which characterize the behavior of the general n-mesh system were considered in Chapter 9. The equation for the dissipationless network is the same as the one given there, with the exception that the impedance matrix $[R]$ is equal to zero. We have, accordingly,

$$(2.1) \qquad [Z(D)](i) = (e)$$

for the canonical set of differential equations of the system. In this case the "operational impedance matrix" is

$$(2.2) \qquad [Z(D)] = [L]D + [S]\frac{1}{D}$$

In discussing the solution of the oscillatory network, it is more convenient to consider the various mesh charges as the dependent variables. Since the mesh charge matrix is related to the mesh current matrix by the equation

$$(2.3) \qquad (q) = \int (i)\, dt$$

we may write the canonical equations in the form

$$(2.4) \qquad [L](\ddot{q}) + [S](q) = (e)$$

The general problem is to obtain the solution of the canonical equations (2.4) when we know the arbitrary electromotive forces impressed on the network and the initial charges and currents of the system at $t = 0$. As a step toward the solution, let us assume that the charge matrix is the sum of two matrices given by

$$(2.5) \qquad (q) = (q)_t + (q)_s$$

where we specify that the matrices $(q)_t$ and $(q)_s$ satisfy the following equations:

$$(2.6) \qquad [L](\ddot{q})_t + [S](q)_t = (0)$$

$$(2.7) \qquad [L](\ddot{q})_s + [S](q)_s = (e)$$

That is, the elements of $(q)_t$ are the various transient oscillations, and $(q)_s$ has elements that represent the various forced or steady-state terms.

The Steady-State Solution

Let us assume that the various electromotive forces impressed on the meshes of the system are periodic. If the impressed electromotive forces are periodic functions of fundamental period T, they may be represented within certain restrictions on continuity in the complex Fourier series form:

$$(2.8) \qquad e_k(t) = \sum_{n=-\infty}^{+\infty} a_{kn} e^{jnwt}$$

where

$$(2.9) \qquad w = \frac{2\pi}{T}$$

and the coefficients a_{kn} are given by

$$(2.10) \qquad a_{kn} = \frac{w}{2\pi} \int_0^{2\pi/\omega} e_k(t) e^{-jnwt}\, dt$$

If we introduce a column matrix $(a)_r$ defined by the equation

$$(2.11) \qquad (a)_r = \begin{bmatrix} a_{1r} \\ a_{2r} \\ \cdots \\ a_{nr} \end{bmatrix}$$

we may write the electromotive force matrix in the form

$$(2.12) \qquad (e) = \sum_{r=-\infty}^{+\infty} (a)_r e^{jrwt}$$

We must now solve Eq. (2.7) for the various steady-state mesh charges produced by the impression of the general electromotive force matrix (2.12). To do this, let us assume a solution of the form

$$(2.13) \qquad (q)_s = \sum_{r=-\infty}^{+\infty} (Q)_r e^{jrwt}$$

where $(Q)_r$ is a matrix whose elements are amplitudes to be determined of the form

$$(2.14) \qquad (Q)_r = \begin{bmatrix} Q_{1r} \\ Q_{2r} \\ \dots \\ Q_{nr} \end{bmatrix}$$

Substituting (2.13) and (2.12) into (2.7) and performing the indicated differentiation, we obtain

$$(2.15) \qquad \sum_{r=-\infty}^{+\infty} ([L](-r^2w^2) + [S])(Q)_r e^{jrwt} = \sum_{r=-\infty}^{+\infty} (a)_r e^{jrwt}$$

Equating coefficients of like harmonic terms, we have

$$(2.16) \qquad ([L](-r^2w^2) + [S])(Q)_r = (a)_r$$

Letting

$$(2.17) \qquad [f(jwr)] = [S] - r^2w^2[L]$$

$$(2.18) \qquad \Delta(jwr) = |f(jwr)|$$

and $[F(jwr)]$ be the adjoint matrix of the matrix $[f(jwr)]$ defined by the relation

$$(2.19) \qquad [f(jwr)][F(jwr)] = \Delta(jwr)I$$

where I is the unit matrix of the nth order, we have

$$(2.20) \qquad (Q)_r = \frac{[F(jwr)](a)_r}{\Delta(jwr)}$$

This determines the various amplitudes of the steady-state oscillations of the system. Substituting this into (2.13), we have the steady-state solution for the general periodic electromotive forces (2.12):

$$(2.21) \qquad (q_s) = \sum_{r=-\infty}^{r=+\infty} \frac{[F(jwr)](a)_r}{\Delta(jwr)} e^{jrwt}$$

This solution fails for the exceptional case $\Delta(jwr) = 0$. This case occurs when one of the impressed electromotive forces has a component frequency that is a resonant frequency of the system. By a limiting process, the steady state for a component voltage for which $\Delta(jwr) = 0$ is found to be

(2.22)
$$\frac{e^{jwst}}{\Delta'(jws)} \{[F(jws)]' + t[F(jws)]\}(a)_s$$

where

(2.23)
$$\Delta'(jws) = \frac{d}{d(jws)} \Delta(jws)$$

and

(2.24)
$$[F(jws)]' = \frac{d}{d(jws)} [F(jws)]$$

3. THE TRANSIENT SOLUTION

Having obtained the steady-state solution for a general class of periodic electromotive forces, we turn now to a discussion of the free, or transient, oscillations of the network. These oscillations are governed by the equations

(3.1)
$$[L](\ddot{q})_t + [S](q)_t = (0)$$

To solve this equation, let us assume the solution

(3.2)
$$(q)_t = e^{jwt}(k)$$

where e^{jwt} is a scalar multiplier, and (k) is a columnar matrix of n constants to be determined. Substituting (3.2) into (3.1) and dividing out the scalar factor e^{jwt}, we obtain

(3.3)
$$(-w^2[L] + [S])(k) = (0)$$

If we premultiply both sides of (3.3) by $[S]^{-1}$, the inverse of the elastance matrix, we obtain

(3.4)
$$(-w^2[S]^{-1}[L] + I)(k) = (0)$$

where I is the unit matrix of the nth order. If we let

(3.5)
$$w^2 = 1/m$$

and

(3.6)
$$[u] = [S]^{-1}[L]$$

then (3.4) becomes

(3.7)
$$(mI - [u])(k) = (0)$$

The square matrix of the nth order $[u]$ is the "dynamical matrix." Equation (3.7) may be written in the following form:

$$(3.8) \qquad\qquad [u](k) = m(k)$$

Premultiplying the equation by $[u]$, we obtain

$$(3.9) \qquad\qquad [u]^2(k) = m[u](k) = m^2(k)$$

By repeating this procedure it may be shown that

$$(3.10) \qquad\qquad [u]^s(k) = m^s(k)$$

for s a positive or negative integer.

Now in order for the linear equations (3.7) to be consistent, we must have

$$(3.11) \qquad\qquad |mI - [u]| = 0$$

This determinantal equation will, in general, have n distinct real roots m_j. These are the eigenvalues of the dynamical matrix $[u]$. Every eigenvalue m_j has associated with it an eigenvector (k_j). These eigenvectors satisfy n equations of the form

$$(3.12) \qquad\qquad [u]^s(k_i) = m_j^s(k_i) \quad (j = 1, 2, \ldots, n)$$

where s is a positive or negative integer. This set of matrix equations may be written in the form

$$(3.13) \qquad [u]^s[(k_1)(k_2) \ldots (k_n)] = [m_1^s(k_1)m_2^s(k_2) \ldots m_n^s(k_n)]$$

where the square matrices of both members of (3.13) are partitioned matrices formed from the (k_j) columns as indicated. If we introduce the square matrix $[k]$ defined by the equation

$$(3.14) \qquad\qquad [k] = [(k_1)(k_2) \ldots (k_n)]$$

we may write (3.13) in the form

$$(3.15) \qquad\qquad [u]^s[k] = [k] \begin{bmatrix} m_1^s & 0 & \cdots & 0 \\ 0 & m_2^s & \cdots & 0 \\ \cdot & \cdot & \cdots & \cdot \\ 0 & \cdot & \cdots & m_n^s \end{bmatrix}$$

The matrix $[k]$ will be called the modal matrix; if the eigenvalues m_j are distinct, the modal matrix has an inverse, and by postmultiplying (3.15) by $[k]^{-1}$ we obtain

$$(3.16) \qquad\qquad [u]^s = [k] \begin{bmatrix} m_1^s & 0 & 0 & 0 & \cdots & 0 \\ 0 & m_2^s & 0 & 0 & \cdots & 0 \\ \cdot & \cdot & \cdot & \cdot & \cdots & \cdot \\ 0 & 0 & 0 & 0 & \cdots & m_n^s \end{bmatrix} [k]^{-1}$$

Let us place

(3.17)
$$[A] = [k]^{-1}$$

Then, by direct multiplication, we obtain

(3.18)
$$[u]^s = \sum_{r=1}^{n} m_r^s [u_r]$$

where

(3.19)
$$[u]_r = \begin{bmatrix} k_{1r}A_{r1} & k_{1r}A_{r2} & \cdots & k_{1r}A_{rn} \\ k_{2r}A_{r1} & k_{2r}A_{r2} & \cdots & k_{2r}A_{rn} \\ \cdot & \cdot & \cdots & \cdot \\ k_{nr}A_{r1} & k_{nr}A_{r2} & \cdots & k_{nr}A_{rn} \end{bmatrix}$$

For convenience, let the eigenvalues be arranged in order of decreasing magnitude. We then have

(3.20)
$$|m_1| > |m_2| \cdots > |m_n|$$

Then, when s is a large positive integer, only the terms corresponding to the dominant root need be retained in (3.18). We have, therefore, for s sufficiently large

(3.21)
$$\lim_{s \to \infty} [u]^s = m_1^s \begin{bmatrix} k_{11}A_{11} & k_{11}A_{12} & \cdots & k_{11}A_{1n} \\ k_{21}A_{11} & k_{21}A_{12} & \cdots & k_{21}A_{1n} \\ \cdot & \cdot & \cdots & \cdot \\ k_{n1}A_{11} & k_{n1}A_{12} & \cdots & k_{n1}A_{1n} \end{bmatrix}$$

If we premultiply Eq. (3.16) by $[k]^{-1}$, we obtain

(3.22)
$$[k]^{-1}[u]^s = \begin{bmatrix} m_1^s & 0 & \cdots & 0 \\ 0 & m_2^s & \cdots & 0 \\ \cdot & \cdot & \cdots & \cdot \\ 0 & 0 & \cdots & m_n^s \end{bmatrix} [k]^{-1}$$

Placing $s = 1$ and $[k]^{-1} = [A]$, we have

(3.23)
$$[A][u] = \begin{bmatrix} m_1 & 0 & \cdots & 0 \\ 0 & m_2 & \cdots & 0 \\ \cdot & \cdot & \cdots & \cdot \\ 0 & \cdot & \cdots & m_n \end{bmatrix} [A]$$

If we now consider the matrix $[A]$ to be partitioned into n rows, as shown,

(3.24)
$$[A] = \begin{bmatrix} A_{11} & A_{12} & \cdots & A_{1n} \\ A_{21} & A_{22} & \cdots & A_{2n} \\ \cdot & \cdot & \cdots & \cdot \\ A_{n1} & A_{n2} & \cdots & A_{nn} \end{bmatrix}$$

and let

(3.25) $[A_r] = [A_{r1}A_{r2} \ldots A_{rn}]$

then, by virtue of (3.23), we have the relation

(3.26) $[A_r][u] = m_r[A_r]$ $(r = 1, 2, \ldots, n)$

It will now be shown how it is possible to obtain a row proportional to $[A_r]$ from the column (k_r) in a simple manner.

If we substitute $[u] = [S]^{-1}[L]$ in the set of equations (3.12) we obtain

(3.27) $m_r(k_r) = [S]^{-1}[L](k_r)$ $(r = 1, 2, \ldots, n)$

Now if we remultiply (3.27) by $[L]$, we obtain

(3.28) $m_r[L](k_r) = [L][S]^{-1}[L](k_r)$

If we take the transpose of both sides of Eq. (3.28) and make use of the reversal law for transposed products, we obtain

(3.29) $m_r(k_r)'[L]' = (k_r)'[L]'[S]^{-1'}[L]'$

Since the square matrices $[L]$ and $[S]$ are symmetric, we obtain

(3.30) $m_r(k_r)'[L] = (k_r)'[L][u]$

Comparing Eqs. (3.26) and (3.30), we see that we must have

(3.31) $[A_r] = a_r(k_r)'[L]$

where a_r is a constant.   The relation (3.31) is most useful in obtaining the transient solution, as will be shown.   Since $[A] = [k]^{-1}$, we have

(3.32) $[A_r](k_s) = \begin{cases} 0, & \text{if } r \neq s \\ 1, & \text{if } r = s \end{cases}$

Hence,

(3.33) $(k_r)'[L](k_s) = 0 \quad r \neq s$

This expresses the orthogonal properties of the eigenvectors.

After the above digression into the theory of eigenvectors, let us continue our solution of Eq. (3.1).   The problem has resolved itself into finding the eigenvalues of the dynamical matrix.   These are related to the natural frequencies of the system by Eq. (3.5).   We must also determine the various eigenvectors (k_r) associated with the various natural frequencies.   It is in the numerical simplicity of these operations that the matrix method has distinct advantages.

4. DETERMINATION OF THE FUNDAMENTAL FREQUENCY

We shall now consider a procedure which will yield the fundamental natural frequency of the system.   Let us select an *arbitrary* vector $(x)_0$ and form the following sequence:

(4.1)
$$[u](x)_0 = (x)_1$$
$$[u](x)_1 = [u]^2(x)_0 = (x)_2$$
$$\cdot \qquad \cdot \cdot \cdot \qquad \cdot$$
$$[u](x)_{s-1} = [u]^s(x)_0 = (x)_s$$

Then, in view of Eq. (3.21), we have, for a sufficiently large s,

(4.2)
$$[u]^s(x)_0 = [u]^s \left\{ \begin{matrix} x_{10} \\ \cdot \\ x_{n0} \end{matrix} \right\} = m_1^s \left\{ \begin{matrix} k_{11} R_1 \\ \cdots \\ k_{n1} R_1 \end{matrix} \right\}$$

where $R_1 = A_{11} x_{10} + A_{12} x_{20} + \cdots + A_{1n} x_{n0}$, and we see that for a sufficiently large s in the sequence (4.1), we have the relations

(4.3)
$$\frac{x_{js}}{x_{rs}} = \frac{k_{j1}}{k_{r1}}$$

(4.4)
$$m_1 = \frac{x_{j, s+1}}{x_{j, s}}$$

From the relations (4.3) and (4.4) we determine the slowest natural
frequency given by

(4.5)
$$w_1 = \frac{1}{(m_1)^{1/2}}$$

and the eigenvector (k_1). The row matrix $[A_1]$ is given by

(4.6)
$$[A_1] = a_1 (k_1)' [L]$$

where a_1 is an arbitrary constant.

5. COMPLETION OF THE SOLUTION

Having determined the fundamental frequency w_1 and the eigenvectors
(k_1), we must now proceed to a determination of the overtones and the
eigenvectors associated with the overtones. In terms of the eigenvectors
(k_1), the solution of Eq. (3.1) may be written in the following form:

(5.1)
$$(q)_t = \sum_{r=1}^{n} (k_r)(B_r \sin (w_r t)/w_r + D_r \cos (w_r t))$$

where (k_r) is the eigenvectors of the rth mode and B_r and D_r are arbitrary
constants associated with the rth mode and to be determined from the initial
boundary conditions. Let us premultiply (5.1) by the row matrix $[A_s]$;
then, in view of the relation (4.6), we obtain

(5.2)
$$[A_s](q)_t = B_s \sin (w_s t)/w_s + D_s \cos (w_s t)$$

Then, if the mode corresponding to w_s is absent,

(5.3) $$[A_s](q)_t = 0$$

In particular, if the dominant mode w_1 is absent, the coordinates must satisfy the homogeneous linear scalar equation:

(5.4) $$[A_1](q)_t = 0$$

Now, after the sequence (4.1) has been formed, (k_1) is determined and $[A_1]$ is given by (4.6).

Expanding Eq. (5.3), we obtain

(5.5) $$A_{11}q_{1t} + A_{12}q_{2t} + \cdots + A_{1n}q_{nt} = 0$$

If we solve for q_{1T} in (5.5), we have

(5.6) $$q_{1t} = -\frac{A_{12}q_{2t}}{A_{11}} - \frac{A_{13}q_{3t}}{A_{11}} \cdots - \frac{A_{1n}q_{nt}}{A_{11}}$$

Accordingly, when the fundamental mode is absent, we have

(5.7) $$\begin{Bmatrix} q_{1t} \\ q_{2t} \\ \cdot \\ q_{nt} \end{Bmatrix} = \begin{bmatrix} 0 & -\dfrac{A_{12}}{A_{11}} & -\dfrac{A_{13}}{A_{11}} & \cdots & \dfrac{A_{1n}}{A_{11}} \\ 0 & 1 & 0 & \cdots & 0 \\ \cdot & \cdot & \cdot & \cdots & \cdot \\ 0 & 0 & 0 & \cdots & 1 \end{bmatrix} \times \begin{Bmatrix} q_{1t} \\ q_{2t} \\ \cdot \\ q_{nt} \end{Bmatrix}$$

Now, if we substitute (5.7) for the right member of Eq. (3.8), we obtain

(5.8) $$m(q)_T = [u]_1(q)_T$$

where

(5.9) $$[u]_1 = [u]\begin{bmatrix} 0 & -\dfrac{A_{12}}{A_{11}} & \cdots & -\dfrac{A_{1n}}{A_{11}} \\ 0 & 1 & \cdots & 0 \\ \cdot & \cdot & \cdots & \cdot \\ 0 & 0 & \cdots & 1 \end{bmatrix}$$

Now $[u]_1$ is the dynamical matrix for a system whose fundamental mode is m_2. A sequence similar to that of (4.1) is now set up. This new sequence gives us the first overtone w_2 and the second eigenvector (k_2). From the second eigenvector we obtain

(5.10) $$[A_2] = (k_2)'[L]$$

A condition that insures that the overtone w_2 is absent is

(5.11) $$[A_2](q)_t = 0$$

This equation combined with Eq. (5.4) enables us to obtain a matrix $[u]_2$ which is the dynamical matrix of a system having both lowest frequencies w_1

and w_2 absent.   Continuing this process, we obtain the n angular frequencies w_j and the n eigenvectors (k_r).   Equation (3.31) enables us to find the n modal rows $[A_r]$.   From the eigenvectors we may construct the matrices $[k]$ and $[A]$ which, as we shall see, enable us to evaluate the arbitrary constants.

6. EVALUATION OF THE ARBITRARY CONSTANTS

From Eq. (2.5) we have

(2.5)
$$(q) = (q)_t + (q)_s$$

Suppose the system has the n initial mesh charges at $t = 0$ denoted by the matrix

(6.1)
$$(q^0) = \begin{Bmatrix} q_1^0 \\ q_2^0 \\ \cdot \\ q_n^0 \end{Bmatrix}$$

and the n initial mesh currents at $t = 0$ denoted by the matrix

(6.2)
$$(i^0) = \begin{Bmatrix} i_1^0 \\ i_2^0 \\ \cdot \\ i_n^0 \end{Bmatrix}$$

Then we have from (2.5)

(6.3) $$(q^0)_t = (q^0) - (q^0)_s$$
(6.4) $$(i^0)_t = (i^0) - (i^0)_s$$

where (q_t^0) and $(i^0)_t$ are the transient charges and currents at $t = 0$.   Placing $t = 0$ in Eq. (5.1), we obtain

(6.5)
$$(q^0)_t = \sum_{r=1}^{n} (k_r) D_r$$

This may be written in the matrix form:

(6.6)
$$(q^0)_t = \begin{bmatrix} k_{11} & k_{12} & \cdots & k_{1n} \\ k_{21} & k_{22} & \cdots & k_{2n} \\ \cdot & \cdot & \cdots & \cdot \\ k_{n1} & k_{n2} & \cdots & k_{nn} \end{bmatrix} \begin{Bmatrix} D_1 \\ D_2 \\ \cdot \\ D_n \end{Bmatrix}$$

If we introduce the column matrix of arbitrary constants defined by

(6.7)
$$(D) = \begin{Bmatrix} D_1 \\ D_2 \\ \cdot \\ D_n \end{Bmatrix}$$

then, in view of (3.14), we may write Eq. (6.6) in the form

(6.8) $(q^0)_t = [k](D)$

(6.9) $(D) = [k]^{-1}(q^0)_t = [A](q^0)_t$

Similarly, from (5.1), we obtain

(6.10) $(i^0)_t = (q^0)_t = \sum_{r=1}^{n} (k_r)B_r$

and if we introduce a column matrix of arbitrary constants (B) defined by

(6.11) $(B) = \begin{Bmatrix} B_1 \\ B_2 \\ \cdot \\ B_n \end{Bmatrix}$

we have

(6.12) $(B) = [A](i^0)_t$

From this it is seen that we have the $2n$ arbitrary constants $(D_1 \ldots D_n)$, $(B_1 \ldots B_n)$ determined by Eqs. (6.9) and (6.12).

7. NORMAL COORDINATES

Equation (5.1) may be written in the matrix form

(7.1) $(q)_t = [k] \times \begin{bmatrix} \sin(w_1t)/w_1 & 0 & \ldots & 0 \\ 0 & \sin(w_2t)/w_2 & \ldots & 0 \\ \cdot & \cdot & \ldots & \cdot \\ 0 & 0 & \ldots & \sin(w_nt)/w_n \end{bmatrix}$

$\times \begin{Bmatrix} B_1 \\ B_2 \\ \cdot \\ B_n \end{Bmatrix} + [k]$

$\times \begin{bmatrix} \cos(w_1t) & 0 & \ldots & 0 \\ 0 & \cos(w_2t) & \ldots & 0 \\ \cdot & \cdot & \ldots & \cdot \\ 0 & 0 & \ldots & \cos(w_nt) \end{bmatrix} \begin{Bmatrix} D_1 \\ D_2 \\ \cdot \\ D_n \end{Bmatrix}$

If we introduce the coordinates Q defined by

(7.2) $(Q) = [k]^{-1}(q)_t = [A](q)_t$

then Eq. (7.1) on premultiplication by $[k]^{-1}$ reduces to

$$(7.3) \quad (Q) = \begin{bmatrix} \sin (w_1 t)/w_1 & 0 & \cdots & 0 \\ 0 & \sin (w_2 t)/w_2 & \cdots & 0 \\ \cdot & & \cdots & \cdot \\ 0 & \cdot & \cdots & \sin (w_n t)/w_n \end{bmatrix} (B)$$

$$+ \begin{bmatrix} \cos (w_1 t) & 0 & \cdots & 0 \\ 0 & \cos (w_2 t) & \cdots & 0 \\ \cdot & & \cdots & \cdot \\ 0 & 0 & \cdots & \cos (w_n t) \end{bmatrix} (D)$$

By multiplication, we have the general relations

$$(7.4) \qquad (Q_r) = \sin (w_r t) B_r/w_r + \cos (w_r t) D_r \quad (r = 1, 2, \ldots, n)$$

That is, the motion of any normal coordinate such as Q_s is independent of the motion of any of the other normal coordinates Q_r. The motions of the several normal coordinates Q_r is thus seen to be uncoupled.

8. ILLUSTRATIVE EXAMPLE

To illustrate the above general theory, let us consider the circuit of Fig. 11.1.

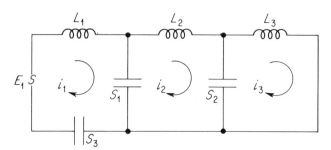

FIGURE 11.1

Let

$$L_1 = L_2 = L_3 = 1 \text{ henry}$$
$$S_1 = \tfrac{1}{3} \times 10^6 \text{ darafs}$$
$$S_2 = \tfrac{1}{6} \times 10^6 \text{ darafs}$$
$$S_3 = \tfrac{1}{2} \times 10^6 \text{ darafs}$$

The inductance and elastance matrices are, therefore, given by the equations

$$(8.1) \qquad [L] = \begin{bmatrix} 1 & 0 & 0 \\ 0 & 1 & 0 \\ 0 & 0 & 1 \end{bmatrix} \quad [S] = \begin{bmatrix} \tfrac{5}{6} & -\tfrac{1}{3} & 0 \\ -\tfrac{1}{3} & \tfrac{1}{2} & -\tfrac{1}{6} \\ 0 & -\tfrac{1}{6} & \tfrac{1}{6} \end{bmatrix} 10^{-6}$$

The dynamical matrix is, therefore,

$$[u] = [S]^{-1}[L] = 10^{-6} \begin{bmatrix} 2 & 2 & 2 \\ 2 & 5 & 5 \\ 2 & 5 & 11 \end{bmatrix} \begin{bmatrix} 1 & 0 & 0 \\ 0 & 1 & 0 \\ 0 & 0 & 1 \end{bmatrix}$$

(8.2)

$$[u] = 10^{-6} \begin{bmatrix} 2 & 2 & 2 \\ 2 & 5 & 5 \\ 2 & 5 & 11 \end{bmatrix}$$

Determination of Natural Frequencies

Substituting the above values of $[u]$ into (3.8) gives

(8.3)
$$10^{-6} \begin{bmatrix} 2 & 2 & 2 \\ 2 & 5 & 5 \\ 2 & 5 & 11 \end{bmatrix} (k) = m(k)$$

If we let

(8.4)
$$\bar{m} = 10^6 m$$

the numerical factor 10^{-6} is absorbed and we have

(8.5)
$$\begin{bmatrix} 2 & 2 & 2 \\ 2 & 5 & 5 \\ 2 & 5 & 11 \end{bmatrix} (k) = \bar{m}(k)$$

The natural frequencies are given by the equation

(8.6)
$$w_r = \frac{10^3}{\sqrt{\bar{m}}}$$

To determine the fundamental frequency, let us form the sequence (4.1). As our arbitrary vector (x_0) let us choose

(8.7)
$$(x)_0 = \begin{Bmatrix} 1 \\ 1 \\ 1 \end{Bmatrix}$$

We then begin the sequence

(8.8)
$$[u](x)_0 = \begin{bmatrix} 2 & 2 & 2 \\ 2 & 5 & 5 \\ 2 & 5 & 11 \end{bmatrix} \begin{Bmatrix} 1 \\ 1 \\ 1 \end{Bmatrix} = \begin{Bmatrix} 6 \\ 12 \\ 18 \end{Bmatrix} = 18 \begin{Bmatrix} 0.3 \\ 0.6 \\ 1 \end{Bmatrix}$$

Now, it is unnecessary to carry the common factor 18 in the further operations, since it is the *ratios* of successive elements in the multiplications that are important.

Dropping the factor 18 and continuing, we have

$$(8.9) \qquad \begin{bmatrix} 2 & 2 & 2 \\ 2 & 5 & 5 \\ 2 & 5 & 11 \end{bmatrix} \begin{Bmatrix} 0.3 \\ 0.6 \\ 1 \end{Bmatrix} = \begin{Bmatrix} 4 \\ 9 \\ 15 \end{Bmatrix} = 15 \begin{Bmatrix} 0.26 \\ 0.6 \\ 1 \end{Bmatrix}$$

and, after repeating the multiplication nine times, we obtain

$$(8.10) \qquad \begin{bmatrix} 2 & 2 & 2 \\ 2 & 5 & 5 \\ 2 & 5 & 11 \end{bmatrix} \begin{Bmatrix} 0.254885 \\ 0.584225 \\ 1 \end{Bmatrix} = 14.43 \begin{Bmatrix} 0.254885 \\ 0.584225 \\ 1 \end{Bmatrix}$$

Repeating the process further only multiplies the column matrix by the same factor 14.43. Accordingly, we need not go any further in the sequence. We then have

$$(8.11) \qquad\qquad\qquad \bar{m}_1 = 14.43$$

and the fundamental angular frequency is

$$(8.12) \qquad\qquad\qquad w_1 = \frac{10^3}{(14.43)^{1/2}} = 263$$

The fundamental frequency is

$$(8.13) \qquad\qquad\qquad f_1 = \frac{w_1}{2} = 41.9 \text{ cycles/sec}$$

The fundamental eigenvector may be taken to be

$$(8.14) \qquad\qquad\qquad (k_1) = \begin{Bmatrix} 0.254885 \\ 0.584225 \\ 1 \end{Bmatrix}$$

The row $[A_1]$ to an arbitrary constant, is given by Eq. (4.6). If we let the arbitrary constant $a_1 = 1$, we do not lose the orthogonal properties (4.6), so we may take

$$(8.15) \qquad\qquad [A_1] = [(0.254885)(0.584225)1][L]$$
$$= [(0.254885)(0.584225)1]$$

Now by (5.4) in any oscillation from which the fundamental mode is absent, we must have

$$(8.16) \qquad [A_1](q)_t = 0.254885q_{1t} + 0.584225q_{2t} + q_{3t} = 0$$

or

$$q_{1t} = -2.29211q_{2t} - 3.92334q_{3t}$$

In this case, Eq. (5.7) becomes

(8.17)
$$\begin{Bmatrix} q_{1t} \\ q_{2t} \\ q_{3t} \end{Bmatrix} = \begin{bmatrix} 0 & -2.29211 & -3.92334 \\ 0 & 1 & 0 \\ 0 & 0 & 1 \end{bmatrix} \begin{Bmatrix} q_{1t} \\ q_{2t} \\ q_{3t} \end{Bmatrix}$$

The matrix (5.9) is now given by

(8.18)
$$[u]_1 = \begin{bmatrix} 2 & 2 & 2 \\ 2 & 5 & 5 \\ 2 & 5 & 11 \end{bmatrix} \begin{bmatrix} 0 & -2.29211 & -3.92334 \\ 0 & 1 & 0 \\ 0 & 0 & 1 \end{bmatrix}$$

$$= \begin{bmatrix} 0 & -2.58422 & -5.84668 \\ 0 & 0.41578 & -2.84668 \\ 0 & 0.41578 & 3.15332 \end{bmatrix}$$

This is the dynamical matrix for a system whose fundamental mode is $\bar{m}_2$.

We again set up a sequence similar to that of (4.1). We again choose the arbitrary vector (8.7). It is unnecessary to compute the leading element of any column, since this is always multiplied by 0 in the succeeding step. We thus find

(8.19)
$$[u]_1 \begin{Bmatrix} 1 \\ 1 \\ 1 \end{Bmatrix} = \begin{Bmatrix} \cdots \\ -2.4309 \\ 3.5691 \end{Bmatrix} = 3.5691 \begin{Bmatrix} \cdots \\ -0.68110 \\ 1 \end{Bmatrix}$$

(8.20)
$$[u]_1 \begin{Bmatrix} \cdots \\ -0.68110 \\ 1 \end{Bmatrix} = \begin{Bmatrix} \cdots \\ -3.1299 \\ 2.8701 \end{Bmatrix} = 2.8701 \begin{Bmatrix} \cdots \\ -1.09049 \\ 1 \end{Bmatrix}$$

After fifteen approximations, the column repeats itself; the scalar multiple is

(8.21)
$$\bar{m}_2 = 2.6152$$

The eigenvector (k_2) is then given by

(8.22)
$$(k_2) = \begin{Bmatrix} -0.95670 \\ -1.29429 \\ 1 \end{Bmatrix}$$

The angular frequency of the first overtone is given by

(8.23)
$$w_2 = \frac{10^3}{(2.6152)^{1/2}} = 618$$

The natural frequency of the first overtone is

(8.24)
$$f_2 = \frac{w_2}{2\pi} = 98.4 \text{ cycles/sec}$$

The row $[A_2]$ is now given by (3.31) to an arbitrary constant; placing this constant equal to 1, we may take

$$(8.25) \qquad [A_2] = (k_2)'[L] = [(-0.95670)(-1.29429)1]$$

The necessary condition that the first overtone be absent from the motion is

$$(8.26) \qquad [A_2](q)_t = -0.95670q_{1t} - 1.29429q_{2t} + q_{3t} = 0$$

or

$$(8.27) \qquad q_{1t} = -1.35287q_{2t} + 1.04526q_{3t}$$

Equation (8.16) gives the necessary condition: that the fundamental mode be absent from the motion. Hence, eliminating q_{1T} between Eqs. (8.16) and (8.27) gives

$$(8.28) \qquad 0 = 0.93924q_{2t} + 4.96860q_{3t}$$

or

$$(8.29) \qquad q_{2t} = -5.2900q_{3t}$$

Hence, for a motion that has the fundamental and first overtone absent, we have

$$(8.30) \qquad \begin{Bmatrix} q_{1t} \\ q_{2t} \\ q_{3t} \end{Bmatrix} = \begin{bmatrix} 1 & 0 & 0 \\ 0 & 0 & -5.290 \\ 0 & 0 & 1 \end{bmatrix} \cdot \begin{Bmatrix} q_{1t} \\ q_{2t} \\ q_{3t} \end{Bmatrix}$$

Now, in terms of the matrix $[u]_1$ as given by (8.18), we have Eq. (5.8) in the form

$$(5.8) \qquad \bar{m}(q)_t = [u]_1(q)_t$$

Substituting the relation $(q)_T$ as given by (8.30) into the right side of (5.8) gives

$$(8.31) \qquad \bar{m}\begin{Bmatrix} q_{1t} \\ q_{2t} \\ q_{3t} \end{Bmatrix} = [u]_1 \begin{bmatrix} 1 & 0 & 0 \\ 0 & 0 & -5.290 \\ 0 & 0 & 1 \end{bmatrix} \begin{Bmatrix} q_{1t} \\ q_{2t} \\ q_{3t} \end{Bmatrix}$$

Let us define $[u]_2$ by the following equation:

$$(8.32) \qquad [u]_2 = [u]_1 \begin{bmatrix} 1 & 0 & 0 \\ 0 & 0 & -5.2900 \\ 0 & 0 & 1 \end{bmatrix}$$

or

$$[u]_2 = \begin{bmatrix} 0 & 0 & 7.8238 \\ 0 & 0 & -5.0461 \\ 0 & 0 & 0.9539 \end{bmatrix}$$

The matrix $[u]_2$ is the dynamical matrix of a system having the fundamental w_1 and the first overtone w_2 absent. Setting up the sequence (4.1) as before, we have

$$(8.33) \qquad [u]_2(x)_0 = \begin{bmatrix} 0 & 0 & 7.8238 \\ 0 & 0 & -5.0461 \\ 0 & 0 & 0.9539 \end{bmatrix} \begin{Bmatrix} 1 \\ 1 \\ 1 \end{Bmatrix}$$

$$= \begin{Bmatrix} 7.8238 \\ -5.0461 \\ 0.9539 \end{Bmatrix} = 0.9539 \begin{Bmatrix} 8.2019 \\ -5.2900 \\ 1 \end{Bmatrix}$$

Discarding the factor 0.9539 and repeating the process, we have

$$(8.34) \qquad [u]_2^2(x)_0 = 0.9539 \begin{Bmatrix} 8.2019 \\ -5.290 \\ 1 \end{Bmatrix}$$

Since the vector repeats itself, it is not necessary to go further, and we have directly

$$(8.35) \qquad \bar{m}_3 = 0.9539$$

The angular frequency of the first overtone w_3 is given by

$$(8.36) \qquad w_3 = \frac{10^3}{(\bar{m}_3)^{1/2}} = 1025$$

The highest natural frequency of the system is, therefore,

$$(8.37) \qquad f_3 = \frac{w_3}{2\pi} = 163 \text{ cycles/sec}$$

The third eigenvector may be taken to be

$$(8.38) \qquad (k_3) = \begin{Bmatrix} 8.2019 \\ -5.2900 \\ 1 \end{Bmatrix}$$

The row $[A_3]$ may be taken to be

$$(8.39) \qquad [A_3] = [(8.2019)(-5.2900)1]$$

From (8.14), (8.22), and (8.38) we may construct the modal matrix

$$(8.40) \qquad [k] = \begin{bmatrix} (0.254885) & (-0.95670) & (8.2019) \\ (0.584225) & (-1.29429) & (-0.52900) \\ 1 & 1 & 1 \end{bmatrix}$$

And from (8.15), (8.25), and (8.39) we may form the matrix $[A]$ given by

(8.41)
$$[A] = \begin{bmatrix} (0.254885) & (0.584225) & 1 \\ (-0.95670) & (-1.29429) & 1 \\ (8.2019) & (-5.2900) & 1 \end{bmatrix}$$

In this particular example, since $[L] = [I]$, the unit matrix of the third order, the matrix $[A]$ may be taken to be $[k]'$.

Completion of the Solution

The steady-state solution for arbitrary periodic electromotive forces is given by Eq. (2.21). Let the steady-state solution be $(q)_s$; then we have the solution

(8.41a)
$$(q)_t = \sum_{r=1}^{3} (k_r)(B_r \sin (w_r t)/w_r + D_r \cos (w_r t)$$

where, if (q^0) and (i^0) are column matrices whose elements are the initial charges and currents, we have

(8.42)
$$\begin{Bmatrix} D_1 \\ D_2 \\ D_3 \end{Bmatrix} = [A]((q^0) - (q^0)_s)$$

(8.43)
$$\begin{Bmatrix} B_1 \\ B_2 \\ B_3 \end{Bmatrix} = [A]((i^0) - (i^0)_s)$$

from (6.9) and (6.12).

Since we know $[A]$, $[k]_r$, and the various angular frequencies, the arbitrary constants are easily evaluated by (8.42) and (8.43) and the solution is complete. The solution is then given by (2.5). The ease by which the natural frequencies and eigenvectors are obtained is apparent from this example.

9. EFFECT OF SMALL RESISTANCE TERMS

Thus far in our discussion, we have neglected the effect of resistances that may be present in the general network. As soon as resistance enters into the problem, and in actual cases it always does, the work necessary to obtain the solution increases considerably. In practice, however, it happens quite frequently that although resistances are present, they are very small and cause only a relatively slow attenuation. Practically every network used in communication theory comes under this category.

It appears logical, therefore, to extend the theory to the slightly damped case. The method here presented will illustrate how the effect of a small amount of dissipation may be taken into account.

10. THE POTENTIAL FUNCTION

In order to obtain the transient solution of the slightly damped case, let us introduce the following functions:

(10.1)
$$A = \frac{(q)_t'[L](q)_t}{2}$$

(10.2)
$$B = \frac{(q)_t'[R](q)_t}{2}$$

(10.3)
$$C = \frac{(q)_t'[S](q)_t}{2}$$

where $[R]$ is a square matrix whose elements are the self and mutual mesh resistances of the circuit. The scalar functions A, B, and C may be called the potentials of the magnetic forces, the resistance forces, and the electric forces.

In terms of these potential functions, the canonical equations of the free or transient oscillations are

(10.4)
$$\frac{d^2}{dt^2}\left(\frac{\partial A}{\partial q_{kt}}\right) + \frac{d}{dt}\left(\frac{\partial B}{\partial q_{kt}}\right) + \frac{\partial C}{\partial q_{kt}} = 0 \quad (k = 1, 2, \ldots, -n)$$

or

(10.5)
$$[L](\ddot{q})_t + [R](\dot{q})_t + [S](q)_t = (0)$$

Let us assume the solution:

(10.6)
$$(q)_t = \sum_{r=1}^{2n} (x_r)e^{mrt}$$

for the set (10.5), where (x_r) are the various eigenvectors and m_r the several modes.

Substituting (10.6) into (10.5), we obtain

(10.7) $$m_r^2[L](x_r) + m_r[R](x_r) + [S](x_r) = (0), \quad (r = 1, 2, \ldots, 2n)$$

for the various amplitudes (x_r) of the several modes m_r.

If we premultiply (10.7) by $(x_r)'$, the transposed matrix of (x_r), we obtain the following scalar equations:

(10.8)
$$m_r^2(x_r)'[L](x_r) + m_r(x_r)'[R](x_r)$$
$$+ (x_r)'[S](x_r) = 0 \quad (r = 1, 2, \ldots, 2n)$$

Comparing the three members of the equation with the potential function (8.36), (10.2), and (10.3), let us introduce the following potential functions for the several modes x_r:

(10.9)
$$A_r = \frac{(x_r)'[L](x_r)}{2}$$

(10.10)
$$B_r = \frac{(x_r)'[R](x_r)}{2}$$

(10.11)
$$C_r = \frac{(x_r)'[S](x_r)}{2}$$

In terms of these potentials, the scalar equations (10.8) become

(10.12) $m_r^2 A_r + m_r B_r + C_r = 0$ $(r = 1, 2, \ldots, 2n)$

Solving for the eigenvalues, we have

(10.13)
$$m_r = -\frac{B_r}{2A_r} \pm \left(\frac{B_r^2}{4A_r^2} - \frac{C_r}{A_r}\right)^{1/2}$$

Now if the network has no resistance, we have

(10.14)
$$B_r = 0$$

(10.15)
$$m_r = \pm \frac{jC_r}{A_r}$$

and we have a solution of the type (5.1) where

(10.16)
$$w_r = \left(\frac{C_r}{A_r}\right)^{1/2}$$

Now, in the case of small damping we have

(10.17)
$$\frac{C_r}{A_r} \gg \left(\frac{B_r}{2A_r}\right)^2 \quad (r = 1, 2, \ldots, 2n)$$

so that

(10.18)
$$m_r = -\frac{B_r}{2A_r} \pm j\left(\frac{C_r}{A_r}\right)^{1/2}$$

In this case, the motion is only slightly perturbed from the undamped case and the solution (5.1) must be modified to

(10.19)
$$(q)_t = \sum_{r=1}^{n} (k_r)e^{-\alpha_r t}\{B \sin\left(\frac{w_r t}{w_r}\right) + D \cos(w_r t)\}$$

where

(10.20)
$$\alpha_r = -\frac{B_r}{2A_r}$$

is the attenuation constant, and the natural frequencies w_r and amplitudes may be calculated as before, since if the relation (10.17) is satisfied the frequencies and amplitudes of the undamped system differ from those of the damped system by quantities of higher order.

11. COMPUTATION OF THE ATTENUATION CONSTANTS

We have seen that if the relation (10.17) is satisfied so that the frequencies of the system may be computed by neglecting the resistance terms, then the solution for the damped case given by (10.19) differs from that of the undamped case (5.1) by the presence of the attenuation constants (10.19). These are given by (10.20). The eigenvectors (x_r) may be taken proportional to the eigenvector (k_r). Substituting these into (10.20), we have

$$(11.1) \qquad \alpha_r = -\frac{(k_r)'[R](k_r)}{2(k_r)'[L](k_r)}$$

The procedure to be followed in the transient solution of the oscillatory network is first to neglect the resistance matrix $[R]$ and to obtain the natural frequencies w_r and the modal matrices (k_r) by the methods of the first part of this chapter.

Then if the relation (10.17), which may be written in the form

$$(11.2) \qquad \frac{(k_r)'[S](k_r)}{(k_r)'[L](k_r)} \gg \left(\frac{(k_r)'[R](k_r)}{2(k_r)'[L](k_r)}\right)^2$$

is satisfied, the solution is given by (10.19), and the various attenuation constants are obtained from (11.1) by direct matrix multiplication.   The rest of the solution proceeds as before.

REFERENCES

1. Frazer, R. A., W. J. Duncan, and A. R. Collar, *Elementary Matrices*.   London: Cambridge University Press, 1938.

2. Pipes, L. A., "Matrix Theory of Oscillatory Networks," *Journal of Applied Physics* (Dec., 1939).

12 THE STEADY-STATE ANALYSIS OF FOUR-TERMINAL NETWORKS

1. INTRODUCTION

In the fields of electric power transmission and communication engineering, the interest is seldom centered in the distribution of current or voltage along the chain of structures which is placed between the output and the input terminals of the circuit. The main interest in a practical case is the actual relation between output quantities and input quantities. From this standpoint, the transmission line or the chain of circuits may be regarded as placed inside of a box containing four terminals. Two of these terminals are designated as the input terminals and two as the output terminals. In this chapter we shall, therefore, consider the general behavior of a general arrangement of linear passive network elements having two accessible pairs of terminals. We shall then consider the general behavior of specific types of structures, such as T networks, π networks, transmission lines, transformers, etc. In this chapter the steady-state behavior of such systems will be considered.

2. THE GENERAL EQUATIONS

Let us consider a general four-terminal network, as shown in Fig. 12.1.

FIG. 12.1. Four-Terminal Network

We shall assume that the reference directions for voltages and currents are as shown in Fig. 12.1. The four-terminal network will be assumed to

337

consist of an n-mesh network having only two accessible elements, as shown. The voltages E_1 and E_2 are complex voltages produced by sources external to the network, and the currents I_1 and I_2 are the mesh currents in meshes 1 and 2 produced by the application of the external electromotive forces inserted in the sense shown, in series with the two accessible terminals. The internal structure of the four-terminal network will be assumed to be quite general, and the n meshes will be assumed to have complex mesh impedances, Z_{nn}, and complex mutual impedances between meshes, Z_{mn}. The restrictions on the component elements of the network are that they be linear, constant, and bilateral. It will be further assumed that the network is passive; that is, the only sources of electromotive force are E_1 and E_2 produced by external agencies. The canonical equations for the complex, steady-state amplitudes of the voltages and currents of such a network may be written in the matrix form:

$$(2.1) \qquad\qquad (E) = [Z](I)$$

where (E) is a column matrix whose n elements are the n-mesh complex voltages, $[Z]$ is a square symmetric matrix of order n whose elements are the self and mutual mesh impedances of the n-mesh network, and (I) is a column matrix whose n elements are the n-mesh currents of the network. The matrix equation (2.1) is readily obtained by the methods of Chapter 9 for the determination of the steady-state solution of a general network due to the application of harmonic electromotive forces. In view of the symmetry conditions of the mutual impedance elements,

$$(2.2) \qquad\qquad Z_{mn} = Z_{nm}$$

we have:

$$(2.3) \qquad\qquad [Z]' = [Z]$$

where $[Z]'$ is the transpose of the matrix $[Z]$.

In the case under consideration, the system has accessible terminals in only two meshes: the input mesh, which we shall call mesh 1, and the output mesh, which will be called mesh 2. Since the system is supposed devoid of internal electromotive forces, the voltage matrix has all its elements equal to zero with the exception of the first two. If we premultiply both members of (2.1) by $[Z]^{-1}$, we have an explicit relation for the current matrix.

$$(2.4) \qquad\qquad (I) = [Z]^{-1}(E)$$

Let us introduce a square matrix of the nth order $[Y]$, defined by

$$(2.5) \qquad\qquad [Y] = [Z]^{-1}$$

Since $[Y]$ is the inverse of $[Z]$ and $[Z]$ is a symmetric matrix, we have

$$(2.6) \qquad\qquad Y_{rs} = \frac{\text{Cofactor of } Z_{rs}}{|Z|}$$

where Y_{rs} is the general element of the matrix $[Y]$, and $|Z|$ is the determinant of the matrix $[Z]$.   Hence, we may write concisely

(2.7) $(I) = [Y](E)$

From (2.7) we have

(2.8)
$$I_1 = Y_{11}E_1 + Y_{12}E_2$$
$$I_2 = Y_{21}E_1 + Y_{22}E_2$$

for the currents of mesh 1 and 2, and we have the general relation $Y_{12} = Y_{21}$ from the general property, $Z_{12} = Z_{21}$.

In writing the above equations, it has been assumed that the positive currents in each mesh have clockwise directions and that positive electromotive forces tend to circulate positive currents in the meshes where they are applied.   It is easy to see that with this convention of signs, all the mutual impedances Z_{mn} are negative.   In the theory of four-terminal networks, it is convenient to use a somewhat different reference direction for the voltage E_2.   The standard convention is shown in Fig. 12.2.

FIGURE 12.2

Hence, if we write

(2.9)
$$I_1 = Y_{11}E_1 - Y_{12}E_2$$
$$I_2 = Y_{21}E_1 - Y_{22}E_2$$

we conform to the standard reference directions of Fig. 2.2.   Solving for E_1 and I_1 in Eqs. (2.9), we arrive at the standard form of the equations:

(2.10)
$$E_1 = AE_2 + BI_2$$
$$I_1 = CE_2 + DI_2$$

where

(2.11)
$$A = \frac{Y_{22}}{Y_{12}} \qquad B = \frac{1}{Y_{12}}$$
$$C = \frac{Y_{11}Y_{22} - Y_{12}^2}{Y_{12}} \qquad D = \frac{Y_{11}}{Y_{12}}$$

and by a direct multiplication it is seen that we have the identity:

(2.12) $AD - BC = 1$

We note that A and D have the dimensions of pure numbers, B has the dimensions of an impedance, and C has the dimension of an admittance. It may be noted also that since we have not placed any restriction on the number of meshes n or on the internal structure of the four-terminal network other than that the component parts be linear, constant, and bilateral, it thus follows that the relation (2.12) is true in general. This relation holds in the limiting case where the four-terminal network is a smooth transmission line which may be regarded as a circuit of an infinite number of meshes. The general theory thus shows that any linear, passive, constant, bilateral, four-terminal network is characterized by a square matrix of the second order:

$$(2.13) \qquad [u] = \begin{bmatrix} A & B \\ C & D \end{bmatrix}$$

whose elements are related by Eq. (2.12). Such a matrix will be called the chain matrix of the network. The chain matrices of several common structures will be discussed in a later section.

3. ALTERNATIVE FORM OF THE EQUATIONS

The standard equations (2.10) which refer to Fig. (2.2) may be put in the following alternative matrix forms. These other forms are sometimes very useful in certain applications.

$$(3.1) \qquad \begin{bmatrix} E_1 \\ I_1 \end{bmatrix} = \begin{bmatrix} A & B \\ C & D \end{bmatrix} \cdot \begin{bmatrix} E_2 \\ I_2 \end{bmatrix}$$

$$(3.2) \qquad \begin{bmatrix} E_2 \\ I_2 \end{bmatrix} = \begin{bmatrix} D & -B \\ -C & A \end{bmatrix} \cdot \begin{bmatrix} E_1 \\ I_1 \end{bmatrix}$$

$$(3.3) \qquad \begin{bmatrix} I_1 \\ I_2 \end{bmatrix} = \begin{bmatrix} \dfrac{D}{B} & -\dfrac{1}{B} \\ \dfrac{1}{B} & -\dfrac{A}{B} \end{bmatrix} \cdot \begin{bmatrix} E_1 \\ E_2 \end{bmatrix}$$

$$(3.4) \qquad \begin{bmatrix} E_1 \\ E_2 \end{bmatrix} = \begin{bmatrix} \dfrac{A}{C} & -\dfrac{1}{C} \\ \dfrac{1}{C} & -\dfrac{D}{C} \end{bmatrix} \cdot \begin{bmatrix} I_1 \\ I_2 \end{bmatrix}$$

$$(3.5) \qquad \begin{bmatrix} I_1 \\ E_2 \end{bmatrix} = \begin{bmatrix} \dfrac{C}{A} & \dfrac{1}{A} \\ \dfrac{1}{A} & \dfrac{B}{A} \end{bmatrix} \cdot \begin{bmatrix} E_1 \\ I_2 \end{bmatrix}$$

(3.6)
$$\begin{bmatrix} E_1 \\ I_2 \end{bmatrix} = \begin{bmatrix} \dfrac{B}{D} & \dfrac{1}{D} \\ \dfrac{1}{D} & -\dfrac{C}{D} \end{bmatrix} \cdot \begin{bmatrix} I_1 \\ E_2 \end{bmatrix}$$

4. INTERCONNECTION OF FOUR-TERMINAL NETWORKS

The matrix equations of the preceding article may be used to advantage in finding the resultant four-terminal constants when several four-terminal networks are interconnected in various manners. If we consider the interconnection of two four-terminal networks, we see that two such networks may be interconnected to form a resulting four-terminal network in five distinct manners, which we shall consider in turn.

(a) The Cascade Connection

Let us first consider two four-terminal networks connected in cascade, as shown in Fig. 12.3. In this case we have

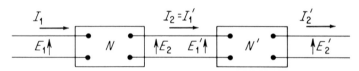

FIG. 12.3. Cascade Connection

(4.1)
$$\begin{bmatrix} E_1 \\ I_1 \end{bmatrix} = \begin{bmatrix} A & B \\ C & D \end{bmatrix} \cdot \begin{bmatrix} E_2 \\ I_2 \end{bmatrix}$$

and

(4.2)
$$\begin{bmatrix} E_1' \\ E_2' \end{bmatrix} = \begin{bmatrix} A' & B' \\ C' & D' \end{bmatrix} \cdot \begin{bmatrix} E_2' \\ I_2' \end{bmatrix}$$

where (A, B, C, D) are the parameters of the network N and (A', B', C', D') are the parameters of the network N'. The currents have the sense shown in the figure. Since for this type of connection we have

(4.3)
$$\begin{bmatrix} E_2 \\ I_2 \end{bmatrix} = \begin{bmatrix} E_1' \\ I_1' \end{bmatrix}$$

It thus follows that if we substitute this relation into (4.1) and (4.2) we obtain

(4.4)
$$\begin{bmatrix} E_1 \\ I_1 \end{bmatrix} = \begin{bmatrix} A & B \\ C & D \end{bmatrix} \begin{bmatrix} A' & B' \\ C' & D' \end{bmatrix} \cdot \begin{bmatrix} E_2' \\ I_2' \end{bmatrix}$$

(4.5)
$$\begin{bmatrix} E_1 \\ I_1 \end{bmatrix} = \begin{bmatrix} (AA' + BC') & (AB' + BD') \\ (CA' + DC') & (CB' + DD') \end{bmatrix} \cdot \begin{bmatrix} E_2' \\ I_2' \end{bmatrix}$$

The four parameters of the resulting network are given by the elements of the square matrix of Eq. (4.5).

(b) *The Parallel Connection*

Let us now consider the two networks N and N' interconnected as shown in Fig. 12.4. Before we discuss this case, a few words of caution may be stated regarding the consideration of more complicated interconnections than the cascade connection. It is obvious that when two four-terminal networks are connected in cascade, then the current emerging from the lower input terminals is equal to the current entering the upper input terminals. Now, in the more complicated cases to be treated, such as the parallel connection, etc., the currents entering the input terminals are not, in general, equal to the current emerging from the input terminals, and the same is true of the respective output terminals. Current unbalance will occur as a result of potential differences existing between terminals to be joined. As an

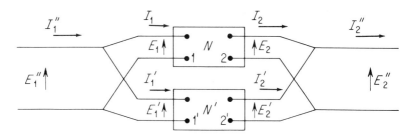

FIG. 12.4. Parallel Connection

example, in the parallel case, suppose that the two input terminals are connected together and that it is necessary to determine under what conditions the assumptions are valid that the entering currents of the output terminals are the same as the currents leaving the output terminals and hence that equations of the type (3.1) hold for each network. An analysis of the situation reveals that the necessary condition is that if the voltages E_{12} and B'_{12} are equal, then there will be no circulating currents which make the equations of the individual networks invalid. The general criterion for no circulatory currents is that no potential difference may exist between terminals to be joined. Returning to the parallel connection, we see that provided there are no circulating currents in the loop $121'2'$, a condition that is insured if $E_{12} = B'_{12}$, we may write the equations of the separate networks in the form:

(4.6)
$$\begin{bmatrix} I_1 \\ I_2 \end{bmatrix} = \begin{bmatrix} \dfrac{D}{B} & -\dfrac{1}{B} \\ \dfrac{1}{B} & -\dfrac{A}{B} \end{bmatrix} \cdot \begin{bmatrix} E_1 \\ E_2 \end{bmatrix}$$

(4.7)
$$\begin{bmatrix} I_1' \\ I_2' \end{bmatrix} = \begin{bmatrix} \dfrac{D'}{B'} & -\dfrac{1}{B'} \\ \dfrac{1}{B'} & -\dfrac{A'}{B'} \end{bmatrix} \cdot \begin{bmatrix} E_1' \\ E_2' \end{bmatrix}$$

for the networks N and N', respectively. For this connection, we have the relations

(4.8)
$$\begin{bmatrix} I_1'' \\ I_2'' \end{bmatrix} = \begin{bmatrix} I_1 + I_1' \\ I_2 + I_2' \end{bmatrix} \qquad \begin{aligned} E_1'' &= E_1 = E_1' \\ E_2'' &= E_2 = E_2' \end{aligned}$$

If we add together Eqs. (4.6) and (4.7), then, in view of (4.8), we obtain

(4.9)
$$\begin{bmatrix} I_1'' \\ I_2'' \end{bmatrix} = \begin{bmatrix} \left(\dfrac{D}{B} + \dfrac{D'}{B'}\right) & -\left(\dfrac{1}{B} + \dfrac{1}{B'}\right) \\ \left(\dfrac{1}{B} + \dfrac{1}{B'}\right) & -\left(\dfrac{A}{B} + \dfrac{A'}{B'}\right) \end{bmatrix} \cdot \begin{bmatrix} E_1'' \\ E_2'' \end{bmatrix}$$

If we call A'', B'', C'', D'' the parameters of the composite system, we have

(4.10)
$$\begin{bmatrix} I_1'' \\ I_2'' \end{bmatrix} = \begin{bmatrix} \dfrac{D''}{B''} & -\dfrac{1}{B''} \\ \dfrac{1}{B''} & -\dfrac{A''}{B''} \end{bmatrix} \cdot \begin{bmatrix} E_1'' \\ E_2'' \end{bmatrix}$$

and if we compare the coefficients of the square matrices (4.10) and (4.9), we have

$$A'' = \frac{(AB' + A'B)}{(B + B')}, \quad B'' = \frac{BB'}{(B + B')}$$

(4.11)
$$C'' = \frac{(A - A')(D' - D)}{(B + B')}$$

$$D'' = \frac{(B'D + BD')}{(B + B')}$$

(c) *The Series Connection*

Figure 12.5 shows the two four-terminal networks N and N' connected in series. If $E_{12} = E_{12}'$, as shown, then $V = 0$ and $I_1 = I_1'$ and $I_2 = I_2'$. We write Eq. (3.4) for the networks N and N', respectively, in the form

$$\begin{bmatrix} E_1 \\ E_2 \end{bmatrix} = \begin{bmatrix} \dfrac{A}{C} & -\dfrac{1}{C} \\ \dfrac{1}{C} & -\dfrac{D}{C} \end{bmatrix} \cdot \begin{bmatrix} I_1 \\ I_2 \end{bmatrix}$$

(4.12)

$$\begin{bmatrix} E_1' \\ E_2' \end{bmatrix} = \begin{bmatrix} \dfrac{A'}{C'} & -\dfrac{1}{C'} \\ \dfrac{1}{C'} & -\dfrac{D'}{C'} \end{bmatrix} \cdot \begin{bmatrix} I_1' \\ I_2' \end{bmatrix}$$

For this connection, we have the relations

(4.13)
$$E_1'' = E_1' + E_1 \quad I_1'' = I_1 = I_1'$$
$$E_2'' = E_2' + E_2 \quad I_2'' = I_2 = I_2'$$

If we add Eqs. (4.12), we obtain, in view of (4.13), the equation

(4.14)
$$\begin{bmatrix} E_1'' \\ E_2'' \end{bmatrix} = \begin{bmatrix} \left(\dfrac{A}{C} + \dfrac{A'}{C'}\right) & -\left(\dfrac{1}{C} + \dfrac{1}{C'}\right) \\ \left(\dfrac{1}{C} + \dfrac{1}{C'}\right) & -\left(\dfrac{D}{C} + \dfrac{D'}{C'}\right) \end{bmatrix} \cdot \begin{bmatrix} I_1'' \\ I_2'' \end{bmatrix}$$

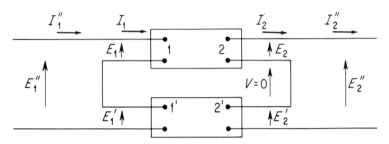

FIG. 12.5. Series Connection

Calling (A'', B'', C'', D'') the parameters of the composite system, we have

(4.15)
$$\begin{bmatrix} E_1'' \\ E_2'' \end{bmatrix} = \begin{bmatrix} \dfrac{A''}{C''} & -\dfrac{1}{C''} \\ \dfrac{1}{C''} & -\dfrac{D''}{C''} \end{bmatrix} \cdot \begin{bmatrix} I_1'' \\ I_2'' \end{bmatrix}$$

Comparing the coefficients of the square matrices of (4.14) and (4.15), we obtain

(4.16)
$$A'' = \frac{AC' + A'C}{(C + C')} \quad C'' = \frac{CC'}{(C + C')}$$
$$B'' = \frac{(A''D'' - 1)}{C''} \quad D'' = \frac{(DC' + CD')}{(C + C')}$$

(d) *The Series-Parallel Connection*

Figure 12.6 shows the two four-terminal networks N and N' connected in series-parallel. To treat this case we write Eq. (3.6) for the networks N and N' in the form (provided that $E_{12} = E_{12}'$):

(4.17)

$$\begin{bmatrix} E_1 \\ I_2 \end{bmatrix} = \begin{bmatrix} \dfrac{B}{D} & \dfrac{1}{D} \\ \dfrac{1}{D} & -\dfrac{C}{D} \end{bmatrix} \cdot \begin{bmatrix} I_1 \\ E_2 \end{bmatrix}$$

$$\begin{bmatrix} E_1' \\ I_2' \end{bmatrix} = \begin{bmatrix} \dfrac{B'}{D'} & \dfrac{1}{D'} \\ \dfrac{1}{D'} & -\dfrac{C'}{D'} \end{bmatrix} \cdot \begin{bmatrix} I_1' \\ E_2' \end{bmatrix}$$

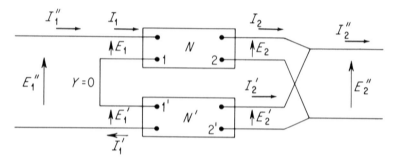

FIG. 12.6. Series-Parallel Connection

The relations between the voltages and currents for this connection are

(4.18)
$$E_1'' = E_1' + E_1 \qquad I_1'' = I_1 = I_1'$$
$$I_2'' = I_2 + I_e' \qquad E_2'' = E_2 = E_2'$$

If we add Eqs. (4.17), we obtain, in view of (4.18), the equation:

(4.19)
$$\begin{bmatrix} E_1'' \\ I_2'' \end{bmatrix} = \begin{bmatrix} \left(\dfrac{B}{D} + \dfrac{B'}{D'}\right) & \left(\dfrac{1}{D} + \dfrac{1}{D'}\right) \\ \left(\dfrac{1}{D} + \dfrac{1}{D'}\right) & -\left(\dfrac{C}{D} + \dfrac{C'}{D'}\right) \end{bmatrix} \cdot \begin{bmatrix} I_1'' \\ E_2'' \end{bmatrix}$$

If we call (A'', B'', C'', D'') the parameters of the composite system, we have

(4.20)
$$\begin{bmatrix} E_1'' \\ I_2'' \end{bmatrix} = \begin{bmatrix} \dfrac{B''}{D''} & \dfrac{1}{D''} \\ \dfrac{1}{D''} & -\dfrac{C''}{D''} \end{bmatrix} \cdot \begin{bmatrix} I_1'' \\ E_2'' \end{bmatrix}$$

Comparing the coefficients of the square matrices of (4.20) and (4.19), we obtain

(4.21)
$$A'' = \frac{(B''C'' + 1)}{D''}$$
$$B'' = \frac{(BD' + B'D)}{(D + D')}$$
$$C'' = \frac{(CD' + C'D)}{(D + D')}$$
$$D'' = \frac{DD'}{(D + D')}$$

(e) *The Parallel-Series Connection*

Figure 12.7 represents the two four-terminal networks N and N' connected in parallel-series. In order to analyze this case, we write Eq. (3.5) in the form (provided that $E_{12} = E'_{12}$):

(4.22)

$$\begin{bmatrix} I_1 \\ E_2 \end{bmatrix} = \begin{bmatrix} \dfrac{C}{A} & \dfrac{1}{A} \\ \dfrac{1}{A} & \dfrac{B}{A} \end{bmatrix} \cdot \begin{bmatrix} E_1 \\ I_2 \end{bmatrix}$$

$$\begin{bmatrix} I'_1 \\ E'_2 \end{bmatrix} = \begin{bmatrix} \dfrac{C'}{A'} & \dfrac{1}{A'} \\ \dfrac{1}{A'} & \dfrac{B'}{A'} \end{bmatrix} \cdot \begin{bmatrix} E'_1 \\ I'_2 \end{bmatrix}$$

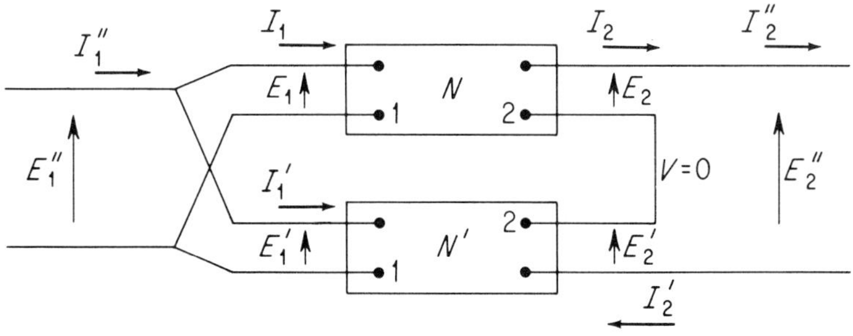

FIG. 12.7. Parallel-Series Connection

The relations between the voltages and currents in this connection are

(4.23)

$$E''_1 = E_1 = E'_1 \qquad E''_2 = E'_2 + E_2$$

$$I''_1 = I_1 + I'_1 \qquad I''_2 = I_2 = I'_2$$

If we add Eqs. (4.22), then, in view of (4.23), we obtain

(4.24)

$$\begin{bmatrix} I''_1 \\ E''_2 \end{bmatrix} = \begin{bmatrix} \left(\dfrac{C}{A} + \dfrac{C'}{A'}\right) & \left(\dfrac{1}{A} + \dfrac{1}{A'}\right) \\ \left(\dfrac{1}{A} + \dfrac{1}{A'}\right) & \left(\dfrac{B}{A} + \dfrac{B'}{A'}\right) \end{bmatrix} \cdot \begin{bmatrix} E''_1 \\ I''_2 \end{bmatrix}$$

If we now let the parameters of the composite system be denoted by (A'', B'', C'', D''), we have

(4.25)

$$\begin{bmatrix} I''_1 \\ E''_2 \end{bmatrix} = \begin{bmatrix} \dfrac{C''}{A''} & \dfrac{1}{A''} \\ \dfrac{1}{A''} & \dfrac{B''}{A''} \end{bmatrix} \cdot \begin{bmatrix} E''_1 \\ I''_2 \end{bmatrix}$$

Comparing the coefficients of the square matrices of (4.24) and (4.25), we obtain

$$A'' = \frac{AA'}{A + A'}, \qquad C'' = \frac{CA' + C'A}{(A + A')}$$

(4.26)

$$B'' = \frac{(BA' + B'A)}{(A + A')} \qquad D'' = \frac{(B''C'' + 1)}{A''}$$

5. THE CHAIN MATRICES OF COMMON STRUCTURES

If we have a network N characterized by the equation

(5.1)
$$\begin{bmatrix} E_1 \\ I_1 \end{bmatrix} = \begin{bmatrix} A & B \\ C & D \end{bmatrix} \cdot \begin{bmatrix} E_2 \\ I_2 \end{bmatrix}$$

then the matrix

(5.1a)
$$[u] = \begin{bmatrix} A & B \\ C & D \end{bmatrix}$$

will be called the "chain matrix" of the network. Several chain matrices of common four-terminal networks will now be derived.

(a) *An Impedance in Series*

If we have an impedance in series, as shown in Fig. 12.8, we have, by inspection,

(5.2)
$$[u] = \begin{bmatrix} 1 & Z \\ 0 & 1 \end{bmatrix}$$

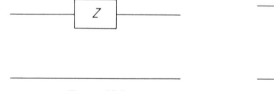

FIGURE 12.8

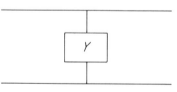

FIGURE 12.9

(b) *An Impedance in Parallel*

(5.3)
$$[u] = \begin{bmatrix} 1 & 0 \\ Y & 1 \end{bmatrix}$$

(c) *T-Network*

(5.4)
$$[u] = \begin{bmatrix} (1 + Z_A Y_C) & (Z_B + Z_A Z_B Y_C + Z_A) \\ Y_C & (Z_B Y_C + 1) \end{bmatrix}$$

This chain matrix may be easily derived by considering the T-network to consist of a cascade connection of the impedance Z_a, the admittance Y_b, and the impedance Z_b and by multiplying the various associated matrices together to obtain the resultant matrix.

(d) *The π Network*

(5.5)
$$[u] = \begin{bmatrix} \dfrac{(Z_B + Z_C)}{Z_B} & Z_C \\ \dfrac{(Z_A + Z_B + Z_C)}{Z_A Z_B} & \dfrac{(Z_A + Z_C)}{Z_A} \end{bmatrix}$$

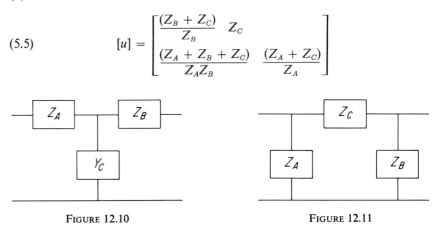

FIGURE 12.10   FIGURE 12.11

The chain matrix of this network is derived by considering the π network to be formed by the cascade connection of a shunt impedance Z_a, a series imepdance Z_c, and a shunt impedance Z_b, and by multiplying together the chain matrices of these respective structures.

(e) *The Real Transformer*

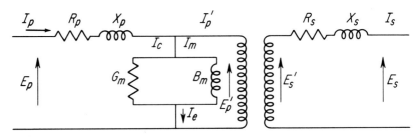

FIG. 12.12. Equivalent Circuit of Real Transformer

The conventional equivalent circuit of the real transformer is shown in Fig. 12.12. Let us use the notation:

N_p = the number of turns in the primary winding.
N_s = the number of turns in the secondary winding.
a = N_s/N_p = the ratio of transformation.
G_m = the equivalent conductance of the magnetizing circuit.
B_m = the equivalent susceptance of the magnetizing circuit.
I_p = the primary current.
E_p = the primary voltage.
I_s = the secondary current.
E_s = the secondary voltage.
I_c = the current representing the core loss.
I_m = the magnetizing current.
I_e = the exciting current.
X_p = the primary leakage reactance.
X_s = the secondary leakage reactance.
R_p = the primary winding resistance.
R_s = the secondary winding resistance.

Now if we let

(5.6) $$Z_p = R_p \mp jX_p \quad \text{where} \quad j = \sqrt{-1}$$

(5.7) $$Z_s = R_s + jX_s$$

(5.8) $$Y_m = G_m + jB_m$$

then the four-terminal network representing the transformer may be regarded as the cascade connection of four individual circuits: the first circuit consisting of a series impedance Z_p, the second of a shunt admittance Y_m, the third of an ideal transformer, and the fourth of a series impedance Z_s.

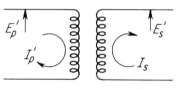

FIG. 12.13. Ideal Transformer

Figure 12.13 is the circuit diagram of the ideal transformer. Since the ratio of transformation is a, we have the equations

(5.9) $$E_p' = -\frac{E_s'}{a} \qquad I_p' = -aI_s'$$

Accordingly, the chain matrix $[u]$ for the four-terminal network representing the ideal transformer is

(5.10) $$[u] = \begin{bmatrix} -\dfrac{1}{a} & 0 \\ 0 & -a \end{bmatrix}$$

Accordingly, if we let $[u]_t$ represent the chain matrix of the real transformer, we have

$$(5.11) \quad [u]_t = \begin{bmatrix} 1 & Z_p \\ 0 & 1 \end{bmatrix} \begin{bmatrix} 1 & 0 \\ Y_m & 1 \end{bmatrix} \begin{bmatrix} -\dfrac{1}{a} & 0 \\ 0 & -a \end{bmatrix} \begin{bmatrix} 1 & Z_s \\ 0 & 1 \end{bmatrix}$$

$$= -\frac{1}{a} \begin{bmatrix} (Z_p Y_m + 1) & (Z_s + Z_p Z_s Y_m + a^2 Z_p) \\ Y_m & (Y_m Z_s + a^2) \end{bmatrix}$$

and we have the following relation between the primary quantities and the secondary quantities:

$$(5.12) \qquad \begin{bmatrix} E_p \\ I_p \end{bmatrix} = [u]_t \begin{bmatrix} E_s \\ I_s \end{bmatrix}$$

and

$$(5.13) \qquad \begin{bmatrix} E_s \\ I_s \end{bmatrix} = [u]_t^{-1} \begin{bmatrix} E_p \\ I_p \end{bmatrix}$$

(f) *The Smooth Transmission Line*

In Sec. 9 of this chapter the four-terminal constants of the smooth transmission line of Fig. 12.14 will be derived. As shown in Sec. 9, the chain

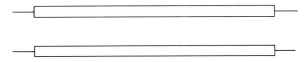

FIG. 12.14. The Smooth Line

matrix of the smooth transmission line is given by

$$(5.14) \qquad [u] = \begin{bmatrix} \cosh \theta & Z_0 \sinh \theta \\ \dfrac{\sinh \theta}{Z_0} & \cosh \theta \end{bmatrix}$$

where θ is the characteristic angle of the line as defined in Sec. 9 and Z_0 is the characteristic impedance of the line.

From the above discussion it is apparent that when the parameters of the individual elements of a simple system are known, then the parameters of a complex system formed by the interconnection of the simple constituent elements may be determined by simple matrix multiplication.

6. THE HOMOGRAPHIC TRANSFORMATION

Let us consider a four-terminal network terminated by an impedance Z, as shown in Fig. 12.15.   We have the general equation

(3.1)
$$\begin{bmatrix} E_1 \\ I_1 \end{bmatrix} = \begin{bmatrix} A & B \\ C & D \end{bmatrix} \cdot \begin{bmatrix} E_2 \\ I_2 \end{bmatrix}$$

In this case we have the relation

(6.1)
$$E_2 = ZI_2$$

Hence, substituting this value of E_2 in (3.1), we obtain

(6.2)
$$\begin{bmatrix} E_1 \\ I_1 \end{bmatrix} = \begin{bmatrix} A & B \\ C & D \end{bmatrix} \cdot \begin{bmatrix} Z \\ 1 \end{bmatrix} I_2$$

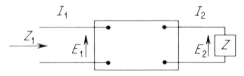

FIGURE 12.15

Now, if we call Z_1 the impedance looking into the network from the left when the network is terminated by the impedance Z on the right, we obtain

(6.3)
$$Z_1 = \frac{E_1}{I_1} = \frac{(AZ + B)}{(CZ + D)}$$

It is thus apparent that the insertion of the four-terminal network transforms the impedance Z into the impedance Z_1 by a homographic transformation. The properties of homographic transformations are well known, and an account of them may be found in any treatise on the complex variable.   The chief properties may be briefly summarized by the following statements:

(a) The homographic transformation when A, B, C, D are complex constants turns circles in the Z plane into circles in the Z_1 plane provided that straight lines must be regarded as degenerate circles. It is this property that accounts for the many circle diagrams that occur in circuit theory.

(b) The homographic transformation is a one-to-one transformation of the complete Z plane into the complete Z_1 plane which leaves the angle between any two intersecting curves unaltered.

(c) The homographic transformation may be generated by an even number of inversions with respect to circles or straight lines.

If we place $Z_1 = Z$ in the transformation (6.3), we shall obtain two different values of Z which will be unaltered by the transformation. These are given by the equation

$$(6.4) \qquad CZ^2 - (A - D)Z - B = 0$$

The two roots of this equation may be written in the form:

$$(6.5) \qquad s_1 = \frac{(A - D) + \sqrt{(A + D)^2 - 4}}{2C}$$

and

$$(6.6) \qquad s_2 = \frac{(A - D) - \sqrt{(A + D)^2 - 4}}{2C}$$

If s_1 and s_2 are distinct, we may write

$$(6.7) \qquad \frac{(Z_1 - s_1)}{(Z_1 - s_2)} = \frac{K(Z - s_1)}{(Z - s_2)}$$

where

$$(6.8) \qquad K = \frac{(A - Cs_1)}{(A - Cs_2)}$$

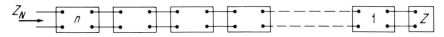

FIGURE 12.16

and K is called the multiplier of the transformation. Now, if we have a chain of n identical circuits all having the chain matrix $[u]$, as shown in Fig. 6.2, then the impedance Z_n looking into the cascade chain from the left is given by the transformation

$$(6.9) \qquad \frac{(Z_n - s_1)}{(Z_n - s_2)} = \frac{K^n(Z - s_1)}{(Z - s_2)}$$

obtained by a repeated application of (6.7). Or

$$(6.10) \qquad Z_n = \frac{Z(s_1 - s_2 K^n) + (K^n - 1)s_1 s_2}{Z(1 - K^n) + (s_1 K^n - s_2)}$$

We shall see in a later section that the quantities s_1, s_2, and K are intimately related to the matrix $[u]$. The problem of determining the sending end impedance of the cascade arrangement of Fig. 12.16 is thus completely solved by Eq. (6.10).

7. CASCADE CONNECTION OF DISSYMMETRICAL NETWORKS

Let us now discuss the problem of determining the voltages and currents along a chain of n identical networks which are arranged as shown in

Fig. 12.17. If we apply the method of Sec. 4(a) and consider the equations for the cascade connection of the element Z_s and the n identical four-terminal networks whose chain matrix is $[u]$, we obtain the following equation:

(7.1)
$$\begin{bmatrix} E_g \\ I_0 \end{bmatrix} = \begin{bmatrix} 1 & Z_s \\ 0 & 1 \end{bmatrix} \begin{bmatrix} A & B \\ C & D \end{bmatrix}^n \begin{bmatrix} E_n \\ I_n \end{bmatrix}$$

The matrix $[u]$ could, of course, be raised to any integral power n by direct multiplication, but such a procedure is tedious; we may, therefore, make use of the basic theorems of matrix algebra. The procedure is similar to that developed in Chapter 4 for the solution of polynomial equations. As a first step in the procedure of raising the matrix $[u]$ to a high power, let us construct the characteristic matrix of the matrix $[u]$. This matrix is defined by the equation

(7.2)
$$[A(m)] = mI - [u] = \begin{bmatrix} (m - A) & -B \\ -C & (m - D) \end{bmatrix}$$

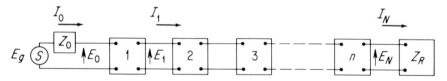

FIG. 12.17. Chain of Dissymetrical Networks

The characteristic equation of $[u]$ is, in this case,

(7.3)
$$|A(m)| = m^2 - m(A + D) + 1 = 0$$

and the eigenvalues of $[u]$ are, therefore,

(7.4)
$$m_{1,2} = \frac{(A + D)}{2} \pm \frac{1}{2}\sqrt{(A + D)^2 - 4}$$

We note that the product of the eigenvalues satisfies the equation

(7.5)
$$m_1 \cdot m_2 = 1$$

and the sum of the eigenvalues satisfies the equation

(7.6)
$$m_1 + m_2 = (A + D)$$

Accordingly, if we let

(7.7)
$$m_1 = e^a$$

where a is a complex number, we have, in view of (7.5),

(7.8)
$$m_2 = e^{-a}$$

and as a consequence of the relation (7.6), we have

$$(7.9) \qquad \cosh(a) = \frac{(A + D)}{2}$$

The adjoint matrix of the characteristic matrix (7.2) is

$$(7.10) \qquad [F(m)] = \begin{bmatrix} (m - D) & B \\ C & (m - A) \end{bmatrix}$$

Let us now form the vector $(k)_1$ by substituting $m = m_1$ in the first column of the matrix (7.10); that is,

$$(7.11) \qquad (k)_1 = \begin{bmatrix} (e^a - D) \\ C \end{bmatrix}$$

Now let us form the vector $(k)_2$ by substituting $m = m_2$ into the first column of (7.10); that is,

$$(7.12) \qquad (k)_2 = \begin{bmatrix} (e^{-a} - D) \\ C \end{bmatrix}$$

Let a square matrix $[k]$ be formed from the vectors $(k)_1$ and $(k)_2$ so that we have

$$(7.13) \qquad [k] = \begin{bmatrix} (e^a - D) & (e^{-a} - D) \\ C & C \end{bmatrix}$$

If we now substitute (7.9) into (6.5) and (6.6), we obtain

$$(7.14) \qquad s_1 = \frac{(e^a - D)}{C}$$

and

$$(7.15) \qquad s_2 = \frac{(e^{-a} - D)}{C}$$

Accordingly, we may write $[k]$ in the form

$$(7.16) \qquad [k] = C \begin{bmatrix} s_1 & s_2 \\ 1 & 1 \end{bmatrix}$$

$[k]^{-1}$ is seen to be

$$(7.17) \qquad [k]^{-1} = \frac{1}{C(s_1 - s_2)} \begin{bmatrix} 1 & -s_2 \\ -1 & s_1 \end{bmatrix}$$

There is a basic theorem in matrix algebra which states that any matrix $[u]$ may be transformed into the form

$$(7.18) \qquad [u] = [k] \begin{bmatrix} m_1 & 0 \\ 0 & m_2 \end{bmatrix} \cdot [k]^{-1}$$

provided that the two eigenvalues m_1 and m_2 are distinct, which in this case places the restriction:

(7.19) $$(A + D) \neq \pm 2$$

The above theorem may be proved as follows: Let the matrix under consideration be

(1) $$[u] = \begin{bmatrix} A & B \\ C & D \end{bmatrix}$$

and the characteristic matrix of $[u]$ be

(2) $$[A(m)] = mI - [u] = \begin{bmatrix} (m - A) & -B \\ -C & (m - D) \end{bmatrix}$$

Let the adjoint matrix of the characteristic matrix of $[u]$ be

(3) $$[F(m)] = \begin{bmatrix} (m - D) & B \\ C & (m - A) \end{bmatrix}$$

Since $[F(m)]$ is the adjoint of $[A(m)]$, we have the relation

(4) $$[F(m)][A(m)] = [A(m)][F(m)] = I|A(m)|$$

where I is the unit matrix of the second order, and $|A(m)|$ is the determinant of the matrix $[A(m)]$. Now, since m_1 and m_2, the eigenvalues of the matrix $[u]$, satisfy the equation

(5) $$|A(m)| = 0$$

we have from (4)

(6) $$[A(m_1)][F(m_1)] = 0$$

and

(7) $$[A(m_2)][F(m_2)] = 0$$

Therefore,

(8) $$(m_1 I - [u]) \begin{bmatrix} (m_1 - D) & R \\ C & (m_1 - A) \end{bmatrix} = [0]$$

and

(9) $$(m_2 I - [u]) \begin{bmatrix} (m_2 - D) & B \\ C & (m_2 - A) \end{bmatrix} = [0]$$

If we let

(10) $$(k)_1 = \begin{bmatrix} (m_1 - D) \\ C \end{bmatrix} \qquad (k)_2 = \begin{bmatrix} (m_2 - D) \\ C \end{bmatrix}$$

then, in view of (6) and (7), we have

(11) $(m_1I - [u])(k)_1 = (0)$ and $(m_2I - [u])(k)_2 = (0)$

Hence

(12) $[u](k)_1 = m_1(k)_1$ and $[u](k)_2 = m_2(k)_2$

These relations may be written in the form

(13) $[u][(k)_1 \;\; (k)_2] = [(k)_1 \;\; (k)_2)] \begin{bmatrix} m_1 & 0 \\ 0 & m_2 \end{bmatrix}$

Now, if we let $[k]$ be a partitioned matrix constructed as follows:

(14) $[k] = [(k)_1 \;\; (k)_2]$

the relation (13) may be written in the form

(15) $[u] = [k] \begin{bmatrix} m_1 & 0 \\ 0 & m_2 \end{bmatrix} \cdot [k]^{-1}$

This establishes the theorem.

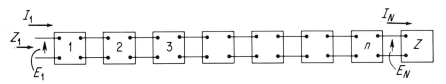

FIGURE 12.18

Substituting in the values of $[k]$ and $[k]^{-1}$ in (7.18), we may write the matrix $[u]$ in the form

(7.20) $[u] = \begin{bmatrix} s_1 & s_2 \\ 1 & 1 \end{bmatrix} \begin{bmatrix} e^a & 0 \\ 0 & e^{-a} \end{bmatrix} \begin{bmatrix} 1 & -s_2 \\ -1 & s_1 \end{bmatrix} \dfrac{1}{(s_1 - s_2)}$

The form (7.20) has the advantage that by repeated multiplication we obtain

(7.21) $[u]^n = \begin{bmatrix} s_1 & s_2 \\ 1 & 1 \end{bmatrix} \begin{bmatrix} e^{an} & 0 \\ 0 & e^{-an} \end{bmatrix} \begin{bmatrix} 1 & -s_2 \\ -1 & s_1 \end{bmatrix} \dfrac{1}{(s_1 - s_2)}$

where n may be a positive or negative integer.

The Iterative Impedances

Let us consider the chain of circuits of Fig. 12.18. If $[u]$ is the chain matrix of the individual identical four-terminal networks of the chain, we have the relation

(7.22) $\begin{bmatrix} E_1 \\ I_1 \end{bmatrix} = [u]^n \begin{bmatrix} E_n \\ I_n \end{bmatrix}$

Let us use the notation

(7.23)
$$\begin{bmatrix} A_n & B_n \\ C_n & D_n \end{bmatrix} = [u]^n$$

Now, if the chain is terminated by an impedance Z, we have the relation

(7.24)
$$E_n = ZI_n$$

If we call Z_1 the impedance of the chain looking from the left, we have

(7.25)
$$Z_1 = \frac{E_1}{I_1}$$

Substituting (7.24) into (7.22) and taking the ratio E_1/I_1, we have

(7.26)
$$Z_1 = \frac{(A_n Z + B_n)}{(C_n Z + D_n)}$$

If we now consider an infinite chain of networks, we may use (7.21) to raise the matrix $[u]$ to a high power. We then have

(7.27)
$$\underset{n=\infty}{\text{Limit}} \, [u]^n = \frac{e^{an}}{(s_1 - s_2)} \begin{bmatrix} s_1 & -s_1 s_2 \\ 1 & -s_2 \end{bmatrix}$$

Substituting into (7.26), we find that

(7.28)
$$\underset{n=\infty}{\text{Limit}} \, Z_1 = s_1$$

In the same way, the impedance of an infinite chain of networks looking at the chain from the right is found to be equal to $-s_2$. These impedances are called the iterative impedances of the network and are denoted by

(7.29)
$$Z_{01} = s_1$$

and

(7.30)
$$Z_{02} = -s_2$$

If we substitute these values into Eq. (7.21), we have

(7.31)
$$[u]^n = \begin{bmatrix} (Z_{01}e^{an} + Z_{02}e^{-an}) & (2Z_{01}Z_{02} \sinh an) \\ 2 \sinh an & (Z_{02}e^{an} + Z_{01}e^{-an}) \end{bmatrix} \frac{1}{(Z_{01} + Z_{02})}$$

Equation (7.31) holds for n either a positive or a negative integer, and is a very convenient formula for the calculation of high powers of $[u]$. If the individual four-terminal networks are symmetrical, then we have the relation

(7.32)
$$A = D$$

and hence

(7.33)
$$Z_{01} = Z_{02}$$

We have in this special case

(7.34)
$$[u]^n = \begin{bmatrix} \cosh(an) & Z_{01}\sinh(an) \\ \dfrac{\sinh(an)}{Z_{01}} & \cosh(an) \end{bmatrix}$$

The case of equal eigenvalues of the matrix $[u]$ arises when

(7.35)
$$(A + D) = \pm 2$$

As a consequence of this, we have

(7.36)
$$Z_{02} = -Z_{01}$$

(7.37)
$$\cosh(a) = \pm 1$$

(7.38)
$$\sinh(a) = 0$$

This case may be treated as a limiting case of (7.31). After this digression into the consideration of the iterative impedances of the network, let us return to the analysis of the chain of networks of Fig. 12.17. Using the notation of (7.23), we have

(7.39)
$$\begin{bmatrix} E_g \\ I_g \end{bmatrix} = \begin{bmatrix} 1 & Z_s \\ 0 & 1 \end{bmatrix}\begin{bmatrix} A_n & B_n \\ C_n & D_n \end{bmatrix}\begin{bmatrix} E_n \\ I_n \end{bmatrix}$$

Now, since we have the terminal condition

(7.40)
$$E_n = I_n Z_r$$

we obtain the following equation for the impedance of the system looking at it from the generator end:

(7.41)
$$Z_g = \frac{E_g}{I_c} = \frac{[(A_n + Z_s C_n)Z_r + (B_n + Z_s D_n)]}{(C_n Z_r + D_n)}$$

To find the general voltage E_k and the current I_k along the network, we write

(7.42)
$$\begin{bmatrix} E_g \\ I_0 \end{bmatrix} = \begin{bmatrix} 1 & Z_s \\ 0 & 1 \end{bmatrix}\begin{bmatrix} A_k & B_k \\ C_k & D_k \end{bmatrix}\begin{bmatrix} E_k \\ I_k \end{bmatrix}$$

Or, on finding the inverse of the resultant square matrix on the right side of (7.42), we have

(7.43)
$$\begin{bmatrix} E_k \\ I_k \end{bmatrix} = \begin{bmatrix} A_{-k} & B_{-k} \\ C_{-k} & D_{-k} \end{bmatrix}\begin{bmatrix} 1 & -Z_s \\ 0 & 1 \end{bmatrix}\begin{bmatrix} E_g \\ I_0 \end{bmatrix}$$

In view of (7.41) and (7.23), this may be written in the form

(7.44)
$$\begin{bmatrix} E_k \\ I_k \end{bmatrix} = \begin{bmatrix} A_{-k} & B_{-k} \\ C_{-k} & D_{-k} \end{bmatrix}\begin{bmatrix} 1 & -Z_s \\ 0 & 1 \end{bmatrix}\begin{bmatrix} 1 \\ \dfrac{1}{Z_g} \end{bmatrix}E_g$$

and we thus have all the relations in terms of E_g and the constants of the system. Substituting the relation for Z_g from (7.41) and carrying out the matrix multiplication, we obtain, after some algebraic reductions, the two following relations for the voltages and currents along the line:

$$(7.45) \qquad E_k = \frac{E_g[Z_{01}e^{(n-k)a} + Z_{02}r_Re^{-(n-k)a}]}{(Z_s + Z_{01})(e^{na} - r_sr_Re^{-na})}$$

and

$$(7.46) \qquad I_k = \frac{E_g[e^{(n-k)a} - r_Re^{-(n-k)a}]}{(Z_s + Z_{01})(e^{na} - r_sr_Re^{-na})}$$

where

$$(7.47) \qquad r_s = \frac{(Z_s - Z_{02})}{(Z_s + Z_{01})}$$

and

$$(7.48) \qquad r_R = \frac{(Z_r - Z_{01})}{(Z_r + Z_{02})}$$

The quantities r_s and r_R are called the reflection coefficients at the sending and receiving end, respectively. Equations (7.45) and (7.46) are very useful for the computation of the current and voltage distribution along the chain of networks of Fig. 12.17.

8. ATTENUATION AND PASS BANDS

The prominent role that the eigenvalues of the chain matrix $[u]$ of the four-terminal networks play in determining the attenuation and pass bands of a chain of such networks will now be demonstrated. Let us consider an isolated four-terminal network, as in Fig. 12.2. Let us also assume that we have the following relations between the output current and voltage and the input current and voltage:

$$(8.1) \qquad E_{n+1} = mE_n, \quad I_{n+1} = mI_n$$

where m is a complex number to be determined. In view of the relation

$$(8.2) \qquad \begin{bmatrix} E_n \\ I_n \end{bmatrix} = [u] \begin{bmatrix} E_{n+1} \\ I_{n+1} \end{bmatrix}$$

we have

$$(8.3) \qquad \begin{bmatrix} E_n \\ I_n \end{bmatrix} = [u] \begin{bmatrix} E_n \\ I_n \end{bmatrix} m$$

or

$$(8.4) \qquad (I - m[u]) \begin{bmatrix} E_n \\ I_n \end{bmatrix} = (0)$$

where I is the unit matrix of the second order. In order for (8.4) to be consistent, we must have the determinant $|I - m[u]| = 0$; if we expand this determinant, we obtain the equation

$$(8.5) \qquad m^2 - m(A + D) + 1 = 0$$

since $AD - BC = 1$. Now Eq. (8.5) is the characteristic equation of the matrix $[u]$, and hence as in Sec. 7, Eqs. (7.7) and (7.8), we may write

$$(8.6) \qquad m_1 = e^a$$

and

$$(8.7) \qquad m_2 = e^{-a}$$

for the two roots of (8.5). The root m_2 is associated with the propagation of currents and voltages to the right, and the root m_1 is associated with propagation to the left. From (7.9), we also have the equation

$$(8.8) \qquad \cosh a = \frac{(A + D)}{2} = b$$

and since, in general, A and D are complex numbers, it follows that b and hence a must be complex. Let us assume

$$(8.9) \qquad a = p_1 + jp_2 \quad j = \sqrt{-1}$$

and let us write b in the polar form:

$$(8.10) \qquad b = b_0 e^{j\phi}$$

where p_1, p_2, b_0, and ϕ are real. Substituting this into (8.8), we obtain

$$(8.11) \qquad \cosh(p_1)\cos(p_2) + j\sinh(p_1)\sin(p_2) = b_0(\cos\phi + j\sin\phi)$$

Equating the coefficients of real and imaginary terms, we have

$$(8.12) \qquad \cos(p_2) = \frac{b_0 \cos\phi}{\cosh(p_1)}$$

and

$$(8.13) \qquad \sin(p_2) = \frac{b_0 \sin\phi}{\sinh(p_1)}$$

Pass Bands

If a is entirely imaginary and hence $p_1 = 0$, then m_1 and m_2 introduce only changes in phase, but no attenuation of the voltages and currents along the chain of four-terminal networks. Placing $p_1 = 0$ in Eqs. (8.12) and (8.13), we find the necessary condition that there be no attenuation. Placing

$p_1 = 0$ in (8.13), we see that since $|\sin (p_2)| \gtrless 1$ and $\sinh (0) = 0$, the only manner that this condition may be satisfied is for

$$(8.14) \qquad \sin \phi = 0, \quad \text{and hence} \quad \phi = k\pi, \quad k = 0, \pm 1, \pm 2, \text{ etc.}$$

This restricts b to real values. Placing $p_1 = 0$ in (8.12), we have

$$(8.15) \qquad |\cos (p_2)| = \left| \frac{b_0 \cos \phi}{\cosh (0)} \right| \leqq 1$$

and since ϕ is restricted to take on only multiple values of π, we must have

$$(8.16) \qquad |b| \leqq 1$$

Therefore, in terms of A and D, we have the following two conditions for a pass band:

$$(8.17) \qquad A + D = \text{Real number}$$

$$(8.18) \qquad A + D \leqq 2$$

If the component parts of the four-terminal network are dissipationless elements, it may be shown that the condition (8.17) is satisfied. The condition (8.18) is true for only certain frequencies. Frequencies for which (8.18) is true are passed, and the others are attenuated.

9. THE SMOOTH TRANSMISSION LINES

The smooth transmission line may be regarded as the limiting case of an infinite number of symmetrical four-terminal networks of the type shown in Fig. 12.19. Let us consider that the transmission line has a series impedance Z per unit length and a shunt admittance Y per unit length. Then we may regard the line to be made up of an infinite number of four-terminal networks of the form in Fig. 12.19. The chain matrix of the T network of Fig. 12.19, which may be obtained by (5.4), is

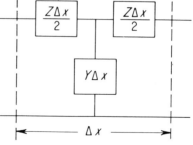

FIGURE 12.19

$$(9.1) \qquad [u] = \begin{bmatrix} \left(\dfrac{1 + ZY\overline{\Delta x^2}}{2} \right) & \left(\dfrac{Z\Delta x + Z^2 Y\overline{\Delta x^3}}{4} \right) \\ Y\Delta x & \left(\dfrac{1 + ZY\overline{\Delta x^2}}{2} \right) \end{bmatrix}$$

In terms of the associated matrix $[u]$ of the above infinitesimal four-terminal network, we may write

$$(9.2) \qquad \begin{bmatrix} E_1 \\ I_1 \end{bmatrix} = \underset{\substack{n \to \infty \\ \Delta x \to 0}}{\text{Limit }} [u]^n \begin{bmatrix} E_2 \\ I_2 \end{bmatrix}$$

where E_1 and I_1 and E_2, I_2 are the input and output quantities, respectively. Since the infinitesimal network is symmetric, that is, $A = D$, we may make use of (6.5), where Z_{01} is given by

$$(9.3) \qquad Z_{01} = \frac{1}{2C}\sqrt{(A + D)^2 - 4}$$

Substituting the values of A, D, and C from (9.1) and neglecting higher-order terms in x, we obtain

$$(9.4) \qquad Z_{01} = \sqrt{Z/Y} = Z_0$$

In order to calculate the latent roots of the matrix (9.1), we use

$$(9.5) \qquad m_1 = \frac{(A + D)}{2} + \sqrt{\frac{(A + D)^2}{4} - 1} = e^a$$

In this case, we have

$$(9.6) \qquad \frac{(A + D)}{2} = 1 + \frac{ZYx^2}{2}$$

Hence, on substituting this into (9.5) and neglecting high-order terms, we obtain

$$(9.7) \qquad e^a = 1 + \Delta x\sqrt{ZY} + \frac{\overline{\Delta x^2}\sqrt{ZY}}{2} + \cdots$$

However, we have the relation

$$(9.8) \qquad e^a = 1 + a + \frac{a^2}{2!} + \cdots$$

Hence, comparing this expansion with (9.7), we obtain

$$(9.9) \qquad a = \Delta x\sqrt{ZY}$$

Substituting this into (7.34), we obtain

$$(9.10) \qquad [u]^n = \begin{bmatrix} \cosh(n\Delta x\sqrt{ZY}) & \sqrt{\frac{Z}{Y}}\sinh(n\Delta x\sqrt{ZY}) \\ \sqrt{\frac{Y}{Z}}\sinh(n\Delta x\sqrt{ZY}) & \cosh(n\Delta x\sqrt{ZY}) \end{bmatrix}$$

On passing to the limit, we make use of the relation

$$(9.11) \qquad \underset{\substack{n \to \infty \\ \Delta x \to 0}}{\text{Limit}} (n\Delta x) = l$$

where l is the length of the line. If we let

$$(9.12) \qquad l\sqrt{ZY} = \theta$$

$$(9.13) \qquad \sqrt{\frac{Z}{Y}} = Z_0$$

and substitute into (9.10), we have the usual relation for the smooth line:

$$(9.14) \qquad \begin{bmatrix} E_1 \\ I_1 \end{bmatrix} = \begin{bmatrix} \cosh(\theta) & Z_0 \sinh(\theta) \\ \dfrac{\sinh(\theta)}{Z_0} & \cosh(\theta) \end{bmatrix} \begin{bmatrix} E_2 \\ I_2 \end{bmatrix}$$

This result is thus obtained as a special case of (7.34) without the use of differential equations.

10. THE GENERAL LADDER NETWORK

The matrix method of analysis of four-terminal networks appears to reach its greatest power in the theory of the general ladder network. A general form of this is shown in Fig. 12.20. This is a generalization of the network

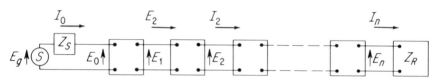

FIG. 12.20. General Ladder Network

of Fig. 12.17 in that we shall now assume the n networks to have different chain matrices. Let $[u]_r$ be the chain matrix of the rth network. We may then write the equation

$$(10.1) \qquad \begin{bmatrix} E_g \\ I_0 \end{bmatrix} = \begin{bmatrix} 1 & Z_s \\ 0 & 1 \end{bmatrix} \prod_{R=1}^{n} [u]_R \begin{bmatrix} E_n \\ I_n \end{bmatrix}$$

If we let

$$(10.2) \qquad \begin{bmatrix} A_n & B_n \\ C_n & D_n \end{bmatrix} = \begin{bmatrix} 1 & Z_s \\ 0 & 1 \end{bmatrix} \prod_{R=1}^{N} [u]_r$$

Then, in view of (6.3), we have the following equation for Z_g, the impedance of the system looking at it from the generator end:

$$(10.3) \qquad Z_g = \frac{E_g}{I_0} = \frac{(A_n Z_r + B_n)}{(C_n Z_r + D_n)}$$

To find the voltage and current distribution at any point of the network, we use the equation

$$(10.4) \qquad \begin{bmatrix} E_g \\ I_0 \end{bmatrix} = \begin{bmatrix} A_k & B_k \\ C_k & D_k \end{bmatrix} \begin{bmatrix} E_k \\ I_k \end{bmatrix}$$

or

$$(10.5) \qquad \begin{bmatrix} E_k \\ I_k \end{bmatrix} = \begin{bmatrix} D_k & -B_k \\ -C_k & A_k \end{bmatrix} \begin{bmatrix} E_g \\ I_0 \end{bmatrix}$$

But, in view of (10.3), we may write

$$
(10.6) \qquad \begin{bmatrix} E_k \\ I_k \end{bmatrix} = \begin{bmatrix} D_k & -B_k \\ -C_k & A_k \end{bmatrix} \begin{bmatrix} 1 \\ \dfrac{1}{Z_g} \end{bmatrix} E_g
$$

We thus obtain the currents and voltages in terms of the voltage of the generator. It may be remarked that this analysis parallels that of the one given for the series identical elements. In that case, the matrix product (10.1) reduces to the matrix power of (7.1). Since multiplication of second-order square matrices is particularly simple, it is seen that the analysis of the general ladder network may be carried out in a most direct manner by this method.

REFERENCES

1. Bartlett, A. C., *The Theory of Electrical Artificial Lines and Filters*. New York: John Wiley and Sons, 1930.

2. Brillouin, Leon, "Les Filtres Electriques et al Theorie des Matrices," *Revue Generale de l'Electricite* (1936), pp. 3–16.

3. Guillemin, E. A., *Communication Networks*, Vol. II. New York: John Wiley and Sons, 1935.

13 STEADY-STATE SOLUTION OF MULTICONDUCTOR LINES

1. INTRODUCTION

The treatment of the transmission line given in Chapter 12, Sec. 9, was based on a consideration of a single conductor and its return. In this chapter the mathematical theory of the propagation of periodic currents over a system of parallel wires energized at its physical terminals will be developed. This is a generalization of the problem of transmission over a line of uniformly distributed resistance, inductance, capacitance, and leakage. It involves the formulation and solution of a set of differential equations, which will be termed the generalized telegraph equations to distinguish them from the well-known telegraph equations which characterize the transmission over a single wire and its return circuit. The method to be followed in this formulation is a direct generalization of the classical analysis of the two-wire transmission line equations to the case of n wires. This classical solution is a generalization of ordinary circuit theory to circuits having distributed parameters and is not exact. To obtain a more accurate solution, we would have to begin with Maxwell's equations and take a number of things into account, such as electromagnetic radiation, proximity effects, terminal conditions, skin effect, etc. An excellent discussion of the limitations of this classical theory will be found in reference 2. An analysis of the approximations involved leads to the conclusion that the errors introduced are of small practical significance, provided that the conductors are wires of small cross section compared to the distance between conductors and that the resistivity of the conductors is much smaller than that of the dielectric in which the conductors are embedded. It is found that in such cases we may specify the system of conductors in terms of its self and mutual impedances to a high degree of approximation.

365

2. THE COEFFICIENTS OF CAPACITY AND INDUCTION

Let us consider a system of n conducting bodies situated in air, as shown in Fig. 13.1. Let Q_i, $i = 1, 2, \ldots, n$ represent the charges on the conductors in coulombs, and let V_i be the absolute potentials of the various conducting bodies in volts. Now, because of the linear relations between potential and charge, we may write

(2.1)

$$V_1 = p_{11}Q_1 + p_{12}Q_2 + \cdots + p_{1n}Q_n$$
$$\quad . \qquad . \qquad . \qquad \cdots \qquad .$$
$$V_n = p_{n1}Q_1 + p_{n2}Q_2 + \cdots + p_{nn}Q_n$$

The quantities p_{ij} are the coefficients of potential and depend entirely on the geometrical arrangement of the conductors. To facilitate the writing of the set of linear equations (2.1), let us introduce the column matrices (V) and (Q), whose elements are the n potentials and charges on the conductors, and

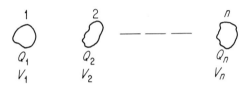

FIGURE 13.1

the square matrix $[p]$, whose elements are the coefficients of potential. It may be mentioned that, in general, $p_{ij} = p_{ji}$, and hence the matrix $[p]$ is a symmetric matrix. Using this notation, we may write the set of equations (2.1) in the convenient form:

(2.2)
$$(V) = [p](Q)$$

If we premultiply Eq. (2.2) by the inverse of $[p]$, $[p]^{-1}$, we obtain

(2.3)
$$(Q) = [p]^{-1}(V)$$

Let us now introduce the matrix

(2.4)
$$[C] = [p]^{-1} = [C_{ij}]$$

The coefficients C_{ij} are called the coefficients of capacity when $i = j$ and coefficients of induction when $i \neq j$. Since $p_{ij} = p_{ji}$, it follows that $C_{ij} = C_{ji}$ and the matrix $[C]$ is symmetric. In terms of $[C]$, we may write

(2.5)
$$(Q) = [C](V)$$

Parallel Conductors

The above relations between charges and potentials hold, in general, independently of the size or arrangement of the conductors. Let us consider a system of n long, parallel, widely separated, cylindrical conductors above an equipotential ground plane, as shown in Fig. 13.2.   Let

d_r = radius of conductor r.
h_r = height of conductor r above ground plane.
$a_{rs'}$ = distance between conductor r and the image of conductor s.
b_{rs} = distance between conductors r and s.

Now if we assume that the ground plane is at zero potential and that the distances separating the conductors from each other and from the ground

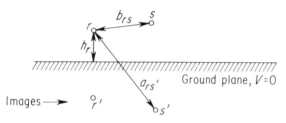

FIGURE 13.2

are large compared to the radii of the various conductors, we have, from electrostatics,

$$(2.6) \qquad p_{rr} = 18 \times 10^{11} \log_e \frac{2h_r}{d_r} \text{ darafs/cm}$$

$$(2.7) \qquad p_{rs} = 18 \times 10^{11} \log_e \frac{a_{rs}}{b_{rs}} \text{ darafs/cm}$$

for the coefficients of potential in this case.

3. THE ELECTROMAGNETIC COEFFICIENTS

Let us now consider the flux linkages of the various conductors by the flux produced as a result of the current flow in the several conductors.   If we let the flux linkage of conductor r due to its own current i_r be $(L_{rr}i_r)$ and the flux linkage of conductor r due to the flux produced by current i_s flowing in conductor s be $(L_{rs}i_s)$, we may write

$$(3.1) \qquad \phi_r = L_{r1}i_1 + L_{r2}i_2 + \cdots + L_{rn}i_n$$

for the total flux linkages of conductor r due to the flux produced by its own current and to the currents flowing in the other conductors.   Accordingly, we may write

$$\begin{aligned}
\phi_1 &= L_{11}i_1 + L_{12}i_2 + \cdots + L_{1n}i_n \\
\phi_2 &= L_{21}i_1 + L_{22}i_2 + \cdots + L_{2n}i_n \\
&\quad \cdot \qquad \cdot \qquad \cdots \qquad \cdot \\
\phi_n &= L_{n1}i_1 + L_{2n}i_2 + \cdots + L_{nn}i_n
\end{aligned} \qquad (3.2)$$

for the total flux linkages of all the conductors. Now, if we introduce the column matrices (ϕ) and (i), whose elements are the flux linkages and currents of the various conductors, and a square matrix $[L]$, whose elements are the coefficients L_{rs}, we may write the set of equations (3.2) in the compact form:

$$(3.3) \qquad (\phi) = [L](i)$$

The coefficients L_{rs} are called coefficients of self-induction if $r = s$, and coefficients of mutual induction if $r \neq s$. For the system of parallel wires over the parallel perfectly conducting ground plane of Fig. 13.2, these coefficients have the values:

$$(3.4) \qquad L_{rr} = \left(\frac{1}{2} + 2 \log_e \frac{2h_r}{d_r}\right) \times 10^{-9} \text{ henry/cm}$$

$$(3.5) \qquad L_{rs} = \left(2 \log_e \frac{a_{rs'}}{b_{rs}}\right) \times 10^{-9} \text{ henry/cm}$$

These values are obtained on the assumption that the current is distributed uniformly throughout the cross section of the solid conductors of radii d_r and that there is no penetration of magnetic field into the perfectly conducting ground plane. The presence of the perfectly conducting plane is taken into account by assuming image currents flowing in the opposite direction and in the same location as the image conductors of Fig. 13.2. The coefficients of inductance have the general property that $L_{rs} = L_{sr}$, and hence the matrix $[L]$ is symmetric.

4. THE GENERAL DIFFERENTIAL EQUATIONS

In order to derive the general equations governing the distribution of potentials and currents in the n-wire transmission system, let us use the notation (all quantities are per unit length):

L_{rr} = the self-inductance of the conductor r.
L_{rs} = the mutual inductance coefficient between conductors r and s.
R_r = the series resistance of the conductor r.
C_{rr} = the self-capacitance coefficient of conductor r.
C_{rs} = the mutual capacitance coefficient between conductor r and s.
g_{rr} = the leakage conductance to ground of conductor r.
g_{rs} = the leakage conductance between conductors r and s.

Let us now consider the current and potential distribution along the rth conductor, as shown in Fig. 13.3. The leakage current to ground and to the other conductors over a length dx is

$$(4.1) \quad i_{Lr} = [g_{r1}(e_r - e_1) + g_{r2}(e_r - e_2) + \cdots + g_{rr}e_r + \cdots + g_{rn}(e_r - e_n)] \, dx$$
$$= [e_r(g_{r1} + g_{r2} + \cdots + g_{rn}) - g_{r1}e_1 - g_{r2}e_2 - \cdots - g_{rn}e_n] \, dx$$

Now if we let

(4.2)
$$G_{rr} = g_{r1} + g_{r2} + \cdots + g_{rn}$$
$$G_{rs} = G_{sr} = -g_{rs} = -g_{sr}$$

we may write (4.1) in the convenient form:

(4.3) $$i_{Lr} = (G_{r1}e_1 + G_{r2}e_2 + \cdots + G_{rn}e_n)\, dx$$

The capacitive current to ground and to the other conductors over a length dx is

(4.4) $$i_{Cr} = \frac{\partial Q_r}{\partial t}\, dx$$

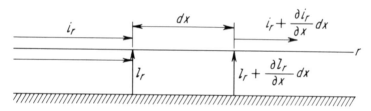

FIG. 13.3. Ground

Hence, if we write Kirchhoff's first law for the conservation of current over an elementary length dx, we have

(4.5) $$i_r = i_{Lr} + i_{Cr} + i_r + \frac{\partial i_r}{\partial x}\, dx$$

or hence

(4.6) $$\frac{\partial i_r}{\partial x}\, dx = -i_{Lr} - i_{Cr}$$

Substituting (4.3) and (4.4) into (4.6), we obtain

(4.7) $$\frac{\partial i_r}{\partial x} = -(G_{r1}e_1 + G_{r2}e_2 + \cdots + G_{rn}e_n) - \frac{\partial Q_r}{\partial t}$$

Now, from Eq. (2.5), we have

(4.8) $$Q_r = C_{r1}e_1 + C_{r2}e_2 + \cdots + C_{rn}e_n$$

If we write

(4.9) $$Y_{rs} = G_{rs} + C_{rs}D$$

where D is the operator d/dt, we may write (4.7) in the convenient form:

(4.10) $$-\frac{\partial i_r}{\partial x} = Y_{r1}e_1 + Y_{r2}e_2 + \cdots + Y_{rn}e_n$$

In a similar manner, by equating the potential at the point x to the potential drop over the length dx and the potential at the point $(x + dx)$ of Fig. 13.3, we obtain

(4.11) $$-\frac{\partial e_r}{\partial x} = \frac{\partial \phi_r}{\partial t} + R_r i_r$$

Now from (3.2), we have

(4.12) $$\phi_r = L_{r1} i_1 + L_{r2} i_2 + \cdots + I_{rn} i_n$$

If we let

(4.13) $$Z_{rr} = (R_r + L_{rr} D)$$

and

(4.14) $$Z_{rs} = L_{rs} D$$

where $D = d/dt$, we may write (4.11) in the form

(4.15) $$-\frac{\partial e_r}{\partial x} = Z_{rn} i_n + Z_{r2} i_2 + \cdots + Z_{rn} i_n$$

There are n equations of the type (4.10) and n more of the type (4.15). If we introduce column matrices (e) and (i), whose elements are the potentials to ground and currents of the various lines, and square matrices $[Z]$ and $[Y]$, whose elements are the operators Z_{rs} and Y_{rs}, respectively, we may write the two matrix equations

(4.16) $$-\frac{\partial}{\partial x}(i) = [Y](e)$$

and

(4.17) $$-\frac{\partial}{\partial x}(e) = [Z](i)$$

These equations are a generalization of the usual equations for the case of a two-conductor line. They will be called the "generalized telegraph equations." It may be noted that since the operators Z_{rs} and Y_{rs} have the property that $Z_{rs} = Z_{sr}$ and $Y_{rs} = Y_{sr}$, the matrices $[Z]$ and $[Y]$ are symmetric.

5. THE STEADY-STATE EQUATIONS

Let us now consider the case when alternating potentials are impressed on the lines at the sending end. Let us assume that the various potentials have the same angular frequency w, but have different phases. In order to determine the distribution of potential and current in this case, we will assume

(5.1) $$\begin{array}{ll} (e) = \text{Re } (E)e^{jwt} & \\ (i) = \text{Re } (I)e^{jwt} & j = \sqrt{-1} \end{array}$$

where e^{jwt} is a scalar multiplier common to all potentials and currents, the elements of the matrices (E) and (I) are functions of x to be determined, and the symbol "Re" means the "real part of." We now substitute these two equations into (4.16) and (4.17), suppressing the symbol "Re." Now from (4.9) and (4.13), we may write

(5.2) $$[Z(D)] = [R] + [L]D \qquad D = \frac{d}{dt}$$

(5.3) $$[Y(D)] = [G] + [C]D$$

Hence

(5.4) $$[Y(D)](e) = ([G] + jw[C])(E)^{jwt}$$
$$= [Y(jw)](E)e^{jwt}$$

Similarly,

(5.5) $$[Z(D)](i) = [Z(jw)](I)e^{jwt}$$

Accordingly, substituting these relations into (4.16) and (4.17) and dividing out the common factor e^{jwt}, we obtain

(5.6) $$-\frac{d}{dx}(I) = [Y(jw)](E)$$

and

(5.7) $$-\frac{d}{dx}(E) = [Z(jw)](I)$$

These two equations determine the complex amplitudes of the matrices (I) and (E) subject to the terminal boundary conditions.

6. SOLUTION OF THE EQUATIONS, BOUNDARY CONDITIONS

Let us consider the schematic diagram of Fig. 13.4. The elements of the matrices $(E)_g$ and $(I)_g$ are the complex amplitudes of the potentials and

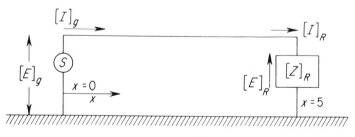

FIGURE 13.4

currents at the generator end, $x = 0$, and the elements of the matrices $(E)_r$ and $(I)_r$ are the complex amplitudes of the receiver end currents and potentials.

In Fig. 13.4 the arrangement has been drawn as if it were a single wire line. This is done for convenience, and it must be realized that the various matrices have n elements. The elements of the terminal impedance matrix $[Z]_r$ represent the various impedance elements from the various lines to each other and to ground. In general, we have the relation

(6.1) $$(E)_r = [Z]_r(I)_r$$

We must solve Eqs. (5.6) and (5.7) subject to the boundary conditions at the terminals. In certain problems of power transmission, the receiving end currents and potentials are specified, and it is required to determine the generator and currents and potentials. In other problems, we are given the generator potentials and currents, and we must determine the receiving end currents and potentials. In still other problems, we are given the generator potentials and the receiving end impedances, and we must determine the distribution of currents and potentials throughout the lines. Equations (5.6) and (5.7) are two sets of linear differential equations of the first order with constant coefficients. The simplest method of solution is to introduce a p-multiplied Laplace transformation with respect to the *variable* x (see Appendix I). Symbolically we write

(6.2) $$\mathscr{L}(E) \doteq (E)_t \quad \text{where} \quad \mathscr{L}(E) = p \int_0^\infty \varepsilon^{-px}(E)\,dx$$

(6.3) $$\mathscr{L}(I) \doteq (I)_t \qquad \mathscr{L}(I) = p \int_0^\infty \varepsilon^{-px}(I)\,dx$$

where every element of the matrices $(E)_t$ and $(I)_t$ are the Laplacian transforms of the elements of the matrices (E) and (I) with respect to the variable x. From the basic theorem involving the transforms of first derivatives, we write[4]

(6.4) $$\mathscr{L}\frac{d}{dx}(E) \doteq -p(E)_g + p(E)_t$$

(6.5) $$\mathscr{L}\frac{d}{dx}(I) \doteq -p(I)g + p(I)_t$$

where $(E)_g$ and $(I)_g$ are matrices whose elements are the values of the variables at $x = 0$. Substituting these transforms into Eqs. (5.6) and (5.7), we obtain

(6.6) $$p(E)_g - p(E)_t = [Z](I)_t$$

(6.7) $$p(I)_g - p(I)_t = [Y](E)_t$$

Eliminating $(E)_t$ from these equations, we obtain

(6.8) $$(p^2 U - [Y][Z])(I)_t = p^2(I)_g - p[Y](E)_g$$

Eliminating $(I)_t$, we have

(6.9) $$(p^2 U - [Z][Y])(E)_t = p^2(E)_g - p[Z](I)_g$$

where U is the unit matrix of the nth order.   Let

(6.10) $$[a] = [Y][Z]$$

(6.11) $$p^2 = m$$

(6.12) $$[f(m)] = [mU - a]$$

With this notation, we have, from (6.8),

(6.13) $$[f(m)](I)_t = p^2(I)_g - p[Y](E)_g$$

We then have, explicitly,

(6.14) $$(I)_t = [f(m)]^{-1}\{p^2(I)_g - p[Y](E)_g\}$$

In order to compute $[f(m)]^{-1}$, we may use Eq. (11.27) of 87, Chapter 4. From the theory of that section, we have

(6.15) $$[f(m)]^{-1} = \frac{[F(m)]}{D(m)}$$

where $[F(m)]$ is the *adjoint* matrix of $[f(m)]$ and $D(m)$ is the determinant of the matrix $[f(m)]$.   Now, if we assume that the determinantal equation,

(6.16) $$D(m) = 0$$

has n distinct roots, m_i, $(i = 1, 2, \ldots, n)$ and the degree of the adjoint matrix $[F(m)]$ is less than that of the polynomial $D(m)$, we have

(6.17) $$[f(m)]^{-1} = \sum_{r=1}^{n} \frac{[F(m_r)]}{D'(m_r)} \frac{1}{(m - m_r)}$$

where

(6.18) $$D'(m_r) = \frac{d}{dm} D(m)|_{m = m_r}$$

Substituting (6.17) into (6.14), we obtain

(6.19) $$(I)_t = \sum_{r=1}^{n} \frac{[F(m_r)]p^2(I)_g}{D'(m_r)(p^2 - m_r)} - \sum_{r=1}^{n} \frac{[F(m_r)][Y](E)_g p}{D'(m_r)(p^2 - m_r)}$$

To obtain the complex amplitude matrix (I), we must compute the inverse transform of $(I)_t$.   This may be easily done by using the transforms

(6.20) $$\frac{p^2}{p - m_r} \doteq \cosh(x\sqrt{m_r})$$

(6.21) $$\frac{p}{p - m_r} \doteq \sinh \frac{(x\sqrt{m_r})}{\sqrt{m_r}}$$

Substituting these values into (6.19), we have

(6.22) $$(I) = \sum_{r=1}^{n} \frac{[F(m_r)](I)_g \cosh(x\sqrt{m_r})}{D'(m_r)} - \sum_{r=1}^{n} \frac{[F(m_r)][Y](E)_g \sinh(x\sqrt{m_r})}{D'(m_r)\sqrt{m_r}}$$

This is a formal solution for the complex current amplitudes along the line in terms of the generator currents and potentials. If we let $\phi^2 = m$, $\phi_r = \pm \sqrt{m_r}$, we see that in this case we have $2n$ propagation constants ϕ_r which merge together to give the solution (6.22). If we have only a single line and its return, then the solution (6.22) reduces to

$$(6.23) \qquad I = I_g \cosh(\phi x) - E_g\sqrt{\frac{Y}{Z}} \sinh(\phi x), \quad \text{where} \quad \phi = \sqrt{ZY}$$

To obtain the potential distribution, we must find the inverse transform of $(E)_t$ of Eq. (6.9). Let

$$(6.24) \qquad\qquad\qquad [b] = [Z][Y]$$

and

$$(6.25) \qquad\qquad\qquad [g(m)] = [mU - b]$$

It will now be shown that the determinant $|g(m)|$ of the matrix $[g(m)]$ is the same as the determinant $D(m)$ of the matrix $[f(m)]$ defined by (6.12). To do so, let us take the transpose of $[g(m)]$ and obtain

$$(6.26) \qquad\qquad\qquad [g(m)]' = mU - [b]'$$

Now, by a fundamental theorem,

$$(6.27) \qquad\qquad [b]' = [Y]'[Z]' = [Y][Z] = [a]$$

since $[Y]$ and $[Z]$ are symmetric matrices. Hence, comparing (6.26) and (6.12), we have

$$(6.28) \qquad\qquad\qquad [f(m)] = [g(m)]'$$

Now, since the value of a determinant is not altered by interchanging its rows and columns, we have

$$(6.29) \qquad\qquad |g(m)| = |g(m)|' = |f(m)| = D(m)$$

It therefore follows that the roots of the equation

$$(6.30) \qquad\qquad\qquad |g(m)| = 0$$

are the same as those of the equation $D(m) = 0$. We may now expand the matrix $[g(m)]^{-1}$ in the form

$$(6.31) \qquad\qquad [g(m)]^{-1} = \sum_{r=1}^{n} \frac{G(m_r)}{D'(m_r)(m - m_r)}$$

where $[G(m_r)]$ is the adjoint of the matrix $[g(m)]$ evaluated at $m = m_r$. Substituting this into (6.9) and making use of the transforms (6.20) and (6.21), we obtain

$$(6.32) \qquad (E) = \sum_{r=1}^{n} \frac{[G(m_r)](E)_g \cosh(x\sqrt{m_r})}{D'(m_r)} - \sum_{r=1}^{n} \frac{[G(m_r)][Z](I)_g \sinh(x\sqrt{m_r})}{D'(m_r)\sqrt{m_r}}$$

This is a formal solution for the complex potentials in terms of the generator currents and potentials. For the case of a single wire and its return circuit, it reduces to

$$(6.33) \qquad E = E_g \cosh (\phi x) - I_g \sqrt{\frac{Z}{Y}} \sinh (\phi x)$$

7. THE DETERMINANTAL EQUATION

Equations (6.22) and (6.32) give the formal solutions for the currents and potentials in terms of the sending end conditions, provided that the determinantal equation

$$(7.1) \qquad D(m) = |mU - [Y][Z]| = 0$$

has n distinct roots $m_1, m_2, \ldots, m_n$. In such a case we have $2n$ propagation constants given by

$$(7.2) \qquad \phi_r = \pm m_r \qquad r = 1, 2, \ldots, n$$

Now, in certain cases of practical importance, it will be found that the determinantal equation (7.1) has multiple roots and that the number of distinct propagation constants is reduced. We will discuss the more common cases that occur in practice.

(a) *Ideal Case, Perfect Conductors, Perfect Ground Conductivity*

In this case we have no energy loss in the lines and no penetration of current into the conductors. For this case, we have, therefore,

$$(7.3) \qquad [G] = [0], \quad [R] = [0]$$

and hence

$$(7.4) \qquad [Y] = jw[C]$$
$$(7.5) \qquad [Z] = jw[L]$$

Hence

$$(7.6) \qquad [Y][Z] = -w^2[C][L]$$

Now, from Eq. (2.4), we have

$$(7.7) \qquad [C] = [p]^{-1}$$

For the case of no current penetration into the conductors, there is no internal magnetic field in the material of the conductors, and hence the factor $\frac{1}{2}$ in (3.4) must be omitted. Comparing Eqs. (2.6) and (2.7) with Eqs. (3.4) and (3.5), we see that

$$(7.8) \qquad [L] = \frac{1}{v_0^2} [p]$$

where $v_0 = 3 \times 10^{10}$ cm/sec, or the velocity of light in vacuum. Hence, substituting (7.8) into (7.6) and (7.7), we obtain

$$(7.9) \qquad [Y][Z] = -\frac{w^2}{v_0^2}[p]^{-1}[p] = \frac{-w^2}{v_0^2}U$$

where U is the unit matrix of the nth order. If we substitute this value of $[Y][Z]$ into Eq. (7.1), we have

$$(7.10) \qquad D(m) = \left(m + \frac{w_0^2}{v_0^2}\right)U = 0$$

or

$$(7.11) \qquad \left(m + \frac{w^2}{v_0^2}\right)^n = 0$$

In this case, the determinantal equation has n equal roots:

$$(7.12) \qquad m = -\frac{w^2}{v_0^2}$$

It is easier to obtain the current distribution directly from Eq. (6.8) directly rather than from the general solution (6.22). Substituting (7.9) into (6.8), we obtain

$$(7.13) \qquad \left(p^2 U + \frac{w^2 U}{v_0^2}\right)(I)_t = p^2(I)_g - p[Y](E)_g$$

or

$$(7.14) \qquad (I)_t = \frac{(I)_g p^2}{p^2 + \dfrac{w^2}{v_0^2}} - \frac{[Y](E)_g p}{p^2 + \dfrac{w^2}{v_0^2}}$$

Using the transforms

$$(7.15) \qquad \frac{p^2}{p^2 + a^2} \doteqdot \cos(ax)$$

$$(7.16) \qquad \frac{p}{p^2 + a^2} \doteqdot \sin\frac{ax}{a}$$

we obtain

$$(7.17) \qquad (I) = (I)_g \cos\frac{wx}{v_0} = \frac{v_0}{w}[Y](E)_g \sin\frac{wx}{v_0}$$

In the same way, we obtain the potential distribution:

$$(7.18) \qquad (E) = (E)_g \cos\left(\frac{wx}{v_0}\right) - \frac{v_0}{w}[Z](I)_g \sin\left(\frac{wx}{v_0}\right)$$

In this ideal case, we have only one propagation constant w/v_0, and the solution is especially simple.

(b) *Transposed Conductors, Ring Symmetry*

In many cases of practical importance, the conductors are identical and are transposed in such a manner that the matrices $[Z]$ and $[Y]$ exhibit so-called "ring symmetry." As a special case, let us consider an impedance matrix $[Z]$ of the sixth order:

$$(7.19) \qquad [Z] = \begin{bmatrix} Z_{11} & Z_{12} & Z_{13} & Z_{14} & Z_{15} & Z_{16} \\ Z_{21} & Z_{22} & Z_{23} & Z_{24} & Z_{25} & Z_{26} \\ \cdot & \cdot & \cdot & \cdot & \cdots & \cdot \\ Z_{61} & Z_{62} & Z_{63} & Z_{64} & Z_{65} & Z_{66} \end{bmatrix}$$

The condition of "ring symmetry" may be easily obtained from the schematic Fig. 13.5.

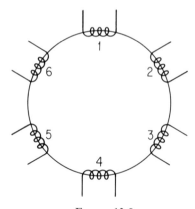

FIGURE 13.5

We now set

$$Z_{rr} = Z, \quad Z_{12} = Z_{23} = Z_{34} = Z_{45} = Z_{56} = Z_{61}, \text{ etc.}$$

In general, the mutual impedances between conductors at equal distances from each other around the ring are set equal to each other. Substituting these relations into the matrix $[Z]$ of Eq. (7.19), we obtain:

$$(7.20) \qquad [Z] = \begin{bmatrix} Z & Z_{12} & Z_{13} & Z_{14} & Z_{13} & Z_{12} \\ Z_{12} & Z & Z_{12} & Z_{13} & Z_{14} & Z_{13} \\ Z_{13} & Z_{12} & Z & Z_{12} & Z_{13} & Z_{14} \\ Z_{14} & Z_{13} & Z_{12} & Z & Z_{12} & Z_{13} \\ Z_{13} & Z_{14} & Z_{13} & Z_{12} & Z & Z_{12} \\ Z_{12} & Z_{13} & Z_{14} & Z_{13} & Z_{12} & Z \end{bmatrix}$$

We see from this that the matrix of the sixth order that exhibits ring symmetry may be specified in terms of the self-impedance Z, and the mutual impedances Z_{12}, Z_{13}, Z_{14}. Now, if the admittance matrix $[Y]$ exhibits the same type of symmetry, then it may be demonstrated that the determinantal equation (7.1) has six *distinct* roots in the sixth-order case. In the general case of n circuits having ring symmetry, the number of distinct roots is n. The importance of the ring-symmetric case is that it may be solved explicitly and may be reduced to the practical cases of transposed circuits as special cases.

Rather than attempting to obtain the various roots of the determinantal equation directly, let us transform Eqs. (6.6) and (6.7) by a certain matrix that diagonalizes the impedance and admittance matrices having ring symmetry. It will be found that this is the basic transformation matrix used in the theory of symmetrical components.

8. TRANSFORMATION OF THE BASIC EQUATIONS

Equations (6.6) and (6.7) will now be transformed by means of the non-singular symmetric matrix $[A]$ defined by

$$(8.1) \qquad [A] = [A_{rs}] \qquad r = 1, 2, \ldots, n, \qquad s = 1, 2, \ldots, n$$

$$(8.2) \qquad A_{rs} = a^{-(r-1)(s-1)}$$

$$(8.3) \qquad a = e^{j2\pi n} \quad j = \sqrt{-1}$$

This transformation matrix $[A]$ occupies a central position in the theory of symmetrical components. The transformation matrix $[A]$ is thus a square matrix of the nth order with the important property that

$$(8.4) \qquad [A]' = [A]$$

where $[A]'$ is the transposed matrix of $[A]$;

$$(8.5) \qquad [A]^{-1} = \frac{1}{n}[\bar{A}]$$

where $[A]^{-1}$ is the inverse of $[A]$ and $[\bar{A}]$ is the conjugate of $[A]$. Let us now premultiply Eqs. (6.6) and (6.7) by $[A]^{-1}$; we thus obtain

$$(8.6) \qquad p[A]^{-1}(E)_g - p[A]^{-1}(E)_t = [A]^{-1}[Z][A][A]^{-1}(I)_t$$

$$(8.7) \qquad p[A]^{-1}(I)_g - p[A]^{-1}(I)_t = [A]^{-1}[Y][A][A]^{-1}(E)_t$$

Let us now define the matrices:

$$(8.8) \qquad [A]^{-1}(E)_g = (E)_{gs} = (E_{gsr})$$

$$(8.9) \qquad [A]^{-1}(I)_g = (I)_{gs} = (I_{gsr})$$

$$(8.10) \qquad [A]^{-1}(E)_t = (E)_{ts} = (E_{tsr})$$

(8.11) $$[A]^{-1}(I)_t = (I)_{ts} = (I_{tsr})$$

(8.12) $$[A]^{-1}[Z][A] = [Z]_s$$

(8.13) $$[A]^{-1}[Y][A] = [Y]_s$$

With this notation, Eqs. (8.6) and (8.7) are transformed to

(8.14) $$p(E)_{gs} - p(E)_{ts} = [Z]_s(I)_{ts}$$

(8.15) $$p(I)_{gs} - p(I)_{ts} = [Y]_s(E)_{ts}$$

Now, the whole purpose of this transformation is that if the matrices $[Z]$ and $[Y]$ have the ring symmetry discussed above, then the matrices $[Z]_s$ and $[Y]_s$ defined by (8.12) and (8.13) are diagonal matrices. It is easy to show that the matrices $[Z]_s$ and $[Y]_s$ have the form

(8.16) $$[Z]_s = [A]^{-1}[Z][A] = \begin{bmatrix} Z_1 & 0 & 0 & 0 & \cdots & 0 \\ 0 & Z_2 & 0 & 0 & \cdots & 0 \\ \cdot & \cdot & \cdot & \cdot & \cdots & \cdot \\ 0 & \cdot & \cdot & \cdot & \cdots & Z_n \end{bmatrix}$$

and

(8.17) $$[Y]_s = [A]^{-1}[Y][A] = \begin{bmatrix} Y_1 & 0 & \cdot & \cdots & 0 \\ 0 & Y_2 & \cdot & \cdots & 0 \\ \cdot & \cdot & \cdot & \cdots & \cdot \\ 0 & \cdot & 0 & \cdots & Y_n \end{bmatrix}$$

The elements Z_r and Y_r are given by

(8.18) $$Z_{r+1} = (Z_{11} + a^{-r}Z_{12} + a^{-2r}Z_{13} + \cdots + a^{-(n-1)r}Z_{1n})$$

(8.19) $$Y_{r+1} = (Y_{11} + a^{-r}Y_{12} + a^{-2r}Y_{13} + \cdots + a^{-(n-1)r}Y_{1n})$$

The relations between the impedances Z_{ij} and Y_{ij} due to the ring symmetry may be substituted into (8.18) and (8.19). Now, because of the diagonal nature of the matrices $[Z]_s$ and $[Y]_s$, the matrix equations (8.14) and (8.15) separate into n scalar equations of the form

(8.20) $$pE_{gsr} - pE_{tsr} = Z_r I_{tsr} \quad (r = 1, 2, \ldots, n)$$

(8.21) $$pI_{gsr} - pI_{tsr} = Y_r E_{tsr}$$

Eliminating E_{tsr} from these equations, we obtain

(8.22) $$I_{tsr} = \frac{I_{gsr}p^2}{p^2 - Y_r Z_r} - \frac{Y_r E_{gsr}p}{p^2 - Y_r Z_r}$$

Eliminating I_{tsr}, we obtain

(8.23) $$E_{tsr} = \frac{E_{gsr}p^2}{p^2 - Y_r Z_r} - \frac{Z_r I_{gsr}p}{p^2 - Y_r Z_r}$$

If we let

(8.24) $Y_r Z_r = a_r^2,$ $r = 1, 2, 3, \ldots, n$

and take the inverse transforms of (8.22) and (8.23), we obtain the following expressions

(8.25) $I_{sr} = I_{gsr} \cosh (a_r z) - E_{gsr} \sinh (a_r z) \left(\dfrac{Y_r}{Z_r}\right)^{1/2}$

(8.26) $E_{sr} = E_{gsr} \cosh (a_r z) - I_{gsr} \sinh (a_r z) \left(\dfrac{Z_r}{Y_r}\right)^{1/2},$ $r = 1, 2, 3, \ldots, n$

The set of equations (8.25) and (8.26) may be written in the following matrix form as one single equation:

(8.27) $(I)_s = [\cosh (az)]_d (I)_{gs} - \left[\sinh (az)\left(\dfrac{Y}{Z}\right)^{1/2}\right]_d (E)_{gs}$

(8.28) $(E)_s = [\cosh (az)]_d (E)_{gs} - \left[\sinh (az)\left(\dfrac{Z}{Y}\right)^{1/2}\right]_d (I)_{gs}$

In (8.27) and (8.28) the matrices with subscripts d are diagonal matrices with elements given by (8.25) and (8.26). The subscript r runs from 1 to n.

If we now premultiply Eqs. (8.27) and (8.28) by the matrix (A), we obtain the current matrix (I) and the potential matrix (E) in the following form

(8.29) $(I) = (A)[\cosh (az)]_d (A)^{-1}(I)_g - (A)\left[\sinh (az)\left(\dfrac{Y}{Z}\right)^{1/2}\right]_d (A)^{-1}(E)_g$

(8.30) $(E) = (A)[\cosh (az)]_d (A)^{-1}(E)_g - (A)\left[\sinh (az)\left(\dfrac{Z}{Y}\right)^{1/2}\right]_d (A)^{-1}(I)_g$

Equations (8.29) and (8.30) give explicitly the complex current and potential amplitudes of the transmission lines in terms of the sending-end currents $(I)_g$ and the sending-end potentials $(E)_g$ when the conductor arrangement has g ring symmetry.

Identical Conductors; Perfect Transposition

In the practical case in which all the conductors are identical in size and are perfectly transposed with respect to each other and with respect to the ground plane, then the elements of the impedance and admittance matrices have the following properties

(8.31) $Z_{rr} = Z_0$ and $Z_{rs} = Z,$ $r \neq s$

(8.32) $Y_{rr} = Y_0$ and $Y_{rs} = Y,$ $r \neq s$

That is, all the self-impedances and self-admittances are identical and all the mutual impedances and admittances are also identical. In this practically important case, Eqs. (8.18) and (8.19) reduce to

(8.33) $\qquad Z_1 = Z_0 + (n - 1)Z \qquad Z_r = Z_0 - Z \quad$ for $\quad r \neq 1$

(8.34) $\qquad Y_1 = Y_0 + (n - 1)Y \qquad Y_r = Y_0 - Y \quad$ for $\quad r \neq 1$

In this case, we have only two propagation constants given by Eq. (8.24).

9. SOLUTION IN TERMS OF TERMINAL IMPEDANCES

The general solutions (6.22) and (6.32) have been formulated in terms of the sending-end currents and potentials. In many practical cases, the receiving-end potentials and currents are specified, and the sending-end potentials and currents are to be determined. To treat this case, it is simpler to measure the distance x from the receiving end, and write

(9.1) $$\frac{d}{dx}(I) = [Y](E)$$

(9.2) $$\frac{d}{dx}(E) = [Z](I)$$

instead of (5.6) and (5.7). If we go through the same procedure as in Sec. 6 to solve these two equations subject to the terminal conditions that $(E) = (E)_r$ at $x = 0$ and $(I) = (I)_r$ at $x = 0$, where the elements of the column matrices $(E)_r$ and $(I)_r$ are the various receiving-end current and potential amplitudes, we obtain the general solution

(9.3) $\quad (I) = \displaystyle\sum_{r=1}^{n} \frac{[F(m_r)](I)_r \cosh(x\sqrt{m_r})}{D'(m_r)} + \sum_{r=1}^{n} \frac{[F(m_r)][Y](E)_r \sinh(x\sqrt{m_r})}{D'(m_r)\sqrt{m_r}}$

and

(9.4) $\quad (E) = \displaystyle\sum_{r=1}^{n} \frac{[G(m_r)](E)_r \cosh(x\sqrt{m_r})}{D'(m_r)} + \sum_{r=1}^{n} + \frac{[G(m_r)][Z](I)_r \sinh(x\sqrt{m_r})}{D'(m_r)\sqrt{m_r}}$

where all the quantities have the same significance as in Sec. 6, but now x is measured from the receiving end. Hence, by the use of (9.3) and (9.4), we may determine the sending-end potentials and currents, provided we know the receiving-end potentials and currents. The general equations (6.22), (6.32), (9.3), and (9.4) may be put into a very convenient form in the following manner. Let us introduce the following matrices:

(9.5) $$[A(x)] = \sum_{r=1}^{n} \frac{[F(m_r)]\cosh(x\sqrt{m_r})}{D'(m_r)}$$

(9.6) $$[B(x)] = \sum_{r=1}^{n} \frac{[F(m_r)][Y]\sinh(x\sqrt{m_r})}{D'(m_r)\sqrt{m_r}}$$

$$(9.7) \qquad [C(x)] = \sum_{r=1}^{n} \frac{[G(m_r)] \cosh (x\sqrt{m_r})}{D'(m_r)}$$

$$(9.8) \qquad [D(x)] = \sum_{r=1}^{n} \frac{[G(m_r)][Z] \sinh (x\sqrt{m_r})}{D'(m_r)\sqrt{m_r}}$$

With this notation, the general equations governing the distribution of potential and current may be written in the form

$$(9.9) \qquad (I) = [A(x)](I)_g - [B(x)](E)_g$$

$$(9.10) \qquad (E) = [C(x)](E)_g - [D(x)](I)_g$$

with x measured from the sending end.   Equations (9.3) and (9.4) may be written in the form

$$(9.11) \qquad (I) = [A(x)](I)_r + [B(x)](E)_r$$

$$(9.12) \qquad (E) = [C(x)](E)_r + [D(x)](I)_r$$

with x measured from the *receiving* end.

Determination of Currents and Potentials, Given Terminal Impedances

Equations (9.9)–(9.12) are useful in determining the current and potential distributions, provided either the sending-end or the receiving-end currents and potentials are given.   In some cases, the sending-end potentials are specified, and the impedances of the various branches of the terminal apparatus are given as shown schematically in Fig. 13.4.   The receiving-end currents and potentials are then related by the relation

$$(6.1) \qquad (E)_r = [Z]_r(I)_r$$

The elements of the matrix $[Z]_r$ are the various self- and mutual impedances of the various branches of the terminal apparatus.   To determine the current and potential distribution in this case, let us place $x = s$ in Eqs. (9.9) and (9.3); we then have

$$(9.13) \qquad (I)_r = [A(s)](I)_g - [B(s)](E)_g$$

$$(9.14) \qquad (E)_r = [C(s)](E)_g - [D(s)](I)_g$$

If we now premultiply Eq. (9.13) by $[Z]_r$ and equate the resulting expression to $(E)_r$, we may solve for $(I)_g$ and obtain

$$(9.15) \qquad (I)_g = ([Z]_r[A(s)] + [D(s)])^{-1}([C(s)] + [Z]_r[B(s)])(E)_g$$

This determines the sending-end currents in terms of the given sending-end potentials and the known constants of the line and the terminal impedance matrix.   To determine the potential and current distribution at any point along the line, it is necessary only to substitute the value for $(I)_g$ given by (9.15) into Eqs. (9.9) and (9.10).

10. GENERAL CONSIDERATIONS

From the above analysis, it is seen that the determination of the potential and current distribution of the multiconductor transmission system is vastly more complicated than that of the simple two-wire line. The problem may, however, be formulated in terms of the so-called "generalized telegraph equations" and solved for the steady state by the convenient use of matrix notation and the Laplacian transformation applied to the space variable x. The equations simplify enormously in the dissipationless case or the cases where the system of conductors exhibits symmetry. In any case, however, the determination of the potential and current distribution is entirely possible, and is reduced to a process of determining the roots of the determinantal equation of the system and to matrix multiplication.

REFERENCES

1. Bewley, L. V., *Travelling Waves on Transmission Systems*. New York: John Wiley and Sons, 1933.

2. Carson, J. R., "The Rigorous and Approximate Theories of Electrical Transmission Along Wires," *B.S.T.Jl.*, Vol. 7 (1928), pp. 11–25.

3. Carson, J. R. and R. S. Hoyt, "Propagation of Periodic Currents over a System of Parallel Wires," *B.S.T.Jl.*, Vol. 6 (1927), pp. 495–545.

4. Pipes, L. A., *Applied Mathematics for Engineers and Physicists*. New York: McGraw-Hill Book Co., Inc., 1958, Ch. XXI.

5. Pipes, L. A., "Matrix Theory of Multiconductor Transmission Lines," *Phil. Mag.*, Ser. 7, Vol. 24 (July, 1937), pp. 97–113.

14 TRANSIENT ANALYSIS OF MULTICONDUCTOR LINES

1. INTRODUCTION

In the last chapter, the steady-state analysis of multiconductor lines was discussed. The steady-state analysis was carried out by assuming a sinusoidal variation in time of the various potentials and currents of the system, and followed the customary procedure of replacing d/dt by jw in the general partial differential equations of the system. To determine the behavior of the multiconductor system subject to the impression of general potentials at the sending end at $t = 0$ is a vastly more difficult task. To carry out this analysis, we must now return to the partial differential equations (4.16) and (4.17) of the last chapter, which we called the "generalized telegraph equations" and attempt to obtain a solution that will satisfy the given initial and boundary conditions.

2. THE GENERAL EQUATIONS

The "generalized telegraph equations" of the last chapter may be written in the convenient form:

$$(2.1) \qquad -\frac{\partial}{\partial x}(e) = [R](i) + [L]\frac{\partial}{\partial t}(i)$$

$$(2.2) \qquad -\frac{\partial}{\partial x}(i) = [G](e) + [C]\frac{\partial}{\partial t}(e)$$

where the elements of the column matrices (e) and (i) are the various instantaneous potentials to ground and currents of the system. The square matrices $[R]$, $[L]$, $[G]$, and $[C]$ are the resistance, inductance, leakage, and capacitance matrices of the system and are defined in Sec. 4 of Chapter 13.

Discussion of the Line Parameters

The formulation of the n transmission-line problem by the matrix equations (2.1) and (2.2) is a generalization of the engineering treatment of the single-line-and-return problems. The complexity of the n-conductor problem is such that an analysis based on the Maxwell field equations is practically impossible; hence, a simplified treatment based on the generalization of the concepts of circuit theory to the case of distributed parameters must be undertaken. This treatment is based on Maxwell's coefficients of capacity and induction. The question of the validity of such a procedure naturally arises. A qualitative discussion of the principles involved is helpful in making clear the approximations which are introduced.

(a) *The Coefficients of Induction*

The coefficients of self- and mutual induction, as given by Eqs. (3.4) and (3.5) of the last chapter, are based on the following assumptions:

1. The neglection of radiation from the system. This amounts to saying that we are dealing with a "quasi-stationary" process and that the displacement current term in the field equations may be neglected.

2. The mean spacing of the conductors is so great that we may neglect the "proximity effect." This effect would tend to disturb the symmetrical distribution of current in the wires on which the calculation of the induction coefficients is based.

3. The "skin effect" is neglected. The factor $\frac{1}{2}$ in the coefficient of self-induction in Eq. (3.4) is obtained on the basis of uniform current distribution inside the conductors. This is correct for solid conductors only for the case of zero frequency. At high frequencies or for travelling waves, the skin effect is so great that there cannot be any penetration of the current into the conductors. Hence, the factor $\frac{1}{2}$ must be neglected in such cases. In the "dissipationless" case of no conductor resistance, the factor $\frac{1}{2}$ must be neglected at all frequencies, since in this case there is no penetration of current into the wires.

4. A perfectly conducting ground plane is assumed. This assumption leads to the introduction of a set of image currents flowing in the opposite sense to preclude any penetration of magnetic flux into the ground plane. Actually, of course, the ground has a finite conductivity and is not homogeneous.

(b) *The Coefficients of Capacitance*

The coefficients of capacitance vary so little with frequency that they may be considered constant even with an appreciable amount of conductor resistance present. Although theoretically the capacitance matrix is given very accurately by the reciprocal of the matrix $[p]$, whose elements are given by (2.6) and (2.7) of the last chapter, the capacitance parameters do vary with frequency or steepness of wave front slightly. This is because the theory does not include the effect of insulators, pins, and cross-arms which are essential to the support of the lines. Metal pins introduce additional lumped capacitance at the supports. The resultant circuit is quite complex and may be approximately represented by a ladder network. There is some evidence that the capacitance coefficients are functions of the potentials of the conductors when the line potentials are above the critical corona potentials; however, it has been found sufficient to take into account the effect of corona by modifying the leakage coefficients.

It may be also noted that in the case of an imperfectly conducting earth, the height to ground of the conductors differs from that of Eqs. (2.6) and (2.7). We must actually take a height above an equivalent conducting mass which represents the effect of the ground.

(c) *The Resistance Coefficients*

The theoretical variation of the resistance parameters with the steepness of the front of travelling waves is due to changes in the distribution of internal flux linkages in the conductors. The transient skin effect tends to crowd the current towards the surface of the conductors. This tends toward an infinite surface density of current for very steep wave fronts. This wave effect, therefore, tends to increase the conductor resistance with frequency over its direct current value.

(d) *The Leakage Parameters*

Below the critical corona voltage, the leakage parameters may be determined by measurement and regarded as constant. Of course, they depend greatly on the condition of the insulation and whether the weather is dry or wet. Above the disruptive corona point, the leakage parameters may be regarded as functions of the line potentials. It is customary, in order to simplify the analysis, to assume certain magnitudes of the leakage coefficients that will give the same energy loss per unit length as the actual corona discharge determined by experiment. The problem is one of the utmost complexity, and the best that can be done is to assume certain values for the leakage parameters that appear reasonable.

3. THE DISSIPATIONLESS CASE

The analysis of the dissipationless case is particularly simple, and since it serves as a model for the discussion of the general case, it will be considered first. The dissipationless case is characterized by the conditions that

(3.1) $$[R] = [0]$$

(3.2) $$[G] = [0]$$

and that there is no penetration of current into the wires, and hence that the factor $\frac{1}{2}$ in the coefficients of self-induction, as given by Eqs. (3.4) and (3.5) of Chapter 13, must be neglected. Hence, in this case, the basic equations become

(3.3) $$-\frac{\partial}{\partial x}(e) = [L]\frac{\partial}{\partial t}(i)$$

(3.4) $$-\frac{\partial}{\partial x}(e) = [C]\frac{\partial}{\partial t}(e)$$

To solve these equations, let us introduce a Laplacian transformation with respect to the independent variable t. To do this, let

(3.5) $$(E) \doteq (e)$$

(3.6) $$(I) \doteq (i)$$

That is, the elements of the matrices (E) and (I) are the Laplacian transforms of the elements of the matrices (e) and (i) with respect to the time variable. If we assume that at $t = 0$, there is no initial distribution of potential or current along the lines, we have

(3.7) $$\frac{\partial}{\partial t}(e) \doteq p(E)$$

(3.8) $$\frac{\partial}{\partial t}(i) \doteq p(I)$$

by the basic theorem giving the transforms of derivatives. Hence, Eqs. (3.3) and (3.4) transform to

(3.9) $$-\frac{d}{dx}(E) = p[L](I)$$

(3.10) $$-\frac{d}{dx}(I) = p[C](E)$$

Eliminating (I) from Eqs. (3.9) and (3.10), we obtain

(3.11) $$\frac{d^2}{dx^2}(E) = p^2[L][C](E)$$

and eliminating (E), we obtain

(3.12) $$\frac{d^2}{dx^2}(I) = p^2[C][L](I)$$

Now in the dissipationless case, we have the general condition

$$(3.13) \qquad [L][C] = [C][L] = \frac{U}{v_0^2}$$

where U is the unit matrix of the nth order and $v_0 = 2 \times 10^{10}$ cm/sec, the velocity of light in vacuo. This condition was established in Sec. 7(a) of Chapter 13. Hence, we have

$$(3.14) \qquad (E) = (A)_1 e^{-ax} + (A)_2 e^{ax}$$

$$(3.15) \qquad (I) = (B)_1 e^{-ax} + (B)_2 e^{ax}$$

where

$$(3.16) \qquad a = \frac{p}{v_0}$$

and the column matrices $(A)_1$, $(A)_2$, $(B)_1$, and $(B)_2$ are matrices of arbitrary constants to be determined from the boundary conditions and the fundamental equations of the system. The elements of the constant matrices are not independent, because Eqs. (3.9) and (3.10) determine relations between (E) and (I). To determine these relations, let us write (3.9) and (3.10) in the form:

$$(3.17) \qquad -\frac{d}{dx}(E) = [Z](I)$$

$$(3.18) \qquad -\frac{d}{dx}(I) = [Y](E)$$

where $[Z] = p[L]$, $[Y] = p[C]$ in the dissipationless case that we are considering. Substituting (3.14) and (3.15) into (3.17) and (3.18), we obtain

$$(3.19) \qquad \{[Z](B)_1 - a(A)_1\}e^{-ax} + \{[Z](B)_2 + a(A)_2\}e^{ax} = (0)$$

$$(3.20) \qquad \{[Y](A)_1 - a(B)_1\}e^{-ax} + \{[Y](A)_2 + a(B)_2\}e^{ax} = (0)$$

Since these equations are to hold for all values of x, the coefficients of e^{-ax} and e^{ax} must vanish separately. Making use of this fact, we obtain

$$(3.21) \qquad (B)_1 = \frac{[Y](A)_1}{a} = v_0[C](A)_1$$

$$(3.22) \qquad (B)_2 = \frac{-[Y](A)_2}{a} = -v_0[C](A)_2$$

Substituting these values into (3.14) and (3.15), we obtain

$$(3.23) \qquad (E) = (A)_1 e^{-ax} + (A)_2 e^{ax}$$

$$(3.24) \qquad (I) = v_0[C](A)_1 e^{-ax} - v_0[C](A)_2 e^{ax}$$

for the transforms of the voltage and current matrices in the dissipationless case. We have now $2n$ arbitrary constants to be determined from the terminal conditions of the apparatus. To determine the arbitrary constants, let us consider the schematic diagram of Fig. 14.1. Let $(E)_g$ represent the transforms of the various potentials to ground impressed on the lines at $x = 0$ and $t = 0$, and let the matrices $[Z]_s$ and $[Z]_r$ represent the operational impedance matrices of the sending- and receiving-end apparatus of the system. We have the boundary conditions:

$$(3.25) \qquad (E)_s + [Z]_s(I)_s = (E)_g \quad \text{at} \quad x = 0$$

$$(3.26) \qquad (E)_r - [Z]_r(I)_r = (0) \quad \text{at} \quad x = 1$$

From (3.23) and (3.24), we have

$$(3.27) \qquad (E)_s = (A)_1 + (A)_2$$

$$(3.28) \qquad (E)_r = (A)_1 e^{-a1} + (A)_2 e^{a1}$$

$$(3.29) \qquad (I)_s = v_0[C][(A)_1 - (A)_2]$$

$$(3.30) \qquad (I)_r = v_0[C][(A)_1 e^{-a1} - (A)_2 e^{a1}]$$

FIGURE 14.1

We now substitute these values into (3.25) and (3.26) and obtain

$$(3.31) \qquad [U + v_0[Z]_s[C]](A)_1 + [U - v_0[Z]_s[C]](A)_2 = (E)_g$$

$$(3.32) \qquad [U - v_0[Z]_r[C]](A)_1 e^{-a1} + [U + v_0[Z]_r[C]](A)_2 e^{a1} = (0)$$

where U is the unit matrix of the nth order. If we now let

$$(3.33) \qquad [K]_1 = [U + v_0[Z]_s[C]]$$

$$(3.34) \qquad [K]_2 = U - v_0[Z]_s[C]$$

$$(3.35) \qquad [K]_3 = [U - v_0[Z]_r]e^{-a1}$$

$$(3.36) \qquad [K]_4 = [U + v_0[Z]_r[C]]e^{a1}$$

we then obtain

$$(3.37) \qquad (A)_2 = \{[K]_2 - [K]_1[K]_3^{-1}[K]_4\}^{-1}(E)_g$$

$$(3.38) \qquad (A)_1 = \{[K]_1 - [K]_2[K]_4^{-1}[K]_3\}^{-1}(E)_g$$

In general, the impedances at the receiving and sending ends and the transform matrix $(E)_g$ of the sending-end potentials are functions of p.   To find the actual current and potential distribution, we must now find the inverse transforms of the matrices (E) and (I) as given by (3.23) and (3.24). This, in general, will be a complicated task, depending on the nature of the impedance operators $[Z]_r$ and $[Z]_s$ and the type of impressed potentials.

In any case, in Eqs. (3.23) and (3.24), the terms containing the factor e^{-ax} represent waves travelling in the positive x direction with a velocity of v_0 and the terms containing the factor e^{ax} represent a set of waves travelling in the negative x direction with a velocity of v_0 as a result of reflection at the receiving ends.   In this ideal dissipationless case there is only one common velocity of propagation, and it equals the velocity of light in the medium that surrounds the transmission-line wires.

Infinite Lines

The case in which the lines are infinite so that there is no reflection from the receiving end is particularly simple.   In this case, Eqs. (3.23) and (3.24) reduce to

$$(3.39) \qquad (E) = (A)_1 e^{-ax}$$

$$(3.40) \qquad (I) = v_0[C](A)_1 e^{-ax}$$

If we impress the sending-end voltages directly on the lines at $x = 0$, we have

$$(3.41) \qquad (E) = (E)_g e^{-ax}$$

$$(3.42) \qquad (I) = v_0[C](E)_g e^{-ax}$$

where $(E)_g$ is a column matrix whose elements are the various transforms of the sending-end voltages.   Now, since $a = p/v_0$, we may find the inverse transforms of (3.41) and (3.42) very simply by using Theorem 9 of the appendix; we obtain

$$(3.43) \qquad [e(x, t)] = \left[e\left(t - \frac{x}{v_0} \right) \right] \qquad t > \frac{x}{v_0}$$

$$(3.44) \qquad [i(x, t)] = v_0[C]\left[e\left(t - \frac{x}{v_0} \right) \right] \qquad t > \frac{x}{v_0}$$

That is, the impressed potentials are propagated without distortion with the velocity v_0, and the current waves are linear combinations of the voltage waves and are propagated with the same velocity and also without distortion. This characterizes the behavior of the dissipationless line only and does not hold for the general case, as we shall see.

4. THE GENERAL CASE

In the dissipationless case discussed above, the analysis was particularly simple, because the disturbances in the wires were all propagated with the common velocity v_0 without distortion. This is a characteristic of the dissipationless case only. Let us now consider the general case. We will find that the general case is one of a great deal of complexity, and we shall here outline a possible method of solution that may be carried out if the importance of the problem warrants the expenditure of effort necessary for its solution.

If we introduce the transforms of the potential and current distribution as defined in (3.5) and (3.6), the general equations (2.1) and (2.2) may be written in the form:

(4.1)
$$-\frac{d}{dx}(E) = [Z](I)$$

(4.2)
$$-\frac{d}{dx}(I) = [Y](E)$$

where the matrices $[Z]$ and $[Y]$ are given by

(4.3)
$$[Z] = [R] + p[L] = [Z(p)]$$

(4.4)
$$[Y] = [G] + p[C] = [Y(p)]$$

Equations (4.1) and (4.2) represent two sets of differential equations of the second order in x with constant coefficients. The elements of the matrices $[Z]$ and $[Y]$ are functions of the complex variable p, but with regard to the integration with respect to x, p may be considered as a constant, as in the usual method of solving partial differential equations by the Laplacian transformation. Equations (4.1) and (4.2) are identical to Eqs. (5.6) and (5.7) of the last chapter, with the exception that now the complex factor jw is replaced by p. As in the last chapter, we could proceed to integrate (4.1) and (4.2) with respect to x in a formal manner, and all the results of that chapter could be used by the mere device of substituting p wherever jw occurs in the resulting formulas. Having integrated Eqs. (4.1) and (4.2) with respect to x and evaluated the arbitrary constants in terms of the boundary conditions, we are then confronted with the difficult task of obtaining the inverse transforms to obtain the actual instantaneous potential and current distribution. The determinantal equation of the system is the same as (7.1) of the last chapter. The roots m_i of this equation are now functions of the complex variable p introduced in the Laplacian transformation with respect to time.

On interpreting the inverse transforms, we should expect to get n *distinct* velocities of propagation in the general case, and we should also obtain the various potential and current waves as linear combinations of the fundamental waves travelling with the n distinct velocities. A practical difficulty in this method of solution is that of determining the roots of the determinantal equation (7.1). Since we have replaced the number jw in that equation by the complex variable p, we cannot use the usual numerical methods for determining the roots of this equation. Accordingly, this method fails when it is not possible to obtain the roots of the determinantal equation by some process of factoring. Alternative devices for the solution of these equations may be set up, but because of the formidable nature of the analytical procedure, we shall not discuss them here. The important feature of the general case is that we obtain n distinct velocities of propagation. We shall now turn to a discussion of the practical case, where the system exhibits a certain type of symmetry.

5. THE CASE OF RING SYMMETRY

In Chapter 13, it was seen that if the conductors were transposed in such a manner that the system possesses the "ring symmetry" defined in Sec. 8 of that chapter, then the general equations could be solved by the simple process of first transforming them by the premultiplication by a transformation matrix $[A]$ defined by Eqs. (8.1) of that chapter. To treat this case, let us premultiply Eqs. (4.1) and (4.2) by the matrix $[A]^{-1}$; we then obtain

$$(5.1) \qquad -\frac{d}{dx}[A]^{-1}(E) = [A]^{-1}[Z][A][A]^{-1}(I)$$

$$(5.2) \qquad -\frac{d}{dx}[A]^{-1}(I) = [A]^{-1}[Y][A][A]^{-1}(E)$$

Let us now introduce the matrices:

$$(5.3) \qquad [A]^{-1}(E) = (E)_s = (E_{sr})$$

$$(5.4) \qquad [A]^{-1}(I) = (I)_s = (I_{sr})$$

$$(5.5) \qquad [A]^{-1}[Z][A] = [Z]_s$$

$$(5.6) \qquad [A]^{-1}[Y][A] = [Y]_s$$

Now, provided that the lines are transposed so that the matrices $[Z]$ and $[Y]$ have ring symmetry as discussed in Sec. 8 of Chapter 13, then the matrices $[Z]_s$ and $[Y]_s$ are diagonal matrices, and their elements are given by Eqs. (8.16) and (8.17) of Chapter 13 with the stipulation that the factor jw of these equations must be replaced by the complex variable p. That is, the matrices $[Z]_s$ and $[Y]_s$ are now diagonal matrices whose elements are given by

$$(5.7) \quad Z_{r+1} = R_{11} + p[L_{11} + a^{-r}L_{12} + \cdots + a^{-(n-1)r}L_{1n}]$$
$$= R_{r+1} + pL_{r+1}$$

$$(5.8) \quad Y_{r+1} = [G_{11} + a^{-r}G_{12} + \cdots + a^{-(n-1)r}G_{1n}]$$
$$+ p[C_{11} + a^{-r}C_{12} + \cdots + a^{-(n-1)r}C_{1n}]$$
$$= G_{r+1} + pC_{r+1}$$

where a is defined by (8.3) of the last chapter. In view of the diagonal nature of the matrices $[Z]_s$ and $[Y]_s$, we may write (4.1) and (4.2) in the form:

(5.9)
$$-\frac{d}{dx}E_{sr} = (R_r + pL_r)I_{sr}$$

$$r = 1, 2, \ldots, n$$

(5.10)
$$-\frac{d}{dx}I_{sr} = (G_r + pC_r)E_{sr}$$

These equations are of exactly the same form as in the theory of the single transmission line; their solution is

(5.11)
$$E_{sr} = K_r e^{-a_r z} + B_r e^{a_r z}$$

(5.12)
$$I_{sr} = \frac{K_r e^{-a_r z} - B_r e^{a_r z}}{Z_{0r}}$$

where

(5.13)
$$a_r = \sqrt{(R_r + pL_r)(G_r + pC_r)}$$

(5.14)
$$Z_{0r} = \sqrt{\frac{R_r + pL_r}{G_r + pC_r}}$$

as the solutions of Eqs. (5.9) and (5.10). We must now determine the $2n$ arbitrary constants K_r and B_r in terms of the boundary conditions at the terminals of the lines.

Infinite Lines

For simplicity, let us first consider the case of infinitely long lines and potentials impressed directly on the terminals of the lines at the sending ends, $x = 0$. Let $(E)_g$ be a column matrix whose elements are the various transforms of the potentials impressed on the lines at $x = 0$. Now let

(5.15)
$$[A]^{-1}(E)_g = (E)_{gs}$$

Now, in the case of infinitely long lines, there are no reflections from the receiving ends, and hence the constants B_r in (5.11) and (5.12) must all be equal to zero. If we now introduce the diagonal matrices

(5.16)
$$[e^{-ax}]_d = \begin{bmatrix} e^{-a_1 z} & 0 & \cdots & 0 \\ 0 & e^{-a_2 z} & \cdots & 0 \\ \cdot & \cdot & \cdots & \cdot \\ 0 & 0 & \cdots & e^{-a_n z} \end{bmatrix}$$

(5.17)
$$\left[\frac{e^{-ax}}{Z_0}\right]_d = \begin{bmatrix} \dfrac{e^{-a_1 z}}{Z_{01}} & 0 & \cdots & 0 \\ 0 & \dfrac{e^{-a_2 z}}{Z_{02}} & \cdots & 0 \\ \cdot & \cdot & \cdots & \cdot \\ 0 & 0 & \cdots & \dfrac{e^{-a_n z}}{Z_{0n}} \end{bmatrix}$$

we may write Eqs. (5.11) and (5.12) in the convenient form for this non-reflective case

(5.18)
$$[E(x)]_s = [e^{-ax}]_d (K)$$

(5.19)
$$[I(x)]_s = \left[\frac{e^{-ax}}{Z_0}\right]_d (K)$$

Placing $x = 0$, we must have

(5.20)
$$[A]^{-1}(E)_g = [E(0)]_s = (K)$$

Hence, we have

(5.21)
$$[E(x)]_s = [e^{-ax}]_d [A]^{-1}(E)_g$$

(5.22)
$$[I(x)]_s = \left[\frac{e^{-ax}}{Z_0}\right]_d [A]^{-1}(E)_g$$

If we now premultiply (5.21) and (5.22) by $[A]$, we obtain, in view of Eqs. (5.3) and (5.4), the equations

(5.23)
$$[E(x)] = [A][e^{-ax}]_d [A]^{-1}(E)_g$$

(5.24)
$$[I(x)] = [A]\left[\frac{e^{-ax}}{Z_0}\right]_d [A]^{-1}(E)_g$$

To obtain the instantaneous values of the potentials and currents of the system, we have the relations

(5.25)
$$[e(x, t)] \doteqdot [E(x)]$$

(5.26)
$$[i(x, t)] \doteqdot [I(x)]$$

Hence, we must compute the inverse transforms of the various elements of the matrices $[E(x)]$ and $[I(x)]$. If we perform the matrix multiplication, we see that each potential and current wave is a linear combination of n waves having different propagation constants and surge impedances given by Eqs. (5.13) and (5.14). If the impressed potentials are constant electromotive forces impressed at $t = 0$, then we must compute inverse transforms of the type

(5.27)
$$e^{-a_r x} \doteqdot u_r(x, t)$$

(5.28)
$$\frac{e^{-a_r x}}{Z_{0r}} \doteqdot w_r(x, t)$$

where a_r and Z_{0r} are defined by (5.13) and (5.14). These transforms are of the same form as those given by Transforms 81 and 82 of Appendix I. We see from these transforms that each potential and current wave is composed of a linear combination of waves propagated with a velocity

(5.29)
$$v_r = \frac{1}{\sqrt{L_r C_r}}$$

where L_r and C_r are defined by (5.7) and (5.8). In the case of perfect transposition, the number of velocities reduces to two and is given by

$$(5.30) \qquad v_1 = [[L_0 + (n - 1)L][C_0 + (n - 1)C]]^{-1/2}$$

$$(5.31) \qquad v_2 = [(L_0 - L)(C_0 - C)]^{-1/2}$$

where L_0 and C_0 are the coefficients of self-induction and capacitance, respectively, and L and C are the coefficients of mutual induction and capacitance per unit length of the lines. If we construct two diagonal matrices of the form

$$(5.32) \qquad [u(x, t)]_d = \begin{bmatrix} u_1(x, t) & 0 & \cdots & 0 \\ 0 & u_2(x, t) & \cdots & 0 \\ \cdot & \cdot & \cdots & \cdot \\ 0 & 0 & \cdots & u_n(x, t) \end{bmatrix}$$

$$(5.33) \qquad [w(x, t)]_d = \begin{bmatrix} w_1(x, t) & 0 & \cdots & 0 \\ 0 & w_2(x, t) & \cdots & 0 \\ \cdot & \cdot & \cdots & \cdot \\ 0 & 0 & \cdots & w_n(x, t) \end{bmatrix}$$

we may write the inverse transforms of (5.23) and (5.24) in the form:

$$(5.34) \qquad [e(x, t)] = [A][u(x, t)][A]^{-1}(E)_g$$

$$(5.35) \qquad [I(x, t)] = [A][w(x, t)][A]^{-1}(E)_g$$

These equations give an explicit solution for the potential and current distribution of a set of long lines having transposition giving rise to "ring symmetry" and having the constant potentials expressed by the elements of the column matrix $(E)_g$ impressed directly on their terminals at $t = 0$.

6. GENERAL BOUNDARY CONDITIONS

Let us now consider the problem of general boundary conditions for the case of ring symmetry. This is analogous to the general case discussed in Sec. 9, Chapter 13. We have now to deal with matrix quantities rather than with scalars, but the formal operations are sensibly the same. If the generator potentials are impressed on the lines through an impedance system having an operational impedance matrix $[Z]_s$, and if the terminal apparatus has an operational impedance matrix $[Z]_r$, then the equations to be satisfied by the transform matrices at the sending and receiving ends are

$$(6.1) \qquad [E(0)] + [Z]_s[I(0)] = (E)_g$$

$$(6.2) \qquad [E(1)] = [Z]_r[I(1)]$$

where 1 is the length of the lines.

Equations (5.11) and (5.12) may be written in the form

(6.3)
$$[E(x)]_s = [e^{-ax}]_d(K) + [e^{ax}]_d(B)$$

(6.4)
$$[I(x)]_s = \left[\frac{e^{-ax}}{Z_0}\right]_d (K) + \left[\frac{e^{ax}}{Z_0}\right]_d (B)$$

where the matrices with a subscript d are diagonal matrices whose elements are given by (5.11) and (5.12).

If we premultiply the boundary equations (6.1) and (6.2) by $[A]^{-1}$, we obtain

(6.5)
$$[E(0)]_s + [Z]_{ss}[I(0)]_s = (E)_{gs}$$

(6.6)
$$[E(1)]_s = [Z]_{rs}[I(1)]_s$$

where

(6.7)
$$[Z]_{ss} = [A]^{-1}[Z]_s[A]$$

(6.8)
$$[Z]_{rs} = [A]^{-1}[Z]_r[A]$$

(6.9)
$$(E)_{gs} = [A]^{-1}(E)_g$$

We may now substitute (6.3) and (6.4) into the boundary equations (6.5) and (6.6) and solve for the matrix of constants (K) and (B). Performing the indicated operations, we obtain

(6.10)
$$(B) = (C_1 - C_1 b_1^{-1} b_2)^{-1} (E)_{gs}$$

(6.11)
$$(K) = (C_1 - C_1 b_2^{-1} b_1)^{-1} (E)_{gs}$$

where C_1, b_1, and b_2 are the matrices:

(6.12)
$$C_1 = U + [Z]_{ss}\left[\frac{1}{Z_0}\right]_d$$

(6.13)
$$b_1 = [e^{-a1}]_d - [Z]_{rs}\left[\frac{e^{-a1}}{Z_0}\right]_d$$

(6.14)
$$b_2 = [e^{a1}]_d - [Z]_{rs}\left[\frac{e^{a1}}{Z_0}\right]_d$$

Having evaluated the matrices of arbitrary constants (K) and (B) we now premultiply Eqs. (6.3) and (6.4) by $[A]$ and obtain

(6.15)
$$[E(x)] = [A][E(x)]_s$$

(6.16)
$$[I(x)] = [A][I(x)]_s$$

The actual potential and current distribution is then given by the inverse transforms of these matrices in the form:

(6.17)
$$[e(x, t)] \doteq [E(x)]$$

(6.18)
$$[I(x, t)] \doteq [I(x)]$$

This is the formal solution for the case of ring symmetry subject to the general boundary conditions described above.   In a practical case, the actual computation of the above procedure may lead to a vast amount of computation, but the solution is entirely possible and may be carried out if the importance of the problem justifies the necessary expenditure of effort.

7. GENERAL CONSIDERATIONS

From the above analysis of the transient behavior of the multiconductor line problem, we see that the formal analytical procedure may be carried out in practically the same manner as in Chapter 13, Section 9.   We find that in the general multiconductor case, the entire procedure is vastly complicated by the fact that we now have many propagation constants.   The ideal case of no dissipation is very simple and leads to one velocity of propagation, as compared to n velocities of propagation in the general case.   The practical case of ring symmetry may be completely solved rather easily because of the particularly simple form that the determinantal equation of the system exhibits in this case.   Cable circuits exhibit this type of symmetry as well as properly transposed systems, and hence the analysis of these symmetric cases has considerable practical importance.

REFERENCES

1. Bewley, L. V., *Travelling Waves on Transmission Lines*. New York: John Wiley and Sons, 1933.

2. Bewley, L. V., "Travelling Waves on Transmission Systems," *A.I.E.E. Transactions*, Vol. 50.

3. Pipes, L. A., "Matrix Theory of Multiconductor Transmission Lines," *Phil. Mag.*, Ser. 7, Vol. 24, pp. 97–113.

4. Wagner, K. W., "Induktionswirkungen von Wanderwellen in Nachbarleitungen," *E.T.Z.*, 1914.

APPENDIXES

1 THE ELEMENTS OF THE THEORY OF LAPLACE TRANSFORMS

The modern theory of the operational calculus which has proved such a powerful mathematical tool in the study of transients in linear dynamical systems is based on the following integral, known in the literature as the Bromwich-Wagner integral:

$$(1) \qquad h(t) = \frac{1}{2\pi i} \int_{c-i\infty}^{c+i\infty} \frac{e^{pt} g(p)\, dp}{p} \qquad i = \sqrt{-1}$$

The integration is supposed to be performed in the complex p plane and the integral is supposed to converge. The following notation is introduced:

$$(2) \qquad \mathscr{L} h(t) = g(p)$$

for two functions related to each other by Eq. (1). Under certain restrictions of the function $g(p)$, the integral (1) possesses the inverse

$$(3) \qquad \frac{g(p)}{p} = \int_0^\infty e^{-pt} h(t)\, dt$$

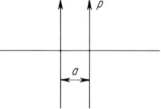

FIGURE A1.1

This integral is known in the operational literature as Carson's integral. Mathematicians speak of the relation (3) as a Laplace transform of $h(t)$ to $g(p)/p$. The relations (1) and (3) taken together are known in the mathematical literature as the Fourier-Mellin integral theorem.

The expressions (1) and (3) are valid if either one of the two groups of conditions A or B is fulfilled.

Conditions A

1. $g(p)/p$ is an analytic function of the complex variable p, having no point of singularity in any finite region situated to the right of the straight line $\mathrm{Re}\,(p) = a$ parallel to the imaginary axis, as shown in Fig. A1.1.

2. There exists a positive number n_0 such that

$$\lim_{\substack{|p| \to \infty \\ \mathrm{Re}\,(p)\, >\, a}} |p^n g(p)| = 0 \quad \text{for} \quad n < n_0$$

Conditions B

1. $g(p)/p$ is an analytic function of the complex variable p, having no points of singularity in any finite region situated to the right of the two straight lines L_1 and L_2 defined by

$$p = a + re^{\pm i\phi} \quad \pi > \phi > \frac{\pi}{2}$$

2. A positive number n_0 exists, so

$$\lim_{|p| \to \infty} \left| \frac{p^n g(p)}{p} \right| = 0 \quad \text{for} \quad n < n_0$$

p is to the right of L_1 and L_2.

Operators satisfying either the conditions A or B are known as restricted operators. The solution of problems concerning dissipative electrical networks is always expressed by restricted operators, but nonrestricted operators sometimes appear as a consequence of evaluating the complete solution by splitting it into parts.

It frequently happens that we must interpret the operational equivalent:

$$(4) \qquad\qquad h_n(t) = \mathscr{L}\, p^n g(p)$$

where $g(p)$ is a restricted operator of class B, but the operator $p^n g(p)$ is a nonrestricted operator, because it increases faster than p as $|p| \to \infty$.

However, it is easy to show that if the integral

$$(5) \qquad\qquad h(t) = \frac{1}{2\pi i} \int_{L_1 L_2} \frac{e^{pt} g(p)\, dp}{p}$$

as defined by condition B converges, then the integral

$$(6) \qquad\qquad \frac{d^n h}{dt^n} = \frac{1}{2\pi i} \int_{L_1 L_2} \frac{p^n e^{pt} g(p)\, dp}{p}$$

will converge for $t > t_0$, where t_0 is positive but arbitrarily small.

Impulse Functions

If we place $g(p) = 1$ in (5), the function $h(t)$ corresponding to the operator $g(p) = 1$ may be shown by the theory of residues to have the following values:

$$(7) \qquad h(t) = \frac{1}{2\pi i} \int_{L_1 L_2} \frac{e^{pt} \, dp}{p} = \begin{array}{ll} 0 & t < 0 \\ \tfrac{1}{2} & t = 0 \\ 1 & t > 0 \end{array}$$

It is thus seen that $h(t)$ is, in this case, equal to the unit function $1(t)$ of Heaviside and we may place

$$(8) \qquad \mathscr{L}1(t) = 1$$

Now if we place $g(p) = p$ in the integral (5), we obtain the following values:

$$(9) \qquad h(t) = \begin{cases} 0, & t < 0 \\ \infty, & t = 0 \\ 0, & t > 0 \end{cases}$$

We introduce the notation

$$(10) \qquad \mathscr{L}\delta(t) = p$$

where $\delta(t)$ is the impulse function which has been so extensively used by the Dirac theory of *Quantum Mechanics*. The function $\delta(t)$ has the property that

$$(11) \qquad \int_{-\infty}^{+\infty} f(t) \, \delta(t - a) \, dt = f(a)$$

where $f(t)$ is a continuous function of t, and

$$(12) \qquad \int_{-\infty}^{+\infty} \delta(t) \, dt = 1$$

The function $\delta(t)$ may be treated as an ordinary function and may be formally differentiated an unlimited number of times. We thus write, in general,

$$(13) \qquad \mathscr{L}\, \delta^{(n-1)}(t) = p^n$$

where $\delta^{(n)}(t)$ is an impulse function of the nth order with the property that

$$(14) \qquad \int_{-\infty}^{+\infty} f(t) \, \delta^{[n]}(t - a) \, dt = f^{[n]}(a)$$

and

$$(15) \qquad \delta^{(n)}(t) = \begin{cases} 0, & t \neq 0 \\ \infty, & t = 0 \end{cases}$$

2 THE BASIC THEOREMS OF THE LAPLACE TRANSFORMS

From the fundamental equations

(1) $$h(t) = \frac{1}{2\pi i} \int_{c-i\infty}^{c+i\infty} \frac{e^{pt} g(p)\, dp}{p}$$

and

(2) $$g(p) = p \int_0^\infty e^{-pt} h(t)\, dt$$

it is possible to deduce some very powerful theorems, which are of the utmost importance in the transient analysis of linear dynamical systems. For simplicity we express the functional relations between $h(t)$ and $g(p)$ given by (1) and (2) above in the symbolic form:

(3) $$\mathscr{L} h(t) = g(p), \quad \mathscr{L}^{-1} g(p) = h(t)$$

We then have the following theorems:

(4) $$\mathscr{L}^{-1} g\!\left(\frac{p}{s}\right) = h(st) \qquad s > 0$$

(5) $$\mathscr{L}^{-1} p g(p) - p h(0) = \frac{dh}{dt}$$

(6) $$\mathscr{L}^{-1} p^n g(p) - \sum_{k=0}^{n-1} h_{(0)}^{[h]} p^{(n-h)} \doteq \frac{d^n h(t)}{dt^n}$$

(7) $$\mathscr{L}^{-1}\left\{ \int_{-\infty}^0 h(t)\, dt + \frac{g(p)}{p} \right\} \doteq \int_{-\infty}^t h(t)\, dt$$

(8) $$\mathscr{L}^{-1} \frac{p}{p+a} g(p+a) \doteq \varepsilon^{-at} h(t)$$

(9) $$\mathscr{L}^{-1}\varepsilon^{-ap}g(p) = \begin{cases} 0 & t < a \\ h(t-a) & t > a \end{cases} \qquad a > 0$$

(10) $$\mathscr{L}^{-1}\varepsilon^{ap}g(p) = h(t+a) \quad \text{if} \quad h(t) = 0 \quad 0 < t < a \quad a > 0$$

(11) $$\mathscr{L}^{-1}\left(-p\frac{d}{dp}\right)^n g(p) = \left(t\frac{d}{dt}\right)^n h(t) \qquad n > 0$$

(12) $$\mathscr{L}^{-1}p\left(-\frac{d}{dp}\right)^n \frac{g(p)}{p} = t^n h(t) \qquad n > 0$$

(13) $$\mathscr{L}^{-1}\int_p^\infty \frac{g(p)}{p}\,dp = \int_0^t \frac{h(u)\,du}{u}$$

(14) $$\mathscr{L}^{-1}\int_0^p \frac{g(p)\,dp}{p} = \int_t^\infty \frac{h(u)\,du}{u}$$

(15) $$\int_0^\infty \frac{g(p)\,dp}{p} = \int_0^\infty \frac{h(x)\,dt}{t} \qquad \text{(an ordinary equality)}$$

(16) $$\lim_{|p| \to \infty} g(p) = \lim_{t \to 0} h(t) \qquad \text{(ordinary equality)}$$

(17) If

(a) $g(p)$ has no points of singularity in any finite region situated to the right of the two straight lines, $L_1 L_2$ defined by

$$p = \varepsilon \pm \delta^\phi \quad \pi > \phi > \frac{\pi}{2} \quad j = \sqrt{-1},$$

(b) the limit of $g(p)$ exists and it tends toward a finite value $g(0)$ when $|p| \to 0$ on to the right of the two lines L_1 and L_2, then

$$\lim_{|p| \to 0} g(p) = \lim_{|t| \to \infty} h(t) \qquad \text{(ordinary equality)}$$

(18) $$\mathscr{L}^{-1}p\int_p^\infty \int_p^\infty \cdots \int_p^\infty \frac{g(p)}{p}\,(dp)^n = \frac{h(t)}{t^n}$$

If

(19) $$\mathscr{L}^{-1}g_1(p) = h_1(t) \quad \text{and} \quad \mathscr{L}^{-1}g_2(p) = h_2(t)$$

then

$$\mathscr{L}^{-1}\frac{g_1(p)g_2(p)}{p} = \int_0^t h_1(u)h_2(t-u)\,du \quad \text{(Faltung or convolution theorem)}$$

$$= \int_0^t h_2(u)h_1(t-u)\,du$$

If

(20) $$g(p) = \frac{S(p)}{Q(p)}$$

where $S(p)$ and $Q(p)$ are polynomials in p and the degree of the polynomial $Q(p)$ is at least as high as the degree of the polynomial $S(p)$, then, if the polynomial $Q(p)$ has the n *distinct* zeros $(p_1, p_2, \ldots, p_n)$ and $p = 0$ is not a zero of $Q(p)$, it follows that

$$\mathscr{L}^{-1} \frac{S(p)}{Q(p)} = \frac{S(0)}{Q(0)} + \sum_{r=1}^{n} \frac{S(p_r)\varepsilon^{p_r t}}{p_r Q'(p_r)}$$

where

$$Q'(p_r) = \left. \frac{dQ}{dp} \right|_{p=p_r} \qquad \text{(Heaviside's expansion theorem)}$$

If

(21)
$$g(p) = \frac{N(q)}{D(q)}$$

where

(a) q is a function of p, $q = q(p)$.

(b) $D(q)$ and $N(q)$ are rational polynomials in q.

(c) $N(q)$ is of lower degree than $D(q)$.

(d) $D(q)$ has n distinct zeros, q_r and $q = 0$ is not a root of $D(q)$.

Then

$$\mathscr{L}^{-1} \frac{N(q)}{D(q)} = \frac{N(0)}{D(0)} + \sum_{r=1}^{r=n} \frac{N(q_r)}{q_r D'(q_r)} \phi\,(t, q_r)$$

where

$$\mathscr{L}^{-1} \frac{q}{q - q_r} = \phi(t, q_r) \quad \text{and} \quad D'(q_r) = \left(\frac{dD}{dq} \right)_{q=q_r}$$

If

(22)
$$g(p) = \sum_{r=0}^{\infty} a_r p^r + p^{1/2} \sum_{r=0}^{\infty} b_r p^r$$

where both series are convergent series in p_r, then

$$\mathscr{L}^{-1} g(p) = a_0 + \frac{1}{\sqrt{\pi t}} \left(b_0 - \frac{b_1}{2t} + \frac{1 \cdot 3 b_2}{(2t)^2} - \frac{1 \cdot 3 \cdot 5\, b_3}{(2t)^3} + \cdots \right) \quad t > 0$$

These basic theorems are very powerful when used in connection with a table of transforms in the solution of transient phenomena. Theorem (20) is the conventional Heaviside expansion formula, whereas theorem (21) is a generalization of the Heaviside formula. Theorem (21) is known in the operational literature as Heaviside's third rule.

3 TABLE OF BASIC TRANSFORMS

This table contains a list of transforms of great value for the solution of numerous problems involving transients in linear dynamical systems. These transforms may be obtained by evaluating the basic integrals (1) or (2) of Appendix 2. The transforms given here are those most frequently occurring in transient problems; a collection of these transforms into a table facilitates the solution of many problems.

(1) $$\mathscr{L}1(t) \doteq 1$$

where $1(t)$ is the Heaviside "unit function" having the values:

$$1(t) = \begin{cases} 0 & t < 0 \\ \frac{1}{2} & t = 0 \\ 1 & t > 0 \end{cases}$$

(2) $$\mathscr{L}^{-1}p \doteq \delta(t)$$

(*Note about notation.* In the following table, the following notation is used: If $\mathscr{L}^{-1}g(p) = h(t)$ then in the table this is expressed as $g(p) \doteq h(t)$ where $\delta(t)$ is an impulse function that has the following properties:

$$\delta(t) = \begin{cases} \infty & t = 0 & \int_{-\infty}^{+\infty} \delta(t)\, dt = 1 \\ 0 & t \neq 0 & \int_{-\infty}^{+\infty} f(t)\, \delta(t - a) = f(a) \end{cases}$$

where $f(t)$ is an integrable continuous function of the real variable t.)

(3) $$p^n \doteq \delta^{[n-1]}(t)$$

where n is a positive integer. $\delta^{[n-1]}(t)$ is the Dirac impulse function of the nth order and has the following properties:

$$\int_{-\infty}^{+\infty} f(t)\,\delta^{[n]}(t - a)\,dt = f^{[n]}(a) \quad \text{and} \quad \delta^{[n-1]}(t) = \begin{cases} 0 & t \neq 0 \\ \infty & t = 0 \end{cases}$$

(4)
$$p^n \doteq \frac{t^{-n}}{\Gamma(1 - n)}$$

except for n a positive integer. $\Gamma(n)$ is the gamma function of the real argument n.

(5)
$$p^{1/2} \doteq \frac{1}{\sqrt{\pi t}}$$

(6)
$$p^{3/2} \doteq -\sqrt{\frac{2}{\pi}}\,\frac{1}{(2t)^{3/2}}$$

(7)
$$p^{5/2} \doteq \sqrt{\frac{2}{\pi}}\,\frac{1 \cdot 3}{(2t)^{5/2}}$$

(8)
$$p^{7/2} \doteq -\sqrt{\frac{2}{\pi}}\,\frac{1 \cdot 3 \cdot 5}{(2t)^{7/2}}$$

(9)
$$p^{-1/2} \doteq \sqrt{\frac{2}{\pi}}\,(2t)^{1/2}$$

(10)
$$p^{-3/2} \doteq \sqrt{\frac{2}{\pi}}\,\frac{(2t)^{3/2}}{1 \cdot 3}$$

(11)
$$p^{-5/2} \doteq \sqrt{\frac{2}{\pi}}\,\frac{(2t)^{5/2}}{1 \cdot 3 \cdot 5}$$

(12)
$$p^{-7/2} \doteq \sqrt{\frac{2}{\pi}}\,\frac{(2t)^{7/2}}{1 \cdot 3 \cdot 5 \cdot 7}$$

(12a)
$$\frac{\sqrt{p}}{p^n} \doteq \frac{(2t)^n}{1 \cdot 3 \cdot 5 \cdot \ \cdots \ \cdot (2n - 1)\sqrt{\pi t}}$$
$$n \text{ is a positive integer}$$

(12b)
$$p^n\sqrt{p} \doteq \frac{1 \cdot 3 \cdot 5 \cdot \ \cdots \ \cdot (2n - 1)}{(-2t)^n\sqrt{\pi t}}$$

(13)
$$\frac{p^2}{p + a} \doteq \delta(t) - a\varepsilon^{-at}$$

(14)
$$\frac{p}{p + a} \doteq \varepsilon^{-at}$$

(15)
$$\frac{1}{p + a} \doteq \frac{1}{a}(1 - \varepsilon^{-at})$$

(16)
$$\frac{1}{p(p + a)} \doteq \frac{t}{a} - \frac{1}{a^2} + \frac{\varepsilon^{-at}}{a^2}$$

(17) $$\frac{p^2}{(p + a)(p + b)} \doteqdot \frac{1}{(a - b)}\{a\varepsilon^{-at} - b\varepsilon^{-bt}\}$$

(18) $$\frac{p}{(p + a)(p + b)} \doteqdot \frac{1}{(a - b)}\{\varepsilon^{-bt} - \varepsilon^{-at}\}$$

(19) $$\frac{wp}{p^2 + w^2} \doteqdot \sin(wt)$$

(20) $$\frac{p^2}{p^2 + w^2} \doteqdot \cos(wt)$$

(21) $$\frac{w^2}{p^2 + w^2} \doteqdot 1 - \cos wt$$

(22) $$\frac{wp}{p^2 + w^2} \doteqdot \sinh wt$$

(23) $$\frac{p^2}{p^2 - w^2} \doteqdot \cosh wt$$

(24) $$\frac{wp}{(p + b)^2 + w^2} \doteqdot \varepsilon^{-bt} \sin(wt)$$

(25) $$\frac{p(p + b)}{(p + b)^2 + w^2} \doteqdot \varepsilon^{-bt} \cos(wt)$$

(26) $$\frac{wp}{(p + b)^2 - w^2} \doteqdot \varepsilon^{-bt} \sinh(wt)$$

(27) $$\frac{pw \cos\phi \pm p^2 \sin\phi}{p^2 + w^2} \doteqdot \sin(wt \pm \phi)$$

(28) $$\frac{p^2\cos^2\phi \mp wp \sin\phi}{p^2 + w^2} \doteqdot \cos(wt \pm \phi)$$

(29) $$\frac{wp \cos\phi \pm p(p + b) \sin\phi}{(p + b)^2 + w^2} \doteqdot \varepsilon^{-bt} \sin(wt \pm \phi)$$

(30) $$\frac{p(p + b) \cos\phi \mp wp \sin\phi}{(p + b)^2 + w^2} \doteqdot \varepsilon^{-bt} \cos(wt \pm \phi)$$

(31) In the following transforms, let $w^2 = w_0^2 - a^2$, $\tan\phi = w/a$, and $(-m)$ and $(-n)$ be the two roots of $p^2 + 2ap + w_0^2 = 0$; then

(32a) $$\frac{p^2}{p^2 + 2ap + w_0^2} \doteqdot \frac{w_0}{w} \varepsilon^{-at} \sin(wt - \phi) \qquad \text{if } w_0^2 > a^2$$

(32b) $$\frac{p^2}{p^2 + 2ap + w_0^2} \doteqdot \frac{1}{n - m}(n\varepsilon^{-nt} - m\varepsilon^{-mt}) \qquad a^2 > w_0^2$$

(32c) $\quad \dfrac{p^2}{p^2 + 2ap + w_0^2} \doteqdot \varepsilon^{-at}(1 - at) \qquad a^2 = w_0^2$

(33) $\quad \dfrac{p}{p^2 + 2ap + w_0^2} \doteqdot \dfrac{\varepsilon^{-at} \sin wt}{w} \qquad w^2 > a^2$

$$\doteqdot \dfrac{1}{n - m}(\varepsilon^{-mt} - \varepsilon^{-nt}) \qquad a^2 > w_0^2$$

$$\doteqdot t\varepsilon^{-at} \qquad a^2 = w_0^2$$

(34) $\quad \dfrac{1}{p^2 + 2ap + w_0^2} \doteqdot \dfrac{1}{w_0^2}\left\{1 - \dfrac{w_0}{w}\varepsilon^{-at}\sin(wt + \phi)\right\} \qquad w_0^2 > a^2$

$$\doteqdot \dfrac{1}{w_0^2}\left\{1 - \dfrac{w_0^2}{n - m}\left(\dfrac{\varepsilon^{-mt}}{m} - \dfrac{\varepsilon^{-nt}}{n}\right)\right\} \qquad a^2 > w_0^2$$

$$\doteqdot \dfrac{1}{w_0^2}\{1 - \varepsilon^{-at}(1 + at)\} \qquad a^2 = w_0^2$$

(35) $\quad \dfrac{p^2}{(p + a)^2} \doteqdot \varepsilon^{-at}(1 - at)$

(36) $\quad \dfrac{p}{(p + a)^2} \doteqdot t\varepsilon^{-at}$

(37) $\quad \dfrac{1}{(p + a)^2} \doteqdot \dfrac{1}{a^2}\{1 - \varepsilon^{-at}(1 + at)\}$

(38) $\quad \dfrac{1}{(p + 1)^n} \doteqdot \dfrac{1}{\Gamma(u)}\displaystyle\int_0^t \varepsilon^{-n}u^{n-1}\,du$

where n is real and $\geqq 0$.

(39) $\quad \dfrac{p}{(p^2 + w^2)(p + a)} \doteqdot \dfrac{1}{w\sqrt{a^2 + w^2}}\{\varepsilon^{-at}\sin\beta + \sin(wt - \beta)\}$

where

$$\beta = \tan^{-1}\dfrac{w}{a}$$

(40) $\quad \dfrac{p^2 + 2w^2}{p^2 + 4w^2} \doteqdot \cos^2(wt)$

(41) $\quad \dfrac{2n!}{(p^2 + 2^2)(p^2 + 4^2)\ldots\{p^2 + (2n)^2\}} \doteqdot \sin^{2n}(t)$

(42) $\quad \dfrac{(2n + 1)!\,p}{(p^2 + 1^2)(p^2 + 3^2)\ldots\{p^2 + (2n + 1)^2\}} \doteqdot \sin^{(2n+1)}(t)$

(43) $\quad \dfrac{p}{(p + a)^n} \doteqdot \dfrac{\varepsilon^{-at}t^{n-1}}{(n - 1)!}$

where n is a positive integer.

(44)
$$\frac{(p - a)^2}{(p + a)^2} \doteq 1 - 4ate^{-at}$$

(45)
$$\frac{p}{\sqrt{p^2 + a^2}} \doteq J_0(at)$$

where $J_0(y)$ is the Bessel function of the first kind and zeroth order.

(46)
$$\frac{p}{\sqrt{p^2 - a^2}} \doteq J_0(iat) \qquad i = \sqrt{-1}$$

(47)
$$\frac{p}{a^n \sqrt{p^2 + a^2}} (\sqrt{p^2 + a^2} - p)^n \doteq J_n(at)$$

where $J_n(y)$ is the Bessel function of the first kind and nth order.

(48)
$$\varepsilon^{-a/p} \doteq J_0(2\sqrt{at})$$

(49)
$$\varepsilon^{i/p} \doteq J_0(2\sqrt{-it})$$
$$\doteq \text{ber}\,(2\sqrt{t}) + i\,\text{bei}\,(2\sqrt{t})$$

where $i = \sqrt{-1}$ and ber in the "bessel real" junction and bei in the "bessel imaginary" function by Lord Kelvin defined by

$$J_0(in\sqrt{ix}) = \text{ber}\,(nx) + i\,\text{bei}\,(nx)$$

(50)
$$\varepsilon^{-i/p} \doteq \text{ber}\,(2\sqrt{t}) - i\,\text{bei}\,(2\sqrt{t})$$
$$\doteq J_0(2\sqrt{it})$$

(51)
$$\cos\frac{1}{p} \doteq \text{ber}\,(2\sqrt{t})$$

(52)
$$\sin\frac{1}{p} \doteq \text{bei}\,(2\sqrt{t})$$

(53)
$$\log\frac{1}{\sqrt{1 + p^2}} \doteq \text{Ci}\,(t)$$

where

$$\text{Ci}\,(y) = \int_{-\infty}^{y} \frac{\cos u\,du}{u}$$

is the integral cosine function.

(54)
$$\cot^{-1}(p) \doteq \text{Si}\,(t)$$

where

$$\text{Si}\,(y) = \int_{0}^{y} \frac{\sin u\,du}{u}$$

is the integral sine function.

(55)
$$\log_\varepsilon (p - 1) \doteqdot -\int_\infty^{-t} \frac{\varepsilon^{-u} \, du}{u}$$

(56)
$$\sqrt{\frac{p}{p + 2a}} \doteqdot \varepsilon^{-at} J_0(iat)$$

(57)
$$\frac{p}{\sqrt{(p + a)^2 - b^2}} \doteqdot \varepsilon^{-at} J_0(ibt)$$

(58)
$$\varepsilon^{-ap} \doteqdot 1_a^t \qquad a > 0$$

where

$$1_a^t = \begin{cases} 0 & t < a \\ \frac{1}{2} & t = a \\ 1 & t > a \end{cases}$$

(59)
$$\frac{p}{\sqrt{1 + p^2}} \varepsilon^{-a\sqrt{1 + p^2}} \doteqdot \begin{cases} 0 & t < a \\ J_0(\sqrt{t^2 - a^2}) & t > a \end{cases}$$

(60)
$$\frac{p}{\sqrt{p + a}} \doteqdot \frac{\varepsilon^{-at}}{\sqrt{\pi t}}$$

(61)
$$p\varepsilon^{-\sqrt{ap}} \doteqdot \frac{1}{2} \sqrt{\frac{a}{\pi}} \frac{\varepsilon^{-a/4t}}{t^{3/2}}$$

(62)
$$\varepsilon^{-\sqrt{ap}} \doteqdot 1 - \text{erf} \left(\frac{a}{2\sqrt{t}} \right)$$

where erf (y) is the "error junction" defined by the integral

$$\text{erf} (y) = \frac{2}{\sqrt{\pi}} \int_0^y \varepsilon^{-u^2} \, du$$

(63)
$$\frac{p^{1/2}}{p^{1/2} - a} \doteqdot \varepsilon^{a^2 t} \{1 + \text{erf} \, (at^{1/2})\}$$

(64)
$$\frac{p^{1/s}}{p^{1/s} - a} \doteqdot \varepsilon^{a^s t} \sum_{n=1}^{(s-1)} \{1 + \phi_n(t, a)\}$$

where

$$\phi_n(t, a) = \frac{1}{\Gamma\left(\dfrac{n}{s} + 1\right)} \int_0^{a^n t^{n/s}} \varepsilon^{-u^{s/n}} \, du$$

(65)
$$\frac{p^3}{p^3 - a} \doteqdot \left(\frac{1}{3}\right) \varepsilon^{a^{1/3} t} + \left(\frac{2}{3}\right) \varepsilon^{-a^{1/3} t/2} \cos \left(a^{1/3} t \frac{\sqrt{3}}{2} \right)$$

(66)
$$\frac{p^4}{p^4 - a} \doteqdot \frac{1}{2}\cosh(a^{1/4}t) + \frac{1}{2}\cos(a^{1/4}t)$$

(67)
$$\frac{q}{q - a} \doteqdot \frac{b}{b - a^2} - \frac{a^2}{b - a^2}\varepsilon^{(a^2 - b)t}$$

$$+ \frac{a\sqrt{b}}{b - a^2}\operatorname{erf}(\sqrt{bt}) - \frac{a^2}{b - a^2}\varepsilon^{(a^2 - b)t}\operatorname{erf}(a\sqrt{t})$$

where $q = (p + b)^{1/2}$ and $b \neq a^2$.

(68)
$$\frac{q}{q - a} \doteqdot \frac{1}{1 - a^2}\left\{\varepsilon^{a^2 bt/(1 - a^2)} + a\varepsilon^{-bt/2}I_0\left(\frac{bt}{2}\right)\right.$$

$$+ \left.\frac{ab}{(1 - a^2)^2}\varepsilon^{a^2 bt/(1 - a^2)}\int_0^t \varepsilon^{(a^2 + 1)bt/2(a^2 - 1)}I_0\left(\frac{bt}{2}\right)dt\right\}$$

where

$$q = \sqrt{\frac{p}{p + b}} \quad \text{and} \quad a^2 \neq 1$$

$I_0(y) = J_0(iy) = $ the Bessel function of the second kind and zeroth order.

(69)
$$\frac{p^{3/2}}{p + a} \doteqdot \frac{1}{\sqrt{\pi t}} + ia^{1/2}\varepsilon^{-at}\operatorname{erf}(ia^{1/2}t^{1/2}) \quad i = \sqrt{-1}$$

(70)
$$\frac{1}{p^4 - 3p^2 + 2} \doteqdot \frac{1}{2} + \frac{1}{2}\cosh(t\sqrt{2}) - \cosh(t)$$

(71)
$$\frac{wp^{3/2}}{p^2 + w^2} \doteqdot \sqrt{2w}\left\{\sin(wt)S\left(w^{1/2}t^{1/2}\sqrt{\frac{2}{\pi}}\right) + \cos(wt)C\left(w^{1/2}t^{1/2}\sqrt{\frac{2}{\pi}}\right)\right\}$$

where $C(y)$ and $S(y)$ are the Fresnel integrals defined by

$$C(y) = \int_0^y \cos\left(\frac{\pi u^2}{2}\right)du$$

$$S(y) = \int_0^y \sin\left(\frac{\pi u^2}{2}\right)du$$

These integrals have been tabulated.

(72)
$$\frac{\sinh(bp^{1/2})}{\sinh(ap^{1/2})} \doteqdot \frac{b}{a} + \frac{2}{\pi}\sum_{n=1}^{\infty}\frac{(-1)^n}{n}\sin\left(\frac{n\pi b}{a}\right)\varepsilon^{-(n^2\pi^2/a^2)t} \quad \begin{matrix} a > 0 \\ b > 0 \end{matrix}$$

(73)
$$\frac{\sinh\{b(p + c)^{1/2}\}}{\sinh\{a(p + c)^{1/2}\}}$$

$$\doteqdot \frac{b}{a} + \frac{2}{\pi}\sum_{n=1}^{\infty}\frac{(-1)^n}{n}\sin\left(\frac{n\pi b}{a}\right)\left\{\frac{c}{c + \frac{n^2\pi^2}{a^2}} + \frac{n^2\pi^2}{a^2 c + n^2\pi^2}\varepsilon^{-\left(\frac{n^2\pi^2}{a^2} + c\right)t}\right\}$$

(74) $\dfrac{\cosh (x\sqrt{RCP})}{\cosh (l\sqrt{RCP})}$

$$\doteqdot 1 + \frac{4}{\pi} \sum_{s=1}^{\infty} \frac{(-1)^s}{(2s-1)} \cos \left\{ \left(\frac{2s-1}{2} \right) \frac{\pi x}{l} \right\} \varepsilon^{-(2s-1)^2 \pi^2 t / 4CRl^2}$$

(75) $\dfrac{\sqrt{PC} \sinh (x\sqrt{RCP})}{\sqrt{R} \cosh (l\sqrt{RCP})}$

$$\doteqdot \frac{2}{lR} \sum_{s=1}^{\infty} (-1)^s \sin (m_s x) \, \varepsilon^{-m_s^2 t / CR} \quad m_s = \left(\frac{2s-1}{2} \right) \frac{\pi}{l}$$

(76) $\dfrac{\sqrt{PC}}{\sqrt{R}} \dfrac{\cosh (x\sqrt{RCP})}{\sinh (l\sqrt{RCP})} \doteqdot \dfrac{1}{Rl} + \dfrac{2}{Rl} \sum_{s=1}^{\infty} (-1)^s \varepsilon^{-s^2 \pi^2 t / CAl^2} \cos \left(\dfrac{s\pi x}{l} \right)$

If

(77)
$$\alpha = \sqrt{(R + Lp)(G + PC)}$$
$$Z = R + Lp$$

$$\frac{\alpha \cosh (\alpha l)}{Z \sinh (\alpha l)} \doteqdot \sqrt{\frac{G}{R}} \frac{\cosh (x\sqrt{RG})}{\sinh (l\sqrt{RG})} - \frac{E}{Rl} \varepsilon^{-(R/L)t}$$

$$+ 2 \sum_{s=1}^{\infty} \frac{(-1)^s l \cos \left(\dfrac{s\pi x}{l} \right)}{s^2 \pi + RCl^2} \varepsilon^{-\rho t} \left[\frac{1}{\beta^s} \left\{ \frac{s^2 \pi^2}{Ll^2} \right. \right.$$

$$\left. \left. + \frac{1}{2} G \left(\frac{R}{L} - \frac{G}{c} \right) \sin (\beta_s t) - G \cos \beta_s t \right\} \right]$$

where

$$\rho = \frac{1}{2} \left(\frac{R}{L} + \frac{G}{C} \right) \quad \beta_s = \sqrt{\frac{m_s^2}{LC} - \frac{1}{4} \left(\frac{R}{L} - \frac{G}{C} \right)^2}$$

$$m_s = \frac{s\pi}{l}$$

(78) $\dfrac{\cosh \{\alpha(l - x)\}}{\cosh (\alpha l)} \doteqdot \dfrac{\cosh s(l - x)}{\cosh sl}$

$$- \frac{\pi v^2}{l^2} \varepsilon^{-\rho t} \sum_{n=1,3,5}^{\infty} n \sin \left(\frac{n\pi x}{2l} \right) \left[\frac{\rho \sin \beta_n t + \beta_n \cos \beta_n t}{\beta_n(\rho^2 + \beta_n)} \right]$$

where

$$\beta_n = \sqrt{\frac{n^2 \pi^2 v^2}{4l^2} - \sigma^2} \qquad \rho = (a + b)$$
$$\sigma = (a - b)$$

$$v = \frac{1}{\sqrt{LC}} \qquad\qquad a = \frac{R}{2L}, \quad b = \frac{G}{2C}$$

$$\alpha = \sqrt{(R + LP)(G + PC)} \qquad S = \frac{2\sqrt{ab}}{v}$$

(79) $\dfrac{\sinh \alpha(l - x)}{Z_0 \cosh (\alpha l)} \doteqdot \dfrac{G}{s} \dfrac{\sinh s(l - x)}{\cosh (sl)}$

$+ \dfrac{2v^2}{l} \varepsilon^{-\rho t} \displaystyle\sum_{n=1,3,5}^{\infty} \cos \left(\dfrac{n\pi x}{2l}\right) \left[\dfrac{G\rho \sin \beta_n t + G\beta_n \cos \beta_n t}{\beta_n(\rho^2 + \beta_n^2)} - C\dfrac{\sin (\beta_n t)}{\beta_n}\right]$

where the constants are those defined for (78) and

$$Z_0 = \sqrt{\dfrac{R + LP}{G + CP}}$$

(80) $\dfrac{\sinh [\alpha(l - x)]}{\sinh (\alpha l)} \doteqdot \dfrac{\sinh s(l - x)}{\sinh sl}$

$-\dfrac{2v^2\pi}{l^2} \varepsilon^{-\rho t} \displaystyle\sum_{n=1,3,\ldots}^{\infty} \dfrac{n \sin \left(\dfrac{n\pi x}{l}\right)[\rho \sin (\beta_n t) + \beta_n \cos (\beta_n t)]}{\beta_n(\rho^2 + \beta_n^2)}$

where the constants are those defined for (78).

(81) $\varepsilon^{-\alpha x} \doteqdot \begin{cases} 0 & t < \dfrac{x}{v} \\[2ex] \varepsilon^{-\rho x/v} + \dfrac{\sigma x}{v}\displaystyle\int_{x/v}^{t} \varepsilon^{-\rho u} \dfrac{I_1\left(\sigma\sqrt{u^2 - \dfrac{x^2}{v^2}}\right)}{\sqrt{u^2 - \dfrac{x^2}{v^2}}} \, du & t > \dfrac{x}{v} \end{cases}$

where

$$\alpha = \sqrt{(Lp + R)(Cp + G)} \qquad \rho = \dfrac{1}{2}\left(\dfrac{R}{L} + \dfrac{G}{C}\right)$$

$$\sigma = \dfrac{1}{2}\left(\dfrac{R}{L} - \dfrac{G}{C}\right) \qquad v = \dfrac{1}{\sqrt{LC}}$$

$I_1(y)$ is the modified Bessel function of the first order.

(82) $\dfrac{p \exp\left\{-\dfrac{x}{v}\sqrt{(p + \rho)^2 - \sigma^2}\right\}}{\sqrt{(p + \rho)^2 - \sigma^2}} \doteqdot \begin{cases} 0 & t < \dfrac{x}{v} \\[2ex] \varepsilon^{-\rho t} I_0\left(\sigma\sqrt{t^2 - \dfrac{x^2}{v^2}}\right) & t > \dfrac{x}{v} \end{cases}$

where the constants are the same as those in (81) and $I_0(y)$ in the modified Bessel function of the zeroth order.

(83) $p\varepsilon^{-\alpha x} \doteqdot \delta\left(t - \dfrac{x}{v}\right)\varepsilon^{-\rho x/v} + \dfrac{\sigma x}{vz}\varepsilon^{-\rho t}I_1(\sigma z) \qquad t > x/v$

where the constants are the same as those given in (81) and

$$z = \sqrt{t^2 - \left(\dfrac{x}{v}\right)^2} \quad \text{and} \quad \delta(t) \text{ in the impulse function}$$

(84) $\dfrac{\rho\varepsilon^{-\alpha x}}{Z_0} \doteqdot \begin{cases} 0 & t < \dfrac{x}{v} \\[2mm] \dfrac{1}{k}\,\varepsilon^{-\rho x/v}\,\delta\!\left(t - \dfrac{x}{v}\right) + \dfrac{1}{k}\,\varepsilon^{-\rho t}\left[\dfrac{\sigma t}{z}\,I_1(\sigma z) - \sigma I_0(\sigma z)\right] & t > \dfrac{x}{v} \end{cases}$

where

$$\alpha = \sqrt{(L_p + R)(C_p + G)} \qquad \sigma = \frac{1}{2}\left(\frac{R}{L} - \frac{G}{C}\right)$$

$$k = \sqrt{\frac{L}{C}} \qquad \rho = \frac{1}{2}\left(\frac{R}{L} + \frac{G}{C}\right)$$

$$v = \frac{1}{\sqrt{LC}} \qquad Z_0 = \sqrt{\frac{R + L_p}{G + C_p}}$$

$$Z = \sqrt{t^2 - \left(\frac{x}{v}\right)^2}$$

(85) $\qquad \rho\varepsilon^{-\alpha x} \doteqdot \dfrac{y}{2t\sqrt{\pi t}}\exp\left(\dfrac{y^2}{-4t} - 2\beta t\right) \quad t > 0$

where

$$\alpha = \sqrt{R(C_p + G)} \qquad \beta = G/2C$$

$$y = x\sqrt{RC}$$

(86) $\qquad \dfrac{\rho\varepsilon^{-\alpha x}}{Z_0} \doteqdot \dfrac{u(y^2 - 2t)}{4t^2\sqrt{\pi t}}\exp\left(-\dfrac{y^2}{4t} - 2\beta t\right) \quad t > 0$

$$\alpha = \sqrt{R(C_p + G)} \qquad u = \sqrt{\frac{C}{R}}$$

$$y = x\sqrt{RC} \qquad Z_0 = \sqrt{\frac{R}{C_p + G}}$$

(87) $\varepsilon^{-\alpha x} \doteqdot \frac{1}{2}\left[\varepsilon^{-y\sqrt{2\beta}}\,\mathrm{erf}\left(\dfrac{y}{2\sqrt{t}} - \sqrt{2\beta t}\right) + \varepsilon^{y\sqrt{2\beta}}\,\mathrm{erf}\left(\dfrac{y}{2\sqrt{t}} + \sqrt{2\beta t}\right)\right] \quad t > 0$

$$\alpha = \sqrt{R(C_p + G)} \qquad \beta = \frac{G}{2C}$$

$$y = x\sqrt{RC} \qquad \mathrm{erf}\,(u) = \frac{2}{\sqrt{\pi}}\int_0^n \varepsilon^{-v^2}\,dv$$

(88) $\qquad \dfrac{\varepsilon^{-\alpha x}}{Z_0} \doteqdot \dfrac{u}{\sqrt{\pi t}}\exp\left(-\dfrac{y^2}{4t} - 2\beta t\right)$

$$+ \frac{u\sqrt{2\beta}}{2}\left[\varepsilon^{-y\sqrt{2\beta}}\,\mathrm{erf}\left(\dfrac{y}{2\sqrt{t}} - \sqrt{2\beta t}\right)\right.$$

$$\left. -\,\varepsilon^{y\sqrt{2\beta}}\,\mathrm{erf}\left(\dfrac{y}{2\sqrt{t}} + \sqrt{2\beta t}\right)\right]$$

where

$$\alpha = \sqrt{R(C_p + G)} \qquad \beta = G/2C \qquad u = \sqrt{\frac{C}{R}}$$

$$Z_0 = \sqrt{\frac{R}{C_p + G}} \qquad y = x\sqrt{RC}$$

(89) $\qquad p\varepsilon^{-\alpha x} \doteq 0 \qquad t < \dfrac{x}{v}$

$$\doteq \frac{\delta\left(t - \dfrac{x}{v}\right)}{k} \varepsilon^{-\alpha x/v} + \frac{1}{k} \varepsilon^{-\alpha t}\left[\frac{at}{z} I_1(at) - aI_0(at)\right] \qquad t > \frac{x}{v}$$

where

$$\alpha = \sqrt{(L_p + R)C_p} \qquad k = \sqrt{\frac{L}{C}} \qquad t = \sqrt{t^2 - \left(\frac{x}{v}\right)^2}$$

$$Z_0 = \sqrt{\frac{L_p + R}{C_p}} \qquad v = \frac{1}{\sqrt{LC}} \qquad a = \frac{R}{2L}$$

(90) $\qquad\qquad \varepsilon^{-\alpha x} \doteq 0 \qquad t < \dfrac{x}{v}$

$$\doteq \frac{1}{k} \varepsilon^{-at} I_0(az) \qquad t > \frac{x}{v}$$

where the constants have the same values as in (89).

(91) $\qquad p\varepsilon^{-\alpha x} \doteq \delta\left(t - \dfrac{x}{v}\right)\varepsilon^{-\rho x/v} \qquad t > \dfrac{x}{v}$

where

$$\alpha = \sqrt{(Lp + R)(Cp + G)} \quad \text{and} \quad \frac{R}{L} = \frac{G}{C}$$

$$\rho = \frac{1}{2}\left(\frac{R}{L} + \frac{G}{C}\right)$$

$$v = \frac{1}{\sqrt{LC}}$$

(92) $\qquad\qquad \varepsilon^{-\alpha x} \doteq \begin{cases} 0 & t < \dfrac{x}{v} \\[2mm] \varepsilon^{-\rho x/v} & t > \dfrac{x}{v} \end{cases}$

where the constants have the values given in (91).

(93) $\qquad \dfrac{p\sqrt{p + 2a}}{\sqrt{p} + \sqrt{p + 2a}} \doteq \dfrac{\delta(t)}{2} + \dfrac{1}{2t} \varepsilon^{-at} I_1(at) \quad t > 0$

where

$$a = \frac{R}{2i}$$

(94) $$\frac{\sqrt{p + 2a}}{\sqrt{p} + \sqrt{p + 2a}} \doteq 1 - \frac{1}{2} \varepsilon^{-at}\{I_0(at) + I_1(at)\} \quad t > 0$$

where $a > 0$ and $I_0(y)$, $I_1(y)$ are the modified Bessel functions of the zeroth and first orders.

(95) $$\frac{p \exp{(-y\sqrt{p})}}{1 + \sqrt{\dfrac{p}{a}}} \doteq \sqrt{\frac{a}{\pi t}} \exp{\left(-\frac{y^2}{4t}\right)}$$

$$- a \exp{(y\sqrt{a} + at)} \operatorname{erf}\left(\frac{y}{2\sqrt{t}} + \sqrt{at}\right) \qquad a > 0, \quad t > 0$$

(96) $$\frac{\exp{(-y\sqrt{p})}}{1 + \sqrt{\dfrac{p}{a}}} \doteq \operatorname{erf}\left(\frac{y}{2\sqrt{t}}\right) - \exp{(y\sqrt{a} + at)}\operatorname{erf}\left(\frac{y}{2\sqrt{t}} + \sqrt{at}\right) \quad t > 0$$

(97) $$\frac{pn\sqrt{p} \exp{(-y\sqrt{p})}}{1 + \sqrt{\dfrac{p}{a}}} \doteq \frac{n(y - 2t\sqrt{a})}{2t}\sqrt{\frac{a}{\pi t}}\exp{\left(\frac{-y^2}{4t}\right)}$$

$$+ na\sqrt{a} \exp{(y\sqrt{a} + at)}\operatorname{erf}\left(\frac{y}{2\sqrt{t}} + \sqrt{at}\right) \quad t > 0$$

(98) $$\frac{n\sqrt{p} \exp{(-y\sqrt{p})}}{1 + \sqrt{\dfrac{p}{n}}} \doteq u \exp{(y\sqrt{a} + at)}\operatorname{erf}\left(\frac{y}{2\sqrt{t}} + \sqrt{at}\right) \quad t > 0$$

(99) $$\frac{pn\sqrt{p}}{1 + \sqrt{\dfrac{p}{a}}} \doteq n\sqrt{a}\left\{\delta(t) - \sqrt{\frac{a}{\pi t}} + a\varepsilon^{at} \operatorname{erf} \sqrt{at}\right\} \quad t > 0$$

(100) $$\frac{n\sqrt{p}}{1 + \sqrt{\dfrac{p}{a}}} \doteq u\sqrt{a}\varepsilon^{at} \operatorname{erf} \sqrt{at}$$

(101) $$\frac{p^2 \exp{(-y\sqrt{p})}}{1 + \sqrt{\dfrac{p}{a}}} \doteq \frac{(y^2 - 2yt\sqrt{a} - 2t + 4at^2)}{4t^2}\sqrt{\frac{a}{\pi t}}\varepsilon^{-y^2/4t}$$

$$- a^2 \exp{(y\sqrt{a} + at)}\operatorname{erf}\left(\frac{y}{2\sqrt{t}} + \sqrt{at}\right) \qquad t > 0$$

(102) $\dfrac{p \exp(-y\sqrt{p})}{1 + \sqrt{\dfrac{p}{a}}} \doteqdot \sqrt{\dfrac{a}{\pi t}} \exp\left(\dfrac{-y^2}{4t}\right)$

$$-a \exp(y\sqrt{a} + at) \operatorname{erf}\left(\dfrac{y}{2\sqrt{t}} - \sqrt{at}\right) \qquad t > 0$$

(103) $\dfrac{p^2}{1 + \sqrt{\dfrac{p}{a}}} \doteqdot -a\,\delta(t) + \dfrac{(2at - 1)}{2t}\sqrt{\dfrac{a}{\pi t}} - a^2 \varepsilon^{at} \operatorname{erf}(\sqrt{at}) \qquad t > 0$

(104) $\dfrac{p}{1 + \sqrt{\dfrac{p}{b}}} \doteqdot \sqrt{\dfrac{a}{\pi t}} - a\varepsilon^{at} \operatorname{erf}(\sqrt{at})$

(105) $\dfrac{pw^{2n+1}\{\sqrt{(p+a)^2 + w^2} + (p+a)\}^{-2n}}{k\sqrt{(p+a)^2 + w^2}} \doteqdot \dfrac{2}{L}\varepsilon^{-at}J_{2n}(wt) \quad t > 0$

where

$$k = \sqrt{\dfrac{L}{C}} \quad a = \dfrac{R}{L} = \dfrac{G}{C}$$

$$w = 2/\sqrt{LC} \quad n \text{ is a positive integer}$$

(106) $\dfrac{p2(2a)^n}{R}\sqrt{\dfrac{p}{p+2a}}(\sqrt{p+2a} + \sqrt{p})^{-2n}$

$$\doteqdot \dfrac{a}{R}\varepsilon^{-at}\{I_{n-1}(at) - 2I_n(at) + I_{n+1}(at)\} \quad t > 0$$

where

$$a = \dfrac{2}{RC}$$

n is a positive integer. $I_n(y)$ is the modified Bessel function of the nth order.

(107) $\dfrac{2(2a)^n}{R}\sqrt{\dfrac{p}{p+a}}(\sqrt{p+2a} + \sqrt{p})^{-2n} \doteqdot \dfrac{2}{R}\varepsilon^{-at}I_n(at)$

where the constants are the same as in (106).

(108) $\dfrac{\{\sqrt{1+a} + \sqrt{a}\}^{-2n}}{\sqrt{(1+a)}Z_1 Z_2} \doteqdot \dfrac{1}{k}\displaystyle\int_0^{\omega_c t} \varepsilon^{-\frac{bu}{\omega_c}} J_{2n}(u)\,du$

where n is a positive integer

$$a = \dfrac{LC}{4}(p+b)^2 \qquad \dfrac{1}{Z_2} = C(p+b)$$

$$Z_1 = L(p+b) \qquad w_c = \dfrac{2}{\sqrt{LC}} \qquad k = \sqrt{\dfrac{L}{C}}$$

(109) $$\frac{w_c}{k} \frac{1}{\sqrt{p^2 + w_2^2}} \left(\frac{\sqrt{p^2 + w_c^2} - p}{w_c} \right)^{an} \doteqdot \frac{1}{k} \int_0^{w_c t} J_{2n}(n) \, dn$$

where the constants have the same significance as in (108).

(110) $$\frac{1}{2} \tanh \left(\frac{Tp}{2} \right) \doteqdot h(t)$$

where

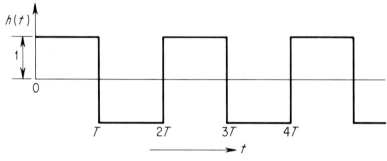

FIGURE 110

(111) $$\varepsilon^{t_1 p} - \varepsilon^{t_2 p} \doteqdot h(t)$$

where

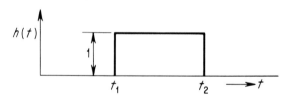

FIGURE 111

(112) $$\frac{m}{p} (1 - \varepsilon^{-pT}) - mT\varepsilon^{-pT} \doteqdot h(t)$$

where

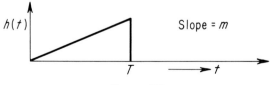

FIGURE 112

(113)
$$\frac{1}{(\varepsilon^{Tp} - 1)} \doteq h(t)$$

where

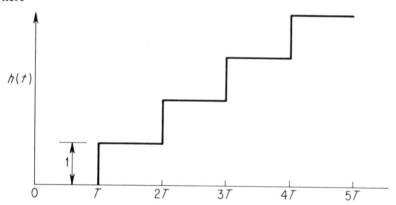

FIGURE 113

(114)
$$\frac{m}{p} - \frac{mT}{\varepsilon^{pT} - 1} \doteq h(t)$$

where

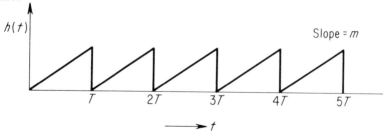

Slope = m

FIGURE 114

(115)
$$\frac{m}{p} - 2mT \left\{ \frac{1}{\varepsilon^{Tp} - 1} - \frac{1}{\varepsilon^{2Tp} - 1} \right\} \doteq h(t)$$

where

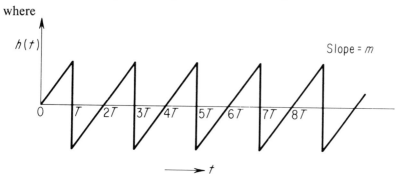

Slope = m

FIGURE 115

(116)
$$\frac{1}{\varepsilon^{pT} + 1} \doteq h(t)$$

where

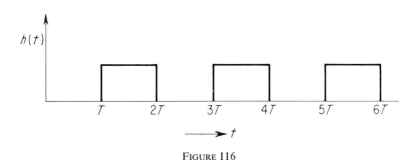

FIGURE 116

REFERENCES

The above table of transforms, combined with the basic theorems of the Laplacian transform theory given in Appendix II, will be found most useful in obtaining the solution of many problems involving the transient behavior of linear dynamical systems.   Any table of integrals listing integrals of the direct Laplacian transformation type may be used to obtain transforms.   Integrals of this type will be found listed in the following works:

1. Campbell, G. A. and R. M. Foster, "Fourier Integrals for Practical Applications," *Bell System Tech. Jl.* (Sept., 1931).

2. Dierens de Haan, D., *Nouvelles Tables d'Integrales Definies*.   Leiden, 1867.

3. Bromwich, T. J. I'a., *An Introduction to the Theory of Infinite Series*, 2nd ed.   London: 1926.

4. Watson, G. N., *A Treatise on the Theory of Bessel Functions*.   London: Cambridge University Press, 1922.

5. McLachlan, N. W., *Complex Variable and Operational Calculus*.   London: Cambridge University Press, 1939.   (Gives an extensive bibliography.)

INDEX

A

Absolute acceleration, 177
Acceleration, 175
Angular coordinates, 173
Angular momentum, 185
Angular velocity, 166

B

Bôcher's formulas, 61

C

Castigliano's theorem, 135
Cayley-Hamilton theorem, 73
  in matrix inversion, 77
  reduction of polynomials, 75
Central ellipse, 40
Change of reference axes, 170
Characteristic determinant, 59
  equation, 59
  function, 39
  matrix, 39
  polynomial, 39
Classical mechanics, 163
Cofactor, 4
Coupled pendulums, 237
Couples, 181
Cramer's rule, 13

D

Damping matrix, 255
Determinants, 3
  cofactor, 4
  differentiation, 15
  elements, 3
  expansion, 6
  minor, 4
  pivotal condensation, 10
  product, 15
  properties, 7
Difference equations, 94
Dissipation function, 254

E

Eigenvalue, 40
  geometrical interpretation, 40

Eigenvalue (*cont.*)
  location, 285
  real symmetric matrix, 49
Eigenvector, 40
  algebraic interpretation, 46
Elastic constants, 120
  equations of equilibrium, 125
  equations of motion, 122
Elasticity, 100
Electrical circuits, 288
  average power, 302
  attenuation constants, 336
  canonical equations, 292
  determinantal equations, 306
  dissipationless networks, 316
  effects of small resistances, 333
  energy functions, 313
  normal modes, 306
  potential function, 334
  repeated roots, 311
  sources with different frequencies, 298
  sources with different phases, 298
  steady state solution, 295
Euler's equations, 189

F

Flexibility matrix, 130
Foucault pendulum, 201
Four-terminal networks, 337
  attenuation and pass bands, 359
  cascade connections, 352
  chain matrices, 347
  general equations, 337
  homographic transformations, 351
  interconnections, 341
  iterative impedances, 356

G

General ladder network, 363

H

Hermitian matrix, 50
Homographic transformations, 351

I

Initial stresses, 154
Iteration, 263

K

Kinematics, 166
Kinetic energy, 177
Kirchhoff's laws, 290

L

Lagrange's equations, 212
  for electrical circuits, 217
Laplace transformation, 401
  tables of transforms, 407
  theorems, 404
Linear equations, 13
  Cramer's rule, 13
  homogeneous equations, 34
Loaded string, 246

M

Mass-weighted coordinates, 224
Matrix, 18
  addition and subtraction, 20
  adjoint, 25
  binomial theorem, 72
  commutative, 57
  diagonal matrix, 31
  differentiation, 88
  division, 28
  equality, 20
  function, 78
  functions and characteristic equations, 83
  hermitian, 50
  infinite series, 66
  integration, 88
  iteration, 266
  linear differential equations, 90
  modal, 47
  multiplication, 21
  nonsingular, 26
  norm, 67
  partitioning, 31
  polynomials, 65

Matrix (*cont.*)
  products, 23
  reversal law of products, 29
  singular, 26
  special matrices, 33
  submatrix, 32
  symmetric, 53
  transposition, 19
  types, 19
  vector product, 163
Matrizant, 92
Maxwell's reciprocity theorem, 134
Modal matrix, 47
  columns, 230
  fundamental properties, 231
Modified structure, 144
  analysis of modification, 155
  flexibility, 150
  modified elements, 147
  stiffness matrix, 157
Moment, 181
Moment of inertia, 179
Motion relative to surface of earth, 193
  near surface of earth, 198
Moving axes, 186
Multiconductor lines, 365
  capacity and induction, 366
  determinantal equation, 375
  differential equations, 368
  electromagnetic coefficients, 367
  ring symmetry, steady-state analysis, 377
  ring symmetry, transient analysis, 392
  steady-state equations, 370
  transient analysis, 384
Multiple roots of characteristic equation, 249

N

Network terminology, 288
Nonconservative systems, 254
Normal coordinates, 221

O

Operational impedance, 292
Orthogonal transformations, 51
Oscillations in a symmetric electrical circuit, 251

P

Pass band, 359
Peano-Baker method, 91
Plumb line, 196
Principal axes of inertia, 179
Principle of minimum potential energy, 136
 of virtual work, 136

Q

Quadratic forms, 53
 transformation to sum of squares, 54

R

Rigid body kinematics, 166
 center of mass, 183
 equations of motion, 183
Rotation of coordinate axes, 165
 successive rotations, 172
Rotation matrix, 44
 invariants, 45
Routh-Hurwitz criterion, 282

S

S-waves, 124
Smooth transmission lines, 361
Spinning top, 201
 precession, 205
 stability, 206
Stiffness matrix, 130
Strain, 111
 energy, 117
 extension, 114
 irrotational, 114
 matrix, 116

Strain (*cont.*)
 potential, 125
 principal, 116
 quadric, 116
Stress, 100
 invariants, 109
 matrix, 102
 principal, 109
 quadric, 108
 shear, 109
 three dimensional, 106
 two dimensional, 102
Stress-strain relationship, 117
Structures, analysis, 129
 displacement method, 151
 force method, 138
 Maxwell's reciprocity theorem, 134
 modified structures, 144
 multiple loads, 132
 strain energy, 134
Sweeping matrix, 267
Sylvester's theorem, 78
Symmetric damped systems, 279

T

Transformation, Laplace, 401
 linear, 12
 orthogonal, 51
Triple pendulum, 270

V

Velocity, 175
Vibration problems, 210
 analogies, 215
 dynamic coupling, 227
 equations of motion, 212
 functions of matrices, 241
 transformation of coordinates, 210
 two degrees of freedom, 218